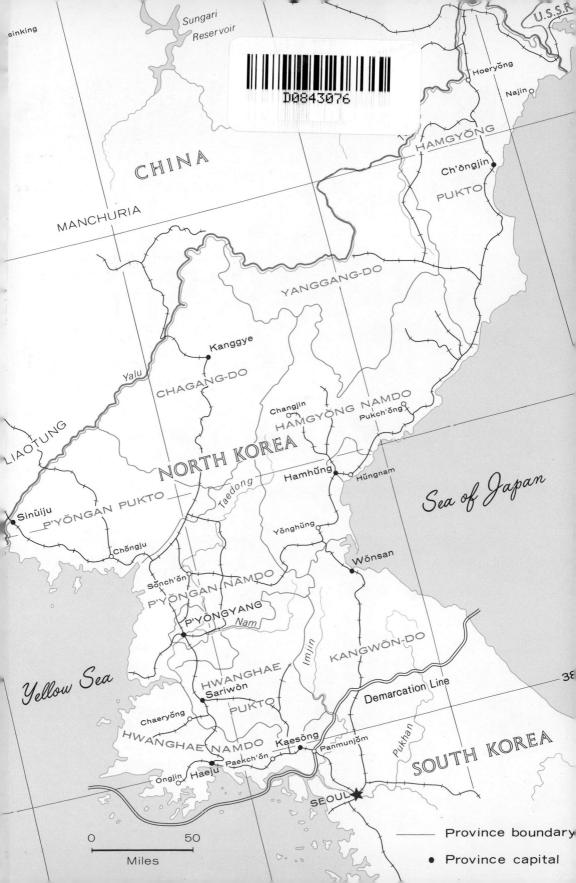

KOREA

The Politics of the Vortex

Written under the auspices of
The Center for International Affairs
Harvard University

KOREA
THE
POLITICS
OF THE
VORTEX

Gregory Henderson

**HARVARD UNIVERSITY
PRESS**

Cambridge, Massachusetts
1968

For Maia

WHO SUSTAINED ME

Foreword by Samuel P. Huntington

The customary style in forewords, I have observed, is nothing if it is not oblique. The foreworder is supposed to ease his readers (who may or may not significantly overlap the book's readers) into an awareness of the importance of the subject of the book, then into an awareness of the importance of the book, and finally into an awareness of the importance — and qualifications — of the author of the book. All this is normally done in a properly decorous and involuted manner, setting well-chosen praise phrases for book and author into appropriately detached and academic-sounding reflections on the existing state of scholarship in the field.

I prefer not to beat around the bush.

Gregory Henderson's book is profoundly important to at least three audiences for at least three reasons.

First, for those interested in Korea, it is the most comprehensive and penetrating analysis of Korean political culture and political development available in English and probably, as far as I can gather, in any other language, including Korean and Japanese. The expert on Korea will find new information on many aspects of Korean development, particularly the period of Japanese rule and the period immediately following World War II. The book reflects the author's almost total immersion in that country for over a decade. Appointed in 1947 as one of the first Foreign Service Officers to specialize in Korean affairs, Mr. Henderson subsequently served over seven years in the U.S. Embassies in Seoul and Pusan and three more years at the State Department in Washington. Although this is his first book, he is the author of a score of articles in Asian and American scholarly journals on aspects of Korean society and culture. In these he has shown himself equally at home with the intricacies of both the ceramics of early Korea and the social patterns of the present day.

The thorough specialist often becomes lost in details. Henderson, however, focuses on one central feature of Korean culture, using it to broaden our understanding of Korean politics and to provide a unified explanation of Korean political development. He finds homogeneity and centralization to be the keys to Korean society much as De Tocqueville identified equality and democracy as the keys to American society. The result in Korea is an atomized society in which individual, family, and clique have gyrated frenetically in a bureaucratic "updraft" that Henderson so appropriately describes as the politics of the vortex. This is a bold thesis and a vivid metaphor. Future scholars may dissent vigorously from this thesis, but few will ignore it.

Second, for those concerned with comparative politics and political development, Henderson's book provides a fascinating case study of what is almost an ideal type, located at one extreme of the homogeneity-pluralism continuum. Henderson wrote his manuscript while a Research Associate at the Harvard Center for International Affairs, 1964–1965. During this period he was a regular participant in the Harvard–MIT Faculty Seminar on Political Development and in other Center activities concerned with political change in modernizing societies in Asia, Africa, and Latin America. In treating Korea, he comes back regularly to many themes that have preoccupied other students of comparative politics. In particular, Henderson provides a balanced appraisal of the advantages and disadvantages of pluralism in the process of modernization. On the one hand, what is good for national integration is not necessarily good for national development. Uniformity does not produce unity, nor consensus cohesion. Homogeneity and centralization have created a system characterized by high levels of social mobilization and low levels of organizational development. On the other hand, Korea has also lacked the traditionalism, unwillingness to change, and nostalgia characteristic of other societies. Korean society is open and dynamic. Striking similarities, indeed, exist between Korean society and American society. The crucial question is: Can Korea adapt to pluralism?

Finally, this book is important to policy-makers, in Washington and elsewhere, who are concerned with producing political order out of economic change and social turmoil. How can political stability be achieved as a highly centralized and bureaucratic society moves into the modern age? One means, common in societies with this type of traditional structure, is the totalitarianism found in China and Russia. Is there any other way of filling the void and stilling the vortex? The question is relevant not only to Korea but to other countries, such as Thailand and Iran, that have moved toward modernity under the auspices of centralized traditional monarchies. Henderson presents a persuasive case for decentralization of political authority and the encouragement of autonomous centers of power at the local level and in the economic sphere. Similar arguments have been made with respect to Vietnam, and, inevitably, concern with that country may motivate many policy-makers to read Henderson's analysis. Vietnam differs significantly, and perhaps fundamentally, from Korea in its religious and ethnic pluralism. But it shares with Korea the experience of being a tribute state to China, a mixed Buddhist and Confucian heritage, and, most important, a tradition of centralized power that has attempted to weaken and destroy intermediary groups. The Vietnamese themselves have become fascinated with the Korean experience, and many Americans have held that the creation of a dominant political party under military auspices along the lines of the Democratic Republican party is an appropriate model for Vietnam. More recently Americans have also begun to stress the need to decentralize power and to develop more vigorous local political institutions in Vietnam.

Henderson has produced a striking interpretation of Korean history, a valuable study in the comparative politics of modernization, and a suggestive proposal for encouraging political stability and pluralistic democracy in Asian and African societies. Anyone concerned with any of these matters would do well to read this volume.

Author's Acknowledgments

This study owes its existence to the Harvard University Center for International Affairs which had faith in the potential value of an inquiry into the Korean political pattern even when no clear theme existed in the author's mind and faith had to be strong indeed. For the lonely and enchanting pursuit of my own researches and thoughts that a Research Associateship at the Center from March 1964 until January 1966 solely enabled, I salute the generosity of the Center, the comradeship of like minds, the fertile ambience of my native Cambridge, and a happy system of patronage that few earlier courts can have equaled. To the Center's Director, Professor Robert R. Bowie, I owe, besides the above, an insistence on analysis over history that laid the keel for this book. Finally, my thanks are due the Center for sponsoring this publication.

There are not many men with whom one can discuss a theme of this sort on Korea near its inception. I am repeatedly grateful for the broad understanding, deep knowledge, and exquisite accuracy of this country's top modern scholar on Korea, Dr. Edward W. Wagner, Associate Professor of Korean Studies at Harvard. First in ideas, then in many criticisms of the manuscript, not unmixed with encouragement, finally in much help with sources and citations he has placed me in his debt. Many as may be the errors — and they are all mine — how many more would there have been had his knowledge not caught them. To Dr. Ki Il Choi of the Economics Department of the College of William and Mary I also owe the fruit of much early discussion illuminated by his constant originality of thought and trenchant metaphor. To Dr. Maner Thorpe, Department of Anthropology, University of California, Santa Barbara, I am indebted for placing at my disposal his unique insights and experience with Korean rural life.

Most of all, this book is the issue of over seven years' service in Korea with the American Embassy: July 1948–October 1950, May 1958–March 1963, years that saw the end of U.S. military occupation, the foundation of the Republic, rebellion, the outbreak of war, the recapture of Seoul, the April revolution that overthrew President Syngman Rhee, the military coup that overthrew his democratic successors, a bewildering suite of disasters and triumphs in Korea's search for stability, integrity, and true independence. A host of Korean friends from every walk of life guided and taught me through these years. They wove for me the threads of what follows, however little they may recognize — or like — the tapestry. Few can be recognized but one thinks of men like Lyuh Woon-hong, with his rich social knowledge, of the late Dr. Yi Sang-baek, of Professors Yi Pyŏng-do and Yi Man-gap, all of Seoul National University, and many more.

For willing help in research and for suggestions on sources my thanks are due to Mr. Kiwon Chung of George Washington University, Dr. Young-ik Lew, then of Harvard and, for generously answering my many bibliographical questions, to Mr. Sungha Kim of the Chinese-Japanese Library of the Harvard-Yenching Institute, to Mr. Joobong Kim of the East Asian Library, Columbia University, and to that *doyen* of Korean librarians, Mr. Key P. Yang of the Library of Congress. For loan of materials I must acknowledge the generosity of the late Mr. William R. Langdon, long Consul, Consul-General, and Political Advisor in Seoul, and Mrs. Langdon, and Richard D. Robinson, Senior Lecturer at the Massachusetts Institute of Technology, who placed at my disposal his unpublished manuscript on the United States occupation of Korea, enabling me to fill a grievous gap.

Once the first draft was ready, others came to my aid: Professors Rupert Emerson and Samuel P. Huntington of the Department of Government, and Professor Benjamin Schwartz of the Department of History, Harvard University, all read the manuscript and made helpful suggestions. To Professor Huntington I acknowledge particular gratitude for guidance in the re-structuring of the chapters.

Finally, to Robert Erwin, Editor of Publications, Center for International Affairs, a long salute for patience, helpfulness, and forbearance with an author hard to rein.

The loneliness of an author in his search for a theme and his labor

Author's Acknowledgments

on a text is more than matched, with less reward, by his wife. To
Maria von Magnus Henderson, then, my deepest thanks for support
so long and so endearingly given.

Gregory Henderson

11 Riverside Drive
New York City
March 1968

Contents

Illustrations
Following page 112

1. Compound of a Korean aristocrat-politician in Seoul, early nineteenth century. From a painting owned by Dr. Yi Pyŏng-do.
2. The Taewŏn'gun (1820–1898), Prince Regent of Korea, 1864–1873.
3. Korean Independence Day outside Seoul's Duksoo Palace, March 1, 1919. Courtesy Dr. Frank Schofield.
4. Song Pyŏng-jun and Uchida Ryōhei, leader of the Black Dragon Society. From Kuzū Yoshihisa, *Secret History of the Annexation of Korea* (Tokyo, 1930), Vol. II.
5. Korean independence leaders Kim Ku, Syngman Rhee, and O Se-ch'ang, March 1, 1946.

KOREA
The Politics of the Vortex

Introduction

The political pattern of Korea has remained, both within Korea itself and abroad, largely uncharted. Where charts are few, perplexities abound and will remain, for no single work can hope to dispel them. Korea has, relative to most developing nations, old literary traditions and an abundance of materials. The task of sifting these, making them available for the wide needs of modern research, and constructing a monographic base to enable sound analysis has only begun, not only for the dynastic centuries covered by long annals but even for recent decades of Japanese administration. The Sino-Korean annalistic historical tradition has dissuaded its scholars from, rather than prepared them for, comparisons and analyses; Western scholarship on the Far East, understandably preoccupied with the almost impenetrable richness of materials on China and Japan and their overwhelming importance, has hardly come to consider the small land between. Even a good, basic, modern history of Korea is still lacking in any Western language.

Under these circumstances, any attempt at a broad analysis of Korea's political culture is temerarious. It must recognize that the conclusions at which it seeks to arrive are tentative, that many will be revised and some refuted. Yet not to attempt a preliminary study is still more irresponsible. Scholars need the stimulation of inquiry as to where the path of their studies may lead. More urgent are the claims of the practical international world. Korea, source of recent war, object of costly international peacemaking and reconstruction efforts, clearly holds immediate interest. Within living memory, Confucian dynasty, colonial administration, American military occupation, autocracy, democracy, popular revolution, and military coup have all beaten like successive waves over the country. Political stability, though temporarily greater, has still not been achieved, nor is an end to Korea's political dilemmas clearly discernible. Nevertheless, the political culture has in some respects proved to be resilient under all these shocks. What should the man actively engaged in international affairs make of this seeming paradox? The diplomat, the soldier, the aid official, the planner, and the teacher have only the present in which to do their work. What they must do will be done before the perfection of the scholarly millennium arrives. This study is also for these comrades.

Korea requires understanding not only as an entity; she must also be comprehended in the framework of political development in general. Over forty million Koreans now live within their peninsula. The critically strategic location of their land is now belatedly, at great cost, recognized, and a moment's reflection should convince the inquirer that their cultural and historical weight is considerable. Korea's claims for recognition by political scientists in fact rest on more than population rank and location. The form her government has often tended to take, that of a centralized oligarchy with an agricultural framework — not a city-state — is a rare specimen in world history. Few if any traditions affecting an entity of this size have operated in so uniform an environment of race, culture, and language, within geographic boundaries so stable or a political framework so enduring. Few states eliminated local power so soon or so completely and sustained centralized rule in such unchallenged form so long. The Korean greenhouse has had several gardeners, but its temperatures have been, on the whole, constant.

Not only is the setting of Korea's political tradition atypical, but the results might, from the point of view of much modern political-development theory, be called unexpected. On the surface, it would seem that Korea early gained that national unity, ethnic and cultural homogeneity, and strong, centralized, uncontested bureaucratic rule for which most emerging nations of the present world still struggle painfully. Other emerging societies might envy such conditions and be tempted to predict for such a nation the possibility of a relatively swift political and economic modernization. Yet Korea missed — or has been slow to attain — the fulfillment of this promise. She failed to use these advantages to solve the political, economic, or military problems of the nation in the initial decades of Western contact. Nor have they seemed of decisive help in easing her path since, certainly not within the democratic system. Political scientists have reason to inquire into the reasons for this apparent failure. The surprising nature of the results of Korea's long-sustained homogeneity and centrality may affect political theory conjuring with the issues of unity and coherence in the political cultures of other developing nations. Is it possible that the unity, centrality, and homogeneity now sought by emerging nations may set in motion, as they did for Korea, a vortex similarly destructive to political amalgamation and pluralism? Must not our understanding of political science extend to an examination of the physics of centralization, a capacity to gauge the forces it forms and to clock the velocities of the tides and vortices to which it gives birth? Are these forces functional or dysfunctional for democratic modernization? When and to what degree?

The problem calls for illustration. In the fall of 1963, the successful leaders of the Korean military coup of 1961 allowed popular elections for the President and the National Assembly to take place under conditions of appreciable freedom. A powerful government party, munificently financed, had been formed and was backed with all the instruments at the government's command. Sentiment critical of, or even hostile to, military government abounded, and the opposition, containing almost all of the country's well-known politicians, was backed by most urban areas and by considerable portions of the press. Opposition supporters knew that they would have many political cards stacked against them by the government and were daily warned that only through unity could they expect to make a strong showing. The opposition not only shared strong antipathy to military government but had, within itself, no great divisive regional, ethnic, religious, class, or ideological differences. Nevertheless, it splintered acrimoniously into eleven different parties, was unable to agree on joint Assembly candidates in almost any instances, ran competing candidates in nearly all districts and, as a result, committed virtual political suicide. The government party received only 33.5 percent of the vote, yet it was able to obtain 110 out of 175 representatives. The opposition, with two thirds of the vote, could place only 65, or little more than one third of the representatives. In 1966, a comparable disability continued to dog opposition preparations for the 1967 elections. The failure, often repeated, of a homogeneous culture with a single, long political tradition to produce voluntary political unity and cohesion has turned a potential majority into a humiliatingly defeated minority and frustrated the expression of majority will, hence of democracy. The fact that this result may remind political observers of France and of some highly centralized bodies politic extends rather than limits its significance.

That such incohesiveness was not primarily the function of transient personalities or tactics or chance is well demonstrated by chapters in Korean history set forth below: the long and painful amalgamative process needed by the opposition against the Liberal party, 1952–1960; the dispersal of conservative forces in the face of extreme competition from communism, 1945–1947; the complete failure to rally effective political opposition to Japan's 1910 takeover despite long, essentially independent traditions, deep-rooted antipathy to Japan, and the presence of only a few thousand Japanese troops in the midst of some thirteen million Koreans. Political incohesiveness against both internal and external threat is a theme of Korean history, chronic, endemic, extreme. It has often frustrated Korean efforts at modernization. To what causes should we look to explain it in a nation which, except for arbitrary foreign dividing of north and south, has been almost completely lacking in objective grounds for cleavage?

I argue here that the unity and homogeneity of Korea acted to produce a *mass* society, much, perhaps, as they acted for the population of the core area of her neighbor, China. By mass society, I mean a society lacking in the formation of strong institutions or voluntary associations between village and throne; a society that knows little of castle town, feudal lord and court, semi-independent merchant societies, city-states, guilds, or classes cohesive enough to be centers of independent stance and action in the polity. Thus mass society consists typically of atomized entities, related to each other chiefly through their relations to state power — a society whose elite and masses confront each other directly, "by virtue of the weakness of groups capable of mediation between them," a society characterized by amorphousness or isolation in social relations.[1]

Mass societies of various kinds are not rare, and most tend toward centralization and autocracy. Korea's mass society is distinguished from others, in this respect, not in kind but in the extreme length to which the tendency has been carried. Compactness of territory, absence of ethnic, religious, political, linguistic, or other basic sources of cleavage within Korea, and a universalistic value system have created a society in which groupings are artificial. Vested interests, religious separations, basic policy differences and ideological divisions tend not to occur and, since they have counted little for so long, tend not to be a relevant part of the political pattern the society has formed. Grouping is hence an opportunistic matter concerned only with access to power for its members, and, because other differences are not present, each group tends to be distinguishable from the others only by the personalities of its members and by their relationship to power at the time. Hence groupings are factional; for the issues and interests that forge true parties from factions are absent from the homogeneous, power-bent society.

The result is a pattern of extreme centripetal dynamics, its intensity heightened by the smallness of the peninsula's dimensions beyond that generally sustainable throughout the vaster mass societies of China or Russia. The physics of Korean political dynamics appears to resemble a strong vortex tending to sweep all active elements of the society upward toward central power. Weak horizontal structure and strong vertical pressure complement each other. Vertical pressures cannot be countered because local or independent aggregations do not exist to impede their formation or to check the resulting vortex once formed. More striking still, intermediary groupings find it difficult to achieve aggregation. Vertiginous updraft tends to suck all components from each other before they cohere on lower levels and tends to propel them in atomized form toward the power apex.

This pattern can be identified in the erosive action of the premodern Korean central government upon the interest groups of the country and, most arrestingly though still somewhat tentatively, upon class structure. The strength of the vortex can be tested by examining the process through which formal immobility was transformed into significant covert mobility. The persistence of the pattern in overt form can be detected in the period from 1880 to 1910; its transformation and expansion through broadened education, industrialization, and urbanization in the late colonial period into the basis of the political and party system after Liberation can be clearly followed; and the effects on it of autocracy, democracy, military rule, and communism in the decades from 1945 to 1965 can be in some degree analyzed.

That such a scheme is ambitious is obvious. Its bounds would exceed the possibilities of exhaustive proof even for societies far better investigated and understood than Korea's. Broad as it is, there are several areas of inquiry that my argument tends to bypass, however, and these areas have usually been judged so important for Korea that account must be taken of their absence.

The first of these concerns the question of foreign influence as a critical formative agent in Korea's history and on her political behavior. It follows from an analysis along the lines above that I believe the prime responsible agent for political phenomena in Korea, both in the past and now, to be an indigenous, internal pattern — prehensile, deep-rooted, and comparatively unchanging — acting in turn on each of the forms of central government that comes within its influence with a continuity that can only be called stubborn. The forms of government adopted or forced on Korea in this process have been largely of foreign origin: Confucian monarchy and bureaucracy, Japanese colonial rule, American military government, constitutional democracy. The weight these foreign loads are felt to have is increased by the fact that Korea is a small country surrounded by more powerful neighbors, hence an environment actually, but even more psychologically, inured to foreign influence and to the inborn conviction that what is native is weak, what is foreign is strong. There also is, and long has been, pride in mastering foreign forms when they work and an equally strong instinct to ascribe responsibility to the policies of foreign powers when they do not.

A country under such conditions paradoxically tends to slight its own internal patterns while overestimating external influence. Koreans habitually interpret the history of their nation in terms of foreign invasion, Chinese domination, Japanese occupation, American sellouts (for example, Theodore Roosevelt), United Nations actions, foreign communism, the Cold War, American foreign policy, and the operations of the American embassy in Korea. To such agencies and causes is often imputed major blame for loss of independence, failure of the independence movement, inability to "protect" democracy, failure to make economic progress, and so forth. As a member of the American embassy staff in Korea for over seven years, I was subjected to such argumentation in memorably heavy barrages. I also witnessed, with greater or lesser intimacy, the operation of American influence on Korea and its politics over a period of some eighteen years. That such arguments have a measure of validity, that substantial American and other foreign influence exists, sometimes in undue degree, is obvious; that foreign influence is on the whole tangential, not central to the fundamental operation of Korean politics is, to me, equally so. Such belief has led to the theme of these pages: a thesis, a theory regarding the underlying nature of the Korean political pattern. History is much adduced to demonstrate the thesis — and is more needed because so little Korean history is widely known. This work however, is not history and, in particular, makes no essay to render full account of all external — or even internal — developments. These pages say little about many instances of foreign influence that others think important; they do so partly to avoid that to which I was officially privy, partly because details must be subordinated to theme. Behind this lies, however, conviction and judgment that external factors are for Korea and her internal courses of secondary importance. If this judgment is wrong, I stand most ready to have it proved so.

Much the same disclaimer, somewhat less confidently fifed, applies to the influence of economic factors. Korea's long and inexhaustible appetite for politics together with her slighting of economic activity and derogation of economic role-players suggests the basic predominance of politics over economics in her system. Of course, politics and economics cannot, in the end, be separated; manifestly, in recent times, the relentless aid of the United States and its inescapable inoculations of material — and also professional — standards and values have affected Korea's political progress. The transfer of influence from the economic to the political arena appears, as these pages are written, to be increasingly vital, and its importance for many decades might well be demonstrated at some length in economic studies of Korea. Such studies must be made. Yet to me the ancient political predominance remains in the culture.[2]

Finally, and of more concern to the modern political scientist, this study concerns itself more with macroanalysis than with microanalysis, primarily with social aggregates and the dynamics of the Korean political system and only rarely with the private socialization process or with psychological interpretations of the individual's political behavior.[3] Systematic attitudinal-behavioral analysis still faces a lack of organized materials regarding Korean child-rearing as well as the political-socialization process. In general, the bridges that social scientists have been able to construct between the psychological and the sociological components of political culture have lacked sufficient structural strength to encourage use of Korea's inadequate materials in this area. Moreover, the extreme centralization and political concentration of Korean culture seem at least as likely to influence the way the Korean child is brought up and politically socialized as is such training likely to be a mainspring of the political pattern. Hence, psychological, like economic, factors appear more functions, less sources, of the fundamental dynamics of the political culture than in more dispersed and heterogeneous communities. Such conclusions and many others, however, are tentative and must wait in the wings until further study brings them to the stage.

I hope that my many Korean friends will not find in the pages that follow what might seem to them a counsel of despair. "If, indeed," they might complain, "we are caught in a pattern, a vortex, which has, through so many and long experiences, not loosened its hold on us, then what is our hope?" To them I would reply that if this study has something true to say, it is not of despair that it speaks. On the contrary, the vortex in which I find Koreans have politically moved is created, not inborn, and springs, in my view, from that lack of "intermediary" groups which betokens mass society. Modernization — with its demands for factory units, exploitation of resources outside the capital, professions and specialists, a multi-functional, multi-centered society — carries within it institutions well adapted for Korea's cure. These innovations can also, of course, fuel autocracy and dictatorship, as in North Korea. There seems fair hope that, in South Korea's case, they will be and already are harbingers of better change. Some half the Korean population has now been educated in a system influenced by the United States, hence one adapted to a plural society. Political change has already come from both students and soldiers produced by the new system; in a society most of which is under twenty, more change of this kind is on its way. The new industrial system with its staffs and multiple loyalties seems cast, if not in a Western image, then with many surfaces bearing the West's chisel marks. Both education and communication are widespread and complex enough to enable increasingly thoughtful Korean responses to new imported values. These modernizing influences exert persistent change on Korea's political culture and bid fair to transform it — sooner, perhaps, than pessimists would predict and, almost certainly, for the better. They can also, by intent and planning, be speeded. In this my hope is firm. It is only that these results lie largely beyond the pattern of the darker years with which the present pages deal.

PART I

Homogeneity and Updraft

1

The Single Magnet

GEOPOLITICS

Smallness of dimension, stability of boundaries, ethnic and religious homogeneity, and exceptional historical continuity mark Korea. With its 85,286 square miles (about the size of Minnesota, of England-Scotland, or of Honshū), the Korean peninsula is barely larger than a medium-sized Chinese province: Kwangtung or Kwangsi. Though not diminutive within the present world community, it is overshadowed by its neighbors. Japan is almost 70 percent larger, China almost 43 times Korea's size, the adjoining Russo-Siberian land mass beyond compare.[1]

Protecting this overawed position, however, are firm boundaries: the sea on three sides and on the other the long northern border formed by two great rivers, the Yalu and the Tumen, whose west- and east-flowing waters rise in the same mountain mass, Korea's highest land. They have bounded Korea since the fifteenth century and, on the west, for some time before. Beyond them, the Manchurian and Siberian vastness has been, until recent decades, lightly and usually impermanently inhabited, a condition somewhat true of Korea's own northeast border region until a century ago.[2] Even today, the tiny eleven-mile border with Siberia runs through swampy ground near the Tumen's broad mouth; neither it nor the rest of the northeast constitutes promising military venue. Land access thus lies chiefly along the lower third of the Yalu in the northwest, where a stretch of low land forms a corridor into the Manchurian plain. The sea, through many good natural harbors, is the main channel of access to Korea, but it was long ignored by the Koreans themselves: maritime activities flourished remarkably less in northeast Asia than in Europe.[3]

Behind its borders, Korea can protect itself by supporting a relatively large population, though its people have recently grown almost beyond its resources. Only one fifth of the land area is easily cultivable, but climate is temperate, water is usually abundant, and growing conditions are generally favorable. The present population of over forty million, product of the relentlessly sensational increases of the twentieth century, would exceed normal security demands and even threaten stability. Even the fairly stable population of around eight million conjectured for much of the Yi period, however, sufficed to prevent easy conquest or, at least, easy continued domination of a land far from China's or Japan's power centers.[4]

Not too much should be made of Korea's natural boundaries, of course. The nations around her have long been larger and, often, more aggressive than she. They carved her strategic position. Her boundaries and army protected the northern Korean kingdom of Koguryŏ in A.D. 598 and 612–614 against China's great Sui forces, but the attempt crucially sapped the strength of the victors as well as of the repulsed. A T'ang Chinese attack of 660 on the southwestern kingdom of Paekche was successful; Liao incursions of 994–1011 penetrated deep, once taking the capital; the Chin threatened the northern borders in the twelfth century; repeated Mongol incursions ended in the complete capitulation of the Koryŏ Dynasty in 1259 and a century of Mongol overlordship. Japanese piratical raids caused great distress in the thirteenth and fourteenth centuries; Japanese invasions in 1592 and 1597 overran and devastated the country; and Manchu invasions of 1627 and 1636 made even quicker work of subjugation. Koreans were made acutely aware of foreign threat and their own weakness.

Increasingly feeling the hopelessness of purely military defense, both polity and culture adopted other means of maintaining essential independence and identity. Some were formal. After the Manchu invasions, a policy of isolation from all other nations except China and minimal relations with Japan was adopted. Yet even in other periods, foreign relations were circumscribed, sometimes almost paranoically.

In earlier centuries, Buddhist and Confucian influence had flowed in together with much other Chinese culture, and isolation was probably chiefly a function of geography and undeveloped communication. But the Mongolian invasion of the mid-thirteenth century brought a more conscious seclusion in the fourteenth century that, despite some liberalization in the first half of the fifteenth century, persisted. From 1609 on contacts with Japan were officially limited to the small port of Pusan, which was sedulously isolated. Even the visiting Chinese envoys were screened from contact with anyone outside a small official group. Resources lay consciously undeveloped lest they attract foreign avarice; the mining of gold and silver was discouraged lest it lead to increased Chinese exactions of Korean products; except during the ninth century, and the end of the eleventh century (with Sung) trade never really flourished; visitors or castaways were hustled out or repelled as rapidly as possible. Warnings against foreign contact became a conventional theme in government councils.[5] No significant minorities of foreign origin could root themselves on Korean soil. Within the fabric of the culture, reactions against "alien" ways worked themselves deep.

Foreign threat also produced both a perceived and a subconscious drive for unity: the Korean house divided could not stand. The northwest had been controlled by Han China as the important colony of Lolang from 108 B.C. to A.D. 313. Thereafter the peninsula had been divided into three kingdoms whose maneuverings to escape domination had invited the rival interventions of both China and Japan. Geopolitics deeply impressed this lesson on later Korean governments. The peninsula was united in 668 and remained, with the rarest and most temporary exceptions, undivided until the foreign-imposed Cold War division hardened along the 38th Parallel in 1945 and in 1953 along the nearby Demilitarized Zone. The northern borders were somewhat fluid until the mid-fifteenth century, but, on the whole, Korea has one of the longest traditions of unity within approximately the same borders of any nation of the present world.

This unity in the face of foreign threat manifested itself historically in terms of extreme, almost constantly increasing centralization. At first as military and control centers of the clans, then by capture, removals of wealth and slaves, then by further concentrations of armed forces and officials, the seat of government assumed unusual size and dominance in national affairs. It is notable that the Silla capital at Kyŏngju, with its population of perhaps half a million, contained a possible 15–20 percent of the total post–seventh-century population; and its remains suggest ambitions to ape T'ang Ch'angan. The Koryŏ and Yi capitals, despite a general lack of urbanization in the culture, hence lesser populations, were almost equally pre-eminent. Local power was, from not much later than the seventh century on, rigidly and almost continuously discouraged. No local center was ever allowed to approach the capital in size. The peninsula, four-fifths mountainous, with high ridges separating different quadrants of the country, sizable rivers, and with over 3,300 islands (636 in South Korea alone inhabited), presented sufficient geographic opportunities for diversity, local powers, courts, castles, and lords.[6] But the cultural pattern did not allow independent or even semi-independent enclaves of importance to develop. The Koreans make much of local characteristics and dialect or accent differences; yet compared to most nations, even of Korea's size, these are remarkably few and narrow: one language is generally intelligible throughout the peninsula, and dialects are, with the comparatively minor exception of that on Cheju Island, close to the national tongue. Cheju, most distant of major islands, alone developed a unique dialect and culture, the social, religious, and, to some extent, political habits of some of its 300,000 inhabitants differing somewhat from those of the mainland. Other islands or high ridges, which Europe would have made bastions moated by sea or mountain, the semi-independent fiefs or alods of barons scornful of a central court, became instead inseparable and largely indistinguishable parts of a homogeneous polity.[7]

Strangely, the challenge of Korea's vulnerability failed to create the response of a lastingly strong military institution and with it an enduring vested interest that could contribute to the variety and strength of the society. Early centuries had contained much military promise. Korea's forces during the fourth through the seventh centuries had sufficed to inflict striking defeats even on the great Chinese Empire and to unite their own peninsula (660–668). The Koryŏ military rose to great influence and power in the eleventh and twelfth centuries in response to repeated incursions of Khitan and Jurchên (Chin) marauders, and the Koryŏ Dynasty arranged its ruling officials into two ranks of civil and military officials called *yangban,* thus implying a certain equality and balance of civil and military power. The threat of military hegemony and its control over foreign affairs brought on a power contest between the two ranks, however, ending in 1170 in Korea's only pre-1961 successful military coup against civilians. This was followed by a century of unstable rule of shogunal type in which power alternated between ten military warlords from six families (1170–1270).[8]

The officials of the succeeding Yi Dynasty (1392–1910) harbored a disturbed historical memory of these portents. They took quiet but extremely persistent steps to see that civilian dominance was secure. After the dynasty's first century, military officials were increasingly barred from high rank. The potent Censorate was, from the beginning, virtually closed to them. The Board of War became mostly civilian, as did even appointments to high-ranking provincial army and navy commands. Military honor and prestige drained away; to be "sent West" (assigned from a civil or "East" position to a military or "West" one) was an omen of departure from the *cursus honori.* In Confucianism's name, unaggressiveness was exalted even when military action was patently necessary. Reliance on China was constantly invoked in defense. Discontent among military men was chronic. Coups were talked of but always forestalled.[9] The result was centuries of appalling military weakness. Japanese invading forces in 1592 took the capital in three weeks and wandered almost at will thereafter, devastating the country. In 1637, the Manchus overran Korea with ease in a month. Such attacks no longer found vested institutions which could effectively mobilize the nation or arouse adaptive powers. In the nineteenth century, fiscal collapse brought still further weakening and an almost total incapacity to resist threat. When formally disbanded on August 1, 1907, the armed forces of a threatened nation of twelve million numbered six thousand largely demoralized men.[10] Meanwhile, in thwarting military group power, the nation had sacrificed far more than defense. She had blocked the emergence of reform and innovation vested within an interest group and thus contributed fatally to the stagnation of an adaptive polity. Unity was thus maintained by an inert homogeneity characterized by innumerable petty quarrels that found no great institutional interests which could override or subordinate them. A curious, fossilized culture, the Yi was at once unitary, acrimonious, and, for important matters, in a seemingly eternal state of suspended animation.

ETHNIC HOMOGENEITY

Ethnic homogeneity was even more fundamental. Koreans belong to the Tungusic branch of the Mongol race. Their language is clearly Altaic, related to Mongolian, Turkic, Tungusic, and Japanese. The peninsula was apparently settled by various ethnic groups deriving from this strain and entering Korea from the interior of northwest Asia comparatively late, probably during or after the third millennium B.C.[11] That other peoples lived in Korea long before now seems evident from excavations at Kongju revealing a well-stratified paleolithic culture. That such peoples may, for a time, have persisted as minorities within the later Tungusic society is not improbable but remains speculative. If so, they have been assimilated without any trace perceivable in the Koreans of today. The Tungusic peoples entered in various waves, some went on to Japan to introduce the *yayoi* culture and become the dominant Japanese stock. Others entered shortly before the Chinese domination of 108 B.C. and, apparently driven south, were absorbed with slight trace.[12] Some survivors of the Lolang colony, which Chinese texts tell us numbered some 257,000 toward the end of its history, seem to have founded Korean families. Though numerically and certainly culturally significant at the time, their absorption appears to have been complete. Even before the seventh century, evidence of great cultural variety within the peninsula — except for that between the Chinese colony and the indigenous peoples — is not very abundant. Different Tungusic ethnic or tribal groups did, however, coexist there, some more closely related to the Manchurian peoples of that time, but with the unification of the peninsula under Silla from 660–668 A.D. the less powerful were either expelled or absorbed.[13]

Later centuries did not add significant ethnic variety. We hear of the families of Chinese diplomats or soldiers occasionally settling in Korea; some Japanese soldiers remained after invasions or raids, at least one Korean clan tracing its origin to them. But ethnically the effect was negligible. Some admixture occurred during the period of Mongol invasion and control; it is well known in the Koryŏ royal family, but bad Mongol-Korean relations must have limited it considerably outside the court. The Jurchên, who controlled the northeastern strip of Korea until the fifteenth century, seem to have exerted fairly marked effect on the character of the Hamgyŏng-do population.[14] Even this has been absorbed. It is now impossible to tell from what part of Korea a Korean comes by his physical appearance. Until about 1890, Koreans very rarely went abroad and, when they did, as captives of Mongol or Japanese, even more rarely returned with foreign spouses. During the Japanese Annexation, a Japanese population that varied from about 150,000 in 1910 to some 700,000 by 1944–45 lived in Korea. Admixture was exceedingly small, and all except a very small number of Japanese wives of Koreans were repatriated by 1947. Before and since, largely for the "security" reasons noted, no ethnic minority of significance has lived in Korea for centuries. Resident aliens numbered only 24,000 in 1960 and have varied little for some time; almost all are Chinese.[15] Korea is one of the comparatively few nations of the world without either ethnic or minority problems. On the one hand, such ethnic homogeneity reduced sources of conflict and tension. But by the same token it eliminated sources of social innovation. Korea lacked the creative or modernizing minorities known to so much of the world. With no minorities to be protected, less need existed for safeguarding rights; and the development of liberal attitudes lacked stimulus.

CULTURE

The culture brought into the peninsula, though more diverse than that of today, partook of much the same relative homogeneity as the ethnic composition. Archeology shows us that, though culture was unevenly developed throughout the peninsula, it was relatively uniform, compared to that in China, Japan, or Southeast Asia, more especially so after about 700 A.D.

Deep religious differences, such as have divided so many nations and influenced their political development, have had less effect on Korea. Shamanism has been and remains the underlying religion of all Korean areas. It has been overlaid first, from the fourth century on, by Buddhism, then, mostly from the fourteenth century on, by neo-Confucianism. The mix has not been entirely even nor the coatings of equal thickness but they have, by and large, been applied nation-wide. Buddhist and Confucian influence is slight in most islands, including Cheju, and is less strong in the northeast and northwest than in the areas to the south, but such differences have never been articulated in major political ways to trouble the unity of the state. Though the Buddhist–Confucian transition was not without acrimony and tension, Korea has known no religious wars and, with the exception of the Tonghak, 1860–1900 — more a sociopolitical than a religious movement — no religious revolts or insurrections; the land has enjoyed throughout most of its history a relatively exemplary religious concord.[16]

The educational and even behavioral pattern has likewise approached national uniformity, probably largely as a result of the Yi governing elite, who made it one of the dynasty's major preoccupations to see the doctrines and especially the behavioral pattern of Confucianism spread and enforced throughout the country. The educational system and the local influence of the ruling class were directed to this end. An astonishingly continuous and widespread system of exiling had the added effect of spreading the court culture and value system into even the most outlying portions of the land. Five centuries imprinted this system deeply upon the whole country. Island and fishing communities, the outcast groups, and, to a lesser degree, the northerners were less deeply indoctrinated than the core of the country, but such variation has had comparatively little political or national significance.

Sinified government magnified unity. Ruling through carefully standardized institutions and relatively uniform means, its spirit was that of a jealous centralism dedicated to the obliteration of any "unorthodox" activities. Not only political but also economic activities that would have encouraged regional growth, the accumulation of individual wealth, or diverse influences from abroad through trade were forbidden or rigidly controlled.

Such regional differences as originally existed were therefore steadily eliminated through thirteen hundred years. A uniform nation-state had been created by at least the seventeenth century, the middle of the Yi period.[17] Moreover, the smallness of the country, certain fluidities in its social system, the rapid appointments and exiles of its officials, the far-flung chain of regional markets, and the lack of internal obstructions as a result of the absence of local or feudal power tended to homogenize the culture. Thus, in contrast to even the unity of Japan, one finds in Korea remarkably few "pockets" of people with deviant ways, living in isolation from the general society.[18] To an extent decidedly exceptional, the sources of unity in Korea are strong. Even today, in keeping with the experience of centuries, potential divisive threats to it come mostly from the capital, not the provinces.

THE EARLY DEVELOPMENT OF POLITICAL CENTRALISM

The national bent for centralization was soon and strongly reflected in the political system. We are far from being able to complete any exact analysis of the initial terms of unity and cohesion, but what we know is of interest.[19] Silla society (ca. 300–935 A.D.) was structured on lineage groups known as "bone ranks," from the chief of which the kings and, originally, queens were chosen. When this rank began dying out, queens, and finally kings, came from the next rank. Officials were chosen from high bone ranks under the kings. "Bones" appear to have been the basis of "Six Groups," which controlled the capital area and, after the end of the seventh century when Silla began a primitive version of the Chinese examination system, dominated its semi-Sinified government bureaucratic ranks.[20] Even local officials were drawn from these central ranks and received their lands, theoretically at least, from government grant. These "groups" were apparently the representatives of the societies of various local areas at first probably drawn by common fighting cause under one banner, then united and formalized around the "Six Groups." Originally non-lineage, they became lineage groups and were increasingly associated with the central government. A bureaucratic system developed such that even examination candidates were limited to hereditary ranks. Merit and ascriptive systems here began their long conflict, but it is the centralizing effect which concerns us. By exam or by incorporating local rank into hereditary central rank, central bureaucracy continually drew the elite away from local concerns toward central government. Except through Buddhist temples, local power left few impressive remains. The immense gulf the Silla tombs show us between the standards of the capital and of the countryside betray the values of the period.

Silla's centralization contained a further remarkable feature. It was not — certainly during the last centuries, perhaps never — lodged in an autocrat. The Silla king was the first among equals, his legitimacy derived from his "bone" status. There is little indication of divinity in rule. In a fashion reminiscent of the Western Tungus, ascriptive leadership groups instead of honored and selected individuals bore what amounted to sovereign powers in council. Each had, on lineage basis, equal qualification and voice, special competence carrying, apparently, small weight. The top council, called *hwabaek*, determined the (non-hereditary) succession to the throne and sometimes exercised a veto over the king's decisions. Reflecting the importance of each element in the central council, discussion was supposed to produce unanimity, and "it was the custom that any single disagreement brought the termination of the discussion on the specific issue . . ." [21] The *hwabaek*, not the kings, may have drawn on religious sanction. We are told that they always met on one of the four "sacred peaks" near Kyŏngju. High-born shamans also played a role in the society, possibly at the level of the central council.[22] Thus the drawing of the elite to the capital was seemingly accompanied by the political and religious institutionalization of their access to power and right to rule. The powers of councilorship added to the lures that brought men to the capital and kept them there more certainly than a royal autocracy would have done. A peculiar system of centralized oligarchy was initiated that has long persisted and may be viewed as the expression of a society demanding in multi-membered councils access of maximum numbers to power; through this device cultural concentration on the values of central rule began unusually early and intensely in Korea's history.

In essence, the Koryŏ Dynasty (918–1392) continued these centralist tendencies.[23] It inherited from Silla and further developed an extensive Buddhist monastic system. This partially counterbalanced the capital with an essentially local force, but these thousands of temples and monasteries were also local representatives of the government; for Buddhism, as the established national religion, became an instrument of rule. Temples existed partly to pray — and even fight — for national security and to communicate support for the Koryŏ throne and its system, and the upper monastic hierarchy was appropriately interwoven with the royal and noble houses of the country. The system was thus reminiscent of that known to pre-revolutionary Russia, to Europe in more distant times, and to Ethiopia today. The temple-monastery was a fruitful institution, useful for both central and local purposes. With its rise and power must be closely associated the capacity of Korean culture to stand close to the forefront of world cultural achievement during much of the Koryŏ period, a position Korea was soon to lose when the Yi rulers weakened Buddhist institutions.

YI CENTRALISM

Centralized council rule continued to characterize the Koryŏ system and was transmitted with little break to the Confucian Yi Dynasty that overthrew Koryŏ in 1392. High council, rejoicing in a succession of titles, continued to be the locus of chief Koryŏ power, and the decisions to call both the founder of the Koryŏ regime and, nearly five centuries later, the founder of the Yi regime to the throne were made by this same highest body.[24] At the same time, as sinification mounted, the central bureaucracy and the examination system became stronger and more formal, and China's powerful neo-Confucianism broadened its influence in Koryŏ's last century (1291–1392).

The Yi Dynasty proved itself the culmination of these long developments. In its 518 years (1392–1910), the already old themes of Korean political pattern and rule received their most enduring institutionalization and were transmitted to modern times, indeed to living memory.

The change from Koryŏ to Yi power was accompanied by considerably more revolution than previous Korean dynastic change. Confucianism, especially in the form expounded by Chu Hsi in twelfth-century China, replaced Buddhism as the state cult, and subservience to the Ming became the state policy of the Yi. The aims of government and its bureaucracy became Confucian; the political qualities of obedience, loyalty, and remonstrance strengthened within the value system. A miniature of the immense impedimenta of the largest and most centralized state on earth ruled Korea. Its five centuries of dominance affected every sphere of Korean life. China's uniquely continuous and mature concentration on the problems of government and social order became, more than ever, the lodestar of Korean political and social stability.

Confucianism was, first of all, a universalistic system. It provided for a comprehensive explanation and rule of life. It penetrated, during its long dominance, every portion of the peninsula and, with differing depth, every level of society. Its terms were resorted to not only for state organization and conduct but for that of family, guild, and clan. In these respects, it resembled the medieval church of Europe. But it differed vitally in its complete lack of division between church and state. Unlike European and even Near Eastern society, the church had no separate hierarchy. The apex of everything was the monarch and the upper bureaucracy that controlled him. Those exercising political power tended, as has been said of China, "to be absolute within their own interpretation of the ethical code." [25] Officials represented this power in the king's name. Unlike Europe's medieval church or, to a lesser degree, Islamic communities, or, perhaps, even Koryŏ Buddhism, the Yi system allowed no institutions outside central government in which moral or religious power could, with any degree of independence, inhere in such a way as to check central power.[26] The system gave the development of pluralism no prop and tended to cantilever society so powerfully toward central power as to induce covert social mobility to reach it.

As in China, Confucianism was built around the "Five Relationships" or "Bonds": father and son, husband and wife, ruler and subject (or prince and minister) elder and younger brother, friend and friend. The first three, the "Three Bonds," were most essential. These relationships formed a chain, but it is pertinent to observe that, when viewed from a "feudal" European or even Japanese viewpoint, the chain was incomplete, if not broken. Strong within household and village, it envisioned a world in which individuals or family heads had direct relationships with the ruler — direct at least emotionally — and it failed to provide guidance in relationships with one's superiors in organizations between the village and the throne or with colleagues in such organizations. Beyond village bonds, it was weak in all representational relationships.

The effect of direct confrontation between ruler and ruled that these relationships adumbrated was reinforced by their dominantly authoritarian nature. All except the last relationship, between friend and friend (the least emphasized), involved inequality and obedience. The obedience of son to father was the core of the system. The enforcement of this obedience and of the relationship lay, in all except rare "state" cases, with the father. Confucianism's numerous texts, even its codes, in Korea as in China, took these relationships as their central theme, constantly comparing one with another and supporting them with an elaborate ethical code accompanied by exacting standards of propriety that approached the force of law. Thus attitudes toward the ruler, toward authority and government, which in a feudal society tended to lie outside the home to be determined by intermediate bodies such as churches, monasteries, schools, guilds and the like, were, in China and Korea, determined within the home and subject to parental discipline. Rebelliousness to political authority was equated with rebelliousness to father. Obedience was deeply ingrained: the government — an encompassing control mechanism built into the home, extending to clan, academy (*sŏwŏn*), or family — organized administration and education so that no large groups could exercise rights and responsibilities except in the prescribed way.

Finally, Confucianism was not only a political and an enforcement system but also a moral, ethical, and religious one. It had strong doctrines and impressive texts, rites, and ceremonies. Yet it had, in effect, no separately structured church. Its theory was of rule by the sage. But the sage was part of an embracing, unitary moral system of which the emperor was high priest. Social progress was, on the whole, felt to take place when the sage correctly perceived the true intent of the classics so as to apply them to the given situation. Individual insights were sometimes respected and occasionally rewarded, but individualism had no place in the system. In essence, such theory strengthened education and individual understanding but made a separate church superfluous and even impossible. The question of whose understanding should dominate and in what degree was decided not by a church hierarchy but by governmental appointment; the ruler was, theoretically, the chief sage, and the wiser the official the higher should be his standing. The ruler was thus the apex not only of the administrative but of the moral and religious system. He was responsible to Heaven for the political-moral tone of the realm.[27] His bureaucrats, ruling in his name, were sanctioned with a double value: the literati were, in effect, administrators, judges, theologians.

The system prevented the strong development of church organization, hence of any church-state contest. It deprived the polity of a powerful rival hierarchy. The bureaucracy became the highest career; its power over all others grew; the centripetal forces of the state multiplied. Buddhism and its hierarchy were forced into the role of the *bête noire* and systematically eliminated as an alternative.[28] The function, for example, not only of the European church but even of Islam and its guilds and associations as pockets in a society that, while "giving unto Caesar," still were able to resist encroachments and make authoritarian rulers pause could not be institutionalized and developed in Korea. Government and administration became entwined with religious precept, departures from it cast in the role of heresy. Innovation and change were thus fettered. On the one hand, lack of alternative careers whetted political concern and contest for power through Confucian doctrinal criticism; opposition criticism was ever present and often vicious. On the other hand, any change involved not just administrative but, in effect, religious struggle. In theory and to some extent in practice, this religio-political combination served to knot society together into an obedient whole. By riveting on government not only political but also moral and religious attentions, it tended to introduce a pattern of deep, emotional concern with politics and to flood administration with political, ethical, almost religious qualms, principles, and grounds for attack. Operating within Korea's confined geography, this pattern induced enormous centralization of politics, administration, values, and even emotion.

Institutional Gaps

To the hierarchical lacunae implicit in the Five Bonds were now added important institutional gaps. From 500 A.D. on the temple-monastery had been the chief institution outside the central government. Thousands of temples had covered the land, scores of great size, apparently surpassing most in China.[29] Often founded by a king or powerful court official, they had been the great developers of the countryside. Through them, regions still remote were first brought under the plough, visited by arts and techniques and assembled into meaningful, differentiated, "modern" communities. Their great ceremonies, like that of the Lanterns or Buddha's birthday, brought remote villages together in rite and feast. They gave to the task of development common purpose and broad association. Their hierarchies united local areas with national purpose as they prayed for defense or were instructed through capital headquarters. Their learned members had not only religious wisdom but knowledge of technique and economics: the planting of upland areas with the mushroom or the teabush, the ever-filled granary for usurious loan against harvest failure, tile and pottery making, community food preparation, wood-carving, weaving, stonework. Institutional lending contracts, some-times under the name *kye*, flourished.[30] In the temples classes were not isolated but brought together for common, indeed frequently for developmental, purpose. Men of all ranks gave their sons as monks. Headed by royal or noble relatives, the temples often were endowed by the government with slaves. For centuries they must have been to Korea not only what the monastery was for medieval Europe but even what, in terms of inter-class cooperation, De Tocqueville found the fourteenth-century courts, assemblies, and semi-independent com-munities to have been for a pre-centralist France.[31] Equality was, of course, absent, but such institutional life, such subordination to a kind of law, the Vinaya, such embracing function made of the Silla and Koryŏ temple a kind of corporate institution similar to the monasteries of the European Middle Ages, sound foundation for more modern institutional life and economic development. When the Con-fucian Yi government ended state support for temples, they declined, and their vitality departed. The vigor Buddhism has retained in Vietnam it has largely lost in Korea.

The Koryŏ regime had established Buddhism as the official, state-supported religion. The Yi stripped it of state support and of all offi-cial role but had no proper substitute. Instead, the dynasty adopted from China the Sung, Yüan, and Ming concept of the *shu-yüan*, a local Confucian shrine with which was usually associated a school educating for the central bureaucracy. Such academies (*sŏwŏn*), be-ginning in 1543, boomed with factional warfare in the seventeenth century; by the end of the eighteenth, some 650 had been spawned, 270 with government sponsorship and lands, others locally sponsored, often by *yangban* clans (those from which officials were drawn).[32] The academy core was the shrine where the portrait and tablet of the patron scholar — usually of the local faction — were ensconced. Lit-erati who had dared oppose monarchs or governing factions were here singled out for enshrinement and emulation. It was a religio-political center, frequently associated with opposition politics. Entry was not completely dependent on *yangban* status; the *sŏwŏn* had some limited social mobility. Yet it was for those who could afford an education, its interests in Confucianism and politics had upper-class connotations, and it was only for men. It held rice lands but showed less economic initiative than Buddhism. Its ceremonies were far smaller, more exclusive and puritanical than those of the temple. It nourished adhesive factional loyalty and the conviction that education has political purpose, but it was rarely in itself an institution effective in checking the government; for that it was too small and had too little hierarchical development, and it was too dependent on its contacts in the capital for power to develop much self-reliant independence. It prepared men for a world where centralized values predominated, a world in which even local status derived from local *yangban* contact with the Seoul world. The *sŏwŏn* was institutionally no substitute for the temple at any time. When even the *sŏwŏn* were, in the 1870's, ordered closed, the countryside became devoid of almost all important institutional life.

Confucianism had the effect of aggravating the problem of insufficient general participation in the dominant value system. Confucian philosophy, religious practice, and theory of government were complex and demanding. Lengthy education and mastery of the Chinese ideographical and textual universe were required for full participation; they were increasingly exalted as the only bridge to power and satisfaction. But few could afford them. Almost the same was true in the religious field. Confucianism's ceremonies were complicated, its equipment private and costly, and public festival and emotionalism were deprecated as "superstitious." Most could not participate; many found the Confucian emotional world jejune. The common people hence tended to go outside the system to shamanism and a popularized Buddhism for satisfaction, risking Confucian "upper-class" condemnation. The institutions that, like the temple, had given even slaves some institutional participation in the dominant values were now undermined. Class and value gaps less typical of late Koryŏ times opened. Jealousy and a feeling of moving toward the top by non-institutional means, hence by individual mobility, was encouraged. Vertical communications were cut in a way that England and Japan were not to know. No hierarchy in whose rites there was popular participation now led in stepped progression from rice field and mountain slope toward royal court. Behind the unity of Confucianism's new religio-political integration lay a gradual process of alienation in values and in society; and behind that, in turn, were stirrings of unrestricted competition. Confucian values challenged and aroused, but the upward path was an individual one for a few through examinations, not one lying primarily through institutions.

In the country the great halls of temples were replaced by *sŏwŏn*, far smaller and self-consciously austere. In Seoul, palace buildings multiplied. The bureaucracy grew with them in impressiveness and elaboration. The attention withdrawn from the countryside devolved on the capital.

The Central Apex

Like the country itself, the administration was unitary and centralized, a pyramid atop the state, the king its apex. The State Council far surpassed in power its Ming and Ch'ing prototypes. Under it came in classic Chinese pattern the Six Boards or Ministries, replete with ministers, vice-ministers, councilors, and secretaries.[33] The Royal Secretariat handled — and sometimes interfered with — the documents flowing to or from the king; rich numbers of tribunals and boards moved off and on the Yi stage.[34] Resonant titles beckoned: First, Second, and Third Mentors to the Crown Prince; Superintendents of Music, of Military Training, of the Royal Stables; Supervisor of Sacrifices and Posthumous Names; magistrates, counselors, bailiffs, inspectors, secretaries, censors, scribes, tutors of every kind. All were scrupulously ranked in nine degrees, each degree itself divided into two classes. Each post was variously colored with profit and prestige, those outside Seoul having often much of the former, less of the latter. The gate to this world was the examination system, demanding and elaborately administered, as ringed with precautions as a papal election, its chief passers honored with royal audience, their village homes specially decorated. The exacting form and elaboration of the bureaucracy was symbolic of its unique place in a state otherwise lacking institutions or, for the most part, even sharp definitions. An ambitious structure borrowed from the most impressive bureaucratic system then known, it embedded in the small Yi state an artificial central weight beyond balance.

The Vortex of Centralism

Toward this central structure, the forces of Yi state Confucianism relentlessly directed all ambition. The examination system attracted and often drained the brightest talent from the countryside. Along with individual ability, the main lines of the chief noble clans, the

Chŏng of Tongnae, the Kim of Andong, and others, moved permanently to the capital and added the name of its streets to theirs: Kim of Ch'angdong, Chŏng of Hoedong. Their clansmen became Seoul men, lived in the capital most of their lives, unless forced out of it through exile or disfavor, fought the battles of the court either as central participants or on the sidelines, and infused their lives with its culture. As Paris was for France, Seoul was not simply Korea's largest town; it was Korea. In the court lay the only drama of the land worth living, the chief rumors worth hearing, the only culture of richness worth enjoying.[35] If one were "called" to Seoul, one stayed or sought to stay, as quickly as possible losing country ties. Conversely, staying too long too far from Seoul was held to be tantamount to forfeiting one's own ambitions and jeopardizing the chances of one's children. Birth in a "remote" place might subject one to unkind gossip if not to political attack. Then and now, one of the chief functions of local gentry (since 1910 local landlords) or such local leadership as existed was to make periodic visits to the capital, maintain a residence there if rich, or, if not, visit with the "highest" friend possessed.[36] As in China, the chief privilege of the local *yangban* was access to the bureaucracy; his real power lay in the knowledge of the magistrate that any exam passer had claims on those in power who passed in the same year as he and that he would not hesitate to press these claims over the magistrate's head. Thus even what passed for local power was central power extended.[37] Even the architecture of the local town seemed structured around communication from the capital as a prayer rug is oriented to Mecca. On the wide porches of its main houses the returned landlord re-enacted for his small-town intimates the daily dramas he had savored in the capital. On their smaller porches the second- and third-hand versions of these tales were re-enacted for the lower circles of rural society. The court became the entertainment of the country. Talents arose with which the culture is still rife: gift for mimicry, appetite for acting, and the gamut of the raconteur's lusts.

As Seoul was heart and brain of the country, so was politics its core, the eye of every Korean storm. Government was not a static, lifeless force. It was the great drama of an otherwise patient or unaggressive agricultural people. It absorbed virtually all the energies of a numerous upper class, either as officials or as active spectators — hangers-on in the houses of the contestants, memorial writers, political teachers in local academies. Looking back on the five-hundred year Yi history, one is hard put to find what else was contributed except that which directly or indirectly fed this drama. Government was a great vortex summoning men rapidly into it, placing them briefly near the summits of ambition, and then sweeping them out, often ruthlessly to execution or exile. Of the patient, seasonal rhythm of the rice fields it had no reck or ken. Excitement pulsated daily, hourly. The Censorate met twice a day. Memorials and remonstrances flowed from it in steady stream. Officials were daily reviewed and dropped. With legal boundaries lacking, few matters were free from contest. The dynasty prated of tranquility, but it lived on agitation and controversy.

An ominous tattoo of accusation was the central theme: the king dared to wound a pig within the palace walls; a minister of the Board of War had conducted business transactions while on a tribute mission; another had a heretical belief in shamanism, or Buddhism; others had deserted a first wife without appropriate reasons, eaten meat in a mourning period, or had been simply — but with as much finality — "interest-seekers." Attacks were the daily meat of court life. Those on His Majesty were slightly oblique — though Louis XIV would not for a moment have stomached them. Otherwise, there were no limits. The king's brothers, his aunts, his brothers-in-law, his nephews, his cousins, the merit subjects he appointed, those whom his father appointed, his officials, their relatives — none were beyond cavil and censure. Formal Censorate accusation, detailed and textually referenced like a legal brief, might reach five separate cases a day. Though the dynasty was, for its length, fairly free of outright coups until its last decades, few governments have been more laden from one end to another with rumors and imputation of plot and crime by association. The vocabulary of accusation and derogation steadily waxed; investigation, public and private, flourished: the nine-hundred-odd fascicles of the Yi annals must be not only one of the longest but one of the most scurrilous written creations of human history.[38]

The eye of the storm was as dangerous as it was attractive. No tally of the lives lost in the purges, royal and factional, of the dynasty has been made, but they almost surely reached the thousands, virtually all victims being of the ruling class. For crimes sometimes as minor as that of spilling wine on the king's robe or taking the "incorrect" side in a dispute, officials would be tortured, beheaded, exposed, dismembered, gibbeted; their property was confiscated, their houses torn down, the sites ploughed over, their brothers beaten, their wives and families turned into public slaves, their relatives deprived of rank and privilege. Sometimes whole noble families would thus be rooted out or would sink into slavery. Between 1495 and 1863 at least sixteen sons and grandsons of kings were condemned to death for treason; most were innocent.[39] Not even the dead were exempt: one monarch, Yŏnsan'gun, pulverized the bones of dead "criminals" and dismembered and beheaded corpses within the grave, penalties well calculated to impress a society entranced with ancestor worship.[40] Yet the higher the risk, the greater the haste to take part.

As participation in the capital was the highest value, so was banishment from it the commonest penalty. Exiling was omnipresent, reaching thousands in every corner of the ruling class, including kings (Tanjong, Kwanghaegun, and Yŏnsan'gun), the highest ministers, and the greatest scholars. It was, in fact, one of the few passes at rural development undertaken by the dynasty, which thus inadvertently conferred on its most distant and least-developed places princes of the blood and their suites, officials of every rank, and scholars of high and low degree. Some places, like the isle of Chindo, received their culture, learning, ideas of cooking, manners, and what slim resources of method an Yi official possessed almost entirely from this source. Yet banishment's hectic pulse fitted it better for inoculating the countryside with capital ambitions than for development.[41] Some victims stayed very briefly before either being recalled (and often promoted) or killed. Some, like the great scholar Chŏng Tasan, lived out much of their lives in exile, producing there in bearable comfort and a peace unknown to the capital nearly all their works.[42] Others eked out an oblivion, fed through holes in their thorn-hedged prison huts. Whatever the tolerance in treatment allowed, the care and feeding of these "visitors from the capital" was of far more concern to local officials than the well-being of the local population.

Subordination of the Economy

Property and the economy were as oriented toward central power as politics. There was no real theory of private property. Indeed, as in many modernizing nations, privacy was regarded as virtually sub-versive.[43] Economic status was based exclusively on political power. The monarch and his officials had first claims on all and could, in theory, distribute and redistribute as they saw fit.[44] Bureaucracy was increasingly a self-serving, not a public-serving, instrument, see-ing the state and its population largely as a farm to be "eaten" and exploited. The first act of the founding Yi monarch was to promul-gate a new land reform based, like the earlier Chinese system of the Sui and T'ang dynasties, on the theory of state ownership. In essence it was not different from the initial land reforms of preceding dynasties. Urban land was similarly treated. Lots for residence in Seoul were awarded by the government in the name of the king; the size of the house, the materials of which it was made, and, to some extent, even the furniture within it were regulated by the rank or status of the owner.[45] Less prestigious stretches of the capital, far from the palace, were set aside for commercial activity by the gov-ernment's "grace and favor." Merchants were not allowed to own rice lands. No concept could therefore develop of land accumulated as a result of personal effort. Since the wealth of Korea was almost entirely in land, this prohibition greatly inhibited the possibility of capital accumulation.

Landed estates likewise had little base for secure or continuous development. Land, owned by the king in theory, had the function of providing livelihood for the peasant and revenue support for officials. The latter were assigned what were, in effect, most of its taxes. They and their descendants usually tried to hang onto it thereafter; local estates and residences and *de facto* private owner-ship did develop. But there was neither legal nor felt concept of *freies Eigentum;* the feeling never died that one's justification for controlling the land lay in capital and court, not in the use one made of property, one's residence on it, or any development effort.[46] As late as 1893, the rebellious Tonghak peasants declared, "We are simple . . . ignorant people . . . and we till the ground of our king to maintain our fathers and mothers." [47] What was needed by the landlord was constant reaffirmation of access to central power. A continuous local position whose development would benefit the de-scendants of the owners — the motivations of a Duke of Newcastle, a Lord of Satsuma, a Prussian junker — had no force in Yi Korea. Few great historic Korean estates lasted even into this century, and none survive today.

Lack of Development

What private initiative in local development did not supply, the government system did not make up. Local areas were, as in the later French monarchy, operated as part of the national bureaucracy, not as an expression of the autonomy of the local community. They were divided into eight provinces, headed by governors whose positions often included that of local military commander. Five cities next to P'yŏngyang in size were headed by prefects. Below these were *pu* (a kind of department), *kun* (counties) headed by *kunsu* (county magistrates), and islands. The last three were in turn divided into townships, or *myŏn*, below which came villages. The characteristic Confucian break between village and formal government came at the township level; above it all officials were appointed by the central government, below it they were informally "elected" by consultation of elders and, sometimes, other citizens and were confirmed by the local magistrates. Over township and village the day-to-day control of the government was, as in China, loose and occasional, informality and a certain superficiality in rule prevailing until the coming of Japanese administration. From the central bureaucratic viewpoint, local jobs enjoyed little esteem. The *yangban* county magistrates under the "law of avoidance" were never of local origin and were changed constantly, frequently being transferred even before arrival on post.[48] Their actual functions were, except in crises, largely confined to major legal cases: these arose rarely since Confucianism encouraged delegation of daily justice and controls to the family. Local clerks (*ajŏn*) were more active, but their work, largely concerned with taxation and *corvée*, could hardly be called prestigious or beneficial to the people. Government was there to exploit; the magistrate "ate the village"; little service was given. As the vortex increased and the number of aspirants surged, exploitation grew ever more harsh.

The auspices for local leadership — hence for the strong individual leadership it might bring to the capital — were adverse. A bright boy went through the examination system and left for the capital. The magistrate by terms of service, the *ajŏn* by status, the village chief by function were all discouraged from aggressive, continuous leadership. Of the thousands of Yi men known to us for fame of some sort, no more than a handful can be classed as local leaders.

Even the great scholars, the "grass-roof protesters" who scorned government service, were more noted for scholarship or moral example than for aggressive local action. Honored, they had little power. Only toward the end, mostly in the last century, did men of the lower classes occasionally find personal and local provocation sufficient to lead a revolt.[49] Until the Tonghak, such leaders were more flashes in a pan of acute economic and social discontent than exemplars of a sound local leadership tradition.

Beneath the county, even to a great extent beneath the province, yawned an administrative and social gap. Villages had only weak, informal horizontal integration with other communities in the same county, virtually none beyond. Confucian relationships gave little incentive for bridging the gap. Regionalism, despite the importance Koreans attribute to it, is weak compared to Europe and Japan. Men have died for Burgundy, York, Venice, and Satsuma; no man ever died for Chŏlla-do. In Seoul, given a strong myth of regionalism, sensitivity to even slightly different accents, and, above all, lack of other associational vehicles, men from the same province do tend to make common cause. Few, however, knew each other at home, and within their province they neither felt nor needed great unity: difference of county, township, and village there loomed large. Local schools inculcated — and still inculcate — no local concerns. The happiness and pride of family and village life made for much viability and self-containment but not for bridges to the society above. Lacking secondary organizations, the Korean state, far more than post-revolutionary France, tended to absorb into itself all organizing activity of a social character.[50] Every lure and ambition urged rural talent to find a place in the central structure. But there was no graduated path: one had to leap. No vicar, no squire, no lord brought to the village Kim the stepped, upward communication known to the swain of Northumberland and Owari.

2

The Traditional Society

Where the intermediate structures of religion, local government, guild, business, or voluntary association are weak, social divisions may constitute the last defenses the community throws up against the extremes of mobility: social atomization and political disorder. The weakness of Korea's intermediate institutions thus leads us to examine the defenses of her social structures and how well they served. For the presence or absence of social barriers will, in the vacuum of other firm institutions, probably largely determine the cohesiveness to which society is accustomed. In mass societies, social mobility will be an important determinant of the formation of parties and political institutions, of the social ends that politics serves and the dynamics it engenders.

The Yi Dynasty formally recognized four social classes: (1) the ruling class, known as the *yangban,* monopolized virtually all government positions and alone had effective access to the more important examinations; (2) the *chungin,* a small "middle" class, consisted of professionals hired at the lower levels of government, chiefly the central government, and viewed as technicians or clerks; (3) the *sangmin* (also known as *yangmin* or *sangnom*) were the common people — farmers, merchants, artisans; (4) at the bottom came the *ch'ŏnmin,* the "low-born," "degraded," or "vile" class, itself composed of several elements, including slaves.[1]

Such a description is the official one of the dynasty, which inscribed these class names on the *hop'ae,* or name tags, that all citizens had to carry with them, made of different materials according to social rank. Scholars have followed this description with more or less minor deviations.[2] But further inquiry casts doubt on the extent to which the sharpness of this description corresponded with the realities of the Yi social system. The grounds for this doubt appear most forcefully in an examination of the *yangban* class.

THE YANGBAN

From the tenth century, the word *yangban* was used to denote the two ranks or "files" (*pan*) of officials, civil on one side, military on the other, ranged ceremonially before the throne. The *yangban* were, first of all, the officials of the dynasty above clerical level. The class was theoretically coterminous with the officer-level bureaucracy. In original theory as derived from China, admission was through a merit system based on passing the civil or, later, military examinations, which came, by the end of the fourteenth century, usually to be given triennially. The monarch's right to appoint men of special merit or deserving family directly was from the end of the fifteenth century increasingly opposed within the government (especially by the Censorate), and recipients of such favor were almost always less highly regarded. The theory was that, outside the royal relatives, success in the examinations was the means of attaining *yangban* status and the consequent right to draw income from a small landholding. The system seemed, on the surface, to intend the reproduction in Korea of the Chinese system of comparatively mobile merit-class rule, divorced from hereditary privilege. Probably the most enlightened system of bureaucratic recruitment anywhere practiced in the world of that time, its possession enhanced Yi Korea's cultural standing in the ancient Chinese world in much the same way that the possession, in appearance, at least, of a modern legal system tends to enhance international standing today.

From the beginning, however, the Korean version worked quite differently from what theory prescribed and, apparently, quite differently from the manner in which recruitment to the bureaucracy seems to have worked in China.[3] The law codes of the Yi period prescribed that the right to sit for the examination should be limited to *yangban* descendants. The Korean version was therefore less a mobility system than China's, and its manipulation produced an inner clique of court "aristocrats" around the throne with a kind of pre-sumptive right on higher position. These were the heirs of the system of the oligarchs around the Silla and Koryŏ throne; they may, in some cases, have been their descendants. Their rights were often pressed through their place on the twenty-one lists of "Merit Sub-jects" that monarchs published between 1392 and 1728, which marked them as men specially entitled to position, land (in most cases, hereditary grants), and reward.[4] Where necessary, the exams could be manipulated to afford the entry of junior members; it is evident from many recorded complaints — among them that of the rebel Hong Kyŏng-nae in 1812 — that they were. The inner clique "aristocrats" further consolidated their position by membership in powerful control bodies like the Censorate, insisting that such priv-ilege be limited to "first-grade clans from . . . ancient Korea."[5] Ensconced in such bodies, they exercised great influence over the appointment process throughout the government and resisted at-tempts, even by the king, to dilute their control. They appear to have been a tight, Seoul-residing, intermarried clique that did its best to sit astride the mobility struggle.[6] A minuscule proportion of the total who in Korea claimed *yangban* status, it was chiefly this small group that deserved the name and might be considered an "aristocracy."

Lesser clans also inhabited the system. The exams, however ma-nipulated, could not be completely controlled; nor was it feasible to fill all positions with members of a tight clique. Most *yangban* clans of any pretension had discontinuous access to power, but their interests produced more rivalry than class cohesion. Many lesser clans, whose exact status at the time of initial exam passing or royal appointment is, especially near the beginning of the dynasty, not always clear, had extremely discontinuous access to appointment thereafter and competed with each other for more bureaucratic power in an atmosphere of bitterness that Korea's smallness did much to enhance. The status of other "middle" *yangban*, however, though originally established by appointment, derived more from repute as exemplars of Confucian morality. Scholars, teachers at local academies, writers of eloquent and upbraiding memorials to the court — these embodied that life of social and behavioral exam-ple which was the theoretical Confucian justification of the class.[7] Where others tended to advance status by accepting appointment, they shone by refusing it. They are the foundation of a long and continuous tradition of intellectual alienation from power whose heirs are today's university professors. They were far fewer in number than their appointment-seeking brethren, though their opinions carried more weight. Together these *yangban* formed a "middle" layer many times the size of the power-holding court aristocrats.[8] Yet it was perhaps not much more than a significant minority among the hundreds of thousands eventually claiming *yangban* status.[9]

To demonstrate from firm data the numbers of persons in these *yangban* categories is not now possible. Tax records seem not yet to have been analyzed to clarify the situation, and other statistics are lacking. Estimates made at the end of the dynasty varied from a total of about 2,000,000 *yangban* down to 89,050 households (possibly, 400,000–450,000 people).[10] The latter, based on a Japanese "survey" of unspecified methods seems to be the only estimate above the purely impressionistic.[11] The differences in these estimates are plausibly explained by a contemporary Japanese observer who gave a comparable figure of 100,000 for total *yangban* around 1910, remarking that if the estimate included *hyangban* or *t'oban* (types of rural squires), semi-*yangban*, and *yangban*-related elements, it might well be between 300,000–400,000 households or some one and a half to two million people.[12] Some less plausible estimates of this mass of semi-*yangban* run still higher.[13]

The inexactness of these figures is revealing. It is clear that, at the end of a long dynasty in which a "rigid" social system is said to have operated, neither the government, the people, nor the *yangban* themselves were in any agreement on how large the ruling class was or who was in it. There was a vague partial consensus that two million people considered themselves — or were thought to consider themselves — *yangban*. This many would constitute a "governing class" of nearly 18 percent of the population — an enormous percentage for a hermit agrarian society with small functional differentiation and limited needs for leadership. The figure is suspiciously large, however, for a class supposedly emergent from approximately 14,000 civil exam passers, many from the same families, and a modest number of military passers during the entire Yi Dynasty.

Since the *yangban* class was observably large, serious disagreement as to its dimensions tended to confuse the definitions of the entire social system and now confuses scholars who attempt to define it. Statistics for membership in other classes are also lacking, and few even tried to estimate their size. Whatever it once had been, the Korean social system became extremely ill-defined; hence it was clearly of very doubtful rigidity or cohesiveness. Yet, in a Korea having few other sources of cohesion and institutional life, lack of these qualities in classes would have important consequences for the society, its leadership, and the viability of its political life. How did this situation occur? To answer such questions leads us to inquire into the putative *yangban* majority and how it came to be formed.

In Chinese theory and, to some degree, in practice, status obtained by official rank was tied to the record of the man obtaining it. It was, of course, remembered by his descendants, but if not renewed by their acquisition of official position, the status withered. The Korean codes seem to lack an official statement of such withering except in the case of titles. Korean titles, like some Chinese but unlike European, lessened one degree with each generation and were extinguished entirely in five generations for the descendants of royal sons, in three generations for the descendants of Merit Subjects.

There was some informal tendency, unsanctioned by codes, for the same to occur to the normal *yangban* status.[14] The status withered, but the claim had to persist; there was no alternative to society's monolithic concentration on the avenues to central power and its privileges. The privileges were succulent: eligibility to take the official examinations and to be selected on passing, hence access to the country's only prestigious career; exemption from taxation; exemption of one's household, including slaves, from military service; special trial privileges, including that of substituting one's slaves' punishment for one's own; the informal function of influencing or moderating the local magistrates' decisions through central connections; and, of course, all manner of social prestige and precedence. The obligations of status, in contrast, were few. The *yangban* had to keep a family record, *chokpo,* and a theoretically strict household registry, at least if he wanted his descendants to pass Censorate screening or to marry "well." He was supposed to know the classics and how to perform rites properly and to maintain certain standards of behavior, the principal one of which was that he was to avoid work and hold himself aloof from members of other classes. In practice, both officially and informally there was great reluctance to relinquish a status so profitable and undemanding.

The problem worked on the society for five hundred continuous dynastic years. Those who thought themselves eligible steadily increased, but the number of jobs that were the formal justification for status apparently remained, until the coming of foreign influence, not much over 1,000, hopelessly few in proportion to the demand. As generations passed, most *yangban* found themselves ever more distant from their ancestor's position and from their own possibility of renewing it. The result on the one hand tended to sanction almost any scheme — influence-peddling, corruption, or even crime, however base — in order to get a government position. On the other, it contributed to the creation of an enormous "in-between" class of shadowy or pretender *yangban*. Many of these had "fallen from the capital" and are often called by Koreans *hyangban* or *t'oban,* "local squires." For modern analytical purposes, this social group (with its upward-rising commoner-born brethren) should be considered distinct.[15] Despite the problem of establishing their identity and although their position was technically uninfluential, consideration of the *hyangban* is crucial for understanding the modern Korean political pattern.[16]

One of the few studies locating this problem and laying bare the pattern of social and political mobility it contains is that of the noted Japanese expert on oriental population statistics, Shikata Hiroshi.[17] The extraordinary results of his examination of Yi local population records, if even approximately acceptable, appear to yield the following conclusions:

1. The total population in the districts for which Shikata found records was relatively stable during the entire century and a half covered, 1690–1858, being slightly lower at the end than in the beginning.

2. Natural *yangban* increase was slight, indeed negligible.[18]

3. Despite these conditions, the *yangban* population of these districts increased in terms of households 623.8 percent between 1690 and 1858. At the same time, commoner's households fell by 50.3 percent, and slave numbers fell 31.2 percent.

4. Hence the *yangban,* who had started out by constituting 7.4 percent of the numerical population in 1690, ended up by being 48.6 percent (70.3 percent of the number of households) in 1858; the commoners, who began by being 49.5 percent of the population, fell to 20.1 percent; and the slaves fell from 43.1 percent of the

population to 15.9 percent in the 1783–1789 period and 31.3 percent in 1858. The rate of *yangban* increase was rather constant, from 80 to 100 percent, in each of the four periods covered. The decrease in commoners, however, rose sharply from only 0.3 percent in the seventeenth century to 50.3 percent in the nineteenth century.[19]

We are thus led to believe that the increase which resulted in the Yi's enormous *yangban* population was, for the most part, not natural but a function of social mobility. The same is true for the decrease in the other two main classes, which Shikata takes generally to mean that large numbers of the slaves and despised groups moved up into commoner status while many commoners moved up into *yangban* status (presumably as *hyangban*). The extent of this movement was so great that, if these figures are in even the slightest way typical, the formal Yi social system may have become the exception and the covert class system the rule. The Yi social system had, in fact, probably a high degree of unacknowledged flexibility in middle levels. Only the upper *yangban* maintained really strict status, and only the hopelessly poor cleaved strictly to low status. The *hyangban*, the rural farmers, and the so-called despised classes could live together, communicate with and even marry each other behind the back of the formalities of law and society.[20]

Other sources shed light on the process. The *Sok taejŏn*, one of the Yi codes, prescribes one hundred strokes or exile for falsifying the census register (*hojŏk*), thus confirming the existence of the practice. The famous Confucian critic Chŏng Tasan (1762–1836) tells us that this penalty was not enforced.[21] It was especially easy to assume the low status of *yuhak* (a first-stage exam passer who had not completed the examinations or a *yangban* claimant who had nothing else to call himself), and the number of these increased markedly in the nineteenth-century period covered by the records. Slaves could also rise by risking their lives or contributing grain in times of national emergency, a practice for which there are many quoted examples, and by agreeing to excessive property exactions by officials (that is, bribery).[22] At the end of the dynasty, official position was more or less openly sold, and even before that letters of investiture (*kongch'ŏp*) were often traded.

The downward path was trodden when the aristocratic or royal ancestor fell from Seoul through exile or punishment or was edged out in factional fights, through long failure of a family to pass the examinations, or through poverty as new reigns and new favorites came. Countless historical instances of such falls, permanent or impermanent, can be cited.[23] *Yangban* status was, at first, prehensilely retained; the family often used it to appropriate what local lands it needed. Gradually, capital connections wore thin; the elite function of influencing or moderating local officials through central connections eroded. Strict marriage custom, avoidance of both work and money, the paraphernalia and food requirements of Confucian ceremony became harder and harder to maintain. Marriage with daughters of other local families, then commoners, finally even slaves, was contracted.[24] Lands were divided or forfeited to the more powerful. Heavy debt brought sale or exchange of status. To thousands — perhaps to more than retained status — a *yangban* past became a dusty record in the family *chokpo* and a hoarse laugh in village gossip. Even those arresting decline, keeping *hyangban* status and becoming rural landlords, rarely clove to the loneliness of aloof status. They shared the gaming tables, the wine pots, the funeral ceremonies, and the commercial opportunities of rural life with *ajŏn* on the way up.[25]

There was thus formed on the lower, rural stretches of Korean society a large and little-described group with limited governmental but with large social influence. It liked to call itself *yangban,* but it was not a nobility, or an aristocracy, or even an elite. It was an organ of mobility which thus could not possess firm ties and loyalties. Nor could it possess firm behavioral patterns that might freeze its mobile function. It melded not only classes but behavior. Communication downward was important to the *ajŏn-hyangban* since only thus could they carry on their rural functions. They also needed to communicate upward with officials. From above, they of course adopted Confucian ideals and behavior, an excellent melding vehicle, as Karl Wittfogel has observed.[26] At the same time, just as the Negro accent drifted upward into southern American speech, so did the spontaneity and some of the naturalness of formerly lower-class behavior seep upward in Korean society through the melding *hyangban* class. We see this pressure for behavioral change in Yi novels and in masked dances that pillory the pretentious, impecunious *yangban* frauds.

As the dynasty's end approaches, the enormous sleeves and hats of the upper class disappear. Once the aristocrat sat sedately on a donkey and was supported on both sides by servants when he traveled. He carried "nothing for himself not even his pipe . . . [for] supreme helplessness is the required convention." [27] Such behavior could not survive modern communication and new values. *Hyangban* and *ajŏn*, asked to fill, from circa 1895 on, expanded economic and political roles, brought with them new behavior. Lower- or middle-class speech replaced the elaborate address forms of deliberately cadenced language. Gregariousness ousted the aloofness once affected from all not within the charmed circle. The *yangban's values* — central power-holding, education — were transmitted downward, new behavior percolated up. As a discrete class, the *yangban* were destroyed. The aristocratic pattern vanished far more completely than that of Europe or even parts of the United States. The divided classes, the molded class personality type, the behavioral marks, and the clear class accents to be expected if a society had maintained a "rigid" class system continuously for five hundred years have been far more completely swept away than in Japan, India, and South America. Talk of class and respect for it became notable by their absence. Economic and modern educational gaps are obvious but beside these what few class differences remain are so hard to spot that the few Koreans interested must usually inquire about them if they wish (usually for marriage purposes) to know. Today extreme spontaneity (*kibun*), gregariousness, and humor mark the social pattern. Aristocratic form, ceremony, and restraint have given way to a middle- or even lower-class, no-holds-barred intimacy. As when found in the United States, the manners, the personality type, and the anti-aristocratic accents themselves suggest the presence of high mobility. For it the *hyangban* were the putative channel.

Such behavioral transmission adds powerfully to Shikata's evidence of the fluidity of late Yi society. Had rigidity been hundreds of years inbred, a continuously governing *yangban* class should have provided a reservoir of accepted leadership, trained, cohesive, confident, and useful for bridging the transitions to modern times. Even in decline, such a class should have exhibited aristocratic behavioral characteristics as a last badge of status, as in the *fin de siècle* society of Proustian France. Instead, *yangban* inflation of numbers accompanied by no advance in role or function eroded the kind of elite defense against the rise of mass values that England and, to some extent, Japan were able to stage. Relatively early, Korea's elite lost the ability to transmit its own values downward or to serve with confidence as leaders. Instead, the invasion of foreign Japanese values and behavioral patterns was greatest among them. Of the descendants of the important old aristocracy today, few play prominent roles and many have emigrated.[28] The failure of Korean society to transmit elite values coherently reflected in a class has largely robbed young Koreans of serious models and ideal types with which to form images of themselves and thus stand armed for their futures. Many young Koreans feel the lack of such models.

Korean clans reflect the same tendencies. Many have developed as covert class mobility channels rather than as unique groups preserving standards and interests peculiar to themselves. Few instances where clans took and were able to enforce common positions are known toward the end of the dynasty or since — many clans, like the Yŏhŭng Min, producing striking divisions over even such issues as opposition or cooperation with Japan. Rather than being units of action or position, they processed mobility; covertness undermined their authority; new entrants compromised their particularity. Monstrous clanopoli, like the Kimhae Kim with their putative several million members, rose to cover mobility.[29] The resulting concentration of half the Korean population under a few family names, so peculiar and unexplained a phenomenon, appears to be in part an effort to cloak with anonymity large-scale upward streaming toward status.

These processes had much to do with the erosion of Korea's leadership. The real leadership class of capital aristocracy was small, isolated, aloof, and vulnerable. The larger "governing" class was, in substantial degree, an elaborate fraud, possessing no leadership or cohesion and, behind behavioral posturing, the most tenebrous class boundaries. The *hyangban* on the downward path might shed aloofness enough to drink with a few neighbors but would still be too self-conscious to make common cause with them in public or speak to them in respectful language. His neighbor, on the other hand, might well be in upward migration, anxious to avoid consolidating himself with the group he was leaving, yet not sure enough of himself to stand firm with the class into which he was surreptitiously passing. Rural drama, masked dances, literature, and nineteenth-century rebellions showed that the rural population had good cause for cynicism and even hostility toward the pretensions of a *yangban* group that not only would not work and could not be officials but that was riddled with members widely known within the tight world of rural gossip not to be what they said they were.[30] As in the France De Tocqueville describes, government was centralized, yet the elements of society failed to cohere. Class or clan characteristics, a sense of community, pride, and loyalty could not solidify. Common interest, goals, and leadership were possible only under those conditions of extreme crisis rare in the placid Yi world. Society developed through merging, not through accommodation, and was thus hostile to making or obeying rules and definitions. Expectation of upward mobility, into lower *yangban* ranks at least, was a mute but powerful social assumption. Thence it fed the dynamics of Korean politics. Atomized, mass streaming toward power, not the formation of groups restraining power and, by both law and social pressures, mediating it, became the *modus operandi* of the social order. In all this, Korea's class system adumbrated her later politics and parties.

THE "MIDDLE CLASS": *CHUNGIN* AND *AJŎN*

If society at the top lacked leadership and cohesion, were there more signs of these qualities in the middle or lower elements of Korean society? Did these other classes play leadership roles, and can they teach us more of the nature of grouping and common action in Korean society?

In any sense understood by the West, Korea — southern Korea, at least — had no middle class. No broad and populous functional or status group with common interests ever established itself between *yangban* and commoners. Korean society was basically a dichotomy between the rulers who had all the rights and the ruled who had all the burdens.[31] The Western and Japanese conception of an influential middle class with its own culture and standards related to trade and commerce was irrelevant to Korea. Merchants were not considered "middle" but were ranked below farmers in the lower commoner fringes. They were few, derogated, and if they shared a quality it was shame not pride.[32]

What middle groups existed were small and had sharply defined functions within the central government, local administration, or the military. As usually defined there were three: the *chungin* (ideographically, "middle men"), the permanent professional-clerical staff of Seoul's ministries and offices; the previously-mentioned *ajŏn* county-clerks; and the *changgyo* professional military officers.[33] All seem originally to have had humble social origin. The *chungin* most probably were descendants of the aristocracy by concubine wives.[34] The *ajŏn* were likely to have sprung from rural commoners or in some cases slaves. The social system permanently pinned these humble origins on the members of these groups by giving them specific, hereditary clerical functions in official life where they could be watched and their mobility curbed.[35] Even in China, professionalism was the disesteemed antithesis of the generalist, aristocratic Confucian *cursus honori;* transplanted, it was particularly derogated in the native Korean ascriptive system, hindering the emergence of the modern specialist. Virtually alone in a bureaucracy of volatile arbitrary appointments, these small clerical groups represented continuity — and, with it, the freezing of status opportunity.

Unlike *yangban* and commoners, *chungin* and *ajŏn* each had cohesion. They had important functions to perform that involved each group in cooperative activity. To perform their interpreting, legal, medical, and astrological professions within the court bureaucracy, the *chungin* required books and learning, often from China; they had a shared interest in professional communication. The results of the Jesuit presence in China were garnered into the fringes of the *chungin* nets; among *chungin* and their circle early Christian converts were made.[36] They had, among themselves, pride in a learning frequently transcending the "clerkish" and superior to much *yangban* scholarship. The *ajŏn* functions were in some respects still more vital and almost as clannish. These clerks constituted the permanent staff of the offices of Korea's 350-odd counties, collected the taxes and impositions, administered welfare measures when disaster struck, assembled and supervised local labor, had all contacts with local gangs, and mediated the country magistrate's sentences. They were the only social group practicing the skills of grass-roots political communication and negotiation needed by a modern, representative system; for the population as a whole, they were the chief daily political communicators of the dynasty.[37] Unrewarded for all this, they supplemented their minuscule salaries not only with extortion but with an informal grain-loaning, banking, and trade business in which they used their own national rural network.[38] Their cohesion derived primarily from the adverse position they occupied within the social system; theirs was not a pride in enjoying sanctioned rewards.

Chungin and *ajŏn* both had strong, though scarcely vaunted, identities. The *chungin* in Seoul purveyed their "clerkish" learning within the same court circle. They lived together in Seoul's central district, deriving from it rather than from their social position their name. To this day one can spot them together at social occasions. Each circle married within itself; each was small. One authority believes there were 10 *ajŏns* on the average for each of the 350 counties.[39] *Chungin* positions were fewer.[40] Group members shared the same plight. Both groups resented the poor price society paid for their skills and the contempt shown to their members by officials. County magistrates, always *yangban* appointed from Seoul, were compared to water in the way they ran through their districts and returned as swiftly to the capital; their *ajŏn* assistants stayed and controlled: "The river flows on," Chŏng Tasan remarked, "yet the stones remain. Clerks are things to fear." [41] Identity was not something to aspire to within the Korean social system. It blocked mobility. To the present, editorials are written entitled "Koreans Do Not Like To Be Identified"; a thousand initially mystifying Korean telephone conversations daily hide the speaker behind "it's me" or "it's Kim."

The cultural barriers against cohesion and identity thus stunted the fulfillment of *chungin* and *ajŏn* and blocked much of their potential contribution for modernization. Both had key social locations, the *chungin* being, in some respects, potentially better located for influence than most of the reform-intent samurai of Meiji Japan. Each Korean group was intelligent, educated, alert, and had some motivation for change. Certainly the *chungin* bore the genes of reform and had for decades before the dynasty's end been behind much of what innovation there was.[42] They were few; but small size in a group of high integration well-located within a society was no necessary disadvantage: those among the samurai who sparked the Meiji Restoration did not draw their fame from their numbers. In fact, in proportion to their size the *chungin* probably contributed more than any other group to Korea's first painful decades of modernization.[43] They provided intellectual and political leadership, one of their number drafting the Independence Declaration.

Ajŏn contributions were also not few. With their unrivaled local knowledge, they soon found, both in the colonial and independence periods, the rewards Yi society had withheld. Taking advantage of *yangban* ignorance of property and local conditions and profiting from the Japanese cadastre of 1911–1918, they were soon numbered among Korea's largest landlords. A Japanese authority observed in 1925 that out of 300 county magistrates of about that time 260 were from the *ajŏn* class.[44] After 1945, democracy provided a highly favorable setting for their skills and connections. Running enthusiastically in countless local elections, they became probably the single most significant political class in reborn Korea.

Yet, though both *chungin* and *ajŏn* did much, they failed to perform the role that the financially poorer, more scattered, perhaps less well-located lower samurai of Japan filled. Fundamentally, this frustrated accomplishment derived from the Korean social tendency to encourage cohesion and identity only in groups with common cause against the value system, thus mitigating against giving these bonds pride, prestige, and leadership. Even the lowliest *ashigaru* among the samurai, poorer and more footloose than *ajŏn* and *chungin*, had pride in his status and gloried in identifying himself. Japan's language and literature, especially its drama, are rich in phrases of self-identification, much as in the tradition of Gawain and Lancelot. No words fell or still fall with such pain on the *chungin* and *ajŏn* ear as those for their groups; in Japan, only *eta* shun identity as they shunned it. This sense of shame prevented their social surfacing in cohesive group form. They sought, rather, to keep their status hidden as they would a personal aberration.[45] Their many contributions have not yet lessened the thrust of this shame. Hence they were and are impeded from acting as groups, from communicating with society as such. The samurai could succeed the *daimyo* as a new, self-conscious leadership class for a modern transition; the *chungin* and *ajŏn* could not so succeed to the *yangban*.

Chungin and *ajŏn* each needed something the other had.[46] The *chungin* lacked local roots, the *ajŏn* influence in the capital. Relative prosperity also blunted the impulse of each for action or the stimulus of their members to see themselves as agents of change. They lacked the poverty goads of most late Tokugawa samurai. By the dynasty's end, *chungin* and *ajŏn* were relatively rich. They needed unity but lacked both the stimulus and the public identity to find it. Their accomplishments became individual not group-supported ones. The failure of the *chungin* and *ajŏn* to structure their private sense of community into a greater public purpose lay at the heart of the problem of the homogeneous society in achieving a diverse and pluralistic community. Korea approached its late nineteenth-century period of historical crisis rich in political ambitions and in individual abilities but without a single group whose pride, repute, and cohesion could spur its members to leadership or rally behind them the nation.

THE COMMONERS

The structural tendencies illustrated within the upper and middle groups found echoes in the classes below them: among the farmers, a tendency toward the generation of a large, undefined "mass" conducive to mobility; in lower groups, a pejorative tendency toward defined, specialized, sometimes cohesive forms.

Farmers, in function if not in class, constituted probably some 75 percent of the population of Yi Korea. They were the only group to enjoy, in fair repute, freedom from any form of deceit or guile.[47] Both in fact and in Yi literature, it was they who were pitied and exploited. As in most societies, they were too scattered to have more than atomized, village forms of self-knowledge or cohesion. This tendency was increased in Korea by the lack of any strong feudal pattern to draw villages together.

Shikata's statistics suggest that the farmers' incohesive world also concealed much mobility. Most of the 48 percent of the *hyangban* recorded by Shikata in his rural townships must have originally been functionally farmers, who tended to merge, mostly upward, with the *hyangban* class. Others, pressed by taxation and military service, often tried to escape obligation within the slave population. Lower *yangban* likewise often became farmers. By the end of the dynasty, the farming occupation no longer corresponded clearly with what had been the farming class, and farmers whose families had never known any other social status than that of farmer may well have become a minority of the farming population. The concealments and tensions accompanying such mobility operated, as among the *hyangban*, to increase the social incohesiveness and incapacity for common action of rural communities.[48] Common action to express grievances came hard. Though estimates in the Dynastic Annals of those without sufficient food rose from 1,691,397 between 1752 and

1781 to 23,334,229 between 1782 and 1811 and 21,674,066 between 1812 and 1840, accompanied with much other evidence of an intolerable deterioration in conditions, farmer action or revolts were slow to start.[49] Despite continuous military weakness and inefficient administration, they were few, isolated, and unsuccessful until the rise of the Tonghak after 1860.[50] Common rural action remains difficult to achieve today.

Merchants, the great majority peddlers, were regarded as belonging, below the farmers, to the lower fringes of commoners. They are said to have constituted only some 6 percent of the population.[51] The lack of a strong Korean merchant class, even compared to China and Japan, is a well-recognized phenomenon, obvious to Western observers of the end of the Yi period.[52] Trade in Korean ships, never common since the tenth century, had been forbidden from 1644 on, and a policy of exclusion was enforced — rigidly except for the Chinese return gifts brought back by Korean tribute missions and a Japanese trading post at Pusan. A particularly puritanical version of the Confucian gentleman's disesteem of worldly goods, fortified by the desire to ward off foreign jealousy, curbed economic activity and placed the little there was under strict surveillance.[53] Mining, a royal monopoly, was limited in kind and amount; the currency system developed late and shoddily, its use not permitted in border regions. There was no center of merchant activity comparable to Canton or Osaka; one town, Kaesŏng, former Koryŏ capital, became known as a merchant hub, but its scale was extremely modest.

More important than policy was the attitude of the society toward specialist activities. Trade itself is not necessarily despised; villagers admire the farmer with sideline skills in bargaining for bulls and probably always have. But the trader-specialist was looked down on as an exploiter and, during most of the Yi Dynasty, could usually not own land. Most trade was confined to a countrywide network of small markets dominated, then and now, by the farmer-trader. Shops were few and small. The best ones were government-controlled, as were most workshops and much of the better production. Squeezed between a generalist value system and government control, entrepreneurship and capital formation never developed until the coming of the Japanese merchant in the 1880's.[54] Merchants above the peddler level were few and had small social influence. Business placed little stamp on institution-forming.[55] In the economic area, the homogeneous society sought to stifle any sources of interest, variety, and diversity.

The largest, best-organized, most influential, and lowest function of the merchant world was peddling. Since most transactions took place — and still do — outside of stores, a network of tens, if not hundreds, of thousands of peddlers plodded with their packs throughout the country, feeding the market network and going from home to home.[56] A large group despised as low-born, sly, homeless outcasts, they had special organizational needs, and the guild they developed was the strongest non-governmental organization during the Yi period; it exists — relatively less prominently — today. Through it, the peddlers developed internal leadership, rules, discipline, particular dress and language, conventions and ceremonies. The members enjoyed powerful internal solidarity, addressing each other as "brother," "uncle," or "nephew." They were important controllers of markets throughout the nation and were to some extent feared. They had the gang behavior of the outgroup. Whenever one was wronged, he would call on the aid of his fellows, whereupon a riot would start and ransom would be exacted. Such tactics still survive in Korea's urban markets.[57]

In the nineteenth century and perhaps even earlier, the peddlers had a special relationship to the government.[58] In armed crisis, the government called on them. Their guilds were often under the orders of censors or inspectors, and they induced numerous local officials to enroll in them as headmen. Their function and organization made them useful spies. Before Japan introduced a postal system, they delivered letters. With them, also, governmental use of tough men of low rank in the form of strong-arm gangs saw its modern political beginnings. On November 21, 1898, the cabinet used the peddlers guild as a *force de frappe* to attack and practically exterminate the liberal Independence Club.[59]

Korean guilds are an interesting example of the widely known function of organization as the weapon of the low and the despised, increasing the social connotation of "lowness" that already accrued to the organizing function within Korean society. Thus guilds, which in Europe served to limit central tyranny, in Korea served as its extension and arm. Merchant activities, which in London, Venice, Bremen, Lyons, Osaka, and Boston built a respectable patrician aristocracy as the spearhead of diversity and private interest within the modern world, in southern Korea were largely a force connoting meanness, gangsterism, and covert collaboration with the government to destroy private interest and, when it appeared, liberalism. Around middle groups no more than upper ones could Korea's sense of community or modernizing leadership be structured.

THE DESPISED CLASSES

The despised classes, or *ch'ŏnmin*, were even less likely sources of leadership. They were treated as if they were outside the society. They were not taxed, only in emergencies drafted for military service, almost never educated, and, except for slaves, usually lived in separate communities.

Functionally, the *ch'ŏnmin* were on the whole the best-defined portion of the population. They are variously divided by writers on Korea but are perhaps most easily seen in terms of (1) those who mingled with the rest of society; (2) those who were outcasts; and (3) those who were slaves. North Korean society had few *ch'ŏnmin* as it had few *yangban*.[60]

The first *ch'ŏnmin* category included Buddhist monks and nuns (allies of the preceding dynasty and victims of the Yi), shamans, buffoons and traveling performers, jailkeepers, fugitives and criminals. The outcasts, known as *paekchŏng*, conformed fairly closely to the *eta* of Japan. They traditionally lived in their own communities, mostly in villages or on the edge of towns; dressed their hair in a certain way and were forbidden the use of normal hats; were almost entirely self-governing, a function they pursued with considerable internal democracy; and performed specialized tasks like basket- and sandal-making, bark-peeling, slaughtering, butchering, removal of carcasses, leatherworking, shoemaking, dog-catching, and the torturing and executing of prisoners.[61] Though formal segregation was declared abolished in 1894, some distinctions and separation of communities live on, as they have on a larger scale in Japan. Several hundred essentially *paekchŏng* communities survive today.[62] Butchers constitute the most important element among them — around 50 percent — and are still one of Korea's most cohesive groups, with electrically swift means of informal price controls operating through hundreds of small stores. The *paekchŏng* were not necessarily poor, and the butchers especially, maintaining good price controls and profit margins, are today comparatively well-off.[63] They remain socially sensitive, after centuries in which they had to perform, almost uncompensated, whatever menial orders *yangban* gave them and to suffer beatings without legal resort. Yet the gap between them and other classes seems informally less great, more bridgeable, than that endured by Japan's *eta* and perhaps always was. Informal avoidance of sharp definition makes Korean society far less exclusive in tone and tendency than Japanese.

Slaves played a relatively lesser role in Yi than in Koryŏ society.[64] They were divided into public and private categories. The former consisted of *kisaeng* (female entertainers), *naein* (court maidens), *ijok* (male slaves), slaves in courier stations, slaves of sheriffs, court slaves, and escaped convicts. Each ministry had some thirty to forty. Public slaves could marry commoners and were paid. Private slaves consisted of those whose forebears had been in the family for five generations or more, those bought at the market place, and those coming from the wife's family at the time of marriage.[65]

By such sharp definitions, the society sought to limit social mobility and inculcate social values on which, lacking strong enforcement agencies, both political and social order depended. Yet the underlying mobility of the society conflicted with this defined system. Sharp variation in the numbers of slaves suggests this.[66] So did the process by which slaves were recruited. Private slaves were usually recruited from commoners and sometimes even from *hyangban* who, pressed by debts, taxes, funeral expenses, and the like, sold themselves into slavery or sought in this status the protection of a powerful noble. Such recruitment resulted in an attitude toward this class significantly different from that of Americans or Europeans toward slaves. They not only became "members of the family," but, having no different appearance or, often, background, found ways for integration within the family or the Korean group. Sons of slave girls were often free on reaching majority, and so, frequently, were second and third daughters, only the first usually inheriting the mother's position. *Yangban* often had sons by slave mistresses and sometimes sneaked these into the family or clan. The children of public slaves who married commoners occasionally seem to have become *ajŏn*. Only in such a way can one explain how, when slavery was "abolished," the slave population tended to vanish so quickly that, miraculously, though it married and reproduced, almost no one claims to be or is even accused of being its descendant among present-day Koreans.[67]

The same can be said about most *paekchŏng* and other *ch'ŏnmin*. After centuries of supposedly institutionalized immobility, they have tended to vanish almost without trace into the vast classless Korean mass. Even protests against discrimination, common at the end of the dynasty and occasional into the 1920's, have almost disappeared. Again, like class movement around the *hyangban*, the formerly lowly have merged, not accommodated. The fact that no accent or behavioral characteristic adhered to them or made it difficult for them to pass into whatever group seemed more powerful is witness to the homogenizing forces of Korean society. A leadership role for them as a group was out of the question. More important, neither their expectations nor the terms of what cohesion they had were such as to enable a force with political potential to rally around them in the post-traditional community.

What was true for any one segment of society was to a significant extent true for all. The inner tendency of society, its dynamics, conflicted with the semblance of order contained in the definitions of the class system. The circle of court *yangban* and beneath them *chungin, ajŏn,* and slaves presented an apparently well-defined and maintained exterior. In fact, however, these defined groups constituted small portions of the social scene. The real tendency of society was to avoid definition, associate it with lower groups, color it with hostility, and transcend it by mobility. Social definition was avoided for the same basic reason that had led the culture to avoid institutionalization and the formation of interest groups. The singleness of value and objective in central power, the lack of diversity to support alternatives, set in motion a strong inner mobility throughout the culture. Such pattern, in turn, created an inner value that deprecated definitions as obstacles to updraft. It is not possible — it may never be possible — to measure the extent of this force with any exactness; argument regarding it is inevitable. Yet it existed, and was apparently so extensive that Korea's social classes lacked real boundaries or cohesion and thus came to afford only weak checks against both social and political atomization.

PART II

The Dialectic of Korean Politics

The astonishing formal continuity of Korean political culture was shattered within the last century. The Yi Dynasty, having enjoyed one of the most prolonged cases of decline and senescence in any history, arrested this process from 1864 to 1874 by the use of political and social techniques that altered the terms of its earlier existence. The forces of mobility set in motion in that decade were subsequently widened in the period of faltering controls that followed it; they were still further extended and confused when, from 1884 to 1910, foreign power increasingly filled the vacuum and master-minded the placing of actors on the national stage. At that point, in 1910 and until 1945, Japan usurped all direction, firmly controlled all access to power, and installed a host of Japanese nationals in all leading roles. Defeated and humiliated, Japan was, in 1945, more than any other former colonial power, cast from both presence and influence over her former colony. Liberation's vacuum of power and direction was filled in the North by the clear-cut programs of Soviet-implanted communism; in the South, an American occupation lacking policy, preparation, and competence made a more desultory imprint. The successor South Korean regimes, while more resolute, have been inadequately rooted; four distinct governments have followed one another, two ousted by revolution and military coup. Political instability has slowly receded but remains. Korea has thus seen, within the span of a contemporary human lifetime, historical changes more frequent and complete than the total of those which history visited upon the peninsula from the seventh to the nineteenth century.

It has not proved easy, even for the Koreans themselves, to salvage from this traumatic scenario abiding meaning. Yet this must be the task of analysis. The more apocalyptic seem the hours of historical drama, the more needed for nation-building is the exorcism and refinement of the turbulence. Despite the rise of unexpected actors, despite conflicting influence of Japanese, Russians, and Americans, despite twists and disruptions in political life, an old theme can still be detected under the new forms: continued and almost exclusive concentration on central power.

3

The Beginnings of Modern Political Mobilization

The chaos of the Yi's last half century (1860–1910) contracted the dominion of the dynasty's formalities and greatly expanded the informal, even the previously covert, trends of Korean society. In these decades, Korea became unsettled and severely shaken by new domestic forces and foreign influences. The traditional structure disintegrated, patterns of power and opportunity that were less new than previously repressed operated to break what institutions and boundaries had existed, and classes formally barred from access to power now started to journey rapidly to it and even to confront it directly. A revolution in political recruitment took place that was perhaps the most essential and permanently important contribution of the late Yi period to modern Korean politics. The formless, fluid tendencies induced by the homogeneous milieu and inculcated in the institutional and class life of the old society became more pronounced and freer of Confucian conventions. Covert interclass mobility became overt and started its role as the dominant source of political recruitment and of the dynamics of modern politics. In essence, these fifty years saw the formulation in increasingly hectic terms of the underlying modern political pattern of an adaptive, as distinguished from an established, society.[1] It was this society whose pattern re-emerged after the colonial interlude and in large part continues today.

Political recruitment and modernization passed through four significant stages during this eventful period — under, successively, autocratic, religious, intellectual, and foreign leadership. Each shed some light upon the nature of Korean political process and each left on this process some mark.

AUTOCRATIC REACTION: THE TAEWŎN'GUN

When the period opened about 1860, the dynasty stood on the verge of bankruptcy and collapse. It had little military power, suffered administrative paralysis induced by divided and conflicting council government, and was threatened by chronic peasant revolt. Foreign rivalry for domination of the strategic peninsula was a small cloud on the horizon in the 1860's but by the 1880's had become a storm threatening the country's existence.

As this period opened, the internal challenges to the Yi provoked sufficient response to give the dynasty temporary reprieve. In 1864, the throne lacked direct heirs, a new king was selected with an almost coup-like rapidity by a dowager queen, and his father ruled the realm for the decade of his minority under the title of Prince Regent, or Taewŏn'gun. This regent, formerly an obscure prince of a cadet line, had been brought up outside the isolation imposed on the immediate royal family, had observed first-hand many of the ills of his society, had had some contact with reformist intellectual opinion, and was possessed of a vigorous, pragmatic determination to see Yi royal rule strengthened and maintained.[2] Of the many reforms he instituted, those relating to the structure and administration of state power most permanently influenced the political pattern.

In succeeding to central power under such circumstances, the Taewŏn'gun faced the typical problems of ruling with a relatively weak legitimacy. His responses were those of a pure, though crafty and intelligent, autocrat. He saw that the country's ancient rule-by-council had almost engulfed the throne, strangled executive power, and brought the country to the brink of anarchy. Aided by the fact that Korean royal power, unlike Japanese, had never been physically separated from rule, the Taewŏn'gun moved to restore its leadership to an extent far greater than the Meiji leaders were to achieve four years later. He made it far less dependent on its councilors, abolishing many councils, pruning others, and defining and concentrating the powers of the remainder.

To make himself independent of the older ruling circles he needed new, counterbalancing forces that would be dependent on him alone.

Although continuing to rely on the ruling Noron and associated Soron factions for most positions, he ended the monopoly of their former hold on office and appointed, for the first time in many decades, members of the opposition Namin and Pugin factions to a few fairly key offices.[3] He also abolished such informal bars as were held to have existed against the appointment or promotion of northerners and, like Louis XIV — and with similar motives — relaxed those against the lower classes.[4] Several northerners were appointed, one of them the son of a public slave. *Ajŏn*, except where notoriously corrupt, were especially favored not only by appointment but by becoming the Taewŏn'gun's special agents, shadow cabinet, and even spies. Criteria for appointment came a step closer to talent, somewhat farther from birth. The abolishing of the *sŏwŏn* (academies) and the tapping by tax and fiscal reforms of *yangban* wealth both invaded old privilege and hastened economic expansion and social change.[5] That he was, as a regent from a cadet line, able to take these steps without effective forces or factional support and yet incur for years little opposition more serious than grumbling is evidence that the *yangban* had begun to abdicate class leadership and had ceased to be a viable interest group or cohesive community ready to defend its own interests and effective in so doing.[6]

Not facing cohesive class opposition, the Taewŏn'gun's strong reassertion of leadership in the "successor behavior" pattern became the magnetic pole around which the myriad iron filings of politics rearranged themselves. For negotiations with the Japanese, he used a *chungin* interpreter; for the governor of Kyŏngsang, a Pugin faction member; for key county magistrates, personal intimates; for shadow cabinet advisors, *ajŏn*; for a private intelligence network, *ajŏn*, peddlers, and a strengthened *oga chakt'ong* (or block unit of five households); for the defense of Kanghwa against the French, peddlers and tiger hunters; for many ministerial positions, Noron.[7] Few had close relations with each other; all had close relations with him. Inspectors and censors he shifted so rapidly (he appointed a new one on the average every twenty days for ten years) as to neutralize their already vapid minatory power. Hence, he operated a kind of dual state of private and official channels, undercut factional power, atomized further the forces around him, prevented the formation of interest groups, and maximized access to power through himself.[8] By these techniques, familiar to many autocrats and later used by Syngman

Rhee, the regent maintained in a milieu of incohesive loyalties a decade of personal autonomy. He was Korea's first master manipulator of the atomized "mass" society.[9]

Yet atomized societies are inherently unstable. In their lack of subgroups and group loyalties lies their evocation to dominators continually to manipulate them. The technique is destructive of principle, and atomized individuals, though sometimes longing for ideology or principle, find difficulty in relating themselves to any such guideline. In confronting an ancient Confucian community, committed to ideals and principle in governing, the pragmatic Taewŏn'gun sacrificed the support of the intellectuals and scholars, much as twentieth-century Korean autocrats were to do. Memorials protesting his power manipulations and lack of principle flowed in. His rule being autocratic, no fruitful dialogue between the literati and the throne ensued. The protests became a flood. Protest found a leader in a country scholar who, in temporary league with the family of the new queen, forced the Taewŏn'gun to retirement at the end of 1873.

Unprincipled the regent's autocracy may have been, but it was the most effective decade the Yi government had seen in centuries. Fiscal and administrative reforms and measures flowed out faster than in any living Korean memory. The leadership of the throne was established. Unfortunately, it was not effectively maintained. The Taewŏn'gun's retirement brought to power a young king as irresolute and wavering as his father had been determined. The strong-minded young queen with her spreading court clan, the Min, dominated the new ruler. The Min clansmen produced in their twenty years of hegemony (1874–1894) no outstanding leaders. A vacuum opened around the throne, to be filled at first with limitless corruption, then, gradually, with foreign interests and advisors. Of these, the Japanese were the most persistent and, ultimately, successful. They dominated largely from 1890, completely from 1900 on.[10] Until the Japanese imposed their own forms, no new pattern arose to block the trends that the Taewŏn'gun and his times had started. The native pattern of mobility unrolled on its own momentum. Recruitment continued to be personally dominated by the king, the queen, and her relatives. Manipulation and lack of principle were more blatant than before; only their effectiveness was gone. The intellectuals continued alienated, but they also could not combine to bring new reforms. It remained for Japan to play the innovative role.

RELIGIOUS MOBILIZATION: THE TONGHAK

While the Taewŏn'gun manipulated the upper levels of society, Korea followed on lower levels a course similar to many other countries then and later: a religious movement arose which, largely in the name of independence from foreign influence, began the organization and political mobilization of the Korean masses. Tonghak ("Eastern learning") was a syncretic revealed religion started by the son of a concubine and a *hyangban* in 1860 in southeastern Korea. Confucianism, by stigmatizing emotional religion as "low-class superstition," had tended to make it an outgroup activity. Monks and shamans were numbered in the despised classes. Yet religion was too popular to be proscribed. Particularly in the absence of other institutions, religions became a natural channel for lower-class mobilization. Under organizers of ability, Tonghak developed an institutional hierarchy throughout the south, spread rapidly among the rural poor, and by 1894 was numbered by some observers at 400,000 members.[11] Though its doctrines contained a new belief in social equality and had some Christian elements, it was not opposed to Confucianism but rather sought a revitalization of the five relationships and of loyalty to the monarch. It was, from the beginning, opposed to foreign influence. Tonghak contained some similarity to the Moslem Brethren movement in modern Egypt and to the Mahdist movement in the Sudan, a similarity later underscored by political history. Desperate economic conditions, rampant government venality, and growing persecution rapidly made it a reformist political movement.

Spokesman for rural grievance to local government and at court, it was at first docile and devoted to monarchy in its petitions. But gradually it developed a Jacobean tone and more open resentment of *yangban* officials. It suffered from failure to communicate upward with the intellectuals, who could have given it better articulation and peaceful channels to the court.[12] When petitions and delegations were not heeded, representatives tried to reach the king directly and demonstrated in front of the palace. When this also failed, pressure for violence grew. One Tonghak group revolted, abortively, in 1871. In 1894, a full-scale rebellion was launched in the southwest, the repression of which brought Japanese and Chinese troops to the peninsula and touched off the Sino-Japanese war. There were instances of killings of landlords and *ajŏn,* burning of their houses, "people's courts," and other signs of class warfare, unique on this scale in Korean history. From 1901 to 1905, the movement supported Japanese intervention in Korea; after that it again shifted to become one of the bulwarks of the 1919 Independence Movement. Its early rebelliousness proved transient. After defeat in 1894, the Tonghak tended to lapse gradually into a classless general politico-religious reform movement. For the masses, however, it had been a traumatic entry to the political stage.

Tonghak in a sense played the role of a religious intermediary between lower-class organization and upper-class insistence on Confucian principle. In so doing it performed innovative political mobilization. Principle as an accoutrement of respectability was the gateway to politics for a group lacking both political power and the social means of access thereto. Religions based on principle thus had an upper-class reference to draw their lower-class memberships toward the political vortex; their hierarchies became channels of political recruitment. Many Tonghak leaders became independence leaders. A movement like that of the Tonghak tended to bear the weight of conflicting and ambivalent demands; "upper" ones of principle, "lower" ones of emotional religion; philosophical ones of goodness and loyalty, practical ones of claims on livelihood and power. Such conflicting demands brought stress and schism.[13] Because the stresses and frustrations of the society were great, religio-political movements were open to violent swings in leadership — now officially political, now adamantly orthodox and cultist. As in the government, the potential solution to these problems lay with intellectual leadership; but, as in the government, the necessary integration did not develop. Consequently, the principles and class cohesiveness with which the movement had seemed to start did not jell into an effective community of national leadership.

The movement demonstrated the rapid emergence of a political mass society. The masses were quickly mobilized and found no institutional or leadership intermediaries between themselves and the throne. The homogeneous fluidity of the society spoke in the rapid shift from docility to revolt, from principle to revenge, from patriotism to, only a little later, support of innovation within Korea by Japan. Not only did values and stands shift within the movement; they shifted from stratum to stratum within the society. The upper-class leaders of the time, the Taewŏn'gun and the Min, ruled by unprincipled pragmatism and lower-class manipulation, connoting in Korean social terms the wile of merchants and, in the cabinet's 1898 use of street force, the strong-arm tactics of peddlers. The lower-class Tonghak spoke in the accents of upper-class Confucian earnestness and social justice. The sans-culottes not the *yangban* in contemporary government, were following in Censorate paths and taking up the cudgels where Chŏng Tasan and the gently-bred opposition reformers of previous centuries had laid them down. "Unprincipled Confucian scholars and *yangban*," the rebels scolded in their rebellion's fourth principle, "shall be reprimanded and reformed." [14] Marxists, successors to much of this moralistic tone, have made much of the Tonghak revolt. Yet the inability of the upper class to retain its values, combined with the high degree of rapid and unstable inoculation of the lower class with upper-class values, points rather to the roller-coaster path values tend to follow in a homogeneous mass society more than to class conflict. Values could not inhere in classes; therefore, political action could not be built around negotiation, compromise, and accommodation. Values and political ideas and actions readily moved from group to group because the people who adopted them belonged to classes and groups that merged. In the beginning the Tonghak movement seemed one of class confrontation, but it too took on the fluidity of the society around it; the fluidity proved more lasting than the class.

INTELLECTUAL MOBILIZATION: THE INDEPENDENCE CLUB

The Independence Club was a small, political-reformist group of intellectuals founded in July 1896 in the shadow of Japan's 1895 victory in the Sino-Japanese war. It was headed by an intelligent and unselfish scion of a provincial *yangban* family, Sŏ Chae-p'il (Philip Jaisohn), recently returned from American medical studies, and by nine other generally upper-class intellectuals, a group that included three more returnees from America. The group founded a newspaper, the *Independent*, written with nationalist zeal in vernacular *han'gŭl* alphabet; had a miniature People's Assembly; sponsored private and public debate on political issues; and held demonstrations for national independence.[15] Critical of the government's ineptness and supineness before foreign influence, the club incurred official wrath. The Prime Minister and some conservative colleagues encouraged a Korean assassin, a soothsayer to Queen Min, and a peddler to whip up the peddler guild against it.[16] These threatened the group in October 1898 and, the next month, raided club headquarters, beat up everyone there, smashed furniture and building, and in subsequent street confrontations beat many members, inflicting several hundred casualties. With that event, the short-lived club was essentially dispersed and disappeared. Philip Jaisohn beat a retreat to the United States, not to return for almost half a century. Syngman Rhee and one or two others went to jail, thence into the Independence Movement.[17] Several others, including the future signer of the Annexation Treaty, Yi Wan-yong, went into the government or into pro-Japanese movements.[18] The Independence Club, essentially Korea's first attempt at a political party, aborted and had no successor.

The brave, tragic transiency of the Independence Club illustrates a number of points concerning the place and the limitations of power of intellectuals in Korean politics and of the movements they generated. First of all they were and are, like intellectuals in most places, a category of people various in origin and disposed to break into factions. The club liberals included a handful of young *yangban*, originally grouped around the former king's son-in-law, Pak Yŏng-hyo, who were infected with early Western ideas. This group later recruited some younger members from Christian schools. But they were, like their Ch'ing contemporaries, an isolated, minuscule group within either *yangban* or intellectual circles; none, for example, of the rural literati who had spearheaded the 1873 attack on the Taewŏn'gun were included. Their reforming efforts made no connections with the Tonghak, despite consistency in many objectives. From this diverse background and motivation, quarrel and disunity erupted even before the club was broken up by force. Han Kyu-sŏl, a former member with bureaucratic ambitions, even joined government-sponsored efforts to destroy it — a decade later, he was Prime Minister.

Second, also not unlike intellectuals elsewhere, Independence Club members were largely isolated and had little influence in their own society. The country literati, spoke in accents of Confucian reform that still had some traction on the public mind. By contrast, despite Club President Yun's harangues, the Korean public was still little prepared for liberal Western ideas, and the Westernized aristocratic group had little popular social rapport.

Finally, the club worked without firm institutional or financial foundations. In a land lacking alternatives to government power, it could not find organized allies, could not suggest alternate reform channels, and had no firm base for educational efforts. Inevitably, it was drawn to criticizing a recalcitrant government that it had no power to oppose. Inevitably, also, the government held the cards not only of force but of lure; none other than an official career was yet imaginable. The club in its own time could be a recruitment channel only by selling out to the government. Yi Wan-yong, first chairman of its executive committee, and Han Kyu-sŏl were both drawn from it by these temptations. Brave and well-placed as its reform efforts were, it was in no position to sustain the political initiatives it began. It had neither ideological nor organizational rootage. Closest of all Korean political mobilization of its time to Western ideals and methods, it was, of the four forms of new leadership then attempted, the least successful.

FOREIGN MOBILIZATION: THE ILCHIN-HOE

The method by which Japan and her allies within Korea succeeded in mobilizing mass political support for the Japanese Annexation of Korea, 1905–1910, is, however we judge its morality, one of the most fascinating adventures in the history of political mobilization in any country. It is, in fact, one of the only instances known to political science of an anti-nationalist mass movement. Because of the understandable objections of Korean nationalists, it is a story substantially overlooked.

In the see-saw of foreign influence, 1884–1904, before which Korea was increasingly helpless, reform-minded Koreans found China most reactionary, czarist Russia not far behind, America disinterested, and the Korean government inept. Only Japan, actively pursuing her Meiji innovations, held much appeal for them. Japan had thousands of immigrants in Korea, an effective commercial network, the most active advisors, and, above all, troops. Most reformists in those years looked to Japan; by and large, Japan gave them support.[19]

Korean society more than ever was a whirlpool without government leadership or cohesive institutions and with deteriorating class and social boundaries.[20] The atomized official world manipulated by the Taewŏn'gun, the restless mass world of the Tonghak, the intellectual efforts of the Independence Club — all had lost their leaders and coherence by the end of the nineties. New men without ties were rising in search of careers. Some came within the field of Japan's power magnet and, lacking any native lodestar, were drawn to it (see Chapter 8).

The coming of the Russo-Japanese War bound together and strengthened these strands. Russia was reactionary and distant. Japan was not only reformist; it was close, its culture and language less alien, its student-exchange program far more active, and its chances of winning strong. As elsewhere, especially in the Middle East, administrative reform from above and the consequent disruption of the traditional social balance ended by facilitating foreign occupation.

In this milieu, several ambitious men of the lower classes began to carve political careers. Song Pyŏng-jun, an *ajŏn's* illegitimate son from the rough northeast, was one. Two others were Son Pyŏng-hŭi, the son of a concubine of a poor, rural southwestern family, and Yi Yong-gu, a poor man's son from south central Korea. These three came to feel that national progress and personal success must be identified with Japan and that Korea should come out positively in her support of Japan in the Russo-Japanese War.[21] Son and Yi were both Tonghak leaders, men of striking appearance, speaking ability, and native energy. They were joined by several members of the defunct Independence Club. Son encouraged and Yi led a political movement within the Tonghak to support Japan. As the accepted leaders of the Tonghak, they found recruitment easy. By 1904, a group of tens of thousands had been formed, mostly from Tonghak rural southern areas. At the same time, Song Pyŏng-jun, who had returned from Japan as interpreter to Major General Otani, Japanese Army Commander in Korea during the Russo-Japanese War, and was backed in his efforts by the Japanese Army, recruited a smaller leadership group centered on Seoul elite that also supported Japan. The group was called the Ilchin-hoe (Advancement Society). Within the year, the two groups had combined under the title of Ilchin-hoe with actual leadership under Song and Yi. Financial aid of 50,000 yen was accepted from Uchida Ryōhei, leader of the Black Dragon Society, who then became an "advisor." [22] Thereafter, the Japanese had a channel of communication to the general society, and the Ilchin-hoe had a lobbying channel within the Japanese-controlled Korean government. It was thus able to place many supporters in important posts inside and outside government and became an important channel for political and social mobility.

The Ilchin-hoe, adopting Japan's aims as its own, issued a manifesto and constantly pressured the government.[23] To symbolize support for reform, its members wore short haircuts. But practical tasks predominated: it mobilized some 270,000 Tonghak and unemployed as laborers or as supply bearers and railroad construction workers for Japan's campaigns in northern Korea and Manchuria.[24] In recruiting these, Song and Yi, in the view of one Korean historian, "convincingly persuaded the masses with the promise that they would be appointed to such governmental positions as governors, magistrates and township heads in addition to the hope of becoming rich when the Ilchin-hoe organized the Korean government."[25] Once organized, the Society, becoming ever more rabidly pro-Japanese, launched a mass movement in support of first the Protectorate Treaty in 1905, then of the abdication of the Korean king, finally in direct support of the annexation of the country by Japan.[26]

The Ilchin-hoe was the first Korean attempt to mobilize mass support for a political party. Indeed, it was Korea's first successful political party. It was a national movement utilizing all the techniques of mass meeting, public speech, posters, large-scale financial support, and lobbying for general national issues. Both Song and Yi, as members of the lower classes, were gifted organizers, ralliers, and public speakers. We read of "a largely-attended out-door meeting . . . at Chemulp'o" with speeches by "the Japanese Consul and others."[27] Another rally of some 10,000 took place in Suwŏn.[28] The Ilchin-hoe set up a company to exploit a seaweed business. It asked the Ministry of Agriculture to recognize a company it organized to cultivate the wastelands. It sent students to Japan "without regard to class." It established a Japanese school in Hamgyŏng Province. It organized in Chinju to prevent attacks on its branch by peddlers "incited" by the Chinju magistrate. It brought the governor of P'yŏngan Pukto to trial and asked the government to dismiss the governors of Hwanghae and the (*yangban*) magistrates of Andong and Chŏnju. The society requested the changing of all government officials and asked to name a slate of its own. It advised the king.

It criticized the cabinet of Pak Che-sun and pressured it to promote the king's early abdication.

Throughout the story of Korea's first political party runs a thread of strong-arm, lower-class methods. Ilchin-hoe arrested people at will who "seem to be inimical to Japanese interests." It brought "six members to court for punishment of illegal acts." [29] It extorted money. It destroyed the magistracy at Paekch'ŏn. It informed on people, especially officials. It forged letters. It employed blackmail. It became so unpopular that people refused to ride in the same boat with one of its speakers, although one observer said that "people are timid since it has Japanese support." [30] Its extremism caused first its separation in 1906 from Tonghak (renamed Ch'ŏndogyo on December 1, 1905), its gradual weakening, and finally its disbandment by the Japanese themselves immediately after Annexation in 1910. Even then, a list dated August 23, 1910, of organizations to be abolished by the new government-general, attributed to it 140,715 members and a hundred subsidiary organizations. Earlier, at its height, before its 1906 split, it claimed a million.[31] Once disbanded, it disappeared completely, never to be revived. Thirty-five years would pass before a Korean party approached it in size.

The Ilchin-hoe is a fascinating example of political mobilization in an emerging nation. Japanese colonial ambitions furnished an issue sufficiently important to require, if not the support, at least the neutralization of the masses. War and railroad building furnished the milieu in which this mobilization could take place. A religious organization supplied a ready-made organizational network. The breakup of traditions let loose new men uncommitted to old groups and values, free-floating and anxious to serve as instruments and leaders wherever power might lie. They gladly broke the ancient Confucian chain of politics. Korea no longer possessed an "establishment." It was becoming an adaptive society but lacked the means and structure to be successfully adaptive. Political leadership no longer had to do with birth, status, education, moral behavior, or literary finesse. It concerned force of presence, skill in public speech, control of organization, striking aim, and effectiveness of action. Agility in changing political horses became far more important than morality and candor.[32] The Taewŏn'gun and the Tonghak had, each in their own way, moved toward this change; still, it came, in the twentieth century's first years, with startling suddenness.

The masses were as unattached, as devoid of loyalties to inter-mediate organization, as were their politically newborn manipulators. "Though the nation came to seem a homogeneous whole, its parts no longer held together. Nothing had been left that could obstruct the central government, but, by the same token, nothing could shore it up." [33] The unattached populace was cheap game. Pay and foreign protection for their livelihood were probably the chief forces mobilizing them. Rallies and speeches provided a sense of excitement and participation to rural people long deprived of these feelings by a puritanical government.[34] Organization was thin, but it had no rivals elsewhere. Understanding of issues ran even thinner, though they were simply and craftily expounded in Song's harangues. That true organizational loyalty hardly existed is shown by the rapidity of the Ilchin-hoe's traceless dissolution. Yet the people were there to be used peremptorily even for extreme causes, even for causes involving the loss of their own independence. They were there to be manipulated by organizations formed above them. Then they were there to be thrown back into political anonymity again like fish too small for keeping.

There is no doubt of the Ilchin-hoe's temporary success; it did much to neutralize any threat of popular insurgence against the coming of Japanese rule. As in many nations that were to emerge in later decades, the sudden direct exposure of the masses brought Caesarism and, in Korea's case, even loss of independence. Korea, from 1890 to 1910, relatively early in her modern period, had already reached that condition of "mass" society that many emerging nations after her were to come to know. She knew it with all its dangerous unexpectedness and instability.

4

Colonial Totalitarianism

DISCIPLINE AND SEPARATION FROM RULE

The administration of Chōsen (1910–1945), as the Japanese called their Korean colony, was a unique experience.[1] With Taiwan and Manchuria, Chōsen was the only important colony of its time to be held by a non-Western power.[2] Colonizers and colonized were racially cousins and geographically neighbors: cultural, political, and historical experiences, though distinct, were not so diverse as those separating most colonies and their masters. Colonial control lasted for thirty-five years — brief compared to many colonies, but uniquely intense. Chōsen was clasped in vise-like grip by the Japanese military with ubiquitous security pre-occupations; the instruments of repression weighed far more heavily than in colonial India, Africa, and Southeast Asia.

Japan's rule of Chōsen was admittedly despotic though purposeful. Long technically under the Bureau of Colonization, which was responsible to the Premier, it was the only Japanese colony over which the Premier was considered not even to exercise supervision.[3] It was ruled by a governor-general formally appointed by the Premier but during the first nine years actually recommended and supported by the *genrō*, Field Marshal Prince Yamagata, who saw to it that high-ranking military officers of his Chōshū clique were honored with this position.[4] The governor-general enjoyed almost complete freedom in administration and, almost to the end, submitted his reports directly to the emperor. As in Taiwan, legislation was enacted by *seirei* and *furei,* decrees and ordinances of the governor-general, almost automatically sanctioned by the emperor through the Premier. The governor-general's legislative powers equaled those of a parliament.

Even Japanese questioned whether legislative authority so despotically exercised by an unelected official operating without a parliament within Chōsen and, until 1919, not even answerable to the Japanese Diet could be regarded as Japanese constitutional rule.[5] With the advent of party cabinets in Japan after 1918 and the political pressures of the 1919 Korean Independence Movement the governor-general's direct dependence on the crown was removed; he became technically a member of the Diet, and his regime became formally answerable to it. Legally, from 1919 on a civilian could have been appointed governor-general. None were; all were military men, mostly on active service. In November 1942, Chōsen was brought technically under the operating control of the Japanese Home Ministry, but since the governor-general continued to be a man of approximately prime minister level, any real personal subordination to a home minister was not to be expected.

In essence, from beginning to end, the theme of rule was the same: stern, centralized, bureaucratic administration without constitutional or popular restraint, its high-handedness justified in Japanese eyes by its efficiency. Chōsen's rule flowed from two related Japanese traditions. One was the tradition of administration already established in Taiwan by Japan's greatest administrator, Gotō Shimpei. Gotō, an especially gifted Meiji civilian leader, expounded the policy of isolating colonial affairs from either bureaucratic or political interference from Japan proper, an insulation he justified on the grounds of the home government's lack of knowledge and insight regarding "local concerns." [6] For such concerns, however, Japanese rather than indigenous administrators were deemed competent. The other chief determinant of the character of Chōsen's rule was the victory of Prince Yamagata's "hard-line" faction with respect to Japan's Korean policy. Through its control of the Katsura cabinets (1901–1906, 1908–1911, 1912–1913) this faction had effectively ended Prince Itō's attempts at "beneficent" control through a technically independent Korean government.[7] The Yamagata-Katsura view saw an independent Korea as a threat to Japan's and the Far East's security, economic administrative development as requiring Japan's firm guiding hand, and complete integration into Japan as the ultimate social goal. It advocated forcible, instant, and complete over-throw of opposition along the lines that were the evident heritage of the theories of Yoshida Shōin. Korean political development was not contemplated. Chōsen was, indeed, an archetype of the administrative state under which politics are intended to wither away. From 1901 on, such views had the virtually undivided support of the Japanese press and public. They set the tone not only of Japanese rule but of the attitudes with which Japanese approached Koreans.[8] This policy formed the logical matrix from which, under the impetus of new militarist expansion in the 1930's, the concept of the cultural obliteration of Korea as an entity distinct from Japan, the extinction of Korean as a separate language, and the end of Koreans as a separate people was born and its implementation begun. Recent colonialism probably contained in neither theory nor practice a policy so radical as this; its effect on an ancient and numerous people of proud traditions could not fail to produce the profoundest sense of humiliation and outrage.

Short of suicidal violence, the Koreans thus had to become accustomed to a rule of complete despotism dedicated to their "Japanization." Despite diplomatic efforts, no foreign nation was willing effectively to espouse their cause. In a sense, they were the only Far Eastern people for whom unchecked autocracy was new. The Manchus had choked the channels of Confucian communication in the Ch'ing Dynasty, shifting Confucianism to obedience to an imperial autocrat.[9] The Japanese had never had much Confucian communication to shift. The Koreans had been accustomed to broader access to rule and to checks on autocracy by government council. Now the whole world of Censorate and Confucian memorializing was gone. Oligarchic centralism was replaced with foreign bureaucratic centralism. At the same time, only with the greatest caution were new channels of communication opened in place of old. The press was crushed: no Korean newspapers were allowed until after 1919, and then the two or three that did publish were strictly censored. Political activity, once the custom of a large class and in recent years rapidly released from class bounds, went underground. In daily life, certainty and security returned for the ordinary, peaceful citizen, but only at the price of resentment, bitterness, and frustration. In the place of the fluid politics and endless discussion of issues once considered the aristocratic birthright came enforcement from capital to village by a bureaucracy equipped with arms, communications, efficiency, and ruthless purpose. Japan's bureaucrats carried Chōsen like a vast tub of water from which no drop was to be spilled. The sense of helplessness vis-à-vis central power intensified. All men became preoccupied with it and divided into those evading it and those seeking to make their way toward it. Neither group was small. Each in its own way was convinced that the government held power and initiative in all things.

The exercise of despotic rule was aggravated and extended by another factor colonially unique to Chōsen and Taiwan: the presence of an enormous ruling Japanese class. Japanese had never historically settled in Korea in any strength. They began immigrating in significant numbers only in the early 1880's. Many were poor folk from Kyūshū seeking economic opportunity. They set up shops that penetrated the local centers in the nineties and by 1905 covered "the country like a network." [10] With the coming of Japanese control and the encouragement of immigration, Japanese "colonizers" swarmed in, increasing from 3,622 in 1882 to 42,460 in 1905, 171,543 in 1910, 336,812 in 1918, and finally 708,448 (or approximately 3.2 percent of the population) in 1940.[11] As a ruling class, the Japanese outnumbered even the *yangban* (minus *hyangban*) whom they displaced. The largest group of them, 41.4 percent (vs. 2.9 percent of Koreans) in 1937 were in government service, occupying almost all important positions. Government offices, in the Korean pattern crowded with hangers-on and favor-seekers, were now, above township level, almost empty of Koreans and ground out distant, stern, ineluctable processes in rooms of low-keyed talk behind corridors little lingered-in. Some 16.6 percent of Japanese residents were in industry, and 23.4 percent were in commerce in 1938.[12] Only 2.6 percent of the Koreans were in industry and 6.5 percent in commerce, while 75.7 percent were still in agriculture at this time.[13] More revealing than the sectoral figures is the fact that, even as late as 1944, 95 percent of gainfully-employed Korean men and 99 percent of the women were laborers.[14] Some 71 percent of the Japanese population was urban, as opposed to 11.5 percent of Koreans. Japanese and Koreans thus coexisted on a completely different economic level. Such differences tended to increase rather than narrow as expansion and war made the Japanese an increasingly prosperous elite while raising appreciably the living standards of only a few Koreans. Koreans watched a rising tide of government and of economic modernization; from full participation in both they were separated by a thick layer of alien elite filling almost all important jobs. It was a phenomenon not often found in colonialism — perhaps the rule of the French in Tunisia offers a rare parallel.

Had the Japanese notion of assimilation been realistic, the distance would have narrowed. Here the Japanese based policy on an inadequate insight into their own society: "it is the particular system or collectivity of which one is a member that counts." [15] The Japanese lived mostly in tight, exclusive swarms in Korea;[16] deprecation of Koreans was part of the ethos of these groups. The few Japanese who disobeyed this separateness tended to become outcasts facing frequent investigations. Despite official "assimilation" pronouncements, there were only 360 mixed marriages by 1924, less than currently take place between a smaller body of culturally more different Americans and Koreans every four months.[17] Despite widespread Korean fluency in Japanese, a surprising lack of Japanese insight into or sympathy for Korean feelings and attitudes was the legacy of this *de facto* apartheid.[18] Koreans for their part, though inwardly hostile, nevertheless showed the usual instincts of colonial subjects in seeking advancement or profit where they were wanted. The difficulty lay in not being wanted. Insulation and alienation from the political process were increased by the thickness and exclusiveness of the Japanese presence. The capacity of Japan to be not only authoritarian but, through intimacy of surveillance and breadth of control, totalitarian was greatly reinforced. It added to the Korean atmosphere of hopelessness. Even Korea's keenest collaborators soon voiced dissatisfaction with Chōsen's first decade.[19]

Economic exploitation added further distance and alienation between the ordinary Korean and his Japanese or Korean collaborating masters. The concentration of landholding in fewer and fewer hands became an almost constant trend. The Japanese, frustrated by the lack of adequate land registration and by undefined concepts of Korean land-ownership, instituted a complete cadastre from 1911 to 1918. Many Korean farmers forfeited their property when, not understanding the new measure, they failed to register or registered incorrectly. Much land whose ownership had been vague, such as *yangban* land registered in others' names, became firmly acquired by Japanese land companies or Japanese or Korean landlords. Firmness of ownership, Japan's need for rice imports, settled conditions, the growth of capitalism, irrigation, and other factors increased yields to landlords and resulted in expansion of their holdings. The percentage of Korean farmers owning no farmland rose from 37.7 percent in 1918 to 53.8 percent in 1932.[20] By 1938, only 19 percent of farmers owned all the land they tilled, 25.3 percent owned some and rented some, and farmers owning none rose to 55.7 percent.[21] In 1942, some 4 percent of "farming households" owned 40.2 percent of all rice paddies, a fair majority of these being Koreans.[22] Gaps of wealth and poverty widened, and there was a steady creation of a rural proletariat. On the one hand, this caused resentment and the emigration of hundreds of thousands to Manchuria and Japan. On the other, land-lessness, more rural schools, expanding communications, and a greater exchange economy all made farmers less self-sufficient, hence less isolated within the economy. Thus farmers came closer to political consciousness at the same time that they were losing or were increasingly alienated from the hierarchical structure through which they might express such consciousness.

Colonial rule brought alienation also from the former Korean governing class. Its members had been too exclusive and incompetent to be popular; now many came into more positive bad odor. Some acquired the reputation of collaborators who in pro-Japanese cabinets until 1910 had sold Korea out. Others sold out when the Japanese, at Annexation, offered eighty-four *yangban* and prominent officials titles with stipends averaging around $10,000 per annum each; only eight refused. It was largely among some of those accepting that any material basis for prominence was retained; almost all others were ruined. In addition, the Imperial Household pensioned off 3,645 Korean officials, selected with a detailed Japanese knowledge of the Korean upper class and its factions.[23] The infiltration and undermining of the leadership class had been, as we have seen, an old and long process. Its final elimination was now extraordinarily thoroughly accomplished. Of all this "leadership class," it is hard to name more than a handful, whether honored by the Japanese or not, who ever again succeeded in exerting leadership roles, became leaders in the independence movement, or thereafter, in the politics of postwar Korea.[24] At least from 1919 on, Korea may be said to have become a country without a leadership class.

Japanese theory and employment of law in Korea, instead of

providing a channel of defense against suppression, added to insulation and alienation from rule. In place of native law, a vastly more complex, codified legal system administered by Japanese professionals was introduced from Japan, where it had been largely copied from European, especially German, law.[25] Only minimal, tangential deviations based on native social traditions and custom were permitted in transferring this corpus to Korea. Some Korean laws were taken over, but these were almost entirely late Yi legislation prepared by Japanese advisors.[26] Otherwise Chōsen's law came to consist of imperial edicts and ordinances enacted either by the government-general or promulgated in Tokyo for Chōsen.[27] Yi law had also been based almost entirely on foreign law, the Chinese. In the beginning, it too must have seemed alien; but with the passing of centuries, the rewriting of codes by Koreans, and the spread of Confucian culture throughout the villages, this alien quality had largely disappeared. Law came in later Yi times to accord with the ethical system Koreans knew in homes and village. It was administered by the county magistrate together with all his other responsibilities. Only a few *chungin* clerks, unknown to the public, were specialists. The "wisdom" of the local official in judgment was the burden of countless folk tales. The German-Japanese system had no such popular relationship, no points of reference in Korean lives; it was the work of overlords and their police. The Koreans saw it and the torture system used against them in the 1912 conspiracy case, the 1919 Independence Movement, the 1918 cadastre, and, indeed, all instances where their interests conflicted with the Japanese. The concept of the consent of the governed or of a system of justice for the individual receded ever farther.

That the judiciary was expanded and professionalized simply added to its sternness, its omnipresence, and its dehumanization. Contact with the legal system, once lax and infrequent, increased. Chōsen was ruled by dictate. Koreans became accustomed to the arbitrary exercise of official power without expectation of official remedy. That this process occurred in modern dress only tended to alienate Koreans from modern systems. Respect for legal or administrative process lay far from the heart of the common citizen. Obedience and law-abidingness, long and strongly inculcated by the local Confucian elite, eroded. Alien and unrespected law could not serve as a barrier to the breakdown of standards and bounds that occurred as elite status deteriorated and died away through class melding and political disrespect. To evade the law or break it now brought applause from many Koreans. A jail sentence, especially for political crimes, was a badge of distinction — and many ordinary crimes could be made to seem political in the telling. Among a people long famous for good manners and conduct, crime, stealing, smuggling, opium dealing, illegality as a way of life, made gradually increasing inroads. Like the child disciplined by an unloved parent, Korean society struck back at its tamers with unruliness. House doors, unlocked in the old days, were locked; broken glass topped the walls of the rich. The bars went up, and with them social isolation.

As the walls rose, so did the instruments of suppression. Expansion of law enforcement started early and progressed steadily. Japanese armed presence in the Sino-Japanese and Russo-Japanese Wars was rapidly succeeded by the Japanese gendarmerie's control of Seoul's police from 1905 on. From 1907 on, the Home Ministry took upon itself complete powers to dissolve and control all assembly through the police. Scattered resistance and local rebellion against the Japanese presence from 1907 to 1911 brought increases in Japanese gendarmes, who were, as Governor-General Terauchi archly put it, "easier to use . . . than police to control a primitive people." [28] Police, however, also increased greatly, as did their powers, not only in security matters but also in registering and licensing schools, soliciting financial contributions, and gathering intelligence. They rose from 678 Japanese police "advisors" and 1,039 Korean policemen in 1906 to 6,222 in 1911 (half Koreans), then to some 14,000 by 1919. In August 1919, as a result of the internal and international pressures generated by the Independence Movement, the gendarmes were abolished, but many of them simply became police. A major network of town and village police stations, telephone-equipped, virtually monopolized local communication until after the Korean War. By 1922, the police had increased to 20,771.[29] The China war brought further accretions until by 1941 there were estimated to be some 60,000 civil and military policemen, or one for every 400 people.[30] For years before the end of World War II, they were the chief controlling agency for politics, education, religion, morals, health, and public welfare, and the chief collectors of everything from population statistics to bribes. The ubiquitousness, the daily sternness of their rule, was in marked contrast to the Yi Dynasty's, which, though at least equally arbitrary, was far more lax.

The effect was deepened by cultural factors. In Japan, use of lower samurai in the police had given it a measure of social respect. In Korea, the police function had been performed by commoners or lower classes. Now it was performed by Japan's short "monkey people" who came from what Koreans conceived to be the end of civilization's line. The thousands of Koreans now attracted to police service were almost always of the lower classes, frequently from the northern provinces. Many had the fanaticism of the *Untertan*. With an enthusiasm to which class hatred was not alien they showed their colonial superiors by their repression of their own countrymen how much Japan could count on their services. In return, ordinary Koreans hated and despised them more than they did many Japanese. For some, police work was a ladder of ambition, a haven to which the free-floating, aspiring low-born, of the type recently in the Tonghak or Ilchin-hoe, could attach themselves. For the ordinary Korean, however, the police represented the ubiquity of colonial bureaucratic oppression, a force far less subtle than Japanese exclusiveness in keeping them from any participation whatsoever in the governing process. Law, even social order, and the police were hated as the props of alien tyranny.

THE INDEPENDENCE MOVEMENT

Repressive bureaucracy and the alienation of Koreans from leadership had two diverse and conflicting general consequences: one unintended and almost immediate, one intended and gradual.

The intended — or at least officially welcome — result was conditioned by the lack within the society of strong secondary institutions, of loyalties, and of leadership groups or classes. The unstable, ambitious, fluid mass society that had already brought forth the Tonghak and the Ilchin-hoe grew externally stabler but inwardly more chaotic throughout the Japanese period. The reimposition of central government strength had, despite all alienation, the effect of assembling around it the iron filings of much of ambitious society, which it subjected to mass organization and manipulation. This outcome was greatly increased by the development of a massive disciplined bureaucracy that, with large resources of Japanese nationals and a capability of integrating many Koreans, was able to control every organization and to effect a totalitarian mobilization of society. This mobilization greatly increased during the period of intensified Japanese war effort after 1931.

The second, unintended and paradoxical result of the harsh removal of Koreans from leadership and rule was the generation of relatively intense nationalist feelings. This nationalist outgrowth occurred less than nine years after Annexation.[31] These opposite but simultaneous gravitations increased both nationalism and participation in the colonial system; both resulted in greater political mobilization but with the certitude of increased conflict.

The generation of nationalism and the history of the Independence Movement are among the few phenomena of Korean history comparatively well described in English.[32] Extreme suppression had created an undertone of heated discontent under the two strait-laced first governors-general. The national movements released by World War I, the breakup of the Austrian and Turkish Empires and of German colonialism, kindled a general atmosphere of nationalist expectation. The funeral of the old king, Kojong, deposed in 1907 under Japanese pressure, brought emotion and crowds of the politically conscious to Seoul as February turned to March, 1919. Leaders or representatives of a number of Protestant, Ch'ŏndogyo, and Buddhist communities met in late February and drafted an eloquent Declaration of Independence, which thirty-three of the leaders (sixteen Christians, fifteen Ch'ŏndogyo, and two Buddhist monks) signed. With all preparations successfully concluded in secret despite the watchfulness of the state and with religious communities throughout the country notified, the Declaration was publicly read in Pagoda Park on March 1, 1919; the signers gave themselves up for arrest; and a peaceful demonstration of thousands of unarmed citizens and students took place in Seoul and many other centers throughout the country. The surprised Japanese, careful not to create a riot by firing into the crowds, followed the demonstration with an orgy of arrests, tortures, and even village-burning.[33] The movement was, on the surface, bitterly and completely suppressed.

Suppression and complete failure to achieve independence led to a sense of disappointment, let-down, even futility. Yet the movement remained in many ways a success, fertile in important political precedents. The forces generated were, for the first time, truly national, as, for instance, the armed insurrections of 1907–1911 had not been. The development of a closely-knit national organization, however temporary, with a local committee in each township acting in coordination, was a performance unmatchable by the hated Ilchin-hoe in its heyday. For the first time widely, schools were aroused and students reasserted their classic role of demonstration and protest in modern times. Largely because of the role of Christianity in education and in the movement, girl students were prominent, and women played parts in the organization, taking their places popularly for the first time on the national political stage. The movement marked the first national response to a Western idea — the first proof in centuries that Korean determination could be national.

Ultimately, its success had deeper springs. Somewhat like Gandhi's movement in India, the high idealism of March 1, its very impracticality, validated the mobilization of a Confucian nation as no armed rebellion could have done and clothed it with an abiding sense of righteousness and faith. As time passes, it seems clearer that nothing else could have succeeded so well. The Independence Declaration was truly eloquent and moving, especially the Korean gesture of signing and reading it in full acceptance of coming arrest. There was dignity and pathos also in the unarmed demonstrations of thousands throughout the country. The minute nation-wide preparations executed without betrayal under the eyes of a police state demonstrated a new confidence and trust. No successful armed rebellion being possible, a peaceful movement, fully justified, led by religious leaders, supported by students, without any touch of selfishness, probably marshaled national spirit as nothing else could. Cruel suppression served only to highlight these qualities and engrave them — and hatred for Japanese methods — into the national consciousness. In its electric spontaneity and almost incredibly swift and secret oral communication, we read the latent strength of the mass society, once an idea that can mobilize it has been planted: a strange strength that then proved invocable even with little leadership. Kept alive by celebration and retelling in after-years, the March 1 movement has woven itself, beyond disappointment, into the heart of the nation. To Koreans, it is the cornerstone of their national politics, one of the few events of their history in which pride is shared and closely felt. For the first time they were united behind an idea, not fragmented by competition for the same power. Perhaps only those who have lived through the kind of suspicion, sycophancy, atomization, and corruption that stamp so much of the politics of emerging nations can quite understand the force of something pure, idealistic, and sacrificial for the rallying of a people.

Institutionally, the Independence Movement found a base like that of similar stirrings in other societies — in religion. Religion was the one "national" institution that the colonial power was inhibited from suppressing. Korean leadership in 1919 hence came from the Christian church communities, especially in areas such as P'yŏngan-do where they had the strength to be centers of community action. It also came from Ch'ŏndogyo groups and rural communities, especially the areas in central and southwestern Korea, where Ch'ŏndogyo had begun the process of political mobilization. Presbyterians predominated among the Christian signers; there were no Catholics (see p. 429, n. 77). The presbytery form of church government had taken root rapidly and effectively within Korea's council tradition and played an important role in generating and making effective an institutional base within the Christian church for the Independence Movement. The strength of presbytery rule is demonstrated by the fact that none of the church signers were, in themselves, leaders of national repute, nor did they or their descendants become so. They were, in fact, more representatives of church communities and presbyteries than individual leaders.[34] It is one of the most important and unnoticed aspects of the Independence Movement that, in and through it, secondary institutions for almost the first time in Korean history played a major, even decisive, role. This was a development of genuine promise for the founding of a pluralistic society.

To sustain a national movement, however, the choice of Christian churches was narrow and not fully representative either socially or regionally; for in neither respect had Christianity developed evenly. Only two of the thirty-three signers came from the eastern half of the peninsula. Religion was virtually the only occupation represented among them in a country where firm adherents of any religion were only a small minority of the population. Even more interesting, through the ascent of religion as the organizational framework of the Independence Movement, the former leadership classes were more or less excluded. Religion in general and Ch'ŏndogyo in particular still had lower-class connotations. Though evidence is still largely informal, so far as can be determined all signers were commoners or members of the middle class. At least two, Son Pyŏng-hŭi (an old Tonghak, then a pro-Japanese leader) and Kim Wan-gyu, were illegitimate sons. At least two were of *ajŏn* or *chungin* background: Ch'oe In and O Se-ch'ang.[35] The rest seem to have been commoners or members of unknown *hyangban* families. Son and the Declaration's drafter, Ch'oe Nam-sŏn, a *chungin*, had approached five highborn ministers of the former Yi cabinet known to have some anti-Japanese sentiments.[36] All had demurred, not for lack of courage (one shortly thereafter joined another aristocrat in open protest against Japanese rule and was imprisoned) but apparently because of the social overtones of the group. The year 1919 marked the last gasp of the old leaders; thereafter, leadership was to come not on a class basis but from commoners' ranks.

The Independence Movement had significant outcomes both within Korea and abroad. Men of strong will from all classes could feel within it common dedication and approximate equality of opportunity. Probably not since the opening decades of the Yi period, when Confucianism had seemed a great, new cause — and even then for more limited class groups — had so many been thus moved by a fresh and common enthusiasm. The movement was a new channel to status and leadership. It had the advantages of the fluid society: new men, new ideas, new forms moving up in a period of modernization. A few new institutions served to provide some unity: the churches, the three Korean newspapers allowed by the Japanese after 1920, and a few private schools. Still, the proportion of the population involved was small. Those giving sustained activity to the Independence Movement probably constituted 5 percent or even less of the population. The others were too isolated or too restricted by the need to make a living to take significant part; and the institutions, influential though they were, were but small islands in the society — small, it turned out, not only at the time but for the future when post-Liberation politics had to be built on them.

It was almost inevitable that the strugglers for independence never objectively had much chance of throwing off the Japanese yoke. Beyond this, however, neither institutional nor social cohesion was sufficient to bear the strains either of modernization or of liberation struggle. In 1927, the Japanese gingerly allowed a kind of opposition party known as the Sin'gan-hoe (New Trunk Society) to form in

Seoul.[37] Ch'ŏndogyo, other nationalist leaders, and members of the newly-formed Korean Communist party put together a coalition to give it unity. Though under constant surveillance, the society served as a limited platform for the airing of some grievances and a clearing house for opposition groups and ideas. When Korean students in Kwangju, South Chŏlla, stirred by an insult to a Korean girl from a Japanese student, rose in demonstrations, the Sin'gan-hoe, mostly underground, helped spread them throughout Korea, eventually involving 54,000 students. This was the only major anti-Japanese incident staged from within Korea between 1919 and Liberation and helped keep nationalism aflame in an adverse time. Yet such limited activities aroused conflict between the leftist elements anxious to pursue them and more conservative nationalists concerned about the maintenance of legality. The society tended to split. Long-range political or social planning was impossible: the nationalist camp was cautious and divided and the Communists would not commit themselves to what they could not control (for the pre-Liberation Communist movement, see Chapter 11). No strong leadership arose to find its way through these problems. By 1931, the Communists, losing hope of domination, voted to dissolve the coalition. Without them, the nationalists proved unable to revive or maintain any strong coalition among themselves. The nationalist movement weakened and regained strength only with Liberation. Such cohesiveness as existed could not bear the burdens of new and differing ideologies, of joint planning against the purposeful Japanese bureaucracy, or of preparation for the formation of more modern institutions. At the time, colonial oppression seemed to be Korea's chief problem; underneath, lack of unity and leadership foreshadowed the future.

Problems more complex and tragic but essentially similar beset exiled Korean independence strugglers. In the spring and summer of 1919, a group of exiled patriots founded in Shanghai a Korean provisional government with a legislative assembly.[38] Represented were diverse Korean communities in Siberia, Manchuria, the United States, and Korea. Some students were sent by the Tokyo community. The President of the Provisional Government, Syngman Rhee, and its ministers differed widely in social and regional background; few of them had even previously met. From the beginning, differing feelings of closeness to Russia or the United States created rifts between their adherents and with those who saw the problem in purely

Korean terms. There was unity against Japan, but that was all. Communication with the sternly guarded homeland or with Korea's scattered overseas communities was difficult. Shanghai, later Chungking, lacked entirely such secondary institutions as church or press to provide seedbeds for unity. One of Korea's major overseas communities — in Japan — was increasingly composed of uneducated men from Kyŏngsang Province or Cheju reluctant to undertake activities that would threaten the livelihoods they were building up within Japanese society. The problem of forging institutions that then had no practical problems to deal with brought out every grain of abstract and moralistic Confucian divisiveness. Consensus was obtainable neither on the establishment of government nor on the independence strategy to be pursued. The issue of royalism and democracy precipitated bitter debate. Intense criticism of "President" Rhee ended in his impeachment by the Assembly in 1925. The selection or maintenance of leadership involved constant quarrel. Falling apart increasingly after 1921, the Shanghai movement soon became hardly more than nominal. In all its history, no foreign government recognized it. Essentially the same fate befell all the societies, associations, and minuscule parties organized among the exiled patriots. Korean Communists were held by some Communists to be a classic of factionalization. Even the small, socially rather uniform Hawaiian Korean community could not keep together. Trial parties and legislatures were discouraging failures, their experiences more divisive than useful for post-Liberation policies. The scattered entities of the Independence Movement seemed to be condensations of the fluidity and divisiveness of the Yi world without offering a solution for its problems.

FORCED MODERNIZATION

The March 1 independence movement proved to be a watershed of more than one kind. For those of exceptional will, it was an open break with Japan. The great majority of the population, however inwardly sympathetic, could not afford such reaction; they had perforce to live and work in the peninsula, very largely on the terms Japan gave them. These terms were Japan's weapon, and she used them. After 1919, she saw that the old methods, employed by the most reactionary members of her society's conservative military fringe, would not work. She altered, though she did not revolutionize the terms. A decade later, under the pressures of continental expansion, she altered them further. The alterations could not bring friendship, true acceptance, or popularity; they did, however, begin to reopen that streaming toward, that competition for, central power that had been the mainspring of the old Korean political tradition. The pattern proved useful for Japan when, after the middle thirties, the militarists swept Japan and Chōsen with her into mass mobilization for war.

The events of 1919 concentrated the attention of Tokyo policymakers on Chōsen for the first time in a decade. The demonstrations chanced to occur in the period of the victory of Premier Hara and the Seiyūkai. Japanese public opinion, always torpid on colonial matters, was not greatly aroused, but Japan was embarrassed by international publicity, and her more liberal statesmen and bureaucrats voiced concern. Admiral Saitō, sensitive and sympathetic, a kind of General Gavin among Japan's military clique, was appointed governor-general and became Korea's best and longest-lasting one (1919–1927, 1929–1931). Instructions were issued to push reforms "in order that all differences between Chōsen and Japan proper, in matters of education, industry, and the civil service, may be finally obliterated. It is the ultimate purpose of the Japanese Government in due course to treat Chōsen as in all respects on the same footing with Japan proper." [39]

Such objectives were not served as hot as they were cooked, but much was done. The gendarmerie was abolished, the police and prison systems improved — as well as enlarged. School regulations were adopted lengthening the course of study, granting wider options in the curricula, permitting religious instruction in private schools, and relaxing the use of the Japanese language in certain subjects. Reports on religious activities were abbreviated. Three Korean language newspapers owned and edited by Koreans appeared, as did in time several journals, including *Kaebyŏk* (Creation) and even the Communist underground *Chosŏn ji kwang* (Light of Korea). The Higher Civil Service and other official and specialist examinations were revised to allow Korean candidacy. A few Koreans were appointed to higher posts, including governor, judge, and public prosecutor. The wearing of swords by civil officials was abolished. The Advisory Council (Chūsūin) with Korean (puppet) members was revived, and local, mostly elected, advisory councils for provinces, prefectures, fourteen municipalities, and townships were provided.[40]

Admiral Saitō appeared determined to make himself the reincarnation in Chōsen of Gotō Shimpei's old "cultural policy" for Taiwan.[41] Some reforms proved of little long-run effect, and yet, by and large, the area in which Koreans could be made to seem to participate in the government, though still confined, widened appreciably. The Admiral well knew that nothing would make Japanese administration popular among Koreans.[42] But his measures did tilt policies enough to end complete alienation and redirect many ambitions toward participation. From his time on, Japanese rule was swallowed with surprisingly little overt Korean protest, bitter as the medicine still was.

Education

More fundamental in increasing Korean participation in their own society was educational expansion. It was not wholly new. Following the abolishment of the *sŏwŏn* in the Taewŏn'gun's decade and the end of the examination system in 1894, Christian schools had begun to fill the gap, gradually from 1885 until 1903, then in a decade of deluge from 1903 on.[43] Koreans, indeed, took their frustrations over impotence and leaderlessness out in these years very largely on education and were swept with a nationwide conviction that only through it could they reassert national pride. With Annexation, the basic earlier Yi pattern of government control over education reasserted itself with all the force of the government-general's growing bureaucratic controls. Under Japanese influence, the elementary school system and the prescription of courses and textbooks was lodged in the Ministry of Education in 1906. Licensing of private schools and imposition of government-improved textbooks came in 1908; schools were required to give all essential information about themselves to the Ministry, which could close them for violating "laws or ordinances." Teachers had to have moral and educational qualifications approved by the government.[44] Government textbooks began to be distributed in 1908, reaching 270,000 copies sold or freely distributed by 1910. Enrollment in government schools increased from 16,000 in 1910 to 95,000 in 1918. Quality also improved: experienced Japanese teachers were lured by the thousands with salary differentials. Thereafter, government control of education was unbreakable; the missionaries, though still significant, especially in high school and college education, became a small, tightly-controlled minority group within the educational system, their schools decreasing to 230 in 1917 and to 34 schools and three colleges by 1937.

Saitō greatly increased this trend. His bureaucrats realized that the only way in which they could hope to maintain control over the loyalties of the Koreans and recruit them into the Japanese imperial system was through educational control both firm and expanded. Koreans enthusiastically welcomed education both for general improvement and as a ticket to the bureaucracy and its values. A start had already been made, but now it was greatly increased. In thirty-one years the number of students at all levels increased over sixteen times, from 110,800 in 1910 to 1,776,078 in 1941.[45] The number of elementary schools increased from one in every three townships in 1922 to more than enough to cover every township by 1945.

Still, over 50 percent of Korean children in 1945 were not receiving "compulsory" primary education, and what was given was almost entirely primary. Only 5 percent of Korean children went beyond. In 1941 there were in higher education, including normal schools and preparatory colleges, 9,565 students of whom Korean students in Chōsen's one full-fledged university, Keijō Imperial (now Seoul National), numbered 304. Besides these, there were, however, thousands of Korean students in high schools, colleges, and universities in Japan — 6,000 in 1936 in all, although this figure did not equal 1 percent of Chōsen's population of college age.[46] At Liberation, little over 20 percent of Koreans had had any formal schooling, as opposed to three quarters of the Japanese population of Chōsen; some ten times the proportion of resident Japanese as of Koreans had secondary education. A study of the 1944 census shows that some 7,733,000 out of a population of 17,000,000 in South Korea were illiterate.[47] Koreans, zealous for education, deeply resented Japanese educational discrimination.

Even so, a great step toward modernization was taken. As with earlier insulation of the Koreans from rule, effects were both intended and unintended. Education was molded in planned uniformity to Japan's purposes. "Common education shall" pay "special attention to the engendering of national [that is, Japanese] characteristics and the spread of the national language [Japanese]"; "the essential principles of education in Chōsen shall be the making of loyal and good subjects by giving instruction on the basis of the Imperial Rescript [of the Emperor Meiji] concerning education." [48] Japanese was emphasized from the beginning. It was increasingly the language of instruction in a school system controlled by Japanese teachers; from 1938 on, instruction could be in no other tongue. Knowledge of Japanese rose from 0.6 percent of fifteen million Koreans in 1913 [49] to over 15 percent of twenty-five million Koreans by 1945, or from ninety thousand to some three and a half million speakers. Every intellectual knew Japanese, and many schooled in the last decade of the regime came to read, if not speak, it better than they did Korean. Rigid indoctrination in Japanese nationalism and loyalty to the emperor was enforced, the loyalty oath having to be daily repeated in Chōsen even though optional in Japan itself.

The system led as naturally to sending sons for higher education to Japan as British colonial education led Indians to London. As Chōsen's economy expanded, thousands went. If successful, the young Korean could take the difficult Japanese Higher Civil Service Examination and, if he passed, demand official appointment. As war expanded opportunity, education found increasingly promising placement. So many Koreans passed as to cause the Japanese private surprise and embarrassment. Many young Koreans became *kunsu* in Chōsen's last years. Lawyers, judges, prosecutors, doctors — all these had their examinations in the Japanese-Germanic tradition. The Koreans tried all of them, and specialization took strides. As in Meiji Japan, the school and examination systems were open without social distinction, though nationalist political activity could militate against educational advancement and only the well-to-do could send their children to Japan. The hectic years of late Yi over, education came to be the only path for ambition, and all good schools were over-subscribed several times. The young Korean was thus thoroughly inducted into the Japanese world. Home education often conflicted, and attitudes toward induction differed. Not a few, however, contrasting indigenous standards with those of Japan, concluded that the path of modernization lay on the whole with the latter. As time wore on, consciousness of independent nationhood slowly receded. For the young, forming one's ambitions in terms of the Japanese world and one's career within Chōsen became almost inevitable, even where resentments and hurt lasted. In the last years there were even some who had to learn for the first time after Liberation a sense of independent cultural identity.

Education, even knowledge of Japanese, however, was a two-edged sword. Japan was one of the greatest publishing countries of the world and the greatest of all translators of Western texts. Schools increasingly used such translations. Development of the paperback early among world nations placed in Korean as well as Japanese hands a wealth of ideas and stimuli far beyond the possibility of narrow Japanese colonialism to contain or repress. Ideas opposed to militarism and colonialism appealed strongly to students who felt resentment at Japan's subjection of Korea and its culture. The effect was increased by trends within Japan itself. Japanese social unrest in the 1920's proved an excellent incubator for hatching Korean revolutionaries. Some radical Japanese teachers, unhappy with the homeland environment, found their way into the Korean educational system and, especially in Seoul and Taegu, spread Marxism and other radical ideologies. Korean students in the non-colonial environment of Japan itself — men such as Yi Kwang-su and Kim Yak-su — were especially likely to become either nationalists or Communists.[50] From 1924 on, leftist students returned from Japan were organized into such groups as the North Star (later North Wind), which introduced communism to young Koreans. Every variety of idea from Christianity to Marxism, socialism, democracy, communism, nihilism, and, under later Axis influence, nazism entered the stream of ideas. The comparative unity of ideas and beliefs that Yi Confucianism had sustained was shattered. The intellectual climate of the state changed rapidly. Ruled by a power that brooked no participation from ordinary Koreans and by means and laws disagreeable to the subjects, the prevailing intellectual attitude toward government became cynical, often revolutionary, nihilistic. No ground for a political belief to unite, motivate, and sustain a nation and its people, even should independence come, was given. Rather, on top of an incohesive society, a diverse, conflicting world of ideas spent itself in arguments that broke on the unyielding reef of the government-general. Bitterness and despair accompanied the expansion of intellectual horizons; such mood spoke in the poetry and stories of the epoch.

Finally, it was also important that the multiplication of schools meant the creation of more institutions. Rooted in the state, they were far firmer than *sŏwŏn* of old, though also far less related to local concerns. Precisely because intermediary institutions were so few and badly needed, schools, especially those above primary school, became, more powerfully than almost anywhere else, the focus of loyalties and of group coherence. Outstanding among these were the student and alumni bodies of Chōsen's private high schools and colleges, both Christian and non-Christian. Given the lack, as De Tocqueville so beautifully puts the plight of the isolated man, of "hereditary friends whose cooperation he may demand or class upon whose sympathy he may rely," school friends, especially high school friends, became the young Korean's lifetime circle, the men he looked to for help to the end.[51] Koreans, feeling largely shut out by the Japanese, here found staging areas for protest and strike, circles where their separate consciousness within the Japanese world could be nourished at the same time that their own induction into the Japanese world was proceeding.[52] Korean leadership reflected these conflicting focuses. It based itself less on academic merit than on artful aggressiveness in outwitting school authorities and doing something "racially conscious" or "independent": preventing, with private threats, the younger classes from applauding during a Japanese patriotic occasion, for example; waylaying a Japanese teacher at night and beating him up; being an athletic hero who outperformed Japanese. Such leadership inspired codes of bravery, heroics, bullheadedness, recalcitrance in the face of authority, competition without restraint or quarter. Career leadership up the Japanese ladders came from impulses opposed to these: obedience to authority, restraint, patience, specialized skills that wore political blinders. School was an exciting *champ de Mars:* a theater of conflicting values, strains, and double standards. It was an immensely important though ambivalent arena between home and career, at once an irreplaceable source of recruitment and integration into the Japanese world and a breeder of opposition and nationalism. Above all, for both patriot and collaborator, it multiplied many times the numbers of those injected, without class boundaries, into the political process.

The Press

A smaller but significant channel of political recruitment opened by Admiral Saitō's reforms was the press. Newspapers, though relatively recent in Korean history, are extremely important.[53] Koreans cite a short-lived attempt at publishing news around the court in 1578, its sponsors soon exiled. But essentially the first modern press appeared in 1883 and for the succeeding twenty-four years advocated reform and "enlightenment." All newspapers were suppressed during the Annexation period, following passage in 1907 of a stern, Japanese-inspired press-licensing law. For a decade, Japanese newspapers monopolized Chōsen — thirty-three of them existed in 1938 — and to the end they dominated.[54] In 1920, however, as a result of the post–Independence Movement reforms, three Korean newspapers were allowed: the *Tong-A Ilbo*, the *Chosŏn Ilbo*, and the *Sidae Ilbo*. Despite many closings, innumerable fines, bans, and seizures and constant harassing censorship, these newspapers continued until 1940, when all were forced to close, leaving the last five years entirely to the Japanese press. The *Tong-A* and *Chosŏn* have continued since liberation to be not only Korea's most important newspapers but among her most important continuing institutions.

The function of these newspapers — and of a few magazines like Yi Kwang-su's *Kaebyŏk* (Creation) — in maintaining national consciousness was great. Despite censorship, they were important forums of public opinion, though demanding an astute reading between the lines. Less obviously, they were important intermediary institutions serving as magnets and meeting houses for those in the nationalist movement. They were financed by men like Kim Sŏng-su who believed in gradual, institutional approaches to eventual independence. They drew together, as almost no other institutions did, elder nationalists like Yi Sang-jae and Yi Sŏng-hun and Korean students returned from study in Japan's slightly more liberal atmosphere or, more rarely, America: men like Chang Tŏk-su, Song Chin-u, Yi Kwang-su, An Chae-hong, Cho Pyŏng-ok, Yŏ Un-hyŏng, Kim Chun-yŏn — in fact, an astonishing proportion of Korea's postwar political leaders, not only of the right but also of the left. The editorship was generally conservative-nationalist, but the staff and even the workers harbored a distinct and rising socialist and even Communist influence. To some extent, publications were nuclei from which political parties were eventually formed and politicians recruited or bred. They even planned political mass meetings, as on April 22, 1924.[55] Besides repression, they had one less inevitable misfortune: unlike the Japanese press in Chōsen, all were centralized in Seoul. There was no local

Korean press to inspire a sense of local pride and community or voice local issues. This failure to hold together local loyalties outside Seoul was an unhappy prelude to the increasing forms of centralization now soon to be strengthened.

Industrialization

For the first twenty years of Japanese rule, Chōsen was looked on primarily as a source of food for Japan's expanding population and as a market for Japanese goods; industry and a middle class were not greatly strengthened. Social mobilization was gradual. In 1931, however, began a sharp change. With Japan's penetration of Manchuria and preparation for further expansion in China, Chōsen became a base for Japanese domination of Asia; her industry and cities were built up, her industrial raw materials exploited, and her communications system, then second only to Japan's in Asia, became Japan's lifeline for continental dominion. After 1938, this expansion greatly quickened with the coming of full-scale war in China.

These developments had great effects on the character of Korean society; more, indeed, than the deliberate changes of the preceding twenty years. They constituted a classic instance of swift social mobilization and the first chapter of a new social, economic, and political upheaval that was to last until after the Korean War.[56] This rapid development, in Japan's rather than in Korea's interest, was undertaken on the basis of a Japanese estimate that the colony had grown sufficiently stable politically to bear the strains of war expansion and exploitation. The estimate proved correct. Japan's war effort was interrupted within Korea by no major incident.

The development of industry is demonstrated in Tables 1 and 2. Andrew Grajdanzev shows that the increase was smaller than it seems.[57] Nevertheless, corrected for changes in the price level, the gross value of industrial production increased over 80 percent in five years. The increase thereafter was steep. Stated yen value in 1945 was about fifteen times the 1932 value.[58] Household industry dropped steadily as a part of total industrial production, from 40.1 percent in 1933 to 24.7 percent in 1938.[59] Heavy industry's share in industrial output, which had been 38 percent in 1930, became 73 percent by 1942.[60] Chōsen's balance of trade (97 percent with Japan) was consistently unfavorable because Japan made Chōsen one of the

Table 1. Development of industrial activity in Korea,
1922–1944

Year	Number of employees (in thousands)	Gross value of industrial product	
		Yen millions	Yen millions corrected for changes in price level [a]
1922	46	223.3	721.7
1929	94	351.5	641.3
1933	120	367.2	520.3
1937	207	959.3	672.0
1938 [b]	231	1,140.1	690.0
1944 (ca)	550	20,500.0	1,376.7

Sources: Andrew Grajdanzev, *Modern Korea* (New York, 1944), pp. 148, 149; Hagwŏn-sa Publishing Company, *Korea: Its Land, People, and Culture of All Ages* (Seoul, 1960), p. 220; Bank of Chōsen Monthly Statistics (Seoul), January 1922, 1929, 1933, 1939.

[a] Corrected by the Seoul index of wholesale prices.

[b] In the same year there were 3,215,000 Japanese workers in Japan, and a gross value of ¥19,667,000,000.

chief repositories of its investments, ¥1,229,417,000 of an export total of ¥3,576,000,000 going there in 1939. Japanese investments in Korea increased from an estimated ¥100,000,000 or less in 1910 to an estimated 5–6 billion yen in 1940.[61] The period after 1930 was charac-

Table 2. Growth of industrial corporations (including mining)
in Korea, 1929–1939

Variable	Year				
	1929	1932	1935	1938	1939
Number of corporations	484.0	563.0	717.0	1,203.0	1,812.0
Subscribed capital (¥ millions)	189.9	260.9	287.9	656.3	728.7
Paid-up capital (¥ millions)	76.7	143.6	198.1	430.1	510[a]
Paid-up capital all corps. in Korea (¥ millions)	310.6	373.3	591.3	1,028.1	1,235.7
Industrial as percent of total	24.7	38.2	33.5	41.8	41.2
Average capital per industrial corp. (¥ thousands)	158	255	276	358	390[a]

Sources: Andrew Grajdanzev, *Modern Korea* (New York, 1944), p. 153; Bank of Chōsen Monthly Statistics (Seoul), January 1939.

[a] Approximate.

terized by the entry into Chōsen of the largest Japanese industrial and trading concerns: Mitsui, Mitsubishi, Sumitomo, Yasuda. Some giant Japanese enterprises such as Noguchi developed primarily in Chōsen.[62] Mining, which increased some 80 to 100 times between 1913 and 1944, saw most of this increase in the last fifteen years. The number of Korean workers in industry and mining doubled and redoubled, becoming some 733,000 within Chōsen by the end of the war, 550,000 plant workers and 183,000 mining workers.[63] Besides these, some 2,616,000 workers were drafted for laboring work in Korea in expanding railroads, and so forth; and another 723,000 were drafted for common industrial labor in Japan and for labor to support the Japanese armed forces in the South Seas. Other thousands went to Manchuria and North China, either with the armed forces or in other capacities.

The process of industrialization offered particular hope for Korea. Good foundations had been laid with a generally successful program of agricultural development. The rapidly increasing population, bright and ambitious, absorbed skills easily, needed employment, and sought the alternative avenues of advancement that industry could offer.[64] Industrial hierarchy and specialization offered potential new sources of order for society. The united peninsula was moderately well endowed with a variety of resources and was well located within the Japanese world for their employment as Manchurian economic development soared. The Japanese contributed some balance to development by locating their industry not in Seoul alone but wherever such resources as tungsten, coal, water power, or fish oil lay. Industry, especially local industry, gave some promise of the development of intermediary institutions and interest groups that might eventually serve not only for economic development but as political barriers to uncurbed central power and, if a new political system came, as the foci of a local representation. Socially, new industry could have bound men in communities of common interest and loyalty and counteracted the tendency toward a mass society.

Unfortunately, Chōsen's industrialization in fact frustrated almost all these benefits and furthered some opposite tendencies. The tempo of growth was hectic. Nameless places, lacking all traditions or ties, mushroomed overnight. Labor was recruited helter-skelter from distant parts, railroads competing with industry in Japan by offering special rates to attract landless southerners to the north.[65] Facilities and resources were overused. Overtime was constant, union activity forbidden. There was no leisure to form new ties. With Japan's defeat, complete industrial collapse drove labor back to other areas or to unemployment; communities became more restless and deracinated than ever.

Even while they lasted, the new industrial institutions had Japanese, not Korean, roots. The Japanese owned 90 percent of the total paid-up capital of all corporations in Chōsen in 1938 and 85 percent of all manufacturing and industrial facilities in 1945 as well as controlling all major banking, insurance, and so on. One Korean economist believes that the Korean share in over-all industrial capital invested in Chōsen in 1940 was not over 6 percent and that nearly 90 percent of money invested in even Korean-operated industry came from Japanese.[66] Only one major textile company and a few other medium-sized banking and other businesses were Korean-owned; elsewhere, Korean ownership was confined to small-scale industry, largely in rice and food processing. Ownership and management were hence alien and, as major firms moved in, tended to be controlled from distant headquarters. Koreans participated only on the lowest rung; discrimination existed down to the foreman level. Under these circumstances, the development of specialization, new hierarchies and respect systems, and the feeling of teamwork or stable career were frustrated. Goaded and overworked as war hysteria mounted, Koreans could hardly feel loyalty to institutions or develop a sense of community. At the same time, this agitated populace had a wide variety of new needs and a new potential to engage in political movements. Atomized and anxious with the collapse of even such associations as existed in 1945, many Korean workers became comparatively easy prey to politics in the form of Communist organization.

A few hopes were fulfilled. As manpower needs rose near the war's end, some thousands of Koreans became well-to-do, a few rich. Hundreds of thousands got their first taste of work in large organizations. Some workers became on-the-job technicians and, as the lack of enough of these was felt, technical education was stepped up, technical middle schools rising from forty-four in 1925 to ninety-five in 1941.[67] The formation of a new middle class was started, though the terms of Japan's industrial and agricultural ownership left it extremely weak. It was the Japanese who constituted almost the entire middle and upper classes of Chōsen, their property the great bulk of vested interest. This was poor auspice for the development of popular respect either for middle classes or for vested interest itself. Koreans of middle-class status thus tended to be more envied than respected; charges of collaboration undermined their effectiveness as an elite.[68] The departure of all Japanese and the forfeiting of their property was thus destined to create a situation far more revolutionary in social, economic, and political terms than took place at the close of probably any other colonial regime, even, perhaps, that in Vietnam.

Communications

Meanwhile, Chōsen was undergoing a revolution in communications. Starting with the opening of the Seoul-Inch'ŏn line in 1899, the Japanese had paid special heed to railroad building, expanding the lines to 6,362 kilometers by 1945 (with several additional new lines 80–95 percent completed by Liberation).[69] The Korean network, concentrated in the north, was second only to Japan's in the Far East, built not only for Chōsen's internal needs but also to service Japan's connections with her expanding Asiatic empire. Roads for motoring were less developed, but Chōsen ended with about 20,000 miles of roads, roughly half of which were primitive tracks and almost none of which were paved. Though the Japanese did most of the traveling, there were over 500 bus companies, 230 taxi companies, and 671 trucking companies in the thirties; most were small, and few survived the wear and tear of World War II. Chōsen ended the war with 230,000 tons of shipping and many port facilities. There was a well-developed network of post offices, 1,031 in 1938 and 670 in South Korea alone in 1945; almost all were equipped to send telegrams. There were over 5,600 miles of telegraph lines and 7,100 telephone lines with some 50,000 subscribers, though only 15,000 of those were Koreans. Broadcasting increased tremendously right up to the end of World War II, with 15 radio stations within Chōsen, 10 of them added since 1941, and some 240,000 radio receivers in South Korea, two thirds owned by Japanese but seized in 1945 by Koreans.[70] Some 200,000 sets had been added since 1938. Thus by 1945 Korea had more radios per population than South Vietnam, Indonesia, Angola, or Kenya were to have by 1959 and more than India, Burma, or Nigeria can be projected to have in 1975.[71] There were 72 theaters in Chōsen in 1937 (as compared to 32,338 in Japan), some 300 by 1945, and 51 cinemas (compared to 94,853 in Japan). There were 20,000 communications employees in Chōsen's government by 1945, 4,000 in top positions being Japanese.[72]

The great majority of these facilities were used by Japanese, but it is still clear that Koreans lived, even before World War II, in an environment of communications and modern stimulation that many emerging nations have not attained today. It is further clear that this environment had been dramatically improved in the years before 1945, helping to catapult a society into the new complexities of modern life. A communications breakthrough was at hand; in it Koreans were beginning to participate more widely and were thus another step closer to large-scale political mobilization.[73]

Urbanization

The boom in industrialization and communication was accompanied by one in urbanization equally abrupt. In 1910, only 11 Korean cities had a population of over 14,000, and their aggregate population was only 566,000, hardly 4 percent of the population.[74] Even this was an increase over urban population as compared to the traditional society, for during most of the Yi Dynasty's 500 years urban residents numbered probably not much over 300,000. Seoul, which had about 103,000 people in 1426 soon after its founding, had 219,824 in a "careful census" taken in February 1897.[75] By 1920 the figure was up to 250,200, by 1930 to 394,200, and by 1940 to 935,500.[76] P'yŏng-yang is recorded by Isabella Bishop in 1896 as "a prosperous city of 60,000 inhabitants reduced to decay and 15,000 [by the Sino-Japanese War]." [77] The *Korean Repository* gives P'yŏngyang and Taegu "about 75,000 each" although the missionary Adams family, arriving at just about that time in Taegu, found that the bicycle they imported was hard to use for lack of roads and paths.[78] Songdo (Kaesŏng) had about 60,000. Four other cities had upward of 30,000, liberally estimated. Inch'ŏn (Chemulp'o) was far under 30,000. Pusan, Taejŏn, Kwangju, Mokp'o, Masan, Kunsan, Hŭngnam, and, indeed, virtually all the later cities of the North, were villages or had not come into existence at all.

By 1939–40, when a census was taken, the population of the above 11 cities had reached 1,916,000, or about 8.4 percent of the greatly expanded total population, having risen by some 91 percent in the four years since 1935.[79] By Liberation, it was well over 2 million in a population of about 26 million. Korea's 6 largest cities more than doubled in size between 1930 and 1940. Some newer northeastern cities like Ch'ŏngjin quintupled in the same period. In addition, in 1940 there were over 50 Korean cities with populations over 15,000, and their aggregate population was 3,012,400 or about 13–14 percent of the population. P'yŏngyang claimed 285,965 inhabitants; Pusan rose from almost nothing in 1875 to 73,900 in 1920 and 249,734 in 1940 (and was to have 1,354,400 in 1963). Wŏnsan's 18,000 had become 80,000 by 1940. Ch'ŏngjin in the north rose from a few thousand to almost 200,000, mostly between 1930 and 1940. Unknown villages such as Taejŏn, Hamhŭng, and Mokp'o became cities with populations ranging upward from 40,000.[80] Not only increased industrialization but also surplus of population on the land, landlordism, and actual rural hunger in the mid-thirties fueled this urban boom. Still further increases occurred before 1945, as war and its industry swept ever greater numbers into cities.

Meanwhile the number of Koreans in Japan — mostly in urban areas — similarly soared. Immigrants rose from 3,630 in 1914 to 419,000 in 1930. The Korean population in Japan, less migratory in the thirties than in the twenties, rose to 456,217 in 1933, 690,503 in 1936, and 2,400,000 by the end of the war.[81] All but about 700,000 of this population returned to Korea after Liberation; few being willing to return to villages, they added with massive suddenness to urbanization.

Even in 1945, none could foretell that urban population would reach 18.5 percent in 1950 and move in the direction of becoming one third of a vastly increased population within the next twenty years, bringing Korea almost abreast of the Soviet Union and ahead of Belgium with respect to proportion of urbanized populace.[82] Korea was undergoing an enormous social revolution that would have forced wide-ranging political change even had a tight colonial regime been allowed to try to retain control.

As with industrial growth, the abruptness of urbanization swept people from all ties and known settings into alien worlds that sought only to exploit their labor and knew no pause in war for social needs. By 1940, 9 percent of all Koreans and 13 percent of gainfully employed men aged twenty to twenty-four were living in provinces other than those where they were born. The percentage was higher by 1945. The province of Hamgyŏng Pukto alone increased its population 29 percent between 1935 and 1940.[83] Before the war's end and increasingly thereafter, urbanization generated its own additions to Korea's rootless mass society as people sought in political movements and demonstrations replacement for the village participation they had known. Pressures for transformation of existing practices and institutions were fast mounting. In such ways, Korean society reached the borders of those prerequisites of disorder in which successful revolution becomes possible.

POLITICS AND MASS SOCIETY UNDER COLONIALISM

First Stage, 1910–1920

The Japanese militarist view of political activity as a meaningless, inefficient, and dangerous nuisance dominated Chōsen from the beginning. The first army autocrats, Terauchi and Hasegawa, had no intention of allowing political activity and, indeed, as Hasegawa said of himself, did "not know much about politics." [84] Strict administration by a bureaucracy appointed by the governor-general, not political parties, was in their view the basis for "orderly" reform and development.[85] During the first decade of Annexation, Koreans were denied all access to political power, had no franchise, and were not even permitted voluntary participation in defense. In Chōsen, unlike Taiwan, many local customs were suppressed.[86] Koreans' first and all-absorbing duty was to be "Japanized." Their second duty was to put their mind on economic development without political distractions.

On the surface, these stern policies bore fruit. The wheels of administration did in fact grind steadily and efficiently without hindrance from public opinion, criticism, or discussion. Agricultural production increased enormously.[87] Many Koreans, apart from resentment at Japan, were left with the impression that the system was, in fact, an efficient and productive one compared to the arteriosclerosis of Yi Dynasty rule by council.

The only political gesture countenanced was the establishment of the Chūsūin, or Central Advisory Council, appointed in September 1910 and composed of sixty-five aristocratic or wealthy pro-Japanese "exclusively chosen from among native Koreans of ability and reputation to give advice whenever the Governor-General chooses to consult it upon administrative measures." [88] The first two governors-general chose not to consult it and, though revived after 1920, it was in thirty years consulted on only some nine matters, all either vague or minor. Factional disputes undermined even these tiny tasks. Its existence only underlined the lack of political communication.

Second Stage, 1920–1931

The reforms of 1920 brought a wary advance toward more political participation. Organizations were allowed to form and meet. Pressure against Christianity was slightly relieved.[89] In the revised local administration system of July 29, 1920, prefectural advisory councils and forty-one *myŏn* (township) and fourteen municipal provincial councils were established. The provincial councils were consultative to the governor-general: two thirds of the members were selected by him from among persons chosen by local councilors of *myŏn*, town, and village; the remaining third were appointed by him. *Myŏn* councils, consultative to the *myŏn* heads, were elected by self-supporting male subjects of Japan who were over twenty-five years of age, had resided in the constituency for at least a year, and paid over ¥5 a year in taxes.[90] The governor-general could deny the franchise to such *myŏn* as he deemed lacking in "adequate capacity for and experience in elections." The council members were then appointed by the *myŏn* heads from "popular spokesmen." Municipal councilors were chosen by a majority of voters defined as above.[91] In further reforms of 1931 and 1933 the advisory councils were given the power to make decisions on matters of local concern, terms were lengthened from three to four years, and two thirds of the members of provincial councils were to be elected by local councils.

Property qualifications disenfranchised all but a small proportion of Koreans.[92] Election interest in purely consultative councils was not high, and the Japanese elections are dismissed as empty gestures by Koreans today. However, analysis of the vote confirms this only partially. Some 70 percent of Koreans possessing the franchise exercised it. Koreans, especially after the 1931–1933 reforms, increasingly voted and ran for office. Koreans could elect Koreans more or less of their own choice and often did. They also sometimes joined Japanese voters in electing Japanese. Parties were not allowed in campaigns, which, accordingly, were bland, in contrast to those taking place in the thirties among the Korean electorates within Japan. The importance of these elections is probably chiefly limited to their serving as minor preparation for postwar elections.[93] They were otherwise of even less importance than the Sin'gan-hoe or the allowance of exploratory political activity to the Communists, both of which adumbrated the difficulties that party activity would entail within the pattern of Korean culture.

Third Stage, 1931–1945

War rather than planned "Japanization" was what made the political difference. A deluge of industrial and communications development and urbanization altered the dynamics and relationships of Korean society and stirred up mass forces similar in kind, though different in origin, from those that colonialism had tried for twenty years to tuck neatly away under the iron lid of discipline. The fluid social forces Song Pyŏng-jun mobilized derived from the breakdown of the *ancien régime;* those of the thirties resulted from over-rapid industrial urbanization. Each was easily manipulated. Where Song used money and charisma, the Japanese used system. Massive policy, army, and bureaucratic efforts regulated virtually all activity. Embryonic totalitarianism was the order of the day; its influence would outlast Japan's Chōsen.

The Manchurian incident brought a tougher breed of militarists and policies to the governor-general's office. General Ugaki moderated the change from 1931 to 1936. In the latter year, the key military extremist, General Minami Jirō, Minister of War and one of the army's Manchurian incident "big three," became governor-general (1936–1942). The gloves were off and stayed off until Liberation. Complete assimilation was rushed as part of the war effort. The Korean language was dropped from courses and soon forbidden in schools and businesses. In December 1936, thought control was introduced and the "thought police" were progressively strengthened. Between 1935 and 1937 the Japanese dissolved all indigenous Korean social and political organizations; even mild political activity stopped; the Korean press was forced to close down in 1940. Suppression intensified. In 1938 alone, 126,626 persons were arrested. All Christian leaders regarded as anti-Japanese were forced to resign, and in 1944 all those under forty-five were subject to conscription.[94] Even the few existing intermediary organizations that could have mediated the naked impact of the government on the population were neutralized or removed

Suppression was accompanied by measures more positive. The militarists wanted more than cowing; they wanted participation. The Spiritual Mobilization League was formed; to achieve mobilization objectives, youth groups and "patriotic" societies of every flavor from the national to the neighborhood level were unleashed.[95] In July 1938, the Patriotic Workers Group of Rising Asiatic Youth was organized in Korea and many members sent to Manchuria as "pioneers," coming back as "spiritual leaders." The same year saw the All-Chōsen Patriotic League and the Chōsen Alliance of Youth Corps. Within Japan, a large Kyōwakai (Concordia Association) was formed to induce Korean cooperation there, with many Japanese police as leaders. Though many Koreans in Japan were hostile, others raised money, gave free labor, and some volunteered for military service, a few writing such requests for conscription in their own blood.[96] The Kyōwakai had some 37 groups under it and by 1943 developed 47 with 1,124 subgroups. The government-general established an office in January 1940 to supply labor forces for the war effort; in June the Volunteer Pioneers' Training Camp was started to train leaders for farm migration to Manchuria and China. October 1940 saw the launching of the Imperial Rule Assistance Movement in Chōsen: Koreans were to be Asia's pioneers. A vast campaign of slogans enjoined everyone to make the last sacrifice for the emperor. Efforts dipped into villages and especially urban neighborhoods. National groups had neighborhood chapters. Local officials down to neighborhood chiefs were whipped into frenetic activity. Rings and gold hairpins were collected for metal. A totalitarian climax to the process of minute social control that had been increasing ever since the Japanese appeared was now reached. It was a far cry from the Yi delegation of village and neighborhood responsibilities to village seniors.

Similar programs swept the army. In February 1938, the Army Special Volunteers Act was promulgated in Chōsen, military training was introduced in all Korean secondary schools in the same year, and Koreans began to be "allowed by special Imperial grace" to volunteer. Over four hundred Koreans were accepted immediately.[97] Equalization of educational facilities was ordered in March. Steps toward compulsory drafting began. Increasing numbers of volunteers were accepted and even more applied.[98] Higher ranks began to be given to those policemen and officials in whose districts volunteering was especially enthusiastic. In 1940 the Asia National Total Mobilization League was organized. A conscription bill for Koreans became effective in January 1944. In November 1942 this "progress" toward assimilation had been marked by a Portuguese-style "end of colonialism." Chōsen (and Taiwan) received the "grace" of administration under the Japanese Home Ministry as major prefectural governments. Under the Koiso administration (1942–1944) residents of Chōsen became eligible to sit in the Japanese Diet. General Abe, last governor-general (1944–1945), appointed six, but the war's end came too soon for them to take their places.

However ruthless, such steps were effective. Chōsen was thoroughly mobilized with minimal disruption. Japanese Home Ministry reports showed increasing satisfaction with Korean participation in the war effort and with the conduct of Koreans in Japan under bombing.[99] Minami — no disinterested source — felt "encouraged by the progress he noted in complete Japanization." [100] In the process, Korean functionaries in the Japanese network learned a technique for mobilization in a mass society they would not forget. They found it, as the Japanese had before them, a substitute for the national, neighborhood, and associational unity that was lacking and for traditions of voluntary participation that, in urban areas at least, had never existed. One did not have to have voluntary agreement; one could create national organizations, fatten them with slogans and handouts, and see them touch every household through bureaucracy's aggrandized hierarchy. It was a world that created its own order and was its own substitution for law. *Yangban* local moral authority was gone; the mass movement took its place.

Pressure of family, of village elders or neighbors, or of church had no power to moderate the extreme behavior that alienation and lack of attachment planted in the atomized urban milieu. New instruments of persuasion rose. Agitators and strong-arm men cared even less than before what others thought of their conduct. Japanese *sōshi*, toughs from the farms of Kyūshū, had played prominent roles in the murder of Queen Min and troubled the diplomatic conscience of Prince Itō. Now they again had their day, and Koreans of their inclination came from countryside to cities. Seeking any employment, they found avenues in the police. The Great East Asia Co-Prosperity Sphere found in them a ready medium to populate Manchuria and North China with spies, opium dealers, brothel operators, and informants; these spawned in the expanding world of force of the late thirties and early forties. Peddler guild, country bandit, and Japanese *rōnin* patterns mingled with half-foreign ideals of complete boss loyalty. Such men hired themselves to the highest bidder. To corral mass demonstrations, exact extra "contributions," intimidate, sniff out and break up any opposition, they were the perfect instrument of violent repression. A force was unleashed in Korea's cities the control of which no man could foresee.

INTEGRATION IN THE BUREAUCRACY AND THE ARMY

Above the masses, integration also expanded. Bitterness at exclusion from bureaucracy had, until the end, been among Koreans one of the most deeply felt of Japan's wrongs. Even by 1907, 40.7 percent of all government officials were Japanese, and the proportion rose constantly for years. By 1927 the total employees of the central government-general numbered some 28,500 Japanese and 16,000 Koreans. Almost all the latter were low-ranking: of 134 officials above the third rank, all but five were Japanese.[101] In 1936 of 87,552 officials in the central government-general and the provincial, municipal, and education offices, 52,270 were Japanese, 35,282 were Koreans, 80 percent of the highest officials being Japanese, 60 percent of the intermediary rank, and 50 percent of the clerks. The war brought changes; at its end, over half of all government officials were Koreans, and more than before were higher on the scale.[102] Universities and semi-government organizations like the Bank of Chōsen provided added bureaucracies. More Koreans went up their ladders in the late thirties and early forties.

By the war's end, well over 10,000 Koreans were serving the Japanese in the civilian and military police — many more thousands if agents were counted. Gone were the early days when the capital had been patrolled by 290 policemen and the whole country by not many hundreds.[103] How out of date seemed Isabella Bishop's complaint that "Seoul is now [1897] . . . much overpoliced, for it has a force of 1200 men." [104] From now on, the state would need curbs for a mass society, and society in its turn used the police as one of the most important channels of mobility for the lower classes. Some Koreans, at great personal cost, refused every offer to serve the Japanese; but for every job the Japanese offered there were many Koreans willing and anxious to serve. Their presence, very largely, made it possible for the government-general to contain — with constant exhortations to wartime austerity — the enormous rise in demand for government and services that wartime mobilization brought.

The army itself illustrated the trend strikingly and with great significance for Korea's future. Its history mirrors the various stages of integration. In 1910, in accordance with the Treaty of Annexation, Japan agreed to integrate certain Korean officers into her own forces. Few of these spoke Japanese fluently or had training equivalent to that of Japanese officers; as members of an alien army, they also were not trusted. All were soon put on the reserve list.[105]

For twenty years after 1910 Japan allowed no more than token Korean participation in the Japanese Army. Those few who were allowed to serve as officers, however — mostly students at the time of the abolishment of the Korean armed forces in 1907 — were more trusted and were given better Japanese training (mostly at the Tokyo Military Academy), and thirty were commissioned as regular Japanese officers. A number became fairly senior as a result of long service, one of them, Hong Sa-ik, reaching the rank of lieutenant general.[106] Others were to become senior officers in the postwar Korean constabulary and armed forces.

From 1930 on, Japan's expansion in Asia and the development of the concept of "comradely cooperation" of all Asian peoples in the Great East Asia Co-Prosperity Sphere brought much greater changes. Japan began, with deliberation, to incorporate Korean officers into two parts of her career system: the regular officers' course in Tokyo and the Manchurian Army. The two were both formally and informally distinct, the Manchurian Army being in fact semi-autonomous and in theory under the Manchukuo emperor. These two strains became the third generation of professional Koreans in the Japanese Army. There was no lack of volunteers. The Koreans were no longer at the bottom of the heap; after 1931 and the Wanpaoshan incident they could look down on the Chinese and become, once they went to Manchuria and China, middle-privileged partners of empire.[107]

Those attending the Japanese Military Academy in Tokyo were the *enfants dorés* of the system. They were selected from well-established schools, usually in Seoul, on the basis of highest standing and leadership promise. A security check was needed to ascertain that none were from families falling under Japanese suspicion. Most belonged to central or southern families, a very few being of *yangban* rank, more of *hyangban* status, some with relatives among the few Korean officers already in the Japanese Army. They were an infinitesimal group within the Japanese cadet corps and totaled, through the years, only about thirty-five to forty, of whom approximately one-half were killed, many as Japanese officers in World War II. None ever defected from any Japanese units; they had elite pride.

The Manchurian Academy was, initially, the continuation of a Chinese military academy run by Chang Tso-lin at Mukden, taken over and continued by the Japanese Manchurian Army after 1931. Japanese, Korean, Mongolian, and White Russian (for the Sungari River area) officer candidates were there added to Chinese in the "Five Races Cooperation" image of the Co-Prosperity Sphere. The academy reflected the independent character of the Manchurian Army, having its own promotion and career system, its own uniforms and insignia, and its own international, intensely anti-Communist, anti-civilian political tone. Its promotion system was somewhat faster than Tokyo's. Training, selection, and career, though comparatively rigorous, were less exacting than the Tokyo course, and until 1939, the Manchurian course ran only half as long — two years. Thereafter the Manchurian Academy moved to the new capital at Hsinking, expanded to meet increasing war needs, and lengthened its course to four years. From 1938 on, the Japanese selected honor graduates of the Manchurian Academy to finish their last two years at the Tokyo Military Academy, although they were viewed as rivals of the Tokyo cadets and housed in separate barracks.

Few Koreans were taken until 1934, but from then on every Manchurian class had between two and thirteen Korean cadets, 1934 and 1939–1941 having the largest groups. Recruitment was especially interesting and quite different from that of the Tokyo course. The Manchurian cadets were almost all poor boys from families with little social standing or previous connection with the Japanese world. With the exception of the future President, Park Chŏng-hŭi, and two other more obscure officers, virtually all were from the four northern provinces of Korea or from Korean families resident in Manchuria. Most were from the province of Hamgyŏng in the northeast, an area considered rough and, until the Manchurian incident, undeveloped, its people formerly without much opportunity. The Japanese searched the schools of this region for especially bright boys who lacked alternative career opportunities. Japanese intelligence took over a former missionary school named Kwangmyŏng at Yongjŏng (Lungchingts'un), a Manchurian rail junction inland from the northernmost part of the Korean border, placed it under a Koreanspeaking Japanese named Hitaka, recruited and gave scholarships to bright boys, and recommended its star graduates to the academy, its second-best to the police.[108] This was an exceedingly effective method of recruitment and integration and is still, by and large, remembered with pride by its graduates.

The Japanese war effort brought still further recruitment. In 1938, the Japanese started a reserve system in high schools and colleges in Japan, Korea, and Manchuria, those joining it becoming either cadet officers or non-commissioned officers depending on examination results. Many Korean students joined when the pressure for officers became intense toward the end of 1943, leading to the conscription of Koreans and of college students in non-scientific areas. Most entrants became officers in January 1944; none, so far as is known, advanced beyond the grade of lieutenant before the war's end. Not careerists, a number deserted and joined the Korean Liberation Army in China.[109] Still another, smaller group was composed of officers or non-commissioned officers who had volunteered as enlisted men under the Special Army Volunteer system of 1938. Still others served as enlisted men, conscriptees, or draftees.

None of these military groups represented Chōsen as a whole; yet the manner in which the Japanese Army recruited Koreans suggests the greater degree and variety of their integration into the Japanese system during the empire's last years. Growing up, also, as stable institutions with internal discipline in the midst of a society increasingly fluid and unattached, these organizations became disproportionately powerful focuses of loyalty and cohesiveness. In this sense, their future roles were already foreshadowed in the last years of Japanese control. Almost alone during those years, outside exile society, they were able to produce a kind of elite. Except among extremists, they were regarded popularly with perhaps less reservation than men of wealth. Bureaucratic achievement retained its value, and many "collaborators" felt that, though integrated, they were bearing a half-hidden Korean flag into the Japanese camp. Except for such bureaucrats, leadership continued to erode. Very few nationalists survived those years of extreme pressure without some tinge of compromise.[110] In view of the weakness of the independence movement abroad, this meant that post-Liberation political parties would have to be formed from leadership largely alienated from the society.

THE FRACTURING OF SOCIETY

Superficially, war shifted people, increased communications, and tended to erode rather than aggravate sectionalism.[111] In place of regional splits came social divisiveness. In this respect wartime mobilization overshadowed by far those few things that were overtly articulated as political during Japan's rule.

Divisiveness was no longer the old divisiveness of factions but based itself on a grievous issue. A small part of society, perhaps under 5 percent, had committed itself to the nationalist movement, hence active opposition to Japan. A small part openly collaborated.[112] Most of the rest of articulate society had been caught up in greater or lesser degree in the mobilizations and career opportunities of Chōsen's last fifteen years. Much as under communism, neutrality was hardly possible. The ubiquity of the regime did not permit silence. Society was for years, until the Korean War placed new writing on the slate, riven with the issue of collaboration.

The issue was bitter but not easy to define. Genuine liking of Japan and its government was really not at its core. The problem was how harshly to judge the individual's atomized tendency to accede to the pressures and lures of government. The bitterness of alien colonialism inflamed this issue, but it remains the chief problem of political choice to this day, different from those years in degree but not in kind. In a society whose Confucian background both predisposes the individual toward central authority and burdens him with moral and ethical condemnation, much agony is generated. On the collaborator issue, except for a few obvious cases, lines were hard to draw. Extreme judgments tended to condemn the entire new elite of bureaucrats and men of property. The Communists made good use of the issue not only to strengthen themselves popularly but also to make themselves the successors in a revolution of leadership. Even moderate opinion, however, condemned signifi-

cant numbers of those with experience and resources and undermined the legitimacy of many leaders who had stayed and tried to
do what they could in Korea. As in so many former colonies in
Africa and Asia, a split opened between the colonial professional,
more integrated into a foreign pattern and looking down on the
unintegrated native, and the potential politician, who shunned such
integration. Suspicion, tension, and backbiting were sown throughout
the society. The new middle class of Korea — unlike the merchants
of London, Boston, or Osaka — lacked all unity. Society provided
little capacity to form the bodies an independent Korea would need.

Meanwhile, underneath the top level, the long history of Japanese
surveillance with its war finale worked its own will on the form of
those organizations outside government mobilization. The Japanese
were superbly informed and had excellent distribution of information within their hierarchies. Korean groupings were in constant fear
of infiltration and discovery. In self-defense, the small group, the
friendship circle, the gang, sworn to brotherhood, became the social
unit.[113] Close classmate ties rose in importance. Society was thus
further fractured. The situation fitted Communist techniques of organization; only Communists evolved effective ways of structuring such
groups within a hierarchy and relating them to higher policy. The
World War II environment nourished the cell.

Much like French colonialism in Vietnam, Japan's dominion in
Korea "brought both exploitation and modernization in a mixture
that is hotly debated and can hardly be unscrambled." [114] The effects
of Annexation on the Korean political pattern were various, and
inconsistent with the plans of Chōsen's bureaucracy. Despite the
massive administrative state, politics did not wither away. Nationalism was created and came to the fore. For the first time the great
majority of Korean society was, by the fact of hated alien rule, given
an idea behind which it could unite. The smallness, the incohesiveness, even the comparative failure of the independence movement
qualified this idea somewhat but could not kill it. The mobilization
of Japan's war years weakened it more. Had the wall against participation remained high and unbridged as before 1920, a strong
and cohesive nationalist movement would, as with the Neo-Destour
party of Tunisia, have been more possible. Increased chance for participation in Japan's system struck a body blow at this cohesion, as
it did in such British-controlled territories as Egypt.

At the same time, within Chōsen, Japan could not give economic progress or modernization a satisfying social or political framework. Bureaucracy and industrialization formed intermediate organizations in more numerous form than any preceding government of Korea, and within them specialization and permanence of career began to be structured; Japan changed the Yi Dynasty's idea of a bureaucracy. It was not a change from a self-seeking bureaucracy to a public-seeking one, for Japan's colonial bureaucrats scorned the well-being of the Korean public. Functionaries did, however, serve Japan's interests instead of their own pockets, and since these interests coincided with development, the expectation of a development-serving bureaucracy was implanted. With the other hand, however, Japan undermined the permanence and effect of the institutions she created by severely limiting Korean access to them and by imposing on them the very hectic tempo of wartime growth. She greatly expanded, through education, communications, urbanization, and industrialization, the numbers of Koreans able to engage in or exert pressure on politics; yet ultimately, in the war years, she set a pattern whereby these forces were more than ever released in fluid, atomized form, without attachments or loyalties, subject to the naked manipulation and mobilization of central government. In World War II she created in Korea a form of colonial totalitarianism little known elsewhere.

Last but very important, by forbidding overt political activity, Japanese colonialism tended to freeze ancient Korean patterns and political instincts in the form that they had taken by the end of the Yi Dynasty. Koreans could not perform their own political experiments on any but the smallest scales for thirty-five years. When Liberation came, the old instincts of uncurbed, atomized access to central power, part Yi, part derived from modern urbanization, were ready to reassert themselves. The colonial period influenced the political pattern, but it did not set it. Above all, it provided for it no satisfying or stable new forms.

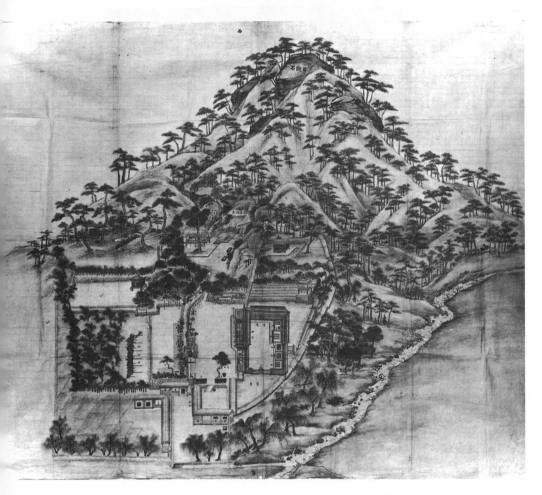

1. Compound of a Korean aristocrat-politician in Seoul, early nineteenth century.

2. The Taewŏn'gun (1820–1898), Prince Regent
of Korea, 1864–1873.

3. Korean Independence Day outside Seoul's Duksoo Palace, March, 1, 1919.

4. The ambitious Song Pyŏng-jun, who identified both national progress and personal success with Japan, stands beside his "advisor," Uchida Ryōhei, leader of the Black Dragon Society.

5. Korean independence leaders, March 1, 1946. Left to right: Kim Ku, Syngman Rhee, and O Se-ch'ang (a signer of the Independence Declaration).

5

The Gates of Chaos

When Liberation came, the tides were at the gates. In the generation of Japan's control, the population had doubled; urbanization, industrialization, education, and communication had multiplied. Alien colonialism had whetted political appetites through repression and economic ones through desire to emulate the colonial power. War brought the further stirrings of mass mobilization. Behind all this stood an ambitious but fluid society without strong intermediary institutions or class identities. Men needed strong leadership: an aroused and impatient people sought a way through a sea of economic and political troubles to new shores. Korea's own institutions had no guidance to give. Instead, direction faltered, and the forces of chaos rose.

THE POLITICS OF INDECISION

On hearing the news of initial surrender negotiations on August 11 and of final capitulation on August 15, 1945, the Japanese government-general under General Abe Nobuyuki (1944–1945) started burning its files. On Okinawa, a successful troop commander, Lieutenant General John R. Hodge, had just been notified that he was to command United States occupation forces in Korea. He did not arrive in Korea until September 7, and it was the next day when, with his staff, he landed and drove to the capital building to receive the surrender from listless Japanese commanders and establish headquarters. Uncomfortably and with different dreams, he was to lie in the still-warm Japanese bed.

The world outside General Abe's windows was a tumultuous one. The war's end and Liberation burst like a bombshell into the Korean world. Less than two years before, hope of freedom had seemed almost gone. Strict isolation, censorship, and intense propaganda prevented forewarning of the end. The Japanese were shocked, almost disbelieving of the imperial radio announcement, fearful of Korean revenge. A Japanese bank president in Seoul dismissed his car, walked alone through the streets to his home, and died of a heart attack. Suddenly, the Koreans were treating Japanese "as foreigners," which was "unbearable." Foreigners indeed, yet comparatively few were molested. The old masters now bowed to Koreans on the streets and kept out of sight. They were soon to be sent home to Japan, stripped of all property.

The Koreans lived incandescent, intoxicating days. The nation took a spontaneous holiday. The Japanese gave workers a year's pay as good-will money. Students, workers, Kims and Lees of town and village, trooped the streets behind hastily scrawled banners and slogans. Liquor vats, Japanese and Korean, were opened and dispensed. Concealed Korean flags were whipped out. Banned newspapers celebrated and reopened; new ones sprouted. At private parties, dignified professors stripped and danced in Bacchic glee.

General Abe took immediate steps to form and turn over powers to a transition government. His hope was that, in exchange for authority, he could obtain assurances of minimal security for Japanese lives and property in Korea until the incoming forces arrived.[1] He did not have many groups he could approach who were moderate, commanded respect, and wielded informal power. One of the few was the Posŏng group, chiefly composed of landowners in the southwest's rich Chŏlla Province and headed by Kim Sŏng-su. The Posŏng group's rise from rural squiredom to urban industry, publishing, and educational leadership brought institutional bonds to political group cohesion. About August 12, Endō Ryūsaku, Abe's Secretary-General of Political Affairs, sought to see Kim Sŏng-su's chief lieutenant, Song Chin-u, to transfer to him administrative power. An approach was made through Endō's subordinate, Director Nichihiro of the National Police. Song refused even to see Endō on the ground that authority for the transfer of such powers would devolve on the Americans.[2] Since leftists accused rightists of collaboration, Song also had special cause to avoid any inference of being Abe's puppet. In addition, he is known to have believed that the legitimacy of the Korean Provisional Government should not be prejudiced by an interim Korean government. Song's cooperation being important, however, Endō then sought, on August 14, to contact Kim Chun-yŏn, Communist apostate who was now one of Song's closest associates, hoping to persuade him.[3] Kim, coached by Song, also refused to see Endō. Finally, on the night of August 14, Endō made contact with Lyuh Woon-hyung, who visited Endō's residence at 6:30 on the morning of August 15 together with An Chae-hong, a moderate. Lyuh, a charismatic leader of immense energy, personal magnetism, and speaking ability who had taken part in the Provisional Government briefly as a Communist in the early 1920's, agreed to assume administration conditional on the release of all political prisoners, the turn-over by the government-general of sufficient rice stocks to feed the Korean people for three months, freedom of speech and the press, and non-interference with Korean political movements or with the organizing of laborers and youth.[4] In return, Lyuh promised that the existing government structure would not be dissolved and that the greatest restraint of violent reprisals against Japanese life and property possible under the circumstances would be provided. Lyuh was given the necessary authority and may have been given or offered a subsidy.[5] Lyuh and his younger brother, Lyuh Woon-hong, set about that same night drawing up a tentative plan of organization for a ruling committee, the Committee for the Preparation of Korean Independence (CPKI), as they called it, which would include rightist and leftist nationalists and Communists: Song Chin-u, An Chae-hong, and other rightists and moderates were to be asked to join. The next day, Endō called Lyuh and said that the United States would occupy only the Pusan–Mokp'o areas in the extreme south and that the rest of the peninsula would be occupied by the Russians. This accorded with Soviet entry into Korea, already begun on August 12, and with many popular rumors, apparently planted by the active Soviet consul-general in Seoul, Alexander Polianskii, and his inflated staff of thirty-six Russians.[6] Assuming that the Soviets would control, Lyuh then removed Song and other conservatives and rightists from his government plans; only one moderate conservative, An Chae-hong, temporarily remained in the CPKI as vice-chairman.[7]

For a few glorious days there had been unity, determination to join hands and march toward a new future, selflessness, generosity.

As returnees streamed in, now joined with refugees from Communist occupation in the north, high school girls came out and cooked rice for them. Hospitals worked night and day with volunteer effort. Throughout the nation, in towns and even counties, men of property set up committees to form high schools or makeshift schooling in the conviction that education would best build the nation. A very few out-and-out collaborators fled to Japan; many others were careful not to show their faces and wondered what would happen to them. Otherwise, all seemed equality and brotherhood. If the mass society could be rapidly mobilized by colonial masters for war, could it not develop better unanimity for independence and peace? Would the very lack of entrenchment of interests not help it?

For a brief moment, it had seemed that this would be possible. Korean postwar politics was formally reborn on August 15 with the launching of Lyuh's Committee. It was soon known by a title formally adopted three weeks later: the Korean People's Republic. Lyuh had wide repute and, as a dynamic liberal nationalist of forensic powers, large-chested and handsome, enjoyed a wide student following. The Committee quickly started to absorb the energies of much of the politically conscious community, at first almost regardless of political background. Newspapers began to spring up and broadsides to be published; but, almost unnoticed, the first die of internal political division had, in fact, been cast. Lyuh's group, though still containing moderates in local areas, was tilted left. Leading members of the Committee were leftists. Until the reappearance of *Tong-A Ilbo* on December 1, 1945, most of the press leaned left and behind Lyuh. On August 16, the initial leftist twist became a swing when some 10,000 prisoners of the Japanese were released from jails in South Korea.[8] They were political prisoners including many, probably most, of the country's fund of Communist leaders then resident south of the 38th Parallel.[9] The next day, August 17, senior Communist Pak Hŏn-yŏng himself arrived from Kwangju, Chŏlla Namdo, where he had worked as a bricklayer, carrying party instructions purportedly emanating from Moscow. Though Lyuh struggled to live up to his word and personally used his influence to discourage reprisals, hotter elements began burning Shinto shrines and beating Japanese policemen. Belatedly realizing that they could turn over command to Americans instead of Russians, the Japanese government-general now tried to clip Lyuh's wings by reducing his "government" to a "public safety committee" and restoring some muscle to Japanese power by quickly transferring 3,000 armed Japanese soldiers into the police force. The official Japanese *Keijō Nippō* newspaper, still publishing, came out against Lyuh on August 20.[10] It was too late. For effective curbs, the hour had passed.

Announcements and world news now made it plain that the United States would land in Korea and that the area of its control would be greater than Endō had been led to believe. The 24th Corps in Okinawa, after considerable difficulty, managed to obtain a weak radio signal with General Kozuki of the Japanese forces in Seoul. From Okinawa and from Tokyo broadcasts Abe's staff learned of the 24th Corps' plans and were told that the government-general should remain in control, maintain public order, and keep demonstrations to a minimum until the American landings. This news emboldened the government-general; it knew it had less to fear from Americans than Russians. The rightists, excluded from Lyuh's government and timorous of Communist hegemony, took courage, and Kim Sŏng-su's Posŏng group made an initial, abortive attempt to form a party on August 27.[11] Internal politics, lacking its own cohesion, had already begun looking to foreign leads.

Without moderate influence, the Lyuh group drifted farther left. By August 28, Pak Hŏn-yŏng had not only established himself as uncontested Communist head but was assuming ever more power within Lyuh's group; the position of liberal elements was becoming untenable. Issues of violence and of policy with regard to the incoming Americans were coming to the fore. On September 3, three moderate leftists were ousted from the Central Executive Committee of the People's Republic and shortly joined the conservatives.[12] On the seventh, Lyuh himself was attacked by terrorists while on the point of designating a cabinet and had to take a complete rest for twenty days.[13] His power was exercised by Hŏ Hŏn, later a North Korean leader, then a non-Communist, left of Lyuh. Korean nationalist unity continued evaporating at the top even among leftists. Nevertheless, operating in both North and South, pretending to act in the name of the Korean Provisional Government and in *de facto* control, the Republic had come far closer to legitimacy than any other group. It had, indeed, no rivals in the first three weeks of Liberation.

Its standing was a natural outcome of the political and economic release of Korean Liberation. Rarely has a nation been so suddenly, so radically stimulated toward revolutionary political and economic development and almost all possible manner of accompanying property and social change. Liberation seemed its immediate cause. Underneath, psychological attitudes toward the Japanese overlords revolutionized expectations in Korea more intensely than they were stirred in other colonies. Ambitious, and with their own long political and cultural background, Koreans did not regard Japan's economic achievements as products of a completely different, alien race unattainable by Koreans; rather, they looked on Annexation as a chance usurpation by a culture similar, if not inferior, of a position of pride and place rightfully Korea's. The material and educational attainments of the 700,000 Japanese they saw among them were hence powerful goads to emulation, accompanied with unquestioning cultural confidence that the job could easily be done. Such feelings became easy prey to the promises of extreme and revolutionary programs. Among them, Lyuh's group best captured these impulses, the cohesive Communist organizational core then allied to it seemingly serving as a needed magnet and instrument of planning.

The presence of Japanese throughout the country and a growing educational and communications system helped activate widespread local political initiatives by the People's Republic. The administrative, transportation, and communication networks were soon commandeered. People's Committees became rapidly established all over the country. The representatives of the People's Republic told the Americans at their September 8 harbor meeting that 135 local committees had already been established. Most were formed spontaneously by groups of prominent local citizens in order to replace the Japanese with a temporary local administration, release local prisoners, oust former collaborators, and, in some cases, provide for coming land reforms. In a revolutionary time, many of these were leftist; where Communist cells or leftist revolutionary or workers' committees existed, initiative often passed to them. Elsewhere farmers' organizations took hold. Some were headed by conservative elements, sometimes Christian pastors.[14] More were motivated by desires to lower rents and redistribute land. Distrustful of the local police, many established their own Peace Preservation Corps of white-shirted young men. These controlled, with varying degrees of strictness, most rural areas from August into November or even December.[15] Beatings of rightists, occasional killings of Japanese police, the "collection" (extortion) of taxes, and interventions, usually against landlords in landlord-tenant disputes, took place though people were generally well-behaved. The committees in each county (in North as well as South Korea) selected representatives for a provincial assembly and started, still with considerable spontaneity, to construct a national government. For all its roughness and its semi-captivity to Communist organization and method, observers generally conceded that rapid local participation was at work. Political communication and participation in government were unfrozen with remarkable heat and speed.

Though formed with little central direction, the CPKI in Seoul regarded all these committees as organs of its government. On September 6, hastening to legitimize itself before Hodge's landing, it summoned a "congress of the people's representatives" in Seoul that over a thousand delegates, many from the country, attended. A tight, leftist-controlled core had prepared all plans. In rapid-fire fashion, a Tentative Government Organization Law was passed, fifty-five representatives for a People's Legislative Committee were elected, Lyuh was made chairman, Hŏ Hŏn vice-chairman, and to them was delegated the appointing of a cabinet. The title of People's Republic was proclaimed. Lyuh admitted that the delegates, who had no part in planning the "congress," knew little of what was happening. Through haste, prior planning, and lack of any parliamentary tradition, the Communist group increased their hold. Even Lyuh, abed with his wounds, had little control over the appointing of his own "cabinet."

The Independence Movement was still the source of legitimacy. In accordance with almost universal sentiment, the Republic adopted a surface coating of the Korean Provisional Government. Syngman Rhee was appointed President, Lyuh Vice-President, Hŏ Hŏn Prime Minister, Kim Ku Minister of the Interior, Kim Kyu-sik Foreign Minister, Kim Wŏn-bong Minister of War. All were abroad and out of communication. In their places, almost all vice-ministers and other ministers were Communist or extreme leftist. Neither Rhee nor Kim Ku would have approved the list. Propertied Koreans now knew that they were staring confiscations and probable People's Court procedures in the face if the People's Republic became sovereign.

Within the first month, the country had been politically split open: unevenly — to the Communists went the share of the lion.

Liberation inevitably brought confusion. But there had also been, at first, some attempt to find political order. The Japanese government-general probably made the best attempt it could to establish a reasonable transition; but its powers were emasculated and its information on Allied plans necessarily inadequate. Lyuh's exclusion of rightists and moderates would, probably, have caused trouble ultimately whatever happened, but meanwhile the People's Republic had made genuine progress in setting down local roots and achieving a degree of legitimacy. Thus far the actors, whether Abe or Lyuh, worked with knowledge, labored or instinctive, of the Korean milieu. They could appraise the formlessness of the society, its unbridled ambitions and concentration on central power and the lack of any organizations within the country to which leaders could turn to mediate the atomized upward flow. Each probably inwardly recognized that the government-general had stood not only against Korean political maturity but also against Korean political chaos.

The colonial regime had been high-handed and unpopular. Yet there was no denying its professional efficiency. Japan's objectives were clear; they were unswervingly backed by the home government, were supported by virtually all Japanese, and understood even by the Koreans who opposed them. The colonial regime reckoned with its own unpopularity with the Koreans and set up bureaucratic control and information systems which, after 1919 at least, proved more than adequate. No power that had ever ruled in the peninsula had been so superbly informed; no power since — in South Korea, at least — has come up to the standard the Japanese set.[16] Their rule had a quality not only of complete control but of complete assurance. Theirs had always been, within Chōsen, a politics of design and decision.

General Abe and his files, his agents, and his decisiveness were in their final hour. The Americans now brought to Seoul a government that was the government-general's antithesis. The GI's lacked background even for a routine Korean situation. They were not in a position to analyze the social mobilization they saw nor judge its consequences. They had no files; indeed, they had no information to put in them. They had agents, but few spoke Japanese and almost none Korean. They had no selfish aims; indeed, they did not have aims at all, lacking policy. In them was thus no basis for decisiveness. This vacuity of knowledge and intention, surrounded by a milieu where all sought central power without other attachments, was to determine the Korean political future more crucially than any intentional American kindness.

The incapacity of the United States to take positive action in Korea was a "tradition." Secretary of State William H. Seward had flirted with forcefully establishing American influence there after the massacres of Catholics in 1866, while the Alaska purchase was under negotiation, and backed away.[17] Chargé George C. Foulk and Minister Dr. Horace N. Allen had pleaded in vain with the State Department to make greater American commitments. Theodore Roosevelt was at least decisive; but his was the negative decision to forswear influence and to give Japan's dominion the nod.[18]

With the end of the war and the diversion of policymakers' attention elsewhere, the old ghost of indecision reawoke. The Cairo Declaration of December 1943 was to make Korea independent, but "in due course." No firm consensus had been reached about when independence was to come or in what stages. A trusteeship or period of "tutelage" or "apprenticeship" usually spoken of as four-power, was to run anywhere from five to forty years, but no one thought seriously about its nature.[19] With the U.S. and the U.S.S.R. confronting each other at the 38th Parallel and MacArthur refusing to share the occupation of Japan, all thought of four-power or apparently even three-power cooperation disappeared.[20] A lack of serious interest in American commitment to Korea was displayed at Potsdam on July 24, 1945, by General George C. Marshall in a crucial conversation with Red Army Chief of Staff, General Aleksei I. Antonov.[21] But shortly thereafter W. Averell Harriman and Edwin W. Pauley from Moscow and even James F. Byrnes counseled greater U.S. commitment in Korea.[22] The decision to propose the division of the country for surrender as "a temporary military expediency" and to draw the 38th Parallel as a surrender boundary, taken, last-minute, in a hectic, evening planning group meeting in the Pentagon on August 10, can be regarded not so much as a compromise with the Soviets as one among Americans — between the hawks and doves of the time:

Harriman, Pauley, Byrnes, and company on one side, Marshall and the Joint Chiefs on the other.[23] The Soviets themselves had, until the way was opened to them by American indecision, shown little of their later stubbornness about Korea.

Surrender and the postwar period brought scant advance in decisiveness or policy. American responsibility and decision-making for Korea were, until August 1947, almost unbelievably divided and confused. Since the occupation was "military," responsibility for it was lodged in the War Department, which contained no one interested in Korea or knowledgeable about its problems.[24] Unaccountably, in the twenty months since Cairo almost no preparations had been made.[25] Secretary of War Robert P. Patterson and most of his staff were known to feel that Korea was a sideshow in which they were extremely reluctant to become "mired down." [26] They filled the halls of policy with a Teddy Roosevelt-like obbligato that the U.S. lacked vital interests in the Korean peninsula and should get out. The Department of State was meanwhile assigned responsibility for the development of American policy in occupied areas.[27] Despite Patterson's pleas, however, Byrnes "opposed the efforts of the War Department to transfer to the State Department control of our occupation organizations in Europe and the Pacific." [28]

To help State, an army brigadier general, John Hilldring, was brought in as Assistant Secretary of State for Occupied Areas. He and his staff were able but also lacked Korean experience or knowledge. The focus of their interests was Germany and Japan. Korea was placed in an "occupied" category when, in fact, the Cairo Declaration should have indicated that it be separately handled as a "liberated" area.[29] The higher rank of General Hilldring over John Carter Vincent, Director of the Office of Far Eastern Affairs, additionally served to impede the development of initiative from the latter office as did the growing tide of civil war in China, to which Mr. Vincent, a China specialist, now had to devote increasingly agonized attention.[30]

Below Vincent, the Japan-Korea Secretariat was presided over by a Japan expert; here also, Japan was writ large, Korea small. The top-ranking Korea expert was a former U.S. Navy lieutenant who had never been in Korea, pretended to no expertise thereon, but had nevertheless been catapulted into the breach. SWNCC (State-War-Navy Coordinating Committee) had to clear all policy. All "major" matters were cleared additionally with the U.S. representative on the Far Eastern Commission. Then came MacArthur and his staff. MacArthur had all powers of government in Korea vested in him until August 8, 1947; never until a year after that time did he set foot in his fief.[31] Hodge had to clear military questions with both MacArthur and the Joint Chiefs of Staff. The experience of being under the most senior and one of the most meddlesome generals of the army would not have inspired bold initiatives in any officer in Hodge's position. If Hodge felt that all these elaborate and interlocking firmaments of power revolved chiefly with confusion and delay and had no polestar for him or for Korea, he must be forgiven.

Chaos was probably aggravated by the man selected for command in Korea. Two qualified generals were considered but had to be dropped.[32] Choice was made at the last minute by the sheerest expediency. Shipping was short. The occupation must come from a place as near Korea as possible. Time was shorter: the Russians began entering Korea on August 12. The closest large unit was the 24th Corps of Okinawa, six hundred miles away; it was accordingly jumped on as the appropriate unit for occupation, and its commanding general, Hodge, went along with the package. A tough, hardworking, decisive combat general from an Illinois farm, risen from the ranks without benefit of a West Point education, unintellectual and without the slightest pretensions of qualification for the political nature of his job, General Hodge was very possibly the first man in history selected to wield executive powers over a nation of nearly twenty million on the basis of shipping time. Asked to do the job, he worked himself to the bone; nor is history likely to judge him as severely as it may some of his Tokyo and Washington superiors. Ultimately, largely through fumblings and failures of nerve in those cities, the Korean command became for him and many other conscientious Americans a well of bitterness.

Gotō Shimpei must have shuddered in his grave. His sensible ideal of appointing good administrators, supporting them, and allowing them to manage their own problems except when they needed help sank beyond all sight in the bewildering and inhibiting channels of American communication and policy, ending in an uninformed, largely incompetent command. Washington's methods created much of the kind of governmental confusion Japanese colonialism regarded as its mission in Chōsen to correct. Had the United States deliberately set out to reproduce within its system the divided responsibilities and conflicting factions of Yi council government, it could scarcely have contrived a more faithful American version. Such qualities were once more to preside over the rebirth of the kind of politics they had encouraged before 1910.

Hodge was given little support. He had to request a State Department political advisor. A Class 2 foreign service officer came without either clear directives or staff; Hodge soon sent him back when he found him lacking in Korean experience and of little use. Hodge's first chief assistant was a general chiefly famed for football prowess at West Point. No civil-affairs teams landed with him, and for the first five crucial weeks the Command had to manage one of the world's most delicate political environments with tactical forces, the Sixth, Seventh, and Fortieth Infantry divisions, that had scarcely even heard of the country they were occupying.[33] When the first civil-affairs units did arrive on October 20, they had been trained for the Philippines, many having gone through nine months of training, largely combat, with no more than a single hour's lecture on Korea.[34] Later units, when not trained for the Philippines, were trained for Japan. Organizationally within Korea, civil-affairs and other Military Government work was long hindered by strict supervision which the tactical forces, USAFIK (U.S. Armed Forces in Korea), long exercised on USAMGIK (U.S. Army Military Government in Korea). Unbelievable delays took place because of needs to clear every Military Government step with uncomprehending tactical officers of short-term Korean assignment. The result was mutual frustration and antipathy. Selection of officers and men for such duty was faulty. Rapid demobilization was the first commitment of every man; until then, USAFIK's emphasis was on keeping its 72,000 men healthy and out of trouble. Strict non-fraternization orders kept even responsible Americans from ascertaining the situation, helping American political objectives, or making the kind of contact and friendships necessary to build confidence in the U.S. presence. The effect was to combine "friendship" with information-collecting in CIC (the army's Counter-Intelligence Corps), human relations' least amiable handmaiden. For replacements, Korea was "end of the line" where Tokyo often sent its poorest — and sent them slowly.

A man such as Hodge, once selected, needed above all guidance and policy. U.S. policy channels were better suited to prevarication and delay. On landing, Hodge had no more than "a draft directive which did not include specific recommendations as to immediate steps to be taken in political and economic matters." [35] MacArthur's General Order of September 7, 1945, spoke politically only of protecting Koreans "in their personal and religious rights." [36] The State Department added only "the eventual reconstruction of political life on a peaceful and democratic basis" and even this muted paean came later.[37] Surrender and repatriation duties were clear, but the government was only "to be conducted in harmony with American policies." [38] Had Hodge not insisted, State would not even have provided an early advisor, and the Command felt State consistently failed to provide basic information on the background of American decisions on Korea. The first policy guidance was not sent until January 29, 1946, and the first detailed political policy directive not until July of the same year.[39] Until then, the situation continued to mirror the statement of the department's chief former Korean consultant that, judging by the documents passing over his desk, "almost no thought at all was given to Korea as a nation of more than 20 million persons." [40] Hodge was, on landing, left with little more definitive than the Army Civil Affairs Manual (again, for occupied, not liberated, areas) telling him that no "organized political groups, however sound in sentiment, should have any part in determining the policies of military government." In general, caution in contact with such groups was urged.[41] Meanwhile, the existing government-general would remain, under Hodge, to be gradually replaced as Koreans were found and trained.[42]

The Koreans were under quite different impressions. Unknown to the Americans, the Korean Provisional Government in Chungking had translated the Cairo Declaration into Korean as soon as it had been issued in December 1943, giving the phrase "in due course, free and independent" the force of "immediately" or "within a few days." Thousands of copies of this translation had been smuggled into Korea in early 1944.[43] The Koreans believed that if they formed a government that cooperated with the limited military objectives of the incoming armed forces, such a government would shortly be in control. Meanwhile, they were anxious to assert their political birthright of maximum access to authority with all speed.

The People's Republic therefore sent an English-speaking welcoming party of three men to Hodge's command ship, when it anchored at Inch'ŏn on September 8, to pledge cooperation.[44] It included the stricken Lyuh's younger brother, Lyuh Woon-hong, a graduate of Wooster College; a wealthy landlord graduate of Brown University, 1905, of moderate political inclinations, named Paek Sang-gyu; and a secretary to Lyuh, also a moderate, named Cho Han-yŏng. Hodge, startled at being faced with a Korean "government" (especially one of this title), lacking instructions, fearing that his visitors were Japanese-sponsored, and reluctant to tip his hand to them politically, refused to see them, though his staff talked to them. He had no way of knowing that this group was a moderate one with which it might have paid to establish good relations.

On setting up headquarters in Seoul after the surrender, Hodge's staff scrambled to find out what the People's Republic was. Lacking any briefing or written references, they sought information from personal sources.[45] These included Korean Christians who spoke English and were friends of a navy commander of missionary background whom Hodge heard speaking Korean and forthwith appointed staff political advisor. Many were American-educated. Able and well-meaning, they were conservative in instinct and tended to be in their later thirties or forties, whereas Lyuh's men were more often in their twenties and more radical. The ideas of these new consultants confirmed the American suspicions aroused at Inch'ŏn. Soon rumors of Communist influence and motivation in Lyuh's ranks reached Hodge, Tokyo, and Washington. To the U.S. soldier, after years of fighting in a simplified world of friend or foe, the "Republic" took rapid shape as foe and rival. Washington, hoping for a coalition government founded under far more U.S. influence, confirmed that "United States policy prohibits official recognition or utilization for political purposes of any so-called Korean provisional government or other political organization by the United States forces." [46] USAMGIK first privately, then publicly castigated the "Republic" and its governmental pretensions. Lyuh could not see Hodge for over a month.[47] Finally, Hodge outlawed the Republic on December 12.[48] In a chaotic situation, the first bid for cohesion had been made by Japanese and Koreans; it had been broken by the Americans.

The price in chaos and discontent now remained to be paid. Members of the Republic who held official posts (mostly in provinces) were summarily fired. Antagonism was created in local areas where the "Republic" dominated with comparative political unanimity. In

Namwŏn, a skirmish broke out when Americans took over from the People's Committee. In Hadong, the "People's Republic of Korea" was reported to have taken over the town and refused to recognize the Military Government. At Ch'angnyŏng, similar groups in an "Independent party" ordered the mayor to dismiss the police so it could take over the town; the police indeed quit.[49] In three east coast counties, where Americans had found it wise to legitimize "Republic" officials, unrest lasted for months, discontent for years. *De facto* control by locally-respected People's Committees of the abortive People's Republic continued in Cheju, Wando, and some other areas, accompanied by an undercurrent of discontent and subversion.[50] The beginnings of a popularly based government had been uprooted. Many alert men who had been encouraged by Liberation to take political initiatives in their own local affairs and who had begun to feel some sort of responsibility now drew back, bitter and disillusioned.[51]

There was nothing to put in its place but armed authority; additionally the Japanese were retained, at MacArthur's instructions. Hodge worked through Governor Abe and Endō until September 12, utilizing some subordinate officials for some weeks thereafter.[52] The tone of Korean welcome quickly soured, the leftists, including the "Republic," were outraged. Hodge was forced to move in embarrassed haste to replace his predecessors. Through the initial blunder, he now could not even retain key Japanese technicians such as were retained by the Communists in the North. By January 1946, only 60 of the original 70,000 Japanese administrators remained; by spring, all had gone.[53] The blunder was perhaps most important for revealing to the Koreans an ignorance and policy weakness they had not known in their rulers since 1910. In this weakness, ignorance, and reliance on contacts with the English-speaking, Koreans saw room to maneuver politically in the ancient game of reaching power by whatever chance connections they could make.

Somehow, avenues for this struggle had to be found, and even the Americans, despite polite protestations of political neutrality, recognized the need for beginning some other process of political cohesion.[54] For Korea's part, it was characteristic of the incohesiveness of a mass society accustomed to central direction to look to the rulers, even foreigners, for cues to follow in reforming politics. Almost alone among newly independent nationals, the Koreans could not look even to the value system of the former colonial master for support since, alone among post–World War I colonial masters, Japan had been defeated and humiliated. With Americans so inept and ill-prepared, Koreans were thus set adrift. Now, with Lyuh and the Communists repudiated, leadership would have to be found elsewhere, among exiled Koreans in America or China. Such leadership was contingent on a decision by the Americans, since only they could grant permission to enter Korea.

Indecision was in fact the hallmark of the Americans, manifested through a series of striking and contradictory actions. Syngman Rhee was returned. The background is little known. The State Department had experience in dealing with Rhee in the long years when it wished to "have nothing to do with" Korean independence. It found him stubborn and intractable. It wished — impracticably, as it turned out — to move toward its initial plans for trusteeship with the Soviets. For that purpose, Rhee's adamant anti-communism seemed less timely to State than it did to Hodge, and Rhee's immediate return under American auspices was opposed. Senior War Department officials lacked strong feelings on the matter, but Rhee had friends in their court, notably Colonel Preston Goodfellow. Hodge also, caught in Seoul's political mires, needed a leader to give a stabilizing influence and personally favored an anti-Communist one to counter Lyuh and the People's Republic. The Korean conservatives around Military Government favored Rhee's return. State's permission was, however, required to give Rhee the formal papers necessary to enter an American-occupied zone.

Colonel Goodfellow and his friends arranged an ad hoc conference on the subject in which they substituted as State's representative the chief of the Passport Division, a lady unconcerned with Korea's complexities who thought the aging exile "a nice patriotic old gentleman." No one representing the Far Eastern Bureau was present. Permission for Rhee's return was quickly granted at this conference, he was hustled out on an army plane, transferred in Tokyo, and arrived triumphantly back in Seoul aboard MacArthur's personal plane on October 16 almost before State policymakers knew what had hit them. His coming was announced with fanfare, welcoming crowds gathered, Hodge reserved a suite for him at the army-occupied Chosŏn Hotel, and, the next morning, Hodge and General Arnold, the military governor, both accompanied him to a press conference.[55]

A welcoming rally was held on October 20. Thereafter an American guard was provided for Rhee, who for a while also received official gas coupons. To Koreans, who knew nothing of the State Department's doubts (State could not clear its doubts through the complex channels of U.S. Korean policy in order to communicate them to Hodge), American policy seemed patent: Rhee was to be the anointed heir of American Military Government. One of the key foreign-policy decisions of the postwar months had, in effect, been made by the chief of the State Department's Passport Division. The good lady was not aware of the resemblance of her recruiting methods to Queen Min's.

The honeymoon was short-lived. Even at the opening rally on October 20, Rhee's speech, immoderately attacking the Soviet Union and the fixing of a border at the 38th Parallel, annoyed Hodge and added to his political problems.[56] State remained displeased but sent no instructions until the end of January. In the leadership vacuum of 1945, Rhee's presence as anointed leader endured. So, also, did American indecision and bumbling. The January 29 instruction from the State Department cautioned Hodge not to associate Military Government closely with either Rhee or Kim Ku. Military Government had to change a course then three months old and belatedly, with somewhat half-hearted support from Hodge, start assembling a coalition under moderate leaders. There was further political confusion, lack of confidence in American leadership, and an implied invitation to the Koreans for a free-for-all.

There remained the Korean Provisional Government (KPG) in Chungking. Its governmental pretensions, though somewhat hollow, still had the greatest claim of organizational legitimacy. It wished to return "to form a coalition government with the patriotic elements" in Korea until a free election could be held under the sponsorship of the Allied Powers.[57] State believed the KPG needed "relegitimizing" by the Korean people and feared it would endanger any chance of agreement with the Russians.[58] Meanwhile, KPG claims to be a government were almost as embarrassing to Hodge as were those of the People's Republic. He was not authorized to recognize any Korean political group. Despite advice from State Department advisors in Seoul that the KPG should be returned forthwith, that trusteeship should be abandoned, and that the KPG should be installed subject to USAMGIK's veto, the return was blocked for about a month until a written promise was extracted from Kim Ku and made to General Albert C. Wedemeyer in Chungking that he and his group would not return as a government. His wings thus clipped, Kim and fourteen of his comrades finally arrived late on November 23 on an ordinary army plane, another fourteen being flown in on December 2.[59] Advance notice was not given; interviews were, at first, allowed only with the foreign, not domestic, press, thus infuriating Korean newspapermen. Kim and the KPG were treated far more warmly than Lyuh Woon-hyung, but Rhee got there first by a month and caught the inside track. He occupied it, however, alone, as a prima donna operator, without organization. It was the role he loved, but Koreans would have preferred him in a governmental setting. Unwillingness to give the KPG any legitimacy, coming after the brush with Lyuh, robbed politics in South Korea of its best chances of initial, non-Communist cohesiveness, did much to destroy the leadership built up in the Independence Movement, and reintroduced chaos into non-Communist Korean politics.

The American command, having removed the only existing sources of political unity, now began to face the prospect of soon going into trusteeship negotiations with the Russians, who had made great strides toward forced political unity in North Korea under communism. In some dismay, Hodge sought to begin reassembling the political picture. On September 12, 1945, he declared that he would "consult" only with "organized political groups." General Arnold followed this up with the statement that "small political parties should group themselves into larger organizations according to their objectives."

Such unification was described as "a necessary preliminary to political maturity." [60] Hodge and Arnold were imagining a country like their own: strong, diverse local traditions, private interests, and multitudinous institutions grouped to exert pressures from below on central government. They would perhaps have liked to see a kind of Constitutional Convention. They had no appreciation of the degree to which Korea's intense centrality and homogeneity, its mass society, inhibited the formation of institutions, no concept that the basic pattern with which they were dealing was one of atomized merging, not of stands and accommodations. Korea had almost no groups able to establish meaningful platforms and objectives for themselves. To be ordered to cohere was incomprehensible; no one knew what to unite around.

An invitation to consult, on the other hand, was one of the most meaningful directions in the culture. It meant that the central power wanted advice and that the glorious path of access to power and its councils had opened. Dozens were equally qualified, equally eager, to follow it; each felt called on to form an "organized political group" to meet the formal qualification and answer the summons. When Hodge called a meeting limited to "political leaders," 1200 appeared.[61] Until September 1, there had been little but the "Republic" group. When Hodge made his first address in the civic auditorium on September 12, there were already 33 "political parties," many formed that week. By October 10 representatives of 43 were discussing unification.[62] By the time Rhee arrived a week later, he felt it necessary to consult with over 50 political "groups" and "parties." Before October 24, 54 "political parties" had registered with Military Government headquarters.[63] Some 134 registered under Ordinance No. 55 in March.[64] Thereafter, the number spiraled higher. Within a year it was 300. The façade of patriotic unity had shattered. Democratic attempts to obtain coherence and organization had instead resulted in fracturing and unlimited competition.

The Cold War increased the melee. In December, the Korean problem had been discussed at the Moscow Conference of the Foreign Ministers of the United States, the Soviet Union, and United Kingdom and, subsequently, China. The impulse of the United States was still to try to obtain agreement with the Soviet Union on Korea as on "more important" issues; for it a price could be paid — compromise was easier on "side issues." Korea was such — the bottom of this, as of every other, agenda. Agreement was reached to set up a joint U.S.-U.S.S.R. Commission to assist the formation of a provisional democratic Korean government "to guide the Korean people toward full independence." [65] The Commission was to work out an agreement for four-power trusteeship for a period of up to five years. In so doing, it was to "consult" like Hodge but on a grander, international scale.

The assembling of political unity in the South to confront the increasingly massive façade of Soviet-induced unity in the North now became urgent. Political "amalgamation" to prepare for democratic consultation was again the device. To prepare for the Joint Commission, Military Government created the Representative Democratic Council of South Korea on February 11, 1946, a "representative" political body that would support the American view in consultation with the Joint Commission.[66] The Council was intended to bring politics together in common cause. This, however, was to be accomplished by giving each major party four delegates. Korean eagerness for consultation interpreted this to mean that one must form more "major" parties in order to be consulted. Ordinance No. 55 of February 23, 1946, which required all groups of three or more persons designed to influence the political life of the country to register with Military Government,[67] encouraged this tendency by affording almost any small group the opportunity of registering with the government — and registration implied access to power, hence status. Lacking interest groups, one achieved status by calling on classmates or a friendship circle, expressing a view, and dashing off to register as a political party. As democratic technique, consultation was impeccable; one may well ask what else the Commission could have done. For stabilizing the inchoate political pattern of Korea, however, it was classically counter-productive.

U.S.-U.S.S.R. disagreements on whom to consult widened and deepened the fracturing process in internal Korean politics. Only Communists and the far left, on order, supported trusteeship. Rightists formed themselves around opposition to it. The Russians countered by demanding at the Joint Commission meetings of March 1946 that those opposing trusteeship should not be allowed to consult regarding it. Exclusion of rightists would have produced a Communist-dominated provisional government. To prevent this, USAMGIK was further led along the path of the January 29 directive: to try to back moderates and form a moderate coalition. Such steps added to the splitting between rightists and moderates. After breaking down in 1946 on the consultation issues, the Commission reconvened on May 22, 1947, to proceed with consultation with those "who are prepared to cooperate with the Commission." [68]

As the issue broadened, was noted in the world press, and generated correspondence between American and Soviet leaders, Korean politicians of both right and left felt mounting pressures of competition to produce the largest numbers of consultative bodies. More bodies were formed, many by the splitting of old ones. Although this proliferation had little permanent meaning, it tended further to discourage smaller leaders from subordinating themselves to larger ones. Such atomization was increased by the distribution of a Joint Commission form asking the views of each body on the problems the future Korean government would confront and the methods to be used in its establishment. The Chief Commissioner of the U.S. delegation announced that, by June 19, 344 political parties and social organizations in South Korea had got copies of the Joint Commission consultation document.[69] Disparateness of political view, not consensus, seemed to be solicited. Within twenty-four hours of announcement of the terms of consultation, over 80 political bodies and social organizations had sent representatives for the forms. Extreme rightists refused to participate, but, even so, 463 political parties and social organizations — from "Democratic Fronts" claiming millions of adherents to a "Full Moon Mating Society" claiming a handful — submitted applications for consultation; 425 were from the American Zone alone.[70]

Right and left were now split so wide over the Cold War and its local trusteeship issue that a gap for a separate moderate stand opened. The moderates started assembling around the American support of State's January 29 directive. Unfortunately, they lacked all other forms of cohesion. From late September 1945 through 1946 an ant's nest of middle-of-the-road groups developed. Provisional Government leaders like Kim Kyu-sik and Wŏn Se-hun had theirs. Independence leaders like O Se-ch'ang, Yi Kap-sŏng, and Kwŏn Tong-jin had theirs. Moderate nationalists from within Korea like An Chae-hong had theirs. Leftists or those associated with the People's Republic who parted with its Communist-dominated ways — Lyuh Woon-hyung and his friends — had theirs, shifting and combining and splitting. Recording who had joined or quarreled or split was now one of the chief occupations of an expanding press.[71]

In July 1946, the Department of State followed its cautious and belated instruction of January 29 by its first real political directive. This long-awaited document ordered USAMGIK to encourage a coalition of moderates as a first step toward establishing an interim government.[72] The coalition was to be built around Lyuh Woon-hyung and Kim Kyu-sik. The job of carrying out this high policy directive and steering U.S. efforts to corral incohesive moderates between packs of aggressive leftists and rightists was awarded to a second lieutenant.[73] Lyuh's younger brother was persuaded to leave the Korean People's party, which, like its predecessor the Korean People's Republic, had become Communist-dominated. Lyuh himself was gradually nudged into the coalition group. Even Hŏ Hŏn, a decidedly leftist leader, showed up at coalition meetings. The fragile coalition was nursed through repeated Communist and rightist attempts to sabotage it during the summer of 1946. On October 8, 1946, it published seven basic principles for Korean unification. It recommended, at U.S. suggestion, formation of an interim assembly. The assembly it recommended was approved by Hodge, and members were publicly elected and appointed. Coalition leader Dr. Kim Kyu-sik became chairman of the Korean Interim Legislative Assembly (KILA) on December 12, 1946. When USAMGIK embarked on a program of appointing Koreans as heads of departments in the South Korean Interim Government (SKIG) and giving them increased responsibility, a sympathetic moderate, An Chae-hong, took office as Chief Civil Administrator on February 10, 1947. Though rightists and extreme leftists refused to appoint delegates to KILA and constantly harassed it in statements, the coalition continued to register some progress until the summer of 1947, a tribute to the political influence the U.S. could have had through earlier and more forceful exertion.

In July 1947, the frail moderate coalition was overturned. Its platform was based on negotiating unification with the Communists in the Joint Commission; its unity on U.S. support for it and that position. The breakdown of the second U.S.-U.S.S.R. Joint Commission, however, ended all hopes for a negotiated settlement with the North. On July 19, the only hope for forceful moderate leadership also vanished with the assassination, in broad daylight within sight of a Seoul police station, of Lyuh Woon-hyung. U.S. support lingered for a while, and a Democratic Independence party of moderate leaders was formed and backed by USAMGIK in October 1947.[74] But by the beginning of 1948 the U.S. was forced to give up attempts to approach unification through the medium of Korean politics and turned to Rhee to back its new policy of separate elections under the UN. On September 23, 1947, the Korean problem had been placed on the agenda of the UN General Assembly, which in November adopted an American resolution calling for the establishment of a temporary commission on Korea to observe the election of a Korean national assembly. The Soviet Union refused to participate. Committed to internal methods of unification and always opposed to separate elections, Kim Kyu-sik and his fifteen small centrist parties refused to take part. Kim Ku, pushed aside inch by inch in Rhee's rise, allied his Korean Independence party with the centrists in this stand. On

April 22–23, 1948, the two Kims and some of their followers were among 545 delegates from North and South Korea meeting in a futile unification conference at P'yŏngyang.[75] The Americans now labeled their recent allies "blind men" who had been "baited by the Communists." [76] Without part in either the 1948 elections or in the politics of the next two years, the moderates were shunted completely aside in national life. Though to some degree the Socialists from 1956 to 1961 can be considered their successors, no strong, truly moderate political movement has since sent down roots into Korean soil.[77]

The failure of moderates again bespoke the mass society. They believed in the very political diversity Korea did not, in a firm organizational sense, possess. They supported the virtues of a society fitted for this diversity by tolerance and compromise, qualities extraneous to Korea's political traditions. They needed the support of a middle class; Korea had virtually no classes, and what new middle class she had was driven right in fear of communism. The moderates had no newspapers, schools, patrons, no organized loyalty to lean on. Financial support thus also failed. They had no rural following. In the realm of ideas, the Communists had Marxism-Leninism, the rightists could seek some slight bolsterings from Confucianism, but the moderates had no philosophical home on Korean earth. The atmosphere could also hardly have been more adverse. A country intensely repressed, then suddenly released, then caught in the emotions of divisions and the Cold War with altering Communist and rightist purges — this was no climate congenial to moderates. Students, perpetually carrying out demonstrations and strikes, needed stronger stuff for their sallies than lukewarm moderation. A strong moderate cause required the essentially voluntary unity of many individual convictions; only those who have lived in a fractured and incohesive society can understand the anxieties to which it gives rise and which impede convinced, united action. Even Lyuh was too inconstant or too insecure about the narrowness of moderate ground to settle there.

There were other failures. American support came too late. Hodge's support was too lukewarm to seem trustworthy. The jobs that moderates were given were constantly threatened by the rightist-controlled South Korean police, whose threats USAMGIK did little to curb; at their door must be laid Lyuh's assassination and some of the nine attempts on his life that preceded it. In an atmosphere of violence and threat, moderate eschewal of force seemed more weak than principled. Even if supported from the beginning, a moderate political effort was probably doomed in those years. The tragedy was a real one; none who knew Kim Kyu-sik or Lyuh and their great gifts can fail to recognize that they were anguished not only at their failure to put down more permanent roots but at the political atomization to which their failure contributed. The fault lay less with their leadership than with the intransigencies of postwar world politics and the nature and traditions of their own society.

The pattern events were forming was thus clearly established well before the end of the Occupation's first two years. The Americans had destroyed or alienated the chief sources of political cohesion in the country. With Korea, the quandary was especially great because the repudiation of the former colonial power had been unprecedentedly complete. Until late 1948, the United States found no substitute except force. Through supporting first trusteeship, then the moderates, it lost the support of the rightists yet found no way to make the moderate position viable ground for political action. Americans added to the incohesiveness of Korean politics by techniques of consultation and freedom of opinion that were natural to the democratic world but aggravating to the abundant sources of disunity and political competitiveness rooted in Korea's own soil. Equal access to power, easily equated with democracy, provided the same intense competition and mobility updrafts that had troubled the last Yi decades. The inability of society to form viable or defined groups (and the collapse of such classes, values, and groups as there had been) steadily broadened political competition within the society but made cohesive party formation difficult. American indecision and doses of democratic procedure simply led to chaos. The receptivity of the group-consultative pattern to such fracturing is nowhere better shown on a comparative basis than during Korea's immediate postwar years; in no other country entered by U.S. forces at the time did such a political free-for-all take place.

THE SOCIETY OF VIOLENCE

Leaderless indecision had other companions at chaos's gates. The rise of anomic, violent forces now greatly altered the terms and risks of politics.

Population growth was, in those years, more monstrous than anywhere else, except possibly Israel. South Korea's population, estimated to be just over sixteen million in 1945, grew by 21 percent
during the next year.[78] Meanwhile 885,188 Japanese, including a
quarter million fleeing from Manchuria and North Korea, were
repatriated. Prior to 1950, 1,108,047 Koreans, mostly war workers,
returned from Japan, 120,000 came from China and Manchuria, and
1,800,000 poured in from North Korea.[79] Even by the end of 1945
there were 500,000 North Korean refugees in South Korea. Annual
increase of births over deaths continued at about 3.1 percent per
annum. Rural areas were crowded and hostile to immigration. Cities,
which had already boomed during the war, had an enormous additional population, rootless and aroused, dumped into them. Upwards
of a third of the refugee flow went to Seoul. The Nathan Report put
the matter succinctly for those crisis years: Korea "probably has a
more difficult basic population problem than any other country." [80]

Administration virtually collapsed. With the uprooting of all Japanese, routine vanished. No one knew to whom to apply for daily
needs, let alone for mountainous exigencies. The economy, instead of
expanding to absorb this enormous increase, declined, the industrial
sector foundering. Japan and her yen bloc, which had absorbed
96.9 percent of Korea's exports by 1939, 99 percent by 1944, now
took almost none. The war, which had brought most industrial
growth, had also overworked and worn out the facilities it created.
There was now no economic force to repair or even maintain them.
Sources of raw materials outside Korea were cut off; so were the
Japanese factories for which Korea processed. The departure of
700,000 Japanese civilians removed almost all the country's technical
and managerial skills and its industrial capital resources.[81] Nearly
90 percent of industrial property and much of Korea's urban real
property was suddenly unowned and untended and, as enemy
property, it became vested in U.S. Military Government. U.S. troops
neither knew anything about the economy nor were equipped to
operate it. No Korean organizations existed that could even begin to
cope with the problem. Labor forces pulverized and started living
by cannibalizing their plants. The Samhwa Iron Mining Company
was stripped by them and vandals, and several of its furnaces were
ruinously allowed to cool with their charge of molten metals. Mines
all over the country filled with water, some so badly that they never

operated again. Railroads 90 percent complete were abandoned; at least one has only just been finished. Twenty-three-year-old U.S. Army sergeants who had been railroad dispatchers would find themselves managing a cement factory, a chemical plant, a silk mill, and a coal mine.[82] Not until 1947 was there a basic inventory of vested industrial and other properties; no good survey to serve as a basis for rehabilitation had been completed by the Occupation's close.

Though accurate statistics were thus impossible, production by the end of 1948 was probably not more than 10–15 percent of pre-surrender potential.[83] By September 1947, industrial employment had fallen 60 percent since 1944. Indeed, unemployment became so widespread in all fields that SKIG believed that a population rather fully employed in 1944 had only about half its labor force of ten million engaged in gainful employment by 1947.[84] In July 1947, Military Government expressed the belief that the disposal of at least small vested industry to private Korean ownership would be more efficient. Unfortunately, the position was taken that disposal should be deferred until an independent government had taken over; very little was effected. Industry was thus almost wholly dependent on an inefficient government. The relative resurgence of agricultural forces and the sharp decline of industry in the Korean scene from 1945 to 1955 had important political effects and was one significant factor in the rise not only of violence but of the Korean right.

Inflation added to chaos. The Japanese, in a *Götterdämmerung* atmosphere first of war inflation, then of defeat hysteria, had flooded the country with yen, partly to buy protection. In June 1943, under a billion Bank of Chōsen yen notes had been outstanding in Korea; on August 6, 1945, there were four billion in circulation in all Korea. By October, seven billion or more circulated in the U.S. Zone alone.[85] Although production and proper tax revenues were lacking, currency in circulation continued to rise steadily: to 18.3 billion in January 1947 and 33.4 billion in December 1947. The government's overdraft at the Bank of Chosŏn by the end of 1948 stood at 38 billion yen.[86] Retail prices rose 10 times between August 1945 and December 1946, wholesale prices 28 times.[87] Electric motors rose 100 times in two years; carburetors that had cost 20 yen brought 70,000 yen by 1947. The average monthly cost of food per person rose from 8 yen before the war to 800 yen by September 1946. The rise had early been aggravated by USAMGIK's release of controls over grain prices in October

1945. Even where there were jobs, no wages (let alone those in the government bureaucracy) could keep up with prices.[88] Strikes, demonstrations, and angry demands flourished. There was virtually no private entrepreneurship to stem the tide. Japan had almost monopolized entrepreneurship, and only those who had collaborated with her had fortunes sufficient to start or restart any of the enterprises she left behind. Even these few individuals were now threatened by both inflation and charges of collaboration. Though the society was not greatly troubled by wide wealth gaps, the economy was, by the same token, helpless to right itself through private effort. Everything was in the government's hands, and the government was incompetent and directionless.

Fed by these forces, from the late summer of 1945 on, crime rose to frightening proportions. Refugees and repatriates without jobs and without the social restraints of their home communities joined gangs that stole, black-marketed, or pimped in Seoul and Pusan's alleys and marketplaces. Corruption invaded every office. The Inch'ŏn police reported so many thieves that people hardly dared leave their homes.[89] The four thousand new refugees pouring into the South every day hurled themselves against the abandoned and untended property of the Japanese. House-grabbing, squatting, rifling, and machinery cannibalization was endemic. Black markets, hitherto almost unknown, now overpowered legitimate commerce.

Conditions unlike anything under Annexation settled on the country. A *sauve qui peut* nightmare swiftly overtook the bright dreams of Liberation. In an open letter to General Hodge on August 31, 1946, the conservative newspaper *Chosŏn Ilbo* said that "the Korean people are now suffering more than they ever did under the Japanese rule." Thoughts of security, suppression, discipline, police protection preempted all others in the civilian mind. Fears, uncertainties, and distrust were worse than in the late Yi days of Tonghak rural uprisings and peddler gangsterism.

The population caught in these massive dislocations and this wave of unemployment and crime was young; the average age was twenty-one. Those who had sought opportunity in Manchuria or been drafted for Japanese industry or military service were all young, employable men. They now flooded the jobless society. Such few organizations as were starting, police and constabulary, could absorb but a few. As crime rose in the late summer of 1945, so did gangs — among them the Neighborhood Comrades Association and student groups like Lyuh's Seoul Association for the Acceleration of Student Unity. As in the 1890's, but this time unsuccessfully, attempts were made to organize the pushcart operators.[90]

An age of youth groups came to Korea. Most were political, agitational, and, at first, leftist. Several grew out of the Korean Communist Young Men's Association, which had been active in the underground.[91] These at first formed part of the Peace Preservation Corps that enforced, in the name of the People's Committees, what little government existed in the weeks after August 15. Young men grabbed what Japanese arms they could find, filled police stations, patrolled, requested "contributions," intervened in disputes, and hoped for the path to power. Most violent were the Korean Student Bands.[92] These — merged by the Communists, disbanded by Military Government for terrorist activities in May 1947, and re-established as the Korean Democratic and Patriotic Young Men's Union — eventually claimed 780,000 members. In all its guises, this violent assemblage of youth was the strongest arm of the left in South Korea, the principal disseminator of propaganda and instrument of bribery and terror. Similar groups in North Korea became prominent channels of political recruitment for the North Korean regime; the Union would have become such in the South had communism or the left gained supremacy. Even in South Korea, relatively many "alumni" of this Union entered the police and, later, the army.[93] By the summer of 1948, all such leftist youth groups were banned.

The Youth Union, the Cold War, unemployment, and the search for political channels spawned rightist youth groups. Partly for political propaganda and power, partly for simple self-defense against leftist bands, a "youth group" became standard equipment for each political group or important political boss. In the autumn of 1945 local rightist politicians were organizing youth groups around the banners of the Korean Democratic party, the Unification party and, later, the Independence party. Anti-Communist American appointees like Sŏ Min-ho, mayor of Kwangju, were active in assembling youth associations and using them as terror organizations to harass the left.[94] The police, stronger in 1946, supported and recruited for them. Seoul's tough Northwest Youth Association of P'yŏngan-do refugees was used to quell rebellion in Cheju-do, becoming notorious there for its cruel use of bamboo staves. From it, later, came political leaders. Gangster (later Assemblyman) Kim Tu-han had his notorious Great Korea Democratic Young Men's Association and was tried, with fourteen members, for beating two opponents to death. Rhee had his Korean Independence Youth Association. General Yi Ch'ŏng-ch'ŏn, a leader of the Provisional Government and its Kwangbok Army, had his Taedong Youth Corps. Thirty-four such young men's bodies registered before the Joint Commission in June 1947.[95]

USAMGIK itself was not immune to the fever. About the middle of 1946, it set about secretly to form a national youth association backed by some five million dollars in official funds, American Army equipment, and an American lieutenant colonel as training advisor. As head, Military Government selected "General" Yi Pŏm-sŏk, former commander of the Second Branch Unit of the Korean Restoration Army in China. His selection was probably based on the fact that, in China, he had worked actively with American intelligence.[96] General Yi's political philosophy was close to that of the tougher Kuomintang activists. He placed the Suwŏn training center under the spiritual leadership of Dr. An Ho-sang, a graduate of Jena during the Nazi era, a student of Hegel, and an open admirer of Hitler's Jugend.[97] Anti-Communist political indoctrination was part of its training. By July 1947, some 70,000 had received training, and the objective by the end of that year was 100,000. Its purpose was to train men who could, if agreement with the Russians was not reached, act as an anti-Communist Korean army. Secrecy and the Youth Association title were employed to avoid Russian protests. Many of its members did, indeed, enter the armed forces, not a few as officers. In thus backing General Yi and placing in his hands one of the few large, trained, cohesive groups in Korea, Military Government was, in effect, anointing him as one of Korea's most important political leaders. Later known as the Racial Youth Corps, this group lasted until the Korean War under one or another name and, though afterwards broken up by President Rhee, constituted a famous Korean political force for some time. Its loyalties and ties are still not dead today.

Though the youth groups seemed to many foreign observers strange at the time, they now appear almost classically expressive of anomic forces: the availability for mobilization of unemployed, displaced masses lacking all other forms of group life or integration. So long as violence and disorder continued, they flourished in terror and lawlessness, waning only when society settled down after the Korean War. Dependent on illegal funds, youth groups relied on forced or "voluntary" contribution of a kind that rose to amount to almost half of national revenues in 1949. They not only substituted for the lack of more developed political organizations and loyalties; they also increased the tendency to give Korean politics a half underground character so important that the official and the informal systems operated almost as a dual state. Youth groups were among the most important places in which political socializing took place. They played a vital role in the recruiting of both political and military leadership, many assemblymen and generals rising out of them. Japanese group techniques and Kuomintang practices, absorbed in the Independence Movement, exerted obvious influence. Behind these the youth groups reflected modes socially congenial to the Korean scene: great, informal channels of social and political mobility cast in the form of equal groups contending, with an urban roughness and modern urgency, for power. What the Japanese had mobilized with slogans and national organization now rose from the Korean milieu almost spontaneously.

As the forces of violence and disorder grew, so did the police. At the time of the surrender, Chōsen's police force is believed to have numbered, throughout the peninsula, about 23,000, of whom some 9,000, or nearly 40 percent, were Koreans, mostly low-ranking.[98] Through its vast network of stations and communications the police ruled the countryside. In no other established, disciplined bureaucracy of that time did so many Koreans have roots. The collapse of central and local government in 1945 thrust it to the fore. Japan's last police chief in Kwangju correctly judged the stakes when he told the incoming Americans that if police power was invested in the People's Committee and its Protection Corps, all other government offices would also fall to them.[99] American officers, security-minded and sympathetic to the police, lent a willing ear to such advice.

By the beginning of 1946, some 14,000 Japanese police had been removed, repatriated, and replaced by 15,000 Koreans. Security-conscious USAMGIK provided sixty-three American advisors — more than for any other organization — and these advisors constituted an important clique within Military Government. The economic and the thought-control police were disbanded, the sanitary police transferred to the Bureau of Public Health, and certain guard duties assigned to tactical forces, but the police nonetheless grew steadily.[100] Some 85 percent of the Korean policemen in the Japanese force were retained and not only those in South Korea. Many charged with collaboration in the North fled south and were accepted in the force.[101] Many had records of brutality in arresting and torturing their fellow countrymen.[102]

By July 1946, the police numbered 25,000, and their swords and clubs were replaced by American and Japanese rifles and machine guns. The U.S. Army provided vehicles and maintenance for the telephone and radio network.[103] For almost two years, police alone in Korea could regularly bear arms. They were, until the end of 1948, responsible not only for internal order but for security along the 38th Parallel. Their work was active and "fruitful": by mid-1947 there were almost 22,000 people in jail, nearly twice as many as under the Japanese in South Korea.[104] Some confusion exists about their total numbers; for by the end of 1948 the force had increased to 60,000, whereas by September 3, 1948, when turned over to Korean control, the police supposedly numbered only 34,000. In any event the increase was great.

During the Korean War, the force rose to 75,000, then gradually fell to 47,000 in 1956, 39,000 in 1958, and about 30,000 in 1963, since which time police and MP's have again increased. With a cohesive core, the police remained for almost a decade probably the largest group in Korea with its own strong internal esprit de corps, in many ways both contemptuous and resentful of the Korean public and determined, as the Japanese had been, to impose order on an "unruly" and resistant public. They and their gangster hangers-on continued to attract men of the lowest classes who hoped to gain access to power as in the days of the peddlers in the 1890's. Behind their uniforms and arms they could vent their resentments on their fellow citizens. Neither respect for law nor countervailing internal force existed to curb them.[105]

USAMGIK, dependent on a few interpreters, lacking skilled bureaucrats or a political base in the country, was forced to rely on many of the police's "broad functions." Police "investigation" sections were among its important sources of political information and of political action. Blanket instructions to arrest all leftist leaders and agitators were known to have been secretly issued.[106] Evidence had little to do with the cases; sentences, especially on leftists, were awarded on hearsay evidence or testimony obtained by intimidation.[107] Rightist gangster Kim Tu-han, however, got off with merely a small fine for torturing to death two leftist Youth Association members found on April 20, 1947.[108] The police were frequently given power to grant permits for public demonstrations or for the publication and distribution of papers or pamphlets; this power was invariably exercised against leftists. Their guardianship of right-wing leaders when speaking in rural areas was marked; little protection was afforded to leftist or moderate leaders. They likewise were chief administrator of the nation-wide grain collection program, not only collecting the percentage of grain to be turned over to the government at a fixed price for use in rations but also determining, by their presence on local boards, the quotas to be allocated each farmer. In a time of steady and drastic inflation, such powers were enormously persuasive, bitterly resented, and, of course, politically deployed.[109]

Older, unmentioned functions also remained. Torture — kidney-punching, water cure, electric shock (popularly known as "telephone"), hanging by the thumbs ("aeroplane"), enforced eating of hot peppers, and so forth — stayed and grew.[110] So did corruption. Salaries bore no relation to income; in September 1945, the average police pay was ¥140 a month, worth hardly more than $3.00. Large, highly secret funds for intelligence were available with little accountability: American forces found several million yen for such purposes in police safes in 1945. Extortion was, especially in 1946 and 1947, a daily ritual.[111] Even in 1958, "allowances" derived from such "voluntary contributions" were fifty to eighty times greater than basic salaries. Political and economic powers threw such trivia as traffic control entirely into the background: drivers steered by the holes in the road while the traffic police performed continuous whistle rhapsodies and vigorous but irrelevant foot exercises before the public gaze, offering one of the few forms of public entertainment then available. The real powers of the police did not amuse. By the end of 1946, they had become USAMGIK's chief instrument of both rule and political cohesion; dislike of the Americans mounted correspondingly.[112]

One after another, storm clouds had been gathering. Even without the Cold War, internal clash would have come; with it, disruption and revolt came faster. The Communists had been the first powerful master of youth group, gang, and demonstration. As the months passed, they concentrated this power largely in powerful industrial and communications unions. U.S. forces began to build up the police and, eventually, even rival, rightist unions. The hardening of Cold War lines further marked off the field for battle.

On September 24, 1946, the members of the South Korean Railroad Workers Association presented to the Military Government Department of Transportation, their employer, demands for an increased rice ration and pay allowances, for abolishment of wage handouts by the day (designed to enforce attendance), for lunches on the job, and for cessation of reductions in the work force.[113] The requests aroused the sympathy of other workers who were suffering from mounting inflation. They were not answered; Military Government's officers were not accustomed to handling labor demands. The next day, the rail workers started striking. Rail transportation was soon paralyzed. The strike spread to the Printers Union, by September 30 to the Electrical Workers and to many other industries. General Hodge charged on the twenty-eighth that the strike was "fomented by agitators." [114] A labor union formed by rightists moved its workers in, pitched battles took place, the police arrested some 2,000 strikers, right-wing gangs guarded the return to work of some 3,000 right-wing union members, tram-car motormen and conductors struck in sympathy on October 2. The fight was on.[115]

Outside Seoul, it spread rapidly. The collection of summer grains, which was just over, caused great anxieties because the crop fell 40 percent below normal, and the short fall in the approaching rice harvest was expected to be 20 percent.[116] Military Government was determined to perform the job of rice collection and rice price control so as to forestall the disastrous inflationary consequences that followed from its failure to do so in 1945. The police quotas showed partiality to anti-Communists and thus gave leftists incentive to stir up sentiment against the police by spreading rumors that the United States was imitating Japan in syphoning off rice and dumping cheaper grains on Korea.

On October 1 in Taegu, a crowd of two to three hundred citizens participated in a food demonstration. A policeman was seriously injured, and a worker engaged in the current strike was shot and killed. Word spread. By 10:00 A.M. the next day, a huge crowd had gathered. The corpse of the dead striker, dressed in a student uniform, was carried by students and workers through the choked streets, bounced up and down on the stretcher for all to see, and laid on the steps of the police station. A brutal battle between mob and police ensued, many police dispersing in terror. The mob captured the central police station and its weapons and ruled Taegu for hours, searching out policemen in their homes, shooting them, and confiscating the rice they found there. Injured policemen were dragged from their hospital beds and killed. Some doctors refused treatment because of police resentment over loss of control of the Department of Health, which Military Government had made independent. The bodies of some policemen were hacked with axes and knives. The hands of some were tied behind their backs and sharp-pointed slate thrown at them till they fell from loss of blood. Boulders crushed the heads of some beyond recognition. In all, fifty-three were mutilated and killed. At 4:00 P.M. the local American command declared martial law and restored order with American tactical troops.[117]

In the next four days, similar, smaller incidents broke out in dozens of districts, towns, and villages throughout South Korea, mostly in the southeastern area in which Taegu is located. There were mobs of nearly 10,000 at Yŏngch'ŏn, where 40 policemen were disarmed and kidnapped and the police station, post office, and homes of prominent rightists burned. About 2,000 people mobbed Waegwan and cut out the eyes and tongue of its police chief before he was beaten to death with five of his policemen. At Naksŏng-dong, a small rural market, 2,000 rioters with sticks seized the summer grain collection and distributed it. There were pitched battles between rightist and leftist youth groups. Troubles beset Kigye, Sŏngju, and Sŏnsan, Park Chŏng-hŭi's home area. In Sangju, a policeman was beaten and buried alive. Leftist plans to capture Chinju, Masan, and Ŭiryŏng near the southeast coast were foiled by stronger police resistance. In Chŏnju, North Chŏlla, nervous police fired into an unarmed crowd and killed 20, many of them women and children. Troubles spread north, though generally at lower heat. Disturbances took place in Tŏksan, Hongsŏng, and Yesan. At Kaesŏng, on the 38th Parallel, Police Director Cho Pyŏng-ok estimated that some 40 police and an equal number of rioters were killed on October 20. Mutilation and even attempted cremation of the corpses of policemen occurred; thousands of high school and college students walked out in sympathy with the strikers. Leftists claimed the resistance exceeded anything taking place under the Japanese.[118] The country was on the brink of a major rebellion.

Hodge, misunderstanding, looked for Communists. Investigations showed not one North Korean agent identifiable as involved.[119] The Coalition Committee was called, but its recommendations with regard to police restraint and dismissals of police chiefs were ignored. Instead, arrests mounted: by June 1947, there were some 7,000 political prisoners. An enduring pattern of subversion and repression was thus established. From these events, an unbroken chain stretched to the subversive attempts of Communists in later months, the infiltration of the constabulary, the revolt of Yŏsu in 1948, and the rise of guerrilla activity thereafter, which ebbed only in the spring before the Korean War.

The rise of anomic violence was the inevitable result, not of the Cold War as Hodge thought, but of the rushed urbanization, industrialization, and mobilization of 1937–1945, plus the economic collapse, population dislocations, and lack of leadership during the first year of Liberation. The Communists were in a position to help light the fuse. More essentially, however, the October revolt laid bare the dangers of the instant mobilization of mass society. Its bitterness and cruelty underscored the abnormality of the forces such a society contained. Distended urban populations, unrooted in intermediary organizations, felt resentments that could be expressed only in mass activity. The decision neither to recognize nor use the People's Committees nor to find alternate channels of communication with local areas contributed to the unrest. Weak rule likewise re-aroused old instincts to compete for power. But the anomic forces themselves showed the political terms of the society. They were not terms of hopeful auspice for democracy or moderation; and they were there to stay. Partly through American indirection, mostly through the release of almost ungovernable forces, South Korean society stood at the gates of chaos. What powers of coherence would reassemble it?

6

Democracy: Feint, Lunge,
and Parry, 1948–1965

Korea's postwar years can be viewed as a series of attempts to find in various governmental forms the sense of a viable whole that society had lost. Within a brief period of seventeen years, in one or another of the two portions of the peninsula the answer was sought in communism, democracy, civilian autocracy, military dictatorship, and a mixed, limited military-civilian democracy. Much has been learned, some positive, more negative; some progress has been made. Student demonstrations and university closings, election irregularities and the failure of the National Assembly to function because of opposition boycotts remind us, as late as the fall of 1967, that the search is not yet painless.

Disengagement

In the late summer and fall of 1947, the United States reviewed and revised its policies toward Korea. It did so in a mood of pessimism. The first Joint Commission had collapsed without hopeful solution; the collapse of the second Commission in July-August 1947 brought to an end the search for unification or agreement on Korea with the Soviet Union — hence an end to the basis of State Department policy toward Korea from 1945 to 1947. State was operating under adverse domestic pressure because of mounting congressional clamor for re-

---

ductions in army expenditures. There was a widespread feeling, especially in military circles, that American forces were spread too thin. At the same time there were dangerous pressures: the position of the Nationalist Chinese government was weakening and that of the Chinese Communists was strengthening: it was already apparent that the Asiatic mainland would be Communist-dominated. Only conviction that the U.S. possessed in Korea vital interests would justify further initiatives.

State and Defense saw no such vital interests in 1947. Like Theodore Roosevelt in 1904–1905, they decided that the United States could, if need be, do without a fragile, complex, and tangential Korea. They regarded American programs there as an expensive and dangerous diversion. The Joint Chiefs of Staff believed that "in the event of hostilities . . . our present forces in Korea would be a military liability. Authoritative reports from Korea indicate that continued lack of progress toward a free and independent Korea, unless offset . . . in all probability will result in such condition, including violent disorder, as to make the position of U.S. occupation forces untenable." [1] It was therefore determined, as Secretary of War Patterson put it, that the United States should disengage itself from Korea "gracefully" — that is, behind a smokescreen. [2]

The first component of the screen was military. The Korean constabulary was to be rapidly built into an army and expanded: there was disagreement on how much. The Communist threat in China raised desires for containment, hence for greater troop strength in South Korea. On the other hand, a Rhee attack on the North was feared. Intelligence estimates of North Korean troop strength were not, apparently, given much credence, nor were they accurate. The result was a weak South Korean army of approximately 100,000 men with equipment for only about 65,000 men, much of it unserviceable or lacking spare parts, without any tanks, with almost no planes, and grievously deficient in other heavy equipment. [3] This force was vaguely believed, for public consumption, to be sufficient to resist an attack from an estimated 150,000-man North Korean army organized and trained by the Soviet Union, equipped with some 242 tanks, perhaps 211 planes, and far more heavy equipment. [4] In fact, ROK (Republic of Korea) forces were still so badly trained and under-equipped as not to justify rational estimate of capacity to resist attack. [5]

A three-year, $500,000,000 aid program was worked out in the winter of 1946–47, after the first Joint Commission failure, for presentation to Congress; the problem of Korean unification was to be turned over to the United Nations, Korea placed outside the United States defense perimeter, and all American combat troops withdrawn.[6] It was this policy — formulated when Dwight Eisenhower was Chief of Staff and James Forrestal was Secretary of Defense and continued under Dean Acheson — to which Secretary Acheson referred in his famous National Press Club speech of January 12, 1950. MacArthur, surprisingly blind to the strategic importance of Korea for the defense of Japan, wholeheartedly endorsed this plan. He believed the U.S. "did not have the capability to train and equip Korean troops . . . to cope with a full-scale invasion . . . If a serious threat developed, the United States would have to give up active military support of the ROK forces." MacArthur recommended withdrawing remaining U.S. units.[7] The President's advisors concurred.

Hodge did not. He rightly appraised the potentialities of the Korean Army at the time, did not believe that it should be left without an American shield and predicted that U.S. troop withdrawal might bring Communist or North Korean domination of the peninsula. His political advisor, William R. Langdon, likewise opposed handing to the United Nations a problem that he felt to be not broadly international but specifically four-power.[8] In addition, in March 1947, the aid component of the smokescreen almost dissolved. Just before the aid program could be presented, Great Britain notified the United States of its inability to shoulder the burdens of defending Greece and Turkey. The Greek–Turkey aid program was rushed to Congress. At the same time, President Truman quietly informed the Department of State that he could not go before Congress with two large requests; the Korean long-term aid program would have to be dropped. After that time, until the Korean War, "our support for Korea tottered along in an unimpressive, inadequate and sporadic fashion." [9] A decision had been reached: one of the worst, most ambiguous, and later most controversial American decisions of the postwar era. Disengagement took place, but the "gracefulness" was missing: without requisite aid or defense the Korean policy created by Americans was a legless monster from birth. This disastrous error — or series of errors — in judgment, harbinger of more to come in

Asia, occurred at almost the same time as the launching of the Marshall Plan, herald of success in Europe.

The Turn to the Right and Syngman Rhee

The withdrawal policy caused the United States to support whatever anti-Communist strength it could find in the Korean political scene, without squeamishness about the character of that strength. The rise in violence argued not only for a "tough" policy, powerful youth groups, and a strong constabulary but for a government decisive and anti-Communist rather than democratic to wield the new forces of defense and order. The American-supported Korean moderates could not have done this in their prime. Their prime was now well past, and the new policy of separate, UN-sponsored elections spelled the elimination of both them and the Communists, leaving rightists as the only supporters of the new *Realpolitik*. The Department of State, despite many reservations, now moved to support Rhee and the right as the only strength there was.

Meanwhile, the still-secret disengagement policy became reflected in progressive American troop withdrawals from 1948 on. At the National Press Club, Acheson indicated on January 12, 1950, that Korea was not within U.S. defense lines. In May, Senator Tom Connally, chairman of the Senate Foreign Relations Committee, went further.[10] Rhee and the right became apprehensive, then alarmed. The youth groups and police gathered ever greater power. Thus American withdrawal nurtured the fears and forces farthest from making democracy possible at the very time that the Americans were hastily mixing the ingredients of a democratic façade.

Syngman Rhee had already established himself as the uncontested leader of the right and the only man to whom, after July 1947, those disengaging from Korea could turn. He had already become from his landing in 1945 a kind of *deus ex machina*. His anti-Japanese record was unassailable — as even Lyuh Woon-hyung's was rumored not to be. Within top patriotic ranks, only Kim Ku could rival the consistency and forthrightness of this record, and Kim Ku, Kim Kyu-sik, and Lyuh Woon-hyung were all his juniors. He had no deep local roots outside Seoul and, though demanding fealty, could demand it from more men and groups and in a more super-local way than could a leader of strong regional attachments. As a *hyangban,* he belonged to a rather comprehensive and general class, not to an exclusive or small one; he chose his associates accordingly. He had no predacious relatives — indeed, he was almost the only man in Korea who seemed to have hardly any relatives at all — and no Korean in-laws, his wife being Austrian. Few could match his knowledge of the classics of both East and West; his Ph.D. from Princeton had a prestige uncompromised by any corresponding inability to quote classical phrases or handle the brush. None could outact him as shaman in the occult art of dealing with foreigners and their diplomacy, a skill he performed with greater force and independence than his Sinophile ancestors and one greatly valued in a country recently colonial, now again foreign-occupied and threatened with an international trusteeship. The very simplicity of his beliefs — in racial and spiritual unity and patriotism without controversial intellectual fretting — disarmed all but intellectual or leftist opposition. Finally, he was first on the scene, and there was the benediction of American invitation, MacArthur's plane, Hodge's introduction. Thereafter, he never ceased to be front-runner.[11]

He fitted well the rightist-flowing tides. Since he was a consistent and uncompromising anti-Communist, the left and the People's Republic were his main enemies. Against them he was happy to ally with USAMGIK and its police; he used them to prevail. No others were yet ready to stand against him. The Japanese had left a leadership vacuum in Korea. The Korean Democratic party (KDP) had fairly good roots and a friendship network, but it lacked a leader of Rhee's stature and qualifications. The pro-Japanese had no leader they could commit to the front lines. They and the KDP stood in as much need of Rhee's independence record as they did of his skill in dealing with Americans. He, for his part, lacking his own roots, needed theirs. Without them, in a free, national race with the Communists he might have fallen. As Communists were pushed into subversive and violent opposition in the fall of 1946, Rhee's problems eased; they were taken off his shoulders by police and army while he emerged in the guise for which he was best suited: amid chaos, the patriotic symbol of unity, dedicated to the restoration of order in an atmosphere of international respect. To this task he brought qualities the Americans lacked: decisiveness and a direct simplicity of policy. They might not know where their interests lay; his directions he knew. Whatever one's judgments of him, whatever reservations one might have about the sincerity of his interest in practicing democracy, he was the obvious leader. Amid the incoherence of the scene, the American disengagers were fortunate to have as much.

The Democratic Façade

Neither the leader nor the state of Korean politics seemed apt for democratic institutions, and the Americans were in haste to leave. Nonetheless the attempt to assemble democratic institutions was thought necessary. The search for Korean cohesion was over; that for South Korean democracy was on.

The first major new institution was the National Assembly. The military governor first suggested a legislature on June 29, 1946.[12] The suggestion was brought, that summer, to the Coalition Committee, which on October 8, 1946, proposed that an assembly be established. The move was designed to elicit more Korean participation in government at a time when coalition moderates were working with the United States to obtain a trusteeship agreement. On October 9, Hodge declared that the Korean Interim Legislative Assembly (KILA) would be South Korea's lawmaking body, would review appointments, be a forum for free discussion, "foster free expression by the people and . . . be a sounding board for public opinion." All decisions, however, were to be subject to the review and veto of Military Government. Ordinance No. 218, establishing KILA, was released to the press on October 12. Its complete American inception was obvious from the brevity of elapsed time between Committee decision and published ordinance: the American draft originally even bore the date August 24!

The Korean Interim Legislative Assembly was to have ninety members, half elected and half, in a manner quaintly Japanese, appointed. It was intended to enact immediately a general suffrage law that would lead to a wholly-elected body. The elections for KILA were peculiar, however. When the Bureau of Information of USAMGIK's Public Relations Office was asked by the high command in February about plans for an assembly, it had indicated that if there was universal suffrage, there was every indication that the left would triumph. Democratic suffrage was therefore avoided.[13] Each hamlet, village, and district "elected" (or appointed) two representatives of the province by secret ballot. No rules specified who would vote in the initial election, however. The Japanese legislation restricting suffrage to taxpayers remained on the books. In some cases, the township heads, many of whom were holdovers from the Japanese period, simply appointed the elector or assumed the post themselves. No steps were taken to see that a democratic or even a fair election was held. "You know," an American officer serving as chief of a provincial Home Affairs Division remarked to an American correspondent in explanation, "strategically, this is the proper time for the rightists." [14]

Rhee had made summer tours of the provinces, and his own organization, the National Association for the Rapid Realization of Korean Independence (NARRKI) was in control of local administrative offices (see Chapter 11). The elections were rushed to take place within October while the police were in their period of uncontested rule following the quelling of the riots earlier in the month. No suitable publicity or explanation was given to the countryside. The cards were thus blatantly stacked for the rightists. In a country whose first political instincts had tended to support the People's Republic, the right was suddenly seated. Of the forty-five elected representatives, thirty-two were formally termed "rightist" followers of Rhee, Kim Ku, and the KDP; eleven were "independents" of rightist sentiment; and two were leftists from Cheju-do who, on orders from the People's Republic, refused to take their seats.[15] Dr. Kim Kyu-sik, chairman of the Coalition Committee, in a letter of November 5 asked Hodge to invalidate the elections, which "produced impressions of an undemocratic nature and caused disappointment to the people." [16] The elections for Seoul and Kangwŏn province were invalidated as the price for keeping Lyuh in the Committee and Hodge was persuaded to appoint a Committee list of forty-five, thirty of whom were moderates or leftists.[17] The Korean Democratic party thereupon immobilized the newborn assembly with a boycott. KILA, not even convened until December 13, passed no legislation from December to March 8, 1947, and only eleven laws, several trivial and others badly drawn, in the entire year and a half of its existence.[18] The press lost interest, public support was low, and in the next Assembly elections only thirteen of its ninety members were reelected.

The second American attempt to establish an assembly was better known and more reputable but still bore the marks of haste. Abandoning unilateral action, the U.S. dumped the Korea problem in the lap of the UN, and the General Assembly adopted, on November 14, 1947, an American resolution creating a temporary commission on Korea to observe the election for a Korean national assembly "not later than March 31."

The UN Temporary Commission on Korea (UNTCOK) first arrived in Korea on January 12. It was not until February 26, 1948, that the General Assembly Interim Committee's decision permitted the Commission to observe elections in South Korea alone if barred by the Communists, as it was from the beginning, from peninsula-wide observation. The election was announced on March 1 to take place less than two and a half months later on May 9 (subsequently changed to May 10). On March 17, the Commission recommended changes in the election law and in some of the conditions bearing on a "free atmosphere"; changes were made in the police; with breathless speed important legal changes were made in the election law, in criminal procedures, and in repealing some older, more repressive legislation.[19] On April 1 General Hodge issued a proclamation of civil liberties enumerating basic provisions commonly set forth in bills of rights. Some 3,140 prisoners were pardoned on March 31. Between March 30 and April 16, 948 candidates registered for the 200 seats in the National Assembly.[20] Elaborate plans were made for observation, security, and dissemination of information through all available media. Government weekly newspaper circulation rose from 600,000 to 750,000, and in April 5,635,000 copies of one paper containing election publicity were published, many being airdropped in an effort to reach villages.

Violence complicated the problems. The Communists, now hopelessly alienated from the government, put on a concerted campaign of incidents in last-ditch attempts to ruin the elections. On February 6, coordinated violence broke out, evidently planned to correspond with the second anniversary of the North Korean People's Republic on February 9. In one night, 40 locomotives were damaged, within the month over 100 persons (including 33 police) were killed, and more than 8,000 arrests were made. Both UNTCOK and the U.S. were deeply concerned. More was to come. On rebellious Cheju-do, where political sentiment was left of the mainland and where weapons were more plentiful because of the high concentration of Japanese troops surrendering there, USAMGIK's fledgling constabulary had to be deployed in semi-military attacks. In the ten days before the election, 323 persons (including 32 Korean policemen) were killed in many incidents.[21] Director Cho of the National Police was quoted as saying that between March 29 and May 19, 589 persons — including 63 policemen, 37 government officials and candidates, 150 members of "Protective Associations," and 330 "rioters"— had been killed; meanwhile some 10,000 persons were "processed" in police stations.[22]

In consequence, the security forces again rose, and it was necessarily under their eyes that much communication concerning the new "democratic" process of elections took place. From April 16 on, Military Government created a large police auxiliary known variously as the Community Protective Association or the Country Guard Corps. To fill its ranks, the police revived the tactic Japan employed only four years before during World War II's era of "patriotic" organizations and defense efforts. They appealed to all "loyal" youths from eighteen to twenty-five to join it without pay. Accoutred with clubs and axes, they patrolled the villages, proud of the government's "favor" to them and anxious to display their new status by interfering in the lives of ordinary citizens. Cases of police or youth groups beating, threatening, robbing, blackmailing, and removing the ration cards of those who would not register were reported to UNTCOK.[23]

These measures were successful in curbing interference in the elections and inducing voting. They were aided by the improved programs of a USAMGIK grown more competent in its last year. The best of these were agricultural. USAMGIK had, in its first weeks, placed a maximum allowable rent at one third of the crop, as compared to 50–90 percent previously. Few Korean officials made much attempt to enforce the regulation, but it was effective on the former Japanese-held lands vested in Military Government.[24] A fortunate decision to sell these to the tenants prior to the end of the Occupation was at last made in 1947. By September 1948, 487,621 acres had been sold to 502,072 tenants, leaving only some 18,620 Japanese acres unsold.[25] Much of this disposal had occurred just prior to the election. Tenancy was reduced to about 33 percent from about 75 percent in 1945. The terms were equitable. Disposal of these lands did much to reduce rural instability, undermine Communist influence, actual or potential, among the peasants, increase their cooperation with the election process, and arouse expectation, later fulfilled, that Korean landlord-held lands would be disposed of similarly. Responsiveness of mood was swelled by declaring election day a holiday. It was, in fact, a greater festival than any other the Confucian countryside knew, enlivened not only with the presences of all possible officials but even with the faces of foreigners in international teams. All organs of the state, officials, police, newspapers, radio, assured the people that voting was a patriotic duty; they were used to having their landlords go to the government to get them agricultural benefits; they knew Dr. Rhee was the personification of patriotism; foreign guests were bestowing added benedictions; villagers were anxious to see some neighbor honored by contact with the executive — and there was no lack of local citizens vying for the honor. Great publicity and appeals to the police were therefore able to thwart Communist attempts at disruption. The Communists tried to call a strike but failed. Only some 40 polling places out of over 13,000 were attacked. In only two counties of Cheju-do were elections sufficiently disrupted to be called invalid. Some 80 percent of eligible voters registered, and 95 percent of these — some 7,480,000, or about three quarters of the eligible — voted. It proved to be the last internal Communist attempt to take serious action within South Korea on a national scale.

Technically, the elections were therefore a success, even an unpredictably great success. The success came, however, from reasons rather different from any deep comprehension of the process engaged in and its significance. As further elections took place and the press and the political opposition worked on the election theme, this understanding deepened with some speed, but in 1948 such maturing lay well ahead. Meanwhile the farmer voted not to communicate his interests but because the government and its police told him to vote and because he was glad to give an ambitious local man the chance for mobility to central power. Nothing in the preparation or training of the Assembly itself had taken place that would make that body new or democratic in substance (see Chapters 8–9).

The new constitution bore the marks and dangers of similar haste. KILA had long debated a draft, but the acting military governor had vetoed it on the ground that it would "hinder the work of the UN Commission." [26] The end of the elections left a brand new assembly hardly two months to rush to conclusion a constitution substantially different from KILA's draft and needed for the inauguration of the new government on August 15. Long sessions were held, and Korean experts outside the assembly, like Yu Chin-o, were called on to do much drafting. American advice was not intensively sought.[27] Though generally conservative, the assembly members embodied no consensus of constitutional thinking and almost no knowledge of constitutional principles. Rhee used this environment personally to quash the initial plan for a cabinet-responsible system and to substitute for it a strong presidential system with the prime minister retained only as "an assistant to the president." [28] The constitution was adopted and promulgated on July 17, 1948. Where the Yi had given decades, even centuries, to adapting the Ming system, modern Korean legislators gave scarcely as many weeks to hoisting "Western" constitutional democracy on board.

An uneasy mixture of democracy and autocracy emerged. The text pronounced innumerable democratic rights and freedoms. It provided for a system of some checks and balances and separation of powers — more between executive and legislative than between those branches and the judiciary. It professed egalitarianism and even pacifism. In essence, it was a strong presidential system, the chief compromise being the president's election by the assembly. There were discomforting signs that rights, freedoms, checks and balances, and separation of powers were not, even in a formal sense, unequivocally guaranteed. Most civil rights were made subject to the specifications of law to be enacted. The independence of the judiciary was qualified by making constitutional review subject to a constitutional committee in which the executive and members of the legislature took part and on which justices constituted a minority; it was never established, and no laws were ever declared unconstitutional. Judges' appointments were limited to ten years, thus making their renewals subject to the executive. The Prime Minister's appointment and that of the Chief Justice were the only ones requiring assembly approval, and removals of the Prime Minister and all ministers were subject to the President's will alone. No provision was made for the dissolution of the Assembly in case of disagreement with the executive. The Assembly simply had the power not to pass the State Council's program; it did, also, explicitly have the right to pass legislation over Presidential veto. In a manner reminiscent of the Weimar Constitution, the Korean President was given emergency powers "to issue orders having the effect of law."

The legislature thus had surface strength, but its checks on the executive were mostly ineffective. The margin of executive domination was increased by vague language, omissions in the constitution and in subsequent legislation, and a centralism unqualified by the faintest touch of federalism.[29] The constitution, as an American expert predicted even at the time, "could evolve into a government by a strong man or a strong party."[30] In essence it contained many of the same flaws as the Meiji Constitution, which was, in fact, the direct mental reference of the Korean drafters. In granting to the people rights that it then subjected to restraints enacted by law, it only nominally guaranteed them; separation of powers was, in fact if not in principle, rejected. The rule of law in its true meaning did not exist. The compromises between executive and legislative powers also tended to confuse responsibilities and heighten conflicts. But at least power had, on the whole, a firm residence in Presidential hands. The Yi Dynasty's pre-Taewŏn'gun history proved that necessity.

Reform of the executive was critically needed. It was the executive, not the legislature or the judiciary, that Koreans identified as "their" government, when such identification occurred to them; it was also the mirror of the massive inheritance of Japanese bureaucratic control. There was a strong feeling that the government, highly centralized and complex, was "remote," unapproachable, unconcerned with the people. There was likewise strong popular feeling against the government's over-concentration on security and repressive aspects, the police, above all. It was therefore on the executive, its form, personnel, and spirit, that Korean political alienation and the immense pressure for change liberated by Japan's defeat were concentrated.

These complaints should have been translated into important reforms by the postwar governments: extensive decentralization; the strengthening of administration close to the people in county, township, and province; decentralization and reduction of the police when security permitted. USAMGIK had been directed from Washington in 1946 to institute broad programs of economic and educational reforms looking to the creation of conditions favorable to the development of a strong and lasting democracy in Korea. But U.S. military headquarters in Seoul was too poorly staffed, too unaware of administrative needs for reform, too inhibited by colonels interested chiefly in rotation to initiate changes of the kind then being effected in Japan. The foundations of a creative executive were not laid. "The Military Government expects to make no basic change in the Civil Service System established by the Japanese . . ." the opening SCAP (Supreme Commander for the Allied Powers) report on Korea grandly announced.[31]

The initial failure found deepened resonance in the executive USAMGIK created. USAMGIK encouraged giving Koreans governmental participation from the spring of 1946 on. From September 11, Korean directors took over government offices; American directors moved out and became, on the surface, advisors.[32] Almost the only Koreans with experience, however, were those who had already worked for the Japanese. There was neither time nor American skill to train replacements for the massive Japanese exodus. A Civil Service Training Academy was established, starting its first class April 1, 1946, but it was a hasty, drop-in-the-bucket improvisation.[33] Selection was haphazard, and once appointed, any Korean could be removed by Americans and any of his official acts annulled. The Chief Civil Administrator, a Korean, admitted before KILA that he had no control over police acts, nor could he fire police chiefs. Advisors were powerless, but by August 1947 there were still 3,231 of them.[34] There was hence neither confidence nor responsibility. Neither Americans nor Koreans felt able to take innovative steps. Rules for the organization and administration of the Korean Civil Service were promulgated on June 13, 1946, but the old pattern of the Korean bureaucracy could not quickly be broken.[35] Lacking real responsibility or objectives, the USAMGIK Korean bureaucracy returned to its old preoccupations with appointments and dismissals, its old concentration on access to status even though power was gone.[36]

President Rhee, on assuming power on August 15, 1948, wanted to keep this pattern. He could. The withdrawal policy and the more temporary American espousal of rival Kim Kyu-sik had ended any great leverage or influence on Rhee that United States power in Korea might once have exerted. He ended up by owing less to anyone than any other Korean ruler in centuries. He faced, in the beginning, little cohesive opposition and had almost free rein. He chose to revive the Yi concept of a bureaucracy as primarily a political instrument, a sieve through which to process the updraft of ambition rather than a tool of administration. Since Liberation, however, there were far more politics to control and a vast expansion of the numbers engaging in it. To contain a force this strong, the complex bureaucratic structure of the government-general was continued, then doubled and redoubled. By 1953, Rhee employed three times as many officials for less than half the peninsula as the Japanese had for their rule over all of it. He was wary only of the professionalism of the Japanese bureaucratic tradition: it tended toward vested interest formation that might make portions of the executive less dependent on him. In place of reform, Rhee expanded the police and the armed forces and did his best to oppose local government.[37] Officials were now Korean, but this fact did not obliterate popular resentment and alienation: the bureaucracy was still the residual legacy of Japanese colonialism. Rhee's regime supported neither innovative nor democratic concepts; its form was Japan's, its political function and spirit *fin de siècle* Yi.

The effects of this atrophy of innovation on planning and development were corrosive. Control of the channels of access to power was put above all else. Only after this came problem-solving for the new nation. As in prior centuries, professionalism was implicitly discouraged. Advice and council outside the ministries — some of it foreign —tended to be sought and followed. Even when desired by the President, proper delegation of power was impossible, and the President became involved in unending flows of trivia, diverting him and those around him from planning or orderly decision-making.[38] His ministers, also, pressed to dispense their own favors quickly, were overwhelmed with endless lines of suppliants day and night, both in the office and at home, and were otherwise preoccupied with making maximum political and financial capital.

Important administrative tasks languished: land-reform legislation, long in discussion and draft, was not signed and implemented until 1950, four years after the North Korean Communist land reform. Inflation mounted steadily, and no effective measures to come to grips with it were initiated during the regime's first eighteen months, despite official American prodding. Long-range planning was not undertaken until shortly before Rhee's fall. Ministries were discouraged from developing their own identities and interests or any council tendencies. High rank tended to be destructive rather than formative of an elite. Tenure lasted mostly months, sometimes weeks. As in the later Yi period, its brevity, followed by a tenebrous personal future, tended to encourage maximum profiting from office during individual power's brief day. Widespread teahouse rumor credited only two of Rhee's one hundred and twenty-nine ministers with not having made money in office, one through ferocious personal honesty, the other through not having been at his desk long enough. The rumor had small regard for some heroic personal efforts — more frequent at lower levels — to resist the general pattern. But there was much fire under the smoke. It was Rhee's purpose to keep the bureaucracy mobile and dependent on him. Its other qualities followed from that.

Rhee's Operation of the System

On May 27, 1948, the newly-elected representatives of the 200-member National Assembly met in Seoul and elected Dr. Rhee temporary chairman by a vote of 189 to 9. Hurriedly they debated and passed the constitution. On July 20, Rhee was elected President of the Republic of Korea by a vote of 180, 16 members voting for Kim Ku. The Republic had leadership nearly unanimously selected.

Before ten weeks had passed, major trouble erupted. The 14th ROK Regiment, embarking for rebellious Cheju from the south coast town of Yŏsu, mutinied on October 19, and the revolt, fanned by anti-police sentiment, spread. Five towns, two of them large, were captured, and hundreds of citizens massacred after trials by "people's courts." The revolt was put down by October 27, but some two thousand soldiers and civilians had been killed, and much fear and insecurity were sown within the army and among the public.[39] The Yŏsu revolt was found to have been instigated by young officers and NCO's of the ROK Army who had associated themselves with a major Communist conspiracy having one of its chief loci in the officers training class.

These events fed the trend toward autocracy. The government rapidly submitted and the Assembly, in November, passed, with some protest, a National Security Law, then promulgated on December 1. In the name of security, the bill outlawed communism and provided for prosecuting Communists under definitions and instructions to the judiciary so vague as to encourage utilization of the judiciary by the executive to eliminate political enemies.[40] The judiciary as an instrument of executive predominance, not defender of rights or instrument of balance of powers, forthwith became even more active than under colonial rule.

It was reported to the UN Commission that 89,710 people had been arrested between September 4, 1948, and April 30, 1949, of whom 28,404 were released, 21,606 turned over to the prosecutor's office, 29,284 transferred to a "security office," 6,985 transferred to the MP's, and 1,187 were pending disposition; of those turned over to the prosecutor, over 80 percent were declared guilty.[41] Figures of those jailed were not separately announced, but the Minister of Justice stated on December 27 that "jails can accommodate 15,000 but have 40,000 now," and the rice-rationing plans of the Ministry of Finance in the spring of 1950 listed the population of South Korea's 21 prisons at 58,000 persons.[42] Inspections of the National Assembly revealed that 50–80 percent of the prisoners were charged with National Security Law violations. An earlier ration plan of November 1949 had called for the feeding of 75,000 prisoners, a figure probably, however, swollen to allow the police side-income from the sale of extra food.

All the country's major organizations were affected by these round-ups. The Minister of Education on December 7, 1948, ordered the directors of all educational institutions to file detailed personal histories of all teachers with a view to firing "leftists." The army was subjected to terror, some of it necessary, when over 1,500 officers and men (most of the latter NCO's) were required to leave its ranks.[43] Senior officers of the still small constabulary estimated that upwards of one third of the original officer–NCO core were either executed, jailed, or discharged. The press fared little better. Between September 1948 and May 1949, the government closed down seven important newspapers and one news agency. Many reporters were arrested and important publishers and editors removed, mostly under the security laws.

When war began on June 25, 1950, such conditions proved to be no more than prelude. Even behind the battlefields, violence rose, and a society already splintered found itself ever further adrift from rules, law, or the possibility of redress against authority.

In the winter of 1950–51, a National Defense Corps of some 500,000 was hastily recruited from the thousands of young men retreating from the Chinese Communist invasion. The four billion wŏn appropriated to support this force (millions of dollars of which was contributed by the United States) was used largely for bribing assemblymen and for other political and private purposes. On the way south, the Provost Marshal General found large parts of the Corps nearly two weeks without food, suffering from exposure, and many of its members dead from starvation.[44] In April–May 1951, the five military heads of the Corps were tried in military court and shot, and the responsible Defense Minister, long the most powerful man in the country after the President, was sent as Ambassador to Japan in November, his political life ended.

At Kŏch'ang in the central-southern mountains even bloodier events were in store. From the end of the Yŏsu rebellion in 1948 until the spring of 1950, Kŏch'ang's poor farming population had, like much of later Vietnam, been ground between the police during the day and the guerrillas controlling their narrow valleys at night. With the collapse of the Communist forces around the Pusan perimeter after the Inch'ŏn landing of September–October 1950, guerrilla control resumed, fed with some local support. ROK troops found themselves frustrated in getting food or information from the villagers. In February 1951, an officer, under orders, called several hundred villagers together, many of them women and children, "to hear an order." On assembling, they were sprayed with machine-gun fire from prepared positions and wiped out. The Assembly committee sent to the spot to investigate was ambushed by the ROK forces and retreated. Even a decade later, feelings were so bitter that, in the summer of 1960, after the fall of the Rhee regime, the villagers seized the man who had then been a police chief, spread-eagled him, piled leaves underneath, poured oil from a local rice mill, and roasted him as, the newspapers observed, in summer they roast dog.[45]

Such incidents did much to arouse opposition and, eventually, party politics (see Chapter 10). Innumerable others were less horrible but bespoke the atmosphere of a mass society helpless before manipulation and beyond the reach of law. Endless bribery, special licenses for smuggling, misuse of money collected to build the statue of a national hero, arrests of alleged Communists within (and outside) intelligence agencies, confiscations of houses and private property by army officers on the return to Seoul — these set the tone of the times.

Such conditions have always fed autocracy. They then did so through the systematic employ of the judiciary for repression. Judges were supposed to grant warrants of arrest only when the police showed cause. In thousands of requests, however, many without the slightest evidence, no more than a handful of refusals was ever encountered. Genuine anti-Communist sentiment and a kind of common esprit de corps derived from the service of most judges, prosecutors, and police under the Japanese played their parts. So, of course, did the complete lack of any tradition of judicial independence.

Clear intimidation by the executive was still more obvious. Judges and prosecutors were privately warned regarding the conduct of National Security cases, and the reality of these warnings was made clear in the arrest, in December 1949, of twenty-one judges and prosecutors, among them a former vice–prosecutor-general. One of those arrested was stated to be suspected because "he had pleaded for the communists many times." The methods employed can be inferred from the fact that the Minister of Justice, in a press conference of December 27, 1949, felt it necessary to reassure his questioners that when the number of prosecutors increased, they would "strictly inspect the cells where the suspects are detained so that the police will not torture them." [46] Many of the arrested members of the judiciary remained in jail four months without trial. Then in court they were accused *ex post facto* of failing to leave the South Korea Labor party at the time when it was still a legal organization, but their sentences were so light as to imply lack of real guilt. Bureaucrats in other branches of government were similarly dealt with.

The judiciary was then turned against the power of the legislature. The government was scarcely launched before the Assembly tried to take control of collaborators, their trials and arrests, away from the executive. Filled less with legislative spirit than with that of Confucian admonishment, forty-six members on October 13, 1948, introduced a motion proposing withdrawal of U.S. and Soviet troops, another being reintroduced with more backers, but also unsuccessfully, on February 4, 1949. On March 18, 1949, sixty-three members sent a message to the UN Commission urging the withdrawal of U.S. tactical units in Korea, a disengagement then in any case well under way. During the tense spring of 1949, this Assembly recalcitrance reasserted itself in the passage, over Presidential objection, of a local administration bill and the overriding of Presidential vetoes on land reform. In June 1949, two important demands for the resignation of the entire State Council were passed. It was clear to the President that his control was threatened. A young opposition assemblyman was arrested on May 18. On June 26, Kim Ku was murdered by an army lieutenant who, not long after his conviction, was released, reinstated, and promoted to lieutenant colonel. Korean police arrived on the scene with a speed described by the U.S. Embassy expert on the subject as inconsistent with normal Korean systems of communication. Within days, ten more "opposition" assemblymen were arrested, among them the Vice-Speaker, a well-known independence patriot. Other arrests followed until, by October 7, sixteen members, over 7 percent of the Assembly, had been jailed.[47]

Pre-trial process communicated the hopelessness of defiance of executive will: the prisoners were held incommunicado and tortured repeatedly until their trial started on November 17, 1949. The press paid little heed. No voluntary lawyer or civil-rights group then existed to exert influence on this process.[48] Four months passed before the Assembly generated sufficient group solidarity to send to the judiciary a letter urging expedition of the trials on the grounds that "prompt and just trial will afford a good illustration of how the people should behave." [49]

The trial multiplied autocracy's effect. An indictment statement obtained by the prosecutor from confessions made in jail, often under torture, dominated the proceedings. Confessions were "corroborated" by a document seized from the "secret parts" of a woman agent who had never before (as she has never since) been heard of and who, despite repeated defense demands, was never produced in court; no other method of testing the document's authenticity was attempted. Two other "agents" described as having transmitted Communist instructions were never produced, and the one Communist witness introduced, in weakened condition, shed doubt on their role and even their existence.[50] The judge, at the prosecutor's request, turned down thirteen defense requests for witnesses and denied all other defense motions but granted all the prosecutor's requests for witnesses and added another himself, one being a police spy, another a stool pigeon. The most blatant leading questions were employed by the judge in court. Remoteness from facts and subjectivity of evidence requested and judged were almost as marked as in Yi trials.[51] In the summation and judgment of the case, the prosecutor's indictment, based on confessions wrung from the accused in their cells, was almost exclusively used and open-court statements ignored.[52] Trial, in other words, remained an Yi stage on which the moral judgments and insights of officials could be validated and in which no substantial line between judicial process and an executive decision could be drawn. The lack of any effective training or preparation of the judiciary for its democratic function was, here as elsewhere, glaringly revealed.[53]

Such traditions died hard. The Korean War stimulated the process by bringing floods of cases against those arrested on charges of collaboration with the Communist occupiers. By November 1950, the Joint Investigation Committee established for such cases had arrested 16,115 suspects. Over 500 were condemned to death, most, including several of exceptional talent, being summarily sentenced and executed after trials bearing little relationship to justice. Additional tens of thousands — probably over 100,000 — were killed without any trial whatsoever when ROK soldiers and the Counter-Intelligence Corps recaptured such areas of leftist repute as Yŏnggwang (Chŏlla Namdo), Chŏngŭp (Chŏlla Pukto), Kimch'ŏn, Sangju, Andong (Kyŏngsang Pukto), and others. Their story has nowhere been written, but the scars remain.[54]

In May and June of 1952, arrests and trials were again employed, even more flagrantly than in 1949, against the National Assembly. Some forty-five of the opposition Assembly majority — at that time threatening to defeat Syngman Rhee's pending re-election — were taken into custody on their way to the Assembly on May 26, 1952, on the pretext of not displaying identification to the Military Police, and were not released for two days, four being retained thereafter.[55] On June 19, fourteen defendants, half of them assemblymen, were sent before seven military and three civilian judges on charges of "Communist conspiracy" under the National Security Act. Defense lawyers were not made available prior to the trial's recess on June 21.[56] The Home Minister again claimed that the "plot" was discovered when a Communist agent was rounded up with "valuable documents," again never divulged.[57]

Many of the arrested were known anti-Communists. When the attending assemblymen fell below quorum level on July 2, 1952, the Home Minister ordered the number augmented in order to produce a satisfactory vote on the President's constitutional amendments. All though July 3, reluctant assemblymen were herded into the hall. The

Martial Law Commander released on bail almost all assemblymen, supposedly on trial for treason, and marched them to the Assembly hall. On July 4, 1952, the Assembly "passed" the amendments 163–0, crippling its power over the President, with only three abstentions. Only then were charges against most assemblymen quietly dropped. On August 5, the Martial Law Command announced that charges in seven of the more serious cases had been suspended.[58] No political trials of such mass proportions occurred until the revolution of 1960 and the coup of 1961 when the technique was revived. But trials of those prominently involved in various aspects of Korea's political life continued to teach the lesson of autocracy to the end of the regime; they have not yet ceased to inculcate similar lessons.[59]

In many other fields there were signs of progress and hope. In the essential areas of politics and law, however, such was, for the most part, the character of the democracy that disengagement left behind.

The Rise of Tension

Speaking of mobilization of the state for war, De Tocqueville remarked: "The tendency that leads men unceasingly to multiply the privileges of the state and to circumscribe the rights of private persons is much more rapid and constant among those . . . nations that are exposed . . . to great and frequent wars than among all others." [60] America's attempt in Korea to build new cohesion around democratic institutions had, in an embattled place and unplanned setting, been rapidly overgrown by autocracy. Rhee's one-man rule kept stability in the state through revolt, guerrilla action, invasion, war, and loss of most of the country. From 1952 to 1956, autocratic stability was at its height; the pattern of atomized mobility toward central power was checked and, later, mobilized within the Liberal party (see Chapter 10). No one dared threaten or seriously contend for rule. The institutions of democracy were either disregarded, overridden, corrupted, or turned against themselves; the search to plant them had proved a feint, not a systematic effort. It had rained into an ancient sea, and still the sea was salt.

War had important long-range political results, especially in the creation of army power. It had short-range political results as well; it aggravated issues of political stress and provided an environment in which sterner autocratic means seemed more legitimate. Yet war probably did not crucially affect the political story within Rhee's years. The story of autocracy, of reaction against it, of the aggregation of opposition feeling in parties, of the gradual recognition of incompatibility between means and theoretical system, the rise of new urban forces, the eventual overthrow — all very probably would have taken place (in somewhat different form, perhaps) even had no war been fought. On the whole, the Korean political pattern resisted the war's political effects, its technicalization, its professionalization, in the early 1950's almost as it had during the five hundred years of Yi rule.

After 1955, the tide began to turn. Extreme central control concentrated governmental fault, gave surface for attack. The creation of a government party intensified competition for power. Urban discontent then backed the formation and growth of an increasingly cohesive opposition party. The war-expanded armed forces meanwhile provided for the first time an institution and a vested interest capable of semi-independence from the central government. These phenomena occupy separate chapters. Behind them lay the rise of factors more basic to political development than war: the growth of cities, of communication, of education. These remain as fundamental to political pressures in Korea today as they were to the political changes of the later 1950's.

The war had dispersed Seoul's growing population. With the return of peace in 1953 and of the government to the city, growth proceeded relentlessly. The city that had contained in 1930 394,200 people, 935,500 in 1940, and 1,446,000 in 1949, and probably under 100,000 in early 1951 reached 1,242,880 as reconstruction started in earnest in 1954. By the end of the Rhee regime, its population had virtually doubled: in 1960, it was 2,445,400.[61] Urban population in general, which had been 11.4 percent of the population in 1940, was 33.2 percent by 1960.[62] During those years Seoul absorbed one third of the total population increase of the entire nation. Half city, with mounting buildings, streetcars, electricity, taxis, and half macrocephalic monster, growing cancerously in hillside shacks and caves, noisome alleys and settlements without water or electricity, Seoul was itself the inflammatory vortex and symbol of the mass society.[63]

Growth was not confined to numbers of people. Seoul was the seat of reconstructed and expanded facilities of every kind. Above all, it became the nub of a tremendous concentration of the country's communication and educational facilities, consequently the gathering point of most of Korea's intellectuals and of opinion, diversity, complaint, and dissent.

From 1948 to 1960, Korea's college-level institutions doubled, rising from 31 to 62, the number of college teachers increasing from 1,800 to 3,633, and the college student enrollment soaring nationally from 24,000 to 97,819.[64] By 1965, with national per capita income still under $100 a year, one out of every 280 Koreans was going to college (while by contrast in England, with annual per capita income of $1,200, only one out of every 425 was college-enrolled).[65] Secondary schools similarly soared from 97 in 1945 to 166 in 1952 to 357 in 1960. By 1962, there were almost four times as many high school students as in 1945.[66] Of these, Seoul claimed the lion's share, by 1964 having 89 out of a national total of 189 higher educational institutions and 31 out of 49 of the country's recognized colleges and universities.[67] Nearly 90,000 out of a national higher-education total of 138,428 students jammed into Seoul to make it, by 1963, one of the largest educational centers in the world.[68]

It was also one of the most discontented. Figures on employment of graduates vary widely, but by 1964 employment of graduates of higher educational institutions was officially listed as 43 percent, not including those going into the armed forces whose ultimate employment is uncertain.[69] Newspaper and popular estimates are much lower, however. Prominent newspapers have estimated employment rates among college graduates in the kind of jobs they want as not over 10 percent. Even official sources rated the wastage of education as near 50 percent.[70] To obtain a desirable job, the winner might have to compete in up to 34 written examinations against more than 100 other applicants. Indeed, it is evident that, much as in post–World War I Germany but on a larger scale, Korea's students have been entering universities partly to escape or postpone unemployment. Even when a student is employed on graduation, his salary varies between $25 and $60 a month, barely a living wage. Thus, although as many as 40 percent or more may report some sort of employment, it is apparent that much of this is not career employment suitable for college graduates. Even official surveys note that in the field of law, for example, colleges "are producing 18 times as many graduates as the field of work can absorb." [71] Some colleges produce scarcely any suitably-employed graduates. Yet education is the channel of mobility. Its frenetic expansion is symbolic of the unbounded character of the mobility system, and the ambition of its graduates can be dammed only at political peril.

Even in college there is much discontent. The student has been used to an intimate, usually large family circle with clear direction from his father and many to care for him. Projected into a large, overcrowded, impersonal campus, where no senior figures and few people of any sort care about him, the student becomes resentful and discontented. In a survey conducted close to the time of the student revolution by Korea's most distinguished educational psychologist, 94 percent of the 2,400 students surveyed said that they did not have a single "understanding" professor, 91 percent were discontented with the efficiency of prevailing individual guidance, 57 percent showed general dissatisfaction with their college programs, 39 percent felt they were unfit for their present studies, 46 percent completely denied the existence of professors able in individual guidance, 85 percent complained that they had no suitable place to talk with professors individually, 80 percent acknowledged frustration in their expectations of college, and 50 percent judged that the courses they were taking would be of little or no use.[72] This discontent spreads also to the teacher, who is not only underpaid but is swamped with the sheer number of students. Besides no longer exercising the almost parental responsibility for each of "his" student's welfare that he had in the "elite" system before 1945, he rarely has the satisfaction of personal student supporters or student faction as he once had; nor does he feel the emergence of new values or broader social recognition to compensate for his loss of prestige. Here, too, compensation has shrunk.

Basic discontent of this ilk is made more dangerous by the tradition of student demonstration, protest, and guardianship of imported values that has disturbed Korean politics for over four hundred years; it may, indeed, be the oldest tradition of its kind in the world — far older than that of nineteenth-century German and Russian students or of Chinese students in the last decade of the imperial regime. This tradition was especially susceptible to stimulation from the coming of a new political system and theory, for its roots lay in the extreme doctrinaire posture students had imputed to Confucianism within a Buddhist, shaman-influenced society. In like vein, after 1945, universities, more than any other reaches of the Korean social milieu had studied and clung to the principles of democracy. As of old, they regarded themselves as citadels of purity, of ideology, and of conduct in a "dusty" world.[73] They thought of themselves as the "voice" of the people when, under Japanese colonialism, few other channels of expression existed. In the demonstrations of 1946–1947, notably the major one at Seoul National against USAMGIK educational measures, the students felt themselves defenders of liberalism against "dictatorship," opposing the administrative centralization of powers then dispersed among the faculty. Since then, discipline and obedience to faculty and president have been eroded by the "democratization" of the Japanese professor-student relationship. The weakening of the ties within the society, the absence of professorial guidance, and the grim prospect of unemployment all created severe threats to the student's sense of security; the more he felt personally isolated, the higher the value he placed on political principle, on uniting with others and identifying himself with unifying social objectives regardless of risk.[74] Thus Seoul is one of the greatest and most incendiary concentrations of student and intellectual discontent anywhere in the world.

Communications also swelled with the population. Both the number of newspapers and newspaper circulations, overwhelmingly concentrated in Seoul, multiplied. *Tong-A Ilbo*, dean of newspapers, increased its circulation from a low of 17,000 just after the war to a high of some 400,000 in the summer of 1964, much of the increase coming before 1960. Some 600 newspapers and periodicals were registered for publication by May 1960 and the Foreign Ministry later stated that these had risen to "1,444 news media which consisted of some 100,000 reporters" as of February 1, 1961.[75] These forces provided close-in observation seats for the country's all-absorbing political show. They generated a mounting and increasingly hostile urban public opinion that became the vanguard of political change. Such landmark opposition attacks as Cho Pyŏng-ok's famous open letter to President Rhee of June 1957 were given the widest and most sympathetic circulation.[76] The seal of the press's opposition effectiveness was minted in governmental retaliation. In 1955, Taegu's Catholic-run *Maeil Sinbo* was sacked by Liberal party–affiliated hoodlums.[77] *Tong-A* was closed for several months for a typographical error involving the President's title, and *Kyŏnghyang*, most outspoken of Seoul newspapers, was closed down on clearly inadequate grounds in 1959, reopening only a year later with the regime's overthrow. Magazines like *Sasanggye* (World of Thought), for years perhaps the leading intellectual journal in the Far East outside of Japan, greatly widened and deepened opposition attack, despite every obstacle. For all those things that even newspapers could not say, teahouses existed as the political watering places of the intellectuals; they too sprouted from 50 in 1950 to nearly 800 by the end of the regime.[78]

By forced closings, by harassment, by mob action, by discriminatory bank loans, and by the police, the regime did what it could to curb or set bounds to these voices. Yet, as the cities grew, the power of the police to control criticism ebbed. True, gangs and thugs flourished in the atmosphere of corruption and autocracy, but their apparent use by the Home Ministry in shooting Vice-President Chang Myŏn in the hand in 1956 and in sacking the *Maeil Sinbo* in 1955 scared few and only intensified opposition. In the wake of a more urbanized and educated world, the age of political assassinations seemed quietly to pass. Police bore the brunt of forceful control, as before. They had risen to a peak of 75,000 during the Korean War and had played important, largely military roles in the elimination of guerrillas until 1955. The Liberal party needed them and yet could not prevent gradual diminution of their numbers as military needs ceased, reaction to 1951 scandals became a political problem, and opposition members and economic-aid authorities intensified their cries for balanced budgets. On July 31, 1955, Assembly opposition pushed to reduce the police from 46,520 to 40,000.[79] The Liberal party fought off the attempt. By 1958, however, the number was thought not greatly to exceed the authorized strength of 39,000 and is not, on the surface, far above it today. Of the old, Japanese-trained force there were only some 600 left by the later 1950's, but they were largely in key positions, and old organizational traditions were intact. The police remained as faithful and fanatically loyal to the government as they had been under Japan. Surveillance, sudden arrests, unjust trials, trumped-up accusations, threats of all kinds to the opposition, and torture were used, although they created more tension and resentment now, less callow obedience.[80] In the 1950's the place of the police as the nation's predominant force passed to the army, which had absorbed from intimate associations with the UN forces new ethics and standards, regarded police traditions askance, and kept more distance from government and politics. The army's turn would come later. For the time being, its reaction to the Rhee regime was concealed some distance under its surface. Meanwhile, the height of police effect had passed: the very rise of resentment revealed the face of a more sophisticated and urbanized society.[81]

THE LUNGE

Korea's new urban strength fed the springs of opposition and came, as we shall see, greatly to strengthen the party system (see Chapter 10). These concentrations aggravated the tensions of politics, the means used to achieve political ends, and the cycle of retaliations. From 1959 on, widespread national anxiety and restlessness attended the preparation for the 1960 Presidential and Vice-Presidential elections. Rhee, eighty-five years old in 1960, had gradually become senescent. His heir apparent, Speaker of the National Assembly Yi Ki-bung, was so ill with advanced locomotor ataxia that he had to be helped in and out of his chair and had difficulty speaking many more consecutive sentences than the President. They faced in the elections of 1960 relatively strong and well-backed opposition Democratic party candidates. Though Cho Pyŏng-ok died a month before the election, his running mate, Chang Myŏn, stood a still better chance than in 1956. A worried Liberal party, largely led by Chang Kyŏng-gŭn, in a resort to exceptional "loyalty" directed a campaign replete with highly secret plans for group voting, ballot stuffing, and invalidations or removal of opposition ballots.[82] Rumors and reports of such plans had for weeks filled the press, creating much tension. The worst fears were realized in the techniques of election day, March 15, 1960, and their results. Rhee received 88.7 percent of the votes, and, more implausibly still, Yi Ki-bung defeated Chang Myŏn 8,225,000 to 1,850,000.

These events summoned the forces of violence to the stage. Something approaching opposition consensus had already been reached in urban-intellectual opinion. This had been intensified in the case of the students by the forming, during the pre-election months, of small, tight clubs, sometimes with young faculty advisors, meeting secretly with ceremonial oaths; their membership generated fanatical enthusiasm for "saving democracy." Attending such meetings one had a strong sensation of the call to action and responsibility that such cells felt, sensing no other groups in the society to which they could turn. On election day, police at Masan, a small southeast coast city, had fired into a group of disappointed Democratic party supporters, killing eight.[83] On April 11, the bloated body of a young student victim of police torture was discovered floating in the harbor, and this roused Masan to three days of uncontrollable, spontaneous rioting accompanied by further casualties. The news, flooding past censorship, kindled Seoul students. On April 18, the students of Koryŏ University launched a large, peaceful demonstration protesting police violence, asking for cancellation of the elections, and demanding new ones. On their road home, they were attacked with chains, rods, and fists by gang elements called on by the police chief of the Presidential residence. Word of the attack spread like wildfire that night. On the morning of April 19, tens of thousands of unarmed students converged on Seoul's center, in some cases mopping up the unemployed young and shoeshine boys as they went. They had no thought of revolution, but before the Presidential mansion the police fired point blank into their ranks. Many fell. The blood of the fallen students and the enormity and unanimity of the crowd's mass turned demonstration in a few minutes to revolution. When the government reacted with confused vindictiveness, further demonstrations on April 25 and 26 brought its downfall. President Rhee resigned, went first into retirement and, on April 29, to Hawaii, where five years later he died. Speaker and Vice-President–elect Yi Ki-bung committed suicide with his wife and two sons. The Liberal party collapsed as fast and as silently as, on its smaller scale, the Ilchin-hoe had in 1910: not a single Liberal candidate was elected in 1965 or 1967. To those who witnessed it, the unanimity, the spontaneity, the utter conviction that swept Korea's cities in those days will remain unforgettable. It is difficult to believe that more pluralistic societies could create the tone of that emotion. It seemed as if the force of that consensus made up in a few hours for the hesitations, the paralysis of action, the frustration of long years.

The country had been brought to the brink of anarchy. The police, principal target of the demonstrators, were now turned from their burned stations, their morale shattered.[84] The army was intact but, though committed to order, was uncommitted politically. The most serious element of chaos, however, was the fact that the student and urban forces that had initiated the action had neither the organization nor the program needed to restore social order, and the surviving political forces of the country had not been closely allied with them in the overthrow.[85] To what they believed was democracy, the students gave great thrust, but the problem of integrating these active forces with those of orderly government faced the Democratic government that then came to power and has not yet been completely solved by its successors. Inflated student power on the brink of a constantly discontented and swollen metropolis remains a threat to political stability, lessened in 1967–68 but not conclusively ended. It is astonishing what great convictions societies can achieve without being able to create the intrumentalities through which to express them.

It was the fate of democratic power not to contain the forces that gave it leadership. The overturn of the Rhee autocracy brought to the helm a democratic regime that, with its interim predecessor, lasted just under a year. Overturned by a military coup of May 16, 1961, staged by a tiny fraction of the armed forces, its tenure was too brief for final conclusions on what its real political significance and long-term chances of success might have been; it does, however, further illustrate the needs for order and cohesion in Korea's mass society.

The student revolution had implied more than a temporary overthrow of autocracy and police power: it was an avenue to the establishment of a non-autocratic government. The army temporarily missed its bid for power, leftist forces were almost nonexistent; the previous development of a two-party system made it clear that the Democratic party would, in one form or another, be the beneficiary of political change. The clarity of choice seemed fortunate.

Considering the chaotic wake of the student revolution, the transition to democratic rule was at first accomplished with remarkable success. President Rhee had, in the week remaining to him after the April 19 demonstrations, called in an old associate, Hŏ Chŏng, a statesman who had distanced himself from the Liberal party and from all the extreme autocracy of the last period of its rule. He obtained American support at once for an interim government under himself as Prime Minister and Acting President and worked with ability and patience to restore civil process. The Democratic party likewise acted with restraint in not hindering his efforts, as did, in these first months, the students. There was a strong sense throughout the society of the danger of anarchy; the communication system worked well to support this sense and the voluntary restraint arising out of it. With slight leadership, the mass society was able to generate common purpose. This spirit of consensus lasted through the memorable visit on June 19 of President Eisenhower.[86] Its more important results lay in the many legislative accomplishments of those weeks.

On June 15, the Interim Government promulgated important constitutional amendments weakening the power of the President, reinstituting the post of Premier, who was now in charge of administration, and establishing a cabinet-responsible system. The upper House of Councilors was created; the President was to be elected in a joint session of both houses and his choice of Premier confirmed in the lower house. Rights and freedoms were no longer made subject to legal reservation.[87] A new local-autonomy law provided for elections of provincial governors and mayors, which took place in December 1960. A new election law did its best to place elections beyond government interference, and free elections did take place on July 29. In them, the Democrats received clear majorities in both houses.[88] The Assembly was expanded — to 233 members for the lower, 58 for the new upper house — and the power of the legislature was greatly increased. Yun Po-sŏn of the "old" faction was agreed on overwhelmingly as President, now largely a ceremonial office. With much more difficulty, Chang Myŏn was elected as Premier. The long party struggle for a cabinet-responsible system had achieved its goals. A wave of popular, press, and legislative feeling, even among former Liberals, supported this sweeping democratic thrust against autocracy. The stage seemed set for successful democratic government, responsive to public opinion at home, applauded abroad. An atmosphere of hopefulness, even pride, prevailed.

It was not long sustained. The new government's dilemmas lay, in the author's view, primarily with the impact of the democratic system on Korea's particular political-social dynamic, secondarily only with faults of leadership.[89] Even so, such difficulties alone did not end its rule. Democracy did not demonstrably fail: it was overthrown by force.

The first step of the tragedy lay in the impact of a democratic party concept on the Korean mobility pattern. (This question is explored at length in Chapter 7.) The dynamic of atomic, upward mobility conquered party unity: the five-year alliance between the "old faction" and the "new faction," led respectively by President

Yun and Premier Chang, disintegrated under the lures of power. In August, President Yun nominated a member of his faction, Kim To-yŏn, as Premier; the choice was narrowly rejected, 122 to 111. He was then reluctantly forced to nominate Chang Myŏn, who narrowly won, 117 to 107, three votes above the required majority. Democratic process itself here again had disruptive impact as during the period of USAMGIK "consultations." The nation perceived that voting was purely factional. Dr. Chang strove to narrow the split by appointing a "coalition" cabinet with ample "old faction" representation. The old faction, refusing cooperation, openly branded as a "traitor" one of its members who agreed to serve. Backed by the President, it determined to struggle to obtain full power for itself. In September 1960, 86 old faction members split from the Democratic party, forming first a new negotiating group, then an independent "New Democratic party." Chang, left with 95 "new faction" members, lost his parliamentary majority and had to reform his cabinet. By patience, persuasion, the use of power, and financial lures, he raised his plurality to a majority of 118 by October 19, pushing it gradually up thereafter so that he had 133 members to the New Democratic party's 62 by the end of his regime.[90] His position was nevertheless comparatively vulnerable, his leadership by implication impugned, and his regime constantly subject to harassment by a powerful and implacable factional foe that could take advantage of any issue to attack since it was separated from Chang by no issue, program, or ideology. The unity, the viability, the stability of his government was gone.[91] Public disenchantment with the age-old cynicism of this process was widespread.[92]

The persistence of the mobility-toward-power pattern also impaired Chang's appointments and the strength and continuity of his administration. Changes in his cabinet were frequent. As power had to be given to the maximum number of followers, so did financial rewards. Despite Chang's personal integrity, corruption ran unchecked, the election and Assembly confirmation of Premier and President stimulating it. As under the Rhee regime, bribery to evade taxes was common.[93] At the end of 1960, assemblymen had to be bribed even to pass their government's budget. Financial needs had particular effects on the army, since much of the sum needed to pass the national budget bill had to be sweated out of army budget appropriations. The trials of Democratic ministers following their arrests in the military coup that lay ahead tended to confirm their relative honesty, but, as one put the matter privately: "After years out of power, you must expect that many Democratic politicians will take some steps to build up their reserves again." The Assembly in Korea has yet to recover from the poor public image it acquired during those days.

The most unfortunate impact of the Chang government lay in public security. With the police overthrown, conditions bore much resemblance to the chaos of 1945–1946. Until controls were slowly restored, gangs flourished, less massive and not government-supported as in later Rhee days, but more numerous. Middle-class and even poorer citizens felt no protection from them. Stealing increased. In urban neighborhoods, people felt queasy by day, fearful by night. The sensational success of the April demonstrations induced all with dissatisfactions to express them as the students had. Until February 1961, hardly a day passed without multiple demonstrations, some 2,000 of these involving some 900,000 participants estimated as having taken place in the year between revolution and coup.[94] Most were small, few dangerous, and, contrary to most reports, the situation in this regard was improving, not deteriorating, in the final three months of the regime.[95] Yet, meanwhile, public fears had stirred.

Early in 1961, apprehensions were heightened by indications of some leftist infiltration into student ranks and the formation in a few prominent universities of Mint'ong, the National Students Federation for National Unification, a group whose leaders advocated peaceful unification and were, during the last weeks of the regime, trying to arrange a debate with North Korean students. Mint'ong, relatively strongest in the Seoul National University Political Science Department, had been organized in only a small minority of universities by the end of the regime, and its members were small minorities within even those student bodies. It was vocal, however, and growing. The power of North Korea thirty-five miles away, the nervous climate of society and the antagonism and blood between rightists and leftists made Koreans of any prominence abnormally sensitive to the possibility of danger from the left.[96] Destructive riots at Yŏnsei University in October in which the house of the acting president, a well-known American closely identified with Korea, was ransacked, heightened nervousness. Rumor was rife that Communist-backed elements were planning an anti-government uprising in March or April. These months passed calmly, but constant apprehension lay under the surface.

Against this tide of threatening disorder, the Chang regime moved gingerly. It had come to power through spontaneous demonstrations against dictatorship and police oppression. It was conscious to a fault that it lacked the legitimacy to use the instruments against which it and the students had fought. In the last weeks and days of the regime, a new National Security Law strengthening its hand was under way, supported by a new and determined Home Minister. Meanwhile its deliberateness was scored as pusillanimous.

The press, which had become popular in pressuring the Rhee autocracy, now undermined the democratic process it had sponsored. The number of newspapers and periodicals jumped from about 600 to nearly 1,500 during the May 1960–May 1961 period. Many simply made money by selling their right to publish and never printed a single sheet. Some distributed a few mimeographed sheets only. Almost all tried to make money by purveying sensational and often inaccurate information, such as reports of starvation in villages to which the reporter had never been and that, when checked, revealed no such conditions. Almost all were financially weak. Some money supporting a very few publications with a slightly leftist editorial line was beginning to creep in from Communist-controlled sources in Japan.[97] Leftist or not, almost no newspapers had any thoughtful regard or sympathy for the problems the Chang regime was struggling to solve in a democratic framework. They reflected the ingrown spirit of criticism toward government that centuries of poor native government or harsh foreign rule had brought to Korea. Praise from the press was scored as suspicious "truckling"; criticism meant increasing circulation. In press columns the image of a society competing in an atomized way without limit or principle for any sort of political or financial advantage became magnified and distorted. Society's fears deepened.

Doubt and disillusion stirred and grew. In the by-elections of December 25, 1960, when governors and the mayor of Seoul were voted on for the first time in Korean history, an average of only 38.2 percent of qualified voters cast their ballots. National percentages in other elections had run 82–94 percent in previous years and, even in urban areas, always over 70 percent. In the by-election in Map'o, a politically active Seoul district, only 39,430 out of 110,000 qualified voters voted on February 10, 1961, where, out of a smaller population, 55,409 had voted in the 1958 election, 44,857 for one candidate.[98] As passing months softened memories of Rhee repression, people became concerned with "chaos and confusion" more than with the freedoms they had won. Conversations echoed the leitmotif: "Was democracy appropriate for the dangers and tensions of Korea?"[99] Premier Chang did not share these doubts. He felt proud that the Korean people "now enjoyed all the rights and freedom guaranteed by the Constitution."[100] There was some grudging agreement and vague realization that Dr. Chang was somehow, in a democratic sense, ahead of his time and society. Americans, living in closely guarded compounds, also felt the value of the gains and could not fully share the anxieties; their pre-Watts nerves were attuned to a stabler society whose basis such disorders could not threaten.[101] In the final analysis, however, there was little trust and confidence. In a cabinet-sponsored poll taken halfway through the Chang regime among 3,000 people in eight universities, only 3.7 percent unreservedly supported the Chang government; 51.5 percent would wait and see.[102]

The truth was that not enough Koreans were prepared to see any good. The government's able labors instituted financial reform, pushed through a politically controversial but fiscally sound exchange rate and a long-needed amalgamation of power companies, and raised rates for heavily subsidized government-operated services. Emphasis on economic improvement was well-placed. A new National Reconstruction Program held out much hope of greater reconstruction effort. The succeeding military government paid Chang the compliment of furthering all these programs. Yet all involved initial inflationary cost that public opinion was ill-prepared to bear. Most of the reforms made were at an American insistence, economically well-intentioned but politically ill-timed. The Americans had borne the faults of the Rhee regime too long in silence and had belatedly prepared stern demands that were presented only in the last days of that government, hence falling for implementation on the frail shoulders of a regime struggling with post-revolutionary chaos. Pushed slowly through cantankerous debate or heated charges in the Assembly's two houses, these reforms somehow failed to impart publicly the same confidence that the swift acts of a determined executive might have conveyed. The deliberations of a cabinet necessarily painfully conscious of public opinion lacked capacity to symbolize national development with suitable *élan*. Confused cabinet shiftings conveyed the impression of a masque of faint leadership in which political goals faded.

The situation, far from critical, was bright with hope and was strengthening in the spring of 1961. If the Rhee regime had lasted less long, if reaction against it had been less extreme, if a strong Presidential system and a smaller, unicameral assembly could have been retained and a democratic system conducted in Dr. Chang's spirit in this framework, the corner might well have been turned. Even as it was, the system had its staunch supporters. Yet few will deny that the "democracy" of those days encouraged and widened splits, aggravated the power free-for-all, and projected an image of weakness and hesitation where chaotic conditions demanded strength and resolution. In these areas it raised questions concerning democracy in Korea that have yet to be answered. Cohesion by democracy might not be impossible, but its demands are stern.

THE THRUST PARRIED: POLITICS UNDER THE MILITARY

The Coup

Korea's democratic experiment was abruptly ended in the early morning hours of May 16, 1961, less than a year after its start, by a brief and almost bloodless military coup staged by a group of roughly 3,500 men assembled around a core of about 250 officers within a 500,000-man army.[103] Seoul was captured in a matter of hours, other units, notably the First Army, surrendering within the next two to three days.[104]

The nation was taken by almost complete surprise. Talk of coup had been confined to small circles; the successful effort was highly secret beforehand. Popular grumblings had arrived at no consensus on replacing the Democratic government, let alone on the choice of its successor. There were shock and, at first, widespread fears that the coup might have had Communist origin.

It was, instead, a non-Communist, even anti-Communist, reaction to what some soldiers considered the loose controls, corruption, and lack of progress of the Democratic regime.[105] Its core was a dozen or more colonels and lieutenant colonels grouped around a recently fired lieutenant colonel, Kim Chong-p'il, nephew-in-law of coup leader

Park Chŏng-hŭi. Like their spiritual predecessors, the young Japanese officers of the early 1930's, they had a messianic, self-styled patriotism that despised civilian politics and believed that direct, extremist action could perfect the world.[106] The essence of their action lay in tight organization, definiteness of plan, speed of action, and, at first, suppression of democracy.

On May 17, the military junta of thirty colonels and brigadier generals headed by Major General Park Chŏng-hŭi seized control of national affairs, dissolved the National Assembly *sine die*, and, for the first time since the Japanese Annexation, prohibited any kind of political activity. A revolutionary committee announced a platform of six oaths: anti-communism, strong ties with the U.S., eradication of "all corruptions and social evils," the creation of "fresh morale," and the establishment of "a self-supporting economy." It pledged that, "upon completion of the aforestated missions, we will turn over the control of the government to clean, conscientious civilians and will return to our proper duties." [107] On May 19, the revolutionary committee became the Supreme Council for National Reconstruction (SCNR) through which all rule was conducted. The constitution was sidetracked. On June 6, 1961, the SCNR legislated the "Law Regarding Extraordinary Measures for National Reconstruction," which superseded the constitution in essential respects and appropriated executive, legislative, and judicial powers to itself.[108]

Where the Democratic regime's controls had been weak, the coup leaders' were unmistakably strong. Chang and most of his leaders and close associates were arrested. Politicians, linked in Homeric epithet with "corrupt," were anathema. Some 2,014 were arrested within six days; about 17,000 civil servants and 2,000 military officers were either arrested, dismissed, or retired by the summer's end, 13,300 within weeks.[109] Demonstrations were *streng verboten.* Communists real and suspected, including Mint'ong student leaders, were sought out and peremptorily arrested, their crimes, if any, left for later determination. Thugs and gangsters were rounded up and 13,387 confined. Violation of traffic or curfew laws brought arrest. Sumptuary regulations abounded against coffee drinking and, for a while, even nightclub dancing. Forty-nine out of 64 dailies published in Seoul were closed, and 1,170 of the 1,573 dailies, news services, weeklies, monthlies, and other public information agencies in South Korea were deprived of their registration under SCNR Proclamation No. 11, and

Ministry of Public Information Ordinance No. 1.[110] A controlled press and radio network was used to make the citizens feel that their previous apprehensions were now replaced with security and confidence.

The young colonels were disparaging of democracy and hostile to political activity.[111] Like their military predecessors in Korean rule, the Japanese generals of 1910–1945, they believed that discussion diverted action and voting delayed it. Cleaned of corrupt politics, good citizens would revert to leading orderly, well-planned, state-directed, developmental lives. Privately, and often in public, the uselessness of the National Assembly and the superfluousness of endless debate were themes of conversation by the young colonels and their sympathizers. Civil rights attenuated even more than under Syngman Rhee—they were now only guaranteed "insofar as they do not conflict with the fulfillment of the tasks of the Revolution." The Political Purification Law of March 1962 banned 4,367 politicians of previous regimes from politics, at first for six years. These were forced to come to Canossa when the government later relaxed its ban somewhat by inviting them to apply for permission to participate in political activity. Some two thirds did so in the opening weeks of 1963, whereupon the government showed its power by clearing all but 200 on February 27, 1963, including many who had not applied. Most of these 200 were cleared by the end of the year, though a few have remained banned, presumably until the law is due to expire in August 1968. The military government regarded politics as a process to be controlled in careful doses by an executive that, in a faintly populist expression recalling Rhee, would know "the desires and will of the people" and on that basis was qualified to "purify" corruption and turmoil. The rigor of this belief has since been much qualified, but it is still alive.

The judiciary was treated with similarly short shrift. The government appointed a revolutionary tribunal of military officers headed by a coup colonel (later himself arrested and tortured) who shaved his head "until the objectives of the coup had been achieved." Under his aegis, criminal cases handled by courts martial rose from 10,080 in 1960 to 22,195 in 1961 and 35,044 in 1962. The quality of the trials remained that of former days, their conduct still more peremptory.[112]

Local administration and decentralization were again casualties. The results of the recent local elections were, in effect, canceled; no more were held. Mayors of Seoul and cities over 150,000 inhabitants and provincial governors were to be appointed by the cabinet with the approval of the Supreme Council, and the heads of all other local government bodies were to be appointed by the provincial governors.[113] General officers were forthwith installed as governors, and other officers, mostly colonels, were made mayors of chief cities. The ancient centralist tendency of the end of the fourteenth century of reshuffling all property at the start of a new dynasty, which had been reconfirmed by Democratic measures against the profiteers of the Liberal period, was reinstated through stern measures against the "Illicit Fortune Profiteers." A Board of Inspection was set up to investigate offenders. Following a number of arrests, a decision was announced in August to extract some $37,000,000 from twenty-seven businessmen; it was revised in October to substitute for outright confiscation investment in "national reconstruction" factories. This process itself bred corruption, especially when secret sums were extracted from businessmen for the operations of the Korean Central Intelligence Agency: and all members of the junta's own investigation team were arrested on September 25, 1961, charged with accepting bribes.[114]

Military Government Midstream

In respect to its ability to control and direct, the officers' experiment worked. Chapters 7 and 9 explore how the military government used council hierarchy without allowing council delays and how the vast Korean Central Intelligence Agency under Kim Chong-p'il was established to become not only control council but ubiquitous processor of mobility for the thousands now needed to fill the places of the ousted.[115] In the first two years, the main danger courted was internal factional struggle for a control too tightly exercised by the CIA. Otherwise, the old rules of the society worked for the usurpers. No group was cohesive or strong enough to stand against the army in this attempt, none even well-enough rooted to serve as a focus from which resistance could be effectively started. Resentment in upper circles from those hurt was widespread, but it was scattered, and the CIA was there to see that the scattered particles nowhere cohered. CIA's work was well and efficiently done by its thousands, even tens of thousands, of agents and operatives. But it was the society itself that made this work easy. Accustomed to gravitate toward any regime in power, regardless of danger, regardless of principle, most Koreans adapted themselves with relative ease to the coup, just as most had to the Japanese, the Americans, Rhee, and Chang Myŏn.

Nevertheless, it was clear that control of this kind would, in the long run, face a hostile national consensus and that the overthrow of the Rhee regime by such consensus had shortened the fuse that would lead to the explosion. War and American support for the Korean military, not the voluntary internal operation of Korean cultural processes, had made the army pre-eminent. A minority coup, not the desire of the nation, had led to army takeover. No single group could effectively organize opposition; yet neither could such a base of support lead to successful national acceptance of reform, leadership with traction enough for real change. Indeed, reforms floundered. Legislation flowed unceasingly from the tight Supreme Council; new councils were weekly spawned with idealistic titles; from ministries to township offices, army charts blossomed on every wall, and wide-eyed civilian bureaucrats were graced with daily briefings. Appropriate for smaller units and homogeneous commands, these innovations floundered in a civilian world that had never regarded the military and its procedures with either practical or moral respect. On February 18, 1963, President Park publicly admitted that his reforms had failed and that the military "revolution" had not been achieved. The government would be turned over to civilians by summer, and he would not participate in it.

The Changeover

On March 16, the decision was reversed under strong pressure from the Korean CIA and the young colonels. Yet it was still clear that a broader base must be sought. Factional jealousies and threats of counter-coup within the military needed channels of release. A clique within the military was too narrow a base of power to permit stability. There was also constant foreign pressure. Washington had, since the summer of 1961, made its aid conditional on a clear commitment to return the government to civilian control, and the UN Commission had made similar pleas.[116]

To prepare for this broadening of the power structure, a new constitution was drafted by December 1962, calling for the election, within a year, of a President who would head a restored strong presidential system, including the right to appoint and dismiss the Premier and the cabinet without legislative consent. Also provided for was a weak, unicameral legislature whose seats were reduced from 233 to 175 and whose power to revise basic legislation passed by the SCNR was nil. Article 36-3 forbade independent candidacy for the Assembly, and Article 38 stipulated that "a person shall lose his membership in the National Assembly . . . when he leaves or changes his party or when his party is dissolved." [117] This constitution was submitted to national referendum and ratified on December 19, 1962, by 78.8 percent of the voters, a clever, though under the circumstances largely meaningless, technique for legitimacy. On December 27, Park announced that members of the SCNR could run and that the government planned to form a political party. In January 1963 the ban on political activities was lifted.

A government party that had been formed secretly during an entire year of general political ban was suddenly unveiled. An election law and many regulations were promulgated. The old election districts were combined so that former politicians would compete with each other and open more chances for new candidates. A proportional representation system was added, through which 44 of the 175 seats were to be distributed to representatives of parties that had won over three district seats or 5 percent of the vote, each such party to get "distributed" seats in proportion to the vote it had obtained. Thus men without local strength were given a chance to run, splinter parties were weakened, and the margin of victory for the winning party increased. In view of the past connections of some military government leaders and their families with communism, the Central Election Management Committee on September 18 reinterpreted the Presidential anti-slander law so as to prohibit "pointing out any fact openly." Nevertheless, opposition parties were formed, although many of their leaders remained under the Political Purification Law's ban. Strict limitations on political funds were in practice applied far more to opposition than to government candidates.[118] The CIA utilized enormous sums, not only to support its candidates, a number of whom came from its organization, but also to infiltrate the opposition parties with agents who disrupted attempts at unity or to induce added opposition candidates to run, thus dividing the vote. Only thirty days of electioneering were allowed.

Thus "orderly," carefully managed elections to the Presidency and the Assembly took place in October and November 1963. A majority of voters (53 percent) voted for opposition candidates, but due to fracturing, real and induced, the opposition vote was divided so that President Park obtained 46.5 percent and former President Yun, chief opposition candidate, 45 percent. Likewise in the November Assembly elections, the government Democratic Republican party (DRP), though it polled only 32 percent of the votes cast (only 72 percent of the voters participated) won 88 district seats and 22 proportional seats, achieving a good working majority of 110 of the 175 Assembly members (63 percent). The opposition, daily warned in the press of the price of disunity, committed electoral suicide by running multiple candidates in almost every district. The mobility pattern, operating in a homogeneous society without natural centers of resistance to government, won the day for the government. By and large, police interference, force, and ballot-stuffing were not employed. The elections were technically free. Freedom now became a technical, managed matter, manipulated by organization, planning, plot, and guile. An atmosphere of cynicism hung over the new democracy. Such cynicism was unfortunately not dispelled by the elections of May 3 and June 8, 1967. In May, President Park proved a gradually widening popularity by winning fairly a 1,162,000-vote majority over Yun Po-sŏn. In the June elections, however, when the DRP raised its majority to 130 over the opposition's 45, irregularities were both charged by the opposition and admitted by the government. As a result, the opposition immobilized the Assembly with a boycott lasting until late November 1967.

Political Desiccation

To the opposition has fallen the penalty of having to cohere by voluntary means in the mass society. It has been singularly unsuccessful in overcoming old political patterns and giving united embodiment to the considerable hostility of urban sentiment. Sadly split, the "old faction" of the Democratic party, under Yun Po-sŏn, elected forty-one assemblymen. Many of the *ajŏn*-landlord core of the Korean Democrats deserted this leadership for no other apparent reason than to obtain a freer hand in placing their candidates in the running and ran with some ex-military men in a Liberal Democratic party that placed nine; most of its members have since rejoined the main party. The "new faction" of the Democrats, embittered by the opposition of the old faction to their regime, could not unite with them and placed only thirteen. A further opposition splinter under Hŏ Chŏng placed only two. A Liberal party, a splinter of the former one, re-formed, competed, but placed no one. By May 1965, after endless discussions, the various opposition camps coalesced into a fragile unity that was almost immediately endangered by a dispute over what tactics to use in opposing the Korea–Japan treaty. Adopting an extreme course after acrimonious discussion, most opposition members submitted resignations from the Assembly in August 1965. The opposition has so far obtained little impressive public support. Though the chief opposition forces did, with extreme difficulty, reunite in 1967, nine splinter parties remained in the June 1967 elections, and the opposition lost by wider margins than it had in 1963. Strong new leadership that might captain an opposition revival of the kind seen from 1956 to 1960 is not yet in evidence in 1968.

The performance of the government Democratic Republican party is hardly more impressive. United on the surface, it is, in fact, partly immobilized by a split between supporters and opponents of the Kim Chong-p'il–CIA branch of the party. Since the constitution allows neither the Assembly nor parties much power, neither has recuperative or adaptive force. The Assembly is little more than a censorial body with consultative and some supervisory powers. Neither party carries the national weight of the Liberal and Democratic parties between 1956 and 1960. Debate has been de-emphasized as an agency for action. Active groups like the students do not regard the parties and the Assembly as effective channels of communication in the state.[119] In consequence, major issues like Korean-Japanese rapprochement were, until the summer of 1965, brought to the streets in chronic, bitter, and sometimes bloody student demonstrations.[120] Such demonstrations reappeared in reaction to the June 1967 elections. In the absence of political means to solve these problems, government temptation to use increased police power has tended to rise. A politically and economically profitable decision to aid the defense of South Vietnam with some 45,000 troops brought strong U.S. support and, since the last months of 1965, has been a considerable stabilizing influence. Political stability probably remains a surface phenomenon, however, and the possibility of further violence has not entirely passed.

In essence, a modified version of the bureaucratic, economy-oriented, militarily-efficient, depoliticized, rigidly anti-Communist rule that was once Japan's formula for the progress of Chōsen has been reimposed. Present planning functions and 1961–1963 government-inspired national movements, like that for reconstruction, have resembled those of the 1930's. The bureaucracy tends to be little hampered by legislative surveillance. Corruption, having fewer checks, again flourished and became a major issue of the 1967 Presidential election campaign. The various austerities that military government tried to impose to obtain reconstruction have lapsed; the "new morale" has, if ever existent, disappeared, and only the reappearance of economic hope is reviving it in bourgeois circles. Lack of effective representation and communication means absence of the means of calculating the extent of opposition or of long-term subversion. Political solutions being forestalled, the police, the Korean CIA, and the military policy must be kept strong to contain restlessness.[121] From 1965 to 1967, the system has operated, if not always smoothly, with fair stability. By and large, the political system has withstood the strain of the major political issue of alignment with Japan. Whether it could withstand the issue of national unification remains in question. The elections of June 1967 and the long fall boycott of the National Assembly by the opposition have not obstructed the wielding of power, but they have hindered the development of normal politics.

Meanwhile, the economic achievements that were once Japan's special boast in Korea are now the pride of the Park government. Administration has been less hampered, the executive can move faster and more flexibly in execution and in planning. Relying now mostly on traditional civilian bureaucrats, it has put in a more impressive performance recently than have the legislature and the judiciary. Although such large projects as the Ulsan Industrial Center have proved in part hastily conceived, they have tended to inspire an image of purposefulness and to symbolize the national interest more than programs inched through a reluctant and carping Assembly. Economic rewards and values have started to take the place of political ones, much as the old colonial administration intended. Inflation and corruption, by outrunning official salaries and placing the bureaucracy at the mercy of business bribing, have increased the trend toward business and the enthusiasm of young men for entering it in place of government. Interest groups in the economic world appear to be increasing; a few industrial and trading empires are greatly strengthening and now appear to be among the strongest and most permanent institutions thus far created by Koreans in the peninsula. Political interest groups lag. If stability is maintained, a stage of big-business hegemony in conservative politics similar to Japan's in the later 1920's may be reached. Eventually, in natural opposition to this, a strong Socialist party advocating breakup of these units and unification by neutralism is a distinct possibility. Agreement to restore full relations with Japan, consummated in December 1965, is a major step likely to increase both these trends.

As for the underlying pattern of Korean society and politics, improvement over the long run seems possible. It is unfortunate for those interested in the development of liberal democracy under Korean conditions that the democratic thrust was parried and democracy artificially overthrown before it could bring its own adaptations to bear on Korea's political pattern. Nevertheless, it is clear that the military government saw needs that were real, however naively formulated and roughly met. Korea's experience in the years 1885–1910 and from 1945 to 1961 alike emphasize the existence of a vortex pattern of political concentration eroding private or intermediary cohesiveness in the state and impeding the development of stability in leadership and government. Such a pattern perpetuates the conditions of a mass society and frustrates the creation of pluralistic sources of strength and of the professionalism needed for development. Military government has failed to plumb the depths of its vortex problem by decentralization. It has, however, perceived some of the destructiveness of "mass" democracy. Rather heavy-handedly, it has acted to depoliticize and place more emphasis on economic and business development. By so doing, it has taken steps strengthening pluralism in institutions and the values they create. It is unfortunate that neither in 1885–1910 nor in 1945–1961 could Korea find a more natural, politically continuous path to this result. Yet the result has been, in both instances, necessary. However illiberal the forces originally producing it, only on a base of pluralism can the vortex be calmed and a representative, liberal democracy begin to flourish.

The shorter-range course may thus be clouded with dissatisfactions and political tension; but the longer-range view is not without great hope. As political problems in developing nations go, the result, despite all reservations, has been comparatively satisfactory.

PART III

The Continuity of Korean Political Culture

Certain themes emerge from the study of Korean society and politics whether recent or ancient. They are not the immediate and simple derivations of the impact of Sino-Confucianism, Japanese colonialism, American militarism, and democracy. These importations, to be sure, left their mark not only in political theory and organization but even in everyday behavior. Written pledges of belief in them and their influence abound. Behind them, however, seem to lie certain deeper, more enduring, native characteristics of Korean political action. Yi Dynasty faction, the Ilchin-hoe, the Liberal and Democratic parties, and the many other party jetsam of Korea's last twenty years are one definite form, an external phenomenon of these: the peras as Plato would have said. The more permanent, indigenous themes show the stamp of a continuous society, Plato's apeiron. The cultural matrix sets certain bounds on the divergence that imports can effect, just as parenthood stamps children, or as common motherhood does even when the male parent changes. Analytically, it is the apeiron with which we must conjure, for if we treat Korean political phenomena as passing events, we shall abdicate real understanding and, with it, the chance to propose solutions in an organized and far-reaching way.

The overlapping, almost the blanketing, of the native pattern with the extraordinarily pervasive influence of alien Chinese culture makes the quarry of Korean continuities elusive. The present study is in some respects the first attempt, at least outside the Marxist framework, to begin the search in the political field. A number of preliminary conclusions, already foreshadowed in Parts I and II, may nevertheless be stated.

In Korea, as suggested earlier, the imposition of a continuous high degree of centralism on a homogeneous society has resulted in a vortex, a powerful, upward-sucking force active throughout the culture. This force is such as to detach particles from any integrative groups that the society might tend to build — social classes, political parties, and other intermediary groups — thus eroding group consolidation and forming a general atomized upward mobility. The updraft also tends to hinder such develop-

*ments as definition of function, legal boundaries, formal proce-
dures, and specialization. This vortex appears to account in part
for Korea's unnatural retardation in these areas at the same time
that she is developed in personal and family culture, education,
political consciousness, and even urbanization. The overwhelming
problems of power-access that this dynamic creates tend further
to the formation of what might be called broad-surface access.
The function of broad-surface access is to absorb the maximum
number of power aspirants. Because they operate in a homogeneous
environment lacking natural cleavages of issues, color, religion, or
culture, such needs for access produce artificial fissures on the broad
surface of government and contention for it via a series of rival
aspirant councils (or, under communism, factions) battling over
issues generated by contrived hostility and verbal acerbity rather
than by belief or vested interest. Rivals compete for the same
object in the same way without the possibility of negotiated solution.*

*It is temerarious, at this early point, to assert that these and only
these are the apeiron of Korean political culture. Research and
argument are needed to refine them, to add to them, or, perhaps,
to subtract from them. Such theories regarding the apeiron are,
at any rate, postulates of this study, and it is after elaboration of
them that subsequent sections will discuss, in their light, Korea's
efforts at viable cohesion.*

7

Centralization and Political Mobility

CENTRALIZATION

Pre-Modern and Colonial

The roots of Korean centralism, as pointed out before, were ancient and strong. The Yi king's legitimacy derived from that of the Chinese emperor and from the maintenance of proper relations with him. *De facto*, the king was held to mediate between the realm and Heaven. He expressed Heaven's will on behalf of the people. The *yangban* were entitled to resort to the concept of the monarch's responsibility to rule in accordance with Confucian principle and even the popular will, but in the last analysis, no defense against him had clear legality. Property was his to award and, in theory, to withdraw. Access to him and, increasingly, control of his powers was the chief force making the bureaucracy the summit of all personal ambition, power, and status. Ancient as Confucianism was in Korea, it to some extent validated and elaborated native social forces still more antique.

The society lacked clearly defined, separate units to modify or control this central power. No different races or cultures existed to confront each other within it. Religious differences were insufficiently concentrated in any broadly based local or social group to permit the firm formation of cohesive opposition or discrete interest. Exclusion of foreign trade and the control and derogation of commercial functions by the central bureaucracy prevented the development of business classes, ports, or specialization that could serve local strength. Local institutions were weak and diffuse, local administration offered no prestige, and ambitious young men saw no use in associations and careers below the capital. On the whole, the centralizing tendency was increased when, from the sixteenth century on, temple yielded place to Confucian academy as rural Korea's prime institution; or later, when the *sach'ang* (grain storage and exchange units that had been strengthened under the Taewŏn'gun and enjoyed a rather democratic form of local direction) were replaced with Japanese banking and cooperative institutions that, though more numerous and efficient, were not local hierarchies but branches of a national bureaucracy offering ladders away from the rural county.[1] Rapid urbanization and the post-1931 chance to colonize in Manchuria or work in Japan pushed many up these ladders and brought millions out of rural homes. Population pressures, landlordism, drought or flood, and ambition were chief factors in this exodus; the police system was another. Established as *the* institution in an institution-poor countryside, the police could bore into the least detail of village life, stifling initiative and leadership; cities could, in shrouding more secrets, encourage group strength, and dispense scope for the individual. To this day, the coming of an urban visitor to the village evokes the pathetic and almost universal desire of young men of any ambition to leave with the traveler.

Liberation

During Japan's administration, other forces compensated for centralism in part. Mines and fishing multiplied institutions outside cities, and some factories in small towns like Samch'ŏk processed local resources. Local administration and local schools, for Japanese outside Seoul as well as Koreans, improved and a loyal and professional bureaucracy encouraged a greater degree of delegation and local responsibility. Liberation undid much of this work. Factories, mines, and larger fishing organizations, abandoned by their Japanese owners, became vested property even more closely managed by the Seoul bureaucracy than under Japanese centralism. Their importance and productivity declined greatly, further weakening local concerns. The Japanese backbone of such cities as Pusan, Masan, Taejŏn, Kunsan, and Mokp'o melted, leaving them with their cores more removed than Frankfurt's was after Nazi expulsion of the Jews. Japanese bureaucracy was replaced by one newer, less professional, and far less stable to which little delegation of responsibility became possible. Meanwhile, the coming of dependency on American aid, funneled in and through the central government, added to the upward scramble.

War and Postwar

The immediate aftermath of war intensified the process. War dispersed and weakened private groups and almost wiped out private holdings. Churches — one of the few intermediary groups — were often burned and their congregations scattered. Intellectuals were mostly pauperized, landlords deeply hurt. Most land had been distributed in May and June 1950, just before the Communist invasion; such as had not was distributed in the immediate postwar years. By 1957 an estimated 1.5 million farmers had acquired some 1.2 million acres of land on which they had formerly been tenants or farm workers.[2] For three years the farmers were to pay one third of the annual crop to the government, which would pay the landlords back 50 percent on an average annual crop in certificates to be used in industrial investment. This meager compensation was almost eliminated by severe wartime inflation and losses. All but the largest and most agile landowners were pauperized. Farm units shrank drastically. The agricultural population increased to 14 million by 1959, consisting of 2.3 million farm families averaging six persons holding about two acres per farm. Roughly 430,000 farms had under four fifths of an acre. Farms of over seven to eight agricultural acres virtually disappeared. Rural technical development, agricultural loans, storage, and selling problems that had once devolved largely on landlords were now increasingly government functions. Some areas of resentment were removed; but so was a chief source of local political leadership and effective communication with the countryside.[3] The political image of a mass society homogeneous in race and culture, now more uniform in wealth than ever, competing increasingly widely and with fewer distinctions for the same objectives, and more than ever the wards of government power, became deeper engraved. The formation of interest groups and of the issues and compromises that build political systems of democratic type were undermined almost before initiated.

In the industrial field, plants in three quarters of the country were wiped out. Rehabilitation under both the U.S. and the UN now poured into the country hundreds of millions of dollars. Scarcely an enterprise in the country had independent, private sources of help.[4] All aid came through the Korean government. After 1956, access to it was concentrated in the Liberal party. Inflation was constant through 1957 (it had been almost continual since 1945) and was severe after 1950. With property destroyed and inflation rampant, the former wealthier and middle-class families were severely hurt, in many cases ruined. Fortunes were made not in production but in speculation and in foreign exchange, for the legal exchange rate was constantly outstripped by inflation and the President was slow to restore balance. The sale of foreign exchange and of the rights for import became a vast government business, increasingly involving payments to the party and officials. Government loans, especially through the Reconstruction Bank, were the chief source of business funds — and of inflation. Since official interest rates were a small percentage of the 10 percent per month or more payable privately, the proportion of kickback greatly exceeded the official interest charged, decreasing funds available for investment in business.[5] Virtually every procurement operation, whether for money or imported goods, involved bribery. Business, more than ever, became an adjunct of government, and, especially as the Liberal party rose, enterprises became the fiefs of politicians.

Again the domination of central government intensified. Even more than in 1945, almost all vested interests were eliminated and, in effect, nationalized, since under war and aid conditions government control over them became almost unlimited. Corruption expressed these conditions. It too centralizes: money passed under a table cannot be passed from afar. Since in important cases higher officials received a cut anyway, it was cheaper and more effective to be "in at the top." Large firms arose whose growth was associated with their ability to maintain whole groups of key officials within the government, officials whose government salaries — on which they could not live in any case — were but a tiny fraction of what these firms paid them. High turnover among officials only increased these pressures: one's "understanding" with a former official must be urgently renewed with his successor. Such a system made constantly necessary presence in the capital — to repair one's fences and pay hush-money.

Weakness in the rule of law furthered the process. When legal codes and the agencies of their enforcement have meaning, one can transact business anywhere, confident of recourse. Since, however, the legal system offered the citizen no defense against political and economic pressures, all business came to depend on personal relations and venue to the central bureaucracy. Such factors greatly increased during the last years of Liberal party dominance and were again fed in the 1961–1963 period by the operations of the military government's CIA.

To an extent even greater than during Yi times, Korea developed into a capital-concentrated society. Under the Japanese, independent businessmen and officials of importance could develop careers in provincial cities and port towns; within the indigenous system, every headquarters and every ambitious man must be in Seoul. Not being seen in Seoul acquired tones of disfavor. To live in the provinces meant disgrace; even being there for longer than the most transient vacations — usually spent at resorts with other Seoul people — seemed subtly sullied with a pale, exile-like cast. Through the long, consistent march of such developments, Korea became as centralized as it is possible to imagine a modern culture to be.

POLITICAL MOBILITY: THE PATTERN IS SET

No satisfying alternatives to participation in central power remaining, it became the sole aim of the ambitious to employ any means to stream toward it.[6] The preoccupation of the culture therefore became the surmounting of the barriers erected to limit access to power. This cultural concentration was the more exclusive because external threat or larger international issues so rarely mobilized national and common effort.

Education

Since the main path to power access led through the examination system to the central bureaucracy, education had been, for roughly a millennium, a chief hurdle. This fact determined governmental policy toward the education system and infused schools with politics. From the fourteenth century on, the National Academy was maintained; its top staff and head were career officials of the central government, the highest titular ones holding concurrent Censorate or official literary positions.[7] The academy's function was to train *yangban* for the examinations and career bureaucratic service. Since it had an enrollment capacity of not much over two hundred, competition to enter was intense, often involving factional maneuverings.[8] This system, in slightly modern dress, together with the feverish competition associated with it, has been retained in today's Seoul National University.[9] The original academy students regarded themselves not only as a specially-privileged elite but almost as already part of the governmental system with semi-consultative rights. Academy students ruled much of their own intramural affairs, could collectively memorialize the throne, and from the fifteenth century on occasionally took to the streets in demonstration.[10] They were sometimes aroused by "senior" academy alumni within the administration to do so.[11]

The early causes that students espoused were significant. Fifteenth-century Korea was locked in a major attempt to adopt a new foreign system and reform a Buddhist state in a neo-Confucian image. The *yangban* and the council forces engaged in this conversion with an enthusiasm bordering on the fanatic. The students, sons of *yangban* elite, played the role of urging the extremer, "purer," doctrinaire forms of the new dogma on a society that they regarded as too slow-moving. The academy students repeatedly demonstrated against Buddhist tendencies throughout the century, even when the country's greatest monarch, Sejong (ruled 1418–1450), was friendly to Buddhism. Hundreds made joint pleas in 1492. They supported the extreme Confucianist reforms of the young official Cho Kwang-jo, and when he fell in the purge of 1519, they "forced their way through the gates of the palace compound and carried to the very door of the king's residence their lamentations and protestations that the accused was innocent." [12] In December 1873, when the remonstrator Ch'oe Ik-hyŏn memorialized against the Taewŏn'gun, the entire student body of the academy left their school in excitement over the issues of Confucian relationships involved, three being banished.[13] Students played active political roles in supporting "justice," often in terms of the theory and dogma of a political system artificially adopted from a "superior" nation. Their zeal for implanting foreign values has, at least occasionally, marked Korean students apart from those of China, the United States, and England, who operate within the internal — or at least the more internalized — values of powerful states.

The political system Japan brought to Korea was certainly not voluntary; it was also doctrinally threadbare and lacking in theoretical appeal. Though some students nonetheless equated it with modernization, they would not demonstrate for it except in government-inspired assemblages. Their own voluntary efforts brought them to the streets to oppose tyranny and support nationalism, as in the demonstrations accompanying the 1919 Independence Movement and the 1929 Kwangju student incident. Again the tradition of deep student involvement in politics and the function of the student in protest was upheld. But in these cases, it was more consonant with many other anti-colonial student movements, including the Chinese.

These traditions have converged in post-Liberation Korea. In the leftist-rightist struggles of 1946–1947 and in the protests against both Syngman Rhee and the Park Chŏng-hŭi governments, the issue of tyranny was inherited from colonial times. In the anti-Rhee and anti-Park struggles, the fifteenth-century student role was, in addition, strikingly revived. Student banners constantly espoused the cause of a pure democracy whose tenets must be "sincerely" upheld. Again the students were cast in the role of supporters, sometimes extremist supporters, of an imported political system whose progress in the indigenous culture they regarded as too incomplete. Probably nowhere else in the world is there so ancient and continuous a tradition of student demonstration, memorializing, and active participation in national politics as in Korea. The extremeness of this tradition bespeaks the national concentration on access to central power, the key role of the educational system therein, and the intellectual tensions aroused when a small nation adopts foreign systems.

Educational expansion also played a key role. The National Academy and the four other official Seoul academies could not accommodate the expanding *yangban* ranks in their rush for power. The local academy (*sŏwŏn;* see p. 27) was the attempt to broaden the upward flow. Education being the main path of access, political factions chose or started rural *sŏwŏn* that could support their bureaucratic-political aims with memorializing and with money from tax-free lands; from them, factional adherents, backed by successful alumni seniors in or near the bureaucracy, could pass the examination and be placed in the government.[14] The vital nature of what was involved is shown in the *sŏwŏn's* extraordinary proliferation: some 650 by the end of the eighteenth century, 270 with some government sponsorship and lands. Though actual placement in the bureaucracy was unlikely for most graduates, the *sŏwŏn* widened opportunity by tapping local men and not always requiring strict *yangban* status.[15]

With the abolishment of the *sŏwŏn* by the Taewŏn'gun by 1872, the door closed. The Academy was also in decline. Education ceased to play a primary role in determining access to power. This role was revived by the Japanese, however, largely in the decade of Saitō's administration in the 1920's, when Koreans became eligible for passing the Higher Civil Service examination and when Keijō Imperial University was established (1926) as the main portal of Chōsen's bureaucracy. Seoul National University has succeeded to this role. It and Korea's sixty-five–odd colleges and universities, mostly built since Liberation, have sought to widen the portal to official power much as the *sŏwŏn* sought to do from 1543 to 1800. Higher education remains the main avenue of mobility, its gates pushed ever more open.

Status Fluidity

Before education's modern expansion as the highway of mobility, its portals were widened by another force whose background requires social explanation. Education by itself was too indiscriminate a system of political recruitment for a dynasty so concentrated on official power. The Yi codes therefore specified, as the Chinese had not, that *yangban* lineage be a requirement for sitting for the literary examination. The Censorate scrutinized the lineage records of all those who were to be placed, frequently blocking appointment. Combined with the examination, status provided a sufficiently controllable hurdle to regularize political recruitment for five hundred years and constitute a keystone of the stability of the dynasty.

The pressures the vortex built up were, however, immense. Educational restrictions had partly crumbled with the establishment of *sŏwŏn* and with factional interference in the examinations. The old rules of lineage now also faced the same upward pressures. The secret of the strategy against these rules lay in the fact that Korean society was too homogeneous and un-feudal to limit access by criteria of race, religion, or the possession of estates and local power and therefore had to choose criteria that were subject to training and imitation: education, manners, dress, and the like. Outright falsification of family records (*chokpo*), the basis of the lineage system, was also practiced. Pressures for access to central power brought covert social mobility, great and possibly massive in dimension. (See Chapter 2.)

Covert mobility, proceeding at least from the period of the Japanese invasion of 1592–1598 on and made easy by the extensive loss of records taking place at that time, had three centuries of gradual expansion in which to eat away at the status system and train ever more levels of society to join a progressively less delimited race for central power.[16] The Taewŏn'gun began to open the door officially to the new classes. His new recruitment was small, however. The court *yangban* could have stopped it had they retained real power as an interest group. They grumbled but did not stop it. The new monarch, Kojong, followed an erratic pattern of appointments that included lower-class men. The official abolishment of class distinctions for appointment purposes was one of the more important reforms of 1894. Instituted at Japanese bayonet point by a rubber-stamp Korean "Deliberative Council," such measures should have become a dead letter if the system they reformed had been healthy. Instead, several important forced reforms had immediate and lasting effect.[17] The careers of such lower-class men as Song Pyŏng-jun and Yi Yong-ik show that some confidence in political judgment and a feeling of qualification to compete in politics had already begun to penetrate the lower classes. The lid was off. There began, on a scale affecting the whole political process, an atomized, uncurbed streaming of ambitious individuals from almost all classes toward central power, their access determined by personal favor often generated by the quixotic and the opportunistic. In the legal sense it was new, but the social process was old. Had it in fact been new, the *yangban* would have turned and fought it. The ease with which Korean society, with a suddenness unknown to modernizing Japan, absorbed the nullification of class distinctions can be explained by the probability that this equalization was, in fact, the surfacing of a covert process long operating, at least in the *hyangban* areas of the society. A struggle for power wide-open enough to include some ambitious men from varied social levels had already acquired a kind of legitimacy, informal though it was. Democracy was to give to this legitimacy new luster.

Informal power-access processes are rarely described and need the color of illustration. In essence, they are still the center of the Korean political process. The culture even institutionalized such melding rise so as to give it a subtle but definite support. Within and beside the gates of the Yi Korean upper-class compound (see Fig. 1) were chains of small rooms for all manner of servant, political messenger, major domo, impecunious relative, eager country scholar, tutor, and "eating guest" (*sikkaek*), the last a role demonstrating the inclusiveness, warmth, eagerness, opportunism, and undefined functions of Korean life. The ambitious young man from the provinces with some note of introduction, the son of a favorite *kisaeng* (female entertainer) of the family head, the graduate of a *sŏwŏn* connected with the ancestor of the house — these might attach themselves, hoping by brightness of appearance to be received, by loyalty of service to be retained. (Regarding the retainer system, see Chapter 12.) The value system condemned stinginess, and what was stingier than keeping from the wide door of a wealthy house those with some introduction willing to serve and needing to eat? The times also favored such access. Liberal ideas were creeping in, and opportunity was spreading downward. At the top, men needed more personal supporters. The support of factions had gradually dried up by the later nineteenth century, and, with the ingrown enmities of a five-hundred-year-old dynasty added to the frictions of new ideas, new foreign temptations, and new economic patterns, even clans were losing their unity. More than ever, even the *yangban* had to count on himself: that meant counting on his household.

One day in the 1870's or early 1880's a husky, handsome youth walked into the compound of the king's cousin, Min Yŏng-hwan, who, already at the age of twenty-three had been appointed Minister of War.[18] The youth had come to Seoul from Changjin, in Hamgyŏng Province, roughest and most remote region of Korea. He carried a note from his *kisaeng* mother, the mistress of his *ajŏn* father, a tax collector in the province. He had himself helped his father in the collecting of taxes when he was sixteen and had learned the techniques and rewards of popularity by burning some tax claims, thereby helping a hundred debtors enjoy the new year.[19] Hanging around the *kisaeng* and hoodlums of Seoul in young manhood, he absorbed the lower-class skill of making quick friends with anyone and watched gangs form and operate as no aristocrat could.[20] From his years on the streets came the instincts of the ward politician and skill in the ways of informal, fluid organizations. Reportedly stimulated by being a young hanger-on in the welcome given the first Japanese envoy, General Kuroda, in 1876, he learned some Japanese in 1879.[21] Endowed with handsome appearance and native ambition, the boy attracted the young prince, who took him in as a *sikkaek* in the Min compound. Min soon saw to it that his guest was appointed a *chusa*, a clerk in the Interior Ministry, and also, reportedly, a military officer.[22] Neither position should have been so easily open to a boy from the North on the lower commoner fringes; but already patronage outbid class. The boy's name now first began to be known. It was Song Pyŏng-jun (see Fig. 4).

The bitter struggles of the time opened opportunities for him. In 1885, after the Min defeated the reformers of the 1884 coup, they dispatched their young handyman to Japan to assassinate "progressive" coup leader Kim Ok-kyun. Ever flexible and impressionable — he had no reputation or family status to validate, no caste ties to Confucian "principle" — Song fell under Kim's influence and, instead of killing him, became his sworn comrade.[23] When he slipped back into Seoul, he was arrested by suspicious Queen Min, argued his way out through his princely protector, and shortly afterward became a magistrate, supposedly still a position only awardable to the noble class. Still Min-backed, he was included in the suite of Prince Ŭihwa, a concubine son of King Kojong, on his visit to Tokyo in 1894. It proved his first "in" with the royal family. Assuming a Japanese name, he remained in Japan for ten years, returned to Korea as interpreter for Major General Otani in the Russo-Japanese War in 1904 and found a Japanese compatible with his personality and background, the Black Dragon Society leader, Uchida Ryōhei, an impulsive lower-class activist. His labors with Yi Yong-gu under Uchida founded the Ilchin-hoe and, with it, mass politics in Korea.

Riding on the crest of Japanese collaboration and political leadership, Song was in a good position to regard with equanimity the suicide of his patron, Min Yŏng-hwan, in despair over the Korean loss of independence in 1905. He solaced himself by assuming some guardian functions over the estate, with a considerable part of which he subsequently absconded. He was quickly appointed Minister of Agriculture, Commerce, and Industry in the Yi Wan-yong cabinet of 1907, actively campaigned within the cabinet and outside through the Ilchin-hoe to give increased powers to the Japanese resident-general (he was a signer of the agreement of July 24, 1907), then to urge outright annexation by Japan. Probably no other Korean — and very few Japanese — played a more effective role for Annexation. He was rewarded with the title of viscount in 1910 and was later made a count. He interested himself in industrialization and died, hated but full of honors, in 1925.

Song was neither alone nor unrepresentative of his age. Yi Yong-ik, an illiterate of the meanest origins, who was found by Horace Allen sweeping floors, was able to deliver messages between the queen and the king during her escape from Seoul. On the strength of this, he became Treasurer of the Royal Household, in charge of all mining rights, the king's personal financial counselor, economic czar of the country from 1900 to 1904, and was thereafter briefly War Minister and Minister of Finance. Along the way he acquired the country's largest fortune, founded the Posŏng educational institutions (including the present Korea University), and started the first printing company in Korea.[24] In much the same manner, Hong Ke-hun, a low-ranking soldier who carried the queen out of the palace in the anti-Japanese revolt of 1882 became Minister of War. Still another individual, Yi Pŏm-jin, illegitimate son of a general by a *kisaeng* mother, was allowed to take the exams before 1894, rose to Minister of Justice in 1896 and became Minister to America, Russia, France, Austria, and Germany — all because his house happened to be the one in which the queen first hid when she escaped from the palace.[25] Yi Kŭn-t'aek, a Ch'ungch'ŏng-do boy who met the queen when she was in exile in his village, became twice Minister of War and a viscount and apparently manipulated the peddler's guild to crush the Independence Club.[26]

Such careers illustrate more in the political process than the occasional breaching of the last formal barriers. With them begins the process of the bridging of such remaining gaps as covert social mobility had left between the elite and the commoners. Kojong's court portended the loss of any leadership identity based on cultural values, the substitution for them of opportunism and dramatic versatility. The "new men" began to carry mass standards to the highest places; elite and non-elite became more similar and more directly dependent on each other. In his Ilchin-hoe, Song Pyŏng-jun broke with the process of enlisting elite support in factional form and began direct appeal to "common bases of response among large numbers of people." [27] A man fresh from a new society, with quite new behavioral norms, Song was free from the restraints, the habitual orientations of his bureaucratic *yangban* predecessors, was, as Max Weber would put it, "foreign to all rules." [28] The old elite dallied and could never make up their minds. He always knew what he was after, no matter how dastardly others held it. The son of a British Prime Minister, speaking of those same years in England, should better have been describing Korea: "the day of the clever cad is at hand." [29] Yet the new cads became the new leaders and put change in motion. Hated as he was, Song was still the first of Korea's modern politicians, and, however silent Koreans now choose to be about him, the meaning of his role in Korean society has not lost its significance.

The Influence of Christian Churches

While the last barriers were being breached above, new ladders of mobility were being placed against the walls below, though the men on them did not always scale them to the summits of government. Language — English as well as Japanese — was one channel. Foreigners were known to have contact and even influence at court, and Western prestige was high after Japan's victory over China. Men like Syngman Rhee and Kim Kyu-sik went to missionary schools like Pai Chai less for their Christianity than to look for political position through English. Enrollment at Pai Chai declined when English was de-emphasized; in 1905, within a day or two of enrollment, "half the school had gone elsewhere in search of English." [30]

But religion, though scorned by the aspiring politician, advanced the humble. Conversions among the 30,000 of Seoul's outcast butcher class soon became "one of the most remarkable features of evangelical efforts in and around the capital." [31] A converted butcher named Pak spread ideals of Christian liberty and social freedom widely; under his influence the outcasts petitioned and were given improved social and political status in the reforms of 1895. "Conversion" became tremendous among men of the North who felt deprived of the *cursus honori*. The *chungin* were influenced.[32] The students of the Yesu Kyo Hak Tang (Christian School) were selected "according to the destitution of the class from which they were drawn." [33] Here, as at the top of government, recruitment was haphazard: "poverty . . .

brought the girl to us"; another was "picked up out of the city wall by Dr. Scranton." [34] An official would send his concubine. "A large proportion of the first Christians were household servants, language teachers, colporteurs and teachers in schools who received compensation or salary." [35] Religious rites had their appeal and importance, but missionaries also ran organizations — schools, hospitals, churches — which, compared to the decaying institutions of the country around them, were relatively well-financed and expanded rapidly after 1903. The missionaries, sympathetic with the underdog, were in complete charge of their own ladders. Houseboy and stray waif, colporteurs and *paekchŏng*, if bright, could run up these ladders better than the next man, and did.[36] *Yangban* still avoided the church: Confucian class and value systems mixed with it poorly; avoidance of labor and the cultivation of physical immobility rasped with the Protestant ethic of the sacredness of work.

As the church in Korea grew and Koreans rose in responsibility within it, Japanese control of the country tightened. The tense coexistence with Japan influenced the church's growth. Haphazardness in recruitment gradually gave way; men now made their churchward way with greater political motivation. The church, though under suspicion, was also a rarity in not being minutely Japanese controlled. Here Koreans were freer to develop their own leadership over large numbers of people.[37] From minister or YMCA secretary to political leadership — if Japanese occupation ever ended — seemed an easy step. The churches, besides helping fill the religious vacuum, became nuclei of the Independence Movement, hence, of political action. Cho Pyŏng-ok, Independence leader, Home Minister, Presidential candidate, presents a picture of himself as a "political-Christian." [38] Even Lyuh Woon-hyung studied at the Korean Presbyterian Seminary. Many political sprouts were planted in Christian seedbeds. A majority among the thirty-three patriots of 1919 were Christian ministers or leaders. Others became government or party leaders after Liberation. Churches reached down into society and gave men political as well as religious ladders; for a while, they were almost the only cohesive element.

A SOCIETY ADRIFT

For twenty-five years after 1885, institutions and groups were eschewed in the atomized struggle for association with central power.

The characteristic institution of the age was *ppaek* (patronage).[39] The updraft was too capricious and personal to permit more substantial bonds. Fourteen uprisings between 1880 and 1894 remained local despite the nation-wide nature of the grievances. Only the Tonghak finally, with religious fanaticism, brought some unity. Court *yangban* had lost their traction on society and ability to rally. Prince Min Yŏng-hwan, handsome member of the most powerful of private clans, cousin of the king and nephew of the queen, minister, general, well-educated, liberal of mind, uncorruptible, an observer of the West and its ways, lacked none of the class, personal, or official attributes of Korean leadership.[40] He prevailed on one hundred former officials to assemble at the palace in November 1905 to protest the signing of the Protectorate Treaty. They appeared in full regalia, a splendid sight under the November skies, and yet they simply staged a protest sitdown strike in front of the palace. "Store keepers put their shutters to mark their mourning," but they did not join the officials.[41] The petitioners were prevented by Korean police under Japanese orders from meeting in a store. There were mobs who the signing officials felt were more likely to attack them than to join in protest. There were still six battalions of Korean troops; one almost shot the Foreign Minister, and two years later, many among them would revolt. But none now made common cause, though Min was a general and had twice been Minister of War. The *yangban* had become more impotent than the nobility of France in 1788: "ostensibly the high command of a great army, but actually a corps of officers without troops to follow them." [42] The nation surrendered with hardly a shot. Min had no one to lead. He went home and committed suicide. "I know that my death will accomplish nothing," he wrote in his beautiful script, "and that my people will be lost in the coming life and death struggle, but seeing that I can do nothing to prevent this by living, I have taken my decision." [43] Nothing to which his leadership penetrated had cohesiveness: not his court *yangban* class or bureaucratic associates, both split on the issue of the Protectorate; not those who served on the local estates he never visited; not the soldiers for whom he was theoretically a general; not even his clan, many of whom in a few years would accept Japanese titles. Far more than Japan's bullying and her 8,000 troops, the atomized upward streaming, with its hemophilic consequences for Korean social coagulation, had led to foreign annexation by depriving society of the instruments of resistance. It had, in fact, more than Japan herself, destroyed the two vital components of a nation: the national integrity and the viability of social institutions.

What worked instead was the man in power who used it as a lure for individual atoms: Uchida for Song Pyŏng-jun and Yi Yong-gu; Itō for Yi Wan-yong and Cho Chung-ŭng. Without hierarchical or even comradely ties, loyalty and patriotism had nothing to adhere to. *Ppaek* was color blind; it did not demand that a man be Korean or Japanese, moral or immoral, only that he personally have power and bestow it. For subversion it was better than bayonets and left less telltale marks. The Japanese, though moving toward more formal recruitment, still used it. Yi Kyu-wan, poor country boy, picked up in the wake of Marquis Pak Yŏng-hyo's hunt through his village and later recruited by Itō, obeyed the genrō's advice: "If you can't read official documents, you can depend on smart advisors." By obeying the Japanese, he became Bureau Chief in the Privy Council in 1907, Governor of Kangwŏn-do for eleven years, of Hamgyŏng Namdo for the next six, and advisor to the Oriental Development Company.[44] His family, which included a son-in-law who was a minister and office chief under Rhee, has, since this hunt, not lost its prosperity.

Divorced from groups, causes, ideals, and their pressure for rationality, atomized mobility brutalized all talent and ambition. Men sold friends, honor, and nation for power, yet stood always on the edge of the abyss. The psychology of this plight explains much of their erratic and cruel behavior. Imprisonment, exile, and assassination were endemic; it was as much in fear of each other as of the Japanese that some sided with Japan as a force to tame these dangers.[45] The queen who dominated the politics of most of the age was cut down by Japanese and Korean thugs in her own palace and burned, some say while not yet dead: one finger alone remained for burial. Kim Hong-yuk, a Vladivostok-born commoner, hired as Russian interpreter and catapulted from there to become the Secretary-General of the cabinet and, in 1898, Vice-Minister of Education, was within weeks charged with conspiring with the king's cook (to concoct opium coffee to serve the court), carted to jail, and knifed before sentence could be given: "the dead bodies were dragged into the busy street of Chongno as if they were dead dogs and cats and beaten and stoned by passers-by."[46] Prime Minister Kim Hong-jip suffered an equally grim end. One of the few men who in the dynasty's last years symbolized all that it claimed to stand for, a high aristocrat, son of a minister, descended from royalty of the eighteenth century, brilliant, reputable, a chief negotiator in treaty after treaty signed with the United States, France, Great Britain, and Russia, he was the first Korean to hold the new title of Prime Minister and, before the end of 1896, had held it three times. When the king hid himself in the Russian Legation on December 28, 1896, Prime Minister Kim, against the warnings of Japanese and Korean officials, set out in his palanquin to bring him back, determined that "I will not let foreigners save my life." [47] On the main street of Seoul he was stoned to death by peddlers and hoodlums stirred up by the pro-Russian faction, the corpse lying untended for hours. His widow starved herself in lamentation.[48] Two other cabinet ministers were also killed, one at his country house. Without the loyalties that intermediate associations form, an irrational and arbitrary cruelty blackened the drama of the vortex. High office, virtually unrelated to public service, could be achieved only through intrigue, exploitation, and violence, and those who seized office expected to be struck back at when the chance was given. Not even the most conscientious could expect to find in it a kindly death. Still men rode into the eye of the storm.

Japan's Attempts at Order

Colonial sternness after 1910 tried to curb the pattern of late Yi decades. Ordered bureaucracy, not personal rule and influence, became the theme of power. Strict examinations controlled most entrances to higher levels; generally, they were scrupulously administered. Government offices were closely policed and, for the first and last time in Korea, cleaned of office-seekers. Administration and education established a world of professions, with promotions gained chiefly by competence, not favor. Education was re-established as the chief path to power; though limited for Koreans, its great expansion widened access on a rational, non-class basis. The Koreans, quick to learn and to observe the currents from above, adapted themselves to the new world with some speed. Yet for them this sort of sanitized world, unvalidated by any morality or philosophy inspiring Korean respect, inhabited largely by foreign men and ideas, brought alienation and despair as well as modernization.

The updraft was still there, and centralization became even more prevalent. The bureaucracy enormously expanded, its tasks multiplied. From performing lethargically the simple and unchanging roles of a uniform agricultural society, it became the agent for the modernization of an increasingly complex state. The few thousand jobs of even the late Yi Dynasty rose steadily to over 90,000, including some 45,000 Koreans. Even though Japanese blocked much of the way, the road had become so widened that many times the number of Koreans could have some government position, however lowly, by the end of the Japanese period than could have had it before the Japanese came. By 1927, there were 28,500 Japanese and 16,000 Koreans in the central government-general alone. (See page 106.) Some alternate business and social organizations were set up, but most were oriented to the central government; their attempt to wean Koreans from politics to the practical and the productive largely failed. The police and intelligence agencies constituted an avenue of upward mobility for thousands of the lower class. Despite clear discrimination, stimulation to get into the educational system and from it to compete for government position increased, its lures deepened among the formerly excluded classes. Even while curbing access, the Japanese intensified the potential struggle for power. Meanwhile, Japan's freezing of the practice of politics gave no rein to political modernization. Increased competition by the old means was held in check only by the colonial presence.

Chaos Returns

Setting up headquarters in Seoul, Hodge's staff scrambled to find out what the strange land and the People's Republic were. Their scramble touched off the old pattern's return. The Americans had no bureaucratic plans or discipline for Korea. Lacking any briefing or written references and any firm contacts, they sought vital policy information from chance, personal sources. The first consulted seem to have been the Americans' Japanese predecessors.[49] The first principal staff political advisor, a navy commander whose family had been missionaries in Korea, was selected from a visiting naval vessel because Hodge happened to overhear him talking Korean with a sidewalk vendor in Inch'ŏn during the first days of the Occupation. First Korean visitors to Hodge's headquarters included a liberal sprinkling of the commander's friends, many well-to-do and conservative contributors to missionary work. From among them, Hodge chose an interpreter; he sat three years at the general's door as a policy and personnel advisor and sifter of visitors, his considerable influence vastly inflated in Korean minds. He was intelligent and well-meaning. He had a good Harvard and Syracuse education. His method of selection, however, was not a far advance on Uchida Ryōhei's choice of Song Pyŏng-jun. Under the circumstances, perhaps, it could not be.

Military Government surrounded itself with men similarly recruited. The core was American-educated, missionary-connected; since proselytizing had been most successful in the North, many were Northerners newly risen in the religious and educational channels. English was an important criterion; those closest to the Americans were among the thirty to fifty fluent English-speaking Koreans available in early Occupation days. Recruitment method recalled that used by the Japanese for Cho Chung-ŭng: an exam-passer in 1883, Cho was advanced under Itō's patronage to ministerial — and eventually to noble — rank largely because of his mastery of the Japanese language. But since the Americans had far less experience in Korea than their Japanese predecessors had even in 1905, they leaned more blindly on their Korean choices. USAMGIK became known all over the peninsula as "the interpreter's government."

Japan's departing 700,000 left a firmament of tens of thousands of jobs sparkling above Koreans. Authority for two years was largely represented by war-weary U.S. officers yearning for home and administering a "policy" without long-range aims or short-range methods. Recruitment returned Korea to late Yi excesses run wild. American combat commanders counting the days until demobilization found themselves provincial governors or heads of ministries. Corporals suddenly commanded chemical plants and textile factories. Lt. Leonard Bertsch, an Ohio lawyer, later debarred, became chief negotiator and political policy administrator for a nation. Koreans had only to approach with a jauntiness attractive to Americans, and the firmament was near. "As we left the Chosŏn Hotel, a colonel approached Bertsch with a radiant smile. 'Say,' he said, 'I understand you're recommending men for the Interim Legislature.' 'Yes.' 'Well, I know a wonderful guy. His name is Rah, and he is the President of the Horse Racing Association. He wants very much to serve in the Legislature. You will do me a great personal favor if you meet him.' 'OK,' said Bertsch. 'Send him to me with your card. I'll talk to him.' " [50] Mr. Rah was in. When the Korean War came, the same pattern re-emerged. The mayor of P'yŏngyang, during the brief occupation of that city by UN troops, was selected by an American colonel who, seeing a group of respectable-looking Korean civilians by the side of the road, asked the one with a necktie if he would like to be mayor. When the incredulous man understood the question, he accepted. There was no telling how far even a houseboy might go. A catch-as-catch-can, happy-go-lucky opportunism ruled those tumbled years, reminiscent not only of Uchida Ryōhei's era but also of the more ancient society of 1259–1354 when Mongol overlords, less light-hearted but personally transient and similarly ill-informed, picked leaders and staffs and sowed disunity. No more than the Mongols did the Americans pause to consider how greatly the impact of such recruitment on Korean political culture would feed the vortex of attraction to central power and contribute to a degree of instability worse than even the ends of the previous two dynasties had known. Nor did any American acquire sensitivity to the fact that such selection, with its easy tolerance, its built-in color blindness to friend and foe, undermined the possibility that American aims in Korea could be seriously regarded. Mr. Rah's race track was, in the end, only a free-for-all.

The Way of Autocracy

Dr. Rhee, though no athlete, liked to preside over race tracks when they were political. He was far more professional in his judgments of people than his American predecessors and had far better advice to turn to. His ideas of an executive, however, were basically late Yi: streams of aspirants depended on him alone for advancement and, through the frequent shifts he made, were rendered addedly incapable of attaching themselves to an interest group. The first nonroyal Korean chief of state, he had, like the Taewŏn'gun, successor problems and behaved in some respects like the old regent. Among contemporaries, Rhee invites comparison to Haile Selassie, another forceful leader with initially fragile claims to the throne.

The pattern was set with the first cabinet, announced on August 4, 1948. With one minor exception, a man dismissed within a few weeks, there was no hold over from USAMGIK's department heads.

Rhee's most important official, General Yi Pŏm-sŏk, Prime Minister and Minister of National Defense, was in charge of the USAMGIK-supported Racial Youth Group and was thus leader of one of the nation's few large and important loyalty systems. Rhee's first decision was to destroy him, his second to prepare for that by giving him high place. Having used appointment to bring General Yi within his own loyalty sphere, Rhee could in 1949 order the Racial Youth to amalgamate into a larger National Youth Corps with different leadership, thus beginning the process of its breakup without risking effectively-led opposition. This accomplished, General Yi could be used as a scapegoat for the troubles of the army after the Yŏsu revolt. He was dismissed from his defense post in February 1949 and as Prime Minister in April 1950. In the early summer of 1952, Rhee again made him Prime Minister for three months in order to generate the extreme measures needed to crush the political opposition. Having served this purpose, General Yi was cast away into complete and lasting retirement, drained of almost all the power and prestige he had commanded four years earlier.

In somewhat similar fashion, Rhee's 1948 appointment of a former Communist, Cho Pong-am, as Minister of Agriculture is hard to view in any other way than as an effort to forestall his later emergence as an important rival. After he later became an opposition Presidential candidate, head of the Progressive party (an opposition socialist group), and a leader of proved ability, Rhee had him executed in 1959.

Rhee's attempt to appoint as Prime Minister Yi Yun-yŏng, chairman of the Chosŏn Democratic party, chief political grouping of the cohesive North Korean refugee group, was in part, a bid for its support, but it was likewise a conscious attempt to weaken Northerners by introducing factional disagreements regarding Mr. Yi's pro-government role; the resulting splits undermined the political development of one of Korea's potentially most adhesive and discontented sectional interest groups. Aware that these motivations rather than Yi's ability lay behind the choice, the Assembly rejected Yi as Prime Minister three times between 1948 and 1952.

Rhee's tactics in thwarting the Korean Democratic party and keeping its members out of his cabinet despite its importance and support belongs to the story of political parties. For the most part, remaining cabinet members were personal adherents of the President, completely dependent and with few qualifications for the jobs they held. The *Tong-A Ilbo* declared the President had "gathered around him a weak, poorly-suited group" and expressed "disappointment." [51] Even the cautious UN Commission reported "widespread criticism . . . and the feeling . . . that the President had failed to utilize fully the best talents available." [52] Hardly had he started office than the President fell into the appointment-dismissal pattern of his ancestors (see pp. 236–239). In less than twelve years, Rhee consumed 129 ministers and prime ministers. The bureaucracy itself swelled to over 300,000 by 1953 to accommodate the power race. For the undivided peninsula Japan had used 95,385 officials as late as 1938.[53]

The persistence of an ancient and inappropriate Yi pattern showed what pressures were fundamental to the society. The peninsula was no longer isolated. High performance was called for. Yet it was control and manipulation of the updraft that still had priority. Theory of government, clothes, entertainment habits, education, currency, even speech changed in Korea, but recruitment, leadership, and elite-formation were in essential process what they had been. Almost to the present, most of the nation's frail resources of trained talent continued to be swept in and out of office so quickly as to leave no accomplishment; then they retired early and stagnated, unable to accept "lower" employment.[54] They rose and fell with a suddenness, an irrationality, an exciting mysteriousness, an intricacy of *ppaek*, an insouciance of professional attainment redolent of the Korean past.

Democracy and Mobility

Once the underlying pattern is understood, the impact of democracy upon it becomes more predictable. "Democracy" multiplied the hopes of access, swelled the numbers intent on joining the free-for-all, and in the initial stage undermined whatever weak forces of cohesion there were. It was nonetheless gladly received both as the prestige system from a larger culture (Confucianism's successor) and because it seemed to legitimize the rights of mobility so essential to the culture. Korean intellectuals welcomed the new doctrine they knew the Americans would bring to Korea. Ever since the Versailles Treaty and the start of the Independence Movement, the word "democracy" had gained currency to express what great Western nations felt new nations should achieve when they were able to express their "self-determination." The increase in radio communication that accompanied the war multiplied the word's use as soon as Liberation dawned. It was 1945's universal password, equated with the concepts of freedom and equality that were the themes of the Korean Declaration of Independence. It was on everybody's lips: Communists, the People's Republic, the rightists, the radio, even before the Americans with their radio programs came.[55] All spoke of freedom of expression' and assembly. There was little to read on what these concepts meant; past experience, necessarily in non-democratic environments, and a few words from missionaries provided the only guides. Only a tiny number of travelers had ever known any other kind of "freedom" than the comparative chaos and lack of efficient administration regnant throughout most of the century before the government-general. Then one could memorialize or, through channels of chance contact, attain the ideal of consultation and power. Now one needed no rank, class, or qualification. Education was helpful, but an anti-Japanese act done in fact or "in one's heart," the founding of a school, a foreign degree, or simply "strong determination" provided "equal" tickets to the race that democracy seemed to urge each man to join. "Liberty," coming after the comprehensiveness of Japanese repression, was taken to promise public debate and demonstration without reserve to everyone with patriotic passion. Demonstrators daily roamed the streets in 1945, and the plaza by Seoul's station echoed to harangue. Freedom and democracy added to indecision in rule, to erratic appointments, to the difficulty of subordinating anyone to a group or reconciling anyone to patience with another's leadership. New, Western-born invitations had been issued for the old game.

The election process added powerful stimulants. Technically, the vast publicity campaign of 1948 worked well: people knew how to vote. More than this, the election and the visits of UN Commission members, officials, and campaigners to villages had on the rural population much the same effect Elton Mayo observed in his experiments in the Hawthorne Electric Company and in those previously performed in an American textile factory: men were stimulated because they were given the feeling that responsible people cared about them.[56] The enthusiasm the UN Temporary Commission on Korea (UNTCOK) noted for the election was real, but it was not primarily that of a people determined to communicate wishes through representatives; rather, the people took pleasure in finding that a government which had long ignored them now suddenly honored them with contact and communication. Later, when publicity declined, enthusiasm declined with it, though the police still made voting a duty. In a sense, however, elections did give villagers a sense of participation, and the traditions and stories of the rural scholar whose studies were rewarded with government service anchored this sense within the culture.

Any man of ambition now hoped that he might win political recognition as the scholar had in legend. First Liberation, then the Assembly, now elections revived political activity to its pre-1910 role as the most honorable and exciting occupation a man could have, the symbol of his standing and respectability in the community. The meaning of a vote to express wishes might be thinly understood, but the value of sending a local son to the capital through the examination system could be transferred with lightning speed to the value of sending him by election.

Elections had a place as an emendation of the ancient system, but within the social structure they tended to extend a revolution. Former upper-class behavior now became a block and liability for the "democratic" political career. Touring through benighted villages by jeep or on foot, shouting at commoners with microphones, gesticulating with contagious persuasiveness, propagating slogans on coarse paper with indifferent calligraphy, mixing intimately with high and low — all this was lower-class or, at best, *ajŏn* behavior. It was precisely what the *yangban* had eschewed.[57] Except in the most conservative communities, one needed, like Song Pyŏng-jun, little more than ambition, energy, guts, and token backing of almost any kind to run.[58] Rice-mill owners, wine brewers, farmers with large holdings and small (after land reform, all holdings were small), former *myŏn* officials, county clerks, men returned from the wars, representatives of prominent clans, village leaders, men with relatives in the capital, those frustrated by failures in everything else — all ran.

Sometimes as many as 20 candidates competed in a single district. Altogether 2,209 competed for 210 seats in 1950. The vibrancy of the struggle could be sensed in the bands of candidates painfully toting precious loudspeakers over dusty roads from village to village and in the sums they spent: 20,000,000–50,000,000 wŏn in the cities (then equivalent to about $20,000–50,000 apiece), 5,000,000–25,000,000 wŏn in the rural areas — this in a country where the average individual's annual income was hardly over 70,000 wŏn ($70).

In this free-for-all, the *ajŏn* were best placed. Only they had traditionally enjoyed a local political function; those established as local landlords, became, perhaps, the sole group that, almost *qua* group, enjoyed more local political participation and success than any other. But they were of course a small minority in the total; the nets of political contest caught fish of every school, almost all as individuals. Parties had no local bases of formation and were not until later to be of great importance (see Chapter 10). Even after they started, from 1954 on, to curb chaotic, atomized access, the problem remained acute enough to lead Korea's military politicians to ban independent candidacy entirely. The dampening of access-mobility through party currently deprives politics of much of its glow; for mobility is basic to Korea's pattern, and the explosive nature of that atomic flow remains recalcitrant to the disciplines of organization.

BACK TO SCHOOL

As democracy has increased the forces of political mobility, so the impact of urban growth, of a more modern economy, of aid, of growing administrative complexity, has acted to increase the weight and the lures of both the capital and the central bureaucracy in national life. Business firms and their headquarters nuzzle against it; Seoul lies in the country's economically least-endowed area, but proximity to bureaucracy remains more important than nearness to resources. Informal paths of access still abound, reminiscent of Song Pyŏngjun's day, but increasingly they have come to lead through one gateway — the educational system and especially its higher reaches.

Education in Korean society has to withstand tremendous cultural pressures. These are demonstrably not the pressures of utility or need. Less than half — in any suitable positions, under a third — of the recipients of higher education can be employed and many of these not in the jobs for which they were trained. The pressures are cultural and essentially ancient. Access to central power demands education, and ambition knows no other avenues. Seoul's acres of castellated college fortresses repeat, in more centralized form, the boom and surplus of *sŏwŏn* in the middle Yi period.[59] The Japanese, by formally reimposing higher education as the highway to an expanded bureaucracy while maintaining it primarily for themselves, only added zest to Korean appetites.[60] The need to train for modern techniques has expanded, complicated and centralized the result.

The cumulative effect of all these influences has been one of the most sensational educational explosions anywhere in the postwar world. Only one university — Keijō Imperial, the present Seoul National — existed in Korea in 1945. There were 19 high schools of *gymnasia* type, a few using the title of college. By April 1946, these had become four-year colleges, and more had already been added to make 26 colleges and other higher educational institutions with 940 teachers and 9,562 students.[61] By 1962 there were 85 colleges (regular or junior) and universities of one sort or another containing 128,557 students, and roughly an additional 10,000 students were attending the three military academies, the National Defense College, the General Staff College, the War College, the Merchant Marine Academy, and several theological seminaries, mostly in Seoul.[62] Despite government efforts to reduce college enrollments by one third, higher institutional enrollment had increased to about 150,000 by 1965.[63] The scale of expansion below college has been hardly less great. At the end of World War II, there were only 139 middle schools with 88,000 students; by 1960, 665,630 middle-school students were studying in 1,165 schools.[64] Total secondary schools increased 10.52 times from 165 in 1945 to 1,738 in 1961.[65] By 1966, there were 5,125 primary schools with 4,914,343 students; in Seoul alone, graduates of primary schools operating in shifts increase currently at the rate of some 30,000 per year.[66]

No less telling than this extraordinary pressure for improvement and expansion is the financial burden. The Ministry of Education estimates that in 1961 college students spent an average of 16,200 wŏn ($123) each just for schooling, which came to a total of 2.28 billion wŏn ($17,640,000).[67] This amount, spent privately, represented close to 20 percent of the estimated 11.9 billion wŏn then in circulation. In addition, 560 million wŏn ($4,300,000) was appropriated by the state treasury to finance the operation of national universities and colleges. Added to this are private gifts, missionary contributions, American aid, income from foundations and investments, and supplementary sums customarily demanded from the students' parents. On top of this the old parents-to-teachers fees, "abolished" by the military government, have been generally replaced by fund-raising foundations which, in high schools at least, demand 2,000–3,000 wŏn or more each three months. Even with this expenditure teacher pay is so poor — for many not more than the equivalent of $1.00 a day — that a few teachers have committed suicide on grounds of poverty, a phenomenon previously unknown. Private scholarships are few, though fee exemptions have grown so that they covered 27,710 students as of 1964.[68] The educational path to the vortex assumes enormous financial proportions in the nation.

These pressures descend with crushing impact on the Korean family. All parents believe that the future of their children depends solely on their education. But since the employment rate of those graduating even from college has been, at most optimistic estimates, not over 44.6 percent, and since only graduates of top universities — usually Seoul National — are taken into the government, the future also depends on the quality and repute of their school. The financial and educational struggle to enter the best schools — virtually all in Seoul — approaches hysteria. Many a family borrows beyond conceivable capacity to repay, mortgaging all property, skimping on food and clothing, making desperate sacrifices. In the villages, ambitious farmers sell not only cattle but sometimes house and land to send one son through college.[69] Maternal pleas for loans are relentless, often resulting in scenes of high emotion and broken friendships. The child is driven to almost constant study, and every crucial entrance examination becomes a shattering emotional crisis.[70] The mother accompanies the child to the examination place and waits outside until it is over. Even a high-ranking father will not leave the country during the time when one of his children undergoes such an ordeal. Failure to obtain admission to the proper institution occasionally leads to the breakdown of child or mother, or even suicide. Bribery to repair a bad showing is common.[71] College presidents, meanwhile, have become the gilded circle of Korean society, frequently occupying larger homes and finer automobiles than cabinet ministers and enjoying a degree of permanence in job unknown to the political world.

Yet, as we have seen in examining the pressures behind the April revolution, though society places no limit on competition, jobs for the competitors hardly exist. Cherished government jobs or higher business positions absorb no more of the educated than the bureaucracy could of the graduates of eighteenth-century *sŏwŏn*. A prominent newspaper notes that, of the 38,000 estimated graduates for 1965, "a recent report shows that banks, state-run business firms and newspaper companies can absorb about 1,000 graduates for the white-collar jobs," the government many fewer.[72] Wages even for the employed can hardly support life, those for researchers in the Atomic Energy Institute, for example, recently reported as being often as low as 5,500–8,000 wŏn per month, or, after automatic deductions, some $15.60 to about $27.00 per month.[73] The limited job opportunities genuinely offered in the open market can probably be filled with the graduates of the top half-dozen universities, or 7 percent of existing colleges and universities.

The vortex, drawing ambition through the educational sieve, thus results in a frustration more intense than that known almost anywhere. Thousands of unemployed students must go back to their families. The family closes its ranks behind its "surplus" son; it is an institution with centuries of experience in caring for its own in a world of too many contenders for limited positions. If lucky, the student joins his father's or a relative's firm as a supernumerary. (Recently, some college graduates have even signed up to mine coal in the Ruhr, though educated Koreans normally display marked reluctance to do manual work.) Lacking employment, the graduate wangles pocket money for the endless pool halls, tearooms, and theaters that absorb the idle, meanwhile hides his face at home a great deal, keeping to a small circle, sometimes trying graduate school or, if possible, education abroad. Since education increases instead of eliminating competition for central power, *ppaek* must continue to play its role in connecting graduates with their objectives. The student thus frequently tries to attach himself to a politician, serving more or less without compensation in the hope that if his patron comes to power he will be able to get more permanent employment. Such job-seeking has been a constant threat to the stability of bureaucratic employment, and the society has developed the belief that it is "unfair" for one man to "eat the cake" of employment too long. Job-seeking absorbs much of the government time of all officials, especially senior ones. Lack of opportunity to participate in society saps the unemployed's sense of worth and capacity to form any positive conception of himself, pride, or self-control. He is readily attracted to mass movements or the substitution of others' judgment for his own. Despite these ills, his family will insist on marrying him off to produce an indigent family of his own, dependent on his parents, on his older or younger brothers, or on friends and connections. So custom contributes to population increase and further unemployment, which now embraces some 2,722,000 persons, or 26 percent of the total labor force.[74]

There is little that is remarkable — and very much that is admirable — in the desire of Koreans to rise and improve themselves and to see that this rise is not confined to a privileged few. The results also hold, in part, great promise. The enormous rise in literacy from some 15 percent in 1945 to some 70–80 percent by 1966 and the enrolling of more people in primary schools by 1967 (over 3.5 million) than there were Koreans with any education at Liberation provide a vastly improved climate for modernization and, though less certainly, democracy.[75] Even the frustration of so large an educated population is a step toward modernization; it is also an open invitation to international society to make the best use of this resource for development elsewhere. If drives for education, even frenetic ones, are, as widely believed, a pre-condition of modernization, Koreans are among the world's most ambitious peoples. What is more remarkable about the pattern and has made it difficult to harness is its marked atomization and the almost uniform velocity of its tempo toward the same goal from all over the social map. Korean postwar education displays both the difficulties as well as the advantages of the pattern in its irrationality and abnormality.

The abnormalities of vast excess education, covert mobility, and the consequent extreme instability of Korean appointments constitute an important key to the nation's character. They damage society with waste and frustration. Such voluntarily imposed damage is difficult to explain without postulating its cause in cultural drives or needs of overriding importance. Clearly, in Korea's case these needs are not those of education. They are those of mobility. The tumorous spread of education and its clustering in the capital, which has been turned into probably the world's greatest producer of unemployed graduates, betray the single-mindedness of the culture's concentration on access to central power and the inner *élan* of its decision that this access be unusually broad and mobile. Much as Yi court *yangban* willingly endangered the country's security by not supporting a military force that might, conceivably, have unseated them, so Korea today willingly endangers its own security in order to feed its mobility updraft. Seoul's 90,000 higher-education students have done what neither North Korea nor communism have been able to do: overturn a Korean government and chronically threaten its successors. In this phenomenon, likewise, the mobile intent of the culture inheres.

8

Functional and Organizational Diffusion

If a vortex pattern predominates in a society, bringing with it high mobility and high interchangeability, then we would expect to find its imprint below, as well as above. We would expect to find groupings formed with highly elastic boundaries and little disposition to hierarchy or specialization so that men can leave them easily for higher places and shed identity in order to function interchangeably. If one is to rise as Song Pyŏng-jun rose, it is easier to leave behind in Hamgyŏng-do no responsibilities or loyalties. If one's prime aim is to use votes from a market community to become an assemblyman, rather than to gain satisfaction from its environment and bonds, then it matters little that the only hierarchy leading one out is rough, ganglike, and unruly. Answering these needs, Korean lower organizations assume such character, which the history of the culture likewise has reinforced as it has, in turn, been shaped by it. In Korea no castle towns, guilds, trading ports, or merchant societies firmly established themselves so as to develop armorers, dyers, merchants, and the specialization, hierarchy, and loyalty that characterize Japan or Europe. Undefined organization, fluid function, resistance to rules and law, and transient occupancy reflect the society, form the milieu in which its work is performed, and support with their transiency the upward-propelling forces.

INDIGENOUS ROOTS

The Village

The search for this pattern leads to village and market place, speculative though the significance of these visits must remain. In such places, also, we see the form organization takes when it is closest to the people, farthest from influence of Chinese, Japanese, or American culture.

Part of Korea's homogeneity still derives from the village. Sixty percent of the population still lives there, and the number of villagers has risen to over sixteen million in South Korea, three million more than lived in the whole peninsula in 1910. Within living memory, the rural percentage was 80 percent or more, and therefore most of the present urban population was village-reared. It would not be true to say that all the villages are just the same.[1] With regard to origin, there are *yangban* clan villages, like Hahoe, Kyŏngsang Pukto, from which many officials came, and there are those from which came only one *yangban,* whose descendants live there. Landlord villages may be found, whose master was more rural investor than official. Commoner villages are sometimes dominated by one family, more often split among several. Some villages were settled by former slaves, by fugitives, or by the outcast *paekchŏng.*[2] With respect to more contemporary features, one may note villages with tight organization and villages with loose organization, some speaking with pride of their "democracy." [3] Certain villages are leftist in sentiment, others rightist. There are poor ones and rich. Within a generally homogeneous milieu, even at the larger village level, cliques and factions, microcosms of Seoul politics, form. As in upper politics, they substitute for the more natural, functional lines of cleavage the society lacks: bitterness and backbiting serve the function of division and rallying cry. As in Seoul, they are the real units of action and mutual protection.[4] These and a hundred other differences form the texture of society's distinctions, and partly because the spectrum of differences is comparatively confined, knowing none of the enormity of a Moslem–Hindu confrontation, these small distinctions are the ones by which villagers live, over which they quarrel, and about which they speak among themselves.

But though the villages are not all alike, neither do they form a pluralistic society. Few are the differences of function, production or occupation, and "vested interest." Differences based on division of labor are rare; and when they occur, someone is being despised and wishes he could lose the brand of deviation in a sea of the norm: the village of potters, for example, often Catholic and now many fewer than in former centuries; of bamboo-weavers near Tamyang, also relatively reduced in numbers; of fishermen, of course. To the outside eye, the despising is not very blatant — the average traveler may neither see nor hear of it — but it is there. Its unseen strength is great. Just after Liberation, thousands of Koreans who tried to return to their own villages from Japan went back to Japan again rather than face village raillery at the differences in habit or speech they had adopted.

The homogeneous norm is a force of great strength, and there are signs, as in China, that such force increased during the very centuries when rival feudal *han* were crystallizing new local identities and sponsoring new products in Tokugawa Japan. Large local institutions have withered. The great temple and the rarer surviving *sŏwŏn* stand almost empty. Small local schools or, sometimes, churches form such institutional focus as remains. The size of the temple hall is a mute reminder that great institutions once flourished on country soil. Communities were once brought together for miles around. Products were exchanged, and loans were made. Men mingled in the wineshops and at the bull auctions. Bonds of belief were cemented in great community rites. The loss of diverse communities has not yet been recovered by the culture. The tale is told more surely in ceramic wares than if a historian had written it. By 1800, most of the variety expressed in fifteenth-century bowls, which bore a hundred sorts of local glaze and design, had been eliminated; and today one can find little more than the homogeneous *kimchi* (pickled vegetable) pot. The Japanese type of community, with its legends of outcast descent, its special pottery, unique designs, particular rope or paper lamp, condiment or dress, much of it the product of years since the fifteenth century, has been left behind in Korea's history. Likewise the equivalent of Japan's pockets of rare dialect or vocabulary are hardly known in the peninsula: there are a very few large and defined major dialect regions, but a homogenizing process has almost eliminated the peculiar dialects of small areas. Now thousands of radio amplifiers installed by the military government's National Reconstruction Movement, the national education system, as well as banking and cooperative connections with national institutions, push the unitary process relentlessly.

Upward homogenizing has long been supported by forces deep within the internal village pattern. Just as the bamboo-weaver or potter or any other specialist is despised, so also the farmer is a staunch generalist, performing all rural functions, bargaining in the market place, making something special only in spare winter leisure, and taking a dim view of those who do otherwise; "specialists" are called *chaengi* from government bureau down to slum alley, and few words in the language are freighted with more eloquent derogation. At home, except in the remotest communities, each wife makes her own *kimchi* and long-stored sauces. She borrows labor for this, and lends her own hands to her neighbors, but hardly any woman makes a product for more than one household. When market takes place, wife, husband, or both may go, open a stall, spread a mat, sell what can be sold, bargain, and then come home. Function and labor are widely borrowed and lent, a process with little friction where skills are maximally homogeneous and interchangeable. The Korean rural market has for centuries resisted the tendencies of many markets elsewhere to develop full-time trades and secondary orientations.

The Urban Market

The urban market has been for centuries the largest of the institutions of Korea that exist between village and central government. It is in the market that the continued influence of rural pattern on urban can still be most clearly seen and also where a form of organization little influenced by Chinese or other imported patterns can be felt. Markets exist in each city, and in each city they are, probably, the single form of economic activity bringing most people together. Seoul itself has many, but among them the ancient markets around the East and South gates of the city are the greatest; their names run through every Seoul household's daily talk. No one has ever counted the tens of thousands whose hub of livelihood they are.

They are the macrocosm of their rural brothers: an enormous, dense tangle of tiny shops, booths, tents, and streetside displays selling untold products directly to customers or jobbing for Seoul's more permanent outlets.[5] They are the centers where the uncounted thousands who have neither capital nor connections can start their way up or try to earn support. Here local produce dealers and middlemen, collecting anything from eggs to PX supplies, pushcart men, booth operators, small money lenders, messengers, gangs — all needing each other yet without the resources of hire — gather and live. No one thinks of the market as an institution or a power group, though such, in some ways, it is. It has no formal uniting organization, no constitution, no real over-all directors, no single legal entity. Groups that possess these things, consciously or unconsciously imitating the West or Japan, rise and die daily in Korea's urban world. Markets alone have survived a life of hundreds of years with no end in sight.

Within them are certain formal organizations, but these are of comparatively small importance. In the East Gate market, a cooperative association collects a small amount of money from each shop under the pretext of a cleaning charge and rents for the government the land along a filled-in stream bed the government owns. More typical are the thousand small merchant or peddler chains of the market, each partly competitive and partly cooperative, partly loyal to the cause of the market as a whole but mostly determined to widen its own share therein.[6] A group of merchants selling the same product compete with each other, sometimes bitterly. Yet if one of their number is threatened with bankruptcy through ill luck, other members of the group will lend him money, often without the signing of any paper. If he is threatened with gangster extortion, the others may band together to give him some protection. If a government policy restrictive of their product is enforced, the group will unite to protest it. Political matters may be mutually discussed if they concern group interests sufficiently. Each knows that, in his uncertain world, he may need the others' help and acts accordingly. Once or more a year, these small "associations" go together on a country outing and, armed with ample liquor to sweeten small differences and female companions (never wives) to provide music, they rehearse their common causes, joke (or fight) over their differences, and, to the insistent drum and high-pitched female voice, lift arms and legs in the dance that is part of every true Korean. Little else in their still quite fluid world gives them chance for leadership or urges them toward joint expression of view. It is the type of organization that furnishes little barrier to despotism. Traditional community it is, but it highlights the country's lack of secondary orientation and of traditional authority below government itself.

The urban market is not untouched by specialization and by the formation of larger identities around expanded urban economic functions. The Japanese affected it little, though by handling commodities like textiles themselves they tended to concentrate its functions on foodstuffs. With Liberation, the Japanese textile trade collapsed and the P'yŏng'an Province refugees, skilled in market activities, moved in, making the market the textile retail center of the country. The great Yŏngnak and East Gate church communities, built in or near the market, became other great centers of the P'yŏng'an world and gave the refugees of that area cohesion and communication greater than South Korean groups possessed. They became famous for mutual help and loan activity. As their mercantile infiltration proceeded, they acquired some control over rice storage and sale and with it one of the few strong, nonviolent weapons that unofficial Koreans have against the government. Thus Liberation added some specialist character, some degree of interest group distinction to the amorphous Korean market world. Yet the change has been limited. The fundamental character remains the same. Amalgamation of small unit to larger has taken place in some textile units, but it is rare. Even the entrepreneur who has money rarely uses it to absorb or amalgamate. He does not avoid this through ignorance. He has seen the Japanese, knows what larger units are, and has watched their efficiency. He eschews large organization because his is a different world. The relationship of superior and inferior is relished less, even among the humble, than in Japan. The larger unit must also combat the encroachments of desperate competitiveness with few reserves. The government, politicians, youth groups, veterans' associations, gang leaders, beggars, one's own expanding household, one's children's school, and one's own wide circle of poor relatives with their needs for weddings, schooling, and funerals all vie with each other for whatever a man has, some not without force and blackmail. In such a world the larger shop front, the greater enterprise, presents less the image of efficiency than a broader target for exaction. Even if one can live financially with increased extortion, the owner must ask himself whether he wishes to part with the many increased hours he and his employees must spend to fend off such pressures.[7]

The small shopkeeper seems, after all, happier. She can shake her head with conviction when the exactor approaches. Sitting with one helper or her grandson beside her and her goods, she can call at countless other traders around her, at the pushcart man struggling in mud before her, share the gossip of the capital, feel the pulse of its emotions. The warmth of endless voices and familiar sights, people and smells, supports her, as if part of a vast family, allowing her almost to forget the costs she cannot meet when midnight curfew and cold force her to shut up her stall and plod home.

The Urban Neighborhood

Something of the same limitation on common action pervades the urban neighborhood. The poor must live cheek by jowl. Occasionally, communities of beggars, thieves, or black-marketeers exist with the same degree of intimate cohesiveness that their outcast forerunners, the *paekchŏng,* had. If they see a policeman in search, they will not help him. Threatened eviction or slum clearance gives ground for common action. There is much knowledge and intuitive grasp of each other's problems. Yet again, Korean sociological researchers have themselves been astonished at the lack of cohesiveness in most poor urban neighborhoods. "In Japan," one researcher noted, "in slum areas, the emphasis is on living together, sharing kitchens, toilet, water system and even beds. But in Taegu, despite the narrowness of living space, residents generally have their own houses," and the emphasis is not on living together.[8]

The sources of disunity frequently revolve around food. Centuries of village experience in natural or human calamities that frequently brought communities to starvation or the eating of bark have given rise to strong emotions regarding the division of food, powerful sentiments that "justice" demands that food be shared, bitter jealousy and complaint when it is not. The lesser degree of such feelings in Japan can probably be traced to the presence of stronger local powers who could be responsible for minimal local livelihoods. To some extent, such sentiments extend also to money, jobs, housing, education, and so forth. Pressure to share food and to share "good fortune" is the warp of emotional strain in many Korean communities and is nowhere more powerful than among groups in constant need and almost constant hunger.[9] Hence the procuring, preparation, and consumption of food take on certain aspects of secrecy. This is especially true in urban areas where food is procured outside the immediate community. Caution is crucial in crowded urban neighborhoods in which no one can share with all, and, since ties are mostly new and weak, the limits of sharing are hard to draw. Intimacy and cooperation among families thus becomes largely the degree to which they share the purchase, preparation, and eating of food, especially of any delicacies such as fish, wine, or bean paste. In better-class Korean dwellings, the inner court has the function of shielding food information from the curious world, but the poor house can keep no such secrets, and its reputation of "generosity" or "stinginess" is made—more usually lost—by what is shared. A survey conducted in Taegu in 1963 found that, of 120 poor families, 55 had no close relationship with any other family, 51 had it with only one family, 11 with two, and almost none with more. Reportedly, 77 families did not share food, 34 shared it with only one other family, and few with more. As many as 82 families invited no neighbors for major occasions of joy and sorrow.[10] Thus a sharing that would have been taken almost for granted in village life seemed, in new suburbs, almost positively avoided. Cohesiveness is hindered by fear of the consequences of the too-great intimacy and sharing of rural life; voluntary associations thus very rarely have neighborhood roots; despair and apathy are the slum's expression where social protest is not.[11]

Poverty faced in this comparatively isolated fashion with a loneliness alien to the normal rural tradition results in underlying unhappiness, strains, and antagonism in Korean urban life. Markets and crowded alleys stage chronic donnybrooks. There is an inability to cohere, take common stands, and develop accepted leadership. The attitudes formed in this environment are not those leading to the rational solution of problems. The jealousies and divisiveness that Koreans themselves articulate on higher political, economic, and social levels undoubtedly have their origins partly in these patterns, so close to basic village life but aggravated when the rural family transfers to the poor urban community.[12]

Seoul has, of course, groupings of more definite and cohesive character: churches like that of Pastor Han, minister of Yŏngnak Church, center not only for Christian faith but for P'yŏngan Province refugees burdened with social and employment problems; the YMCA, the YWCA, the Red Cross; and the city's innumerable schools and colleges. The tightness and formality of organization of all of these, founded under direct or indirect Western influence, emits some "smell of butter" (unaccustomed Western taste). Islands of cohesiveness in an otherwise mass society, new urban institutions, these and their leaders tend to dominate far larger areas of the lives of those who belong than they would in a more pluralist milieu. Their rarity and formality, subjects them, from above and from below, to special pressures.

The Urban Gang

Such "islands" are, however, places whose cohesion is associated with definite leadership, like that of Yŏngnak's Pastor Han. Market, neighborhood, and even many a village cannot achieve a sufficient area of agreement, common aim, or cohesion to produce voluntary ways of selecting leaders to represent them in communicating interests upward. Nor do they articulate their functions in a hierarchy or develop orderly differential relations. Hence, there tends to be formed between them and the forces of government unmediated confrontation. The gap is often filled with gangs, partly an aspect of mobility, partly one of amorphous organizing, which can carry out autocratic government demands on the community and substitute force for more formal institutions. Young men, spirited but unemployed, put themselves under bosses demanding instant obedience and loyalty. In backhanded tribute to these un-Korean organizational qualities and to the lowness of the calling, these leaders are often called by Japanese names, like "Aomatsu." [13] Each has top confidants, under them lesser ones in a strict hierarchical loyalty fitted for sudden action. The boss may connect with the world of political protection and assassination (like assemblyman Kim Tu-han), with former police bosses (like No Tŏk-sul), or with certain market groups. Experts in squeeze and blackmail, their intimate knowledge of market or neighborhood becomes the indispensable tool of autocracy. After one gang leader, Ko Hŭi-du, was arrested one night in the fall of 1948 and his tortured corpse was picked up by his wife at the police station the next day, General "Snake" Kim Ch'ang-yong of CIC, expert on the underworld, wrote in his "Secret Diary":

> Ko Hŭi-du was the Chairman of the Wŏnnam-dong Association, the Chairman of the Tongdaemun Branch of the Civil Defense Corps, the Chairman of the Supporting Society for the Tongdaemun Police Station and the Chairman of the Judicial Protection Committee. Such were the titles he had on his name card. Ko was the representative of the stallkeepers operating along the bank of the Ch'ŏnggyech'ŏn streamlet under the jurisdiction of the Tong-

daemun Police Station. He was the virtual leader of thousands of young men. In some respects, the man who holds the control of Tongdaemun and Ch'ŏnggyech'ŏn can be regarded as the practical dominator of Seoul.[14]

General Kim erred chiefly in one respect. Gang and boss are less dominators than they are the instrument of domination in government's confrontation with the masses. Most famous of the recent gang operations was the one conducted by Yi Chŏng-jae, as member of the Ich'ŏn gang looking for *ppaek* to the police chief of the President's residence, Kwak Yŏng-ju. The Ich'ŏn gang operated in the East Gate market with the backing of the Liberal party and the cooperation of Im Hwa-su. It collected rents, by terrorists tactics if necessary, for a major private tract of land in the market place, gave a large portion to the Liberal party, kept more, and turned the remainder over to the "owner," the Kwangjang Company, which at least felt itself then protected from further exactions. Its funds were, reportedly, one of the Liberal party's largest single sources of revenue. This particular gang, important in attacking Koryŏ University students on April 18, was overthrown with the revolution. Gangs came in for opprobrium as the rotten core of the Liberal party system. Gang elimination became one of the objectives of the military coup, and control was firm for many months. Less is now heard of them; but gangs rise and fall with political and economic tides, and it is doubtful whether massive unemployment, unbroken traditions of exaction, and endless needs for "protection" will yet permit their final exit.

More, perhaps, than any other institution — if institution they can be called — markets and neighborhoods are the microcosms of the Korean world. They eschew obvious unity or any specialization or division of labor that leads to hierarchy, leadership, or cohesion. Yet they have a subtle and intertwined communication system that can, in a crisis, lower or raise prices, control the groups that operate from it, generate widespread political opinion, back it with gossip and threat, powerful and elusive. A Korean market — and neighborhood — is, on the surface, incohesive, too scattered for coherent policy, too unorganized to be effectively mobilized for specific short-range issues. Hence it is tolerant, on the whole, chary of committing itself. Market groups did not strike out at either Japanese or Liberal party control but adapted to both. Members are too near existence's edge for striking stength. Each is like an anemone, anchored lightly to his own rock yet swaying constantly with subtle and immediate responsiveness to the same tide. The market is sensitive to every rumor or pressure, avoiding unity when it can be avoided, espousing it when clearly needed, and exerting it as a kind of massive opinion, backed with pricing and rumors of cornering rice markets. Its strength is not for the issue or the moment. The loyalties and commitments it offers the individual last without being deep, providing him with little base of attachment to the society, much exposure to its upward vortex. The strength of the markets lies in suppleness, ambiguity, and lasting power. For it is in groupings like these, not in strict hierarchies and with clear-cut issues, that Koreans have sought and, by and large, still do seek, to operate.

IMPORTED PRESTIGE CULTURE: THE GOVERNMENT

The top of the traditional society was under direct influence from China. Official organization could not be diffuse, because it had not been left to develop by itself in accordance with Korean ways but was copied directly and almost exactly from the elaborate and generally rational Chinese bureaucracy. The Board of Rites had to function like its Chinese counterpart, and if questions arose, there were books to be consulted and court counselors and censors to admonish. Questions of jurisdiction and function did arise frequently under the Yi and were, at least sometimes, solved with some sense of organizational discipline. *Yangban* power was lodged in councils such as, successively, the Censorate, the Pibyŏn-sa (Border Defense Council), and, to some extent, the Kyujang-gak (Royal Library). These, however, showed a marked tendency toward generalized power that interfered with defined function and, with time, also shifted, slowly, from one board to another throughout the dynasty, displaying some surface similarity to the amorphousness of lower groupings. By and large, Chinese governmental structure was the forerunner of Japanese colonialism and the American army in that it was imitated in form rather than spirit. All three brought their disciplines to the society from outside.

The Generalist Bureaucrat

In many respects, the Sino-Korean prestige pattern reinforced the generalist instincts of village and market. This influence was especially noteworthy and has been particularly lasting in two areas: avoidance of functional or career specialization and a related reluctance to be judged by systems and specialists; a consequent resistance to systems of rational or institutional justice, a lack of respect for procedures, and little sense for the separation of powers.

The Confucian emphasis on the generalist is too well known to need elaboration here. The ideal was a society ruled by sages each one of whom had absorbed the same corpus of classical learning, passed the same literary examinations, and was considered competent to embark on a career in almost any avenue of government or to be a counselor or memorial writer qualified to admonish on any social or administrative question. Specialists were, in general, derogated and confined to clerkish posts. China was a country large and varied enough to make a certain degree of specialization nonetheless possible: it was also subject to sufficient military, foreign, and, from its canal system, even engineering pressures to encourage some degree of specialization within a generalist system. Korea, unstimulated by Chinese varieties, relying on Chinese military and diplomatic support rather than on her own, and too small to generate administrative or water-control problems of China's scale, lacked such pressures and could cling to generalist Confucian theory with far greater literalness.[15] An official could be transferred anywhere at any time. In Korea's case this interchangeability was piquantly mixed with the pressures of extreme updraft in an ever more determinedly mobile society. Thus generalist *allowance* of interchangeability became in Korea an institutional imperative to change assignments rapidly to provide status for the maximum applicants. The resulting incredible shortness of job tenure became the *reductio ad absurdem* of a generalist bureaucracy: virtually all concept of bureaucracy as an arena of accomplishment vanished, and its function dwindled to that of providing status and rewards for its holders.

Discontinuity of Appointment

With the Korean bureaucratic tenure system we again approach the culturally abnormal. Only at the beginning of the Yi Dynasty and with the rarest exceptions thereafter did a man fill his office long enough to be effective. It appears that only in the reign of Sejong (1418–1450), probably the dynasty's most nearly effective, did continuity of service characterize a period; one High State Councilor, Hwang Hǔi, broke all records by serving for twenty-three years, from 1426–1449. The rule, however, was discontinuity. Even the first king changed his Chief Censor 1.7 times a year, his son changed him an average of three times a year, and in 1400 and 1406 there was an average of one Chief Censor every sixty days. The rate did not noticeably slow thereafter: the average was 3.6 a year under much of the seventh sovereign, 2.5 a year under the ninth, and 4.2 a year under the tenth, 6.6 per year in the first twelve years of the eleventh, and thereafter for decades an average of 4.7. In the factional years of 1571–1574, there was an average of a new one almost every month.[16] Nor did this hectic pace, by that time maintained for almost two hundred years, slack thereafter. The Taewǒn'gun, apparently in order to emasculate Censorate complaints and power, replaced the Censor-General 183 times between January 13, 1864, and December 16, 1873, an average of one every twenty days for nearly ten years! In this same period beginning in the 1860's, the Inspector-General, another leading Censorate official, was replaced 193 times.[17] During all these periods, the younger censors and inspectors had terms of duty hardly less hectic, frequently being censors for ten days, then magistrates for three months, then royal secretaries for fifteen weeks, and so on. In contrast, officials in the parallel institutions in China usually remained in office closer to two or three years and sometimes approached careers of specialization in Censorate functions.

The Censorate was admittedly the firing-line. Yet other administrative positions were almost as unstable and discontinuous. The third king reshuffled his Board of Punishment thirteen times in two years. Time and again biographies of Yi officials carry the records of as many as a hundred or more assignments during an official career of some thirty years, interspersed with retirements, periods of mourning, and other such interruptions. The famous Yulgok was Grand Censor twice, each time for a few days; Minister of Finance and Director of the Office of Special Counselors for a few months; Minister of Justice a few weeks; and then Minister of Defense, in which office he was vilified until he soon resigned.[18] The Lord Mayor of Seoul was changed approximately 1,375 times during the 518 years of the dynasty — about once every 130 days for over half a millennium, presumably a world record for any culture.[19] In twelve years between 1850 and 1862, over 442 provincial governors and magistrates as well as military commanders were charged with being corrupt and were dismissed, 140 in Kyŏngsang-do and 105 in Chŏlla-do alone.[20] A newly appointed official was often lucky even to reach his provincial post before being transferred or dismissed from it.

The trend reached delirium proportions in the closing years of the Yi. The breakdown of the social system and the opening of office to all classes in 1894–95 led to the widespread sale of rank to enable lower but monied classes to enjoy legal claim to *yangban* status. By *ch'aham,* or "borrowing brevet rank," a man could, for a consideration, be gazetted to one post from which he resigned the next day. He was then technically eligible for other appointments and received the privileges and exemptions of his purchased rank.[21]

The effect on even those supposedly performing duties amidst this mad game was startling. In the same decades when, across the channel, Matsukata Masayoshi was rounding out eight years as Finance Minister, Yamagata Aritomo four as Home Minister and three and a half as Prime Minister, and Oyama, Iwao, and Masatake Terauchi nine each as War Minister, Pak Che-sun, one of the most important Yi career officials of his time, treated himself to fifty-four posts between entering service in 1883 and the end of the dynasty twenty-seven years later. He was, *inter alia,* Councilor of the Household Boards for eleven days; Vice-Minister thereof for two weeks; Deputy Governor of Seoul for two months; Vice-Minister of the Board of Rites, of Public Works, and of the Board of Revenue for a month each; Governor of Chŏlla-do for one month and of Ch'ungch'ŏng-do for four; Minister of Agriculture, Commerce, and Industry for five days. He served as Minister of Foreign Affairs three times, twice for a month each. He was Ambassador to the Philippines for a month (this in an era of slow boats!), and Deputy Prime Minister for two months. Signet of specialization, he was, for two months, appointed a lieutenant general.[22] These were major administrative posts for which the incumbent had important responsibilities in a time of almost continuous crisis and danger for the Korean state, years in which two wars and a major rebellion were fought over it and in which the country's earliest modernization was supposed to take place.

Japan's professionalized bureaucracy interrupted the pattern, but, as we have seen, it returned with independence. Within six months of taking office, Rhee had changed half his ministers. Thereafter, changes were relentless. Vice-ministers, regarded as alter egoes of their ministers, changed with them. So, until the middle fifties, did many bureau chiefs and other underlings, then regarded as personal appointees of ministers, not as irreplaceable possessors of professional qualification. In less than twelve years, Rhee ran through ministers at the rate of more than ten a year.

Revolution failed to break the pattern. Indeed, it worsened it. None of the ministers of the Rhee government had been kept by the Interim Government except the three appointed in Rhee's final days. Even during its 112 or so days in office, ministerial changes were rather frequent. When Chang Myŏn assumed power, all these short-lived ministers were again replaced. In lower ranks, the Chang government fired 2,213 officials, many recently appointed by the Interim Government. Thereafter, Chang changed his ministers at the most rapid rate known up to that time since the end of the Yi Dynasty, some remaining in office only a few weeks or even days. There was a new Minister of Home Affairs in each of the first four months of the government. In the government's eight short months there were twenty-eight ministers and painful, noisy cabinet reshufflings. January 1961 was spent in constant bickering until a new cabinet of close Chang supporters was formed. Younger members of his group were still dissatisfied, and he was rumored to have offered them another cabinet reshuffle in the spring.[23] Though elections of governors and mayors were held, Chang's democracy was so bemused by central politicking it had no time to build up local democratic strength or effect meaningful decentralization. The coup also failed to modify the pattern. For the first years of military rule, changes of ministers, advisers and even Supreme Councilors were almost as frequent as before, and penalties for those dropped became decidedly more extreme; imprisonment and even torture were visited on many who were dropped from high posts. Since the elections of 1963 and the "civilianizing" of government, however, there have at last been signs of change and President Park has made a conscious effort to stabilize the bureaucracy. It is probably too soon as yet to say whether this influence will prove lasting. But it appears that a degree of quiet has been, at least temporarily, reached.

A pattern so frenetic strikingly demonstrates the bias of the culture. It also operates to destroy or to prevent the consolidation of groups, bonds, personal powers, and vested interests in any province, ministry, or board. Until 1910, five hundred years without dynastic change saluted its success. The pattern operated to prevent the strong growth of all subordinate offices, inhibited the formation of identity or discipline within them; the resulting frustration of interest-development represents an essential inner consistency with the ancient political pattern of the culture.

Rules and Law

Just as official careers were all "general," law in the Sino-Korean concept tended to be less sharply differentiated from general ethics and from other functions of government than in the West. The ruler was responsible to Heaven (in the Korean case, to the Chinese emperor) for seeing that social order harmonized with the *lex naturalis*. He and his officials taught by virtue, precept, and example how this obedience to Heaven was to be incarnated in human action. The *li* (Korean *ye*), rules governing the five great human relationships, were the chief path to harmonious conduct and had, in effect, the force of law. If family and clan heads fulfilled their roles of instruction and example, a Rousseau-like state of absence of law and government was supposed to prevail. Only when they failed was the law required as the extension of the ruler's attempt to harmonize society. Such "administrative" law was regarded as "sacred" and ruler-formulated but better not used.[24] Hence all men tended to avoid resort to law as a slur on their reputations and, in effect, a reflection on their ruler. Those appearing in courts were regarded not as defenders of their rights but as quarrelsome, unruly, and in need of better education. Just as the general function of an official was to be an example, so a legal judgment was regarded as largely a matter of ethical instruction that was the "duty" of the official. Chŏng To-jŏn, a famous early leader of Korean Confucianism, put the case well: "The sage proclaims law not to rule with law but in order to rule without the help of law." [25] The family pattern supported this. Delegation to the family head or enforcement of conduct, hence of most law, trained men to expect personal, familial enforcement and to abhor judgment by systems or specialists. Gauged by a long record of internal peace, the system worked. Law was little invoked between individuals — only as a means the government used to justify its persecution. In daily matters, the *li* provided good, built-in measures of local self-policing. Social discipline and law-abidingness marked the Yi scene more than they have characterized that of modern Korea. Yet it was an attitude that reinforced men's insecurity before the personal judgments of others and inhibited the development of any system of rational or institutionalized justice.

The concept of harmoniousness can be regarded as impeding the development of Sino-Korean law and of the formal rules on which large organization is based. "Harmony" renders constitutional differentiation unnecessary; it obstructs the development of legal distinctions and the formulation of exact rules. It likewise tends to frustrate the development of the concept of reservation of powers. Individual rights are at the mercy of a magistrate who arbitrates a concept essentially mystical and undefined. For citizen or employee there is no more exact resort from the arbitrary than complaint of violation of a general ethic. No rules of evidence develop. Defense or defense counsel are alien since they "interfere" with the "duty" of the magistrate to give moral exhortation. Within a society in many other respects advanced, the Sino-Korean legal system remained a pocket of underdevelopment, essentially stagnant. It laid society open for manipulation by such a ruler as Syngman Rhee and failed to provide the basis for stable, viable authority.

With respect to law, Japan brought important changes to Korea. An impressive legal system, largely copied from French and Prussian models, was imposed, and some concept of living in accordance with law was implanted. For the first time, Korea had professional lawyers, and, with the graduation of the first class of the Law College of Keijō Imperial University in 1930, a few Koreans were among them. By the end of Japan's rule 15 percent of judges, prosecutors, and members of the bar in Chōsen were Koreans.[26]

Japan's legal system survived her defeat and remains substantially intact today. Behind the impressive externals, however, the system and the concepts it might have forwarded remain in large part alien to the life around them. Koreans regarded Japan's law and its administrators as an instrument of oppression to be avoided where possible. This attitude has not been erased by the use to which the system was put since Liberation both by some U.S. Military Government officials and, more especially, by the governments of Rhee and the Korean military officers. The constitutional concept of an independent judiciary, an essential part of the balance of powers, has never developed. Both judges and prosecutors reserve their loyalty for the government rather than any professional standard, and they regard the role of a non-governmental defense counsel as an intrusion on their official moral and status function. Prosecution has long been and still is considered tantamout to guilt.[27] American Military Government introduced the detention warrant, provision of defense counsel, bail, and the writ of habeas corpus. But lack of time and skill frustrated any such systematic overhaul as took place in Japan. Methods to oversee effectiveness were not devised, and all innovations were usually circumvented in practice. They were further undermined by the conduct of trials taking place during the Military Government period, either before inexperienced American army officers or in Korean courts whose conduct was ineffectively reviewed.[28] The Americans were not even able to control improper legal practices by Korean institutions they had founded. An official U.S. historical work noted: "Ordinarily the constabulary had no authority to arrest law-breakers but it consistently ignored this lack of legal right, making arrests at will and searching without warrants." [29] Trials were conducted in more or less open obedience to executive desire to obtain conviction regardless of procedure. Vague, institutional evidence similar to that employed under the Yi Dynasty was used (see Chapter 6). Neither a sound legal tradition nor esprit de corps within the judiciary developed. The law and the judiciary, instead of becoming one of the chief checks on executive power, became one of the chief instruments of autocratic dominance.

The Specialist Dilemma

We have traced the fundamental generalist character of Korean society in village, market, neighborhood, bureaucracy, and judiciary. At all levels, special skills and innovations leading to deeper occupational concentration are neglected, thwarted, and denigrated. The farmer does not want to be a *chaengi*, the market seller on the whole eschews the expansion of a special line, the bureaucrat seeks maximum access through his ability to replace anyone. At the same time, the generalist personality is one of versatility, breadth, complexity, and strength — one closer to the older American and Russian frontier ideal than to the feudal-specialist emphasis of the Japanese or Germans. From village farmer to prime minister, the Korean must be able to do many things to avoid being a *chaengi;* he must learn and adapt quickly and his interests must range widely. He is not only enthusiastic and quick but insatiably interested in everything around him and in everyone else's business. This leads him to competitiveness and tangle with his fellows, yet also to an interest in local and public affairs. His interest in such questions relates primarily to his personal opportunities for a new and higher role, not to improvement of the common weal. Nevertheless, his adaptability could be harnessed for development, and his wide-ranging interest would seem to give much basis for democratic citizenship.

Certain well-established prestige units like the Bank of Korea after Liberation retained the modernized colonial pattern and became breeding grounds of bureaucratic leadership. The post-1955 economic reconstruction forced certain more practical organizational arrangements on the country. Since the stepping-up of the war in Vietnam, integrated business empires of the *zaibatsu* type have been expanding, and the experience of working in large-scale organizations is increasing. It appears likely that the old pattern is beginning to yield.

The farmer is rapidly finding that his income is maximized by specializing in growing fruit in vinyl houses or experimenting in special crops. Expanding textile production and motor traffic makes more specialists in the market place. In the bureaucracy, the technical requirements of administering American aid and of accounting for it to a specialist American aid mission have, since the Korean War, largely swept the generalist out of the economic ministeries. Surging universities have promoted specialist training. Seoul National University's Engineering College has taken the place of its Law and Arts and Sciences Colleges as the chief locus of prestige as the specialist gains ground on the generalist. Still, trade schools have encountered notable difficulties in increasing their role despite government support. In the last few years, mostly after 1960, increase in industrial production and exports and the founding, under American AID university contracts, of business schools have increased respect for business and engineering specialization and employed larger proportions of specialists in these than in any other areas.

On the other hand, specialists, especially in the technical and scientific areas, still feel they do not command sufficient prestige, influence, or reward, and scientific research has not flourished.[30] Among more than one hundred nations that send students to the

United States, Korea has the second worst known record in getting her specialists back. Some 80–90 percent either leave after returning or do not return at all.[31] The only country with a worse record is Korea's generalist mentor, China. Beneath the surface of a changing society, market and village and neighborhood retain prehensilely the patterns of the past, and old ways reproduce themselves. Development of the specialist, of rules, of law, of organizational discipline, and of the institutions that can use these attainments has been one of Korea's most grievous problems; even today, it delays the progress of her modernization.

9

Factionalism and the Council Pattern

THE LONG TRADITION

The atomized updraft toward central political power seems to impede the cohesion of society below the vortex crest, but it leaves unsettled the form the molecules will take on reaching the top; we can thus far only assume that the seats at the top will be hot, the streaming molecular, and the pressure of maximum access great.

Korea for centuries, as described previously, was a monarchy in the Chinese pattern, the king deriving his legitimacy from Peking's emperor, the court and bureaucracy cast in the Sino-Confucian image. Beneath this exterior, however, Korea, at the top as well as further down in the society, preserved a more ancient pattern with its own dynamics, logic, and history. A particular intensity of updraft was part of this pattern, but this updraft tended to demand its own kind of room at the top. The room it created was council rule. Councils, common to most societies, have a role in Korea which appears in some respect peculiar and rooted in the very beginnings of the culture.

Early in the peninsula's political history — perhaps as early or earlier than the *hwabaek* (Council of Elders) of seventh-century Silla or the Six Groups, a tendency to form and rule through council under weak individual leadership emerged (see pages 21–23). Council, not throne, appeared to have religious sanction; the ideology of kingship is threadbare compared to that of China and Japan.[1] Council control may originally have been a kind of representational system for tribal alliances formed through military need. But its imprint is not a passing one, for we see it echoed in the elders' meetings that have immemorially controlled most villages and in the pattern of consultation demanded by most organizations and associations of the society as they operate even today.

During Koryŏ rule (918–1392), decision by clan chiefs moved closer to formal governmental institutionalization. A high council of civil and military officials, under various names, decided or confirmed everything of importance.[2] Even when military coups from 1170 on brought new blood to the ruling upper stratum, the council tradition itself seems hardly to have faltered. It was expanded and formalized in 1279 as the Office of Joint Councilors. Under Mongol control of Korea (1259–1354), the Korean monarchs were made Mongolized puppets and lost much internal prestige. Foreign policy and tribute questions remained in Mongol hands, but the council seems to have come to exercise much of the internal power that the monarchs, often held hostage, could not wield and that the Mongols had neither the desire nor the continuous institutional structure in Korea to maintain.

Councils formed the chief instrument of transition for the new Yi Dynasty in the last decade of the fourteenth century. The Office of Joint Councilors, supporting General Yi Sŏng-gye, joined other officials in petitioning General Yi to accept the throne and drafted and sent the crucial message to the Ming emperor informing him of the event and attempting the delicate task of gaining his understanding and assent. The Ming reply was sent, not to the new Korean king, but to this council office. The participation of much of the nobility was specifically cited as justifying the request. The support of the Koryŏ noble councilors was, *de facto*, the "Mandate of Heaven," the legitimization of the new ruler. For the following half millennium, weak kingship and the force and variety of aristocratic councilor rule are probably the characteristics that chiefly distinguish the Korean government of the Yi from its Chinese model. The contrast with autocratic Ch'ing government was especially marked.[3]

The Censorate

Though council rule shifted from time to time to bodies of different titles and stated responsibilities, its most portentous institutionalization was in the Censorate. In origin a special organ of Chinese government, the Censorate was based on the Confucian belief that ruler and officials alike stood in constant need of criticism by high-minded scholars duty-bound to point out conduct and moral decisions based on Confucian precept. Only the *yangban* had the qualifications to criticize king and government, and they had, in some respects, the obligation to do so.[4] Though such criticism could also reach the court outside hierarchical channels through memorializing, its formal embodiment in the Censorate carried particular prestige, and recruitment for it was scrutinized with sedulous care to determine family background, high academic standing, and absolute probity of behavior.[5] The Censorate "was charged with criticizing public policy, scrutinizing the conduct of officialdom, rectifying mores, redressing public wrongs and preventing forgery and fraudulent misuses of credentials." [6] It offered daily Confucian critiques to the monarch, served as a channel of complaint against government officers, and also had certain police and judicial functions, partly exercised by bailiffs. Since, however, it had no active administrative responsibilities, it was free to criticize without fear of being asked to implement. Full of idealistic, often doctrinaire Confucian zeal, part legal chamber, part theological council, the Censorate was an ideal rostrum for a captious and persuasive vocation. Censors displayed ingenuity and learning in ferreting out fault or dangerous tendency and in buttressing their arguments with passages drawn from nearly two millennia of Chinese social and governmental criticism. They represented a striking device for the political recruitment of intellectuals and the political channeling of intellectual criticism: the institutionalization of the obligation of intelligence and learning to find constructive social and political purpose. A censor could even be punished if he failed to warn, to criticize, or to advise.

The Censorate was the node not only of government but also of the value system and the mobility that grew out of it. It was a key posting station on the inner-track *cursus honori*. At the bottom, it absorbed star Confucian zealots fresh from the National Academy; these new alumni continued to communicate with the students and could use them as a memorializing and demonstrating pressure group. Meanwhile, senior censors could influence upper government ranks. They sought and gained allies: the royal secretaries, the Academy of Talented Scholars, the Office of Special Councilors, and the Office of Royal Lecturers, which dinned Confucian lessons matutinally into the monarch's ear.[7] All could draft memorials and conduct virtual work strikes until their point was gained.[8] The government was sown with their personal adherents, classmates, relatives, or plain colleagues wedged into all boards and offices. Farther inside, the censoring grip extended to the king's apartment; so long as the censors' allies, the historians, held in their hands the brass ink slab of their office, they could oversee every royal meeting, hear every royal word. The monarch had no control over what they wrote or where it was stored, any more than he controlled *yangban* support for the son he designated as successor.[9] The censoring right carried the implication of daily, almost hourly, access to the royal presence. As the function spread, the monarch found himself hardly able to perform the most personal functions without the surveillance of court attendants.[10] The king was never able — he was never permitted by the *yangban* — to develop important council instrumentalities of his own as did his Ming and Ch'ing superiors. The Chinese practiced, under the Ch'ing, rule authoritarian to the point of dictatorship. The Koreans approached the condition of council dissent without rule. Royal power was checkmated, executive action itself hamstrung; even high officials were so hemmed around with remonstrance that, after the restoration of the supervisory powers of the State Council of 1516, even the High Councilors, the regime's chief executives, were scarcely allowed to exercise their role.[11]

No office of these allied consultative organs considered that it had important specialist functions limited to itself to perform. The relative smallness of the government and the comprehensive administrative nature of Confucian doctrine encouraged everyone to concern himself with all important governmental questions. Councils tended to press equal and limitless claims. So did the aristocrats who composed them. In developing a system of generalized council control, a kind of oligarchical rule within an important agricultural society, Korea produced an excrescent rarity within the ranks of the world's known governments.

Yangban control through council enjoyed long historical continuity although the councils wielding power changed. The preceding description applies better to the first hundred and fifty years of the Censorate (*ca.* 1395–1545) than to later centuries. Council power showed some tendency to shift from one body to another through Yi times, a process eased by the non-specialization of most bodies. After the middle of the sixteenth century, for some two centuries or more it rested largely in a body originally concerned with defense called the Pibyŏn-sa; thereafter powers tended at least partially to shift again toward the Kyujang-gak, a body whose name designated a royal library. Since the real functions of these bodies became exceedingly generalized as soon as they succeeded to real power, their control mechanisms were generally similar. Together they formed a chain of council control lasting until the nineteenth century.

Results

Paradoxically, despite the length of time that this process lasted, the Yi controlling councils did not accrete into lasting institutions with firm form, defined functions, articulated objectives, and hierarchical-loyalty systems of their own. The role they played might originate in a fairly specific, imported, formal function like the Censorate, but the Korean trend was ever toward vagueness of definition, functional generalization, amorphousness of form. By way of comparison, the character of Tokugawa organization with its sense of hierarchical place and of language, costume, and art each separate and specific for its own role was essentially as lacking in the Korean hierarchy as it was in Korean village and market. Most of the councils lacked their own ideas and programs. Dogmatic Confucian insistence on rule by the sages (that is, *yangban* literati), rather than the monarch, provided in the first thirteen decades a council rallying cry that had much the ring of a real political opposition. But even this cry grew indistinct as the dynasty wore on. Lack of particularity impeded the formation of opposition.

Leadership within councils was, on the whole, outstanding by its absence. The inner assumption was the equal right of each individual within the group to have access and voice. Since it was also supposed that opinion must be unanimous, disagreement could tie up decision indefinitely. For a few years before his execution, Cho Kwang-jo (1482–1519) provided some exception. In general, however, insistence on equality of voice expressed itself in chronic derogation and antagonism to any signs of strong leadership either within the council or, when an outstanding councilor tried to carry out the executive functions under the monarch, within other reaches of the bureaucracy. There was thus a marked tendency to pillory anyone who showed a tendency to follow the "authoritarian" lead of the king or that of a powerful official. Such men were tagged in the council with opprobrium: as, for example, were those who allied themselves with the "dictatorial" monarch, Sejo (ruled 1455–1468), the "three evil men" who served the powerful High Councilor Kim Al-lo (1481–1537), and others who served the energetic factional chief and official Song Si-yŏl (1607–1689), or, later, the nineteenth-century regent, the Taewŏn'gun. The same sort of hostility toward authority was expressed in the twentieth-century National Assembly against Syngman Rhee and, to a lesser extent, Park Chŏng-hŭi. Yet comparatively few antagonists came forward to serve as leaders themselves; they preferred the cover of a group from which to exert their right to attack leadership. The uses of leadership had not arisen in local fief or guild or army nor in any sufficient pressure of practical emergency. Council government, lacking urgency of task, proved unable to provide a milieu in which these lacks could be made good.

Beginning with the first century of Yi rule and increasing thereafter, the process of decision-making became choked, and even routine executive acts were impeded. If the king tried to rule, the Censorate accused him of "arbitrary decisions." He could not, for example, even worship Heaven without being accused of *lèse majesté* to the Chinese emperor. The third monarch, T'aejong, became so wroth at Censorate obstruction clothed in Confucian moralisms that he refused to do reverence to the tablet of Confucius enshrined at the National Academy.[12] The fourth monarch — Korea's greatest — got no further than sending incense to a ceremony for Heaven, even this achievement requiring much tact and perseverance in the face of entrenched council opposition. The seventh king, most autocratic of all (and therefore pilloried in the official histories) eventually forced the issue and worshiped in person. After his death in 1468, no other monarch ever dared broach the subject: the Altar of Heaven was dismantled, not to be rebuilt until the Japanese insisted on it in 1897 (to the delectation chiefly of tourists). Harassed by the impossibility of their position, the first three monarchs retired considerably before the end of their lives, and the desire of the fourth, Sejong the Great, to do so or even to delegate functions to his crown prince was blocked by Censorate forces of the most insistent kind memorializing over thirteen years (1437–1450). Sejong stayed on, but his last days were clouded with hostile student demonstrations. A century of such tensions ended climactically when these obstruction tactics kindled a towering paranoia in the tenth monarch, Yŏnsan'gun. Striking out against council forces, he slaughtered scores of scholars and Censorate associates, even beheading the corpses of dead ones in their graves. Having united the literati against him, he was deposed in a coup of 1506 and died in exile two months later, cause unknown. Thereafter until 1864 no king put up decisive opposition to the councils.

Expansion of the Censorate function and of the consulting groups mounted as *yangban* population rose. By the middle of the nineteenth century, there were nearly seventy bureaus, committees, and councils: of Merit Subjects, Minor Merit Subjects, Royal Lectures, Royal Household, Royal Clan, Royal Kinsmen, Royal Sons-in-Law, Special Tribunal, and so forth.[13] Since no monarch was threatening enough to unite the *yangban,* they had only themselves to fight for power: the conflicting and cacophonous middle and late Yi world of divided and ill-differentiated councils choked administration. No decisions of the king or any single council were immune. Any matter could be questioned, usually in accordance with Confucian precedent, and had then to be exhausted in discussion. As in ancient Korea, if opinion was split, the matter would be stalemated.[14] Executive decisions were almost impossible to reach, were subject to constant attack, were not official until every barrage had been traversed. Above all, they were never final, since the Censorate — or any senior memorialist — could always display learning, importance, and "loyalty" by re-opening attacks on them. New departures were the inevitable victims, and abuses could not be corrected; in the end, more and more officials despaired of raising substantial or even theoretical questions at all, and government became a function of attacking and defending the routine and the personal.

For example, though the land system began to break down and require reform soon after the start of the dynasty, it remained on the books almost unchanged more than four hundred years, resulting conditions becoming increasingly desperate.[15] The resettling by Koreans of fallow, fertile lands along the Yalu was debated for centuries without substantial effect.[16] Re-surveys of land were called for, but even these were rarely accomplished, and, by the end of the dynasty, no survey had apparently taken place for a century.[17] The military system stood the tests of some hundred and twenty years but then declined so sharply that Yulgok (Yi I, 1536–1584), one of Korea's two most famous philosopher-officials, sensing its weakness in relation to rising Japanese strength, called for drastic reform in 1583, less than ten years before the actual Japanese invasion. Despite royal support, an opposing faction blocked the proposals. The imposition of a military tax in 1616 caused such distress that peasants became slaves to escape it. Although reform was proposed in 1702, discussion went on for almost half a century before, in 1751, the tax was halved rather than abolished. Until the Taewŏn'gun's autocracy finally breached council obstructionism, no action at all was taken to impose a needed household tax or to halt the deterioration of the relief grain system.[18] Only autocracy and foreign control were capable of breaking the pattern and introducing adaptive forces. In succession, both came. The wonder is not that they came but that so purposelessly disputatious a system of government could so long have endured.

REACTION UNDER THE TAEWŎN'GUN, THE JAPANESE, AND THE AMERICANS

The Taewŏn'gun mounted the first force since the fifteenth century to breach the council pattern. He clearly established the throne's leadership and authority, made councilors subordinate, and emasculated Censorate powers. The Japanese in turn virtually abolished them. Within the government-general, councils advised most timidly, for Korean opinion was subordinated to an enlarged, alien, specialist bureaucracy and to formal law; powerful council in the old pattern was unthinkable. Korea enjoyed fifty to seventy-five years of largely enforced vacation from council rule.[19]

As we have seen, despite a respite and the substitution of effective bureaucratic administration, the council instinct did not disappear entirely during the colonial period. It persisted in traditional village controls and in such new organizations as church presbyteries, schools, and newspapers. Such modern forms utilized the council pattern largely subconsciously but successfully as a chief source of strength. Council was still a logical repository for the upward flow of atomized individuals. Society had not yet produced sufficient interest groups and specialization to substitute more hierarchical, professional, and autonomous channels of leadership.

Diffusion of authority appears to follow from the internal logic of the atomized upflow; for if this dominates the culture, then it matters more that the maximum number be able to participate in authority than that the authority itself be definite and clear. As we approach the question of the combination of this pattern with democracy, it will be well to remember that the Koreans do not tend toward council procedure because they "like" this form in a positive sense or because they hold any concepts of exactly what council shape is requisite for an orderly state, and certainly not because they regard council as representative of the body politic. Rather, the atomized updraft that comes to them as naturally as breathing requires a broad surface that will give maximum, equal contact with power to the greatest number; concentration of power, strong leadership, is inconsistent with the physics of this tendency and is thus resented as "unjust." So long as authority is diffuse and contact maximal, the question of what kind of council operates does not disturb the pattern. Hence council form can shift and change in almost the same amoeba-like way that other native organizational forms like the market can. This cultural characteristic may help explain why, in the two decades after Liberation, council rule and democracy could cohabit without marriage and why the council form itself could shift from Assembly to political party to CIA while remaining acceptable to the public and true to the pattern.

That being said, it is not hard to understand how, after Liberation, "democracy" was mistaken by Korean politicians for another opportunity for council government. Laborious preparation and training — and comprehension of the problem — were needed to school the Koreans in understanding the differences between council rule of the Yi type and that under a responsible representative system. USAMGIK had no time and no skill to understand the nature of the problem or to provide the training. When assemblies were constituted from 1946 on, council forces reawakened.

Signs of council rebirth can be traced from the first day of "democratic" assemblies in Korea. Hodge's unilateral appointment of forty-five liberals — with some leftists — to counterbalance the extreme rightist result of the elections for the Korean Interim Legislative Assembly (KILA) was interpreted by the rightist majority as a "dictatorial act" fully equivalent to the more extreme royal or regent action that had brought council protest. Schism yawned between KILA conservatives and moderates. Personal attack, charges of collaboration, protest, departures from the hall in dudgeon were enacted in place of legislation. No bills were passed for three months.[20] Factional behavior tends to give the embarrassing of opponents precedence over issues of substance: thus the conservatives on January 26, 1947, passed an anti-trusteeship resolution that had no chance of practical result but embarrassed Kim Kyu-sik and the moderates and, of course, Military Government. Another such hypocritical resolution sought to investigate accusations in rightist newspapers of Chairman Kim Kyu-sik's complicity in the sale of bogus stocks.[21] Resolutions criticizing and advising the executive were more characteristic of the Assembly than its eleven bills, several trivial or poorly drawn; more time was spent worrying about executive acts than performing legislative ones. The public, in response, re-elected only thirteen of KILA's ninety members. Men began to remember that dictatorial government had, for all its repressiveness, at least been effective. The arguments of the 1961 coup's young colonels were already beginning to appear on Korea's wall.

COUNCIL AND THE KOREAN NATIONAL ASSEMBLY

The traditional council nature of the new National Assembly elected in May 1948, was confirmed by two developments: the character of the elections that produced it; and the nature of its position in the government of President Rhee.

In its representative roots lay the only real initial hope of immediate contrast between Yi council and the democratic assembly. Yet it was these roots that were weak. The elections provided choice in a reasonably free atmosphere but their haste of preparation left no time to establish the concept of election as a means and as a beginning of communication between the Korean individual and his government; voting to a villager was little more than the chance to reward a national or local worthy with a personal avenue to power. Except for national questions like agricultural prices and the need for expanded irrigation, localized interests rarely exerted influence on the daily work of the Assembly or served as basis for groupings, parties, programs or legislative compromise. Once elections were over, communication between assemblymen and their districts tended to cease except for the performance of personal favors involving the bureaucracy. The Assembly floated free above Korean society without natural pressures from underneath to control, check, support or, sometimes, even notice it.

If understanding of the Assembly's function was weak in the Korean individual, it was little stronger in Korean society. The Censorate institutionalized in the capital a function that even an educated farmer's son could exercise within his rural home; though obedient, he, too, could "remonstrate" and advise his father. This understanding of function lay behind the support the Censorate had, on occasion, been able to call on from the students of the National Academy. To this had been joined, earlier in the dynasty, class interests of the *yangban* vis-à-vis the monarch that gave the Censorate bureaucratic and academic allies. Understanding of constitutional and legislative functions had no such roots in the Korea of 1948. Nor were the new representatives a natural social group of a sort that could form alliances of any permanence. Student support for a modern, democratic institution remained almost the only active possibility.[22] By and large, from 1946 through 1954, the press and some pressure from urban and international opinion were the only elements even faintly encouraging the Assembly to act as a modern legislative body.

If the Korean and his society provided little interest and control over the Assembly, the same could not be said of Rhee. In influencing the drafters of the constitution to adopt a strong executive instead of the cabinet-responsible system many assemblymen had hoped for, Rhee, in addition to a self-interest, instinctively felt the old issue of council versus concentrated authority that Yŏnsan'gun, the Taewŏn'gun and even the Japanese had faced. Like Yŏnsan'gun's old advisor No Sa-sin in the last years of the fifteenth century, Rhee stood against the council tendency of native forces and insisted that power must have, both in constitutional provision and administrative fact, a clearly designated residence in the Korean executive.[23] If it did not, endless altercation and debate would paralyze administration and the attention of the entire government would be riveted not on rule but on access thereto. Yet democracy demanded, as Confucian rule had not, an assembly with power both to legislate and to check the executive and these demands corresponded strongly with politicians' ancient council hopes. Their hopes, however, were not backed with the vision of a state whose powers were balanced. They wanted small part of specialist legislative function. Their taste was to exercise, in modern dress, the Confucian right to criticize and the Korean council right to impede executive action and to rule. Rhee knew this but offered little acceptable alternative. The confusion of these three political traditions, the Chinese, the Korean, and the American, converging in the Assembly, intensified inefficiency and strife.

The history of the Assembly from 1948 to 1952 was replete with these tendencies. Legislation was again comparatively neglected. Again, advisory resolutions poured forth — on dismissing collaborators from the bureaucracy, on agricultural management, flood or drought "counter-measures," on foreign affairs. The Confucian advisory resolution supplanted or obscured the task of legislation. The Assembly also showed a chronic tendency to summon ministers or the President before it for questioning, censor them by resolution, or demand the resignation of the cabinet, a right it constitutionally lacked.[24] It delighted in the establishment of "investigation committees." In all such acts, the Sino-Korean censor moved, not the Western legislator. The executive felt hampered and harassed but rarely improved.

The attempt to revive the Korean tradition of council control over the monarch quickly bred institutional warfare in the new Korean government. As soon as independence came, the Assembly found resolution and inspection insufficient and moved to assert control over the "recalcitrant" executive. In August 1948 it passed the National Traitors Law providing for the arrest, trial, and punishment of those charged with having collaborated "viciously" with the Japanese. Hundreds of the wealthy, the aristocratic, the intellectually prominent, and even those active within Korea in the Independence Movement were implicated, including key government officials. The Vice-Minister of Commerce and Industry, for instance, was forced to resign. Especially hounded were police chiefs, the key men in Rhee's chain of security. The law was spearheaded by younger opposition assemblymen in the spirit of Cho Kwang-jo and his young Confucian colleagues; they employed the issue to attack the President, who was known to have obtained political and financial support from collaborators. Having reason to believe it could not trust the government to implement this law, the Assembly forced through legislation to establish a special committee, special courts, special investigators, prosecutors, judges, and even police responsible to it for implementation. (The Censorate had also had special bailiffs.) The President objected, but knowledge of public support induced him to promulgate the bills. From January to June 1949, arrests took place almost daily, important policemen were detained by the Assembly's "Special Police," special trials were held, sentences imposed, and the prospect of further action under Assembly control unfolded endlessly. If such council rule was pushed, the functions of the executive and the judiciary would both be usurped.

The national police, with Presidential encouragement, struck back.[25] In late May 1949, a series of arrests of assemblymen on grounds of "communism" began. A National Enlightenment Association, evidently backed by police and other affected groups, held inflammatory public meetings against the assemblymen on May 31 and June 2, marching on the Special Investigation Committee. The Assembly in turn arrested three Association leaders and two metropolitan police chiefs on charges of "anti-nationalism." Fifty national police retaliated on the sixth by raiding the Committee's headquarters and arresting and mauling the Special Police, whereupon the President on the same day issued an order dissolving them. The Assembly requested the resignation of the cabinet; this could be, and was, ignored. The Assembly was then left weaponless and naked to inevitable revenge from the executive and the judiciary. Arrests of its members started, eventually sixteen assemblymen being taken into custody through June and into July. Kim Ku, now an opposition leader, was murdered. The Assembly was, for the time being, cowed. The special courts and trials petered out. Trials to convict the assemblymen themselves began, replete with suspicious "evidence." Rhee, using police and judiciary, had won the first round of the contest by manufacturing charges and employing force — much the same tactics that had been used against Cho Kwang-jo and his colleagues in 1519.[26]

Council thrust and executive parrying or counter-thrust dominated the next three and a half years. In the year before the Korean War, the Assembly rebid for control through its legislative function. It passed land-reform and local-autonomy bills that it knew Rhee opposed. The President, without basis in constitutional procedure, passed them back without veto but with "suggestions" for their amendment or remarks on their "untimeliness." When the Assembly returned the bills, the President reacted by vetoing land reform and not implementing local autonomy and, when the veto was overridden, delayed land reform until May 1950, a year later. The government even found means of evading Assembly control of the budget: by 1949, the United States Economic Cooperation Administration (ECA) estimated that half the state revenues derived from "voluntary contributions" over which no budgetary control could be exercised. If these were insufficient, inflationary bank drafts were produced.

Executive evasion, illegality, or force only strengthened the Assembly's determination to gain the upper hand. A resolution to revise the constitution to establish a cabinet-responsible system was introduced and voted down early in 1950, but the Assembly's cause was aided by the elections of that year, in which many moderates won seats and Rhee's overt supporters fell from fifty-six to twenty-four.[27] The new Assembly, meeting six days before the outbreak of war, was already taking steps to place a new constitutional amendment on the agenda when Communist invasion postponed it.

War sharpened but did not change the executive struggle with council. The coming of massive U.S. and UN military and relief help raised the stakes of power, with Rhee the winner and Assembly appetite to usurp portions of his power whetted. Inflation, corruption, and scandal swelled; they and Rhee's increasingly contemptuous treatment created an anti-Rhee majority and a double-barreled threat: the Assembly might either pass its amendment or vote Rhee out in the cameral Presidential election scheduled for June 1952 (see Chapter 7). The President realized that his hour had struck and that the only permanent way out of the dilemma was to combat council thrusts by a permanent council bodyguard of his own — eventually the Liberal party (inaugurated on December 23, 1951; see Chapter 11). He likewise introduced his own amendments for popular reelection of the President. These the Assembly resoundingly defeated 143–19 on January 18, 1952, by springing them through a vote before Rhee could apply arrests and mob threats. The Assembly then, on April 19, 1952, introduced its amendment for cabinet responsibility. On May 14, the administration countered with amendments for the popular election of the President and Vice-President.

A second round of Yŏnsan'gun force occurred. On May 24, Rhee appointed as Home Minister General Yi Pŏm-sŏk, then Vice-President and co-founder of the Liberal party, youth-group leader and activist. Martial law was at once declared. Civil power was laid in the hands of the Provost Marshal General, Major General Wŏn Yŏng dŏk, who had special motives for placing his considerable craft and intelligence at the President's command.[28] On the basis of being under the direct command of the President, Wŏn claimed the right to arrest anyone. He immediately announced restrictions on the press, the right of assembly, personal movements, and possession of firearms. In the next two days, 50 of the Assembly's 183 members were detained, 45 for not having proper identification. The Assembly could produce a quorum but not the two thirds needed for a vote on the constitutional amendments. Arrest, trial, and daily mass demonstrations mounted. On May 28, shops, markets, and even schools were closed to permit a four-hour demonstration for Rhee's re-election. Mysterious, previously unknown gangs like the Paekkŏltan (White Skeleton Corps) arose at the call of Yi Pŏm-sŏk to create "popular will" and terrorize the Assembly. For the first time there were rumors that elements high in the Korean military might join the opposition in a coup.[29] The Assembly opposition pleaded with the American embassy to "save democracy." Most of the embassy staff were sympathetic, but the American military, its policy powers ascendant in war, opposed any move to "rock the boat." Jacob Malik, the Soviet representative in the United Nations, had indicated on June 23 Communist willingness to seek a "peaceful settlement." The State Department's probing reply was made on June 28.[30] Washington was more impressed with the need to move toward settlement of the war than to overthrow existing Korean leadership and welcome a democratic government of unknowable stability. The State Department decided against change. On being informed of this, the Assembly, its arrested members officially released and marched to the hall for the purpose, voted the President's amendments. Rhee soon thereafter won 86 percent of the vote in the elections of August 5, 1952: there was still little popular support for Assembly rule. The second major round in the battle between council and monarch had been fought, and council had lost. Institutionally, the defeat was decisive. Thereafter, council struggles largely shifted from Assembly to political party.

A body not effectively representative that chronically tilted counciliarly with the executive lacked both ancient defenses and modern ones. The executive used its own channels to manipulate the people against both the Assembly and individual members. Neither the public nor the press took interest in the 1949 trials of the assemblymen nor saw their institutional significance. The army gave the institution little support: it foiled by trickery the 1951 attempts of the Assembly to investigate such scandals as the massacre at Kŏch'ang (see page 164). Local voters failed to support the assembly in its 1951–52 attempt to wrest power from Rhee; in the by-elections of February 1952, Rhee's Liberals gained three of eight seats, while his Assembly Liberal opponents did not even run. Provincial and local assemblies, at government behest, obediently filed petitions for the "recall" of local representatives who opposed Rhee.[31] Rhee's national organizations easily mobilized both anomic and voting strength crucial to Rhee's victory over Assembly opponents in May and June of 1952; the incorporation of these organizations into the Liberal party was, from the beginning to end, one of its chief sources of strength. When the chips were down, the Assembly remained, even more than its council predecessors, a negotiating and censorial group high above a population willing to vote for candidates but not to support the Assembly's power, integrity, or survival as an institution.

Even in its internal characteristics, the Assembly resembled ancient councils. It had their liquidity, amorphousness, lack of leadership and program. Few assemblymen belonged to any common organization; there were so few to belong to. No ethnic ties and few religious affiliations could serve as bonds. Only the old council rallying cry against dictatorial rule could rouse the Assembly, and even that was ineffective until the creation of political parties. Occupational bonds were not culturally honored. Individuals flowed from one group to another as petty issue or opportunity beckoned (see pages 288–290). When the President threatened or offended the Assembly's *amour propre*, some group cohesiveness formed; when the threat lifted cohesion disappeared. Real shows of government force, as in the summers of 1949 and 1952, brought capitulation. Democratic reinforcement of the council principle of equality of voice hindered formation of leadership of hierarchies, since assemblymen, like their *yangban* predecessors, were reluctant to subordinate themselves to anyone "more equal" than they. For all his stature and brilliance as intellectual and speaker, Dr. Kim Kyu-sik fell victim to this tendency in his failure to lead KILA effectively: constant rightist "revolts" undermined his leadership. Assemblymen looked to Rhee for leadership during the few weeks of constitutional drafting, but as soon as he became President, they began to resent, criticize and rebel against him. The father figure of 1948 became the enemy figure of 1951–1952. It was not until 1952, after shearing the Assembly of much of its power, that Rhee could build a firm supporting group within it. For all his personal forcefulness, Shin Ik-hŭi (Shinicky) as Speaker and Assembly leader also largely failed to conquer council's ancient tendencies and establish consistent, effective leadership, his own group, the Korean Nationalists, being as incohesive and amorphous as any. Just as the nation found it could not use Prince Min Yŏng-hwan in 1905, so the Assembly from 1946 to 1953 saw around it leadership personalities but no leadership. Councils wished to govern, but they could not create in political life that hierarchical subordinate and loyalty that society itself lacked the structure to teach them. The faults of council hence became central to the frustration of democracy.

With its defeat in the 1952 battle and the passage of the President's constitutional amendments of 1952 and 1954, the Assembly ceased temporarily to play a role of independence or control and lost much of its significance as a council institution in the Korean tradition. The overthrow of the Rhee government and the passage in 1960 of constitutional amendments establishing a parliamentary system brought a brief and unprecedented strengthening of its formal function, but by this time the chief council roles had shifted to political parties. The Assembly under the parliamentary system, furthermore, tended to have its censorial teeth somewhat drawn by its position of responsible support for the cabinet and administration. Premier Chang Myŏn, a notably undictatorial man, provided no threat stimulating Assembly development, in the nine months of its existence, into a separate interest group. Its bicameral division likewise impeded the building of a separate identity.[32] The 1962 constitutional amendments of the military government sheared the Assembly of most real powers and left it with small prospect of recovering a council role under these constitutional terms; indeed, repression of the kind of rule it represented was one of the junta's original motives for seizing power.

Recalcitrant as these tendencies have been to change, the pattern may eventually alter. The Assembly's chance to develop as an institution lasted only fifteen years, a tiny segment in Korean history's long span. Its start was unusually mismanaged and ill-prepared by the United States. Had USAMGIK employed even a fraction of the kind of preparation Great Britain gave the parliaments of her colonies before liberating them — training in ceremony, sound rules of debate and procedure, planned contacts with the legislators of older democratic nations, and so forth — the result might have been different. Even so, as Korean society changes, interest groups strengthen, the products of a new educational system come to the fore, and a more favoring atmosphere than at present is provided, future assemblies are likely to break with the pattern and prove more viable.

Meanwhile, however, council rule shifted elsewhere.

THE LIBERAL PARTY AND
THE CENTRAL INTELLIGENCE AGENCY

In some respects, the Liberal party (1951–1960) represents the most massive example so far known in Korea of council rule. It developed council traits outside the Assembly, however, and so its story belongs primarily to the next chapter. It also incorporated these traits in strict subordination to the executive of which it was, in all but name, a part. It therefore defended the government from remonstrance instead of remonstrating.

These exceptions noted, we find the stamp of the council tradition in the party's sheer lack of all particularistic and group sources of strength. Both its individual members and its units were atoms in the vortex. The Liberals consequently lacked any particular social or class flavor. More striking still was the complete generalization of function and aims reflecting diffusion of power through a council body. Its interest in legislation was mild. By contrast, it rejoiced in the widest range of management: dictating loans, supporting industrial fairs, dominating school boards and churches, running charities and banks, operating newspapers, government businesses, and even gangs all over the country. Through these means, as well as through controlling much recruitment to power, it wielded more conclusive bureaucratic as well as political controls than its council predecessors but wielded them in an atomic pattern of much the same kind.

The Liberal party, however, effected more departures and innovations in council rule than did the earlier Assembly. Unbound by legal restrictions on its form and with far more sources of power, hence responsibilities, than a Yi council, it expanded into a hitherto unknown organizational complexity and developed an elaborate hierarchy and leadership. Under a National Party Convention, a Central Executive Committee and a Central Committee, subordinate committees of Home Affairs, Foreign Affairs, and so forth, covered every phase of government. To solve its enormous business and financing problems, it even developed, toward the end of its power, greater liaison with economic specialists, one of the first entries of specialization into Korean politics. Rhee's unswerving support of Yi Ki-pung provided clear and continuous leadership, and this leadership, by appointing the heads of numerous committees and shifting power among them, was able to maintain far firmer discipline and controls than previous councils or factions had known.[33] To fight the factionalism that was endemic in it as in the ancient world of council, the party instituted an abnormal, almost military emphasis on loyalty. But at least some hierarchy and a modicum of specialization had been forged to deal with the problem. For all its faults, it represented for Korean council behavior an impressive advance.

The military coup, in ending the 1960–61 Assembly, cut through a democratically dressed council rule. The coup colonels thus played, by different methods, the same role that the Taewŏn'gun, the Japanese, and Syngman Rhee had all, in varied ways, performed. Yet the junta's nature and its needs for government paradoxically caused restoration of council rule of a different stripe.

This restoration did not concern the bodies that the military named "council." The junta was, of course, itself organized into councils — the Supreme Council, with elaborate clusters of subordinate councils descending from it controlled by key military men and organized to direct and "clean up" the bureaucracy. Although this function represented a reimposition of council rights to inspect and censor, its organization and spirit reflected the normal disciplinary instincts of the military and were a far cry from council government in the Korean tradition. It was quite unlike traditional regimes in the definiteness of its authority, its speed of action instead of endless debate, and its wide use of university specialists and former bureaucrats. These and such enormous groups as the National Reconstruction Movement — which bore an unspoken similarity to the Rural Reconstruction Movement of General Ugaki in the early 1930's — did provide at a lower level the increased political participation that the council form had given during Yi times. Most committees and movements under the military, however, were hasty, considered inefficient, declined before the end of the military phase of government, and lapsed with its passing at the end of 1963.

Military government left behind one lasting institution, however, that is, unconsciously, far closer than its formal governing bodies to the council tradition: the Korean Central Intelligence Agency (CIA). Established immediately after the coup by Lieutenant Colonel Kim Chong-p'il, nephew-in-law of General Park it was the citadel of power for the "young colonels," mostly of Kim's officer-training class, whose ideas, ambitions, and discontent sparked the coup. It was a vast control and censoring organization, located, like the Yi Censorate, outside most formal operating responsibility but in hourly critical and advisory contact with the governing organs and having the power to threaten and disrupt their proceedings. In it as in the Yi councils, caste, now military, substituted for specialist skill. Its powers were vast, vague, and spread among the thousands who sought access to power through it. Since Kim and his colleagues had long experience in intelligence work, the CIA replaced ancient vagueness with modern secrecy and added investigation, arrest, terror, censorship, massive files, and thousands of agents, stool pigeons, and spies both at home and abroad to its council powers. In history's most sensational expansion of council function, it broadly advised and inspected the government, did much of its planning, produced many of its legislative ideas and most of the research on which they were based, recruited for government agencies, encouraged relations with Japan, sponsored business companies, shook down millionaires, watched over and organized students, netted over $40 million by manipulating the Korean stock market through cover brokers, and supported theaters, dance groups, an orchestra, and a great tourist center.[34] From its chrysalis arose the government's political party, the Democratic Republicans (DRP) and CIA agents, in Kuomintang-Communist fashion, formed a strong secretariat core with the intended function of manipulating those selected as representatives. Party, government, army — indeed, all society — were capped with a vast council cover amoebically enlarging itself, ranging in undefined ways through all control and discouraging all other forms of access and of amalgamation. A military chrysalis gave the CIA council form at least the veneer of a more formal internal organization and hierarchy. On the other hand, secrecy is perhaps the ideal addition to council rule's impulse to wield authority ubiquitously without paying the price of responsibility. In this sense, CIA and its relationship to President Park is closer to Yi council in its relationship to the king than either the assembly or the liberal party were. In combining the Liberal party's council innovation of elaborate hierarchical organization and loyalty with its own secret G-2 camaraderie and the ideals of nationalist revolution, CIA has made a definite, though covert and dangerous, innovation in Korea's long struggle for internal cohesion.[35] Other cultures resort to Peróns or Nkrumahs for their dictatorships; Korea with its atomized updraft spreads tyranny through council.[36]

THE FACTIONS

Traditionally in Korea the scramble for place that leads to council government periodically bloats the top councils until they no longer afford sufficient power to their members. Hence the repeated forming of factions competing for the same objective without differences of class, religion, interest, or ideology.

After innumerable splits and recombinations, the *yangban* in the last two centuries of Yi rule more or less stabilized around four firm factions known as the Sasaek, or Four Colors.[37] The struggle of these groups to control the bureaucracy and its councils long constituted the main activity of Korean politics.[38] It was the particular characteristic of these groups that, lacking all fundamental distinguishing features or vested differences, they were forced to seize on picayune differences, often artifically contrived and then inflated in order to produce splits, battle lines, and a spirit of contest. Toward the beginning, to be sure, policy positions of substance were the occasional grouping agent: in the 1580's, for example, when appraisals of the strength and aggressiveness of Japan and the needs for strengthening Korean defenses were argued, or in the 1620's and 1630's when Ming decline and Manchu aggrandizement factionalized a "China-recognition question" fully as painful and immediate as that faced by the United States since 1948. Such issues, soon passing, were replaced by altercations over factional punishment, support for *sŏwŏn*, and whether the period of mourning for a queen should end within a year of her demise or extend beyond it.[39] Distinguishing colors were selected and worn by members of the faction or their wives, sometimes until the turn of the present century. Separation was enforced by strict marriage rules, factional members marrying only within their factions, sometimes to the point of damage to the strength of their stock.[40] Many refused to speak or have any social intercourse with members of other factions.

This pettiness was abnormally intense. In fact, like other abnormalities, it reflected emotional needs generated, in this case, by the underlying physics of the society. Groups might be necessary to produce maximum access and issues were needed to activate and maintain the groups, but if the culture did not contain the basis for producing issues or divisions of sufficient strength, minor ones had to be seized and forced to parade stridently as if in major roles. The atmosphere of politics was thick with evil rumor, back-biting and imagined plot. Such phenomena were not the product of chance or the simple results of child-training but were necessary gestures in the drama of producing hostility and cohesiveness against enemies in a culture where issues and distinctions do not give either hostility or cohesiveness sufficient substance.[41]

Once enmity was created, no compromise was possible; power, not issue, being involved, neither arbitration nor conciliation could arise. Crises such as the Japanese or Manchu invasions did not assemble forces of adaptiveness or cohesion. The conduct of war became factionalized; at war's height successful generals who aroused ministerial jealousy would be defamed and killed even when such action cost the country its defense. Korea's greatest hero, Admiral Yi Sun-sin, was one of many such victims. Toward the end of the dynasty, naked political control became the only goal, and factions no longer even bothered to maintain nominal unity on internal or external problems. Concentration was on methods, which were extreme; every ruse or device was used to come to power and every cruelty and oppression was visited on the vanquished faction. During the long period of struggle, thousands of scholars lost their lives. The centuries-old outcry of reform scholars against factionalism could not stop it. In the stultification and ultimate collapse of effective administration throughout the nation, one can trace the extent to which the country was willing, quite consciously, to hurt itself by factional struggle, hence the extent to which factionalism and council rule were essential to the dynamics of the culture.

Inevitably, with the resurrection of the indigenous political pattern in 1945, factionalism was reborn. The innumerable small groups and cliques spawned from the moment of Liberation on were one of the chief ingredients of the chaos of the time and are still recalled by observers as one of the most extreme instances of the factional milieu ever known to political scientists. The early Assembly likewise was infested, political groups forming, splitting, dying, and re-forming. When Assembly power began to be transferred to the Liberal party, factionalism broke out there, the constant accompaniment of power.[42] Yi Pŏm-sŏk's Racial Youth Corps group, vital in the early days, had to be purged, a "new" faction being formed at this time in contradistinction to an "old" faction rooted largely in Kyŏngsang Province.[43] In the 1954–1955 period, the designations were the "leadership" and the "non-leadership" factions. In 1957–1958, issues of dictatorship within the party came to the fore, and factions formed between Chang Kyŏng-kŭn and Im Ch'ŏl-ho on one side and Yi Chae-hak and Kang Sŏng-t'ae on the other, becoming so bitter over the expulsion of the smuggler-politician Yi Yŏng-pŏm that Speaker Yi Ki-bung had to purge the headquarters. In the summer of 1958, a "young" faction combined with a "hard" faction to advocate that more extreme measures be taken against the opposition than Yi Ki-bung's "moderate" faction thought desirable.[44] Names differed, but the phenomenon persisted. The Liberal party had become the main route to power for the ambitious. Yet no specialist qualification, cohesiveness of subordinate group, important issues, or clear vested interests existed to produce order and objectivity in attaining this access. Again small issues had to be seized on and inflated in order to produce and arm the battle lines.

Among the military, factional conflicts were even more violent. The CIA, as chief processor of the greatest number of applicants for power, found itself in the shoes of the Liberal party as a generator of factionalism. In the first week after the coup, members of the fifth officer class, apprehensive over the near power monopoly of the eighth class (of CIA boss Kim Chong-p'il) approached the military government's first Supreme Chairman and Prime Minister, Lieutenant General Chang To-yŏng. All were arrested on counter-coup charges on July 3, 1961. Other coup attempts, real or rumored, followed from groups of Hamgyŏng officers, air force officers, and obscure — and sometimes fictitious — mixtures of military officers and civilians. Eleven men were arrested in January 1962. On June 1, Kim Chong-p'il announced the smashing of a far larger "coup attempt" including some Democratic party officials. On June 17, thirty-three more persons were arrested. Chang Myŏn himself was, with patent lack of evidence, tried for "conspiracy." [45] Some meetings of the Supreme Council took place with pistols on the table as military factions supporting or opposing the CIA fought. Kim Chong-p'il was twice forced into exile — February 25, 1963, and again in September 1964. Chairman Park grew so sick of the bickering that, on February 18, 1963, he publicly announced and later swore by oath that he would turn over the government to civilians by summer and not participate in it if civilian leaders would make certain pledges to insure stability.[46] Though shortly rescinded, his oath was eloquent testimony to factionalism's strength. Of the original members of the Supreme Council for National Reconstruction (SCNR) of May 1961, more went, at one time or another, to jail or exile than remained in power. Two more rumored coup attempts, both involving former military associates of the military government, have gone through the courts. Not a single counter-coup has broken into the open, but factional instability was rife until 1965. Army control simply aggravated the traditional power struggle; only a large measure of civilianization has gradually but increasingly since 1964 quieted the extremes of the contest. Meanwhile, factionalism continues, into 1968, to decimate the civilian political opposition.

CONCLUSION

We have traced something of the past, the rebirth, and the apparent unconscious continuation of council rule and its factional derivatives. Others may argue over whether the phenomenon exists, or they may call it by other names. Those admitting its existence may still be puzzled to explain the cause of its rise and long hold on Korean society. Some may be moved to explain addiction to council instead of individual dictator in terms of a reluctance by individuals to assume responsibility, a deep-rooted instinct to protect initiative in a society whose political penalties have been extreme. Such an explanation will have to tap more psychological springs of conduct than this study finds possible. The field remains wide open and proponents of other theses should bring their theories forward. I feel the presence of council rule more as a safety valve relieving some of the pressure built up by the upward streaming of the homogeneous society; for the force of that upflow is, as anyone who has seen it can testify, singularly great. Censorate, Assembly, Liberal party, and CIA all seem to me called into existence in response to such needs. The Assembly illustrates the instinct to assume the role even when it means sacrificing democratic and constitutional function and popular support. Finally, council partakes of the generalization of Korean power, its refusal to accept definitions, its resistance to order. It reflects the fact that considerations of power, not function, pervade the society. In few societies are power-holders specialists; in part, consequently, Korea's council instinct is a natural, almost universal one. Yet in Korea these qualities have an unusual degree of persistence, and the form they take has the society's unique stamp. As the farmer will not be a *chaengi,* as the market resists form and tries to resist specialization, as *ajŏn* and innkeeper turn their faces from their titles and long to escape the identity of their function, so also at the top of their society does the controlling body assume general form, eschew definitions and limitations of function, even shroud itself in secrecy, and so protect itself from attack and clothe itself in the ancient image of omnicompetence.

PART IV

The Search for Cohesion

Since 1880, Korea's traditional ruling class has disappeared. The country has been colonized, occupied, ravaged by war, and shaken by repeated major changes in government. It can be argued that the events of so stormy a period in themselves abort leadership and splinter society. On the other hand, we know that unstable government and a poorly integrated society likewise existed during the abnormally protected Yi period. The external drama of modern Korea may then be less important than the inner necessities of the culture in accounting for the incohesion of a homogeneous nation. The formation of more or less identical factions and councils that compete despite the absence of natural cleavage or issue creates its own inner demand for hostility. When to this hostility is added the fundamental component of atomized mobility — when, for example, a man will always place his personal desire for power above the value of remaining with his group and helping it gain power — a political culture is produced in which groups are perceived by the participants as unworthy of loyalty or continuity. As a result, the effort to form groups and keep them intact becomes one of the most frustrating and repetitious tasks of the culture.

If this is true, then the study of the paths taken to achieve cohesion will be a significant part of Korean political analysis. Since Liberation, long and varied but thus far abortive attempts at cohesion by political party have taken place. North Korea has made a painful, on the surface, at least, successful attempt to achieve a degree of cohesion through the forced disciplines and extreme measures of communism. In the South, some cohesion has been achieved through the armed forces created through the external factors of war and intensive American efforts. If cohesion is ever in the long run to flourish, however, it must do so through multiple power centers and decentralization that could tend toward dispersing the vortex. The creation of a pluralist society would be the most important "modernizing" step Korea could take. The rise of business and industry during the Vietnamese War period gives hope of such development.

10

Political Parties

THE NEED FOR PARTIES

The search for cohesion in 1945's formless world met little likelihood
of speedy response. With the exception of communism and the
People's Republic, soon suppressed, no organizations of permanence
and hierarchy funneled aroused public opinion into the channels of
government. Even the traditional vertical communication had been
seriously disrupted, as the October 1, 1946, rebellion demonstrated.
The swollen cities were inhabited by mass society in one of the most
aggravated forms then known to any nation. Youth groups, friendship
circles, agitational political cliques, and vast but vague "Fronts"
formed and reformed, subject to manipulation by leftists, police, gang
bosses, and ambitious landlords. Democratic institutions had no time
to take root. Manipulative autocratic control was at first the dominant
form, perhaps inevitably; history may well have to account it fortunate that, in those chaotic years, power devolved on a man of Rhee's
considerable acceptability and skill.

Autocracy could not, however, be the answer for long, though Rhee
tried until 1951 to make it so. Liberation, a diverse experience for
every nation, was for Korea the signal for political competition unusually determined and widespread. Thousands wanted to make
their way toward central power and felt more or less equally qualified
to do so. The scrambling scarcely had limits during the chaotic
period of American occupation. One-man manipulation might work

for a society less politically aroused or a country with more sub-group satisfactions, but no one leader or patron could provide suffi-cient power-access to satisfy Koreans. At the same time, council struggle was mostly an impediment to what needed doing in the country. Institutions for self-government were required. A semi-modern economy had to be reassembled along lines that would allow peaceful land reform, and the competition of communism had to be met. After decades of subjection, the national ego stood in need of repair.

The aggregates that formed in this context were called "political parties," although neither native nor foreign scholars can readily define what that means in Korea.[1] Like the characteristic entities of Korean society, parties are mostly fluid, rootless associations among opportunistic individuals. They share the molecular and the incohe-sive aspects of Korean grouping. In some respects, the result is curiously like the American party system as interpreted by Lord Bryce: "Tenets and policies, points of political doctrine and points of political practice have all but vanished . . . All has been lost, except office or the hope of it."[2] And, in fact, the lack of ideological, class, ethnic, religious, or philosophical difference between the Liberal and the Democratic parties in Korea and the Republican and Democratic parties in the U.S., with the resulting intensification of the struggle for office, certainly suggests intriguing similarities.[3] Yet, starting from societies worlds apart in the variety of intermediate organizations they support, the two party systems in the final analysis have few common bonds. Korean parties are formed as grudging and pre-carious expedients by individuals who would rather reach power by themselves. Party purpose is not rule, it is access to rule.

PARTY FORMATION

Perhaps the best established mechanism for achieving cohesion in Korea in 1945 was communism; no group rivaled the Communists in discipline and hierarchy. If not opposed by USAMGIK, the Com-munists probably would have come to dominate the Korean political scene south as well as north of the 38th Parallel. Communism is our separate concern in Chapter 11. The failure of non-Communist leftists and moderates (a far less promising source) to find cohesion has already been described, together with the causes that explain why the rightists alone ended up with the key political amalgamation in the South (see Chapter 5).

Liberation found the rightists considerably more surprised and unprepared than the Communists. A few moderate nationalist leaders, informed by clandestine radios of the march of events, had some days' forewarning of the end. Yet they possessed no operating organization. The Sin'gan-hoe movement of the early 1930's had failed, and Japanese militarist stick-and-carrot policies, besides banning political associations, had left too little non-Communist unity to maintain even a clandestine party. Organized nationalism within Korea was confined to churches, a few schools and newspapers, and, since these were largely eliminated as opposition sources by 1940, in the last years, almost entirely to friendship groups. With Liberation, churches were preoccupied with expansion, physical facilities, and social welfare; they remained important opinion-formers, but the legalization of politics absolved them of much of their 1910–1945 political role. High school and college classes were vital centers for friendship and employment and hotbeds of political thought, but violent splits between right and left precluded any widely agreed-upon stands. The police were cohesive, organized, and had political interests; but, as Liberation dawned, 60 percent of the members were repatriating to Japan, public antipathy to the Korean police's support of colonialism was high, and their political alliance with the right was not yet visible. Non-Communist Korea in 1945, with one exception, lacked candidates for political cohesion.

This exception lay in a group of landowners and their associates whose roots were in the rich, southwestern province of Chŏlla-do.[4] These men likewise shared class and, in many cases, family ties. They came from that "in-between" class in which *hyangban,* successful commoner, and *ajŏn* coalesced. It was a partly new, partly traditional group that had fattened on the agricultural development and stable rents of the Japanese years, which had been especially rewarding in Chŏlla-do. The help both wealthy and not so wealthy members of the group had given each other during the chronic crises of rural life further bound them together. Through the long days of enforced colonial rest from politics, they had visited at each other's country homes, played Korean chess together, attended each other's funerals and weddings. Theirs was a conservatism born not only of rural property but in common memory of reaction against the lower-class

Tonghak rebellion, which rose from their soil and had even killed *ajŏn* in their area. Half consciously, they saw rural Communists and the post-Liberation People's Committees around them as its heirs. Their numbers were small — a few dozen or scores of families at most. But they had wide knowledge of their districts. Their *ajŏn* relationship bound them to one of Korea's few cohesive social groups and the only one trained in the function of rural leadership.

Little of this background appeared on the surface. During Chōsen's industrial expansion successful members of the circle became identified with modern business. Several invested in the new Seoul newspapers allowed by Governor-General Saitō. Not all such investments were successful, but they brought this group to Seoul and increasingly into the orbit of nationalist politics and large enterprise. In Seoul, they became known as the Posŏng Group.

The leader and core of the group was Kim Sŏng-su (1891–1955). An early sixteenth-century ancestor of his had been an esteemed, though not high-ranking, *yangban* official, but the family had not held high office since. Descending to *hyangban* status, the Kims had made money by lending, then bought land and increased it greatly in the Japanese 1918 cadastre. The family had long enjoyed a comfortable income, but its sizable wealth is believed to date largely from after 1900. Kim Sŏng-su had been adopted by a wealthy and childless uncle, thereby minimizing the divisions of his own and his brother's inheritances. Modest and gregarious, he assembled a circle of loyal friends, helped them when needed, added younger adherents through a private scholarship program, and profited from the financial advice of his associates.[5] He and his brother, using their landed wealth, founded or strengthened in succession several of the most significant enterprises owned by Koreans during the Japanese administration: the *Tong-A Ilbo* newspaper, from 1920 until today the nation's largest and most respected Korean-language paper; Kyŏngsŏng Textile Company, founded by Kim Sŏng-su but later the domain of his brother, one of the few larger industrial enterprises in Chōsen that were Korean-owned; Posŏng High School (now Koryŏ University), founded by the flamboyant Yi Yong-ik, a Horatio Alger–like figure of the late Yi period, but endowed and expanded by the Kims and their friends; Chungang Primary and Middle Schools, then as now outstanding in Korea.

Though successful financially, these enterprises were more important for bringing together in cooperative pursuits an ever-wider circle of men of different class background and from different, mostly South Korean, areas — men loyal to Kim and, often, to each other.[6] Such unity was alien to exile groups or even Communist subversive cells, which lacked the immediate practical objectives of running enterprises and hence factionalized over small or doctrinal issues. As a friendship circle, the Posŏng Group probably outperformed all others, including the Communists, among whose leaders friendship was rare. It has now changed and its force has ebbed, but is still felt. Though less cohesive in the 1963 elections, it has been almost the only non-Communist group capable of sustaining consecutive political activity over a twenty-year period.

Yet even at its height the Posŏng Group as a basis for political action had drawbacks. It was a species of miniature private Yi Dynasty government, the various Kim institutions acting like governing councils, the men of these councils essentially equals. Kim was patron and the summit of the personal loyalty system; but he did not impose, he harmonized. Benevolent, good-humored, good-willed, exuding a myopic homeliness, Kim did his job far better than most Yi kings. His group was effective where the Yi system was not because it was not — at least until Liberation — called on for functions beyond friendship bounds and needed no strict rules or exact discipline. Its policy did not require swiftness, precision, or originality. Elaborate philosophy, dogma, the need to convince large groups were extraneous to it. Years of struggling to run institutions under Japanese domination had given it a vivid sense of the values of independence and nationalism; its social and financial background inculcated respect for conservatism, private property, and enterprise, and the nature of its organization gave it practice in the give-and-take of opinion and a distaste for the dictatorial. When Liberation propelled it into the political world, its policies came to be formed around these instincts. That land and industrial reform should be accomplished not by confiscation but with compensation to Korean owners was its policy from the start, perhaps the chief stand that gave any specific substance to the rightist label; otherwise, it advocated reform and independence much like other groups.

The landlord core of the Posŏng Group of course made it vulnerable to accusations that its chief political interests were material. In a Korea 70 percent landlord-owned, this charge could not be taken lightly. An American inquiry into conditions in Chŏlla-do (September–October 1947) revealed that 60 percent of the civil cases in one district concerned suits between owners and tenants.[7] Beleaguered by leftists before 1948, the Kim friendship circle's attitude toward the general public was hedged with defensiveness, even suspicion. The members were tempted to see Communists under every bed and to equate the public with something that should be controlled. The Korean War eliminated any overt Communist-leftist sentiment, but the Posŏng Group's minority complex remained latent behind outward assurance. Meanwhile, suspicion and tight friendship made the group slow to absorb the outside allies it needed.

Had a leftist trend with Communist backing continued, Kim Sŏng-su's group might have remained a friendship circle without chance for political sallies. Its first attempt at political organization on August 27, 1945, before the American landing, met with dissension and failure. On September 4, after hearing MacArthur's Proclamation No. 2, it held a further conference. The presence of Americans and their evident distrust of the People's Republic further emboldened it. On September 9, the day after surrender, Kim's brain-trust lieutenant, Song Chin-u, issued a statement criticizing the People's Republic.[8] Finally, on September 16, the Korean (Han'guk) Democratic party (KDP) was formally inaugurated.

That political assets so small in scale ranked so high in the Korea of 1945 is probably the most telling sign of the lack of cohesion underlying Korea's ancient unity and homogeneity and the breakup of such ancient forms of integration as she once had. The road from the Posŏng circle, however institutionally buttressed, to national political leadership was still long. It could not be taken without forceful leadership, and it could not be taken on the basis of business interests alone. Too few in the nation could conceivably identify with southwestern landlord interests of *ajŏn-hyangban* background.

The KDP had first to find leadership outside its ranks. Kim Sŏng-su was an able behind-the-scenes group leader, but he had neither the characteristics nor the desire to be a public figure. Since internal politics was dominated by Communists and leftists, and the Posŏng Group needed Independence Movement legitimacy which it did not have, its only course was to ally itself with the conservative block of the Korean Provisional Government, with which, however, it lacked close bonds. It shared the vague public hope then current that the

KPG would return as a government and that Rhee would somehow become its President. Events frustrated this hope. Rhee returned first, got the inner track, nudged KPG President Kim Ku and his circle aside, and emerged as front-runner without the exile group. Meanwhile, on December 30, 1945, the KDP's political champion, Song Chin-u, fell before an assailant suspected to come from Kim Ku's camp.[9] When returned patriot Kim Kyu-sik's USAMGIK-backed bid also failed — he was in any case too liberal for the Posŏng Group — Rhee became the only contender for alliance with the KDP and political leadership.[10]

Both Rhee and the KDP needed identity for national leadership. Neither had ideology, and Rhee had, at first, no organization, circle, or local roots. The immediate post-Liberation emphasis was on unity. Unity without any dominant group meant umbrella councils with all existing groups represented. If one came to such councils with sharp group identity, like the Communists, one negotiated on that basis. But if one came to councils or conferences without a point of view, one had to acquire *in fora* the identity one did not have. One had to make issues, even where few existed, in order to be known for a stand different from another's; oratory, contention, quarrels, fighting became the dynamics needed to establish identity. It had been so with Yi Dynasty factions, which had no more separate identity than slices of an orange. It was true again now. This situation dictated the tactics of both Rhee and the KDP.

Within a week of Rhee's landing, on October 23, a "unity" meeting took place in the Chosŏn Hotel. It was an important early step in the political amalgamation process. It resulted in a sprawling committee: the Central Council for the Rapid Realization of Korean Independence. The Communist leaders, like Pak Hŏn-yŏng, and leftists Lyuh Woon-hyung and others were absent because of the extreme anti-Russian tone of Rhee's October 20 speech, but Rhee solicited their participation through a joint statement of objectives stressing rehabilitation and early independence through U.S.-U.S.S.R. assistance, and they joined by the end of October.[11] Fifty-seven different political factions and five major parties were now tucked under the quilt. But when, in a meeting of November 2, Pak Hŏn-yŏng mildly declared that division and trusteeship were not serious problems and a resolution was issued the next day expressing gratitude to the Allies but saying that they should withdraw once a government was estab-

lished, Rhee, the KDP, and the right repudiated this stand. An issue
to establish identity was necessary, and the more inadequate the
ground, the sharper the need. The Communists then withdrew. A
few days later, Lyuh and the People's Republic group, disgruntled
at rightist actions and at their too small minority representation on
the Council, followed suit, broad-chested Lyuh stalking out at a
meeting of the newly formed executive committee. At the end of the
month, Rhee publicly voiced to leftists "the last and only chance to
reform their attitudes" by "giving up the idea of starting a so-called
communist revolution." [12] The era of blanket coalition was over, more
or less for good; but the rightists began to have a clear enemy and
sharper identity to begin building unity around. No compromise
would have provided that. Rhee's alliance with the KDP began to
solidify.

The arrival of the exile group helped at a crucial time. Kim Ku regarded Pak Hŏn-yŏng as a traitor to the Provisional Government and
aligned himself with the right. "Councils of State" began to be held,
and pamphlets listing the "Government's" fourteen points were circulated in its name. Conservatives announced a national conference
to support the Provisional Government to take place on January 10.
In this very period, USAMGIK banned the People's Republic (see
Chapter 5).

To achieve real consolidation, vague anti-leftism was not enough.
Too much identification with an unpopular foreign occupation was
also not desirable. A new issue was needed. On October 20 John
Carter Vincent, Director of the State Department's Office of Far Eastern Affairs, publicly launched the idea of an Allied trusteeship for
Korea.[13] It was the main provision of the Moscow Conference, announced December 27, in regard to Korea. The KDP, Rhee, and Kim
Ku all promptly seized opposition to this as the main plank in their
platform and formed an anti-trusteeship committee. The initial danger that the Communists would spoil rightist monopoly of this issue
by themselves condemning trusteeship was averted when, at the turn
of the year, instructions came from Moscow. (The word arrived in the
middle of a Communist anti-trusteeship demonstration, changing it
to pro-trusteeship in midstream!) The commotion over trusteeship
diverted attention from collaboration, the left's chief bullying stick,
gave those tainted with its mark a new, patriotic image, and tended
to disarm charges of subservience to USAMGIK. Since trusteeship

could be made to seem to threaten as well as delay independence itself, violence and demonstration could be launched to oppose it, fragmented anti-Communists could seek unity and coalition in it. Moderate An Chae-hong's Nationalist party expressed readiness to dissolve and form a united party under the KDP banner in early November. On December 4, nineteen small groups and "parties" joined the KDP. Provisional Government allegiance brought some forty lesser groups to the fold. On December 15, many of Korea's wealthiest men formed themselves into an Economic Contributors' Association to provide money for the Provisional Government with Rhee as agent.[14]

The amalgamation of political groups even led to a phenomenon rare in Korea: the formulation of programs. On December 21, nine days before his assassination, Song Chin-u clarified the KDP's program over the American-controlled radio station. Except for anti-trusteeship, compensation for landlord-distributed land, and less mention of collaborators and their punishment, it was a government-centered, socialist program much like that offered by any other Korean group at the time, the Communists included. Rhee's program was similar. In a broadcast on February 6, 1946, he advocated confiscation of Japanese and Korean traitor-owned lands and their redistribution to small farmers; nationalization of "all heavy industry, mines, forests"; government control of interest rates; food rationing; tax exemption for the poor; compulsory education; state control of medicine; minimum wages; social security. With respect to industry, Rhee's program was even more socialist than that advocated by Pak Hŏn-yŏng.[15] Rhee similarly pronounced advocacy of democracy, opposition to dictatorship, socialism, and communism, and even, *mirabile dictu*, support for "liberalism" and civil rights.[16] The discrepancy between his actions and his programs and beliefs interested him not in the slightest. Graduate training at Princeton under Woodrow Wilson notwithstanding, he remained throughout his life fundamentally uninterested in programs, theory, or even systems of politics.[17] Intellectually, his statements interested no one; they merely communicated singleness of purpose, hence Korean leadership that could cover many myriad groups. No Communist, let alone American, was as simplistically agile — and effective.

The rapid political aggregation of November–December 1945 had effect everywhere. At the top, Hodge felt weakened and needed a straw: his strong anti-trusteeship stand had been completely ignored by Washington and overthrown at the Moscow Conference, all without even explanation to him.[18] Below, myriad Korean friendship circles scanned the political heavens nightly to discern what rocket might take them upward. On February 14, 1946, Hodge formed the Representative Democratic Council that Rhee's circle had recommended to him as his new advisory group; he appointed Rhee its chairman. Rhee was now Hodge's chief advisor among politicians, with all the power-access this betokened. At the bottom, insouciant toward programs but sure they had found the path to power, the smaller leaders were negotiating to join the larger bandwagon and engineer consolidations themselves in order to gain more place. Independence Declaration signer Yi Kap-sŏng's new Korean Nationalist party, for example, absorbed smaller groups in December and was ready for bigger things. On February 8, Rhee formed his own cover council, the National Association for the Rapid Realization of Korean Independence (NARRKI). It was distinct from the KDP but long cooperated closely with it to gain an independent South Korea under rightist rule.[19]

Like all previous Korean political organizations except the Tonghak, NARRKI and the KDP were formed from the top down. NARRKI now sought local roots. In February and March of 1946, Rhee conducted a highly successful six-week barnstorming trip through South Korea's rural counties. Here his decision to ally himself with the KDP paid dividends: police and rightist youth groups associated with the KDP and landlord interests did their job well to prepare a good reception. The right for the first time began to have impressive national consolidation and feel under it the local roots that had heretofore belonged to the People's Republic alone. In the next two years, this strength enabled Rhee and the right to resist and outlive American support for the fragile moderate coalition and, in 1946 and 1947, to organize an ultimately successful campaign against the continuation of American military occupation and for the establishment of an independent South Korean government. Except for the great rise in police power and its fervency in the rightist cause following the October 1 riots, Rhee's political base was now essentially formed.

By October 1946, NARRKI claimed a nominal membership of seven million. It outstripped the Provisional Government. It and the

KDP were the chief organizations bringing Rhee to power. Independence achieved, its name was changed to the National Society in August 1948, and, as such, it survived until the overthrow of the Rhee regime in 1960. It is the ancestor of the Liberal party and a kind of stepfather of the Democratic Republican party of the mid-1960's. As such, it warrants examination.

NARRKI was the incarnation of Rhee's ideal of a patriotic society, mystically united, with which he could manipulate a mass society without the interference of interest groups. Its ideas were limited to the vaguest anti-communism and "unity." Other issues were all occasional, mostly negative, and concerned only capital politics: anti-trusteeship, the Cold War, anti–Joint Commission, "recall" of recalcitrant assemblymen, and the like. Rhee, not really wanting NARRKI to be a party, did not permit its leaders to stand for election in the name of the organization. Formed at the top as a leadership faction with local roots as an afterthought, it reflected the society's high degree of centralization and extreme lack of local sources of power. It used the KDP's *ajŏn*-inherited network, but its contrast with the strong local cells of Korean rural communism or the immediate, spontaneous participation of local elements in the formation of the People's Republic was sharp. It had no programs, ideology, or vested interests of its own, nor did it represent or encourage local ones. Its leader was a man who wanted to command, not be told. It was a confederation of personal followings motivated at the top by the subleader's desire for position and at the bottom by the local man's desire to climb the ladder to the capital. Yet it was too vaguely organized and general in its relationship to Rhee to provide any more definite access to power than his whim dictated. Despite its history of fourteen years, the National Society was no closer to real political rootage at the end of its history than at its beginning. Like its predecessor, the Ilchin-hoe, and its successor, the Liberal party, it vanished overnight, hardly with trace or mention, when the apex power on which it had depended was no longer there to legitimize its followers and activate its leaders.

In 1946, a Korean leader interested in constructing a party supporting him in the coming assemblies and serving as a regular recruitment channel could have forged the nation's abundant talent into a strong institution. There was pressure on Rhee to that end. Such a step would, however, have been an innovation; society was too atomistic to produce cohesive parties on its own initiative. And Rhee was not an innovator. He wanted to rule by opposing interest-group formation essentially as Korean councils had always ruled. So he let things rest with his National Society and would not have further allowed or encouraged political aggregation had war and opposition, in 1951–1952, not forced it on him.

His anti-party rationale was expressed in the only philosophy, the only approach at ideology to come from him or his circle. Expressive at once of himself and of the mass society over which he presided, *Il Min Chu I*, or "One People Principle," was formulated by him and one of his chief political lieutenants during the 1946–1947 period. It was populism, simple and unadorned. Its corny name was taken from Sun Yat-sen's *San Min Chu I*, and it posited a "will of the people" that incarnated the national will. The nation's weakness was ascribed to "individual attitudes asserting special interests." "Our supreme objective is to carry on our affairs by sacrificing everything and uniting into one." [20] Special interests were said to deny the true soul of the nation, transmitted through heredity, which longed for unity of action and will. The aim of leadership was to nourish, embody, express, and execute the national consciousness and will. Rhee even went so far as to advocate equality between the sexes and the elimination of class distinctions in the name of this simplistic, mystical "national unity." [21] *Il Min Chu I* was briefly promoted in pamphlets distributed to NARRKI's local branches, and Rhee referred to it in speeches.[22] With the coming of comparative unity under Rhee in 1948, however, it was for the most part discarded.[23] This ineffective and poorly disseminated "philosophy" never mobilized the population. Hardly more than a handful of people around Rhee seem ever to have believed in it; it was the mockery of most intellectuals.

Like Sun Yat-sen's *San Min Chu I*, Rhee's *Il Min Chu I* lacked any program implementation. It was the vehicle of a charismatic leader calling for simple-minded faith. It specifically left its leader free to concentrate attention on remoter objects like Japan, North Korea, and international conspiracies, rather than on living conditions and daily repressions at home. It embodied the worst features of the Korean pattern: complete centralization of power, resistance to vested and class interests that might enrich the society, preference for "patriotism" or vague moral qualities rather than expertise and experience, for acts performed with moral motives rather than rational system.[24] In short, regardless of how shallowly Rhee and his followers planted it in Korea, *Il Min Chu I* fitted a mass society.

It thus revealed the ideological poverty of the nation over which Rhee presided, a poverty made harder to bear in light of the intellectual substance the traditional society once had. Even in anti-Communist South Korea, *Il Min Chu I*'s contrast with Marxism was striking. In a nation of Confucian background, absence of a moral motivation that men could take seriously undermined pride and responsible participation. Constant repetition of the words "patriotism" and "sacrifice" without ideology induced cynicism and continued the habits of evasion resorted to under colonialism. Austerity drives and even simple savings plans foundered on this same reef. Communism found in South Korea no doctrinal rivals, a partly-outworn Confucianism no replacement. In Korea, as in Taiwan, Japan, and Vietnam, politics and society still suffer in much these same terms from the absence of ideological power to evoke participation in politics.[25]

In the practice of state affairs, the absence of ideology and definition broadened powers of personal leadership already unrestrained by constitution or law. Rhee was his own legitimacy; only through him was unity conceivable. Any concept of sharing of powers was alien to his view of the state, honest or loyal opposition incomprehensible. Persons or groups, including the National Assembly, who expressed views or attempted to legislate programs contrary to "the popular will" were branded as "self-seeking plotters," "usurpers of the people's rights," those who "have not learned the lesson of subordinating parts to the greater whole," and of course "Communists." [26] It was this concept of national sovereignty that Rhee used in all his major battles, particularly with the National Assembly, that was a leitmotif of the trials under which he tried its members, and that led to his advocacy of referendum to settle disputes and of popular election of the President in the 1951–1952 political crisis. It was his only ideological weapon in crushing any attempts at alternate leadership. During the Rhee age, Rhee was the state.

ELECTIONS AND FLUIDITY

It was the mark of the fitness of Rhee's views to his society that the Korean rural population essentially agreed with him.[27] The popular vote exerted little pressure toward political aggregation in the early post-Liberation years.

The reason lay in a non-Western conception of representation. Centralized society had accustomed the local landlord, whether *hyangban* or, later, *ajŏn* or rural capitalist, to going to Seoul to argue for better local administration, storage of grain, roads, and prices. There was no institutionalized means of controlling his opinion, but the practice of fairly fluid class boundaries in the *hyangban* stratum made him accessible, and the farmer gladly served a landlord who could ably speak in the capital for local benefits. With some frequency such men or their descendants were in fact selected as assemblymen from 1946 on, especially where land holdings were large, as in Chŏlla-do. No concept of voting for a man as a member of a group existed, however. In a homogeneous country, localities shared most problems, but there was no traditional organization like the local overlord, the fief, or the castle town that provided local loyalty or group traditions. Nor were there local religions, ethnic groups, or business interests of broad common interest.

The value system, indeed, imposed obstacles to group formation. In court society, groupings and factions were derogated politically by Confucianism as bands of "self-seekers." Tight organization outside the family had lower-class connotations of "gang" or outcast village. Such interest groups as existed — fishermen in ports, peddlers in market towns, artisans such as the bamboo-weavers in Tamyang — tended to fall under these categories. The concept of an interest or pressure group purposing to accomplish general social good was virtually unknown. Language emphasized this feeling. Koreans use behind-the-back low talk to describe members of functional occupations like peddlers, *ajŏn,* monks, soldiers, police, fishermen, and weavers — their words derogating both specialization and interest-group aspects and connoting ganging up to take advantage of others, sometimes even stealing, preying on, or cheating.

Social good supposedly derived from the example of the virtuous individual. Most honored was the learned and exemplary men who kept his skirts clean in "retirement" and participated politically by refusing appointment and voicing a "grass-roof protest." Transferred to modern elections, this meant that one usually did not elect the most admired exemplar to the hurly-burly of democratic politics (he probably would not run) but kept him in a kind of treasured reserve.

One also did not elect the *yangban* as such, since his values did not fit elections. On the other extreme, one did not, in the early years, elect a group or party member, since this was "gangism." One actually elected a kind of middle person but nevertheless one who received his qualification as an individual, not a group member, usually as a result of previous participation in some form in public life: a former county chief, police chief, clerk, independence leader, official, active local landlord. Bearing such status with "dignity" was the local form of being a "great man" for political purposes, and "great men" did not form gangs. They maintained their "cleanness" and "sincerity," and guarded their integrity by not consorting with others. In addition, status accreted within a party would tend to give one "great man" an unfairly great chance at power. There were usually several, more or less equally qualified. It was fairer to change one's "great man." [28] The patterns dominant in most rural areas hence were more adverse than helpful to party development.

Candidacy in the beginning was decided not by parties but by individual application. There were no primaries. Parties could not, in early elections, repudiate those individually registering as their candidates or conversely even force their own candidates to declare party affiliation. Few, perhaps hardly more than 5 percent of the electorate, voted on the basis of party or affiliation in the 1948 and 1950 elections.[29] Nearly half the members of the first National Assembly, 85 (by some other calculations 102), were independent, and 55 more were semi-independent, belonging to the National Society, which did not nominate candidates officially.[30] Some 29 others belonged to the Korean Democratic party, 19 to various youth corps.

Parties became important only in Seoul. None had programs or ideas of substantial difference, but voting for a bill was quite different from voting for a candidate; with the former, consensus increased power, and membership in a group maximized one's chance of power access, either by joining the government and being rewarded with a ministry for oneself or one's friend or by joining the opposition and improving chances of capturing the government citadel and rewarding followers wholesale. Hence, between the 1948 and 1950 elections, many independents gathered themselves into the Korean Democratic party, which rose from 29 assemblymen to 68 by May 1950. Even more — often over 70 — joined a fairly nebulous new Korean Nationalist party headed by the Assembly Speaker, Shin

Ik-hŭi. By the end of the first Assembly, the 102-odd independents
had dropped to 29. Parties hence originated in the capital as factions
providing alternate — and opportunistically shifting — ladders to executive power, not as bodies concerned with separate legislative
function. They had no local functions, and, by the same token,
localities had few local demands to make on them or expectations to
communicate to them.

The elections of 1950 reiterated the voter's preference for non-
affiliation. In this election, many prominent moderates who had boy-
cotted the 1948 elections became candidates, mostly as independents.
Almost all were elected, despite intimidation by the police and arrests
of both candidates and their campaigners.[31] The election clearly
showed the unpopularity of most of the candidates who had aligned
themselves either with the government or with the Korean Democratic party. The latter fell, according to Assembly reports, from
68 assemblymen to 24 (other sources give 15). The National Society
fell to 14, the pro-administration Ilmin Club to 3. The Korean Nationalist party fell from 71 to 24. Independents increased to 126,
60 percent of the Assembly. Only 31 assemblymen were re-elected.
Again, when members reached Seoul, party designations increased.
Those usually voting with the administration reached 65. In 1951–
1952, KDP and other opposition members reached a majority of the
210 members. From December 1951 on, the Liberal party was formed
and rose. At the end of the Assembly session in 1954, independents
had dropped by more than half to 60; 99 were members of the government Liberal party, 20 members of the Democrats, and 27 taken
by the Communist invaders to North Korea. Korea's early Assembly
experience showed that parties were formed in the capital and
eroded by the rural voter.

The "merging, not accommodation" characterizing Korean parties
connotes their function as channels of access to power for the elected
individual. Since there is little advantage to standing for office as a
member of a group and since grouping as a function has long enjoyed
low Korean prestige, politicians lack group morale or cogent reasons
for remaining united. The politician feels free to shift allegiance as
he views his chances for access to power altering. There are no local
brakes on such transfer of allegiance, since parties have so little local
function or meaning. The internal walls of parties are thus weak;
condemnation of the "betrayal" of the group by the individual or of

its rupture by splits lacks force. The myriad schisms of the post-Liberation period thus continued in the Assembly. Soon after the 1948 elections, thirty members of the National Society shifted into a new pro-administration group called the Ilmin Club. Hardly had the new Korean Nationalist party been formed in late 1948 when one section split away to join the KDP. In 1962 "inside" Liberals crossed over and became "outside" Liberals. Even after a two-party system became established, Democrats and Liberals defected to each other. After 1954, the scale of party border-crossings diminished, but it remained a powerful force both inside and outside the Assembly so long as freedom to change allegiance remained. It was, indeed, so extreme as to inspire legal action against it. Before the election of 1963, to dampen "political confusion" the military government wrote into its National Assembly Law a prohibition on changing of party affiliation within the National Assembly. However inappropriate legal action may be for a malfunction basically socio-political, the law tacitly recognized that Korean parties had been better fitted for the shifting nature of factional fights, for a society of social mergings, than for the forwarding of principles or programs.

Even when they had legitimate vested interests, the reluctance of Korean parties to incorporate them as the basis for action has been astonishingly characteristic. The Democrats had a group interest in preventing confiscatory land reform. When they were strong and influential, the Assembly on June 21, 1949, forwarded, with little Democratic dissent, a land-reform bill the President himself considered too inequitable to landowners and vetoed. One somewhat more favorable to landowners was eventually passed and signed on March 25, 1950. Meanwhile, it was the show of power between the President and the Assembly — in vetoing or overriding the veto — that interested the KDP, not the question of the vested interest of their members. Similarly, leniency toward collaborators might have been considered a legitimate Democratic party political interest.[32] Yet it was the President who defied the Assembly in insisting on this leniency in the spring of 1949. The only "interest" that Democratic assemblymen or any others would fight for had to do with their own power: such matters as the implementation of bills duly passed or the operation of the parliamentary system in their favor. One is hard put to cite, in all the fourteen years of Assembly history, instances in which a party with particularistic interests was willing to stand and make an issue of them. Local landlord or class ties were kept almost secret, used only to structure informal agreements, aid the introduction of a new recruit, or spice with intimacy the flavor of social gatherings. They were not the objects of party policy or the *raison d'être* of party existence.

Even if one makes allowance for the fact that colonialism tended to undermine the legitimacy of vested interests and thus encouraged public figures not to stand on unpopular questions, it is still significant that Korean society always seems to have expected retreat on such issues. German society would not have expected the same of her Buddenbrooks, nor Britain of her mercantile interests, nor the Continental Congress of the merchants of Philadelphia or Boston. Such important political phenomena go down to important springs in each culture. In Korea, vested interests in property, in traditional sources of wealth and income, were weak, ill-defined, subject constantly to the fluctuations of central power and to the forces of the vortex updraft leading to it. They were like stunted bushes clinging to a canyon wall, not like the luxuriant deep-rooted trees that European and American culture could plant in the ground of its mercantile societies. Under such circumstances, they could acquire little of that assertive pride and confidence in rights that inspired property-holders in mercantile European or American society. Even the phrase "vested interest" has, in Korean, a borrowed, untranslatable cast. Property and rights to it share the fluidity of the society. Grouping for the purpose of promoting property rights tends to make a party ineligible for sustained popular support in much the same way that solidification of functional-class groups made the latter ineligible for mobility and limited their influence in Yi Dynasty culture. Yet this lack of vested interests condemns Korean political parties to transiency.

THE COHESION OF STRUGGLE

Political cohesion of a temporary kind was nevertheless achieved. Its outward form was even impressive. It came not as a result of increasing vested interests but through the completely internal process of rising power struggle within the vortex. Cohesion thus became a function of access-mobility pressures, the very factor that, at more normal intensity, produced atomization. The most massive war in

Korea's history flowed over and around it, but political aggregation was self-induced, not war-created.

An initial type of cohesion clearly was forming even before the Korean War began. The Democrats had supported Rhee into the Presidency. They expected to be rewarded; indeed, they expected to rule in a cabinet-council system with him playing the role of Yi monarch. They lost when Rhee insisted on the Presidential system. They then expected association in rule through important appointments to the government. In this he also disappointed them. When Rhee formed his first cabinet, Kim Sŏng-su was given no post, and only members on the KDP tangent, like Foreign Minister Chang T'aik-sang, were rewarded. Power appeared to go elsewhere to the strong-arm youth corps groups under Prime Minister Yi Pŏm-sŏk; this group controlled the Defense and Home Ministries as well as the Prime Minister's post. Rhee said little; he simply did not want to share power with a cohesive group rooted deeper than he was. He kept most Democrats out of key positions and sent the KDP police director of USAMGIK, Cho Pyŏng-ok, out of the country as an ambassador.

The Democrats considered themselves betrayed. Their organ, *Tong-A Ilbo*, voiced their complaint (see Chapter 6). Blocked in seeking bureaucratic position, they sought power through the Assembly, revived their policy of amending the constitution to provide a cabinet-responsible system, absorbed new members to their cause, and moved, from late 1948 on, steadily toward becoming the Republic's first opposition party. In the KDP convention of October 21, 1949, they revised party programs and platforms toward this end. At first, the issue of parliamentary power lacked wide public appeal, but it had power to attract assemblymen, and it soon began to get urban support as an "anti-dictatorship" issue. As Rhee fought the Assembly on popular issues like punishing collaborators, land reform, local autonomy, and retaliations following the Yŏsu rebellion, both sources of support began to increase. In February 1949, Speaker Shin led a large part of his seventy-member confederation of minor politicians, the Korean Nationalist party, into the KDP which, now renamed the Democratic Nationalist party (DNP), became the first Korean group formed with the explicit purpose of being an opposition party. Although its own formal ranks thinned in the elections of May 1950, it had excellent chances for increasing them through the many newly-elected opposition independents. Until 1952, it remained the strongest, most cohesive, and stable political force in the Republic. In the six days of meetings before the second Assembly had to flee the Communist invasion of June 25, 1950, the DNP and its allies were already taking steps to reintroduce their constitutional amendment. War discontent bid fair to strengthen their hand.

The prewar period also saw the beginnings of political amalgamation on the government side. In 1949, Rhee ordered all youth groups combined into the Taehan Youth Corps, all unions into the Korean Federation of Trade Unions. These steps were probably motivated by desire for improved control. They led directly into party politics in 1951, when both organizations were used as foundations for the Liberal party. Meanwhile, Rhee moved quietly to give support to that portion of the Korean Nationalist party that had not moved with Speaker Shin into opposition. This rump group remained the largest in the Assembly until the 1950 elections and tied with the KDP in electing, with some government support, twenty-four members in May 1950. It played a key role on March 14, 1950, in the defeat of the first constitutional amendments for a cabinet-responsible system, was active in purging Democratic associates from the police, encouraged some forays into political interference, and instituted the so-called Political Action Corps scandal to discredit some of its opponents as Communists.[33] Party amalgamation was rather rudimentary; the Nationalists' resort to force and plot was a transparent substitute for cohesiveness. Nevertheless, amalgamation and political escalation had progressed.

The Korean War had surprisingly few immediate basic political effects. The enhanced political position of a swollen army lay a decade ahead. Communist invasion and occupation eliminated leftists, heightened anti-Communist feeling, and further weakened the independence of businessmen and the middle class, but the pattern of political struggle and its objectives remained unchanged and even its course largely unbroken. That an immensely destructive war, raging over three fourths of the country, altered so little Korea's political pattern demonstrates how deeply it is engrained.

War did, however, quicken and intensify political development. The headlong abandonment of Seoul, revenge consequent on its recapture, military reverses, spiraling inflation and corruption, and the outbreak of crime and scandal along the fringes of the military added fire to opposition determination and opened prospects of increased popular support. Until the middle of 1951, the President had hoped to regard the DNP as a disgruntled partner in a kind of coalition government. He had even appointed several of its associates to ministerial posts. After the extreme disclosures and criticism of the Defense Corps and Kŏch'ang incidents and the election of Kim Sŏng-su as Vice-President, however, they were dismissed (see Chapter 6). A purge of other Democrats began, and a state of hostile confrontation became recognized.[34] On August 15, 1951, Rhee declared political war to emasculate the Assembly's power over the executive. He announced his intention of proposing a constitutional amendment for direct, popular election of the President and another for the formation of a bicameral legislature.[35] To obtain these, he knew, would involve struggle requiring more organized political force than he had: a political party. On August 15, 1961, he announced in a public speech:

> One more thing I should like to say. Thus far it has not seemed wise to form any political parties, for our people had to have time to learn that political parties should stand for great principles and not simply form organizations to grab power by fair means or foul. But the time has come when we must organize a national party based upon farmers and laborers who will band together to protect their own interests and the real interests of our nation. The great masses of our people do not own newspapers or maintain public spokesmen. Their wishes are often ignored and sometimes forgotten.[36]

This party, he added on August 25 in *Il Min Chu I* accents would "hold the national weal as its supreme objective free from partisanship." One-party rule was clearly ahead, but at least a party had been forced on the suprapartisan President.

Once started, its growth was predictably sensational. It had ready-made government channels. For five months all announcements concerning it emanated from the government's Office of Public Information, and police communications facilities were available for its more urgent business. Beginning with a directive of April 1952, the police were ordered "to investigate severely" all political opponents. Above all, Rhee's party had ready-made organization: the National Society, the Taihan Youth Corps, the Taihan Women's Association and the

Federation of Korean Trade Unions, although founded on a supra-partisan basis, quickly turned themselves into supporters and, while remaining legally separate, used their friendship circles to create intertwining parallel hierarchies throughout the country.[37] Local branches flourished overnight, glad to make their members eligible for higher office by campaigning in favor of the President's new amendments, demonstrating, and in some cases terrorizing potential opponents. In organization and partly in spirit, the new party's tactics reminded many of Chōsen's patriotic organizations mobilizing Koreans to win for Japan in World War II.

For a while, such tactics also built up opposition. Pro-government assemblymen formed their own party rather than join one committed to oppose Assembly power. Some joined the opposition because of objection on principle to the methods employed. Even Rhee supporters joined in defeating his amendments 143 to 19 on January 18, 1952. Mass demonstration, terror, and finally martial law and arrests forced Rhee's desperate opponents to appeal to army leaders for a coup and to the Americans for support for "democracy." Universities, in Pusan exile from their Seoul campuses and drained by the draft, were too weak for a stand in the army-dominated milieu. There were no other forces to turn to. The populace disliked the struggle but was distracted by the war and could not stand against all the forces of a war-armed and foreign-backed government. On July 4, 1952, arrested opposition assemblymen who had threatened to block Rhee's re-election were marched to the hall so that they could join with their colleagues in obediently voting for the President's amendments ending most of the legislature's power.

The Liberal Party

The Liberal Party, inaugurated on December 23, 1951, was the image of *Il Min Chu I* and the undifferentiated society. As a state party, it also bore much resemblance to the Republican People's party of Turkey and to the Partido Revolucionario Institucional of Mexico, though it lacked even the façade of revolution. Its enormous hierarchy of council clubs drew membership from every cranny of mass society. In its leadership mingled *yangban* like Yi Ki-bung, *ajŏn* descendants, Japanese bureaucrats of every origin, and the lowest commoners, like the notorious Yi Yŏng-bŏm.[38] There was no orderly recruitment; few leaders were even chosen from the ladders of the national organizations. Regionally, the party included pieces of almost everything except the Chŏlla-do and P'yŏngan-do middle-class groups belonging to the Democrats. If any group typified the inner circle, it was of former officials, central or local, of the Japanese regime, not so high-ranking as to be termed collaborators nor so low as to be excused from any colonial disobedience. They had the instincts of minor functionaries called to control: cautious and lacking in initiative in every respect except deference to authority and guardianship against enemies; in such matters, endlessly watchful and solicitous. Even they did not form a lodestar. The party was at all levels a rootless and patternless mingling of social, regional, and associational groups and individuals on which naked authority alone was likely to impose order. Belief and ideology were, of course, not present to play a binding role. The party expressed only a Perónist-like reiteration of faith in Syngman Rhee.

To the internal requirement of blind loyalty was added the explicit external function of defending the executive from opposition, from public discontent, and from the aggregation of any interests in the body politic. No loose confederation of leaders and cliques could suffice to shield a government beset by war and chronic economic crises in a milieu rich in corruption and opportunism. A tighter organization therefore evolved, a vast hierarchy of councils and control bodies. But this elaborate structure lacked a new or modernized function. It had the traditional ones of watchfulness and control. Its means and actions were thus also retrospective, impelling it backward into the traditional *modi operandi* of the Korean council past: its vast hierarchy became a sieve through which a society lacking vested interest and professional ranks could be swept in and out of position and thus manipulated and controlled.

For seven years these attributes worked effectively. In 1954, the Liberals became the first party in Korean history to receive an absolute majority, 114 representatives out of 203. In 1958, this majority edged up to 126. The Liberal faithful were supplemented by enlisting additional members from the ranks of independents, who, as two-party rule rose, dwindled from their majority in the first elections to 68 in 1954 and 27 in 1958. The rarer independents became, the higher was the price of their sale. The Democrats, reduced in the 1954 elections to 15, were almost eliminated as serious political contenders from 1952 to 1955. The one-party system took hold. Even thereafter, until the revolution of 1960, Liberal dominance was politically assured. The party's chairman became the Assembly's speaker. Strife with the executive ended. Until 1958, party and Assembly almost seemed to merge; both were consolidated as the political arm of the executive. This was control of a closeness and thoroughness then unknown to an independent Korea, whether since Liberation or before Annexation.

Liberal organization was impressive, but the party did not employ this structure for communication, policy-making, and debate (see Chapter 9). It was always a control mechanism, established to monopolize the political powers of the state.[39] Under its moderate leader, Yi Ki-bung, primarily political means to this end were preferred. But the function also demanded non-political force in case political means failed. Such force the Liberal party, from its violent birth, carried always within its structure: a series of strong-armed gangs, toughs, and bosses, direct or collateral descendants of the youth groups unleashed in 1952.[40] Behind its candidates at the polls stood the police, and the locking of the opposition in the Assembly basement on December 24, 1958, showed that they stood behind its representatives even on the floor of the Assembly. In the Liberal party, Japanese-type controls were wedded to Yi council function. When force was not used, political corruption won.[41] Democratic representation dried up or devolved on the weak opposition.

At the bottom, even in the villages, there had been hope that a politically oriented and increasingly literate public would begin to create from the successful formality of elections real channels of communication for their feelings and grievances. The delay of reform, the wake of war, and the opportunities of reconstruction made such communication urgent. Some participation took place through lower channels of the Liberal party's large hierarchy; the village roots were weak, however. There, the police were strong. They now had access to higher power through former policemen, like Han Hŭi-sŏk, sympathetic to their interests and high in Liberal councils. Increasingly, they substituted for political communication. Villages in the last two years were often made to vote in groups under the suitable guidance of a police-supervised "group leadership" system. In 1960, police-encouraged patriotic armbands were widely worn to the polls as a sign of allegiance. Wholesale ballot-stuffing and the arrest or intimidation of opposition campaigners grew. On the one hand, this made official Liberal candidacy so valuable that party discipline could be exacted in return. On the other, the emptiness and cynicism of voting and "representation" were now the chief qualities communicated to the villagers. Voting had had only two full elections to put down roots before the Liberal party age. Through 1967 elections directed by police or adjuncts to them constituted the dominant voting experience. Democratic expression, which many hoped might gain slowly even in the villages, suffered a blight from which it has yet to recover.

The blocking of local administration also reduced political communication.[42] American Military Government had been too weak and irresolute to implement its own local-election ordinance. Rhee now strongly resisted developing local administration on grounds that it might become too independent. He returned the local-autonomy bill passed by the Assembly in 1949 an unprecedented three times, two returns being clearly unconstitutional. War caused further delay. When elections were held in 1952 and again in 1956, national organizations could easily apply official pressure on lower levels, and Liberal party officials were overwhelmingly returned. For a while, the party tried to push local elections, confident of their control. It also passed legislation establishing local agricultural banks and cooperatives. Rhee constantly told his ministers, however, that he could not trust "dishonest politicians" who would use such institutions to "sew up" local districts and come to power — independently of his favor.[43] Some agricultural banks were eventually established, but, until the last day of the regime, no cooperatives. As the unpopularity of the Liberal party grew, it came to share the President's views. In the December 24, 1958, incident it railroaded through an emasculation of the local-autonomy law whereby mayors and other local officials were to be appointed rather than elected. Liberals immediately used the occasion to remove from office all opposition block chiefs in Seoul.[44] Again, there was to be control, not communication or new participation or interest-group formation. Political cohesion had taken form, but the form was frozen.

The Assembly itself froze. The opposition alone used it significantly as a sounding board for complaint and occasional sponsor of "emergency resolutions." Effective action was limited largely to fairly revealing annual inspections of the executive and, under Yi Ki-bung's moderate influence, compromise on some bills like the election law. The Liberal party preferred the controlled channels of its own organization and of the police to Assembly debate. Laws were drafted largely by the executive and passed with little change. The influence party representatives had, the satisfactions they derived, stemmed not from the Assembly but from their influence on the bureaucracy — the local projects they could wheedle from the national budget, the applicants they could place, the business or other favors they could grant. If the executive, as happened with agricultural cooperative legislation, did not concur with the Assembly, the Liberal party had to be loyal and back down. The function of assemblymen shriveled. Fifty of the party's so-called "built-in voting machines" gave not a single speech in two years following their election in 1954. Parliamentary debate dropped far behind the press as a channel of popular communication or effective democratic instrument. The December 24, 1958, railroading through of twenty-two important laws in one sitting was the logical climax. That the Assembly has, persisting into 1968, become a listless body of semi-executive functionaries is largely the outcome of its Liberal party transformation into a subordinate council rather than a democratic body. To this basic pattern, in even more extreme form, the military regime's semi-civilian successors have returned.

Finally, the merging of executive and legislative power had the effect of inoculating the bureaucracy against criticism and change, corrupting it, and thus destroying its reputation with the people. As the President aged, the party increasingly took on his recruiting functions and, in the last years, succeeded in appointing and keeping key members in office. This improved bureaucratic stability encouraged a trend toward specialization, especially in the economic areas, and gave promise of forming an elite.[45] In general, however, the party pressured the bureaucracy chiefly for placement and money, and its presence sheltered the government in such a way that the great talent available in party ranks simply stagnated.[46] There was, until the last two years, no long-range planning. Old faults became ingrained, and corruption spread and deepened everywhere.[47] Like the jealous civilian officials of Yi times, those of the Liberal party produced outer stability at the cost of too sedulously protecting the institutions of the state. In a period of dangerous political disintegration, this historically repetitive effort was natural. Its ultimate effect, however, was to fan the winds of vortex to a force that homogeneous society could summon no powers peacefully to referee or control. This vortex drained attention from the countryside and reinforced the culture's concentration on capital politics to the detriment of economic and social development. It thus created ever larger grievances.

The Later Democratic Party

The Democratic party incorporated fewer traditional aspects than its Liberal antagonist. Its role was newer. As an opposition party in a classless society it had no alternative but to communicate instead of control and to do this by the instruments of politics instead of force. It faced the problem of maintaining unity against government persecution and yet accomplishing this by democratic, voluntary, associational means.

The Democrats reached their nadir in 1952, defenseless against force and mass movement, the 1951–1952 chances for parliamentary government gone. Surveillance developed such wartime severities that the party had to initiate a three-level system of overt, confidential, and covert membership. Its leaders were harassed. Cho Pyŏng-ok, for example, was arrested in 1953 for supporting the American armistice stand, and his house was vandalized by thugs. The old Democratic leader, retired Vice-President Kim Sŏng-su, paralyzed and dying slowly in Taegu, said despondently to American visitors: "All Americans claim they deplore, and yet you do nothing about it. People in Korea and the rest of Asia are now convinced that what you want here is dictatorship, and you have given no indication to the contrary." [48] Before the end of the second Assembly in May 1954, Democratic Nationalist assemblymen had fallen from forty to twenty, their non-party allies also gone.

Violence against opposition and autocratic control did bring eventual allies and cohesion, however, just as they had after Yŏsu and the Assembly arrests of 1948–1949. The first allies to join were large numbers of men from the provinces of P'yŏngan in the northeast under the leadership of Chang Myŏn.[49] Their northern background had given them unusual sources of cohesion. They were not used to deserting their region for the capital, since there had been few officials from the province and very few *ch'ŏnmin*. Favorable location along the trade routes to the continent and the stimulus of discrimination within the Yi system had given them ambition, better distribution of wealth, and exceptional stimulus for economic progress, modernization, and change — hence for education and Christianity. Missionaries had found in this province one of the single richest opportunities for propagation anywhere in the world. Through them, the P'yŏngan middle class of the province developed the closest educational ties with the United States, the greatest entrée to democracy and its ideals of any Korean group. Such P'yŏngan men had had their own independence leader, An Ch'ang-ho, and had been bound with him in a cultural group, the Hŭngsa-dan (Young Korea Academy), seeking to inculcate the ideals of independence. An and Rhee had complex exile roots of antagonism. Hostility had increased when the American Military Government, which utilized many Hŭngsa-dan men, parted ways with Rhee. The feud was continued by Rhee, who followed his ancestors' policy of appointing few men from the north. The group, joining the Democrats from 1952 on, was a natural antagonist to Rhee, his methods, and his control of the channels to power.

The two opposition groups were not, however, entirely compatible allies. The P'yŏngan group and the Chŏlla-do "old" Democrats (now known as the "old faction" as opposed to the "new faction" of Chang Myŏn) had little in common except antagonism to Rhee, desire to have a cabinet-responsible form of government, and certain prejudices in favor of the encouragement of private property and laissez faire. In religion, in ties with the Independence Movement, in class, in occupations and sources of wealth, in region of origin, in ties with the United States, they were widely diverse, even antagonistic.[50] Crisis and persecution kept them together for years. But when power came to them, they split almost immediately, in a form sufficiently deep and enduring to undermine their own government and cause the defeat of civilian rule in the 1963 elections.

Though semi-separate entities, they were, each group within itself, islands of political cohesion, lodestars for the other leaders and nuclear groups that gradually joined. Except to bridge the two groups, they needed less than the Liberals emphatic strictness of organization and fanatic exhortations to loyalty. Democratic policy was not dictated by any single leader: hierarchy did not enforce obedience. Policy was decided in conference with lengthy give and take. On the one hand, this made for delay and for continual struggle over the awarding of positions among "old" and "new" factions, sometimes, as in 1954, so severe as to hinder the party from getting even such committee chairmanships within the Assembly as it might have received. On the other hand, "equal voice in council" also had its attractiveness and drew to it men of strong opinion, able and persuasive in debate. Lawyers found here a fitting milieu and remained an occupational group generally close to the party. On the whole, compromise was developed, the November 1953 convention being marked by this quality and starting the party back to influence from the depths of its 1952 defeats.

More than the attractions of democracy, the chief consolidating force for the Democrats lay in the continued repressive or extra-legal tactics of the Liberals. On September 6, 1954, the Liberal Assembly vice-chairman announced the defeat of the second Presidential amendment by a vote of 135 out of 203, 136 being the two thirds needed. When the Assembly reconvened, it was declared that the amendments had passed, 135 being counted two thirds by rounding to the nearest decimal place.[51] Enraged, the Democrats walked out. All but one independent now joined them against the government. When they returned, they soon gathered under the banner of a new negotiating group, the Comrades Association to Safeguard the Constitution (CASC), formed in December 1954 with some sixty members and much public and press sympathy.

This impetus led to plans for the formation of a new opposition party to unite all non-leftist opposition elements. Severe democratic difficulties impeded progress toward this goal. The DNP and the alliance-tending North Korean refugee Chosŏn Democratic party were both split into pro-amalgamation and anti-federation factions. There was continual disagreement on whether to admit Cho Pongam's Socialists. Formation of the party preparation committee was painful initially and produced subsequent defections. This time Rhee did not provide the impetus of oppression but cagily waited for opposition efforts to fall apart. In May, a second nine-man committee had to be formed to organize politicians outside the Assembly, and soon it too had to be revamped. The courting of the new U.S. ambassador by some members of the committee led to further troubles.[52] In June, the group moved toward appointing advisors. In July, a two-hundred-member preparatory committee met for additional recruitment, drafting, and compromises so that the maximum number of leaders and factions could be included with a minimum of hurt feelings. Even so, twenty-eight of the original sixty-one Assembly members of the original CASC left the party before its September inauguration. Democracy, in stressing "equalities," added to the factional pains of a culture that had lost its social criteria but not its ambitions for place in council.[53]

After many postponements, the new Democratic party, third of its line, was inaugurated, September 19–20, 1955. True to its semi-coalition character, it was headed by a five-man Supreme Committee with a larger Standing Committee under it. Its structural hierarchy, otherwise not unlike the Liberal party's, was based on a "core unit," a kind of cell with not less than twenty members. This unit, lacking reliance on the police, was perhaps somewhat stronger than the Liberal cell, but it remained essentially weak compared with the Communist cell of 1945.

In the middle levels of the society, however, the Democratic party began to gather strength. It rose on a new surge of Korean urban forces. The Korean War, even more widely than Japan's Asiatic war, had swept people from village areas into the larger communities of refugee shelters, often into towns and cities. Again, it knocked people from their niches, changed old ways, introduced new discontents. Even those who returned to the villages returned more politically conscious. Many did not return. By 1955, with the war two years past and the government again in Seoul, the swollen cities were undergoing reconstruction and the press was growing. Repression, corruption, and inflation now had loci of concentration and aggravation. Public reaction against them and corresponding sympathy for the opposition markedly increased. Taken out from under war news the Assembly's voice — and even opposition negotiations — sounded louder.

By March 1955, 112 Democratic core branches out of an eventual 203 had been established, and the party claimed some 300,000 formal members. A Civil Rights Protection Committee was an innovation popular in the cities. Elections showed the results. Though Rhee's re-election in 1956 was a foregone conclusion, his majority fell from 80 percent to 56 percent. Urban votes were crucial in electing Chang Myŏn Vice-President over Rhee's picked Vice-Presidential teammate and heir apparent, Yi Ki-bung. Shin Ik-hŭi, the DNP Presidential candidate, died of a heart attack a week before the elections, but the Seoul crowds his rally attracted on the banks of the Han River, between 100,000 and 200,000, were estimated as the greatest in Korean history.[54] The results showed in the subsequent elections. Starting with 15 assemblymen in 1954, the Democrats increased to 46 before the 1958 elections, and in these they raised their number of representatives to 79. They thus began to be able to threaten the smooth course of government legislation. Among their new numbers, 23 were from Korea's five largest cities, from which the Liberals elected only 5. In Seoul, the opposition captured 15 out of 16 seats, and no Liberal candidates whatever were elected in Taegu and Inch'ŏn. Many of the urban opposition assemblymen were among the Assembly's ablest representatives and led eloquent and well-publicized attacks on the regime's autocracy and corruption. They carried out filibusters, sitdown strikes, and even a "sleep-in." Toward the end of the Rhee regime, an urban consensus against the government was achieved despite arrests, threats, economic favoritism, and surveillance.

The Two-Party System

The 1956 and 1958 elections were revolutionary. For the first time in Korean history, elections had been dominated essentially by party politics. For the first time, genuine groundswells of popular opinion and participation had taken place. Intellectuals all over Korea hailed the appearance of a two-party system, a deepening understanding of opposition, an apparent distinct coming of age in democratic politics.[55] Foreign observers likewise felt a wave of encouragement, a few because of the belief that a two-party system fits a homogeneous environment, more because they saw in this development the image of their own American society.

The hopes of permanence and success for the two-party system proved premature. The vortex so centralized the governmental system that acceptable alternatives to political power could not develop. Politically, two-party amalgamation succeeded in raising public participation in political decision; but this commodity was already common. It had educated the public a little with respect to "undemocratic" acts and civil rights. Yet the very quality of political concentration that the two-party system can exert to draw disparate entities together in a state that is diverse contains harmful tendencies where a state is homogeneous, over-centralized, and over-politicized. In the Korean environment, democracy tended merely to add to mobility, political excitement, and concentration on central power. Ideological or substantial program differences were absent, and no third force or party grew strong enough to make a difference.[56] The opposition did come more successfully to symbolize adherence to democracy; the Liberals increasingly seemed to stand against its methods. Underneath, however, both were motivated by desire for power, not by reform or program. The public suspected that the Democrats' allegiance to democratic process had a power motivation that would, in the long run, force them toward a system of Liberal party type to protect their interests if they assumed power. In essence, therefore, the struggle could be and was viewed as one between two groups of rather similar people scrambling for power for the same reason. The hope of gradual democratization arising from the struggle against authoritarianism was fragile.

THE FAILURE OF PARTIES

With the Democrats' overwhelming post-revolutionary victory in the July 1960 elections, the major characteristics both of national politics and of the Democratic party rose to the surface. Those Democrats not personally close to Chang now saw that, with a party majority so large, their chances of access to power through the party were minuscule. Only personal closeness to the party leader would count. The fragile unity of the Democratic party, which was based primarily not on positive belief in democratic programs but on opposition to the Liberal party and the governing system, began to disintegrate. With the collapse of the Liberal party and the Rhee government, the mainspring of cohesion disappeared. Now, also, the faults of the party's original construction showed: a marriage of convenience between two interest groups, not a unity of belief and loyalty. The pressures and incentives for unity now came only from public opinion. To party members, concern over personal access to power meant a struggle between the party's two component parts. In the late summer of 1960, the two parties split.

The events of the summer of 1960 confirmed an ancient Korean political rule. As in the old days with the attempt to establish firm classes, it remained true that the unity and cohesion of groups must yield to the demands of individuals or subgroups for access to power; there is a deep cultural aversion to firm bonds lest they impede equal mobility. To this ancient pattern Chang's government was sacrificed; for with the defection of the "old" faction, the unity, the viability, and the stability of his government vanished, and its end was foreshadowed.

Meanwhile, another attempt was being made to reappraise the situation and, with it, the party system. This came from the army and was centered in the young colonels dedicated to "order." They viewed the splits and maneuverings of Korean party government as chaos. Their reaction to party politics harked back to that of the Japanese in 1910, many of whom, like Terauchi, were army men. In their view, professionals who knew what was good for society must rule unimpeded by argument and obstruction. Politics was evil, but if necessary to prevent the lid blowing off or to erect an internationally legitimate façade, it must be planned and rationed by a central power, not left carelessly to the popular will.

After the army seized control and found that foreign and domestic pressures would not permit a total ban on politics, the colonels followed through on their political planning. In the early part of 1962, a year before the official ban on political activities was lifted, the Korean Central Intelligence Agency started intensely secret but quite systematic attempts to form a political party that would continue and further the military government's program and be responsive to its leaders even when military rule lifted. Certain key CIA former military officers were in charge of the new party project; they recruited civilian university friends to help them. Political-science teachers were, in some instances, plucked from the streets at night and "persuaded" to participate.

The new party, named on its public emergence the Democratic Republican party (DRP), reflected much of the same Communist-Kuomintang type of organization as its Liberal party predecessor. The party was organized from the top, with Park Chŏng-hŭi as party president and under him a chairman who might or might not have personal importance. Below this level came a strong planning committee, followed by a hierarchy of councils, provincial chapters, and election chapters. The party was provided with a permanent administrative secretariat, originally paid by CIA funds, its staff drawn from the armed forces, the universities, the press, and the fringes of the former political parties. Originally, each of the hundreds of election districts was supposed to have four of these secretariat members, provincial offices eight. This permanent core, recruited and paid by CIA, was responsible for searching out suitable candidates, instructing them in the government's — or the CIA's — wishes and seeing that party discipline was maintained. Members of this secretariat were wont to talk privately about the plans of the CIA to create "puppets."

Every CIA activity had the imprint of the long experience of its leaders in Army Intelligence. Party formation was no exception. Research groups were set up to study the political problems and methods involved, and the secretariat was to accumulate detailed files and become intimately familiar with all possible candidates and with the exact political complexion of each district. Personal weaknesses were carefully noted as means for control, character assassination, blackmail, or political defeat. No previous political group — not even the Liberal party — had ever before been graced with this professionalism of political approach. These innovations had their curious breeding ground in American G-2 techniques, well learned by Korean officers, and in Japanese bureaucratic colonialism: Park Chŏng-hŭi and Kim Chong-p'il were comparatively undisguised admirers of Japan.

CIA's unusual political attempt was rewarded with at least partial surface success. Rumors of CIA council plans and power spread all over Seoul; again, many broke away from their niches and streamed toward power. Numerous would-be politicians saw no other feasible way to gratify their ambitions than through CIA channels. Especially to the younger, a party was a means of fast, personal access to power. "I want to be an assemblyman, and if I want to stay in politics, this is the best way for me to do it" was the kind of remark often heard even from those acknowledging the cynicism of the process. Some joined with motivations similar to those with which many Germans of the 1930's entered the Nazi party: we don't like it, they might argue, but the only way we can influence it and gain greater power for civilians is by entering and working from the inside. In a manner quite reminiscent of the Liberal party, but with mostly younger men, the DRP scooped up free-floating elements from all over the social map — former officers and intelligence agents, former bureaucrats now unemployed, those on the fringes of the former parties who now wanted roles front and center. No cohesive force or interest group formed any basic bonds among these entities. On the whole, their only characteristic was that they had participated little or not at all in previous banquets of central power. Moreover, the covert nature of the CIA political chrysalis provided little for pride to rally around. Instead, factional splits in the 1964–1965 period divided and, to a significant degree, immobilized the party. One large group has remained faithful to its Kim Chong-p'il–CIA background; another, unwilling to assume the status of CIA robots, has opposed it. The constitution has prevented the formalizing of this split by providing that those who repudiate their party lose their seats.

The "rationing" of politics has thus far enfeebled parties even more than in Liberal days. The Democratic Republican party obeyed the government in passing the treaty with Japan, but it has failed to use its large majority to initiate or alter important or constructive legislation. Despite many DRP surface resemblances to the Liberal party, the government has used bureaucracy, CIA, and army, not party, as its primary control mechanisms. A lighter and more covert brand of oppression has given opposition parties less to rally themselves and public opinion around. They have made valiant efforts to cohere but their unity is fragile and far from effective. The 1967 elections reverted to manipulation, corruption, and new lows in political behavior. The resulting five-month opposition boycott of the National Assembly prevented its operation until late November 1967. Public dissatisfaction has therefore had no normal political channel and has tended to become either apolitical and apathetic or rebellious, like the students in their chronic violent demonstrations of 1964–1965.[57] Neither reaction leads to political stability. Economic strides, unhindered by excessive delay or debate, have been possible, and the Vietnamese War has greatly increased them. With faint overtones of the Japanese era, an atmosphere of greater economic interest and activity has been achieved by tapping off some of the elements producing political vortex. The race between economic progress and political discontent is on; the former has, up to 1968, gained over the latter. As of 1968, little sign that either economic growth or political discontent will lead to large, vital political parties is visible. Political parties as a major source of hope have faded, and this part of democracy's experiment in Korea appears, thus far, to have failed.

CONCLUSION

Political parties in Korea have, besides the traits noted at the beginning of this chapter, taken certain characteristic forms.

The chief basis for party formation has been initiative from above, the result of the chief executive's or his associates' interest in the placing of some feasible limit on the unusually broad and intense competition for position that besets Korean politics or in accomplishing some high policy objectives. The first example of this type was Korea's initial political party, the Ilchin-hoe, 1903–1910; in its case, the "power above" was Japan and her puppets within the late Yi cabinets. The second example was probably the Communist party as it developed in North Korea from the time of Liberation on; we will consider this briefly in Chapter 11. The third was the Liberal party. The fourth was the Democratic Republican party. In addition to these, the National Society, with Rhee as the effective politically-governing force, can be viewed as an organization of this type.

Thus far, the party formed from above would appear to be the type most natural to and successful within the Korean political scene. Judged by success in context, all parties so formed have had great achievements. The Ilchin-hoe helped to pave the road to colonial annexation, in some respects with astonishing smoothness. The Communists amalgamated all political forces in North Korea ruthlessly but with efficiency, continuity, and a resulting political stability. The Liberals achieved a power monopoly from which no political group, only revolution, could dislodge it. The DRP passed its initial tests with a success hard to predict from the unpopularity of its origins and remains politically dominant today. All such parties tend more or less strongly toward power monopolies and authoritarian methods; all make use of the controls of the government or power that forms them. They are characteristic of a mass society; for in them individuals are related to each other only by way of their reaction to the common authority of the state, and the elite are selected and fixed through cooptation by virtue of a state monopoly of the means of coercion and persuasion.[58]

The second type of party appearing in Korea is the party formed as a reaction against and in opposition to the first. The initial *raison d'être* for such a party lies in the fact that the government can provide access to power and hence glory in life for only a small percentage of those desiring it; the rest, feeling equally qualified and hence, by inference, deprived of a "right," must organize to obtain it. The main force for the accretion of such a party lies not in the cohesion of a subgroup or in the force of self-generated interests but in the governmental and government-party power hostile to and repressive of the ambitions of many individuals. Out-factions in the middle Yi Dynasty had some of these characteristics, but the Democratic party in its several forms has been the great modern exemplar. The effect that the threat of the Communist party had in molding the Democratic party during the latter's first two years can be cited as an alternate form of this pattern; in this instance, the force came from outside the South Korean government but was only partly non-governmental.

The third Korean type would appear to be exemplified by the Communist party as it existed during the Japanese occupation and in South Korea in the two years following Liberation. In this case, the party makes systematic use of the local molecular instincts of Korean grouping in cells and employs strong ideology, indoctrination, and hierarchical form to make the molecules cohere and to limit their mobility. The long history of Communist failure in the 1920's and 1930's to prevent this form from factionalizing and the ultimate failure of any South Korean group of this type to accomplish cohesion demonstrates the extreme difficulty of forming parties in Korea by this method, a difficulty probably generic to extreme mass societies. Indeed, the success of the South Korean Labor party (SKLP) itself was a transient and very partial one: it, too, became a faction in the North Korean world; it, too, had factions within itself. The strength and comprehensiveness of Communist ideology aided the SKLP; but its temporary success in South Korea was largely a function of the party's ability to harness the emotional drive of opposition to colonialism. In North Korea, communism's success was less popularly based and was that of an official government party.

Molecular groups with party signposts, such as registered with the Joint Commission or have reappeared since, need not be considered parties in a serious sense, nor should such groups as the Korea National party or the Federations assembled by the military government or Kim Kyu-sik. Parties associated with single charismatic leaders — as the Independence party of Kim Ku came to be and such as Lyuh Woon-hyung and his brother, Chŏn Chin-han, Yi Pŏm-sŏk, Kim Chun-yŏn, and others tried to form — have fared poorly in Korea. Strictly speaking the Liberal party's success resulted less from Rhee's personality and charisma than from his monopoly of government power. The lack of success of personally led parties relates partly to the Korean council tendency to share top power and not rely on the single leader, partly to the lack of organizational or class seedbeds for leadership in the Korean cultural environment. Rhee has been, thus far, virtually the only exception to this rule.

It is especially interesting to observe that even when, as with the Democratic party, genuine interest groups are present in Korea, they tend to have little importance as a party develops; if they expand, such organizations attract recruits not in terms of special interests but with respect to chances for power. The Korean Democratic party in 1945 sprang from the Chŏlla-do landlord group of Kim Sŏng-su but the Democrats took their character not from their attitude toward land reform or industrial ownership but from the exigencies of their struggle against Rhee and the Liberals. Their espousal of "democracy" and of the cabinet-responsible system was meaningful only in terms of their struggle for power — it was without significance for their own vested interests. Again, in the "old" and "new" factional rupture of 1960, the split lay not along interest lines but along those of the access of individuals or molecular groups to power and jobs through personal association. Ideology, ideas, and programs likewise have little political importance in the culture except where an alien creed under alien training makes a determined break with native patterns (as has been the case with communism). Representing no interests, lacking ideas, Korean parties are transient. They form and disperse readily. Rapid party formation and dissolution, as in Pakistan, is not politically uncommon, but world history must contain comparatively few examples of large dispersals so rapid and so nearly complete as those occurring in the fall of the Ilchin-hoe in 1910 and the Liberal party in 1960. There is little reason to believe that the Democratic Republican party, if separated from power today, would find an end much less abrupt.

On balance, Korean parties have been ineffective in adding to the cohesion of the nation and comparatively unimpressive in the creation of an elite. To legislation, to welfare, to the economy, to the stability of the country, they have contributed little. A cohesive party is out of place in the upward mobility pattern of the society. There are no permanent party cores, no party professionals, little loyalty to parties in their own right. Parties have added to consciousness and criticism of government, have helped prevent the perpetuation of authoritarian rule, have aided the change to a cabinet-responsible system. But, compared with the efficiency of development, investment, management, and bureaucracy under the colonial system, the part played by the representational process has been chiefly obstructionist: all these functions have, in part because of party influence, been less efficient. The long-sought cabinet-responsible system and the expansion of the legislature with an upper chamber in 1960 contributed to confusion and instability rather than to constructive modernization. Both have been abolished, and the return of neither is desired.

Most basic of all, genuine concern and interest in parties tends to be limited to Koreans with an eye on the main chance. They are instruments not of communication but of climbing. And though parties everywhere exist at least partly for climbing, vortex politics in Korea makes this objective unusually exclusive and intense. To speed up the social and political updraft, to increase opposition in the spirit of the Censorate, is not what Korea needs. Until vested interests — especially local vested interests — appear that demand communication and pressure on the central government, until parties represent such interests sufficiently to forge ideas and programs, and until a party career is viewed as an honorable alternative to central power, Korean party politics will not emerge from stagnation.

11

Communism

A harsh but apparently effective way of subduing the atomized struggle of post-Liberation Korea was provided by communism. It was provided in two quite different forms: the opposition communism of colonial Chōsen, which grew, mostly in South Korea, to be the indigenous communism of immediate post-Liberation Korea; and the official communism imported into North Korea by the Soviet Union with its occupation forces, implanted and backstopped during the first three or more crucial years and continued in power thereafter. For Westerners, separated from these movements and lacking first-hand information about them, any treatment of the subject must be considered highly tentative.

THE COMMUNISM OF OPPOSITION

Koreans were among the first peoples of Asia to come into contact with communism, and its spread among them was, initially, quite rapid. Koreans, atomically mobile toward opportunity abroad as to their own centrality, had spilled across the northeast border into the Maritime Province in large numbers from the time of the Taewŏn'gun on. After Russians and Ukrainians, they eventually became the third largest ethnic group in the Soviet Far Eastern Republic, numbering from 200,000 to 300,000.[1] Communism established rapport with many such Koreans, not only because of its summons to revolution and anti-colonialism, but because of Korean political and military identity of interest with the attempt of the new Bolshevik state to dislodge Japan from its post–World War I position in the Maritime Provinces.[2] The Irkutsk Communist party had a Korean section by January 22, 1918, and a Korean Socialist party was founded at Khabarovsk in June 1918, changing its name to the Koryŏ Communist party on January 10, 1921. The latter, well-organized and Moscow-financed, grew rapidly in Shanghai, Korea, and Manchuria, enrolling many in the Red Army branches in fifteen Siberian and Russian cities by the autumn of 1922.[3] The Soviet alliance of 1918–1920 with Koreans was its first with any Asian people. The movement spread rapidly among the 600,000-odd Korean residents in southeastern Siberia, then the largest Korean group outside Korea. For these Koreans who were, in large part, rootless exiles, knocked from their social and village niches, without effective political alternatives in the anti-colonial fight, communism offered a haven of ideological surety, revolutionary doctrine, blueprint for progress for a society whose old forms they scorned, confirmation of the classless society they almost had, promise of minority autonomy for them within the U.S.S.R., and eventual independence for their homeland. In addition, immediate military tasks and a sense of participation with the new, consolidating Bolshevik forces attracted the Koreans of that time.

The consolidation, initially so massive and spontaneous, covered over too many separations and sources of rift to last. They were compounded, as Confucian rifts had been compounded, with doctrinal quarrels of the kind that give functional quarrels an appearance of deeper validity within the fluidities of mass society. There were nationalist (and internationalist) Communists (some originally connected with the Shanghai government, most soon hostile to it); Irkutsk Communists (increasingly supported by the Comintern and ably backstopped by Comintern Far Eastern Secretariat chief Shumiatsky); Communists primarily bound by internal Korean allegiances; Russianized Korean Communists; Manchurian residents and guerrillas of all colorations; students and workers in Japan; older Koreans with community *positions prises;* younger, drifting Koreans with nothing to bind them; opportunist, dilettantist, intellectual Communists; and the factionalisms of rival friendship circles. Inevitably, the movement split and factionalized. Yet, unlike other movements, it had the basic sinews needed to overcome such ruptures in the end: organizational techniques; the active — if sometimes confused — support of the Soviet Comintern; financing, training techniques, arms, and endless numbers of potential recruits needing a militant and ideological home.[4] Spilling severally across Korea's borders, the movements of Siberia and Shanghai, plus leftist students returning from Japan, became the main sources feeding the internal communism of Chōsen after 1925, when these three streams precariously united and the first Korean Communist party was organized in Seoul.

Within the worlds of Korea, Japan, and the Provisional Government based in Shanghai, opposition communism was, despite many difficulties, one of the more nearly sustained, if not cohesive, movements of the anti-Japanese milieu. Such cohesion as it had came not only from superior support but, like the later Democratic party's, from having strong enemies to unite against. On occasion ready to follow the Leninist doctrine of joining bourgeois movements to dominate or destroy them, leading members joined the early Korean Provisional Government (KPG) and were its most persistent disrupters. Between Communists and largely nationalist guerrillas there was soon blood. On June 26, 1921, a battle between Irkutsk Communists and Manchurian-Siberian-based Korean guerrillas flamed at Alekseyevsk (Svobodnyi), north of Blagoveshchensk; six hundred Koreans were killed, and the non-Communist Korean Volunteer Army withdrew, weakened almost fatally.[5] The establishment of the Koryŏ Communist party in January 1921, and the diversion to it of Comintern funds that the Provisional Government, probably mistakenly, regarded as intended for itself, was an important factor in the KPG's turmoil and decline after 1921. From then on, the splits ran deeper still. Kim Ku's Korean Independence party and the remains of the KPG kept up a kind of running battle with Korean Communist groups. Rifts between Yi Tong-hwi's Koryŏ Communists and the Irkutsk group grew. The latter not only won at Alekseyevsk but was strengthened by the First Congress of The Toilers of the Far East in Moscow, January 1922, virtually the only effective and outspoken international support the Korean independence movement received; thereafter the Irkutsk Korean Communists were an important arm of Bolshevism in the Far East, were well-supported and grew rapidly in Manchuria, Siberia, and North China in numbers and military might far outstripping the impoverished KPG. Probably only the factional difficulties with the Shanghai Communists prevented the Fourth Congress of the Comintern from recognizing an Irkutsk Korean as an official delegate. The Chinese Communists, of course, espoused the cause led by the Irkutsk Communists. The growing gap between the Chinese Nationalists and Communists deepened the Korean political chasm. Rival youth groups and military forces were established in the war years, those of the Communists being considerably the larger and more effective. This division, together with effective Communist efforts, prevented wartime recognition by the Chinese and, possibly, other governments, which would have given the KPG status and support in the postwar world.[6] Inside Korea, disruption similar to that visited on the Provisional Government split the Sin'gan-hoe (see Chapter 4). Even Japan and Los Angeles witnessed leftist-rightist splits among Koreans.

The terrain between leftist and nationalist lines was strewn with a disarray of stragglers, moderates, and would-be compromisers. These were years of political doubt, unfamiliar philosophies, and intellectual dilettantism. There were, besides Irkutsk and Shanghai Communist groups, nationalist-minded Communists like Cho Pong-am and Kim Chun-yŏn, intellectual Marxists like Paek Nam-un and Yi Ch'ŏng-won, and variegated communistic or socialist-connected nationalists hoping for compromise and unity like Cho So-ang, Wŏn Se-hun, Lyuh Woon-hyung, and Chang Kŏn-sang, as well as Communist students, later apostates, like Kim Yak-su.[7] These were interwoven with every variety of instability and opportunism. Nationalist circles soon contained those divided about whether to ally with, oppose, or just keep away from Communists. Wrangling in Shanghai especially, but Seoul as well and even Tokyo, over questions of correct stance took up time that should have been alloted to practical issues or immediate or long-range planning. No substantive task evoked common action: the Japanese played their game cleverly after 1919 and provided few dramatic, repressive issues to rekindle unity. Communism thus in a way acted as a divisive force, making hopes of post-Liberation agreement dimmer, not more bright. Nationalist-Communist hostility and all that lay between had a quarter-century of uncompromising bitterness behind it before Liberation. As with Chinese Communists, the fight against nationalists and compromisers was as much a cornerstone of Korean Communist cohesion as the struggle against Japan.

Korean Communists needed all the sources of unity they could get. The movement cut its way aslant through the ranks of society, dividing classes, communities, villages, clans, and even families. Few major groups did not eventually have their Communist members, even if only a few. The doctrine entered aristocratic doors through education appealing to Confucian doctrinal instincts. It did, after all, have objectives — more specific ones than the nationalists advocated. It posited not only independence from Japan but also the establishment of workers' and peasants' power under a proletarian dictatorship. It promised land, labor, and thoroughgoing reforms. No competing philosophy seemed to fill the framework of an ideology that brought all areas and functions of life to bear on questions of welfare and the state. Sometimes, even elder sons of main lines were affected; more often, it was younger sons or those descended from concubines of main branches — people who could add social grievance to the brew of educational ideas. Sometimes villages would be split down the middle. Some of the sons of the middle class or of independence leaders like Ch'oi Nam-sŏn were affected. Lower-class boys on the way up were often attracted. Inroads were made among farmers in southern Korean districts with heavy absentee landlordism like Chŏlla-do and such landlord areas of Kyŏngsang-do as Andong, Kyŏngju, and Sangju. Finally, as industrialization shifted to higher gear, a few converts began to be found among the "proletariat." [8] Contrary to Marxism but consonant with its practice, adherents were likely to be those without strong class ties. *Paekchŏng* and *chungin* provided few converts but much of the rest of the fluid social milieu made the classless qualification easy.

The pell-mell urbanization, hectic industrialization, and grand recruitments of Japan's war world intensified classlessness. Again, men unglued from their social contexts and resentful of their second-class colonial status sought aim and association. The larger groupings of the time — students, soldiers, youth groups, factory workers, miners — made constantly growing targets for the Communist organizers. The strong-arm gang element of city or rural toughs was the last to be admitted but came to prominence when violence began to be employed in early 1946. The chaos following colonial collapse and the U.S. failure to fill the vacuum tended to darken the night around whatever light communism could provide. A disjointed world threw its jetsam up for membership. Few recruits were independent thinkers or profound doctrinal students; rather, they were "angry young men" without faith in their own surroundings, rebellious against the

Japanese and contemptuous of Korean collaborators, finding in a vague mingling of Marxism, communism, and a wave-of-the-future view of Soviet force and propinquity the only convincing projection of a national future.

For this jungle of Communist groups outside Korea and varied social jetsam inside, every source of unity had to be sought; none was likely to suffice. From April 1925 until the end of 1928, a succession of four more or less united Korean Communist parties, operating despite the closest Japanese surveillance, propagated Communism within Korea and achieved Comintern recognition. Yet even these efforts yielded to renewed factionalism and the third party was largely destroyed by it. The society did not produce adequate variety and compromise for orderly elite formation. Factionalism was equally rampant — largely between Irkutsk and Shanghai but with many minor variations — outside Korea almost from the birth of Korean communism on. "Over the years, as you well know, factional disputes have taken place in many Parties. There are Parties which have achieved a certain amount of notoriety in this respect such as the American and Polish parties, but the Korean factions hold the record." [9] Leaders advanced, changed, and fell. The movement needed not only the tightest internal organization but the force of external hostility to find cohesion.

This it got. The Manchurian incident ushered in deepening, then complete, political suppression; Communists were endangered, jailed, their movement banned. Increasing Japanese oppression and rising collaboration made clear targets for the Communists' hostile bows. As external challenge rose, internal cohesion had to be the response. Japanese police efficiency made a national Communist party headquarters in Korea impossible from 1928 until Liberation. The movement had to scatter and thus lost in effectiveness, but the dispersion at least dampened factionalism. Danger brought the cell to peak effectiveness. Each member had to pass through a special selection process. Each had to have special qualifications, one or more sponsors, and further approval by a local committee. Sponsors were made responsible for the recruit's subsequent behavior. Each cell member was responsible for the actions of the others. Organized in groups of three or more members, cells were further bound by ties of secrecy, consciousness of oppression, and conspiracy.[10] These somehow substituted for the satisfactions of cult and ceremony that Confucianism had purged from the culture. Outside Korea's border, where one could fight — as in Kim Il-sŏng's guerrilla group — it was much the same. Warfare there imposed drastic organizational discipline. There, as in the cell, one could sublimate the rebelliousness nurtured in the passé strictness of a Confucian household or take out the frustration of an uprooted loneliness; there one could sense unity and the track of a goal unsensed by native village or town. The smallness of the cell or guerrilla group, the tightness of its loyalty echoed special needs of the culture: of such stuff must the house forces of thirteenth-century Koryŏ have been sewn; it ran through kinship and village council meetings and was incarnate in Korean rooms themselves — small, dark, their space contracted by the needs of floor heating, settings for intimate contact, elbow-jostling, conspiratorial discussion.

Important to organizational discipline was acceptance of a largely secret hierarchy, unknown to the cell member; only ignorance and the tested loyalty of a minimum number could protect the party from the refinements of torture. Above the cell rose an elaborate, covert hierarchy to supreme headquarters. Its form was imported, but it was a complete administrative world like the old dynasty's and echoed its power. Each cell, after Liberation, was represented in a district committee. District committees led to party conventions, provincial assemblies, and provincial committees. Above flourished the National Convention with its Central Inspection Committee and the controlling Central Committee with its bureaus and executive sub-committees appointing chairmen of Publicity and Propaganda, Labor Unions, Farmers' Affairs, Women's Affairs, Party Practice, Mobilization, Finance, Culture, and Information. There were many underground schools. After Liberation, many southern young men went north for leadership training. Efforts in training were made to counteract the old lack of professionalization.[11] Here, above all, was an attempt to inculcate the stepped progression that the Korean world had lacked.

Before Liberation, such Communist organization as could be sustained nourished itself with strikes, work stoppages, small-scale sabotage. Liberation brought the clover days. The Central Committee and Provincial Assembly held meetings every three months. There were constant meetings, self-criticism sessions, expositions of ideology, inculcation of the party line. Some intellectuals objected to being inculcated with views by those they regarded as inferiors; some, originally excited by theory and argument, only now faced the cold fact that party decisions must be unequivocally obeyed. Later, with the rise of youth-group terror, shakedown, smuggling, and counterfeiting, still more of the fine edge was dulled for the idealist. But most members, anxious to avoid being sentenced to the quiet tenor of rural life, were attracted to the argumentative interweave of program, action, and doctrine; to emotional discussion of "proper spirit," "how one should act toward the people," what sources of unity one should draw on; to righteous indignation at oppression, intellectual absorption in ecumenical dogma. Such themes had exciting newness in a form especially piquant with reference to the Confucian tradition. Drawing men out in such talk kindled the zest for no-holds-barred intimacy, released tensions, and acted as catharsis of the private animosities that smolder in the repressed and ingrown atmosphere of the Confucian home. The village Communist, despairing of the apathy around him, drew pride and hope from his party's careful controls, programs, and intimate concern for those below. Men drawn from an incohesive, fractious society felt the breath of participation in something larger than themselves. Those who feared a life gagging in isolated, unchanging community life sensed in the unseen hierarchy the ampler tides of the capital's heady and mysterious big-time. Communism might be against tradition, but its challenges and excitements were those of the tales all boys were told of the old dynasty: the hard, glorious path of gift and will leading to the antechambers of power, the endless drama and entrancement that courts, of kings or communism, know. But now the path seemed more marked with definite stages and opened the way for those with "qualifications" in place of *ppaek's* patronage.

From 1938 on, discipline and a hierarchy increasingly removed by secrecy from factional strife had begun to produce one of the first well-organized elites Korea had known in many decades. Though revolutionaries, these men partook strongly of the character of bureaucrats. The post-Liberation Communist Central Committee was composed largely of middle-class intellectuals, often with long prison records, one or two with baptism in the March 1 movement. None reflected the new personality more than the acknowledged leader, Pak Hŏn-yŏng, about forty-seven, from rural Koch'ang in North Chŏlla, essentially an internal Communist, though, as a student of An Pyŏng-ch'an, a man with well-laid Irkutsk connections.

Self-effacing, soft-spoken, mildly scholarly, excitable, he had the character of a minor bureaucrat, even a drugstore clerk; his personality fitted the sources of his leadership: constant obedience to his superiors and to every twist and turn in the party line and a regard for seniority within the movement that almost bespoke European socialism. His type stood in stark contrast to the personalities of his rightist or even leftist antagonists like Lyuh, possessors of the charisma, free-wheeling presence, and public-speaking skills needed for the atomized mobility race. When Pak's legitimacy was in doubt, the resort to secret bureaucratic hierarchy was always there. On August 17, 1945, he first came to Seoul from brick-laying in Chŏlla-do and immediately established himself by carrying party lists, plans for reorganization and, above all, rumored (but unsubstantiated) Moscow instructions.[12] On September 12 he revived — and was elected chairman of — the Korean Communist party. Significantly, he headquartered it in Seoul, not in P'yŏngyang. In the latter place, he and the party might have had better protection by the Soviets, and there his group would have been in a good position to achieve leadership of the north. When challenged by more dynamic leaders, as he was by the Yenan Communist Han Pin, who established a rival Sinmindang party in Seoul in February 1946, he regained control by slinking off to P'yŏngyang and reappearing with Russian support. He was like the Ŏsa, the Yi monarch's secret inspecting agent. Korean rightists had no recourse to such persuasive techniques. They had to fight it out below from the beginning: Uncle Sam had, except through the negotiating Lieutenant Leonard Bertsch, little taste for the *deus ex machina* role or its contributions to order in the political process.

With such ideas and organization, Communists and their affiliates became major heirs of the sudden release from Japanese repression, the many stimulations World War II brought to Korea. Their revolutionary ideas well suited a milieu in which most of the country's property was suddenly made ownerless by Japanese departures. From the day of Liberation, they made extremely rapid popular gains, at least until the trusteeship issue of January 1946.[13] From roughly 4,000 members at Liberation, Pak claimed 29,000 Communist members on March 1, 1946, including regular members and candidates for membership in South Korea.[14] Military Government itself estimated 15,000–20,000 Communists during this period.[15] Affiliates and front groups, however, numbered in the hundreds of thousands and claimed millions, organized in galleries and tiers of organizations so supernumerary and overlapping they put even the Boards of Council of pre-Taewŏn'gun days to shame.[16] The Democratic People's Front by February 14, 1946, embodied over ninety leftist political parties, labor unions, and social and fraternal organizations. The Central Standing Committee stood above the Democratic People's Front. Under the Front came twelve major organizations like the All-Korea League of Cultural Organizations, within which there were twenty-two suborganizations like the Korea Industrial Technicians' Alliance. The Alliance in turn contained seven subordinate units.[17] Even through imported forms, communism was expert in appealing to Korea's access-to-power, government-by-council theme.

Communist policies also reflected advance planning and, with some exceptions, a systematic direction that few rightists had. Special instructions were issued in August 1945 to proselytize in the villages. Youth groups were formed and soon started terrorizing Japanese and "collaborators." Neighborhood security units — sometimes one rightist and one leftist in each neighborhood — attacked each other and took turns shaking down the residents. Police, jails, guards, and constabulary were all systematically infiltrated. Most newspaper staffs except *Tong-A Ilbo* were leftist-inclined, and one, the *Hai Pang Ilbo*, was an official Communist organ until closed by Military Government on May 18, 1946; then the *Chosŏn Inminpo* and the *Hyŏndai Ilbo* became semi-official organs until the military governor closed them in turn on September 6. For many months they served as effective organs. Military Government, in contrast, never had a newspaper to speak for it.

Income also aided Communist consolidation. In the weeks immediately following Liberation, People's Committees in North and South collected taxes; they also took over from the Japanese and ran many factories, the proceeds going to the Committees and to the leftist unions that had been one of the important sources of revival in former Japanese plants in postwar Korea.[18] The wealthy, both Japanese and Korean, thinking only Communists would occupy Seoul, paid protection money to Communist organs and youth groups. One industrialist paid ¥2,000,000. The large Soviet Consulate-General in Seoul, never closed by the Japanese during the war, provided funds. After Liberation, large amounts of Bank of Chōsen yen were removed by Soviet military authorities and distributed to supporters. Smuggling was rife over the hardening 38th Parallel. Finally, counterfeiting was resorted to, and the key counterfeiter, Yi Kwang-sul, provided nearly ¥2,500,000 to the party between November 1945 and May 6, 1946, when American investigators broke in on the scene of counterfeiting in Seoul's Chikazawa Building. The resulting revelation of the illegal and foreign-controlled nature of communism, heavily publicized by Military Government, lost the Communists considerable prestige and support.[19]

Korea's opposition communism had a double death. Personally a moderate with initial flashes of friendliness for Military Government, Pak was inevitably driven by the Cold War and perhaps in part by the instructions of his Soviet and North Korean bosses into increasingly adamant, then violent opposition.[20] Hodge and his police then turned on the Communists and rooted them out, Rhee's new government pursuing the remnants and banning the party on December 1, 1948. Some remained underground, at least until the Korean War. One former Korean Communist theorizes that Pak's anxiety about the destruction of his forces in South Korea and his assessment of their backing by South Korean opinion was largely responsible for initiating the Korean War, but it seems doubtful that Pak any longer commanded such decisive influence by then.[21] Pak and his main supporters escaped to the North. But here his error in having so long remained in the South became apparent: Kim Il-sŏng was successfully consolidating power. Pak's seniority over Kim Il-sŏng in the Communist movement now threatened Pak more than Kim. Pak's potential became, as it would have in the days of Yi factionalism, the crime unforgivable. The Sixth Plenum of the Central Committee, August 3–6, 1953 (a week after the conclusion of hostilities), ousted Pak and his group from the Korean Workers party, and in subsequent courts-martial he and ten others were sentenced to death. Sometime before December 1955 Pak was executed — ironically on the pretext of his being an "American spy."[22] The chapter of Korea's "native" communism ended with him.

Despite its ultimate end, Pak's opposition communism had its hour. In Liberation's opening months, it was *imperium in imperio* in South Korea, unquestionably the country's most important single political force for at least the first year. Violent, disruptive, and illegal activities were, as American authorities constantly publicized, a part of its strength.[23] Such authorities notwithstanding, these activities were not its basic component. Communism was the first Korean unit to force its way through the pattern of chaotic, atomized mobility in Korea's Liberation period. Its technique in doing this was in many ways politically more engrossing than that used by the army-backed North Korean Communists and by the South Korean Democratic Republican party or the police-backed success of the Liberal party. In some respects, Pak's anti-colonial communism can probably be called the most balanced attempt so far to found a Korean political movement with both strong high support and strong local roots; the latter were probably more strong and real, less opportunistic, than any developed in Korea thus far by an opposition party. The cells of neither Liberals nor Democrats have shown the cohesiveness and strength of Communist cells. With such a rootage, the party's history of over twenty-five years became probably the longest of any political party movement in modern Korea. It was the first successfully to use a bureaucratic hierarchy to limit atomized mobility and to produce an elite by rational means. Pak Hŏn-yŏng may be reckoned the first modern Korean political figure so produced.[24] Yet, more comprehensively than the Ilchin-hoe, communism used an intricately stepped hierarchy to appeal to the mobility pattern. It likewise made skillful use of the council pattern, innumerable committees and fronts rapidly broadening political participation. The Communist party went Confucians and Christians one better by using dogma, strong discipline, and the attraction of a transcendent objective as organizational glue.[25]

Despite foreign dictation, violence, and the ruthlessness that stood ever ready to sacrifice the individual, the party's effects were great. Lyuh Woon-hyung, with all his great appeal and charisma, waged a running battle with it for leftist control for years and lost. From Sin'gan-hoe down through the moderate coalition and many a small moderate or socialist party, the Communists tremendously damaged those whom they could not subvert. Intellectually, the party attracted many of Korea's best minds, in the South, perhaps, especially: here seemed to them to be a governing process determined and viable but also sustained with ideas, opportunities for protest, and hopes that went beyond mere racial hatred. Nothing else in the Korean political scene then or in South Korea now has had that appeal. Among all conservatives and the great majority of the middle classes, the

Christians, and the propertied, communism inspired fear and alarm. It was probably the first and greatest force driving Korea Democrats and many of Rhee's allies themselves to concerted political action. In the opposition it aroused as well as the allegiance it rallied, communism was unquestionably the chief cohesive force of Korean politics during American Military Government. In the final analysis, however, the assets of communication, voluntary association, and rational elite formation that it possessed turned out not to be the crucial assets to possess; Korea's unlimited centralization placed forceful central power, however obtained, in a position to outbid all other advantages. Pak himself undoubtedly blamed "American imperialism" for his failure. In fact, it appears that, even had the "loss" of South Korea not occurred, the communism the Soviets brought and imposed from above would have dominated and obliterated the home-grown product, much as the Democrats in South Korea had to yield first to the Liberals, then to military coup. Except that under communism, the player only strikes out once; or, at least, stays struck out longer.

THE COMMUNISM OF THE STATE

The communism introduced into North Korea by the occupying Soviet forces and successfully nurtured by them illustrates political cohesion quite different from its home-rooted predecessor. Its political methods are basically more nearly similar to those of the Liberal party and the CIA in South Korea than they are to the communism of 1925–1945. What was done in the North, however, amounts to the most drastic and massive example of the party induced from above that is so far known to Korean political experience.

The Soviet Union declared war on Japan August 8, 1945, and entered Korea by August 10–11, rapidly overrunning most of the northern half of the country. On the surface, therefore, Soviet occupation appeared to have offered far less opportunity for preparation than did the United States occupation.

Soviet actions suggest that, in fact, Russia had given considerably more advance attention to her North Korean occupation than American authorities had to their zone. How long-range such efforts were, who captained them, and under what orders are questions to which the answer is unknown in the West. They had, however, the marks of purposeful effectiveness. This is the more remarkable when one considers the far greater disruption of the war on Soviet society and the far greater relative distraction that her problems in Europe posed for her at the time. Perhaps the Soviet Korean minority had a more effective link with Soviet policymakers than the American Koreans had with the State and War Departments. Possibly the continuity of a considerable Soviet representation in Seoul throughout World War II may also hold a key to this problem.

The Soviet Union faced her Korean occupation with at least one asset far richer than that of the United States. Instead of the U.S. population of some 10,000 Korean-Americans, the U.S.S.R. had a native Korean population of several hundred thousand and had already picked several thousand of these, including a leadership group sometimes called "the forty-three," to accompany Soviet troops into Korea to help them actively with the establishment of a Communist regime.[26] These Soviet Koreans, the most famous of whom is Panmunjŏm negotiator General Nam Il, were from the beginning highly placed; many of them were vice-ministers in real charge of ministries. They were trusted and well-used, despite the fact that none except former Vice Premier Hŏ Ka-ŭi is known to have had a prominent position in the Soviet Union before the war and none except possibly Kim Il-sŏng is known to have held a rank higher than captain in the Soviet forces.[27] They were faithful apostles of a foreign power in its attempt to impose communism from above — most held Soviet citizenship. They had no significant native roots.

With these forces came a fairly successful but still relatively obscure partisan leader, thirty-three years old, a man active in the 1939–1941 period in the Manchurian and Korean border guerrilla fighting of the Chinese Communist–controlled Northeast Anti-Japanese United Army and possibly active as a guerrilla for four or five years before 1939. His real name was Kim Sŏng-ju, but he assumed for leadership purposes the name of Kim Il-sŏng, an appellation associated with a famous legendary guerrilla fighter and taken as a pseudonym by several comparatively minor Korean Communists. As commander of the 3rd Division of the 2nd United Army and later commander of the 6th Division of the 1st Route Army — divisions that did not usually number over a few hundred effectives — Kim led various attacks within Manchuria and over the border into Hamgyŏng Province until, about 1941, Japanese strength greatly reduced guerrilla activities. Through these operations, a group of roughly fifty surviving partisan fighters became bound to him by strong personal ties. Between 1941 and 1945, Kim, who retreated to the vicinity of Khabarovsk and possibly entered the Soviet Army, acquired, for the first time, Russian links. The Soviets picked Kim, for reasons still obscure, to receive a hero's welcome in P'yŏngyang on October 10, 1945, then to head the North Korean branch of the Korean Communist party, and finally to lead the People's Interim Committee which, from early in 1946, began to function as a Communist government under the Soviet occupation.

Although the Committee was obviously a puppet government, the Russians were able, by their control of Soviet Koreans, to establish the appearance of giving their Korean protégés greater power sooner than the Americans felt able to give it to Koreans in their zone.[28] Parties and a "Democratic Front" were formed; "elections" (with 99.6 percent voting and 97 percent endorsing the official slates) were held in 1946; a convention of People's Committees met in February 1947 to create a People's Assembly and elect a Presidium and Supreme Court. Political activity was dominated by the North Korean Workers party (NKWP), which was founded through Kim Il-sŏng's efforts in July 1946. It grew to 360,000 members in 1946, 750,000 in 1948, 1,164,695 in 1956, and to 1,311,563, or about 12 percent of the total population of an estimated 10,700,000 by 1961.[29] Uniting with the remnants of the South Korean Labor party (SKLP), it became the Korean Workers party (KWP) in June 1949. Through it, Kim separated the Yenan and other Communists in the North from control by Pak Hŏn-yŏng's Korean Communist party in Seoul. Well connected in Russia and China, the NKWP-KWP grew in power as well as in numbers and became the spearhead for rapid land reform, 1945–1948, and collectivization, carried out partially under Chinese auspices in the wake of the war, 1950–1958. Such expansion is, or at least was, undoubtedly a political shell, not entirely unlike the Liberal party's rapid aggrandizement after 1951. But it should be seen as a hard shell, built with power and maintained with iron methods and consistency. It has been a classic organization for presiding over a mass society, directing, coordinating, and supporting all governmental and non-governmental organizational activity under a unified chain of command. "The pervasiveness of its influence resulted in a fusion of public and private activity." [30]

Communism eventually showed experience that the Liberal party lacked in maintaining itself as a political shell of groups attached by force and power lures, but even it had striking failures. The Korean War, the considerable collaboration of North Koreans with the invading UN forces, and the mass migrations to the South of over a million people revealed the hollowness of this early growth. In his speech of December 21, 1950, before the Third Congress of the Communist Party Central Committee, Kim Il-sŏng voiced bitter criticism of poor performance and weak discipline among the party cadres, even admitting that some North Koreans had collaborated with the enemy.[31] Extensive propaganda and "political education" were needed to overcome this lack of "revolutionary consciousness." Postwar chaos helped correct the deficiency by destroying most previous barriers to the induction of the population into mass groups, unions, and youth groups in the cities, cooperatives in the country. By August 1958, the entire farm population of North Korea had been brought into cooperatives.[32] Radical collectivization eased communication problems and made propaganda activities more effective.

Meanwhile a government-controlled educational system, unusually thorough and extensive even for Communist societies, was instituted, including a seven-year compulsory system of education and an extremely large, tuition-free university system of, in 1961, 97,000 students in 78 universities of whom 65 percent were either technical or engineering students.[33] Many thousands have also been trained in other Communist countries, but, unlike South Korean students abroad, almost all seem to return for productive placement in the economy. Adult and, of course, teacher-training programs are also intensive. Ideological training and a kind of Nationalist-Communist indoctrination conceived by Kim Il-sŏng in the later 1950's aim at filling the formerly hollow political shell with devotion both to Marxism-Leninism and to Korea as a unique Communist society. The failures of the early system are well shown by the three-four million estimated to have fled it between 1945 and 1951. The thirteen million left today cannot flee, and we cannot know what their feelings are. Certainly they are highly mobilized, if not motivated. They are closely watched in, outside Albania, the narrowest and most intolerant of all Communist states. The fruits of technical training are also, to a degree, undermined by the periodic purges affecting technicians and based on political or doctrinal cause.[34] Whether, in the long run, a society increasingly educated can continue to subject itself to such controlled uniformity remains to be seen, but signs that the system has not worked since 1951 have been kept mostly under the surface.[35]

Throughout this growth, Kim Il-sŏng has kept his seat. Such continuity has taken concerted power. The Soviet attempt to impose him and his group on Communists of diverse background in the context of a political-vortex society inevitably aroused bitter factionalism ("sectarianism," as Kim calls it), which for years threatened the state. At the outset, 1945–1946, there were five of these well-defined factional elements: (1) the Manchurian guerrilla faction, including several non-guerrillas who joined Kim later; (2) Koreans of Soviet residence and/or citizenship; (3) the "Yenan" group associated with the Chinese Communists, mostly in North China; (4) the Communists on the spot in North Korea around the time of Liberation; and (5) the domestic South Korean Communists, the South Korea Labor party of Pak Hŏn-yŏng.[36] Draconian measures were needed to quell the severe contest for central power among these groups, especially since the Soviet-chosen elite was initially the weakest domestically. Group 4 was eliminated by purge and even assassination, mostly by the end of 1946. Pak Hŏn-yŏng and his followers, Group 5, were tried in 1953 on charges of war defeat and American espionage, even less credible than those lodged against the 1949 assemblymen by Rhee; Pak's execution was announced in December 1955. Between 1956 and 1958, Group 3, the powerful Yenan faction under several of North Korea's most senior independence leaders, was swept from power; and, for a year from the autumn of 1957, a ruthless bureaucratic purge affecting much of the central bureaucracy was carried out; much as a fifteenth-century minister might have been reduced to slavery, so was Ch'oe Ch'ang-ik, former Vice-Premier of North Korea, sent to work in the mines. Purge of the Soviet Koreans, Group 2, was gradual. The great Hŏ Ka-ŭi's censure was followed by suicide as early as 1951. His successor as Vice-Premier, Pak Ch'ang-ok, was purged in 1956 for criticizing Kim Il-sŏng to Khrushchev, his wife being reduced to a common laborer. Most "Soviet" Koreans were out of significant positions before 1962, some recalled to the Soviet Union. In 1962, a purge in the Korean Writers Association affected many writers and intellectuals. Kim Il-sŏng's increasing independence after 1956 made it as difficult for the Soviets to succor their supporters in Korea as it had been for the Chinese Communists to support theirs. Such careers recall, within Korean communism, the fall of Yi Tong-hwi, whose funeral in 1935 no Irkutsk Communist would attend, or the degradation of his able lieutenant, eloquent Comintern speaker Pak Chin-sun, reduced to rags and peddling in the streets of Moscow.[37] Strange echoes, these were, of so many late Yi Dynasty careers.

Since that time, the partisan group has occupied fourteen of the sixteen chief political posts. Its control increased in 1961 and again in 1966 when all prominent non-partisan group members of the Political Committee were eliminated from the party leadership and replaced with members of the partisan group.[38] Its control has become so assured that it has felt able to appoint medium-ranking members of purged factions to middle bureaucratic positions. The consolidation of all political elements into the Korean Workers party has accompanied such steps. Kim Il-sŏng, now over twenty years in power and still young, has never been effectively challenged, remains unchallenged today, and can thus count himself one of the current world's senior political leaders. That this continuity has been achieved by a man who started without an independent political personality or record of any stature and was asked to preside over a political-vortex society with no lack of more deeply-rooted rivals for central power makes an interesting study in the fruits of a consistent, unwavering autocratic policy operating in an otherwise fluid social context. Despite inevitable differences of system, his success constitutes a trenchant commentary on vacillating USAMGIK's failures.

The economic accomplishments derived from this dictatorship have, at least until recently, seemed impressive.[39] It appears from analysis of economic data, even allowing for some exaggeration in Communist claims, that the GNP per person in North Korea was about 73 percent of that in South Korea in 1949 and was over 150 percent by 1962. It has presumably fallen somewhat below 150 percent since. Consumption in North and South appears to be about the same, but North Korea has, until recently, saved upward of one third of her GNP, investing most of this in industry, while South Korea has until recently saved and invested almost none of hers, allocating in 1963 only about 15 percent (most of which came from foreign aid) for industry.[40] In the North, enormous emphasis has been laid on creating and maintaining heavy industry, two thirds of North Korea's annual imports consisting of industrial machinery and industrial raw materials as contrasted with 20 percent for South Korea, 80 percent of whose imports were, before 1962 at least, consumables.[41] The rate of economic growth in the North was about 14 percent after the Korean War, roughly three times that of South Korea, until 1963. The gap has since, however, greatly narrowed and, more recently, been closed or even reversed. The Northern rate for 1963–64 may have been less than twice as great as that in the ROK; South Korean performance in 1964–65 improved somewhat and, since then, considerably, attaining a 13.4 percent GNP increase in 1966, with an 8.4 percent increase estimated for 1967, an average rise of 8.4 percent from 1962 to 1966,[42] and exports of $250,000,000 in 1966, almost ten times the level of the later 1950's. From 1963–64, aid to the North from both the U.S.S.R. and Communist China has halted, though in 1967 some military aid has been reported reinstituted. P'yŏngyang has not published official growth estimates since 1964 and has had to postpone the end of its Seven-Year Plan from December 1967 to the end of 1970: it is thus widely felt that growth rates have fallen considerably. Reliable travelers report little North Korean economic progress from 1963 to 1967. It thus appears that, in 1966, growth rates in South Korea, largely thanks to the Vietnamese War, may for the first time in many years (probably, in effect, the thirty-five years since the post-1931 Japanese industrial build-up in Chōsen) have exceeded those in North Korea. The Republic of Korea can answer with a fairly confident "no" the rhetorical question of her own Foreign Minister at Geneva in 1954: "Has not our economy been shattered beyond repair?" [43]

Nevertheless, North Korean achievements remain considerable. North Korean international trade has been much pushed and includes at least nine countries beside the Communist bloc. Population density in 1960 was about 80 per square kilometer in North Korea, about the same as in 1945, whereas South Korea in the same year had 250 per square kilometer, about 50 percent more than in 1945. With about three times as much cultivated land per person as South Korea and as much or more productivity per person, North Korea has a labor shortage, has imported nearly 100,000 Koreans from Japan, and is in a good position to offer jobs to some, at least, of South Korea's estimated two million unemployed. These accomplishments have been the fruit of considerably more planning than South Korea has had until very recently, seemingly better staff work, and greater continuity in government. Examination of personnel changes shows that the old-fashioned, faction-managed bureaucracy has apparently become, since about 1960, an increasingly professional, modern, multiple-function government.

The official communism of North Korea is a striking illustration of a phenomenon already exemplified by the Ilchin-hoe in 1904–1910: the ease with which a party can grow and dominate when imposed from above on Korean society, even when that imposition comes from a foreign source. The Soviet Union could impose its own communism under leaders of its own choice on North Korea even without utilizing the more powerful personalities in its armory. Once power was established, the official party was not abandoned, like the Ilchin-hoe, but multiplied, and when the hollowness of the resulting mass party was revealed under wartime pressures, it was given unusually intensive buttressing through collectivization, propaganda, and state-controlled education-indoctrination. No final judgment on the result can be passed, but the cohesion achieved through communism seems, on the surface up to now, impressive. Communism can impose sacrifice for modernization that South Korea cannot, at least in peace, accomplish. North Korea appears to have made better use of her foreign aid, accomplished greater and better-planned industrial and productive expansion, and achieved, on the surface, far more political stability than the Republic of Korea — to the extent that it is possible to compare a totalitarian society with a partially free one. Professionalization has apparently been more quickly created and, to judge by the results among foreign-trained students, with decidedly more discipline and success.[44]

Such development has affected the factional pattern. The trained young North Korean is not able to drift to the capital, attach himself to a patron, form part of a factional pressure group, and shop around for the best bureaucratic opening. His training is determined by the state's technical requirements; he is assigned and understands that his access to the central bureaucracy lies where the government tells him it lies. He knows no freedom, and his personal growth may, in the process, be cramped and limited. Yet at the same time, it seems also possible that the growth of a multi-functional, multi-centered, professional society is being advanced, and perhaps the first means of breaking the classic pattern of factionalism around the center power vortex has been found.[45] Views will sharply differ as to whether the result is worth — let alone justifies — the price, but the North Korean experiment may sooner or later exert influence on South Korea. Indeed, through the close observation of North Korean communism by Kim Chong-p'il's intelligence circle, it already has. It will be one of the main challenges of South Korean society to limit the degree of such influence and, perhaps, exert some of its own by the construction of an improved social and governmental framework within South Korea.

The enormous southward flow of refugees has certainly sufficed to show that the price exacted is harsh. Very likely it remains so, though the controls of government for the past fourteen years have prevented many signs of unhappiness or unrest from rising to the surface.[46] There seems, however, a fair chance that some strain and restlessness may grow. A Red Guard–army incident against Kim Il-sŏng was reported in Peking in February 1967. Increases in the standard of living and in consumer goods recently and a rapidly expanding educational system may eventually bring to the surface among North Korean students many of the same signs of restlessness and desire for more freedom of contact and inquiry that now motivate Soviet students. North Korea's rigid uniformity in a way conforms to the society's basic homogeneity; but Kim Il-sŏng's extremism and autocracy produce constant sub-surface restlessness and doubt as to the extent to which a fruitful scientific and technically advanced society can subordinate individual abilities and private motivations. In addition, though discipline has been exacted on the ordinary rungs of the access-to-power pattern, the top rungs will one day have to be reclimbed, and, when they are, foreign Communist power is unlikely to referee succession problems as before. The guerrilla as manipulator of a mass, homogeneous society involves some anomaly. He has succeeded in squelching the disruptive effects of the council pattern that Communist committees might have brought. But younger men, schooled to bureaucratic and industrial committee work, may wish to revive the old pattern in new form and, through it, challenge one-man leadership. It is unclear whether the creation of large industrial units outside P'yŏngyang has had any substantial decentralizing effect that might permanently sap the central power vortex: most evidence thus far points to Kim Il-sŏng's increase of centralization. So long as the North Korea state remains rigidly centralized, tensions accompanying any transfer of power will be intense. When such strains or such transfers arise, North Korea may suffer from the effects of a system that, by its very rigidity and continuity, has deprived the society of South Korea's variety of political experience.

Prediction is, in any case, not the business of this study. What is evident is that 1945's desperate needs for cohesion did find in communism an answer, viable at heavy cost. Communism profits from the ease with which a Korean party can be formed from above. The dictatorial pattern can take advantage of the terms of the society: centralization maximized by homogeneity and lack of intermediate associations. The positive effectiveness of communism in North Korea has certainly been aggravated by other factors. Unusually great war destruction and population dispersal made the destruction of the old society exceptionally complete and eased the introduction of new, mass-organized, propaganda-ridden state units. Unlike Eastern European societies, the North Korean population has been allowed no interlude of freedom within almost anyone's memory. Without such conditions, Kim Il-sŏng's problems would have been greater. Yet would their effect have been decisive? Even without them, the stark fact remains that communism arose, in Russia, in a mass society and has shown itself most successful, as in China, in grafting itself to others of like ilk. Its success in North Korea is an additional test of the thesis that Korea strongly shares these mass characteristics.

12

The Military

THE BACKGROUND

Among Korean institutions, the military stands unique. No other cohesive and mature group approaches its size of some 600,000 men, some 530,000 of them in the army.[1] The army has been longest subjected to a consistent discipline and, since the Korean War, to a rational educational process. No civilian group or institution has come close to it in the development of a definite and comparatively fairly administered career service. It is the only Korean group on which Americans have succeeded in concentrating sufficient funds, training, advice, and attention over a long enough period to achieve effective influence. The army has demonstrated more sharply than any other major group the cleavages and internal dynamics of Korean factionalism. Yet it was also the only Korean institution to generate the cure — the means gradually to begin the laying of broader bases for organizational unity. The confidence thus created was at work in the military coup of 1961 and the establishment of military hegemony over government and politics.

Strong armed forces, as we have seen, are unusual in the context of the past several centuries of Korean history. The 1961 coup was the first time in eight hundred years that the military had been cast in a renovating role (see Chapter 1).

Korea suffered much both in weakness and arrested development from the long Yi policy of stunting the military; for on the eve of its long historic somnolence, the military was a promising institutional alternative for the diversification of society. A century before the military coup of 1170, the official histories tell us, the central army was already disorganized, inadequately supplied, and undercut by desertion.[2] Its breakdown was followed by the rise of more local forces based on personal loyalties. The strong men of the coup of 1170 and their successors who ruled until 1270 owed their strength to their "house armies." These proved prime instruments of social mobility, being composed of "house pages," expanded by local retainers, by farmers forced off the land by taxes or invasion, and by slaves, then numerous. The retainers were known as *mun'gaek*, "gate guests." Each private house came to power and ruled through them. Through them, even a slave like Kim In-jun (alias Kim Chun) could rise to supreme shogunal power. His successor, Im Yŏn, was also of humble origin and worked his way upward largely by physical strength and ambition. This disordered century was the closest Korea was to come to the praetorian and also to the feudal world. The military and their private armies, not the government, represented the vigor and power of the age. Official, Chinese-influenced institutions waned, native loyalties rose, and, in some fields, economic productivity as well as destruction flourished. The official history tells us: "When they sent our troops to ward off the Khitan, the skillful and brave soldiers were all the *mun'gaek* of the Ch'oe's, while the government army was weak and unable to be used." [3]

Unfortunately for Korea's development none of the feudal elements was to coalesce and last. The Yi, remembering only the chaos and the dire results of overthrow of civil rule, lastingly repressed the military and usurped its top positions. Since civil officials learned notoriously little of military matters and no one was allowed to remain in any post long enough to acquire expertise, the decline of the entire military establishment — forts, equipment, training, and morale — proceeded with rare reprieve throughout the dynasty. At its end, Japanese subversion of what remained of Korea's "armed forces" was comparatively simple and almost complete. When formally disbanded on August 1, 1907, they numbered only 6,000 men, and only one battalion in Seoul and a few troops in Wŏnju and on Kanghwa revolted.[4] The insurgency between 1907 and 1911 was mostly the effort of poorly armed, scattered farmers. Rarely has a people so numerous and of such distinguished heritage surrendered so easily. Anti-Japanese resistance in Manchuria and China was carried on by many brave Korean guerrillas, but no Korean Army worthy of the word existed from 1907 until 1946.[5] After 2,000 years, Korea was left almost without a living military tradition: a strange backdrop for Korea's flourishing military of today.

The present Korean Army, then, has no relation to the ancient armies of the peninsula. Instead it illustrates the difficulties of organization-building in many emerging, former colonial countries: without control over their own traditions, such countries must copy institutions from abroad. Sources of disunity are thus multiplied at the very time that unity is most needed. Korea's army was melded of several different influences, almost entirely foreign. Embedded within these, however, were the tendencies to make of these foreign origins factions and, within factions, to construct friendship groups that in times of chaos or indecision became strong. The Korean War, however, forced the belated application of enough training and discipline to overcome these informal divisions. Through overcoming them, the Korean Army became the first Korean organization we know of that eliminated most of the sources of fluidity and disunity within Korea's mass society. It became the strongest organization of the country and acquired therewith that vested interest which the Yi civilian rulers had for centuries maneuvered to prevent. The army was thus able to overthrow civilian democratic rule much as Yi officials had feared that it would overthrow their Confucian hegemony. The military forces serve as the great example in Korea, so far, of the crucial role in her society that developed interest groups and their accomplishments can play.

Japan's military system was the main initial precedent. We have seen that her career training institutions, especially the Imperial Defense College in Tokyo and the Manchurian Academy, trained several dozen Korean officers who were to become the elite of the new Korean Army. From the twenty Tokyo-trained officers who survived World War II, the *enfants dorés* of the system, came five of the first seven Chiefs of Staff and three of the Ministers of Defense between 1948 and 1961. The air force has been especially dominated by the Tokyo group, which had better social background and firmer roots in South Korea than any other. The Manchurian officers, numbering over forty World War II survivors, were the second best-trained group. Mostly bright boys of poor families from North Korea, especially Hamgyŏng-do and Manchuria itself, they were an especially ambitious close-knit circle, providing many of the leaders of the ROK Army.[6] The student officers (*hakpyŏng*) formed another group within the Korean armed forces; many joined the Korean constabulary in 1945–1946 and, through brightness, adaptability, and fluency in English, performed excellently, five of the six Chiefs of Staff from 1960 to 1966 being drawn from this circle. Many *hakpyŏng* felt that their civilian education gave them a better "moral" background than that of the Manchurian officers. Though *hakpyŏng* had common sympathy through sharing common status, they had come from widely scattered schools and colleges, had not known each other intimately, and therefore lacked the possibility of forming cohesive factional bonds of the kind the Japanese and Manchurian groups could form through common institutional experience.

Still another, smaller group was composed of officers or NCO's who had taken advantage of the Special Army Volunteer System of 1938 to volunteer for the Japanese Army without particular prior educational experience. Two Chiefs of Staff, Ch'oe Kyŏng-nok and Song Yo-ch'an, came from variants of this group. "Volunteers" had usually served most of their careers as enlisted men or NCO's.

Still another group consisted of enlisted men who had served under the Japanese as conscripts. Some of these, lacking other professions, joined the constabulary, initially as enlisted men, entering officer training course classes on recommendation from late 1946 to early 1948 and particularly dominating the third and fourth classes (April and September, 1947). This was a group of somewhat lower prestige.

In addition to this complex of Japanese veterans, there was a contingent of Korean officers who had served either with the Chinese Army or with the Korean Liberation Army in China, usually the former. They trained in many different places, some having been recruited by warlords. The largest group was probably composed from the hundred young Koreans trained at the Loyang branch of the Chinese Military Academy in accordance with an agreement between Kim Ku and the Chinese nationalists in 1933.[7] The Korean Volunteer Corps in North China later absorbed the leftist Korean military elements, the non-Communists being absorbed largely by Kim Ku's Kwangbok or Restoration Army, which was founded on September 17, 1940, with some 200 officers and men and grew to a possible 3,600 by August 1943.[8] The Japanese-trained circles regarded with some suspicion the large number of "Chinese generals" who emerged from this environment. Many of the latter were older, lacked the rigorous training given in Japanese institutions, and, as some other officers put it, "were honored more for their patriotism than for their military preparation." They laid great stress on "spiritual" and "patriotic" factors, an ingredient more needed in the confused early constabulary days than in the actual combat of 1950. None became Chief of Staff, and many retired soon after the Korean War. They were, in fact, a kind of out-group within an army whose leadership was dominated by the Japanese-trained.

Finally, from the time of the seventh officer candidate class in 1948 on, young Korean civilians, including many of the new college graduates, were recruited for officer training. Since the Korean War, Korean high-school honor graduates have been the exclusive source of cadet material. During the war, however, such officers were still only at very junior levels.

Such were the groups from which the Korean officer corps came to be composed and on whom it relied for leadership for the first fifteen years. During at least the first ten years of that time, the inner story of the Korean Army became really the story of the power and inter-relationships of these groups. American Military Government, lacking depth of understanding or adequate preparation for its task, devised no adequate institutional framework through which these diversities could be overcome. The Korean War introduced more disruption. During those years, the Korean Army provided perhaps the clearest picture of subgroups and their struggle that we can conveniently see within Korean society.

THE CONSTABULARY

The Factions Form

With the coming of Liberation, the officer groups moved homeward from service that had spread them all the way from Japan to the South Pacific. Except for the Korean Volunteer Corps and the Manchurian guerrilla groups, drawn to Soviet-occupied North Korea, almost all converged on Seoul. Many of the "Manchurian" officers attempted to visit their homes in the North but were accused by the incoming Communist troops and native leftists of being "collaborators," and all except a handful felt obliged to flee south. Few had any roots in South Korea. Most officers and soldiers, outside the Japan group, even lacked any suitable channel for ambition, because they came from modest rural or small-town backgrounds and had never had any career but the military. Hence, almost all flocked to the constabulary when it was founded, and, since they had no sources of help in South Korean society, formed a tight group to provide such help for themselves. Like other refugees, they headed for houses of their native provincemen until finding quarters of their own, thus strengthening provincial ties.

Had a larger organization been set up with definite aims, educational purpose, or appealing ideology, it could have attracted many and begun the process of breaking down clique opportunism. None was, and so each group set up its own office or association. One called the Preparatory Unit for the National Defense Forces formed around the second-generation Japanese-trained officers. There was an office for the Kwangbok Army, a Naval Defense Corps for former naval personnel (of whom there were few), an Association for the Establishment of a Korean Air Force, a Student Officers Association, and many others, one former Chief of Staff describing them as "innumerable." This atomization was further complicated by the rightist-leftist split, so that, for example, returning student soldiers were soon greeted with two *hakpyŏng* associations, one leftist, one anti-Communist.[9]

One early attempt was made — by the Communists — to set up an organization embracing all officers; it briefly attracted considerable support. An able young captain of the Manchurian Air Force named Pak Sŭng-hwan, who had made contact with the Yenan Communists during the last stages of the war, flew a plane into Seoul in August and, apparently under instructions, set up an "Officers Association" for all ex-officers. This association early manifested ideological tendencies. Lectures and discussions resolving current questions along Communist lines were conducted. Many younger officers, including some from the last three Tokyo classes and many of the Manchurian seventh class, graduating in 1940, became faithful members and began establishing political connections with the People's Republic and the politicians around Lyuh Woon-hyung.[10] Most non-leftist officers tended to believe in political neutrality and in distancing themselves from political matters. The Communist group was almost alone in its use of politics, ideology, and indoctrination to create a unit crossing the lines of friendship circles and previous affiliations. With the establishment of the constabulary in January 1946, the

Officers Association was banned, Pak went North in December 1945, and ten others followed in the next weeks to become founders of the North Korean "People's Army"; later, reportedly, these met death by purge. Many of the association, however, joined the constabulary, which had not yet instituted security checks; within it they recommended leftist enlisted men to officer classes, especially the third and fourth, and, using this group, became the core of the Yŏsu rebellion, the defections to North Korea of the battalions of Major Kang T'ae-mun and Major P'yo, and other subversive trouble within the Korean armed forces in the 1947–1948 period.[11]

Most ex-officers had been too well indoctrinated with Japanese or Kuomintang anti-communism, confirmed by their experience in the initial liberation of North Korea, to be attracted leftward. For them another avenue soon emerged.

By November 1945 General Hodge and his staff in Seoul had seen enough of chaos in the South and Communist intentions in the North to make strong and repeated pleas to Tokyo and Washington for the creation of a Korean military defense unit. Unfortunately, both MacArthur and Washington, anxious not to arouse the Russians, demurred, and a modest, almost surreptitious, plan for a constabulary-type police reserve was substituted, what little was done being almost entirely on the initiative of Hodge and his staff.[12] This desire to do something that would not annoy the Russians, plus lack of equipment, books, training, or American personnel willing to stay with the job militated against the establishment of a proud cohesive organization.[13]

Still, a start was made. Notices welcoming all experienced comers were posted, and candidates flocked in on January 14, 1946. Instead of purposeful Japanese elite recruitment, procedures consisted of "a brief interview with an American officer" (through an interpreter), the filling out of a questionnaire, and a medical examination. As an official U.S. history puts it: "recruiting standards remained low, and reasonably healthy applicants had little difficulty in enlisting." [14] No American officer concerned had, at the time, any concept of the complex background of the men and groups with which he was dealing.[15] Except for a devoted young officer named James Hausman, few stayed to find out. American officer interest in the spring of 1946 was concentrated on returning to the U.S. for discharge. "In less than seven months there had been five [U.S.] Directors of National Defense and three of the changes occurred in the 11 April–1 June period." [16] This did not prevent Americans from having their own favorites and refereeing the promotion process: those without "background" or education in the Korean sense sometimes got ahead through their patronage. Americans had far fewer selfish and ambitious purposes than Japanese of the 1901–1910 period, but the channel of recruitment they operated recalled that through which Uchida Ryōhei brought Song Pyŏng-jun and Yi Yong-gu to power during the dawn of Japanese control. To arm the men, Japanese rifles were scrounged and machine guns "reliberated" from Americans who had taken them as souvenirs.[17] Indoctrination was nil; Korean officers long argued in vain with successive American advisors about the need for some ideological content, some sense of higher objective, even an appropriate emphasis on loyalty, in military training.

The first course was simply called — and simply was — an English Language Training Course. Training itself was simple. "The purpose of the school was not to teach the Koreans English but to teach them basic military expressions *in* English." [18] Korean instructors were lacking, and manuals were skimpily translated until the Korean War and the postwar period; Americans taught through interpreters, drawings, and sign language. The whole effort was rudimentary for many precious months. As late as November 1946 the entire constabulary had only 143 officers and 5,130 men.[19] The Constabulary Training Center failed to function as anything more than an elementary officers training class through the spring of 1949. In the words of the first commandant of the Korean Constabulary Officers Training School: "The contents of the course were mainly close-order and combat drills, together with tactics which were taught by means of [informal and ad hoc] translations of the American Field Manuals." [20] As late as 1949, some officers still conducted drill by Japanese methods. By the time of the Korean War, only sixteen of the ROK Army's sixty-seven battalions had gone through the battalion stage of training, none had gone through regimental training, and even the company and platoon training was not completed.[21] Moreover, for many months the fledgling force functioned chiefly as warehouse guards subject to popular grumbling that it was a mercenary and puppet group. Not until 1955 did a Korean class with first-rate officer training graduate.

The organization reflected these meager institution-building methods. It is chiefly a tribute to the intelligence and patriotism of the Korean officers and NCO's that the force became as good as it was.

Administration was, from the beginning, essentially American because all material came from U.S. supplies. Thus adaptability to American procedures was important, and this suppleness the younger officers had in fuller measure than the older ones. Except for expediency, however, Korean officers had little reason to take the training they received with the seriousness they had taken the far more professional training Japan had given many of them. Moreover, induction to the early constabulary classes had been on a "first come first serve" basis, with seniority determined more by chance than by ability, knowledge, or experience. Japanese ranks and training remained the prestige system under light American veneer; a senior from Japanese days was regarded as a senior even when he happened to have entered the American service later and had lower rank. Japanese cadet classes, lasting two to four years under strict discipline, continued to be the centers of the friendship and loyalty structure; the American-sponsored officer training classes, lasting, until the Korean War, only six months or less in an atmosphere of improvisation, could not replace them despite every informal attempt to build up the newer relationships. The older groups therefore survived as centers of communications, recruitment, and loyalty. Through them, until about 1949, was decided who among the former officers should be allowed lateral entry and at what rank, what discipline should be meted out when an officer was found involved in corruption or subversion, and who should be given the key assignments in personnel, operations, or the main field or supply commands. The positions where such decisions were made were, as in the Yi government, the objects of extreme factional maneuvering. Through a multitude of small decisions, informally mediated within these groups and then negotiated with the usually innocent American advisors, the factional leaders ran the constabulary and, later, the army.

The Nature of Constabulary Factions

The factions, little disturbed by newer discipline, preserved many traditional characteristics. Confucian and military ideals combined to produce a strong tendency toward recruitment by seniority within them.[22] As elsewhere, decisions were made by group consultation cast somewhat in terms of the "elder to younger brother" Confucian relationship. Hence the senior classes of the officers trained in the 1930's and 1940's tended to be the "older brothers" of the system and the focus of the decision process.

Each group also developed its top leader. He was a senior member of the dominant circle and one who had "demonstrated ability" by an especially brilliant career within the Japanese system. A sword received from the Japanese emperor in recognition of his ability — such as one factional leader possessed — was at least as useful for legitimizing his position as an act of Korean patriotism or participation in the Independence Movement would have been. Ability to communicate with Americans, acquire their confidence, and adapt to their ways also contributed to leadership status. Much as in Korean political life, such leadership was almost never dictatorial. The leader was first among equals in a council-consultation system.

Each important group member tended also to be the leader of his own personal faction within, sometimes partly outside, the group. His success in his personal leadership role contributed to his faction's strength but also tended to make him somewhat more independent of its consensus. As his personal clique developed, it became a matter of particular subtlety and complexity to decide under what circumstances he would join his faction or its leader in a given decision and under what circumstances he would oppose or demur. Those competent to predict such questions — which were often crucial, especially in matters of punishment, counter-action or coup — were few and were themselves a kind of elite in the Korean world whether Korean or, as very rarely, foreign. Such prediction required the constant communication, knowledge, and gossip for which in former times the private *salangban* (gentleman's parlor) of the Yi and now the thousand tearooms of Seoul are famous. This type of decision-making with its ancient council echoes appears to be deeply associated with the indigenous culture. The Japanese world knows no such leeway from — or within — group decisions and has correspondingly less need for the gossip and judgments that surround them.

The complex recruitment and composition of these personal army factions reflects important facets of Korean social process. In every significant circle, factional behavior tends to the obtaining of government power through personal or factional rather than institutional channels; it thus contributes to the vortex of centralization. Within the constabulary, the original company commanders of 1946 were encouraged to recommend suitable NCO's for officer training. Lacking other avenues and loyalties subordinates competed intensely for such recommendations. Within as well as outside the army, the "recommenders" soon acquired their own staffs, drivers, and orderlies bound to their own persons. In the pioneering organizations of the time, the personally recommended rose fast. Kim Ch'ang-yong ("Snake" Kim), who had been a rough enlisted man in the Japanese MP's, was recommended for officer training in 1946 and ended up as Lieutenant General, CIC Commander, and Rasputin of the realm within eight years; he was murdered while still in his early thirties. One driver for a new lieutenant and company commander in 1946 found himself become a brigadier general, member of the Supreme Council, and Director of the Korean Central Intelligence Agency by 1961–1963. Both "Snake" Kim and the driver who steered himself to a generalship had been unknown, poorly educated boys from the lowest social ranks. Such personal recommendations for entry dominated the years from 1946 to 1949. By this time such appointees, their loyalty further deepened by the need for their boss's support in getting favorable assignments, had formed considerable factions. The climbs of the Song Pyŏng-juns and Yi Kyu-wans, liberated from even the few limits of occupation days, were now not the exception but the rule of power access.

Below clique and faction, on their lower fringes, were the "retainers" — were and in part still are, for the pattern in Korea and its army is not yet dead. Late Koryŏ "gate guests" had become private armies; through the centuries the classical form of the upper-class Korean house institutionalized this process by a long series of rooms, largely to accommodate retainers, running along the sides of the compound on either side of the gate (see Fig. 1). Servants have been agelessly ubiquitous, and, as a military or civilian leader rose in importance, he added to these "assistants" orphan relatives, poor wards, or connections.[23] The higher officer — often even the ex-general — had his own jeep and military or ex-military driver. An active general's aide usually housed with him and often became a member of his family, his career from then on typically linked so that he rose with his master, or left the service if his master "had trouble." A former NCO or policeman who had close bonds and lacked his own social base might continue to hang on, running errands, accompanying the general's wife shopping, affording extra protection when needed, and delivering confidential messages or money. Important civilians attracted the sons of impoverished farmers, gentry, or relatives without much to occupy them on the land; all thought of the master's house as their Seoul pad, their place for a lift-off. They came unsolicited, almost beyond avoiding. Such men constituted the lower reaches of any personal faction, performed its humbler chores, and supplied its voracious needs for communication.[24]

The retainer has remained an important part of the color of the crowded, chatty, dramatic Seoul milieu. He belongs to the elastic obligations of the great man; his compensation is irregular, and he expects to profit from his master's success. His presence is a daily reinjection of his master's will toward power. He does not demand moral perfection or financial impeccability; indeed, the sense of excitement important to his existence has derived largely from secret visits to the master's intimates, financial trips to friends, or assignations with concubine or mistress. At best, the retainer has a loyalty stout and unswerving. For better or worse, he has endowed Seoul with much of its furtive and conspiratorial atmosphere. He uses polite language that the master returns with low. Yet he is not in any north European sense a servant.[25] He does not bow or scrape. The hissing of the prewar Japanese he regards with hilarity and disdain. He is a trusty, dependent on his master but nonetheless with a free-swinging sense of his own dignity and importance and a ringing claim to the day's title of humor. The Japanese had small chance of reforming him; his is the clay of another world. Yet, for all its humor and color his has been also a tragic world. Like the factions themselves, the retainers have represented attempts to give minimum insulation, irreducible protection from authorities or other hostile power. In them something of the emotional satisfaction of the Korean family seeks continuance. Yet the vehicle protects weakly, and there remains something immature about clique emotion for all its warmth. The road of the retainer and clique member is rocky and usually, in the end, bitter. The system substitutes with a pathetic inadequacy for the defenses and bonds of institutions.

Ppaek is therefore vital. From factional circle down to personal household, power is not a contribution to a formal, hierarchical organization rewarding through qualification and aimed at national objectives, but has, by and large, remained the capacity of a leader to place and protect the members of his personal group and provide them with the access to power and to a lesser degree the material needs considered the prerequisites of success. High position and title are, in themselves, honored, but if one listens to the ways in which admiration for them is expressed, one finds in them little concern with problem-solving, much concern with the ability to accomplish personal objectives. Those who, like one famous and rigorously honest former Prime Minister, operate outside such concepts, find themselves praised by students and idealists for their "purity," by Westerners for their probity, but regarded by others as amusingly naive, lacking real power and the sinews of action.

Similarly, members of groups view and often judge the operations of the state in a highly personal way. Political approval is likely to be awarded in accordance with the nearness of access of the group leader to power. Words equivalent to "qualification" or even "virtue" are those used, but they are not taken seriously by men involved in the power struggle. "Justice" is far more the fulfillment of the group's wishes than the achievement of legal process. By the same token, those outside have no rational criteria for curbing their own claims on power but engage themselves in instant criticism of those who hold it and struggle by any means to hold it themselves. Such processes have long been close to the society generally, but it is in the army that they could be most clearly seen. Thus in the army, the bitter struggle for the Chief of Staff position that took place throughout the 1950's was as good or even better an illustration of the Korean political process than the operation of political parties themselves.

WAR SWELLS THE FACTIONAL PATTERN

War aggravated the factional system.[26] Floods of supplies and equipment rained down on Korea. Strict control and accountability broke down; loss by black-market sales could be attributed to enemy action. Formal American attempts to control were blocked by language and the thousand channels of evasion. American views of equipment as "expendable," "off-duty" sales to the black market, and "informality" in using jeeps to transport girl friends created unfavorable comparisons with the strict discipline of Japanese use of equipment and a weak climate of respect at the top. From the beginning, salaries in the armed forces had had no relationship to expenses. Spiraling war inflation made this worse. Prices rose 750 percent in Seoul in the first year of the war, a phenomenon on which the 50 percent rise in prices in Vietnam during the first eighteen months of American buildup provides an ironic perspective. Surplus Japanese equipment in 1946 followed by American relief and constabulary proximity to warehouses had long set a pattern of selling goods and relief rations to live, sometimes with the tacit consent of American military counterparts. When such sources were not available, the Special Service fund and most intelligence funds had to be used to supplement salary. Moreover, the American supply service was long defective in not providing sufficient spare parts and repair facilities for equipment. Gas had to be sold to acquire spare parts. The Americans privately admitted lack of funds and equipment for barracks construction, paper, and soy sauce. Much illegal cutting of forests and operating of small factories went on to supply such needs. Often the origins of these activities were both necessary and well-meant. But they contained within them no objective delineation of the bounds between honesty and dishonesty. One could no longer judge a man on whether or not he did these things —virtually all senior officers had to perform some such functions so that their subordinates, as well as they, could live — it became a vague question of how much, whether it was shared or not, whether the purpose was "normal" or for enrichment. The informal factional pattern placed value primarily on ability to take care of one's loyal subordinates; the more one took, the better one could support greater circles of one's men. On this stage, the great corruptions of the early 1950's were performed. Koreans had always known corruption, but its extreme form, its more prehensile pattern, arose inside the Korean Army and at this time. Its hectic embrace has not yet been wrenched loose from Korea.

Factionalism battened on war and corruption. War magnified the mistakes of inexperienced officers, and corruption added to the constant need for the factional leader's protective cloak. The severer the misdemeanor, the greater the claim of loyalty once protection was given. The guilty were prime recruits for a faction. This had been true even when some key officers were protected as a result of the investigations of subversion following the Yŏsu rebellion. Now an officer who had defected in 1946 to the North Korean Army to avoid sentence for having sold a truckload of blankets was reinstated by his factional leader, then Chief of Staff, when he again defected South. Another was reinstated despite the fact that he deserted in the face of the enemy, taking with him a jeep. Many were protected in the face of charges of misappropriation of funds, improper use of vehicles, and so forth. Meanwhile, the Chief of Staff's needs for a faction to fight for his preservation of office in the face of expanding malfeasance likewise grew. Matters leaking into public knowledge or reported to the President through the Counter-Intelligence Corps (CIC) had to be "explained" to the accompaniment of suitable presents to those surrounding him and, on occasion, cabinet members.

Forces of this kind could not be confined to upper officer circles; they affected the army organization to the bottom, and, since most young men passed through the army, they merged with the morale of the nation.[27] The details of gasoline selling or absconding with budgeted funds were hidden from the men, but the effects fell on them. Because gasoline had been sold, recruits at the huge Nonsan training center were forced to walk when their schedule called for trucking.[28] In the worse units, food was chronically short and men continuously hungry because leakage was so constant. If the recruits did not bring a rough equivalent of $50 in cash with them for their three-month training, they could scarcely get through their course. The money went to members of the "gangs" who came to control the training units: roughnecks who joined the service together from one locality in the hope of control and profit. More adept than the naive farm boy or middle-class recruit at the arts of bribery and the less subtle ones of manhandling, they quickly formed liaisons with their superiors, took the recruits' money in return for weekend leave, food, a blanket or other "privileges" (for which American support had, of course, already been given), passed a portion of it on and kept the rest. In return they became squad leaders. In "the graveyard of Korean youth," the sacrifices of institutional interests for personal mobility roosted in the lowest as well as the highest places.

Most deleterious was the corvée. Budgeted funds, largely provided by the U.S., for construction work to be performed by outside hired labor, were often instead split up among key officers, a process into which factional alignment was subtly interwoven. Unknown to the sleeping American advisors, the recruits of Nonsan or the enlisted men elsewhere would then be taken out at night to do the construction work without recompense and after a full training day, a system curiously overtoned with the Koryŏ "public slave" system. Without either sleep or sufficient food, training could not be absorbed. Hundreds of thousands of young men passing through such experiences came into greater or less contact with these conditions as the army grew from little over 50,000 in late 1950 to the 655,000-man ROK Army whose support was authorized by President Eisenhower on May 14, 1953, and attained soon after the armistice in July.[29] As the soldiers were mustered out, knowledge of the system was spread throughout the country. It was a factor in low public morale and in the creation of public sympathy for change. Most infected by this sentiment were the students, who knew that they would have to face such conditions on or before their graduation, and the young officers, whose better training and discipline came into increasing conflict with this more ancient — and seemingly unyielding — way of life.

As the army became the country's most important source of funds, its connection with politics constantly escalated in such forms as an alliance between the Defense Minister, the Chief of Staff, and the chairman of the Liberal party. Cases like that of the illegal sale of U.S.–imported cotton to provide the Liberal party with political funds came increasingly to light. No one will ever be able to compile the astronomical rise in the income and expenditure of the Chief of Staff in these years, or the multiplied demands on factional channels that it brought: key income-producing jobs had to be assigned to the "trustworthy"; financial communication requiring full confidence grew. Assignments and promotions followed these masters like a faithful dog. Factionalism and corruption were twins.

The ascending spiral rose from 1951 on, to the highest reaches of the state. From it came much of the politics of those years. Rhee realized that the war-swollen army, no longer separable from politics, must be employed. He had created neither factionalism nor corruption, but he was skilled in using them to establish firm controls. His strategy was to prevent the accretion of any single faction or leader in control. His tactic was to play the chief army groups off against each other by encouraging their struggle for the Chief of Staff and other key positions. His technique was to use corruption, its investigation and punishment, as the periodic means of effecting changes. His instrument was the Korean investigation agencies.

From 1949, after the Yŏsu rebellion and the evident need for full-scale investigations of subversion, the Korean CIC, in the rough young hands of "Snake" Kim, had grown. With the rise of corruption in the wake of the war, it acquired, almost overnight, immensely swollen opportunities for self-enrichment, not only from payoffs, but because investigation could uncover the houses and other properties of Communists who fled North and identify the abandoned housing of departed American personnel; these its officers were then able to confiscate. Rhee greatly increased these powers by giving his "Snake" direct Presidential access. He was aware, however, that the power thus bestowed also required curbs. He thus called into being a countervailing force, that of the Joint Provost Marshal General Command (JPMGC) under Lieutenant General Wŏn Yŏng-dŏk, grey eminence of the 1952 political incident. CIC, the JPMGC, and the Chief of Staff, all with access to the President, none fully controlled by the other, set up a triangular power struggle among themselves of unparalleled bitterness from 1951 to 1956; its path was strewn with increasing rival tension created by uncontrolled surveillance of the Chief of Staff under conditions in which he was inevitably vulnerable. Such surveillance led, obscurely and ineluctably, to the murder, in January 1956, of "Snake" Kim, and this to the trial of those accused of murdering him — a trial of exceptional length rife with revelation of military corruption. The trial and the pattern that led to it brought in suite the increasing disillusionment of younger officers with the state of the army. The results of the old pattern had gone far enough to rock the nation. A crisis in morale among the young and better-educated elements of the country developed that, almost to this day, has inhibited its full confidence.

PROFESSIONALISM AND REFORM

The New Training

The murder of "Snake" Kim and the trial of those accused of it may be taken as the high watermark of the old pattern. Already reverse tides were rising that were to change both the Korean Army and its historical destiny.

The start of these tides predated the outbreak of war. With the coming of Korean independence in the summer of 1948, most of the former officers and NCO's who were suitable officer material had joined the constabulary. On December 15, 1948, the constabulary officially became the Korean Army. In 1948–1949, the first officer classes, recruited primarily from among new civilian sources, went through the Officer Training School as its seventh and eighth classes. Some of the graduates were still NCO's and some were from Yi Pŏm-sŏk's Racial Youth Group, but many were civilian students. The eighth class reflected the belated desire of the United States to build up the new army rapidly after March 1948 in order to attempt to bring Korean forces to the level where they could "safely" replace the American forces, whose withdrawal took place from late 1948 until the end of June 1949. Rapid recruitment outside factional channels in the constabulary now jammed 726 members into the seventh and 1,801 members into the eighth class (graduating in several increments). The total number of officers graduating up to that time had been 1,379; of these many, some sources believe almost one third, were either killed or discharged during or following the Yŏsu rebellion and the Communist conspiracy case.[30] In consequence, the seventh and eighth classes more than tripled the existing officer corps, largely with new blood unconnected with factions. The new officers came primarily from South Korea or, if from North Korea, had far weaker factional ties there than their predecessors enjoyed. Differences in education were less great than among early constabulary officers. From the spring of 1948 onward rapid conversion of the constabulary from a police reserve force to an army took place, brigade headquarters were activated, technical services started, a weapons school set up, and equipment increased; the American Provisional Military Advisory Group founded with 100 advisors in August 1948 had 241 by April 1949 and some 472 by the end of 1949.[31] By 1949, training, for the first time, began to emerge from the primitive and makeshift. A Command and General Staff College opened in September 1949; other schools were started; and, by the end of 1949, 13 schools were operating for armed forces totaling almost 100,000. The first Korean officers to study in the United States left in 1948 and 1949, and another group of 33 officers, present at the March–June 1950 U.S. troop exercises in Japan, became the first Koreans closely to observe how U.S. Army units operated in the field.[32] Less than three weeks before the North Korean invasion, the first of Korea's four-year Military Academy cadets started training; most were to die within the month in a futile, heroic attempt to stem the North Korean drive near their school grounds. It was a brave beginning, but a beginning only: that, by the Korean War's opening, no artillery field manual had yet been translated or, in any language, printed in Korea was illustrative of a thousand professional shortcomings.

Time ran out on these early attempts to create an army in South Korea worthy of the name. American judgment that Korea's troops were capable of resisting Northern aggression proved clearly and tragically mistaken. Underprepared and badly underequipped, they were quickly defeated in the war's opening days. UN forces had to carry the brunt of the fighting until they could be reformed. When they were, corruption and factionalism hampered their effectiveness.

Yet Korean-American efforts to form effective armed forces were, from 1951 on, sure-footed, and ultimately they succeeded. War had vanquished American inattention to Korea. There was new determination that the mistakes which had brought defeat must be redressed. Lack of training, especially the integrative effect of training on military units, was singled out as chief cause. MacArthur cautiously, Generals Ridgway and Van Fleet far more enthusiastically, put high-powered support behind new training. Military advisors were raised to 746 by the end of 1950, to 1,055 by August 31, 1951, and, on paper at least, to 1,953 in early 1952.[33] The opening of negotiations at Panmunjŏm in July 1951 provided the first opportunity to proceed with training plans with deliberate thoroughness. MacArthur and Truman had agreed on a 10-division, 250,000-man Korean Army during the Wake Conference on October 15, 1950; war, it seems, had changed the general's estimates.[34] Training deficiencies were to be corrected. Toward the end of 1951, the Korean Army's service schools were re-opened, re-equipped, and greatly expanded in facilities and in advisors. Specialist training was expanded; tanks and artillery were provided for the first time on any significant scale. Korean officers were sent now by the hundreds to study in American service schools. Increasing numbers were trained in the next decade, so that by 1959 approximately 10 percent of all Korean officers had some U.S. training. Their adaptability to American ways and their English (the latter more a problem than the former) had improved from fighting side by side with entire American units; indeed, the wartime presence of up to 350,000 American troops in South Korea, giving it a temporary U.S. population considerably larger than and more than twice as dense as Nevada's, provided a massive impulse toward linguistic and cultural Americanization for the army as it did for the country in general. On January 1, 1952, the Korean Military

Academy re-opened for the first four-year course that was to see completion. Thereafter, as peace returned, recruitment and training steadily became more subject to standard procedures, career specialization progressed, and promotions, particularly at the middle and lower levels, were less subject to personal influence and favoritism. With the retirement of the last great factional leader as Chief of Staff in early 1959, the pattern of top factional control and maneuvering greatly declined at the top.

The over-all effects were gradual, but a few were at once apparent. The leading citadel of the new institutional values was the Military Academy. It was consciously and closely modeled on West Point. Its cadets were now selected by rigorous examination. All expenses were borne by the army. The curriculum was rigorous, exams were frequent, and their results posted. The staff was increasingly professional. Exacting discipline, parades, and ceremony were used to inculcate institutional values and pride. The finest senior officers were selected as superintendents. Even more striking were the cadets themselves. Without factional ties when they entered, intensely conscious of the vortex of corruption around them, they used the institution and its rules and the four years of close companionship it gave them to form a solid phalanx of resistance to corruption, favoritism, factionalism, and politics. Each day, they swore an oath against these "evils." The extent to which the evils were ingrained outside endowed the internal bond with fanaticism. When a senior officer, known, incidentally for his integrity, once sent a present of cigarettes to the academy, the cadets refused them to a man. Another divide was crossed when the son of Speaker Yi Ki-bung was forced out of the academy for failing examinations, despite political pressure to keep him. Stern moral standards maintained among the cadets were important in this decision. They kept a close, almost puritanical watch on themselves and all around them, observant of the slightest infraction of what became even more their code than the academy's. In its early years the academy became a kind of island off Korea's moral coast, governed by standards quite different from those of the society around it. Its graduates were eagerly sought by those officers wishing to "regularize" the functions of supply, quartermaster, and budget. Though only about 175 graduated each year from 1955 on, their effect on the army constantly grew, was influential by 1960, and has increasingly set more army standards with each passing year.

It has acquired precisely those characteristics that Korea has not previously given her groups: cohesiveness, unity, pride, loyalty, principle, special character, and strict code. And it has shown the immense influence a well-formed institution can have when set athwart the fluidities of a society.

The content of certain advanced courses enhanced the army not only as an institution but as one with critical distance from the rest of society. The Command and General Staff School at Chinhae, led continuously from the time of the war until that of the revolution by the admired leader of the "Japan group," Lieutenant General Yi Chong-ch'an, laid great emphasis not only on modern management procedures but on concepts of patriotism, spirit of service, loyalty to the service, and avoidance of politics. Virtually all officers had to attend it before achieving senior rank. Such requirements together with more regularized promotion led to a feeling of career elitism that nothing in civilian Korea provided. The courses of the National Defense College also gave officers entrée into economics, political science, national development, and the broader terms of the army's role in world strategy and national defense. The graduates of this course, all senior officers, acquired strong impressions of the possibilities of the nation and the limitations of the existing political system. Most concluded that the civilian governments of Korea were performing inadequately. After graduation, these officers talked far more in political terms than before about the solutions to the problems around them. New management methods gave them added criteria for criticism. They became the only group outside the government seriously development-minded. As the political situation grew more confused, some of these officers felt both a greater capacity and more responsibility for improving the situation. Senior officers remembered the violent reaction of younger Japanese officers to Japanese civilian politics and the coups of the early 1930's. Thus training combined with other forces to give the army a national and an incipient "savior from destruction" image of its own role.

Reaction to Politics

The force behind this image was increased not only by the mounting corruption of the end of the Rhee era but also by the unremitting political pressures emanating from the Liberal party vortex. The army was increasingly asked to deliver the soldier vote for the government. One Chief of Staff was appointed partly because the percentages of pro-government vote in an area he had commanded had been particularly high. The 1959 elections, conducted among soldiers within their compounds, were a widely recognized perversion of the voting process that delivered virtually unanimous majorities for the government in all except a very few army polling places. Such interference did not take place during the post-revolutionary period, but more minor infractions did. Some army commanders were asked, especially during by-elections in 1960–1961, to allow special campaigning in or near their compounds under conditions giving preference to Democratic candidates. The increasingly rapid reshuffling of Chiefs of Staff following the April revolution — there were four within a year — reawakened a pattern of intense competition for that position and encouraged close relations between politicians and generals that aroused strong disapproval in lower ranks. Many officers expressed fears that rivalry for political power would destroy the integrity as well as the neutrality of the army. Many generals and colonels were given the impression that, on their increasing visits to camps and installations, politicians within and outside the Defense Ministry treated the military as their subordinates.[35] It also became known that the Democratic party, sore pressed for money to buy Assembly votes for the passage of the budget, was pressuring military leaders for funds. A decade earlier, matters more serious than these would have been regarded as inevitable. From 1960 on, such interference was not swallowed, however, and it stimulated military plotting. The student revolution temporarily forestalled coup, but the resentment transferred itself to the faults of the Chang regime, relatively minor though these were.[36]

By 1959, these new pressures, starting near the bottom, were making themselves felt at the top. Lieutenant General Song Yo-ch'an, who came from no important faction, was appointed Chief of Staff to replace the last retiring major factional leader. He brought with him as aide the top honor graduate of the first four-year class. General Song took some of the first steps to free the army from the hold of the old personnel and the regional and 2 factional affiliations. He purged a considerable number of higher officers — most of whom were known for corruption, factionalism, or both — and was only restrained from above from purging more.

Even when the glacier began to move, it was hard to judge its weight. Discontent now became concentrated on the promotion system. The immense expansion of the army had, by the middle 1950's, brought virtually all able and many mediocre surviving members of the first four classes and many from the fifth to General officer rank. But at this point it appeared that army expansion was over for good, and there were even rumors of possible troop reduction. The classes just junior to the fifth, especially the gigantic eighth class, looked upward and saw its access to higher rank blocked by men often only two or three years senior, less rigorously selected, sometimes less well trained, often inferior in higher education, frequently without more experience.[37] In addition, many of these seniors had sacrificed their moral prestige by corruption and factionalism. The younger officers expressed their dissatisfaction in idealistic, developmental, "save-the-society" terms.

The purges of 1959 were insufficient to appease these claims. More removals were suggested by the Defense Minister of the Interim Government but were blocked, largely by the American Command, which took the view that such removals would reduce the efficiency of the army by eliminating men of experience and training long before normal retirement age. Senior American officers, their contacts largely monopolized by English-speaking Korean generals, failed sufficiently to sense the weight of the promotional pressures and other dissatisfactions from below.[38] By March and April of 1960, plans for a military coup had already been drawn up; their fruition was forestalled by the student revolution. On September 24, 1960, there was an important storm signal. A dozen lieutenant colonels (ten of them from the eighth class) and four colonels burst into the office of the Chief of Staff to demand his resignation and the removal of many senior ROK officers.[39] The officers involved were arrested for insubordination in December 1960, no action was taken on their request, and most, including their organizer, Lieutenant Colonel Kim Chong-p'il, were dropped from the service.[40] Certain members of this group, plus Major General Park Chŏng-hŭi, the uncle of Lieutenant Colonel Kim's wife, an officer known for financial probity, became the core plotters of the coup that approximately 250 officers and some 3,500 men out of a 500,000-man army successfully staged on May 16, 1961.[41]

The coup was thus a movement with several motivations, some

deep and important, others near the surface and more petty. However one rates these, the reaction of a younger group against a discredited older pattern had much to do with the coup's capacity to gain acceptance sufficient for survival. The "inevitability" of which its leadership so often spoke lay not in the faults of the civilian regimes that preceded it, faulty as they were, but in the war-propelled rise of the military and the disciplined American-supported institutions that accompanied it. These made the Korean Army an unrivaled holder of skills, managerial techniques, specialization, and newly acquired ways of building and maintaining institutions. Training programs heightened military consciousness of national development more than the abstract, academic, Marxian-economics-influenced programs of civilian institutions. Having acquired in Korea, for the first time since the thirteenth century, a position as the most dominant organization, the army found ample grounds for dissatisfaction; as with its Koryŏ predecessors, these lay partly in hostility to political tampering with its integrity. As important as the army's size and its self-imposed "savior from destruction" image were the surface tensions generic to many armies but here found with Korean acuteness: the wartime army had been a ladder of extremely rapid fulfillment for the ambitious who lacked other privilege; now this ladder was blocked at the very time that frustrated ambition could combine with national sentiment. The coup had ambivalent scores to settle.

Further Reaction

The accomplishments and failures of the young colonels' démarche on the national stage deserve discussion elsewhere (see Chapter 6); on much of their action the books are not yet closed. Since the beginning of this role, however, the army itself has still further changed.

On coming to power, the coup leaders indulged in one of the greatest purges of Korean history both inside and outside the army. Inside, 2,000 senior officers, including 55 of general rank, were dismissed, many being temporarily jailed on charges of varying validity. Most coup participants were promoted two ranks before "retiring" as assemblymen, cabinet ministers, or officials of the Central Intelligence Agency. All leading participants shortly became brigadier generals (General Park reaching four-star rank within months), and many eighth class members were likewise elevated. With these steps and subsequent arrests and retirements following coup plots, virtually the entire senior level of the Korean Army, Navy, and Air Force was removed from active service. Meanwhile, the four-year academy graduates, reaching the field ranks, have steadily increased their displacement in the army scene.

The role of the military in politics has been marked by steady discussion and controversy within both the armed forces and the general society. Military rule is now a phenomenon common to many developing countries, but it has occurred in few, if any, with such adamant traditions of civilian rule as Korea's.[42] Controversy continues today. Although the results are, as noted, mixed and have hardly fulfilled the moral promises of revolution, military cohesion and its gifts of organization and planning have offered much to the nation, much that should not have remained isolated in military compounds alone. Moreover, the high concentration of talent and training within the military, in a society lacking other major institutions, is likely to continue as long as tension — currently conflict — in Asia swells Korea's armed forces. The Korean CIA has been one of the mechanisms for bringing military talent to bear on the state and bids fair to have lasting influence. Its distance from control by law or popular will not only strains the polity but highlights a problem still unsolved: by its authoritarian nature, military power has proved, in Korea as elsewhere, an inadequate vehicle for advancing the rule of law, for subordinating itself to constitutionality, or, by these tokens, permitting the advance of private values. As government has become elected and "civilianized" since 1963 and coups have died away, however, the symbiosis of military and civilian talent seems, despite tension, neither barren nor unhappy. War in Vietnam is doing what war in Korea could not — it has removed some of Korea's army from Korea while encouraging the buildup of industry and entrepreneurship. In these senses cohesion by the military has, in its new-found broader social roles, added a measure of abiding achievement.

The result has steadily altered the older military pattern. The flamboyant days of factional leaders with their retainers and cliques, their personal and council controls, have gone. With them has disappeared a certain brand of decisiveness and leadership, but institutionally the change has led to greatly increased, quieter professionalism and stability. Factionalism is no longer spoken of as before, though the four-year classes retain a marked degree of cohesiveness. The chief disturber of rational promotion and access to power among the military, as elsewhere, has probably been the Korean Central Intelligence Agency, and its role is now more limited.

More changes lie ahead. Present General officers remain an "in-between" group, not fully in communication with their seniors or their juniors. Better trained than the former but far less well-trained than the latter, they do not represent the army's total belief in reform; nor did their actions while in power exhaust or satisfy all the pressures for change and improvement that the army contains within it. The four-year graduates were not consulted and, for the most part, did not approve the coup, although the Academy cadets were eventually induced to form a parade in its support.[43] These graduates have quietly led a political decontamination program of their own, a movement to disentangle the army again from politics. The coup's leaders have not been able to resume military commands, though some wished to; meanwhile their influence within the government they captured has gradually declined, and much of the corruption and confusion they fought to oppose has returned. Within the army, there still remains some distance between those who joined the coup and those who did not; the former, many of them either promoted out of the army or ousted, are fewer than ever. Trouble from such sources is still a possibility. The factionalism of constabulary days, however, has passed with the retirement of nearly all former senior officers.

On the whole, it appears that the army, in its transitions both from factionalism and from political control, has survived successfully and is gradually resuming a more normal role in the life of the country. So long as the military objectives in Vietnam, to which the Korean Army is now importantly committed, last, they may also have some depoliticizing effect.[44] Whether the new body of the well-trained and disciplined can keep the army at this task, whether the army will be inveigled by Korean civilian leaderlessness to recommit itself politically, or whether it can continue to solve its own career problems without new entanglements remains for future history to tell.

Its current extremely low pay levels are likely to test both the honesty and the political neutrality of its officers.[45] Its future influence bids fair to be both more cautious and more mature than in the past, reflecting the men trained to a new respect for institutions.

The army, first among the nation's bodies and more than any of them has learned to place some institutional limits on the unlimited atomized competition for the highest posts that has been Korea's chief hereditary disease. In so doing, it has demonstrated the role of well-established institutions in displacing a mass society.

13

The Choice: Cohesion through Decentralization

Nations newly independent normally incorporate pressures of disunity: differences of race, language, religion, natural conditions and occupations, and the expression of these in strong local powers or sub-cultures. New national leaders in Asia and Africa long for greater homogeneity, ease of central control, relaxation of local power. Other nations from Ethiopia through much of the Near East and South America would break the grip of an ancient nobility or landed oligarchs powerful either locally, centrally, or both; in any case, entrenched.

From this majority of the emergent, Korea stands apart, almost alone.[1] Her troubles are the opposite. Homogeneity, centralization, unity of experience are still a source of strength, but they are also a source of her chief problem: the mounting of cohesive, professional institutions to accomplish political, economic, and social change. Homogeneity that should, logically, have aided has hindered. By leaving no natural cleavages to group around, it has increased the atomized dependence of society on central power and delayed the formation of bases for representation. It has set men and their molecular circles against each other in a universal stream toward a single pole. What disturbs this atomized mobility, the culture has consistently rejected: feudalism in the formative centuries, specialization in bureaucracy, firm classes in society, differentiation of product in material culture, and, in all things, vested interest. Central power, then, tends to take over the group-forming function; but since

---

it has no firm roots, neither can the groups that it forms. Liberal or Democratic Republican Party, National Society, Taehan Youth, Korean Federation of Free Trade Unions, Spiritual Mobilization League, Ilchin-hoe share the same characteristics that pervade the organizations of the culture in village, market place, or neighborhood. An amoebic character is what Korean organizations must have in order that they or the men in them may participate in the upward streaming toward the central apex that is, outside the family, the culture's one great commitment. Only mobility shapes them, not function; they are not hierarchical, not retentive of any self-contained principle, not abiding ground for the formation of leadership. Leadership, formed above, is condemned to rootlessness and transiency; the lower society lacks acquaintance with it, remains divorced from it. Whatever is not personal in the process of representation has an alien cast. This isolation of power that is then chronically seen as dictatorial is not caused by ideology — communism or fascism — or by the personalities or ambitions of Kim Il-sŏng, Syngman Rhee, Park Chŏng-hŭi. Indeed, the nature of Korea's political melee tends to make ideology, platform, personality, and leadership largely superfluous to the central race. Consequently Korea's long and intense political history has no important native philosophy and remarkably few enduring or dominant political personalities. What happens outside the capital is likewise extraneous; hence development dissociated from central interests gets short shrift.[2] All values devolve on central power, for which ever-increasing numbers compete without power bases, sources of stability, or alternate means of satisfying ambition. The society has its own shape, and this shape is the towering cone of a vortex.

Such form has been here traced only for Korea; the record should so stand. Yet the question inevitably arises as to whether such vortex form belongs to Korea alone. One can be fairly confident that it does not. No other nation is likely to possess all those qualities that appear to attach a vortex of quite this form and strength to Korea's political dynamics; but a number of nations have mass societies long capped by centralized systems — China and Russia most prominently. For them, vortex analysis is likely to have interest even after enormous differences in size and uniformity have been counted. Even for heterogeneous states that neither mass societies nor ancient centralism have inhabited, new states in Africa and elsewhere, the dangers of vortex politics may contain pertinent warnings. Trends toward dismantling tribal and other traditional forms of cohesion are every-where enthusiastically pursued. Highly centralized systems are being built as rapidly as possible where localism and variety once stood. Behind them, societies with broad susceptibility for adaptiveness and mobility strain at new starting lines. For such new states, political updrafts destructive of intermediary groupings, of parties, of representative political systems may soon bring problems where dilemmas of quite opposite kind existed within living memory. In their hopes for unity, their drive for centralism, their confidence in homogeneity, new nations should carefully weigh such potentialities.

To be sure, other factors than homogeneity and centralization have added their influence to the formation of Korea's vortex. Many causes similar to those operative in other nations acted to unravel the bonds of Korea's classic integration, intensify incohesiveness, and introduce the modern threat of chaos. The historic breakup of the traditional society, the erosion and final collapse of its legitimacy, the imposition of successive foreign patterns, the presence of a multiplicity of models (Chinese, Japanese, Russian, American) all jostling each other for influence, the disruptions of war, abrupt industrialization, urbanization, and the rise of new roles and ways of life — all such forces unmesh the integrative fibers of any society on which they work. They have worked on Korea and we have traced some of their effects. An entire study could justifiably devote itself to explaining wholly in these more conventional terms the disintegrative phenomena with which these pages have conjured.

After all, the presence of diversity is no panacea. Differences of caste, class, language, and religion may provide the basis for a stable multi-party system. But to be institutionalized such a system requires permanent or enduring loyalties that such distinctions, in themselves, by no means always provide. Diversity may encourage contention and disharmony without necessarily affording the ground for cohesion. Each political system contains the germs of its own problems.

When these concessions have been argued and their validity assessed, the importance of homogeneity and of the updraft formed by the physics of centralism in a homogeneous society still does not yield much ground. When one examines, as we have in the early chapters, the symptoms of the traditional society and its collapse, it appears that tendencies within the society itself, not primarily Japan or even the cataclysm of modern times, set in motion the forces of incohesion.

The traditional society had long been lethargic, and the threads of incohesion are traceable some distance back within it. Although the updraft may not originate from the society's homogeneity, clearly Korea lacks those sources of schism which might form resistance to atomic upward flow. Colonial occupation, urbanization, industrialization, the chaos of Liberation, and the incompetence of the United States in setting a new pattern have all added their contributions. Yet they only furthered a process apparently begun even before the traditional society collapsed: the form political cohesions took in Korea when they came and the difficulties they encountered seem to have old shapes even when they have new velocities and, in part, new causes. Below swarmed amorphous groups from which the central draft constantly detached particles; between swirled a swift upward spiral of the kind Song Pyŏng-jun climbed, where no intermediate cohesions are possible. Above swayed the mushroom cloud of high council, providing maximum access surface for particles and capping the vortex. So again, modern cataclysms return us to the pattern, and we find that, though causes similar to the plights of other developing societies have attached themselves to Korea, ancient cultural continuities lie at its core. Education, expanding communication, and specialization may do much to cure those symptoms that have become more internationally familiar. But it is to the continuous core of Korea's own difficulties that we must address ourselves for more essential remedy.

The most obvious cure for centralized homogeneity lies in diversity. As a possible answer to vortex politics, heterogeneity is, to be sure, not lacking in quandaries; the construction of loyalties in intermediate groups may or may not prove politically effective or viable. Yet here, though we can give no completely reassuring answer, there is hope. In essentially heterogeneous nations like India and Nigeria, the inner pattern tends to be one concentrating on the integrity and even separateness of its parts; and only forces largely artificial and extraneous to the pattern seek change in unity. In such nations, heterogeneity will be opposed by modernizing forces because it is an impediment. In Korea, opposite conditions pertain, and, as the society comes to see more clearly the vortex forces that have, in the past, frustrated its modernization, heterogeneity can appear in the guise of progress and cure. If society perceives that diversity has so important a function, there is more hope that heterogeneous units will develop loyalties and integrity to fulfill this function and thus be able to play significant political roles. Koreans may find encouragement for this process in examining the role that such intermediate institutions as the temple-monastery played in the past in raising Korea nearer to the front ranks of world culture than she has since come. They may see in the building of industrial complexes — especially in local areas — the modern equivalent of this force. If education can implant under-standings of this sort instead of multiplying discontent, it will achieve something of the modernizing role political scientists wish to attribute to it.

No other medicine seems to go straight to the disease. Each form of cohesion that is tried at the top in central government is caught in the tug of the updraft. Changing the form of what presides over the society is no remedy. Indeed, each attempt to alter the top tends to attract more attention to it, increase the vortex toward it, and thus worsen the disease.

Authoritarianism, as under Syngman Rhee, whether in its first stage of authoritarian-personal control, or in its subsequent stage of author-itarian–mass party, is a vortex-accelerator creating tension.[3] It stim-ulates mobility demands but cannot satisfy them, as was evident in the discontent of Seoul shortly before the student revolution. It adds political grievance by its incompatibility with ingrained Korean expectation that top power, once gained, should be delegated to councils for sharing; by incompatibility with democracy; and by lack of any compensating ideology, idea, scheme, or program that might substitute an artificial cohesion for the one society lacks.

Korean society instinctively harbors a warm spot for democracy and egalitarianism because they are eminently compatible with the mobility pattern. This very fitness, however, overstimulates mobility, opening avenues already wide still wider. Democracy in Europe served to break down barriers between classes and vested interests that already possessed strong identities; it led them to play roles in one polity. In Korea democracy tends to interdict identities and interest groups whose formation was vital for the society; where leadership is, as a result, weak, egalitarianism seems to make it weaker. As in other monistic societies, democracy in Korea, to the extent that it has been tried, has tended to corrode essential authority and give rise to insecurity and chaos.

Power under the military brings some disciplinary, cohesive, and possibly professional effects to the political pattern. By being the country's only major cohesive interest group, however, to the extent that it monopolizes power the military again intensifies the vortex and, as an authoritarian force, tends to create the same jealousies and tensions as its authoritarian predecessors. These it complicates by the dangers of further military involvement and counter-coup. Despite the fact that army intervention in state power has, in Korea, brought much success since the "civilianization" of the post-coup government, military talents and powers would be better located outside the center of state authority. Indeed, the more successful the coup's successors have become, the farther has the military itself retreated from the center of formal governmental power.

Communism offers a monolithic answer to the problems of cohesion but chiefly through completeness and ruthlessness of control. It gives the satisfaction of seeming to provide both organizational and ideological antidotes for the instabilities, discontinuities, and uncertainties of a mass society. Such antidotes tend to be reinforced, in North Korea's case, by the reassurance brought by alliance with the powers dominant on the Asian mainland, reviving the security Korea has felt in the past through association with more powerful continental neighbors. In essence, however, communism does not change but further intensifies the centralization pattern. Thus it postpones rather than heals the instability that succession problems are likely eventually to create and does so under a cloak of harshness. Initially, plans and investment gains are comparatively unencumbered with opposition. Austerity and savings can be enforced, comprehensive industrial and social changes achieved. But there is question as to whether the system offers enough flexibility for the long-term growth of a complex industrial society. Already, Communist economic achievements compared to those in the Republic of Korea seem less impressive than they appeared in 1962. Whether North Korea can bear the strains of making the kinds of adjustment it may soon need remains uncertain. Its application southward appears now out of the question. Communism is incompatible with the desires, recent traditions, and present ties of South Korea and would involve staggering human cost. The human cost of communism in North Korea has been extremely high; transferred to the South, it would be enormously raised.

Solution to the basic problem therefore does not seem to lie primarily with central government, nor with changing or tinkering with its forms. Nor does it lie with the mystique of a "human revolution so that our people would stop telling lies, cast away the habits of sycophancy and indolence . . ." [4] Such Confucian reveries lack method and starting point. Neither North Korean communism nor South Korean civilized military rule fit the terms of the updraft equation. A vortex problem can be solved only in terms of the creation of alternatives to central power, by decentralization. If cure is sought, there is no alternative but to move toward a pluralist society.

Largely unplanned steps toward this end have been taken. But, in all probability, cure will be nowhere in these terms systematically sought. The North will attempt to persevere with a Stalinist version of communism, perhaps "thawing" a bit as rising education and eventual aging of leadership force changes. South Korea seems likely to continue with a democratically tinged authoritarianism, publicly tolerated when successful, unstable when beleaguered. Meanwhile it will wait for the current rise in business and industrial forces to create new power centers that may, if time allows, permit a democracy more liberal and representative.

Yet Korea can exercise choice and even what De Tocqueville called "art" to hasten a pluralist day. The vortex pattern may be a hereditary disease, but it is one of the society, not the blood: it can be combated, even healed. Modern Korea possesses abundant agents for such healing change. Korea's very lack of class and vested ties makes its society extraordinarily open and empty of entrenched resistance to change. At the same time, education and the expectation of mobility are pervasive positive stimulants. Even Korea's own generalist pattern of concern with everybody else's business is subject to transfer toward vibrant democratic interest in public affairs. Impatience and discontent are abundant and nest in urban storm-centers. There is much intuitive realization that lack of intermediate organization makes government remote and renders social ties weak. It is clear to many that the state cannot organize with effectiveness the intimate daily lives of its citizens and, lacking other units, these remain unsatisfactorily ordered. Empty of firm attachments, people readily turn elsewhere, migrating to Japan, the United States, or wherever else they can. Since few outside the village feel effectively subject to group censure, the city dweller turns easily to corruption, crime, black-marketing, or other forms of *sauve qui peut*. Even when he joins government or other groups, his allegiance tends to be weak, his shifting from group to group rapid: the reality of personal collaboration must lie forever outside the sphere of political, administrative control, and no other control has survived Confucianism's erosion. Without intermediate bonds or satisfying differential relations, the urban individual all too often unburdens discontent in a conversational life of irrational vindictiveness.[5]

Yet from this very discontent sprout the yeasts of change. Education, by its very inflation, creates tens of thousands of alert citizens who realize that they cannot be absorbed by a lone vortex. Low morale, psychological depression, the permanent migration of some 80 percent of American-educated Korean students, abnormal pressures for other emigration, chronic student demonstrations — these reflect the discontent that may lead to change: to use of the adaptiveness implicit in Korean society, and to exploration of new alternatives to central power. Business, industrialization, and specialization have all grown — in the *zaibatsu* form of a few rich companies, sensationally so since 1963. Businessmen, specialists, even young officers, the Military Academy graduates, discontented with the politicizing of part of the army, know that change will come with more such growth and support it. These elements want both new satisfactions alternate to central government power and the economic and political consequences, the socially integrative possibilities, of a pluralist society. Their satisfaction with the present semi-authoritarian government is incomplete; they are impatient with the slow pace of change, and anxious to avoid communism. In the liberal democratic alternative lies the only long-range likelihood of satisfying these aroused forces.

If solution is to arrive in time to forestall instability, the rather undirected progress now being made should be hastened. The prescription calls for gradual dismantling of the vortex while keeping essential central governmental and planning functions. Power and economic activities can be considerably dispersed functionally and decentralized geographically.

A gradual and systematic program of transferring to local governments much administration now handled centrally should be undertaken, including, perhaps, more budgetary and even police controls. "If the presently developing countries are to move on from their present transitional stage to full modernization, all of the barriers between the city and the countryside need to be broken down, including the human barriers . . . There is a need for the privileged, the educated, the modern young people to leave their cities." [6] The first stage should involve the buildup of provincial administration; a second stage might transfer some provincial administrative functions to the county level, either the present counties or perhaps, as more viable units, the combined counties that form the new electoral districts. Steps should quickly be taken to elect all key local officials, many of whom are still appointed. Local education committees, abolished after the military coup, should be re-established. Private business should be encouraged by the completion of the sale of government-held enterprises, by support for projects and aid executed by private American business with private Korean business rather than through the AID mission and the Korean government. [7] Some special remission of part of the first year's taxes should be given to new enterprises locating outside rather than inside Seoul. Projects linking or otherwise benefiting local areas should be given priority, as has been done in the recent completion of the rail line linking the two south coast provinces. If necessary, loan rates of banks outside Seoul might be made a fractional percentile cheaper than in Seoul. The President should set aside one or more days a week when he agrees to see no one except businessmen or representatives from local areas. Korea might well experience from thus decentralizing the management of the economy successes as great as Yugoslavia's in her recent dispersal of the Soviet type of centralism.

The strengthening of local participation in local administration and in development could be encouraged by the formation of Development Advisory Councils essentially similar to those adopted with some success by Pakistan in 1959. Each *ri* (village) should elect its own representatives to a township (*myŏn*) council; the chairman of each such council, together with one of two centrally-appointed members with some technical qualifications should compose a similar council at the county (*gun*) level; and the chairmen of these (who cannot be government appointees) plus a small minority of government officials should in turn compose provincial councils whose eight chairmen, plus not more than four important government officials, should compose a national headquarters. The formulation of works and reconstruction projects should be done at the provincial level primarily on the basis of major council proposals, with county council review. A combination of local and national sources could provide financing as in Pakistan. Since imports under U.S. Public Law 480 have substantially damaged the rural economy, it would be appropriate for such revenues to be a major portion of the funds needed. The 600,000-man military, which now monopolizes PL 480 counterpart funds and which has, except for the two divisions sent to Vietnam, 1965–1968, been non-combatant for a decade, could eventually be the source of such funds by reductions of 20–30 percent when early 1968 security concerns aroused by a ten-fold increase in North Korean infiltration, and by the capture of the *Pueblo* and the guerrilla assassination attempt against President Park, shall have abated. The army would still remain considerably larger than the ten divisions and 250,000 men envisioned as adequate for it by General MacArthur and President Truman in October 1950 and would suffice for any troubles it would be asked to face alone.[8]

The township councils could do much to bridge the gap between the government and the village by assuming duties relating not only to works and reconstruction projects but also to the adjudication of disputes at the village level, village sanitation, record-keeping, voter lists, and minor matters of local security. The police force could then, as often proposed, be considerably reduced. Responsibility for local affairs would be put back into the hands of the village leaders from whom the Japanese colonial regime removed it. Central government representatives would no longer be the omnipresent instruments of supervision and oppression. Local leaders, whose lack of responsible tasks since 1910 has set them adrift to Seoul, would be put productively and locally to work. Farmers' sons who have been given college education but have had nothing to return to could find some scope for their talents. Their education could be put to work to narrow the gap that continues to exist between the alien legal and administrative systems — essentially still of colonial form — and the habits and ways of life of the villagers. Every attempt should in this way be made to tap the human resources and local initiative evidenced in the first post-Liberation weeks but never since well employed. Decentralization should in this way be conducted in the spirit of eliciting greater social participation.

The educational system should likewise be girded to the decentralizing task. In place of a uniform curriculum similar to the French, each local college or university should be required to give courses on the traditions and local problems — including agricultural — of the province in which it is located, as well, of course, as present courses concentrating on Korea as a single nation and culture. Even on the level of secondary education, children should form an appreciation of the place of agriculture and of local areas in the life and progress of their country. If possible, local high schools and colleges should also include training courses specifically to forward local projects such as land reclamation and its technical and social problems. The staff for such courses could also advise on local project priorities. If these universities were not strong enough to generate effective training, a National Development Academy might be considered, but only following maximum efforts to make a local system work.

To attract local initiative, such councils should also be ladders to success above; for regardless of what measures are undertaken, a relatively strong central government is necessary both for Korea and for development and will continue to have tremendous draw. The differential relations that council ladders build are also necessary to form leadership in local areas. The fact that the chairmen of the lower bodies will sit on the next higher will start the hierarchical pull. It would not seem advisable to have these units the basis for the election of the President and the National Assembly, as in Pakistan, since the Korean election system is relatively well-established among a well-educated populace. It may, however, be possible to stipulate that the proportionally-elected segment of the National Assembly be selected by the political parties from among the elected members of the Development Advisory Councils. Some local leaders would thus find themselves drawn to the capital, but they would have gotten their fingers dirty in a piece of local social mechanism and would rise more on the basis of demonstrated performance than hitherto; the number so drawn would be too small to constitute a drain. The combination of economic and political incentives may be even more important — for a society so politically motivated — than it is in Pakistan and may guard against the failure that largely overtook Korea's military government's recent experiment with a National Reconstruction Movement. Meanwhile, human resources will be more fully engaged outside the capital, and the concentration of all values on Seoul will begin to be rivaled by local activity claiming the interest and allegiance of ambitious men.

We can tally few disadvantages to a scheme of this kind. There are few countries where great increases in local power can be taken with so few risks as in Korea. Korea already has her basic road, communications, and even irrigation network. The costs of decentralizing are not impractical. Men and education are super-abundant. The nation knows no separatism; in seventy years, only a single instance of rebellion — on Cheju Island — has had any strong local coloration. Police under provincial instead of Home Ministry controls would not challenge national security; Korea's army, perhaps the largest and most effective possessed by any nation of her size, amply guarantees this and would do so even if reduced 20 to 30 percent. The reforms would not dismantle the strength needed by central government in an emerging nation: Korea's unity and homogeneity is too entrenched. Rather, decentralization will use these qualities to broaden the economic and political process.

Such steps would be no immediate cure for instability in central government. Decentralization would, however, gradually remove pressure from the central power vortex. Its particular objective would be to create alternate bureaucracies and areas of endeavor with local roots and satisfactions not obtained from competition for central power. Though much of the latter would remain, it would begin to be colored with qualification obtained in local position and local performance and would be stabilized by being passed through local hierarchies.[9] Gradually, local and private vested interests would come to be the basis of representation in national politics and in the formation of parties. Rivalry, competition, struggle would, of course, not cease; they might even increase. But they would be rooted in interests and the issues arising from them, less in the atomic desire of individuals to propel themselves upward. Korea would begin to have *representation* and, with it, sight of a solution for the fissiparous political trauma noted in the Introduction. The suicidal struggle of opposition leaders and nuclear groups for leadership in the 1963 election that has continued even through the 1967 election and thereafter would be replaced by a struggle of men representing issues and interests that could be rationally debated and shaped by compromise into a party platform. The Yi and post-Liberation struggles of individuals for the same position — subject to no such compromise and without useful political issue — would gradually be dissipated.

Whether decentralized or not, the dispersal of power to strong business and industrial enterprises could be an important part of the process of creating alternate interest groups and channels for ambition. Their economic necessity is clear to all: South Korea cannot hope to support with any acceptable standard much more than half its population of over thirty million without industrial production and foreign trade. These are the chief hope of a viable future for Korea. The extreme concentration in state hands of almost all important industrial properties, the reluctance of those in power to stand aside from industry, the political appointment of managers and staff, the centralizing instincts of the culture, the shortage of managerial talent, and virtual absence of private industrial capital have made the establishment of private business slow and difficult. It has proceeded in stages. Management largely politically appointed and inept is being exposed and replaced by the growth of large private economic units recalling — and partly modeled after — the Japanese *zaibatsu*. Strength in small and medium-sized business lies largely ahead. Large economic units — the creation of such men as Yi Pyŏng-ch'ŏl (sugar, woolen textiles, foreign trade), Chŏng Chae-ho (cotton textiles), and others in cement, glass, milling, and machinery — are probably a necessary, possibly even a desirable, intermediate development stage. Such units of size have already made possible Korea's profitable economic involvement in the war in Vietnam and have usefully explored the possibilities of foreign trade.

Concentration of the *zaibatsu* type reflects the downward development of business from government control rather than its upward growth through entrepreneurship. Large size is not only a function of the need to concentrate capital and talent for business but also a necessity for dealing with the government. Only with size of capital and breadth of contact and influence within government offices has it been possible to obtain access to more capital, foreign exchange, and import privileges at acceptable rates and to protect these favors from investigation and blackmail once obtained. These *zaibatsu*, built to coexist beside the power vortex, have created the first strong Korean private bureaucracies. The linkage between these firms and the government has been, and continues to be, largely corrupt. Such corruption, however, has also connoted the rise of business values, the growing influence of larger companies, in a government-oriented state. *Zaibatsu* size and influence better symbolize the break with the values of the past than small units could. As political life has become more unstable and careers within it decreasingly profitable and respected, the prestige of work in the bureaucracies of private enterprise has risen and with it the quality of the men they employ.[10] In any country, this is counted a modernizing step; in Korea, it will be — indeed, has already become — of especial significance.

The rise of major business will, of course, bring its own dangers. A stage in which, as in Japan in the 1920's, these economic units come to control parties and exercise more influence over politicians than parties themselves is not unlikely. Gaps between wealth and poverty, not thus far as characteristic of Korea as of many colonial countries, are already being created, and more can be expected. Such gaps, taking place in an overpacked Seoul of over 4,000,000 people, may prove explosive. The extent of Korea's mobility pattern has resulted in a politically excitable society, hence one in which discontent is contagious. Business does not have sufficient prestige to protect itself from these threats. Yet the long-term benefits of business growth have much hope of outrunning political dangers. Eventual *zaibatsu* breakup is not improbable, but meanwhile big-company success will demonstrate the vitality Korea can achieve through the step-by-step dispersal to alternate groups of values and achievements now centrally and governmentally concentrated.

The pluralist society created by these power distributions may be cantankerous, but the nature and effect of conflict and competition will be altered. Privacy of interest, the values of privacy — an area whose cultivation is a pre-condition for democracy — will have some base from which to assert themselves. By emphasizing interests other than simply avidity for central power, Koreans will tend to build these interests, take pride in and derive satisfaction from them. They will interest themselves seriously in protecting them not only from other units but from the state; from this source will come initiative for law and legal process, enthusiasm for the restraint of government rather than for its aggrandizement. Serious private interests will become, as they became in Europe, some check on corruption, a force for the transforming of bureaucracy from the self-serving to the public-serving. Variety of interest will create many centers and hierarchies of elites and counteract the tendency for all decision-making to shift toward the national center or for all men to aggregate around it and form factions to fight for it. Cohesive interests will tend to create issues instead of personal rivalries, positive identities and loyalties rather than the martialing of common cause behind the hostile tissue of rumor and gossip. Conflict of issues and interests, even if heated, will encourage negotiation and compromise rather than deadlock fighting for the same power by men without alternatives. It is on the anvil of pluralism and probably, in the long run, on it alone that the vortex and factional patterns will be shattered.

Modern times have thus far brought largely trauma to Korea. The days when a placid agricultural people could exist, insulated from change behind the protection of the Chinese Empire and a hermit policy, have disappeared, almost beyond memory. Her cloaks withdrawn, Korea has stood during a hundred years in the midst of a melee of great nations, a small land, enfeebled by a social and political pattern adequate only for unchallenged isolation. The last eight decades have led her through a phantasmagoria of misfortunes. Artificially divided, proximate to the Sino-Soviet split and to China's renewed alarums, Korea stands on the borders of contention still. That through it all she has survived and even strengthened will remain a lasting tribute to her people, indeed to the capacities of man himself. South Korea has seen many failures. Yet, when viewed comparatively in the company of new nations, she seems relatively better educated, faster developing, and even politically freer and more stable than most others, despite war, division, extreme overpopulation, and a paucity of resources.

For further progress in a situation still dangerous, change of pattern is needed. Much will come naturally, and, for it, modernization offers Korea particular hope. Industry, mining, trade and their far-flung units, new groups and roles for specialists, new occupations are opening to her sources of diversity that her traditional culture closed. The mass nature of Korean society has hitherto been a detriment to the cohesiveness and confidence needed for change. Yet once the path of progress is clearly perceived by the public, mass society will have its advantages. Mobility beckons to ambition, inspires great creativity; both have long been Koreans' birthright. If Koreans lack the cohesiveness and loyalties of previous attachments, they also lack the traditionalism, the resistance to change, the nostalgia that the world of class and feudalism brings. Korean society is an unusually open one. Americans, living in a dynamic society geared to high material productivity and constant economic change, have reacted by an emphasis on material values and a readiness to adapt to new groups. Koreans have lived in an almost equally dynamic political society; they have a similarly high capacity to inhabit different kinds of political systems, adapting themselves to new groupings, contexts, and changes. This dynamic character, untrammeled with much commitment to their past, should serve them well in forging the kind of pluralist society they need. In this new, more varied world built by their intelligence and freedom will lie their salvation.

Notes
_____
Index

Notes

INTRODUCTION

1. William Kornhauser, *The Politics of Mass Society* (Glencoe, Ill., 1959), p. 228. My definition of mass society owes much to Kornhauser (pp. 31–32, 228, and *passim*) and his concept has greatly clarified my materials. I did not, however, read his book until the completion of my own first draft indicated to others that my materials tended to confirm the pattern he describes. For insight into the dynamics of centralization and the political effects of the lack of secondary powers, no one has surpassed Alexis de Tocqueville. Cf. his *Democracy in America* (New York, 1945), I, 89ff, 99–101, II, 304–348; *The Old Regime and the French Revolution* (New York, 1955), pp. 137, 170, 189, 204, 206, 210–211.

2. The author is not without economic supporters for his theorem. The National Economic Board of U.S. Military Government in Korea had this to say in 1947: "If ever the behavior of a people were conditioned, not to say determined, by non-economic forces, those people are South Koreans today." U.S. Military Government in Korea, *South Korean Interim Government Activities* (USAMGIK Report No. 25, 1947), p. 1. It is quite possible that economic motivations are, especially since 1964, becoming more important than they were twenty years ago.

3. For the importance of psychological approaches to political culture, see Lucian W. Pye and Sydney Verba, *Political Culture and Political Development* (Princeton, 1965), pp. 7–10, 551–554, and *passim*.

CHAPTER 1

The Single Magnet

1. This disproportion of size has become aggravated by the division of the country in 1945. The Republic of Korea (South Korea) has an area of 38,031 square miles, the Democratic People's Republic of Korea (North Korea) an area of 46,768 square miles, the Demilitarized Zone between them, controlled by neither, an area of 487 square miles. Article on Korea

in *Collier's Encyclopedia* (New York, 1965), XIV, 145. *Korea Annual* (Hapdong News Agency: Seoul, 1966), p. 265, gives 38,035 for South Korea.

2. Cho Ching-yang (Ching Young Choe), "The Decade of the Taewŏn'gun" (unpub. diss., Harvard University, 1960), I, 237–249. The great usefulness to me of this excellent thesis is acknowledged with a gratitude that Dr. Cho's sad early death deprives me of the chance to express more personally.

3. See, for example, the eighteenth-century reform writer, Pak Che-ga, *Pukhak-ŭi* (Discourse of the learning from the north), B:19a–20a: "However, for nearly 400 years since the founding of the present dynasty, our country hasn't had a single ship that traded with foreign countries" (cited *ibid.*, p. 60).

4. Shannon McCune, *Korea's Heritage* (Rutland, Vt., 1956), pp. 57–58. Yi Dynasty figures record over seven million in 1693, 1789, and in a somewhat better census of 1807. These are probably underestimates related to governmental inefficiency or shortfall in taxes; no one knows by how much they are short. By the time a better Japanese estimate of 1910 was made, the population had reached some 13,300,000. Since improvement in health standards had occurred only since 1885, one may speculate that the actual "normal" Yi population may not have been much lower than eight to ten million.

By the end of 1962, the South Korean population was estimated at 26,248,250, or 693 persons per square mile as against Japan's density at that time of 669 persons per square mile (Bruce M. Russett *et al.*, *World Handbook of Political and Social Indicators* [New Haven, 1964], pp. 18–20). The population has increased, at least until recently, at the rate of about 2.9 percent per annum and is over thirty million as of spring 1968. The end of 1967 ratio of about 768 people per square mile is already one of the highest densities in the world and the highest per cultivated acre of almost any nation beyond city-state size in the world (Russett, p. 146). Kim Il, First Deputy Premier of North Korea, announced the North Korean population figures in a speech of September 16, 1961, as 10,789,000 (Key P. Yang and Ching-boh Chee, "North Korean Educational System: 1945 to Present," *China Quarterly*, 14:136 (April–June 1963). This figure is roughly confirmed by other kinds of announcements and estimates and is to be preferred to that given by Russett, who uses South Korean figures of doubtful accuracy. *The Europa Yearbook, 1967* (London, 1967), II 726, gives 11,568,000 for the population of North Korea as of December 1963. Population increase in the North being at least as great as in the South — it was somewhat greater before World War II — the North Korean population as of the end of 1967 must be estimated at about thirteen million. The total population of the Korean peninsula will thus be forty-three million by the middle of 1968, and more than two million Koreans live outside the peninsula.

5. The point about deliberately unused resources is made by Edward W. Wagner, "Korea" (mimeo, 1961), p. 20. For citations of council (especially Censorate) warnings against foreign contact or actions outside Korea, see Prof. Wagner's "The Literati Purges" (unpub. diss., Harvard University, 1959).

6. Home Ministry Statistical Bureau, *T'onggye yŏn'gam* (Statistical yearbook of the Republic of Korea; Seoul, 1960), p. 41. Edward W. Wagner, "Korea," p. 14, a reliable source for information in this chapter, gives 3,300 islands, as does *Korea Annual, op. cit.*, p. 265, which notes that islands form 3.4 percent of the total Korean area (more, presumably, for South Korea).

7. Diverse usage of islands was, at various times in Korea history, tried but always later abandoned. The entire court retreated to the island of Kanghwa during the Mongol invasion of 1231–1232, remaining there with 100,000 former inhabitants of the Koryŏ capital until 1270–1273. William E. Henthorn, *Korea: The Mongol Invasions* (Leyden, 1963) gives a good account. The ninth-century "fabulous adventurer and merchant prince" Chang Po-go (Edwin O. Reischauer, *Ennin's Travels in T'ang China* [New York, 1955], pp. 287ff) based his commercial and diplomatic empire on the island of Wando. Revolting palace guards built a formidable base first on Chindo, then on Cheju. None of these attempts toward island separatism or separate power survived, though the government maintained important defenses on Kanghwa throughout later centuries. Islands differ from the mainland chiefly in that they — or their inhabitants — are despised, and men of status do not wish to live there.

8. For much of this material, I am grateful for the excellent study by Henthorn, *op. cit.* The interpretations, however, are generally my own. The Mongol invasion and occupation of Korea at this time caused terrible deprivation and suffering, the *Koryŏ-sa* claiming that 206,800 Koreans were taken prisoner in the winter of 1254. *Koryŏ-sa* (History of Koryŏ); Yonsei University ed., 1955), I, 488.

9. Thus the official annals for 1519, a year of grave political tension, tell us: "Certain military officials are deeply resentful at these men [young Confucian pacifist officials] and are plotting to kill them all. If the government does not take action first, then I fear there will be grave disorder." This passage, from *Chungjong sillok* (The annals of King Chungjong), 37:27ab (1425.1.16), is cited and translated by Edward W. Wagner, "The Literati Purges" (Unpub. diss., Harvard University, 1959), p. 419. For what I learned from this dissertation and from conversations with its author, I acknowledge great debt to Professor Wagner.

10. Recruitment stopped about 1840. The navy, glorious in the 1590's, was almost non-existent in the dynasty's last two centuries. Irregular forces of peddlers and tiger hunters had to be called on to drive off a French force of about 600 men in 1866 (Cho Ching-yang, *op. cit.*, pp. 281, 289–291.) The extraordinary lack of attention to Korea's military weakness in explaining her absorption by Japan is a fallacy of the same dimension as that in Douglas S. Freeman's analysis of reasons for Robert E. Lee's defeat, which failed to mention the presence of the Union Army.

11. Gregory Henderson, "Korea through the Fall of the Lolang Colony," *Koreana Quarterly*, 1.1:147–168 (1959). Thus far an extensive paleolithic phase has not been firmly established in Korean archeology but recent excavations, especially at Kongju, appear to establish its existence and even begin to give it some structure.

The Koreans constantly speak of a "history" of 4,300 years. In any legitimate sense, their history begins in Chinese records of the last few centuries B.C. The first identifiably Korean surviving records date from the beginning of the fifth century, notably the stone inscription recording the exploits of King Kwanggaet'o of Koguryŏ (A.D. 392–413).

12. Archaeology shows that at least one pocket of a people using Ordos art forms remained in the Naktong valley during the Lolang period (108 B.C.–A.D. 313). See Umehara Sueji and Fujita Ryōsaku, *Chōsen kobunka sōkan* (Survey of ancient Korean culture; Kyoto, 1947), I, plates 25–26, figs. 117–125. An earth-pit tomb minority people, probably the Yen, also are identified in Korea in Lolang times. See Kim Wŏn-yong, "Bronze Mirrors from Shih-Erh T'ai Ying-tzu, Liaoning," *Artibus Asiae,* 26.3/4:207–214 (1963).

13. Gari Keith Ledyard, "The Korean Language Reform of 1446: The Origin, Background and Early History of the Korean Alphabet" (unpub. diss., Columbia University, 1965), Chap. I, p. 2n5, relying apparently largely on linguistic evidence and citing Yi Ki-mun, *Kugŏsa kaesŏl* (Outline history of the Korean language; Seoul, 1961), pp. 44–72, and "A Genetic View of Japanese," *Chōsen gakuhō* (Journal of the Academic Association of Koreanology in Japan), 27:94–105 (April 1963). The fact that Koreans are strongly exogamous may be another factor increasing their cultural homogeneity. George P. Murdock remarks on this trait among East African hunters in *Africa, Its Peoples and Their Cultural History* (New York, 1959), p. 62.

14. We are told occasionally in the Yi records of officials of Jurchên and even Uighur descent, and the founder of the Yi Dynasty seems to have been unable effectively to deny that he himself had some Jurchên blood. See Wagner, "The Literati Purges," p. 275; Son Po-gi (Sohn Pow-Key), "Social History of the Early Yi Dynasty, 1392–1592" (unpub. diss., University of California, Berkeley, 1963), p. 205. The latter work is an unusually good Ph.D thesis by a Korean history professor of Yonsei University who has excellent command of the original source materials. He mentions that many men who, like the Yi founding monarch, Yi Sŏng-gye, stemmed from Hamgyŏng Province had Jurchên blood. The *Sejong sillok* (The annals of Sejong), 27:10a (1425.1.16), states that Sŏl Mi-su, a minister of the Board of Rites under King T'aejong, was of Uighur origin and his ancestors served Genghis Khan. Sŏl's brother, Chang-su, was still better known.

15. The Chinese population may be somewhat understated, but it is certainly small, indeed, one of the very smallest anywhere in any Asian country. There is very little intermarriage with the Koreans.

16. For over a century from the founding of the Yi Dynasty in 1392, the Confucian aristocracy pushed hard for extreme anti-Buddhist measures which the early Yi kings, notably T'aejong, feared might bring revolt. Royal influence slowed these excesses somewhat, and, though Buddhist discontent was aroused, revolt was prevented. Buddhist temples fought bravely for the country against the Japanese invasion of 1592.

17. Yi In-yŏng, *Kuksa yoron* (Discussion of national history; Seoul, 1950), pp. 114–115, described the reign of King Sejong (1418–1450) as being the threshold of such national cultural unity. His estimate is very conservative; even by the eleventh century the formation of a homogeneous nation-state can be said to have been well advanced compared

to most nation-states that survive today. Regional variety in such products as pottery was fairly great through the sixteenth century but has become remarkably homogeneous since.

18. However, Herbert R. Barringer gives an interesting description of Samgak-dong, a community located on the North Kyŏngsang–Kangwŏn border that constitutes a remote pocket of Hamgyŏng dialect, building style, and attitudes. "Increasing Social Scale and Social Character in Korea" (unpub. MS, 1966), pp. 14–20.

19. Sources on Silla history are poor. The two major surviving histories of the era were written in the middle of the twelfth and thirteenth centuries, long after Silla's final fall early in the tenth century. For discussions of these patterns of Silla culture, see Suematsu Yasukazu, *Shiragi-shi no shomondai* (Studies in the history of Silla; Tokyo, 1954), Pts. I–IV, VI. I am also grateful to Edward W. Wagner for discussion and lecture notes about the Silla period. Hatada Takashi, *Chōsen-shi* (History of Korea; Tokyo, 1951), pp. 47ff, contains an interpretation of Silla.

20. The term "bone ranks" is evidently a translation of the Mongol word *yasun* used in Mongol and Chinese texts referring to Mongol ethnic groups or social class; the term refers to groups of common origin and ancestry, smaller than clans and more defined. The original kingly "bone" was known as the "holy bone." The concept is also related to the term *kabane* (corpse or bone) similarly used for social groups in ancient Japan. See Yang Lien-sheng, "Marginalia to the *Yuan Tien-chang*," *Harvard Journal of Asiatic Studies*, 19:49–51 (1956).

21. Son Po-gi, *op. cit.*, p. 128. On council rule, see Chap. 9 below.

22. C. Hentze, "Schamenkronen zur Han-Zeit in Korea," *Ostasiatische Zeitschrift*, 5:156–163 (1933), identifies the golden crowns from non-royal but high-ranking Kyŏngju tombs with shamanism. The Confucian or Buddhist believers who wrote histories of the Silla era generally suppressed references to shamanism.

23. The Koryŏ period, itself an impressive continuity of 474 years, introduced a new capital site but comparative few political or social initiatives. The changes of chief significance occurred during the troubled second half of the dynasty (1170–1392). These were ushered in by the successful military coup of 1170, which saw a confused kind of praetorian-shogunal rule established for a century. Before the end of that period, Mongol invasions engulfed and eventually subjugated an impoverished land. The period from 1170 on was marked, on the whole, by some decay of central power and even by the relative rise of subordinate institutions (temples, semi-independent military commands, and local artisan workshops). Alone within an over-all history extraordinarily distant from feudalism, this period is marked with at least incipient feudal characteristics. The interruption of the dominant Korean historical pattern was temporary, however; the chaos of the time did not permit the rooting of strong, permanent local or secondary institutions. With the Yi, particularly after the comprehensive destruction accompanying the invasions of Hideyoshi's forces, Korea's dominant pattern of central strength and weak local development was resumed. Cf. Hatada, *op. cit.;* Yi Pyŏng-do (Yi Pyeng-do), *Han'guk-sa Chungse-p'yŏn* (History of Korea: the Middle Ages), and other standard sources; and Kang Man-gil, "Chosŏn chŏn'gi kongjang-

go" (Investigation of artisans in the early Yi period), *Sahak yŏn'gu* (The study of history), No. 12:1–72 (Sept. 1961).

24. Son Po-gi, *op. cit.*, pp. 129–131. Among the names were *to p'yŏngma-sa, to p'yŏngŭi-sa sa,* more informally, *hapchwa,* and, after 1279, the equivalent of Office of Joint Councilors. On the rise of such councils and their activities, see pp. 22–23 below.

25. Edwin O. Reischauer and John K. Fairbank, *East Asia: The Great Tradition* (Boston, 1958), p. 30.

26. The National Academy seems at times to have made a partial attempt to use remonstrance institutionally to pressure central power. The Academy was, however, an integral part of the governmental system, was confined to Seoul and was miniscule in size.

27. Technically, the Korean king, ruling under the Chinese emperor, was responsible to him, and the emperor alone was responsible to Heaven for the Chinese realm and its tributary states. This point was the subject of much argument between Yi kings and their officials. Although this subordination was of psychological importance to the court, which thus spent much time looking over its shoulder to Peking, and of theological importance within the Confucian system, in fact the emperor almost never interfered in Korean practical affairs. Moreover, since popular loyalty went to the king automatically, the emperor's technical competence was of concern only to high officials.

28. Shamanism had long been completely divorced from government: its past official roles, if they ever existed, had been forgotten. Buddhist involvement in government had been great but largely in teaching and advisory capacities; the temple hierarchy and that of the state were, on the whole, distinct, as was Buddhist religious doctrine, from most of the daily requirements of administration. Such divorce did have exceptions in Koryŏ. Buddhist priests and their temples were regarded as playing key roles in praying for the defense of the country and thus averting invasion. Temples were — and continued in the Yi to be — significant military centers of warrior monks. There was some involvement in the country's taxation system. Major Buddhist festivals had national status.

29. Charles Gernet, *Les Aspects Economiques du Bouddhisme* (Saigon, 1956), p. 8, tells us that very few of the largest Chinese temples harbored as many as 300 monks or nuns. The great stone receptacles built for the daily washing of the temple rice that still exist in a few major Korean temples and date from the Silla period suggest that these temples numbered their inhabitants in the thousands.

30. The *kye* is a group loan agreement still very common, in different forms, in both rural and urban Korean life. The descendants of the famous Confucian sage Chŏng Tasan, living in Kangjin, Chŏlla Namdo, where he was exiled, still possess the *kye* agreement that he signed with the neighboring temple of Mandŏk-sa in the early years of the nineteenth century.

31. Alexis de Tocqueville, *The Old Régime and the French Revolution* (New York, 1955), pp. 15–17, 41.

32. Gregory Henderson and Key P. Yang, "An Outline History of Korean Confucianism," Pt. II: "The Schools of Yi Confucianism," *Journal of Asian Studies,* 18.2:272–273 (Feb. 1959). (This journal is henceforth cited as *JAS*.) See also Yu Hyŏng-jin (Yoo Hyung-jin), "Intellectual His-

tory of Korea from Ancient Times to the Impact of the West with Special Emphasis on Education" (unpub. diss., Harvard University, 1958). In sequestering lands from taxation and in draft-evasion practices, the *sŏwŏn* seem to have given considerable impetus to civic irresponsibility.

33. W. H. Wilkinson, *The Korean Government: Constitutional Changes, July, 1894, to October, 1895* (Shanghai, 1897), pp. 11ff. Mr. Wilkinson was Acting British Consul-General in Korea during the period of the reforms. His volume contains an excellent factual description of both the old and the "new" (1895) Korean governments with all titles given in both Chinese characters and English.

34. The general form of administration remained fairly static during the Yi Dynasty. However, changes did occur and special boards were created and abolished from time to time. The above description is therefore general. The State Council is here described as it was founded in the fourteenth century. Other offices are mostly noted as they were before the reforms of 1895.

35. The court was, however, frequently deprecated by Koreans themselves as inferior to that of China, from which it was borrowed. The massive absorption of even many of the intricacies of Chinese culture was encouraged by the high concentration of Yi culture in the capital. A more dispersed culture would have retained more native roots.

36. There appear to have been comparatively few locally resident landlords in earlier times; at all times absentee landlordism was common.

37. For the same thing in Ch'ing China, see Ch'ü T'ung-tsu, *Local Government in China under the Ch'ing* (Cambridge, Mass., 1963), pp. 174–177.

38. The considerable talent for investigation and spying exploited by the Japanese in Manchuria and China and vigorously by Communists and South Korean authorities alike since 1945 had a natural seedbed in this long-sustained Yi milieu.

39. Cho Ching-yang, *op. cit.*, p. 119.

40. For a detailed exposition of such punishments during the purges of the literati in 1494 and 1504, see Wagner, "The Literati Purges," esp. pp. 170–228. The punishments meted out at that time are conceded to have been the most extreme in Yi history. Though more lurid than the average, they differed from them only in detail and extent. The essential system of punishment and especially the peculiarly Korean exile system went on virtually to the end of the dynasty, the cruel punishments both the prince regent and Queen Min inflicted on each other's adherents in the last quarter of the nineteenth century being especially notorious.

41. In this respect Yi banishment practices somewhat resemble the current brevity of visits to underdeveloped countries of American aid officials and academic development experts.

42. For details of the life and works of this great scholar-official, see Gregory Henderson, "Chŏng Ta-san, A Study in Korea's Intellectual History," *JAS*, 16.3:377–386 (May 1957).

43. See, for modernizing nations, David E. Apter, *The Politics of Modernization* (Chicago, 1965), p. 454.

44. The basic resemblance of the Yi reform to the nationalization of all land called for by the Communists in 1945 is startling. A roughly com-

parable — though more feudal — system operative at the present time is that in Ethiopia.

45. Lots were limited in size to from 67 meters square for the highest royal princes down to 8.6 meters for commoners. The lowest proper aristocrats (*yangban*), officials of the seventh rank, and the sons and grandsons of former high officials received 30 meters. Certain colors were also reserved for palace or court use. City Government of Seoul, *Keijō fu-shi* (History of Seoul City; Seoul, 1934), I, 146, is an excellent source of information on ancient Seoul and Japanese Keijō.

46. The derivatives of such concepts in the value system are endless and fascinating. One senses that the holding of property too long without power responsibilities is disesteemed in Korean society and considered "miserly," a concept more opprobrious and far more broadly employed in Korea than in the West. Even property itself may have slight cultural shades of immoral coloring. The *Li Chi* (Record of ritual classic), for example, a model for Yi Dynasty as for Chinese behavior, states that during their parents' or grandparents' lifetimes, children may not possess property of their own. The holding of private property by a son while living with his father was a punishable offense in Sino–Korean law (see Ch'ü T'ung-tsu, *Law and Society in Traditional China* [Cambridge, Mass., 1961], pp. 25, 29–30). Ostentation was constantly condemned by the Censorate even with regard to a comparative simplicity of life that a noble of Louis XIV would have scorned. The long, generally peaceful centuries of the Yi have transmitted to us objects of an astonishing austerity of taste.

47. Benjamin Weems, *Reform, Rebellion and the Heavenly Way* (Tucson, 1964), p. 29. From a Tonghak declaration posted on the gate of the governor of Chŏlla in 1893.

48. According to E. Barker, *The Development of Public Service in Western Europe, 1660–1930* (New York, 1944), p. 20: "Frederick William I [of Prussia] would never station an official in his native province lest he should forget his primary loyalty." Japanese *bakufu* also used rotation of officials as a means of enforcing loyalty, but neither they nor Western autocrats eliminated local development.

49. Prominent examples were Hong Kyŏng-nae, in P'yŏngan Province, 1811–12, and the religious-social leaders Ch'oe Che-u and Chŏn Pong-jun of the late nineteenth-century Tonghak.

50. Emile Durkheim, *Le Suicide* (Paris, 1930), p. 446.

CHAPTER 2

The Traditional Society

1. See Edwin O. Reischauer and John K. Fairbank, *East Asia: The Great Tradition* (Boston, 1958), p. 428.

2. Some writers — e.g., Ko Chae-guk, "Yangban chedo-ron" (Thesis on the yangban system), *Hakp'ung* (Academic traditions), 13:62–69 (June 1950) — postulate an essentially two-class system with *chungin* and their country cousins the *ajŏn* as adjuncts of the *yangban* in the task of rule, the *ch'ŏnmin* and the *sangmin* together being the ruled class. Others add

the *ajŏn* as a separate class or see the *chungin* and the *ajŏn* essentially as members of the *sangmin* class, not because of their function but because of their technical social status in the Yi system. Yi Sang-baek (Yi Sangback) in *Han'guk-sa Kŭnse chŏn'gip'yŏn* (Korean history: early modern times; Seoul, 1962), p. 306, cites Yi Chung-hwan, an eighteenth-century scholar, as grouping *ch'ŏnmin*, commoners, and *ajŏn* together as *hain* or lower men.

3. The extent to which the examination system in China constituted a mobility erosive of established classes and vested interests continues to be disputed. The dispute has hardly begun with regard to Korea. It has been assumed that the examination system inhibited, virtually prevented, social mobility in Korea. Legal provisions bore out this contention in part, but the case has yet to be convincingly demonstrated by biographical study of the passers. These came in fact from over 600 clans, an impressive spread. The far more rigorous surveillance over lineage exercised by the censoring bodies in Korea than in China additionally argues, however, that Korea's mobility was — or at least became — more restricted; more clans were represented before 1606 than were represented in the three centuries thereafter.

4. For these lists, see *Han'guk-sa sajŏn* (Dictionary of Korean history; Seoul, 1959), p. 40.

5. Son Po-gi, "Social History of the Early Yi Dynasty, 1392–1592" (unpub. diss., University of California, Berkeley, 1963), p. 332.

6. The dimensions of this problem can be indicated by some statistics (*ibid.*, pp. 143ff). Some 561 clans, a very large number, provided higher civil service (literary) examination passers between 1392 and 1606. Of these, only 73 (13 percent) produced members appointed to the three High State Councilor posts, and many fewer produced men in these positions with any substantial period of service. Some 46 clans produced 56.5 percent of the total leadership of the boards in that period, and only 15 clans controlled more than 56 percent of total tenure in councilor office, producing an average of nearly 10 councilors apiece. The Tongnae Chŏng clan, one of the greatest of the inner-circle *yangban* families, produced highest-level appointees for 33 to 36 years of that period. Several of such clans, like the Kim of Andong, strengthened their hold through royal marriages. Much work remains to be done in identifying this inner-clique aristocracy.

7. See, among others, Tanaka Tokutarō, "Chōsen no shakai kaikyū" (Korea's social classes), *Chōsen* (Korea) March 1921, p. 56, quoted in Shikata Hiroshi, "Richō jinkō ni kansuru mibun kaikyū betsuteki kansatsu" (An examination of the population of the Yi period by social classes), *Chōsen keizai no kenkyū* (Studies of the Korean economy), No. 3:373–374 (1938). In certain respects, as the scholarly and behavioral exemplars of the national religion in local areas and as wielders of local political influence, the local scholar *yangban* occupied a position not unlike that of the *marabout* in Senegal and Moslem West Africa.

8. For a vague notion of their numbers and of total *yangban* numbers, see notes 10–11 below.

9. The royal clan had an anomalous status and role within *yangban* groups. Since the first king had eight sons, the second fifteen, the third

twelve, and the fourth about twenty — all before the middle of the fifteenth century — the royal clan soon achieved enormous strength.

By custom, its members could not hold important office, yet were titled for three generations and enfeoffed, forming a semi-feudal component within the centralized bureaucratic system. With the fifth generation, they dropped from the royal household and became mere Yi clansmen. They were then free to take the civil examinations and accept office. Many did; indeed research is now beginning to show that despite a 150-year-late start (five generations), over twice as many royal Yi clansmen as members of any other clan passed the highest civil service exam. Still, the proportion was apparently extremely small. Yi clansmen passing the civil exams, even including those of non-royal descent, were on the order of 800 out of some 14,000. (For the above information, I am grateful to Dr. Edward W. Wagner.) Yet the sons of Yi kings through the fifteenth century alone numbered some 72 (*Han'guk-sa, Yŏnp'yo* [History of Korea, chronological tables; Seoul, 1959], pp. 350–359). Mathematically, the theoretical potential for the descendants of these alone might, by the mid-nineteenth century, be initially assumed to number 72 to at least the sixteenth power (number of generations between 1450 and 1850), or something on the order of a billion times the number of seconds ticked off since the earth's creation! Clearly the survival and reproduction rates, inter-marriage, the "loss of ancestors" phenomenon, etc., drastically, to say the least, reduced this inundation. Yet the number, including of course the descendants of post–fifteenth-century monarchs, must have been high in the hundreds of thousands if not into the millions. The Yi clan numbers in the millions today. Of these, it is safe to say that most are impoverished, many have become simple farmers, even more have lost effective contact with their class. There appears to be little positive evidence that royal descendants were able to hold onto large lands for many generations after the original grant: their ability in this respect was far less than that of European or Latin-American aristocrats. The Yi clan, despite numerous officials, thus also shared the frustrations of general *yangban* society, which saw ever-multiplying numbers competing for an essentially unvarying number of positions. It was to this group and these frustrations that Syngman Rhee and his family were heir.

10. W. E. Griffis, "Japan's Absorption of Korea" (in unnamed American journal included in Korea pamphlets collected by E. G. Stillman and dated October 1910 in Widener Library), states that the *yangban* numbered "400,000 or, with their families, nearly 2,000,000." Joseph H. Longford, *The Story of Korea* (New York, 1911), estimates the number similarly at 20 percent of the population, or 2,000,000. Other estimates hover around 18 percent. Despite their talent for statistics and the greater number of their residents in Korea, Japanese enjoyed little more success in estimates. Kikuchi Kenjō, a contemporary observer, estimated the Seoul population in the early 1890's at between 200,000 and 250,000, of which he thought the *yangban* population was seven-tenths or between 140,000 and 175,000. (*Chōsen ōkoku* [The kingdom of Korea]; Tokyo, 1896), pp. 59, 72, 77. In contrast, Taketsugi Ouchi, writing later, estimated the *yangban* population of Seoul in the period 1900–1910 at only 10,000 out of a total 200,000 city population. "Richō maki no nōson" (Farming

villages at the end of the Yi Dynasty, *Chōsen shakai keizai-shi kenkyū,* 1.6:231–295 (1933).

11. Based on a preliminary census made by Japan, *Nihon Teikoku dai sanjū tōkei nenkan* (Japanese Statistical yearbook; 1911), p. 947. (The first census using local police in villages did not take place until 1930.) The Japanese statisticians said little about the criteria they had used in determining whom to count as a *yangban.* However, Professor Zenshō, publishing this same figure with tables elsewhere, clarifies it somewhat by breaking it down as 15,758 households of central and local government officials, 54,217 households of *yangban,* and 19,075 of literati. Zenshō Eisuke, "Richō Matsuyō no kokō" (Population at the end of the Yi Dynasty), *Chōsen* (Korea), No. 151:41–65 (Dec. 1927). Since Zenshō is the leading Japanese scholar of Korean population statistics, his figures probably come closest of any to being meaningful.

12. Ōuchi, *op. cit.,* p. 236. The average household was then vaguely considered to have about five members.

13. Kim Yŏng-mo, "Han'guk sahoe ŭi kyŏngjejŏk Elite ŭi hyŏngsŏng kwajŏng" (A study of the formation of economic elite in Korea; unpub. paper, Seoul National University, 1962), expanding the statistics in Shikata, *op. cit.,* Appendix 1, to national dimensions, postulates that the *yangban* may have reached 44.6 percent of the households and 48.6 percent of the population by 1853, or upwards of five million.

14. Cf. Ch'oe Nam-sŏn, *Kosa t'ong* (Cultural history of Korea; Seoul, 1943), p. 188; Imamura Tomo, *Chōsen fūzoku-shū* (Compilation of Korean customs; Seoul, 1914), pp. 19–20.

15. The *hyangban* have been neglected in Korean studies. It is easy to deduce that the interests of the social system and of this "in-between" class itself lay in obfuscating its existence. The theory of the dynasty was that position brought status; but it was in the interests of all concerned to pass over the fact that this connection did not and could not exist for most *yangban.* The *hyangban* constituted a semi-concealed class living in uneasy and ambiguous relationship with its own value system. Had the dynasty attempted to enforce abandonment of such an ambiguous status, national unrest would probably have resulted. National internal security hence probably rested partly on the class's concealment and only sporadic attempts were made to investigate corners of the situation (see Ch'ŏl-chong's 1962 reforms, note 21 below).

16. The Korean system was the reverse of feudalism. One did not acquire local power and on that basis demand a voice in state councils; one lost power in the capital and on that basis sought to get by and keep out of the way by living in the country. The persistence of this attitude continues to hinder local development.

17. Shikata, *op. cit.,* pp. 364–481. Shikata was a professor of economic history at Keijō Imperial University, Seoul. His central interest was Korea and "among the economic historians, his documentation is fullest and his knowledge of Korea most impressive" (Hilary Conroy, *The Japanese Seizure of Korea, 1868–1910* [University Park, Pa., 1960], p. 445). His study has not been made available in any Western language or work, nor do its results appear to have been used in any study published in a Western language. In the 1930's, Prof. Shikata found original population

registers of five rural townships (*myŏn*) in southeastern Korea, located in the same county with the city of Taegu, containing relatively high-quality population and household registry statistics for 1690; 1729 and 1732; 1783, 1786, and 1789; and 1858. A full analysis of these statistics should be reserved for a more specialized study. The sample is, of course, extremely small and local. For various historical reasons, the mobility situation in the area represented may have been somewhat higher than the national average, but no reason is currently known that would make it unrepresentative in any extreme degree.

18. The *yangban* household averaged about 3.6 persons during the periods studied by Shikata, excluding the *yangban's* concubines and their children, who often outnumbered the legitimate families but were legally ineligible for their fathers' status. Natural increase in "legal" *yangban* was hence negligible. The average commoner's household had about four members. Slaves were exceptional. Because of consolidation of slaves into large establishments, the numbers in slave households rose from 5.1 and 6.0 in the first two periods to 14 in the third and 93.7 in the fourth. (Shikata, *op. cit.*, p. 389). Since *yangban* were not eligible for taxes and conscription there is no apparent motivation for an artificial statistical reduction in the numbers of "legal" *yangban* indicated in each household. It should be observed that the increase in *yangban* indicated does seem suspiciously low, even allowing for the exclusion of their concubine children. A small adjustment would, however, not affect the general validity of these observations.

19. Yi Man-gap of the Sociology Department of Seoul National University in an entirely separate study made among 336 respondents in six villages in Kwangju and Yongin counties fifty miles southeast of Seoul before 1960 found that "among the whole respondents 44 percent are of *yangban*, 52 percent are of *sangmin*, while 4 percent are of *ch'ŏnmin* and unidentified." Prof. Yi's methods stressed oral field research rather than documentary genealogical study. We can assume that most former *ch'ŏnmin* had succeeded in melding with other classes in his area. Otherwise his results are strikingly consonant. Yi Man-gap, *The Social Structure of Korean Village*[s] (Korean Studies Series, No. 5; Seoul, 1960), pp. 3, 12–13, of the English summary.

20. Mobility probably was not as great in areas like Seoul and Ch'ungch'ŏng-do, where many *yangban* kept concentrated social watch, or in the north, where class differences were less; but there is no *prima facie* reason to doubt that mobility on something like this order characterized other areas. It is difficult to draw other conclusions by visiting Korean villages today — even some supposed to contain *yangban*. The pattern of easy social intercourse is more striking by far than it is, for example, in Japan. From high to low, sons or daughters are lent to serve in neighbors' houses or kitchens during celebrations, and wives, regardless of "status," dressed in indistinguishable informality, help in the fields. Village life has changed only slowly in Korea; there is little evidence of social revolution in rural life. Had a spreading class of hundreds of thousands of *yangban* maintained rigid status throughout the land within living memory, we would not expect to find rural life cast in such easy informality of mold. (For some of the above observations I am indebted

to Dr. Maner Thorpe, University of California, Santa Barbara, who lived in a Kyŏngsang-do village for over a year in 1962–63.)

21. Shikata, *op. cit.*, pp. 394–395. Shikata cites Chŏng Yak-yong (Tasan), *Yŏyudang: Mongmin simsŏ* (A true guide for governing the people), VI, 10. In the same passages, Chŏng speaks of the "universal pretense at being scholars" of slaves entering the local examination places; of widespread changing of the names of fathers and ancestors, all of such changes successful in a generation or two. The second of King Ch'ŏlchong's national reforms in 1862 was "to investigate the false descendants of merit subjects and of members of the royal clan" (Cho Ching-yang, "The Decade of the Taewŏn'gun" [unpub. diss., Harvard University, 1960], p. 92). Penalties for commoners and slaves taking the examinations are referred to in Yi Sang-baek, *op. cit.*, pp. 278–279.

22. Shikata, *op. cit.*, p. 399, cites a passage from the earlier literatus Yi Su-gwang (1563–1628): "Just because they helped a little in the war effort by providing a few bushels of wheat, medical care or delivering a letter, poor and unworthy fellows rose from mixed origins to cabinet ranks, slaves to the principal first and second grades."

23. Cf. Edward W. Wagner, "The Literati Purges" (unpub. diss., Harvard University, 1959), *passim*. The 1498–1519 period Dr. Wagner covers was rife with families disgraced and enslaved. The family of the patriot Kim Ku would appear to be an example of this. It was reportedly descended from Silla kings and kept some status in the capital until the early Yi Dynasty. An ancestor was then executed on a charge of involvement in lèse-majesté and the family fled to Hwanghae Province, where its members performed the "mean" occupation of tilling military fields and acted as commoners to conceal their crime: Kim Ku, *Paekpŏm ilchi; Kim Ku chasŏjŏn* (Memoirs of Paekbŏm: autobiography of Kim Ku; Seoul, 1947), pp. 3–4. Another example is the Yi family of Mangho-ri, Yŏngam, Chŏlla Namdo, whose ancestor, an impoverished *hyangban*, decided to make bamboo combs for a living "rather than disgracing his family name by engaging in other lowly manual labor." The family has made combs ever since. Ye Yong-hae, *Inmun munhwa-jae* (Masters of cultural heritage; Seoul, 1963), pp. 409–410.

Obviously no accurate figures on the size of the *hyangban* class are available. If one accepts the Zenshō figures of 15,558 government official households plus 54,217 other *yangban* households as being essentially the *yangban* in the proper sense of the word and places the remainder of a total of 300,000–400,000 or more as being in greater or lesser degree "in-between," one may have a vague idea of the dimensions of the problem by the end of the dynasty.

24. The ancestor of Syngman Rhee, several generations removed from both the crown and the present day, is reported to have married a slave. (Conversation with Sin Hŭng-u, childhood friend of Rhee.)

25. The difference between theory and practice in status behavior in Korea is well illustrated by usury. Theoretically, *yangban* were supposed to be as distant as possible from money. In fact, even public officials widely practiced usury, as the report of Nam Ku-man, the Inspector-General to the monarch Hyŏnjong (1641–1674), attests (*Hyŏnjong kaesu sillok* [Revised annals of Hyŏnjong], Book 12, 1664. Rice loaned

in the spring bore 50 percent interest when it was returned in the fall. Interest of 20 percent a month was declared legal in the *Sok taejŏn* code of 1744, but rates were sometimes as high as 100 percent per month. This widely-practiced contradiction ate away at the fabric of the social system. It is interesting here to compare the remarks of the famous Ch'ing literatus, Ku Yen-wu, about a Chinese *hyangban* equivalent, the *sheng-yüan,* or low-degree holders and their behavior in this area of class mergings: "It is the *sheng-yüan* who associate with the clerks — some of them are even clerks themselves . . . it is the *sheng-yüan* who visit the yamen and interfere with the administration of the government . . . [and who] rely on their influence to be arbitrary in the villages." *T'ing-lin wen-chih* (Collected works of T'ing-lin [Ku Yen-wu]), 1:20a-b; cited in Ch'ü T'ung-tsu, *Local Government in China under the Ch'ing* (Cambridge, Mass., 1962), p. 177.

26. Karl A. Wittfogel, *Oriental Despotism: A Comparative Study of Total Power* (New Haven, 1957), p. 351.

27. Isabella Bird Bishop, *Korea and Her Neighbors* (London, 1898), pp. 113–114. Such behavior could obviously not have distinguished the *hyangban.*

Korea's classes merged far more than France's. Yet De Tocqueville describes a somewhat similar process of merging. "Basically all who ranked above the common herd were of a muchness; they had the same ideas, the same habits, the same tastes, the same kind of amusements; read the same books and spoke the same way. They differed only in their rights." Alexis de Tocqueville, *The Old Regime and the French Revolution* (New York, 1955), pp. 77–81.

There was, however, much aping of the Sinified superficialities of *yangban* behavior by those usurping their status, much as in inter-caste movement in India where "Sanskritizing one's customs and rituals amounts to claiming ritually higher status than has been granted by local opinion" and "was an accepted mode of social mobility in the caste system." M. N. Srinivas, "Social Change in Modern India" (paper for the International Conference on Comparative Research on Social Change and Regional Disparity within and between Nations; Delhi, India, 1967), pp. 2–3. The author is Professor of Sociology, Delhi University.

28. These generalizations apply more to the court bureaucrats than to the provincial scholars. The latter retained and transmitted scholarly values and have continued to have much influence on local education and behavior.

29. The Kimhae Kim clan, largest in Korea, was unrepresented by a single High State Councilor during the 518 years of the Yi Dynasty and was poorly represented in other positions, though its descendants, like most other Koreans today, claim *yangban* status. The enormous number of Kim in Korea (some 24 percent of the population) reflects how over generations persons who formerly had names associated with the lower classes or who had no family names at all sought a cover name under which to creep into the clan system. The Kim, of course, also had aristocratic clans like those of Yŏnan, Andong, Ch'ŏngp'ung, Kwangsan, Sunch'ŏn. The larger of these, like the Andong and Kwangsan Kim also contain many members of background other than *yangban.* Some smaller clans, such as, for example, the Yŏnan Kim, appear to have maintained

better clan discipline and to be more representative of the old upper classes. See Kim Yŏng-mo, "Yijo Sam-Uijŏng ŭi sahoejŏk paegyŏng" (The social background and mobility of state ministers of the Yi Dynasty), *Han'guk sahoehak* (Korean journal of sociology), 1:38–57 (Nov. 1964). See pp. 45–46 of this article for a list of the clans holding the High Councilor positions.

30. The masked dances of Hahoe, Andong, a *yangban* village, provided an outlet for satire aimed at *yangban* pretensions. See Pak Chi-wŏn (1737–1805), *Yangban-jŏn* (Tale of a *yangban*; Seoul, 1947). Puppet plays, the Sandae Masque Dance, the O-gwang-dae (Masque of the Five Clowns), the Pongsan Masque Dance, and even the stories told by rope dancers on their ropes, all have such themes. (See Ye Yong-hae, *op. cit.*, *passim.*)

31. Yi Sang-baek, *op. cit.*, p. 306. Prof. Yi is a distinguished sociologist and his description of Korean social classes is probably the most authentic recent one.

32. This situation may not have been precisely true in P'yŏngan-do, where class differences were fewer and merchants relatively more active. A clear picture of social structure in north Korea has yet to be painted.

33. It is possible that modern social analysis may add other middle groups to these such as concubine children (*sŏja*) and the merchants along the northwestern trade routes, who seem to have had special and less covert group feeling. Virtually nothing seems to be known about the *changgyo*. That they were lower-ranking military officers is observed in a footnote, p. 386, by the editor of the *Taejŏn hoet'ong* (Comprehensive [institutional] codes; Seoul, 1960), a compendium of major laws of the Yi period. Professional lower-ranking military officers must have been an extremely frustrated group in a society determinedly anti-specialist and anti-militarist in which most of even the military plums went to civil bureaucrats devoid of military knowledge. The apparently small size and importance of this group appears to reflect this role. There seems to be some evidence, however, that the government recruited *changgyo* from among sons of concubines. The military, but not the civil, examinations were open to the concubine-born class. Yi Hang-bok, famous Vice-Premier during the late sixteenth-century Hideyoshi invasion, once quipped when his servant did not respond to his call that "he must have gone to take the military examination." Thus it seems even slaves may have taken it, though the story claims these to have been unusual circumstances. Yi Sang-ok, *Han'guk ŭi yŏksa* (Korea's history; Seoul, 1963), X, 232.

34. Concubines are, in Korean as in most other societies, a sign of wealth and status. The higher the *yangban* house, the more likely it was to have concubine children and in greater numbers. Royalty was especially so prone, royal sons of recognized concubines usually having status, titles, and, not infrequently, inheriting the throne. Such royal sons were essentially outside the normal standards of the Yi system. One is tempted to compare — and to contrast — the *yangban sŏja* with bastardy in Renaissance Italy. In doing so, however, it is clear how much more openly acknowledged and proudly cared for were the bastards of Italy and several other European societies of the day. On the other hand, Korean *sŏja* are not properly described as illegitimate; though discriminated against, they and

their mothers had a recognized status; indeed, this fact may have helped the formation from them of a special class.

35. The *chungin* were specialists in eight strictly defined fields, which, in rank order, were: (1) interpreters for spoken Chinese (all officials knew the written language), Manchu (or Jurchên), Mongol, and Japanese, in that rank order; (2) legal assistants, attached to the Bureau of Crime to give officials of the Board of Punishment advice on the exact penalties to be prescribed, together with the Confucian (usually Chinese) precedents therefor; (3) astrologers to help designate propitious days for ceremonies and beneficent locations for royal burial sites and advise on geographical and astronomical matters; (4) medical doctors, primarily for the palace but secondarily for outside practice and, by extension, herbalists; (5) accountants; (6) copyists or secretaries; (7) artists to draw the maps, charts, plans, and court portraits; (8) the supervisor of the government's one hydraulic clock. See Koh Hesung Chun, "Religion, Social Structure, and Economic Development in Yi Dynasty Korea" (unpub. diss., Boston University, 1959), p. 82. Mrs. Koh's description of Korean social structure is probably the best in English so far. To it I acknowledge much debt.

36. Gabriel Lee, "Sociology of Conversion: Sociological Implications of Religious Conversion to Christianity in Korea" (unpub. diss., Fordham University, 1961), p. 27. The first arrests of Catholics were made in 1785 at the house of the *chungin* interpreter Kim Pŏm-u. The presence of interested *yangban* at the meeting indicates inter-class social intimacy.

37. "Tax Collection in Korea," *Korea Review*, 6:367–368 (Oct. 1906). See also "The Ajŏns," *Korea Review*, 4:249–255 (August 1904), and 6:367–376 (Oct. 1906). These unsigned articles were written by Homer Hulbert, who, fortunately, recognized the importance of *ajŏn* functions. "They are the only students of political economy," he observed. They "have more local influence in every line than do any other class of people." "To them, the people instinctively look for help and suggestion." Mr. Hulbert personally observed *ajŏn* functions in the last decades of the Yi Dynasty. For an interpretation of their opposite numbers in Ch'ing China, see Ch'ü T'ung-tsu, *op. cit.*, pp. 36–55.

They also form an interesting comparison with the provincial intendant (and also subdelegates) of the old French monarchy whose status and power were higher but who were young men "of humble extraction" who actually handled practical provincial matters despite the presence as "Governors" of members of the old order. Alexis de Tocqueville, *The Old Regime and the French Revolution* (New York, 1955), p. 35.

38. Hulbert in the 1904 article, *op. cit.*, describes their salary as only $6.00–$8.00 (American) per month. W. H. Wilkinson, *The Korean Government* (Shanghai, 1897), p. 139, quotes the *Government Gazette 158*, Oct. 24, 1896, as giving the annual salary for head *ajŏn* at $125.00 and for "writer *ajŏns*" at $72.00, essentially consistent with Hulbert. The county magistrate at the same time got $600–$1,000 per year.

39. If these numbers, given by Hulbert in "The Ajŏns," *op. cit.*, are at all accurate, they are startlingly small compared to China, where Ch'ü, *op. cit.*, indicates that there were anywhere from 100 clerks in a small *hsien* to 1,000 in a large, 700–800 being customary.

40. The *chungin,* ineligible for the higher civil examinations, took a

special technical exam every three years. One source lists forty-six passing, another sixty-five, the largest number being for interpreters. See Yi Sang-baek, *op. cit.*, p. 291; Yi Pyŏng-do, *Kuksa taegwan* (General survey of national history; Seoul, 1958), p. 357; Center for National History, Seoul National University, *Kuksa kaesŏl* (Outline of national history; Seoul, 1954), pp. 395–398.

41. Cho Ching-yang, *op. cit.*, pp. 181–182, citing from the *Mongmin simsŏ*.

42. They were prominent allies of the opposition Namin faction in pressing for reform through writings of the Silhak School of practical learning. The Namin, out of power since the end of the seventeenth century, had seen many of its supporters slip to *hyangban* status in which alliance with *chungin* for social causes was easier. Two *chungin*, Yu Tae-ch'i and O Kyŏng-sŏk, were teachers of Korea's first prominent reformer, Kim Ok-kyun. They had good upward communication through their friendship with a royal son-in-law. As an example of inter-class intimacy, cf. *chungin* O Se-ch'ang's friendship with royal son-in-law Pak Yŏng-hyo as reported in *Korea Review*, 6:238 (June 1906).

43. They continue to contribute in the novels of Pak Chong-hwa, the scholarship of Hong I-sŏp, the painting of Ko Hŭi-dong (d. 1965), the political and cultural activities of recent Prime Minister Ch'oe Tu-sŏn, and many others. They remain a well-to-do middle class in Seoul. Their homes, their taste, and their work show native Korean cultural tastes and interests at a level no other group has been able to maintain. The great collector, Chŏn Hyŏng-p'il, though originally of innkeeper-merchant origin, moved in their circle and came well to represent their cultural standards.

44. Inaba Iwakichi, *Chōsen bunka-shi kenkyū* (Studies in the history of Korean culture; Tokyo, 1925), p. 87. Because of the covertness within the Korean class system, such evidence is very difficult to get. Inaba compares the *ajŏn* to the Meiji samurai.

45. This sense of shame in facing identification divides Koreans and Japanese. For example, both countries have innkeepers, but their attitude toward being called innkeepers differs. Japanese expect to be innkeepers for generations and pride themselves in so being, as Germans would, out of a sense of "calling." Koreans do not expect to be innkeepers (in classical parlance *kaekchu*) for generations. There is no honorable calling except officialdom and all harbor the hope of leaving their occupation and becoming upwardly mobile. Korean innkeepers hence shun calling themselves *kaekchu*. It is a term which others use behind their backs. Much the same is true of the terms *ajŏn* and *chungin* as well, of course, as such "lower" terms as *paekchŏng*.

46. Mrs. Koh, *op. cit.*, p. 100, comes to somewhat similar conclusions: "The *chung'in* had motivation for change without the means, while the *ajŏns* had the means without the motivation."

47. Lee Chong-Sik, *The Politics of Korean Nationalism* (Berkeley, 1963), p. 12.

48. Such conclusions affect primarily causes and issues whose locus was beyond the village. Village communities themselves usually had tight organization, and cooperative groups aiding the farmers with seasonal and financial problems flourished.

49. Cho Ching-yang, *op. cit.*, p. 27. The figures no doubt include many

cases of the same person hungry in successive years, but a rise in critical need of something like this order certainly occurred.

50. One fairly serious revolt took place in the northwest in 1812, lesser ones in the south in 1818, 1820, and 1827. General spontaneous uprisings involving over 100,000 people in five provinces took place in 1862–63 (*ibid.*, p. 63). The scattering of villages and the conservatism of rural life also operate in Korea, as elsewhere, to pacify or discourage group action countering the authorities.

51. Ch'oe Ho-jin, *Kindai Chōsen keizai-shi* (Modern Korea's economic history; Tokyo, 1942), pp. 15ff.

52. Among them, Bishop, *op. cit.*, makes many comparisons gathered from her own travels in China, Japan, Korea, and elsewhere.

53. The Yi glorification of poverty was bitterly attacked during the dynasty by some reformist scholars, notably Pak Chi-wŏn (1737–1805), who contrasted unnecessary Yi austerity with Ch'ing China's relative progressiveness and prosperity.

54. Cho Ki-jun (Zo Ki-zun), "A Study of Capital Formation in Korea (1876–1910)," *Journal of Asiatic Studies*, 6.1:1–54 (May 1963). In some respects, the Japanese, from circa 1880 to their takeover of Korea, 1905–1910, played a commercial and modernizing role in Korea not dissimilar to that played by the Chinese in southeast Asia.

55. The government maintained a few specialist stores for cotton, silk, linen, paper, etc., run by a minuscule special class of government agents. Originally, there had been a group of tribute dealers, called *kongin*, but these were abolished in 1609. There were virtually no private commercial houses except in Kaesŏng, P'yŏngyang and, reputedly, Chaeryŏng. These few towns developed clerks called *ch'ain*, corresponding to the *bantō* in Tokugawa Japan; they also had some repute and pride. More numerous were middle-men or brokers: *kaekchu, yŏgak*, and *kŏgan*, running inns which served warehousing and primitive banking or brokerage functions. Many of the Kaesŏng traders were descendants of the Koryŏ royal house, which the Yi had bitterly persecuted — a comment on trading as an out-group function. Cf. Koh Hesung Chun, *op. cit.*, pp. 135ff; Cho Ching-yang, *op. cit.*, p. 180.

56. Pak Wŏn-sŏn, *Pubosang* (Peddlers; Korean Studies Series, No. 16; Seoul, 1965), p. 12 of the English text, states that "the Peddlers had several thousands of branches throughout the country in addition to a magnificent headquarters in Seoul, with a membership of 2,000,000 people." Although it is difficult to believe these statistics, the article is of interest.

57. For observation of late Yi guilds, see Homer Hulbert, *The Passing of Korea* (New York, 1906), pp. 231, 268.

58. Pak Wŏn-sŏn, *op. cit.*, pp. 5–7 of the English text. Legends linked the peddlers in special relationship to the dynasty's founder. They often fought for the dynasty more valiantly than the government's troops.

59. Lee Chong-Sik, *op. cit.*, p. 66. Rhee, whose fight against the peddlers on that day first brought him prominence, was to end his political career sixty-four years later when Seoul's students rose the day after gangs headed by his followers had attacked them.

60. For the first and third groups, Koh Hesung Chun, *op. cit.*, pp. 103–109. For the paekchŏng, see an excellent article by Herbert Passin, "The

Paekchong of Korea," *Monumenta Nipponica*, 12.3–4:27–72 (Oct. 1956). See also Ri Sei-gen (Yi Ch'ŏng-wŏn), *Chōsen kindai-shi* (Modern history of Korea; Tokyo, 1956), pp. 114, 302.

61. Dogs were, of course, eaten. The placing of a number of Korea's arts and crafts within the domain of outcasts hindered craft development under the Yi and has complicated the problem of saving many crafts today.

62. Some 50,000 such communities were enumerated at the time of the 1894 reforms, but Dr. Passin, *op. cit.*, considers the real number closer to 70,000. An enumeration of 1932 listed 34,152, all but 8,212 in southern Korea. Again, according to Passin, *op. cit.*, p. 60, this was too low an estimate.

63. Impoverished *yangban* on occasion borrowed money from *paek-chŏng* — another illustration of the non-equation of wealth and social rank in the value system.

64. Slavery had played a relatively more important role in Koryŏ society than in the contemporary societies of Sung and Yüan China and Heian Japan, and slave revolts considerably affected later Koryŏ history.

Slavery varied greatly under the Yi, 360,000 public slaves being recorded in the late fifteenth century and 370,000 being used toward the end of the sixteenth century by the central government alone. Following the population reduction resulting from the Japanese invasions of 1592–1598, slavery declined, enslavement of males was usually forbidden, and only some 50,000 slaves, mostly female, were recorded at the end of the nineteenth century (Passin, *op. cit.*, p. 57). Slavery was "abolished" in 1886, and re-abolished in the reforms of 1894. In isolated areas, a few people still live voluntarily in an essentially similar status even today, though legally the status is long dead.

65. Koh Hesung Chun, *op. cit.*, pp. 107–108. At first, only *yangban* could own private slaves and have public slaves assigned to them. The boundaries between the two often became blurred, as in the case of land. In addition to slave categories (known as *p'alban*, or "eight socially-degraded groups"), there were also the *ch'ilch'ŏn*, or the "seven lowest official occupations" — official messengers, guards, watchmen, oarsmen, sailors, torch guards, and post couriers. Such positions were often held by the "socially degraded."

66. Shikata, *op. cit.*, p. 415.

67. The patriot Kim Ku, in his autobiography, *op. cit.*, pp. 3–4, admits that after his family lost status (note 23 above), its members were mistreated by neighbors. It is evident that the family regarded themselves as commoners but was regarded by others as below commoner status. Such an admission borders on the outside limits of Korean frankness on the subject.

CHAPTER 3

The Beginnings of Modern Political Mobilization

1. For this antithesis, see Elton Mayo, *The Social Problems of an Industrial Civilization* (Cambridge, Mass., 1945), pp. 11–12.

2. The best English source on this period is Cho Ching-yang, "The Decade of the Taewŏn'gun" (unpub. diss., Harvard University, 1960),

esp. Chap. IV, pp. 99–249. I have drawn on it for information but not necessarily for interpretation. Cho sees the Taewŏn'gun primarily as a reformer. In my view, the Taewŏn'gun was not a man devoted to reform as such but a decisive, essentially conservative pragmatist, determined to do what had to be done if Yi rule and, therewith, the fortunes of his house were to be maintained.

3. The Noron (Old Doctrine), Soron (Young Doctrine), Namin (Southerners), and Pugin (Northerners) were the most important factions during the Yi period. They formed during the sixteenth and seventeenth centuries, and faint traces of the close ties that built them may be found even today. See Key P. Yang and Gregory Henderson, "An Outline History of Korean Confucianism," Pt. I, *JAS*, 18:94–98 (Nov. 1958), as well as Chapter 8 below.

4. The dynasty's founder, himself a northerner, is reputed to have enjoined his descendants not to appoint northerners, who were, like the early Yi leaders, ambitious and aggressive. Though recent research is making it clear that residents of the northern provinces constituted at least 15 percent of the highest civil exam passers after 1600 and in the last Yi century possibly matched the north's population ratio, there was much complaint of discrimination and widespread feeling that it existed. Undoubtedly some did, especially in promotion.

5. See Yi Sŏn-gŭn, *Han'guk-sa, Ch'oegŭnsep'yŏn* (The history of Korea: the recent era; Seoul, 1961), pp. 151–223.

6. Though the Noron Min and their portion of the faction profited from the Taewŏn'gun's overthrow and abetted it, theirs was not the frontal attack that overthrew it; this came from a strait-laced Confucian country literatus and his disciples who had little or no social or factional connection with the inner Noron circle.

7. See, for example, Cho Ching-yang, *op. cit.*, pp. 432–433. The Taewŏn'gun's overthrow finally came at the hands of disunited enemies whose chief weapon, in the last analysis, was that the king had reached his majority.

8. The Taewŏn'gun was careful to use his appointees as hand-picked individuals, not as group members.

9. Cf. William Kornhauser, *The Politics of Mass Society* (Glencoe, Ill., 1959), pp. 32, 128: "Deliberate atomization is a technique of total domination." See also Zbigniew K. Brzezinski, *The Permanent Purge* (Cambridge, Mass., 1955), *passim*.

10. The story of these years is effectively told in one of the few top-flight studies of Korea by a non-Korean: Fred H. Harrington, *God, Mammon, and the Japanese* (Madison, Wis., 1944).

11. A convenient, recent, and generally reliable description of the Tonghak, relied on here, is Benjamin Weems, *Reform, Rebellion, and the Heavenly Way* (Tucson, Ariz., 1964).

12. Use of *hyangban* as a communication medium was, however, attempted. Among others, the petition to the king of 1893 was presented by *yuhak* (exam graduates not appointed to position), according to *ibid.*, p. 25.

13. While the second Tonghak leader stressed religious cohesion, his subordinate revolted in favor of social and political action; the movement split over this difference.

14. Weems, *op. cit.*, p. 40, quoting point 4 of Chŏn Pong-jun's 12-point code. Chŏn was of *ajŏn* background.

15. For example, speaking to an audience of 3,000, Club President Yun Ch'i-ho (later baron in the Japanese nobility) accused the Korean government of conscienceless concessions of natural resources to foreign governments. See Mun Chŏng-ch'ang, *Kŭnse Ilbon ŭi Chosŏn ch'imt'al-sa* (History of modern Japan's plundering of Chosŏn; Seoul, 1964), p. 546.

16. One of the conservative instigators was Min Yŏng-gi, a relative of the liberal Min Yŏng-hwan, who was much interested in the club's activities. The former accepted a Japanese baronetcy; the latter committed suicide in protest against Japanese control. Clans, even powerful ones, were not units of common interest.

For details of how the peddlers were used, in a way parallel to the incident of April 18, 1960, see Kim Yŏng-gŏn, *Chosŏn kaehwa pidam* (Hidden stories of the enlightenment of Korea; Seoul, 1947), pp. 59–71; Hosoi Hajime, *Chōsen tōchi shinri no komponteki henkō ni kansuru ikenshō* (Views on the basic changes in the psychology of Korean government; Tokyo, 1924), pp. 19–20, 23–25.

17. Syngman Rhee, recruited to the club while a Paejae School student, first came to public attention for his leading role in the fight with the peddlers. The club was his first political activity.

18. Yun Si-byŏng, Yu Hak-chu, Yŏm Chung-mo, and Yu Chong-sik all joined Song Pyŏng-jun in the pro-Japanese Ilchin-hoe in 1904. Though opposed to all foreign domination, many members tended to believe the Japanese more reform-minded than other foreigners — another cause of internal dispute.

19. The most extensive and conscientious account in English of Japan's role during these years is Hilary Conroy, *The Japanese Seizure of Korea, 1868–1910* (University Park, Pa., 1960).

20. The reforms forced by the Japanese and backed by their troops during the 1894–95 Sino-Japanese War period included many provisions abolishing all class privilege both in the governmental and the social fields. Japanese bayonet-point reform methods gave these little legitimacy; nevertheless, the legal ending of such privileges had lasting effects. This fact is evidence that the society itself had already moved, informally but far, toward their abolishment.

21. Weems, *op. cit.*, pp. 52–53. Weems contains the most detailed summary so far in English of the rise of the Ilchin-hoe. The *Korea Review* of the period 1903–1906 also contains comment and information. Korean sources include Yi Sŏn-gŭn, *Han'guk-sa Hyŏndaep'yŏn* (History of Korea: modern times; Seoul, 1964). The Japanese sources hereafter cited are of interest in view of Japan's intimate involvement. But probably none are without some bias, whereas the Weems account is generally straightforward.

22. The amount of aid was ostensibly equivalent to $25,000 but in actual purchasing power was closer to $50,000. It bought a lot more than it would now.

23. See Weems, *op. cit.*, and Kunio Ōhigashi, *Yi Yong-gu no shōgai* (The life of Yi Yong-gu; Tokyo, 1960), p. 9. The author of the latter work is the son of Yi Yong-gu and writes in defense of his father. The first

four manifesto provisions were forwarded from Japan by Son Pyŏng-hŭi; the fifth was added after the Tonghak merger with Ilchin-hoe.

24. Since at least half of these are said to have been recruited in P'yŏngan Province, where Tonghak strength was weak, many must not originally have been Tonghak believers. It is interesting that Tonghak strength, once almost entirely southern, decreased in the South and grew in the North to such an extent that the successor Ch'ŏndogyo Church claimed in 1946 that over 80 percent of its strength was in the North (Weems, *op. cit.*, p. 90). It would be interesting to know whether this change in membership was begun by the recruitment process in the Russo-Japanese War. Estimates drawn from Ōhigashi, *op. cit.*, pp. 44–46; Kuzū Yoshihisa, *Nisshi kōshō gaishi* (History of Sino-Japanese negotiations; Tokyo, 1938–39), p. 21 — an official Black Dragon account of Japan's continental diplomacy. Payment is said to have come largely from the Ilchin-hoe, only partly from Japanese Defense Ministry sources. It is an odd illustration of the role of communications in political development that railroad workers (mostly A-frame bearers and peddlers) seem to have constituted the majority of Korea's first political party.

25. Ri Sei-gen (Yi Ch'ŏng-wŏn), *Chōsen kindai-shi* (Recent Korean history; Tokyo, 1956), p. 308. Mr. Yi is considered a Marxist historian and is now in North Korea.

26. The first of these campaigns eventually brought, in 1906, a split with Son Pyŏng-hŭi, who had favored Japanese victory in 1904 but opposed Japan's absorption of Korea.

27. *Korea Review*, 5:32 (Jan. 1905). The editors of the *Review* (it was largely a personal organ for Homer B. Hulbert) were consistently and openly hostile to the Ilchin-hoe from the beginning, considering it violent and opportunistic. Yi Yong-gu had strong anti-Christian motivations, favoring revival of the ancient Eastern heritage along lines that prefigured the East Asia Co-Prosperity Sphere. (Conroy, *op. cit.*, pp. 413–438). The meetings and movements referred to are drawn *passim* from Korean press items appearing in the *Korea Review*.

28. *Korea Review*, 4:556 (Dec. 1904). Press quotations presumably brought by Hulbert.

29. *Ibid.*, 5:191 (May 1905).

30. *Ibid.* In its arrests, pressures, and extortions — indeed in its whole "dual state" methods — the Ilchin-hoe bore a striking resemblance to the activities of the Korean Central Intelligence Agency, 1961–1964.

31. Cited in Kim Chong-ik, "Japan in Korea, 1905–10: The Techniques of Political Power" (unpub. diss., Stanford University, 1959). *Korea Review*, 4:512 (Nov. 1904), always hostile to the group, scoffed at this claim but admitted "there can hardly be less than 50,000 of them."

32. With the exception of Syngman Rhee, whose part in late Yi politics was brief and minor, it is hard to think of a single Korean political figure of consequence who maintained a steadfast and consistent political course during these years. Son Pyŏng-hŭi was an early patriotic Tonghak adherent. He became a Japanese agent (cf. Japan Foreign Archives, *Chōsen dokuritsu undō mondai ni kansuru sankō shiryō* [Reference material concerning problems of Korean independence; Tokyo, 1922], p. 102), then a pro-Japanese politician. Gradually, however, he swung against the

Japanese and ended up a nationalist leader in 1919, dying in 1921 after medical release from a Japanese jail. Yi Wan-yong was successively pro-American, pro-Russian, and pro-Japanese. Even Song Pyŏng-jun started with a pro-Min, pro-Chinese assassination attempt before supporting Japan. The Tonghak movement itself incorporated these twistings and turnings in being first anti-foreign, royalist, and anti-aristocratic; then pro-Japanese and anti-royalist; then anti-Japanese and pro-independence. Its shifting relations with Japan form another striking parallel to Mahdist hostility toward and then support of the English presence in the Sudan in roughly the same period.

33. Alexis de Tocqueville, *The Old Regime and the French Revolution* (New York, 1955), pp. 210–211, describing the social situation brought about in France by the time of the French Revolution. De Tocqueville would have had no difficulty in discerning the aptness of his phrases for Korea's condition.

34. Confucianism had long and successfully fought against most of the popular ceremonies and festivals that had brought men together in local cooperation and provided feelings of emotional participation.

CHAPTER 4

Colonial Totalitarianism

1. "Chōsen," the name picked by the Japanese, was an old term (in Korean, "Chosŏn"). In view of the essential differences between Korea as a colony and Korea as an independent country, Chōsen will be used in this text for Korea from 1910 to 1945, less for philological accuracy than for the need to give verbal distinction to these differences.

2. Manchuria, although technically administered through the puppet emperor Pu Yi, can be viewed as a military colony run by the Japanese Army. Taiwan was a normal though intensely developed civilian colony, and elements of both patterns were present in Chōsen. South Sakhalin (Karafuto) had also been administered as a colony before its incorporation into Japan proper, as had Kwantung before merger with Manchuria.

3. Noboru Asami, "Japanese Colonial Government" (unpub. diss., Columbia University, 1924), p. 18. A useful factual study, although Dr. Asami lacked first-hand contact with Korea and its attitudes.

Among Japanese sources, the critical review of the period by Hatada Takashi, *Chōsen-shi* (History of Korea; Tokyo, 1951), pp. 203–224, is considered fair by many Koreans. The best English-language source for the period is still undoubtedly Andrew Grajdanzev, *Modern Korea* (New York, 1944). In general, Japan had a virtual monopoly on the serious study of Korea during the period of her administration.

4. Asami, *op. cit.*, p. 23. In a speech at the Saiwai Club in Tokyo on June 5, 1914, Viscount Gotō Shimpei attributed his own appointment as President of the South Manchuria Railroad to Yamagata's support. Yamagata's influence is one factor in the stability of appointments to the governor-general position and the unusual isolation of the affairs of Chōsen from Japanese politics. The first appointee, Field Marshal Viscount Terauchi Masatake, 1910–1916, a soldier from youth, had been known

for his autocratic suppression of civil liberties even in Japan. The second, General Hasegawa Yoshimichi, 1916–1919, former commander of Japanese troops in Korea, followed Terauchi's policies with little change and even greater narrow-mindedness. The contrast between these autocrats and the governors-general (mostly civilian) of Taiwan is one cause of Korea's greater nationalism and anti-Japanese feeling. Taiwan's lack of an independent political tradition is, of course, more fundamental.

5. The basic issue was, for example, raised in the Diet by Ōishi Masami in March 1911. See Lee Chong-Sik, *The Politics of Korean Nationalism* (Berkeley, 1963), p. 91, citing Shakuo Shunjō, *Chōsen heigō-shi* (History of Korean annexation; Tokyo, 1926), p. 822. Japanese public opinion on Korea was generally inert, however, and interest in such questions was confined to a few lawyers and politicians.

6. Asami, *op. cit.*, p. 14. Gotō, however, played the key role in persuading the military on Taiwan to restrict itself to military affairs and permit the establishment of an administration of professional bureaucrats. This never occurred in Chōsen. Gotō was aided by the fact that Taiwan, unlike Korea, was an inappropriate gateway to the continent for Japan, hence less militarily strategic. In addition, no civilian personality of Gotō's eminence ever appeared on the Japanese administrative scene in Korea, nor did any able civilian administrators acquire with their governors-general the unique relationship of Gotō with General Kodama in Taiwan, which provided the opening wedge of civilian hegemony.

7. It was Katsura who in 1905 had suggested establishment of the Protectorate (Lee Chong-Sik, *op. cit.*, p. 72). See also Hilary Conroy, *The Japanese Seizure of Korea, 1867–1910* (University Park, Pa., 1960). Conroy stresses not factional dichotomy within Japan but the susceptibility of "realists" to descend to reactionary and even brutal methods under the pressure of "security" interests. Conroy also rightly stresses the influence of the Black Dragon Society–Ilchin-hoe extremists on the development of the finally dominant view, an influence aided by a mass society.

8. Kim Chong-ik, "Japan in Korea, 1905–10: The Techniques of Political Power" (unpub. diss., Stanford University, 1959), pp. 70–71, cites the *Kokumin Shimbun* (National newspaper) of April 7, 1905, as being a semi-official reflection of the Yamagata faction view that Japanese policy should "insure the integrity of the Korean territory as essential to our own independence and to preserve order, insure safety, reform the administration, open up the rich resources and develop the industries of Korea under our protection . . . [also] to treat Korea as an inseparable part of our own country." The editor further stated that Korean and Japanese interests were "synonymous." For Yamagata's view that only the annexation of Korea and her economic development could insure safety for Japan and peace for Asia, see Tokutomi Iichirō, *Kōshaku Yamagata Aritomo* (Prince Yamagata Aritomo), cited in Tyler Dennet, *Americans in Eastern Asia* (New York, 1922), p. 100.

9. David S. Nivison and Arthur F. Wright, *Confucianism in Action* (Stanford, 1959), p. 222.

10. Homer Hulbert, *The Passing of Korea* (New York, 1906), p. 287.

11. Chōsen Government-General, *Chōsen jinkō genshō* (Chōsen's population phenomenon; Seoul, 1911), pp. 103–104; Grajdanzev, *op. cit.*,

pp. 75–76; Kaizōsha Publishing Company, *Chōsen keizai nempyō* (Economic annual for Chōsen; Tokyo, 1939), pp. 445ff; *Chōsen ni okeru naichijin chōsa shiryō* (Chōsen economics yearly; Japanese in Korea Research Material Series, No. 2, 1923), p. 4. The broad and deep penetration of Korea and its rural areas by a culturally related people who then represented only a medium stage of development affords an interesting and rather rare experiment in the development process. Despite reservations expressed here, it was not ineffective.

12. Grajdanzev, *op. cit.*, p. 79. When not otherwise specified, Grajdanzev is the source for most of the statistics in this paragraph. Irene Taeuber, *The Population of Japan* (Princeton, 1958), p. 188, gives 20 percent in "public service" and 27 percent in "technical and clerical" services — most perhaps government-connected — in 1944.

13. Despite every inducement of grants, subsidies, low-interest loans, etc., the number of actual Japanese farmers who settled in Korea was about 4,000. There were some 40,000 Japanese (including non-gainfully-employed family members) engaged in landlord or land management activities according to Grajdanzev (*op. cit.*, pp. 79–80). Japanese physical penetration of Korea was rather thorough; Japanese could be found in small towns or even completely rural areas in many parts of Korea, more commonly where the best land was. In addition to the readier communication that larger landholding provided, the Japanese not only introduced police and the communications accompanying them into virtually every village but an excellent network of agricultural experiment stations and extension services. Indeed, among colonial countries, Chōsen came to possess one of the best systems of rural communication. Without this inheritance, it is difficult to conceive that independent Korea's excessively metropolitan government could have adapted itself even minimally to the needs of the countryside.

14. Taeuber, *op. cit.*, p. 188. The contrast, though marked, was probably less so than that in most Western colonial countries. There were many Japanese of modest circumstances in Korea.

15. Robert N. Bellah, *Tokugawa Religion* (Glencoe, Ill., 1957), p. 13.

16. Between 1904 and 1914, for example, they formed separate Japanese municipalities within Korean cities where they had a strong minority. Twelve of these existed in 1909 and had, under some protest, to be forbidden by the government-general in 1914. Japanese associations and school associations were endemic.

17. On marriages during the Annexation, see Joung Yole Rew (Yu Chŏng-yŏl), "A Study of the Government-General of Korea with an Emphasis on the Period between 1919 and 1931" (unpub. diss., American University, 1962), p. 127. For authority, Mr. Rew cites Yanaibara, *Shokumin oyobi shokumin seisaku* (Colonization and colonial policy; Tokyo, 1926), p. 396.

A body of less than 50,000 Americans produced 1,265 marriages to Koreans in 1964 and 771 in the first eight months of 1965 despite the placing of considerable red-tape obstacles in their path (New York *Times*, Oct. 23, 1965). Such figures are rather typical.

18. Fluency in Japanese was widespread. Comparatively few Koreans, however, learned to speak Japanese with anything like native depth and

skill. The difference between these two levels did not matter for formal or business contacts, but it played its part in hindering the development of intimate social relations. Virtually no Japanese mastered Korean.

19. Song Pyŏng-jun is reported to have once tried to refuse elevation from viscount to count in 1921 on the grounds that "the twenty million Korean people have not been graced by the result of having become subjects of the Japanese emperor, therefore how can we few enjoy that gift?" Yi Yong-gu, bitter at the dissolution of the Ilchin-hoe, refused a title and also a gift of ¥150,000 ($75,000) from Terauchi in return for the services rendered by the Ilchin-hoe in achieving Annexation. Dying in Tokyo in 1912, he is reported by his son to have said: "I was one of the world's damned idiots. I seem to have been cheated after all." Kunio Ōhigashi, *Yi Yong-gu no shōgai* (The life of Yi Yong-gu; Tokyo, 1960), p. 16.

20. Grajdanzev, *op. cit.*, p. 108.

21. Ch'oe Mun-hwan, "A Review of Korea's Land Reform," *Korean Quarterly*, 2.1:55 (Spring 1960).

22. The landowners with over 12.5 acres numbered 89,185 in 1942; the total number of Japanese recorded as engaged in agriculture was 33,638, not all of them landlords. Korean landlords selling land in the 1949–50 land reform numbered 169,803. The average farming acreage of one household at the time was 2.45 acres (one *chŏngbo*), according to *ibid.*, pp. 55–62. Japanese by 1945 held some 25 percent of all Korean farmland, including most larger holdings (see Lee Chong-Sik, *op. cit.*, p. 94). It should be noted that the social composition of the Korean landlord class changed markedly in this period. Comparatively few really upper-class *yangban* seem to have retained substantial holdings, while the former *ajŏn* and a rising group of the enterprising, mostly commoners, greatly increased theirs. This seems to have been especially true in the southwest. At the same time, most *yangban* landlords became separated from politics and hence their ancient status functions. The result was the further breaking down of class lines and the creation of a vague "landlord" class toward which the feelings of the ordinary farmer were, at best, ambivalent.

23. According to Imamura Takeshi, "Hanseikizen no Chōsen" (Korea half a century ago), *Chōsen Kindai shiryō kenkyū shūsei* (Collection of studies on historical materials of modern Korea), 3:167–208 (Tokyo, May 1960), the chief selector was Kuniita Shōtaro, who had lived in Korea since the 1870's and had prepared for Prince Itō a detailed list of the factions existing just prior to Annexation. Imamura, himself a veteran of over twenty years' service in Chōsen, attributed some of the "smoothness" of the Annexation to Kuniita's skill and knowledge. This list of pensioned officials may be the only expert criterion we have for insight into who, as specific individuals, really comprised the "ruling group" within the vast, unfunctional, so-called *yangban* clan. For other sources on the trends and phenomena of this period, see Aoyagi Tsunataro, *Chōsen dokuritsu-sōjō shiron* (Historical background of Korea's agitation for independence; Seoul, 1921), pp. 60–65; Chŏn Sŏk-tam *et al.*, *Ilche-ha ŭi Chosŏn sahoe kyŏngje-sa* (A social and economic history of Chosŏn under the Japanese empire; Seoul, 1947), pp. 50–51. Nevertheless, it would be a mistake to conclude that even these eighty-four, let alone the 3,645, were all neces-

sarily powerful or significant. Rew, *op. cit.*, pp. 106–107, cites documents of the Chōsen Gendarmerie, *Taishō hachinen Chōsen sōjō jiken jōkyō* (Situation of the 1919 uprisings in Chōsen; Seoul, 1919), to indicate that some donations went to *yangban* on grounds of severe financial need and, in consequence, some important *yangban*, affronted by having lesser *yangban* equated with them, became more anti-Japanese.

24. Among the few to be placed in this category are Yi Si-yŏng, grandson of Prime Minister Kim Hong-jip, Minister of Finance and of Justice in the Provisional Government and first Vice-President of the Republic of Korea; Yun Po-sŏn, grandson of a title-holder and President of the ROK, 1960–1962; and Yi Sun-yong, Home Minister, 1951–1952, and near relative to the former ruling family. "Leadership class" in this sentence refers only to those *yangban* families who really maintained access to power.

25. Until the 1930's virtually all judicial officials were Japanese. Even at the end of the Japanese administration, "over 85% of the judges, procurators and members of the Bar Association were Japanese." E. Grant Meade, *American Military Government in Korea* (New York, 1951), p. 132.

26. An example was the new penal code of 1905. Cf. Paul Kichon Ryu (Yu Ki-ch'ŏn), *The American Series of Foreign Penal Codes* (Seoul, 1960), Introduction, p. 1. The Japanese criminal code continued in force until the new code of October 3, 1953.

27. Asami, *op. cit.*, pp. 39–44.

28. Fukuda Tōsaku, *Kankoku heigō kinen-shi* (Memorial history of the annexation of Korea; Tokyo, 1911), p. 627. I have drawn other information in this section from Kim Chong-ik, *op. cit.* Gendarme methods of brutality and torture were well illustrated in the merciless handling of 123 Christian leaders accused, with little evidence, of a "plot" against Terauchi in 1911.

29. Grajdanzev, *op. cit.*, p. 63.

30. George M. McCune, "Korea's Postwar Political Problems" (Secretariat Paper No. 2 at the Institute of Pacific Relations Tenth Conference; New York, 1947), pp. 4–5.

31. There were other proximate factors: the world surge of nationalism following World War I, the Wilsonian pronouncements on self-determination, and the emotions aroused by the death of the former monarch, Kojong (see below). These are of little importance for this study and of a probably overstated importance for the movement itself.

32. Lee Chong-Sik, *op. cit.*, though somewhat weaker on the nationalist movement within Korea than on that outside, is a detailed, objective, accurate treatment.

33. As Lee Chong-Sik, *ibid.*, p. 114, points out, statistics on killed and wounded are divergent. Japanese gendarmerie statistics show 587,641 persons involved, of whom 26,713 were arrested, 553 killed, and 1,409 injured (with 9 Japanese killed and 186 injured). The *Chōsen dokuritsu shisō oyobi undō* (Korean independence sentiments and movement; Investigation Document No. 10, Information Section, General Affairs, Government-General, 1924) p. 102, lists 19,525 as arrested in the March 1 movement, 1,363,900 as participating, 6,670 killed. Nationalist sources for

a slightly longer period show as many as 7,645 Koreans killed and 45,562 injured. Henry Chung, *The Case for Korea* (New York, 1921), p. 346. The 1919 movement was one of the few occasions on which the Japanese were ever caught flat-footed within Korea. In reaction, the Japanese sent six companies of infantry, 400 gendarmes, and later 6,000 soldiers into Korea. For a nationalist account, see Yi Sŏn-gŭn *Han'guk tongnip un-dong-sa* (History of the Korean independence movement; Seoul, 1956), p. 336.

34. This seems to have been less the case with Ch'ŏndogyo, for its mass following created leadership of a stronger individual character but with less representational strength.

35. Kwŏn Tong-jin claimed in court to be a *yangban* and might be considered a minor one; he held the office of *kunsu* (county chief) of Haman and the military rank of captain or major but was very likely a product of upward mobility in the late Yi period. For this and other background information, see Yi Pyŏng-hŏn, *Sam-il undong-sa* (History of the March 1 Movement; Seoul, 1959), containing the court records of the trials of the independence leaders and indicating origin and occupation. Exact social origin has, however, to be inferred from this evidence and checked with informants knowledgeable about Korean society.

36. Marquis Pak Yŏng-hyo, son-in-law of King Ch'ŏlchong; Han Kyu-sŏl, former Prime Minister; Viscount Kim Yun-sik; Yun Yong-gu; and Yun Ch'i-ho. Chōsen Government-General Police Bureau, *Sōjō jiken no gaikyō* (General situation of the riot incident; Seoul n.d.), p. 21.

37. For materials on this epoch in Korean politics, see Lee Chong-Sik, *op. cit.*, pp. 250–260.

38. For the early Korean Provisional Government, see Lee Chong-Sik, *op. cit.*, pp. 129–155, an especially excellent description.

39. Statement by Premier Hara on Chōsen of Sept. 10, 1919, drawn up after discussion with Korean leader Lyuh Woon-hyung (Yŏ Un-hyŏng) in Shanghai. Drawn from Hugh Cynn, *The Rebirth of Korea* (New York, 1920), pp. 166–169, by Donald G. Tewksbury, *Source Materials on Korean Politics and Ideologies* (New York, 1950), pp. 65–66.

40. See Hugh Borton, "Korea: Internal Political Structure," *Department of State Bulletin*, Nov. 12, 1944, p. 580.

41. E. Alexander Powell, "Japan's Policy in Korea," *Atlantic Monthly*, March 1922, pp. 408ff.

42. He so remarked to Dr. Frank Schofield, an associate of the Independence Movement, in a private discussion held during the period.

43. In 1902 there were 63 missionary schools with 993 pupils; by 1907, 508 plus 22 high schools and two theological schools with an estimated 13,288 students under American missionaries alone. By 1909 the Christian College, Union Christian College, and Ewha had made deep marks on higher education. The late Yi government also started many schools, as did some private Koreans. L. G. Paik, *The History of Protestant Missions in Korea, 1832–1910* (P'yŏngyang, 1929), p. 390 and *passim; Kankoku Shisei nempō* (Annual report of the Residency-General, 1910–11; Seoul), p. 244. (Hereafter *Kankoku Shisei nempō*, which became the Annual Report of the Administration of the Government-General from

1912 to 1944, will be cited as *Annual Report of the Government-General by year.*)

44. *Annual Report of the Residency-General, 1908–9,* p. 170.

45. Grajdanzev, *op. cit.,* p. 261; Hagwŏn-sa Publishing Company, *Korea: Its Land, People, and Culture of All Ages* (Seoul, 1960), p. 369.

46. *Annual Report of the Government-General, 1935–36,* p. 88. Then as now, considering the paucity of well-to-do Koreans, the number willing to make sacrifices for the best possible education for their children was impressive. See also Harold B. Peterson, "The Occupation of Korea, 1945–48" (M.A. thesis, Columbia University, 1951), pp. 51–52.

47. Supreme Commander for the Allied Powers (hereafter cited as SCAP), Summation of Non-Military Activities in Korea, No. 7 (Tokyo), April 1946. Many had learned the native alphabet and the simplest reading through rural education classes conducted by Korean students or from village literates. They could not, however, have read a newspaper.

48. Government-General, "Educational Ordinance for Chōsen," in *Manual of Korean Education* (Keijō, 1913), pp. 8–10. The Ordinance was enacted on August 23, 1911. It likewise urged vocationalization and a dual system of education for Japanese and Koreans (i.e., segregation).

49. Grajdanzev, *op. cit.,* p. 269, quoting from a Japanese magazine. Almost no Japanese learned Korean, a fact contributing to the greater Korean skill in language learning in the post-Liberation generation. A Korean could be arrested for speaking Korean in Chōsen in the last year of World War II.

50. Richard H. Mitchell, *The Korean Minority in Japan* (Berkeley and Los Angeles, 1967), pp. 16–21, 25. A Japanese professor of Keijō (Seoul) Imperial University, Miyake Shikanosuke, hid in his house a group trying to re-establish the Korean Communist party; he was arrested. Suh Dae-Sook, *The Korean Communist Movement, 1918–1948* (Princeton, 1967), p. 191.

51. Alexis de Tocqueville, *Democracy in America* (New York, 1945), II, 342.

52. At Chōsen's high schools and colleges there were 20 strikes in 1920, 33 in 1921, 57 in 1923, and 48 in 1925. Suh Dae-Sook, *op. cit.,* p. 137; citing Tsuboe Senji, *Chōsen minzoku dokuritsu undō hishi* (Secret history of the Korean peoples' independence movement; Tokyo, 1959), pp. 160–161.

53. This section is taken largely from Hagwŏn-sa Publishing Company, *op. cit.,* pp. 399–400. Also consulted was a typescript history of the Korean press by Yi Kwan-gu, distinguished senior Korean newspaperman.

54. In 1961 Korea ranked 52nd out of 125 nations and territories in number of newspapers circulating per thousand (64), about the same as Spain. Her rank in 1944 may have been about the same.

55. Lee Chong-Sik, *op. cit.,* p. 248.

56. The last six years of Japanese administration have yet to receive treatment from this point of view. American and most foreign activities in Korea ended with the war, as did most outflow and even some compiling of data. It is the unavoidable but great disadvantage of Grajdanzev that he had no data from the "boom" years, 1942–1945 and virtually none for 1940–1941. The Japanese themselves lost, with Korea, the chance to

look back on this hectic period, and the Koreans, absorbed in their new problems, have not done so. It is an extremely fertile field for the testing of such hypotheses on social mobilization as have been advanced by Karl W. Deutsch, "Social Mobilization and Political Development," *American Political Science Review*, 55.3:493–514 (Sept. 1961). With the possible exception of Manchuria, it is probable that Korea, from 1931 to 1945, encountered more intense social mobilization than any other colonized country.

57. Grajdanzev, *op. cit.*, pp. 148–149.

58. Chung Kyung-cho, *Korea Tomorrow* (New York, 1956), p. 120. For example, the gross volume of manufactured goods rose from ¥327,000,000 in 1929 to ¥1,873,000,000 in 1941.

59. Grajdanzev, *op. cit.*, p. 150.

60. Rew, *op. cit.*, pp. 239–243.

61. For Japan's exports to Korea, see Grajdanzev, *op. cit.*, p. 227; investment increase figures from Grajdanzev, p. 234. The increase would, however, be more than halved by inflation.

62. The so-called "younger *zaibatsu*" — Nissan, Noguchi, and Mori — were especially prominent in the development of both Manchuria and Korea. Obviously, Japan's sensationally successful economic aggrandizement and development in Manchuria in the thirties was a key factor in the creation of Chōsen's economic boom.

63. Rew, *op. cit.*, p. 220.

64. It should be noted that partly by accident, partly by design, Japan's stages of modernization in Korea were (exploitation aside) almost exactly those now advocated as soundest for development: modernization of agriculture; spread of education and communication; industrialization. Korean urbanization and emigration — largely to industrialized areas — absorbed about 85 percent of the population surge of Korea during the 1935–1945 decade. Between 1925 and 1940, emigration absorbed a fourth of the 4.5 million increase. Taeuber, *op. cit.*, p. 188.

65. Mitchell, *op. cit.*, pp. 77–79. Some 660,000 Korean workers entered Japan between 1939 and 1945 alone.

66. Ch'oe Mun-hwan, "The Path of Democracy — A Historical Review of the Korean Economy," *Koreana Quarterly*, 3.1:61 (Summer 1961).

67. Hagwŏn-sa Publishing Company, *op. cit.*, p. 369.

68. Richard D. Robinson, "Korea: The Betrayal of a Nation" (unpub. MS, 1947), pp. 48–49, quotes from an Oct. 5, 1945 manifesto of the Korean People's Republic in exactly this vein. "Wealthy persons and men of political or upper social positions in Korea are naturally pro-Japanese . . . if he was a 'respectable' gentleman he would not be a true patriot."

69. Hagwŏn-sa Publishing Company, *op. cit.*, p. 266.

70. *Ibid.*, p. 405.

71. Bruce M. Russett, *World Handbook of Political and Social Indicators* (New Haven, 1964), pp. 350–351.

72. SCAP, Summation of Non-Military Activities in Japan and Korea," Sept.–Oct. 1945, p. 20.

73. Japan's economic accomplishments in Chōsen were, as noted, done for the benefit of the Japanese and Chōsen, not for the benefit of Koreans and Korea. Nevertheless, Western nations would do well to note that

enough was done at a sufficiently rapid tempo, in a short time, and with a sufficiently massive application of skill, techniques, and capital to constitute a towering (and largely overlooked) reproach to the slower, more desultory efforts of "white colonialism" in almost all its forms and in almost all of the places in which it — for so much longer — operated.

74. Grajdanzev, *op. cit.*, p. 80. The 11 largest cities of 1910 had a population only 17 percent as large as that of Seoul in 1966.

75. *Korea Times,* July 11, 1964. Early statistics must be regarded as approximations. Isabella Bird Bishop, *Korea and Her Neighbors* (London, 1898), p. 34. Undoubtedly the count of 1897 was far less systematic than Japanese police-conducted censuses after 1930.

76. *Korea Times,* July 11, 1964, from Japanese census records.

77. Bishop, *op. cit.*, Pt. II, p. 114.

78. *Korean Repository,* 1:112 (April 1892).

79. Taeuber, *op. cit.*, pp. 187–189, gives Korean urban population as 608,000 in 1925, 890,000 in 1930, 1,245,000 in 1935, and 2,377,000 in 1940. Osaka with some 250,000 was, at the time, the third largest "Korean" city.

80. Grajdanzev, *op. cit.*, p. 80. See also Roh Chang-shub (No Ch'ang-sŏp), "The Study of a Residential Community in Seoul" (Korean Research Center Studies Series, No. 20; Seoul, 1964), p. 177. Urbanization in Korea by 1945 surpassed the level most African and a number of Asian countries have attained today (1967).

81. Mitchell, *op. cit.*, p. 76, citing secret Home Ministry records. Korean labor freed Japanese for the armed forces. Jerome B. Cohen, *Japan's Economy in War and Reconstruction* (Minneapolis, 1949), p. 326, and other sources point out that, in general, Korean labor in Japan and elsewhere was rewarded, not threatened, when war ran up its price.

82. Russett, *op. cit.*, p. 52.

83. Taeuber, *op. cit.*, p. 188.

84. Quoted by Lee Chong-Sik, *op. cit.*, p. 92, from the biography of General Akashi Motojirō, Terauchi's chief aide. Terauchi was Hasegawa's mentor. Dr. Lee believes (pp. 89–90) that their methods were considerably influenced by Russia's techniques in nineteenth-century Poland, which had been studied sympathetically by the autocratic-minded Lt. Gen. Akashi while he was military attaché in St. Petersburg.

85. Japanese theory on this point was not completely monolithic. Terauchi espoused the above *kaihatsu-saku,* or "development policy." Powerful commercial-political groups, which had considerable Japanese government backing, believed in an *iminteki dokusaku,* a policy of assimilation through planned, large-scale immigration of Japanese colonists and importation of Japanese capital. Rew, *op. cit.*, pp. 46ff.

86. *Ibid.,* p. 99, citing Aoyagi Tsunatarō, *Chōsen tōchi-ron* (Treatise on the administration of Chōsen; Keijō [Seoul], 1923), p. 192.

87. According to Japanese sources, some 60 percent of the total arable land of the country was lying essentially uncultivated by the end of the Yi Dynasty and was brought under cultivation in the colonial years. Extension services, new planting methods, and new seed improved rice yields over 30 percent. Many subsidiary crops were introduced, fruit production doubled, cocoon production rose 4500 percent, salt production over 7000

percent, and acreages of wheat, beans, and barley increased several hundred percent — all by 1920. Bank of Chōsen, *Economic History of Chōsen* (Seoul, 1921); E. Alexander Powell, "Japan's Policy in Korea," *Atlantic Monthly,* March 1922, p. 409.

88. Asami, *op. cit.,* pp. 53–54. See also John Kie-chang Oh, "Western Democracy in a Newly Emerging Eastern State: A Case Study of Korea" (unpub. diss., Georgetown University, 1962), p. 155; Borton, *op. cit.,* p. 580.

89. A previous order that would have prevented Christians from giving religious instruction in their schools was withdrawn before it was implemented.

90. All Koreans automatically became subjects and citizens of Japan after 1910.

91. Asami, *op. cit.,* p. 56; Borton, *op. cit.,* p. 580. After 1925 Korean citizens of Japan also had voting rights there as Japanese citizens if they had lived in one spot for a year and were not on relief. By the 1930's Koreans in Japan had become more politically active than those in Korea were allowed to be. Between 1929 and 1939, there were 187 Korean candidates for public office in Japan, of whom 53 were elected. One, Pak Ch'un-gŭm, was elected both in 1932 and 1936. Mitchell, *op. cit.,* pp. 94–95.

92. Virtually all Japanese were eligible, and many of the councilors elected in municipal councils were Japanese, some being elected by more votes than there were local Japanese voters. Rew, *op. cit.,* p. 157.

93. This preparation, though minor, probably sheds some light on why Americans, many of whom believed the 1948 elections to be the first in Korea, were surprised at the ease with which Koreans absorbed them. Protestant Christianity, especially Presbyterianism, had been the first and continued to be one of the most important means by which voting and parliamentary procedure were introduced. Not only did church congregations elect elders, but the church sponsored youth groups who debated and elected their own leaders. This was important especially for the northwest, where Presbyterianism was most flourishing.

94. Korean Affairs Institute, *Voice of Korea* (Washington, D.C.), Vol. I, No. 5, Feb. 12, 1944.

95. For much of this material, see Rew, *op. cit.,* pp. 235–236.

96. Mitchell, *op. cit.,* pp. 71–74, citing secret Japanese Home Ministry records. On the other hand, 165 Korean students were arrested in Japan in 1940 for violating the Peace Preservation Law, and the number arrested in 1941 was five times as great as in 1939 (p. 71).

97. Pak Kyŏng-sik, "Taiheiyō sensōjii ni okeru Chōsenjin kyōsei renkō" (Koreans forced to enter the Pacific War), *Rekishigaku kenkyu* (Historical research), No. 297: 30–46 (Feb. 1965), gives 406 Koreans in military service for 1938, 613 for 1939, 3,063 for 1940, 3,208 for 1941, 4,077 for 1942, 6,300 army and 3,000 navy for 1943, 186,980 army and 82,290 navy for 1944. Those for 1945 are unknown (pp. 37–38).

98. Rew, *op. cit.,* p. 239, quotes Japanese sources as claiming that in 1940 10,000 volunteers were accepted out of 84,000 who applied. The figures do not accord with Pak's.

99. Mitchell, *op. cit.,* pp. 72, 71–73, quoting the Naimushō Keihokyoku

Hoanka (Home Ministry Police Bureau security section). *Chōsenjin kankei shorui* (Security matters concerning Koreans; Tokyo, 1941–42), Library of Congress Reel 215, p. 855.

100. Borton, *op. cit.*, p. 581.

101. Ko Ken-san, *Kindai Chōsen seiji-shi* (Recent Korean political history; Tokyo, 1930), pp. 261–262. In contrast, in about the same period, the number of Americans in the administration of the Philippines dropped from 51 percent in 1903 to 6 percent in 1923.

102. George M. McCune, *Korea Today* (Cambridge, Mass., 1950), pp. 24–25. In 1938 the entire country was administered by 95,385 officials: 59,209 in the central government; 6,289 in provincial governments; 1,085 in county and local districts; 1,985 in school districts and 14,513 school teachers; 188 in the Imperial office (*Annual Report of the Government-General, 1939*). The corresponding number of officials in South Korea alone was 326,591 in 1953 and 237,196 in 1961.

103. Hagwŏn-sa Publishing Company, *op. cit.*, p. 128.

104. Bishop, *op. cit.*, Pt. II, p. 264.

105. The information here given was acquired from senior Korean officers whose fathers or relatives were included in this early military history.

106. Lt. Gen. Hong was executed for war crimes against Allied prisoners in the Philippines.

107. For a recent description of the incident and its effects, see Takehiko Yoshihashi, *Conspiracy at Mukden* (New Haven, 1963), pp. 143–144.

108. Many of the outstanding early leaders of the Korean Army were recruited in this manner, including Prime Minister Chŏng Il-kwŏn and Lt. Gens. Kang Mun-bong, Yi Han-lim, Pak Im-hang, and others.

109. Especially a group with Chang Chun-ha and Kim Chun-yŏp, afterward editors of *Sasanggye* (World of thought), which arrived in Chungking in early 1945. Lee Chong-Sik, *op. cit.*, pp. 226–227. Chang was elected to the National Assembly in June 1967 as a prominent opposition leader.

110. The list of those who capitulated, at least externally, is long. It includes Ch'oe Nam-sŏn (drafter of the Declaration of Independence), Ch'oe In (signer of it), Baron Yun Ch'i-ho, and Yi Kwang-su (gifted novelist whose work greatly raised consciousness of cultural independence). Most were induced to make public statements supporting the Japanese war effort or joined organizations dedicated to Japanese ends. For a fascinating apologia of a nationalist turned collaborator see Yi Kwang-su, *Naŭi kobaek* (My confession; Seoul, 1948).

111. Thus fulfilling Prof. Deutsch's hypothesis, *op. cit.*, p. 501, that rapid social mobilization tends to "promote the consolidation of states whose people already share the same language, culture, and major social institutions" while leading to splits under more heterogeneous conditions.

112. Yi Kwang-su, *op. cit.*, pp. 209–210, estimates the collaborators at "more than 10,000," so that adding their families would bring the total to "roughly a few hundred thousands."

113. Small groups of this kind were also characteristic of Japan, where traditions of tight surveillance operated longer than in Korea.

114. John K. Fairbank, speaking of the French in Vietnam in "How to

Deal with the Chinese Revolution," *New York Review of Books,* Vol. VI, No. 2 (Feb. 17, 1966). Both in exploitation and in modernization, Chōsen's experience was more intense.

CHAPTER 5

The Gates of Chaos

1. Both Abe and well-informed Koreans were aware from August 11 on that surrender was afoot. Despite the highly emotion-charged atmosphere, Abe worked quickly and efficiently to devise plans for the transition. They proved a great embarrassment to the incoming forces. Somewhat similar Japanese last-minute offers of independence to Indonesia and Indo-China had similarly disruptive results. For many of these details, I am indebted to conversation with Kim Sam-gyu and others who took part in these events.

2. Song was then at home, feigning illness, since the Japanese were still busy mobilizing Koreans, and there were strong, not unfounded, rumors that the Japanese were planning last-ditch liquidations of Korean nationalists and intellectuals. The Japanese had arrested about 4,000 Koreans in March 1945, after discovering "some plots." For details on Kim, Song, and their group, see below, pp. 276–279. For accounts of these events, see Kim Sam-gyu, *Konnichi no Chōsen* (Today's Korea; Tokyo, 1956), pp. 20ff, and Morita Kazuō, "Chōsen ni okeru Nihon tōchi no shūen" (The end of Japanese rule in Korea), in Nihon Kokusai Seiji Gakkai (Japan International Political Science Association), *Nik-Kan kankei no tenkai* (Development of Japanese-Korean relations; Tokyo, 1963), pp. 90ff.

3. Kim was a good friend and relative of Kim Sam-gyu, also a former Communist, whose Japanese wife was the cousin of Abe's chief of political intelligence.

4. For this and many other details of this time, the *Korea Times,* an English-language newspaper started immediately after Liberation on September 5, 1945, by a group of graduates of American universities — including Yi Myo-muk, later interpreter to General Hodge, and Dr. Ha Kyŏng-dŭk, first Korean Ph.D. from Harvard — is a primary source, as is the *Keijō Nippō,* official Japanese press organ in Korea. See also Robert Myers' Associated Press dispatch of November 13, 1945, on the People's Republic. A full description of the terms and much of the negotiations is given in Yi Man-gyu, *Yŏ Un-hyŏng t'ujaeng-sa* (History of the Lyuh Woon-hyung struggle; Seoul, 1946), pp. 186–189, by one of Lyuh's partisans. Song's views were expressed in a radio broadcast on December 21 over JODK, the government broadcasting station. He then castigated Lyuh Woon-hyung, Abe's "appointee," for accepting the job.

5. The accusation of a subsidy was later made an issue by Lyuh's enemies. Yi (*ibid.,* pp. 227–228), describes the "rumor" of a "bribe" of ¥700,000 as "groundless" and makes it clear that he and Lyuh thought the planter of the rumor was Song Chin-u. When available, the official records will have to be checked to ascertain whether the Americans corroborated the rumors by querying Endō.

6. Lee Won-sul, "Impact of United States Occupation Policy on the Socio-Political Structure of South Korea" (unpub. diss., Western Reserve University, 1961), p. 55. The Russian staff stayed on in Seoul for the entire war unmolested by the Japanese. It was finally closed and its staff returned to Moscow in June 1946. USAMGIK Summation No. 9, June 1946, p. 18. Its activities during this period have never been divulged. Shortly after August 15, Russian posters appeared in Seoul. No plans for an occupation limited to the southern fringe seem ever to have been formulated by Americans and Endō could not have learned of them directly since he was not in radio contact with Americans until some days later. He could scarcely have been aware of the Joint Chiefs of Staff reply to Secretary of State Byrnes that "in a race with the Soviets we would do well to get even the tip of the Korean peninsula around Pusan." Martin Lichterman, "To the Yalu and Back," in Harold Stein, ed., *American Civil-Military Decisions* (University, Ala., 1963), p. 576. The source of the report Endō heard can only be surmised. Its results were, possibly, tragic, although disagreement on political planning had already begun to appear in informal discussions between leftist and rightist leaders.

7. Yi Man-gyu, *op. cit.*, gives a far less precise account, pp. 203–207, describing Song as reluctant to the point that Lyuh's friends told him to forget about Song. Yi makes it quite clear that Song and Lyuh were, from the beginning, antagonistic. Not all versions of the above events are in. Other observers doubt that Endō purveyed such misinformation and believe that the rightist-leftist split grew out of the past together with a strong general feeling that the Russian arrival in Seoul was imminent; indeed, crowds assembled at Seoul station on the sixteenth to meet the Russians.

8. The estimate is Yi Man-gyu's, *ibid.*, p. 170, but appears to be vague.

9. Lee Won-sul, *op. cit.*, pp. 55ff, cites among these Yi Kang-guk, Yi Ki-sŏk, Chŏng Paik, and Ha P'il-wŏn. Members of a group known as the Seoul Young Men's Association were also freed.

10. On these points, Lee Won-sul cites a report in the U.S. Government archives sent to the State Department by State's political advisor on Hodge's staff, Merrill Benninghof. Richard D. Robinson, "Korea — Betrayal of a Nation" (unpub. MS, 1947), pp. 42–43, offers additional evidence.

11. Kang Chin-hwa, *Taehan Min'guk kŏn'guk simnyŏn-ji* (Ten-year record of the ROK; Seoul, 1956), pp. 186–187.

12. Kim Yak-su, a former Communist, Yi Kyu-gap, and Yi Tong-hwa. Conservative defector Wŏn Se-hun also joined the Kim Sŏng-su group.

13. See Yi Man-gyu, *op. cit.*, pp. 235–236. A group of five attackers, one with a school cap, beat Lyuh and then escaped in a car. After the attacks of August 18 and September 7, Lyuh suffered from severe headaches and insomnia. As in most of the outbursts of those days, the attackers were never identified.

14. Robinson, *op. cit.*, pp. 43–44, and E. Grant Meade, *American Military Government in Korea* (New York, 1951), pp. 54–58, give a detailed description of the formation of the conservative People's Committee in Kwangju, which gradually became leftist as a result of Communist superiority in local organization.

15. In Kwangju, capital of Chŏlla Namdo, "Captain" Kim Suk ruled the city with 6,000 followers until ousted by U.S. troops in early November (Meade, *op. cit.*, p. 70).

16. The Japanese information system was probably an important inspiration for the great efforts of the Korean Central Intelligence Agency to build systematic files after the military coup of 1961. Even authors of Korean origin like Lee Chong-Sik demonstrate that there was very little about the secret anti-Japanese Korean nationalist movement that the Japanese police did not know.

17. Tyler Dennett, *Americans in Eastern Asia* (New York, 1922), pp. 417–421. Seward had proposed joint action, presumably to include an expedition to Korea, with the French. Events fortunately relieved him of the need to pursue this initiative.

18. Fred H. Harrington, *God, Mammon, and the Japanese* (Madison, Wis., 1944), devotes much of his space to this story.

19. Roosevelt had said after Cairo, at the Teheran meetings with Stalin, that it was to be "lengthy" and that Korea would "need some period of apprenticeship before full independence . . . perhaps forty years." Robert E. Sherwood, *Roosevelt and Hopkins: An Intimate History* (New York, 1948), p. 777. At Yalta, he spoke to Stalin of twenty to thirty years. A State Department briefing paper for Yalta supported a four-power trusteeship of Korea "as a single unit until such time as the Koreans are able to govern themselves." See Carl Berger, *The Korean Knot* (University Park, Pa., 1957), p. 38. Apparently, Roosevelt had a false analogy with the Philippine experience in mind, relying excessively on such off-the-cuff judgments. On May 28, 1945, Hopkins, in his talks with Stalin of May 26 to June 6, 1945, spoke of twenty-five years or less but "certainly" five to ten years and added the concept of four-power control. See Herbert Feis, *Between War and Peace* (Princeton, 1960), pp. 115–116. MacArthur apparently succeeded in having the latter idea dropped when he vetoed sharing the occupation of Japan.

20. As late as January 1946, in describing Korean administration to take place under an Allied trusteeship, Acting Secretary of State Acheson, referring to the basic American paper used at the Moscow Conference, said: "It was not discussed in that paper whether the administration should be a government or whether it should be something else." *Department of State Bulletin*, Feb. 3, 1946, p. 155. Exactly when and why China and Great Britain were dropped from participation in Korea has never been precisely explained.

21. George L. Millikan and Sheldon Z. Kaplan, *Background Information on Korea: Report of the Committee on Foreign Affairs Pursuant to House Resolution 206*, House Report 2496, 81st Congress, 2nd Session (Washington, D.C., 1950), p. 3, reporting a statement of General T. S. Timberman before the U.S. House Committee on Foreign Affairs. Marshall said that "all our effort would be placed in the invasion of the Japanese homeland" in answer to Antonov's query on whether the U.S. would support U.S.S.R. operations in Korea. The Russians may have seen from this the presence of a power vacuum they could fill and hence added Korea to their original objective, "the destruction of the Japanese Army in Manchuria." A position in Korea did not seem to be on Stalin's mind

at the Teheran Conference, Nov. 1943. Soon Sung Cho (Cho Sun-sŏng), *Korea in World Politics, 1949–1950* (Berkeley, 1967), pp. 22, 41. See also pp. 50–51. Dr. Cho's is an excellent recent account.

22. Richard C. Allen, *Korea's Syngman Rhee* (Rutland, Vt., 1960), p. 70. Lichterman, *op. cit.*, p. 276, points out that Byrnes wanted the surrender as far north as possible but the Joint Chiefs were dubious of the possibility of getting more than the extreme south. MacArthur seems also to have "been resigned to the loss to Communism of all Manchuria and Korea . . ." Trumbull Higgins, *Korea and the Fall of MacArthur* (New York, 1960), p. 6.

23. R. Ernest Depuy and Trevor N. Dupuy, *Military Heritage of America* (New York, 1956), p. 658; conversation with John Carter Vincent, former Director of the Office of Far Eastern Affairs, Department of State. See also Department of State Publication 7084, *The Record on Korean Unification, 1943–1960* (Washington, D.C., 1960), pp. 44–45, and Cho, *op. cit.*, pp. 46–54. The planning group proposal was made a decision by the State-War-Navy Coordinating Committee on August 11, by the Joint Chiefs and the State Department on August 12–13, and was approved by Truman on August 13.

The particular line at the 38th Parallel was suggested by a U.S. colonel as being a convenient, approximately half-way divisor that would leave Seoul in the South and place the U.S. in as strong a position as possible under the circumstances. Conversation in 1948 with George M. McCune, who was the State Department's specialist on Far Eastern affairs 1944–1945. Under Secretary of State James E. Webb, in Millikan and Kaplan, *op. cit.*, p. 2, likewise makes clear the hectic nature of the meeting. See also Arthur L. Grey, Jr., "The Thirty-Eighth Parallel," *Foreign Affairs,* 29:482–487 (April 1951); and, for American policy during this entire period, Leland M. Goodrich, *Korea: A Study of U.S. Policy in the United Nations* (New York, 1956), pp. 12ff. Roy E. Appleman, *South to the Naktong, North to the Yalu* (Washington, D.C., 1961), p. 3, and Cho, *op. cit.*, p. 52, note that Lt. Gen. John E. Hull and a planning group at Potsdam in late July had determined that a line near the 38th Parallel would be an appropriate boundary between U.S. and Soviet forces. The idea, however, was not discussed in the military meetings of the Potsdam Conference.

24. With the exception perhaps, after the beginning of 1948, of Col. Brainard E. Prescott, former Civil Administrator of the U.S. Zone in Korea.

25. Meade, *op. cit.*, p. 47. Mr. Meade, a Civil Affairs officer of the U.S. Military Government during the opening months of the occupation, has written a conscientious account of the period and its problems. Dr. George M. McCune, then in the State Department, tried in vain to interest decision-makers in the Korean problem. Work on Civil Affairs Handbooks for Korea was reportedly halted by a superior order during this period. It seems possible that American over-estimates of the strength of the Kwantung Army were, in 1944–1945, leading not only to excessive emphasis on the need for Soviet troop help in the area but also to the feeling on the part of some officials that Korea was likely to fall wholly within the Soviet orbit.

26. Conversation with Mr. Vincent. See also Walter Millis, *The Forrestal Diaries* (New York, 1951), p. 273. Secretary Marshall disagreed.

27. Department of State Publication 2794, *American Policy in Occupied Areas* (Washington, D.C., 1947), p. 1.

28. James F. Byrnes, *Speaking Frankly* (New York, 1947), p. 244. Secretary Patterson had more than once asked the State Department to assume responsibility for and control over Korea; he was turned down until General Marshall became Secretary. Richard E. Lauterbach, *Danger from the East* (New York, 1947), p. 248.

29. The distinction never had been and never would be made. As a Marine lieutenant and stockade commander in Saipan during the campaign there in June–July 1944, I forwarded a policy recommendation suggesting that Korean POW's be differently treated from Japanese in accordance with the spirit of the Cairo Declaration. My Marine seniors, who had served in North China, tried to dissuade me from this course, in the belief that Koreans had done the dirty work for the Japanese Empire. Such feeling was a hidden but real factor in early occupation American attitudes and doubtless lay behind the famous rumored Hodge statement of the occupation's first days that Koreans "are the same breed of cats as the Japanese" (Lauterbach, *op. cit.*, p. 201). What is astonishing is that no American critic or intellectual seems to have detected the "occupied vs. liberated" problem either at the time or, for that matter, since.

30. Conversation with Mr. Vincent.

31. Millikan and Kaplan, *op. cit.*, p. 4, quote General Order No. 1, Sept. 7, signed by MacArthur: "All powers of Government over the territory of Korea south of the 38th° north latitude and the people thereof will be for the present exercised under my authority."

32. Lt. Gen. Wedemeyer is said to have been the first with whom the top Korean job was discussed. He was in North China at the time, and the rapid deterioration of conditions there made his experience with that problem too valuable to lose. Choice then fell on another Far Eastern military expert, Lt. Gen. Joseph H. Stilwell; Korea was to have become the headquarters of his Tenth Army. When news of this designation came to the ears of Chiang Kai-shek, however, the Generalissimo sent forthwith an urgent letter to MacArthur protesting the placing of Stilwell on his Manchurian flank and refusing cooperation with him if he was. Stilwell was accordingly dropped. One of the few American generals with a profound sense of the issues of war and revolution in Asia, his judgment of the Korean scene might well have been crucial had health as well as politics sustained him. (Robinson, *op. cit.*, pp. 11–12. Mr. Robinson, an officer of Military Government in Korea, himself read the official reports on this matter. Shortage of shipping may have been another factor. Shipping a corps to Korea drew less on tight shipping than transporting an army.)

33. Military Government was not formally organized until January 4, 1946. Early civil-affairs teams were under tactical forces until that time although, after September 12, under Military Governor, Major General A. V. Arnold. SCAP, Summation of Non-Military Activities in Japan and Korea, No. 4, Jan. 1946, p. 281. Hereafter cited as SCAP Summation by date. Meade, *op. cit.*, pp. 47–52 and *passim,* contains a first-hand observer's detailed account of the difficulties encountered.

34. Lee Won-sul, *op. cit.*, p. 81. Two companies began late and haphazard training for Korea in September but arrived much later (Meade, *op. cit.*, p. 51).

35. George M. McCune, "Occupation Politics in Korea," *Far Eastern Survey*, 15:34 (Feb. 1946).

36. Department of State Publication 7084, pp. 44–46; Millikan and Kaplan, *op. cit.*, p. 5.

37. *Department of State Bulletin*, Nov. 18, 1945.

38. According to Lauterbach, *op. cit.*, p. 199, George M. McCune, in charge of Korean affairs at the time, stated that General Hodge had a draft directive received prior to his departure from Okinawa that "explicitly stated he was to remove the Japanese administrators though retaining for the time the general structure of the government." It failed, however, to give concrete proposals to solve immediate political or economic problems. On balance, it seems not to have been very explicit.

39. Robinson, *op. cit.*, pp. 7, 84, 130.

40. George M. McCune, "Korea: The First Year of Liberation," *Pacific Affairs*, 20.1:4 (March 1947).

41. *United States Army and Navy Manual of Military Government and Civil Affairs* (Field Manual 27–5; Washington, D.C., 1943), pp. 9, 17, cited in Meade, *op. cit.*, p. 60.

42. See, for example, President Truman's statement of September 18, 1945, *Department of State Bulletin*, XLII, 435. Hodge presumably knew from his political advisor that State had not and would not recognize the Korean Provisional Government.

43. Meade, *op. cit.*, p. 44. See also Sumner Welles, *The Time for Decision* (New York, 1944), pp. 301–302.

44. In their desire to be the first to meet Hodge and their uncertainty regarding his arrival, the group spent three days bobbing on the sea, without adequate provisions, waiting for him (conversation with Lyuh Woon-hong).

45. One Joint Army-Navy Intelligence Service report had been prepared in Washington, but it had little information on internal politics. There was extreme shortage of information and even of maps. Desperate, last-minute attempts were made to cull scattered information from Korean prisoners on Okinawa, most of whom were laborers. Harold B. Peterson, "The United States Occupation of South Korea, 1945–48" (unpub. diss., Columbia University, 1952), p. 21.

46. SCAP Summation No. 1, Sept.–Oct. 1945, p. 177.

47. Meade, *op. cit.*, p. 248.

48. Hodge declared that "the activities of any political organization in any attempted operations as a government are to be treated as unlawful activities . . ." (Robinson, *op. cit.*, p. 54).

49. SCAP Summation No. 1, Sept.–Oct. 1945, p. 186.

50. Robinson, *op. cit.*, pp. 47, 55–56; Meade, *op. cit.*, pp. 177, 185.

51. Robinson, *op. cit.*, pp. 56–57. The pattern was diverse, however. Some committees were more extreme than representative.

52. George M. McCune, "Postwar Government and Politics of Korea," *Journal of Politics* 8.3:611–612 (August 1947). The mistake still seems incredible. Korean feelings toward the Japanese were well-known to

McCune, then a State Department advisor, and had been recently detailed by Grajdanzev, whose book had appeared the previous year in New York. Hodge's first political advisor, Merrell Benninghoff, is said to have carried with him when the Command landed a State Department memorandum prepared by George M. McCune recommending that the top level of Japanese officials be jailed, which would enable the Americans to use the technical services of the lower levels in the initial occupation weeks. Benninghoff apparently felt that he operated under too weak directives and in too predominantly military a milieu to allow him to take this memorandum from his pocket and ask for its implementation (conversation with George M. McCune, 1948, and with Shannon McCune, 1967).

53. Robinson, *op. cit.*, p. 14.

54. Col. Brainard E. Prescott, Civil Administrator in Korea, said in the New York *Times,* Jan. 20, 1946, that USAMGIK's "policy is not to mix in Korean politics."

55. Robert T. Oliver, *Syngman Rhee: The Man Behind the Myth* (New York, 1954), pp. 13–15. Dr. Oliver, a warm friend of President Rhee, was his quasi-official biographer and a registered agent of the Republic of Korea in the United States. He had access to many papers and memories of Dr. Rhee not otherwise available.

56. Military Government described Rhee's speech as "unscheduled" (SCAP Summation No. 1, Sept.–Oct. 1945, p. 180).

57. New York *Times,* Sept. 4, 1945.

58. *Department of State Bulletin,* June 1945, pp. 1058–1059.

59. SCAP Summation No. 2, Nov. 1945, p. 183; No. 3, Dec. 1945, p. 187.

60. SCAP Summation No. 1, Sept.–Oct. 1945, p. 178.

61. *Ibid.*

62. *Ibid.,* p. 179.

63. *Ibid.,* p. 20.

64. USAMGIK Summation No. 6, March 1946, p. 2.

65. Department of State Publication 5609, *The Korean Problem at the Geneva Conference* (Washington, D.C., 1954), p. 2.

66. Robinson, *op. cit.*, p. 82.

67. *Ibid.,* p. 88; SCAP Summation No. 5, Feb. 1946, pp. 281–282; USAMGIK Summation No. 6, March 1946, p. 2; also Robinson, p. 88.

68. Letter of Secretary of State Marshall to Foreign Minister Vyacheslav Molotov, May 2, 1947, summarized in Department of State Publication 2933, Far Eastern Series 18, *Korea's Independence* (Washington, D.C., 1947), p. 6.

69. USAMGIK Summation No. 21, June 1947, p. 25.

70. USAMGIK Summation No. 22, July 1947, p. 24, reported that organizations desiring consultation included The Automobile Society of Yi Sang-o and The Youth Organization of Anam St. in Seoul. The original number registering was scaled down. South Korean Interim Government (SKIG) Activities No. 23, August 1947, p. 163, reports 147 parties and organizations listed for consultation, 28 from North Korea and 119 from South Korea.

71. For example, USAMGIK Summation No. 11, August 1946, p. 15, notes: "By the end of August, 86 national and 86 provincial organizations

were registered under Ordinance No. 55. Eighteen other organizations have disappeared through dissolutions and mergers."

72. Robinson, *op. cit.*, p. 130; conversation with officials.

73. Shortly promoted to first lieutenant, Leonard M. Bertsch, a lawyer from Akron, Ohio, and a graduate of Holy Cross and the Harvard Law School, had considerable political and persuasive talents. He performed in this almost impossible situation ably. Having taken the risks he was asked to take, he was then peremptorily shipped home in the summer of 1947 without thanks or a chance to say goodbye to those with whom he had dealt.

74. McCune, *Korea Today* (Cambridge, Mass., 1950), p. 91.

75. Originally, the idea for the conference had come partly from the Nationalist Chinese, especially Ambassador Liu Yu-wan, who wished all political leaders, including Rhee, to join in an Asian-managed unification scheme where Chinese influence could be increased. Rhee, deft in footwork, at first privately indicated acceptance, then ducked out leaving the others exposed and holding the bag. Rhee was the first to blame his former colleagues for accepting. (Conversation with former Joint Commission political advisor.)

76. McCune, *Korea Today, op. cit.*, p. 264. For far greater detail on the election period and the reactions of the participants see also the Reports of the United Nations Temporary Commission on Korea (UNTCOK), UN Document A/AC.19/80 with Addenda and UN General Assembly Official Records (GAOR; hereafter so cited), 3rd Session, Supplement No. 9 (A/575), 1948.

77. In February 1966 there were signs that another middle-of-the-road party would be formed before the next elections, but, with its leader harassed and under arrest during part of the year, 1967 and 1968 have both dawned with little sign of any moderate revival.

78. U.S. Congress, *Background of U.S. Aid* (Washington, D.C., 1949), p. 13. The 1944 census showed 25,900,142 for all Korea. See also USAMGIK, Department of Public Health and Welfare Bureau of Vital Statistics, Census Report, Sept. 1946; SKIG Activities No. 27, Dec. 1947, p. 4.

79. SKIG Activities No. 23, August 1947, p. 3. See also USAFIK, Office of the Military Governor, Summation of Economic Activities, June 1947. Only 60 Japanese remained employed in the national government by the end of January 1946, where there had been 70,000 in civil service in South Korea five months earlier. By February 25, only 6,608 Japanese remained in the U.S. Zone. See SCAP-USAMGIK Summations Nos. 4–6, Jan.–March, 1946; Republic of Korea, Ministry of Foreign Affairs, *Trade Guide to Korea* (Seoul, 1959). SKIG Activities No. 23, August 1947, p. 3, lists 822,380 up to August 1947. It was impossible to keep accurate statistics, for the inpouring came all over the border and "uncounted thousands" went not to refugee camps but directly to relatives or to buildings, mostly urban, emptied by the Japanese.

80. Robert A. Nathan Associates, *An Economic Programme for Korean Reconstruction* (Washington, D.C., 1954), p. 23.

81. The North Korean regime retained sufficient Japanese for minimal industrial requirements. Many Americans felt some should have been re-

tained in South Korea, but after the violence of public reaction to the temporary retention of administrators, USAMGIK felt politically unable to take this step.

82. New York *Times*, August 6, 1946.

83. Charles Clyde Mitchell, Jr., "The New Korea Company Ltd." (unpub. diss., Harvard University, 1949), p. 4.

84. SKIG Activities No. 24, Sept. 1947.

85. *Department of State Bulletin*, Jan. 27, 1946. Meade, *op. cit.*, pp. 115–116, says eight billion circulated by the end of September. Col. Prescott, then Civil Administrator, said in an NBC broadcast of January 19, 1946, that three billion were poured into the economy by the Japanese from August 6 to September 6. Repatriating Japanese tried to run off with some of it.

86. Republic of Korea, *Economic Review of the ROK, 1948* (Seoul, 1949), p. 5.

87. Chang Ki-yŏng, "Haebang toen Chosŏn kyŏngje ŭi silsang" (The truth of the economy of liberated Korea), *Sinch'ŏnji* (New universe), 2.2:51 (Feb. 1947).

88. In 1948 the average government salary was below ¥3,000 per month, whereas the minimum cost of necessities for an average family was ¥10,000 per month exclusive of expenditures for clothing, medicine, or entertainment. Mitchell, *op. cit.*, p. 187.

89. USAMGIK Press Release, Dec. 5, 1946.

90. Justin Sloane, "The Communist Effort in South Korea, 1945–48" (M.A. thesis, Northwestern University, 1949), pp. 145–163.

91. *Ibid.*, pp. 67–69. Robinson claims, *op. cit.*, p. 35, that the association, originally founded in 1920, boasted 30,000 members. Pak Hŏn-yŏng himself started with this group. On the youth corps and terror, see also SKIG Activities No. 27, Dec. 1947, p. 169. SCAP Summation No. 3, Dec., 1945, p. 192, notes that December was the first month since the occupation began during which "an entire week had passed without the occurrence of a single incident to disturb the peace."

92. Meade, *op. cit.*, p. 162. Their first merger produced the Korean Young Men's General Union (which first changed its name to the Korean Democratic Young Men's Union).

93. Meade, *op. cit.*, p. 164, estimates that at one time in Chŏlla Namdo 30 percent of the police were ex–Peace Preservation Corps members.

94. *Ibid.*, p. 163. In a transmogrification of late Yi ilk, Sŏ became in 1965–1967 a leader who at times attempted to assemble socialist forces and advocated contact or negotiation with the North.

95. Robinson, *op. cit.*, p. 258; SKIG Activities No. 27, p. 166. Kim Tu-han, as an assemblyman in 1966, attained latter-day notoriety for the cabinet crisis he caused by dumping a can of excrement on the Prime Minister and other ministers in the National Assembly.

96. Lee Chong-Sik, *The Politics of Korean Nationalism* (Berkeley, 1963), p. 227. See above, p. 215.

97. Robinson, *op. cit.*, pp. 248–250. See also *Far East Stars and Stripes Weekly Review*, June 15, 1947.

98. Some estimates run lower. Lee Won-sul, *op. cit.*, p. 93, gives 20,000. There were about 15,000 in the U.S. Zone. My figures are based on offi-

cial USAMGIK calculations in 1945. See SCAP-USAMGIK Summations, Sept. 1945–August 1946, p. 100, and Summation No. 18, March 1947, p. 19.

99. Meade, *op. cit.*, p. 70.

100. *Ibid.*, p. 120.

101. Lee Wŏn-sul, *op. cit.*, p. 94.

102. Metropolitan Police of Seoul, *Chronological History of the Metropolitan Police Department Territory* (Seoul, 1947).

103. Japanese police had swords. These were replaced in 1945 by billies that so resembled the sticks used by Korean women to beat their clothes that the police were immediately called the "washerwomen." Increased security needs — more than derision — brought rising weaponry. With vast numbers of captured Japanese weapons and large-scale U.S. demobilization, weapons were far more easily provided than any other sort of American advice, aid, training, or even policymaking.

104. International Cooperation Administration, *Report on the National Police* (Seoul, 1957). USAMGIK Summation No. 22, July 1947, p. 34, lists 20,554 in jail in May 1947; SKIG Activities No. 23, August 1947, p. 196, claims 19,777 by July 31; SKIG Activities No. 27, p. 165, however, claims a little over 30,000 prisoners in all Chōsen during the last part of the Japanese occupation, of whom about 16,200 were in South Korea. For police numbers, see Report of the United Nations Commission on Korea, GAOR, 4th Session, Supplement No. 9 (A/936), 1949, I, 22–23. Ten thousand police were in Seoul alone.

105. For some months during Military Government, even the uniforms were Japanese; for the uniform factory had been stripped during Liberation. The police as depicted had changed by 1965. The overthrow of the old police by the student revolution corresponded roughly to the superannuation of most of the senior Korean products of the Japanese force. When the police force reformed, it was, internally, a changed organization and is only gradually recovering its former powers.

106. Robinson, *op. cit.*, p. 142.

107. Robinson cites, for example, the case of Kim Wŏn-bong in March 1947, who fortunately could prove that the speeches the police alleged he made had not been delivered at all. Few were fortunate enough to be able to do this. See also Meade, *op. cit.*, pp. 133–136.

108. Robinson, *op. cit.*, p. 156; SKIG Activities No. 27, Dec. 1947, p. 166. Kim was indicted with fourteen others. USAMGIK, dissatisfied with civilian process, sent the trial to a military commission.

109. Robinson, *op. cit.*, pp. 148–149.

110. Examples abound and are eloquently detailed in *ibid.*, pp. 143–158. Especially notorious was the Japanese police torturer No Tŏk-sul, who "disappeared" before his trial in 1948 on well-founded charges that he had torture-murdered a prisoner and concealed the body under the ice of the Han River (only to have it discovered in the spring thaw). He later ran an industrial fair for the Liberal party. Conversation with Yi Ki-bung, 1959.

111. One police-connected local extorting agency in Taegu in 1945 rejoiced in the title of "Love Your Neighbor Society."

112. Opinions of the place of the police in politics were extraordinarily

frank. SKIG Activities No. 27, Dec. 1947, p. 167, contains the following from the Opinions Bureau of the Department of Justice. "The police are considered to be the one strongly cohesive force in Korean political life and in its reform it must not be weakened too rapidly."

A poll taken by USAMGIK's Department of Information in mid-February 1946 disclosed that only 52 percent of the Koreans polled considered the American administration of South Korea better than the Japanese. The poll was suppressed. (Robinson, *op. cit.*, p. 82. Capt. Robinson was in the Department at the time.)

113. *Seoul Times*, Sept. 25, 1946.

114. *Ibid.*, Sept. 29, 1946; USAMGIK Press Release, Sept. 28, 1946.

115. Robinson, *op. cit.*, p. 161.

116. John Carter Vincent, speech at Cornell University, January 22, 1947.

117. The official account of these troubles, much toned down, is in USAMGIK Summation No. 13, Oct. 1946, pp. 23–25.

118. Lauterbach, *op. cit.*, p. 239.

119. Robinson, *op. cit.*, pp. 162–165; my notes on accounts given by witnesses.

CHAPTER 6

Democracy: Feint, Lunge, and Parry, 1948–1965

1. Reply of September 26, 1947, from Secretary of Defense Forrestal to the SWNCC (State-War-Navy Coordinating Committee) inquiry on Korea, declassified and printed in New York *Times*, Nov. 3, 1952.

2. John Carter Vincent, letter to the New York *Times*, Jan. 30, 1957, p. 28. Mr. Vincent describes the abortive attempt at economic aid at some length in this letter. The request was prepared in his office.

3. Robert K. Sawyer, *Military Advisors in Korea: KMAG in War and Peace* (Washington, D.C., 1962), p. 98. A valuable official source, too little used, on this period.

4. W. D. Reeve, *The Republic of Korea: A Political and Economic Study* (London, 1963), p. 28, citing George M. McCune, *Korea Today* (Cambridge, Mass., 1950), p. 266; also *Korea Annual* (Hapdong News Agency: Seoul, 1966), p. 277. Estimates differed egregiously. The ROK Army Chief of Staff informed the United Nations Commission that the North Korean Army had some 175,000 men armed with tanks and heavy artillery. General Roberts, chief of KMAG (Korean Military Advisory Group), thought total strength was about 100,000 — and seemed not to see tanks (Leland M. Goodrich, *Korea: A Study of U.S. Policy in the United Nations* [New York, 1956], p. 89).

5. For many of these points and their background, see the documentation released during "the great debate" on Korea policy during the Presidential campaign of 1952, much of it, including the correspondence between SWNCC and the Joint Chiefs of Staff of September 1947, published in the New York *Times*, Nov. 3, 1952. For withdrawal and UN election policy, see Truman's statement as quoted in the same issue of the New York *Times*.

6. Sawyer, *op. cit.,* pp. 22–113.

7. *Ibid.,* p. 37, citing CINCFE (Commander-in-Chief, Far East) messages. Despite these seemingly basic doubts, "the President was . . . reluctant to withdraw the last of our troops in Korea until he had the assurances of our top military commander in the FE that he would be entirely safe to do so. In the spring of 1949, he sought and received those assurances" (New York *Times,* July 22, 1952, quoting a speech by Senator Paul Douglas). MacArthur's position and judgments relating to the Korean issue as a whole are clearly in need of searching reappraisal. The brilliance of the Inch'ŏn landing of 1950 pales somewhat beside the thought that probably no war would have occurred and no landing would have been necessary had MacArthur not doubly erred in his judgments regarding ROK Army buildup and, particularly, the withdrawal of U.S. troops. Trumbull Higgins, *Korea and the Fall of MacArthur* (New York, 1960), has well begun this reappraisal.

8. Langdon, letter to President Eisenhower, Dec. 14, 1952. For Hodge's stand, see "Military Situation in the Far East," *Joint Senate Committee on Armed Services and Foreign Relations Hearings,* 82nd Congress, 1st Session (Washington, 1951), pp. 2008–2009.

9. Vincent letter to New York *Times,* Jan. 30, 1957.

10. He opined that Russia could seize Korea at her convenience since Korea was not "very greatly important." Trumbull Higgins, *op. cit.,* p. 14.

11. A poll by *Tong-A Ilbo* on July 23, 1946, showed that, of 6,671 passers-by polled, 1,916 (or 29 percent) thought Rhee would become the first President. Some 11 percent thought Kim Ku, 10 percent Kim Kyu-sik, 10 percent Lyuh Woon-hyung, 1 percent Pak Hŏn-yŏng, 2 percent "others," and 375 "didn't know."

Rhee was a typical *hyangban* from an impoverished and utterly powerless branch of the royal clan; his ancestors had not held office since the fifteenth century. His father was an alcoholic wanderer; his mother took in washing and sewing from the neighbors. (See Sŏ Chŏng-ju, *Yi Sŭngman Paksa-jŏn* [Biography of Dr. Syngman Rhee; Seoul, 1949], pp. 32, 110). He had, to the end, that mixture of unsatisfied pride, ambition, and defensiveness that impelled many *hyangban* upward. He had joined the Independence Club as a young Christian convert from Pai Chai, was arrested when the government broke it up, spent seven years in jail (during which he wrote a popular tract called *The Spirit of Independence*) and was released in 1904 at the suggestion of the Japanese Minister, Hayashi Gonsuke, who simply wished all those released who had been arrested at the instigation of the Russian faction at court: it happened to have been the Russian faction that had broken up the Independence Club. (Conversation with Dr. Hugh Cynn [Shin Hŭng-u], 1959, a childhood friend of Rhee, imprisoned at the same time.) Going to America with missionary help after his release, he received three U.S. university degrees, including a doctorate in international relations from Princeton in 1910. A visit to Korea in 1911 showed he was too closely watched to permit active work, and he made his home in the United States from 1912 to 1945. As Korea's most highly educated political scientist, he was elected, *in absentia,* President of the Shanghai Provisional Government in 1919. He visited it briefly for only six months, December 1920–June 1921, fighting continually with its members and leaving it a largely broken organization over which he never again exerted effective control. (Lee Chong-Sik, *The Politics of Korean Nationalism* [Berkeley, 1963], pp. 148–152). During most of the remaining years, Rhee was not president but chairman of the exile government's commission in Washington, D.C. His campaigns to achieve recognition for this government, although failing, did advertise its cause with some effectiveness, displaying his own gifts as publicist, organizer, and single-minded leader of unshakable self-confidence. Factional warfare schooled him, and he was everywhere at its node because of his insistence on undivided control; but he never lost his leadership image.

12. USAMGIK Summation No. 10, July 1946, p. 12.

13. USAMGIK Summation No. 13, Oct. 1946, p. 3; Richard D. Robinson, "Korea: The Betrayal of a Nation" (unpub. MS, 1947), p. 174. I have drawn heavily on Mr. Robinson's first-hand description of the election of 1946. It should be observed that USAMGIK "surveys" of the time were hardly very sophisticated and that political attitudes in Korea fluctuated greatly from month to month.

14. Mark Gayn, *Japan Diary* (New York, 1948), p. 395.

15. USAMGIK Summation No. 13, Oct. 1946, p. 3, gives very slightly different figures dependent on different interpretations of who was "right" or "independent."

16. Robinson, *op. cit.*, p. 177; *Tong-A Ilbo*, Nov. 6, 1946.

17. For the roster of KILA, see SKIG Activities No. 24, Sept. 1947, pp. 115–116.

18. See Chapter 9. The boycott itself ended but was followed by endless altercation, largely arising from it. The Summations of USAMGIK and SKIG Activities in Korea deal regularly with KILA from the October 1946 report on. Its record was, perhaps, not improved by the military governor's vetoes of KILA's temporary constitution and of its anti-collaborator bill. (SKIG Activities No. 27, Dec., 1947, pp. 147, 152–153.)

19. The chief sources of the 1948 election are the reports of UNTCOK included in GAOR, 3rd Session, Supplement No. 9 (A/575 with Addenda), 1948, and UN Documents A/AC.19/80, AC.19/SC.4, AC.19/SR.33–106, and AC.19/61–95. See also Philip Jessup, "The Question of Korea in the UN Interim Committee," U.S. Department of State, *Documents and State Papers,* 1:92–98 (May 1948).

20. *Historical Record of Assembly Elections* (Seoul, 1964), p. 71.

21. Leon Gordenker, "The United Nations, the U.S. Occupation, and the 1948 Election in Korea," *Political Science Quarterly,* 73.3:447 (Sept. 1958).

22. Cho Pyŏng-ok, *Seoul Times,* June 4, 1948. UN Document A/AC.19/SC.4/20, April 28, details the disorders from February 7 through April 20, 1948.

23. UN Document A/AC.19/SC.4, 1948, reports 16, 18, and *passim.*

24. C. Clyde Mitchell, "The New Korea Company Ltd., 1945–48" (unpub. diss., Harvard University, 1944), p. 33. Mr. Mitchell was a responsible USAMGIK official concerned with the Japanese-held agricultural lands then vested in Military Government.

25. *Ibid.,* p. 131.

26. SKIG Activities No. 27, Dec. 1947, pp. 147, 152–153.

27. American advisors were cautioned to give advice only when solicited, and their talents were only partly employed. One of them, Dr. Ernst Fraenkel, had a profound knowledge of the Weimar Constitution and the historical experience of Germany between the two world wars as well as of American constitutional experience; greater deliberation of pace could have utilized his and other expert talents more fully.

28. Rhee's words, reported by Robert T. Oliver, *Syngman Rhee: The Man behind the Myth* (New York, 1954), p. 272, are instructive: "There was another question which created a strong division of opinion. This was about the premier and the cabinet [i.e., the cabinet-responsible system] . . . [Certain ambitious assemblymen] were about to present a resolution . . . to this effect when I learned of it . . . I explained . . . we should adopt the American system . . . Overnight the Committee changed its recommendation and decided to keep the premier in name but to make him assistant to the president, who will be the real executive head." Rhee was elected unanimously in Seoul (his only opponent had been "induced" under police pressure to withdraw) and became chairman of the Constituent Assembly before his election as president.

29. Local bodies were permitted merely "within the framework of laws and orders" to "perform their administration and such additional acts as are delegated to them by the State" (1948 Constitution, Article 96).

30. Paul S. Dull, "South Korean Constitution," *Far Eastern Survey,* 17.17:207 (Sept. 8, 1948).

31. SCAP Summation No. 1, Sept.–Oct. 1945, p. 177.

32. USAMGIK Summation No. 12, Sept. 1946, p. 99. Summation No. 19, April 1947, pp. 11–12, contains Military Governor General Lerch's statement on Ordinance No. 135, March 15, 1947, turning over appointment responsibilities to Koreans.

33. USAMGIK Summation No. 6, March 1946, p. 5.

34. McCune, *op. cit.,* p. 74. Mitchell, *op. cit.,* contains a vivid picture of the effect of such "Koreanization" on office management at the time.

35. USAMGIK Summation No. 9, June 1946, p. 15.

36. For an excellent description, see Roger Baldwin, "Our Blunder in Korea," *Nation,* August 2, 1947, pp. 119–120.

37. Though USAMGIK had tried in Ordinance No. 126 to provide for local elections, they were never held. A bill to elect local officials was twice returned by the President. Elections for even local councils were not held until 1962, those for mayors and heads of towns and townships not until 1956, the latter again replaced by an appointment system in 1958. (Reeve, *op. cit.,* pp. 72–93).

38. See Oliver, *op. cit.,* p. 277.

39. Sawyer, *op. cit.,* pp. 39–40.

40. Article 1, Par. 2, provided for the punishment of those who "in collusion with a betrayer . . . played leading roles in an association or group established for the purpose of disturbing the tranquility of the nation." Article 11 said, "In case it is deemed proper, the court may suspend pronouncing sentence on an accused and at the same time detain him for re-education," a traditional function of the law as moral education. Article 17 mentioned re-education camps. For the text, see the United Nations

Commission on Korea (UNCOK) Report, GAOR, 4th Session, Supplement No. 9, 1949, II, 32.

41. GAOR, 4th Session, Supplement No. 9 (A/936), p. 28. Also Lawrence K. Rosinger, *The State of Asia* (New York, 1951), p. 149. Figures and interpretations vary somewhat.

42. *Tong-A Ilbo*, Dec. 28, 1948. According to Andrew Grajdanzev, *Modern Korea* (New York, 1944), p. 254, the Japanese seemingly held no more than 10,000 political prisoners and about 20,000 others.

43. Sawyer, *op. cit.*, p. 40, cited a letter from Brig. Gen. William L. Roberts, commanding general of the Korean Military Advisory Group at the time, giving this figure, which is approximate and may be high.

44. United Nations Civil Assistance Command, Korea (UNCACK), Political Memorandum No. 9, August 4, 1952. Also conversation with Lt. Gen. Ch'oe Kyŏng-nok, then Provost Marshal General. Estimates of those who died vary down to 187. General Ch'oe, who personally investigated the incident, believes that the figures were much higher, perhaps over 700. See UNCACK Political Memorandum No. 10, August 27, 1952; United Nations Commission for Unification and Rehabilitation of Korea (UNCURK) Report, GAOR, 6th Session, Supplement No. 12 (A/1881), 1951, p. 18, a notice whose brevity politely defers to the pain of the subject; *Korea Times*, August 13, 1952. I have also drawn on personal accounts of the investigators.

45. The Kŏch'ang (Kuhchang) incident "caused a great shock to the (UN) Commission and is of a nature to impair the standing of the ROK overseas." GAOR, 6th Session, Supplement No. 12 (A/1881), 1951, p. 24. The incident is detailed — largely from the government side — on pp. 22–24.

46. *Tong-A Ilbo*, Dec. 28, 1949.

47. Only thirteen were tried. One was released for the duration of the Assembly session and, on "behaving himself," was not re-arrested; another was tried in a provincial town, given a jail sentence, but reappeared in the Assembly on bail; the third was added late, tried only briefly, and not sentenced at all. For text and signatories of the message to the UN Commission, see GAOR, 4th Session, Supplement No. 9 (A/936), Addendum 1, 1949, pp. 41–42.

48. The press is still ineffective in analyzing trial or pre-trial conduct, but civil-rights and legal-aid or bar groups have developed some effectiveness since the Korean War.

49. Letter of Chairman Shin Ik-hŭi read before the Assembly, Oct. 29, 1949, noticeable chiefly for its strong Confucian tone.

50. Five defendants testified in open court that they had been tortured, and their testimony was never effectively challenged. The details of these trials are taken from the records of two Korean employees of the American Embassy, made separately and checked. Full Korean court records recording all questions and answers were not made. Fourteen hearings were held between November 17, 1949, and February 4, 1950. The Communist witness, Yi Chae-nam, appeared at the twelfth hearing on January 20, 1950. No questions were raised as to whether his weakness was connected with his prolonged investigation by the "police and MP's."

The inference that trials are validations of cultural and political values rather than exercises in justice is increased by the fact that the German-Japanese legal system then in force in Korea does not operate on the theory that evidence obtained outside the court is of greater validity than that obtained within. German criminal procedure recognizes the principle of *Unmittelbarkeit*, and the Japanese Code of Criminal Procedure, then operative in Korea, provided for the right of the defendant to cross-examine each witness by submitting through the court additional questions to the witness, a procedure constantly denied or ignored in these and many other trials. (I am here grateful for the expert opinion of Dr. Ernst Fraenkel, Professor of the Free University of Berlin, then Legal Advisor for the American Embassy, Seoul.)

51. Thus in the eighth hearing, the judge asked a defendant who had held the number 2 during the election: "Your candidate number being 2, leftists disguised as night watchmen beat their sticks twice meaning that leftists wanted their fellow leftists to vote for candidate 2. They also fired signal lights twice with the same meaning. Is this true?" No previous evidence of any sort had been introduced supporting such contentions, and the defendant denied them.

52. The defendants were declared guilty and sentenced on May 14, 1950, to terms far shorter than those appropriate had they been proved guilty. In the light of conversations taking place after their release during the Communist occupation of Seoul, it seems probable that two were guilty, but the others were unaware of any Communist contact. Confession, an expert on Chinese law observes, "makes it possible to determine the degree of repentance of the accused and his moral qualities"; as such, it is much used by the Chinese Communists. Luke T. Lee, "Chinese Communist Law: Its Background and Development," *Michigan Law Review*, 60:461 (Feb. 1962).

53. Mock-court trials as educative instruments were sponsored by the Korean-American Legal Academy in 1947, but the effort was insufficient to have great effect. See USAMGIK Summation No. 19, April 1947, p. 25.

54. Problems of the administration of justice in 1950–1951 were of considerable concern to UNCURK, which detailed many in GAOR, 6th Session, Supplement No. 12 (A/1881), 1951, pp. 20–22.

55. UNCACK Political Memorandum No. 1, June 2, 1952, available at the Library of International Affairs, Chicago. The series of declassified political memoranda, beginning in the summer of 1952 with the one cited here, continued into 1954 and is one of the most interesting and thorough sources available for the period. See also UN Document A/AC.39/Inf. 111/Add. 2, June 27, 1952.

56. *Ibid.*, Add. 5, June 24, 1952.

57. The Korean CIC check told the Americans that evidence of a Communist plot was lacking.

58. The trials of assemblyman opposition leader Sŏ Min-ho, arrested April 24, 1952, on shooting charges, lasted from June 1952 until October 1953 and provided a dazzling display of conflicting sentences and miscarriages of justice.

59. Examples include the trial of Chŏng Kuk-ŭn, 1952–1954, a political newspaperman and associate of former Prime Minister Yi Pŏm-sŏk. Chŏng was hanged after torture so severe that he could not stand for his own

execution, which had to be delayed nearly a month. In 1953–54, Kim Sŏng-ju, briefly a U.S.-appointed "governor" of P'yŏngan Namdo during the weeks of that province's recapture in the fall of 1950, was arrested, tried, and, before sentence could be given, torture-murdered, his corpse being stuffed under the floor of an out-building in the residence of the Provost Marshal General. During 1956–57, Lt. Gen. Kang Mun-bong and other officers stood a lengthy trial for the murder of CIC Chief "Snake" Kim, facing procedures rank with improprieties. In 1958–59, Cho Pong-am, former Minister of Agriculture, former Vice-Speaker of the Assembly, Presidential candidate, and socialist leader, was tried on charges of "communist conspiracy." Although the main evidence was retracted because it had been obtained under duress, Cho was hastily and almost secretly executed. A little later, trials of Liberal party leaders on *ex post facto* charges were conducted, with some reluctance, by the Chang Myŏn government. The military coup of 1961 was followed by trials of its Democratic party antagonists, preceded by fantastic charges and characterized by convictions obtained with marked pressure and irregularity by a specially-designated "Supreme Prosecutor-General." Thereafter, up to the present, factional dissidents like Lt. Gens. Pak Im-hang and Kim Tong-ha, politicians like Yun Kil-chung and Yi Tong-hwa, and political groups like the People's Reform party have been treated to trials similarly characterized by trumped-up charges of conspiracy, remote evidence, deduction from key witnesses not even in the country, torture, confessions, discrepancy between in-trial and outside-trial evidence, leading questions, double jeopardy, and other paraphernalia illustrated in the 1949 assemblymen proceedings. Judging by the recentness of these phenomena, it appears that the judiciary still acts to abet not balance tyranny and will be one of the last groups to bring its practice into consonance with law and constitution.

60. Alexis de Tocqueville, *Democracy in America* (New York, 1945), II, 318.

61. *Korea Times,* July 11, 1964, and April 22, 1965, based on City Hall statistics.

62. Yun Chŏng-ju, "Voting Behavior of Eup Inhabitants," *JAS*, 4.1:5 (June 1962).

63. Even in 1965, water was supplied to only 56 percent of Seoul's dwellings (New York *Times*, Nov. 28, 1965). The *Korea Times*, Feb. 24, 1966, reported that nearly half of Seoul's families were crowded into one or two rooms and that deficiency in dwelling units was likely to increase to a million in ten years.

64. Korean Ministry of Education and National Commission for UNESCO, *Education in Korea* (Seoul, 1962), p. 37.

65. Lee Chang-gun (Yi Ch'ang-gŭn), research member, Atomic Energy Research Institute, Seoul, in *Korea Times*, Oct. 8, 1965.

66. Ministry of Education, *Munkyo t'onggye yoran* (Annual survey of education; Seoul, 1965), p. 194.

67. Lee Chang-gun, *loc. cit.*, p. 28.

68. Seoul had, as of April 1963, the nation's most prominent university, Seoul National, with 11,649 students and graduate students. One public college, 10 private universities, 13 private colleges, 12 junior colleges, the

National Education College, 2 military academies, the National Defense College, and the War College were also located in Seoul. See *Han'guk ch'ulp'an yŏn'gam* (Yearly list of Korean publications; Seoul, 1963), pp. 634–638.

69. *Mungyo t'onggye yoran* (1965), p. 98. Similar figures for 1963 were 30 percent, for 1964, 44.6 percent.

70. *Korea Times*, Nov. 26, 1964. The New York *Times*, Feb. 24, 1966, reported that only 1,200 out of 23,000 college and university students then graduating had found suitable jobs. Paik Hyŏn-gi, "Educational Plans and Economic Plans," *Journal of Social Sciences and Humanities* (Seoul), No. 23:40 (Dec. 1965), states that less than 10 percent of high school graduates are employed or, if employed, work in the field for which they studied. "More than half of the human resources in the secondary education stage is wasted without any result." Dr. Paik is Director of the ROK Central Educational Research Institute.

71. Korean Ministry of Education and United States Operations Mission to Korea, *Report on Survey of National Higher Education in the Republic of Korea* (Seoul, 1960), p. 155. This conclusion would be subject to the reservation that law graduates usually aim not at specialist law positions but at general bureaucratic appointments which would take a somewhat higher number. Other fields of less generalist interest like pharmacology, however, have similar unemployment rates. Science graduates have been recently far better employed, resulting in a trend away from the traditionally favored humanities. Social welfare and business administration are recent fields that have been successful in selling their "product."

72. Chŏng Pŏm-mo, Associate Professor, College of Education, Seoul National University, is the scholar referred to; figures are from his "Summary Report of Research Project: Individual Problems of College Students" (mimeographed, 1960), p. 38.

73. See the statement of the Koryŏ University Student Council, March 30, 1964, regarding its protest demonstrations against rapprochement with Japan: "Throughout the long history of Korea, we 6,000 intellectuals of Korea University have not hesitated to take action whenever dark shadows were cast over the Fatherland . . . We students have struggled to find the ideology of leadership inside the ivory tower because we judged the May Revolution [against the Rhee regime] to be an attempt to purify the national sense of our independence" (*Kyŏnghyang Sinmun*, March 30, 1964).

74. For this phenomenon among U.S. students today, see Dr. Jerome D. Frank, Professor of Psychiatry, Johns Hopkins University, New York *Times*, May 9, 1965. It is essentially the same phenomenon that the rapid urbanization and industrialization of the 1938–1946 period produced in Korea.

75. ROK Foreign Ministry, *Han'guk kunsa hyŏngmyŏng* (Korean military revolution; Seoul, 1961), p. 61.

76. *Tong-A Ilbo*, May 31–June 8, 1957.

77. Two prominent Korean newspapers, the Taegu *Maeil Sinbo* and the *Kyŏnghyang Sinmun* were run by a Catholic foundation, the former with active editorship by a priest. They were probably the two most outspoken

opposition newspapers during the Rhee regime. It is interesting that during the Japanese regime, the Catholics had been known as far less resistant to dictatorial oppression than the Protestants. During the Rhee era, however, there was some tendency for these roles to be reversed.

78. *Korea Times,* April 25, 1964.

79. *Tong-A Ilbo* and *Kyŏnghyang Sinmun,* August 1, 1955, were the only papers to carry the report. The leading Assembly critic was forced to pay bank loans immediately, and the police harassed his subordinates.

80. In early 1957, "Tiger" Kim Chong-wŏn, major perpetrator of the Koch'ang massacre, was back as Director of the National Police. On March 7, 1957, *Chosŏn Ilbo* carried his description of his visit to the bed of the thug who had attempted to murder Chang Myŏn: "Since I was informed by the Director of the hospital that he was in a dangerous condition, I slapped him in the face to wake him up and asked him questions."

81. The anti-police trend continued for a time. The police were virtually overthrown in the 1960 revolution. Many of their older members were fired and replaced with recruits, some of them college graduates, who were hostile to older police traditions. Between 1961 and 1964, the military government relied for its controls less on the police than on its Central Intelligence Agency, which, more urban-oriented and less simple in method, left the countryside with somewhat lighter controls than it had known for several decades. Since 1964, however, police numbers have again advanced.

82. See the official statement in the Foreign Ministry publication, *op. cit.,* pp. 36–37.

83. Stephen Bradner, "The Student Movement in the Korean Election Crisis of 1960" (M.A. thesis, Harvard University, 1963), p. 85. Mr. Bradner, a well-informed personal observer of the revolutionary period, has written the most detailed account available in English of the revolution.

84. A poll of Seoul National University students who participated in the April revolution revealed that 65 percent did so with the motive of "anger at the outrageous police" Kim Sŏng-t'ae, "Sawŏl sipkuil ŭi simnihak" (The psychology of April 19th), *Sasanggye* (World of thought), 9.4:78–85 (April 1961). For the early post-Rhee period, see also John M. Barr, "The Second Republic of Korea," *Far Eastern Survey,* 16:242–249 (June 1960). It should be stressed that the restraint and political maturity shown by the students immediately after the revolution was a key factor in re-establishing order out of threatened chaos.

85. Some banners decrying both political parties were carried by the students.

86. The consensus at the time extended to the Americans. The embassy's swift announcement on April 19 of the need for reform and characterization of the student grievances as "justified," together with private urging of the President to resign, placed it clearly on the side of the changes of those weeks. The revolution was, however, as much of a surprise to the embassy as it was to the students themselves who, on first going to the streets on April 19, had no idea of overthrowing the government.

87. See Reeve, *op. cit.*, pp. 142–143; Han T'ae-yŏn, "Che-i Konghwakuk hŏnpŏp ŭi kyŏnghyang" (The trends of the second republic's constitution), *Sasanggye* (World of thought), 8:165–173 (June 1960).

88. Some 75.1 percent in the lower house, 53.4 percent in the upper. *Central Election Committee Report* (Seoul, 1963), pp. 446–448.

89. Its weaknesses during the Democratic regime are often ascribed to the quality of the leadership of Premier Chang Myŏn and his followers. Dr. Chang was a man without dictatorial instincts who believed in proceeding with caution and much consultation and felt deeply the nature of the democratic trust that had been laid on him. He lacked political genius and boldness but was conscientious, hard-working and intelligent. His cabinet, although far too often reshuffled and overworked, was essentially the most able the country had had. Many excellent programs and changes were instituted, and individual mistakes were relatively minor in scale. The feeling of lack of leadership that certainly communicated itself strongly to the Korean public was, to a considerable extent, the derivative of the particular forms of democracy on which the country had, after the student revolution, decided.

90. The problem of the two Democratic parties remained the really serious one. It should be noted that the collapse of Liberal power brought the partial rebirth of the 1945 trend to form many small parties. Some twelve of these staged beginnings or comebacks during this period. None, however, achieved any major size or effect. The largest, the Socialist party, elected only four lower-house members (1.7 percent), a remarkably poor record considering the leftist fears of the period and the size of previous support for Cho Pong-am. On the whole, neither Communists nor any other leftists succeeded in taking substantial advantage of chaos and freedom.

91. In October, for example, after bitter attacks on Chang's more moderate position regarding the punishment of former high-ranking Liberals, certain members of the opposition aided in inspiring a student demonstration that broke into the National Assembly, occupied the Speaker's platform, and forced his hand into backing unwise *ex post facto* legislation punishing the Liberals. This Restriction of Civil Rights Law No. 587, Dec. 31, 1960, placed 690 persons prominent during the Rhee regime automatically under its provision. (Announcement of Minister of Justice, Feb. 25, 1961). Since those "guilty" could not enjoy civil rights for seven years, the Democrats were, in effect, legally forbidding access to power to their own opposition.

92. A *Han'guk Ilbo* newspaper public opinion poll, Sept. 29, 1960, showed that the government and the Democratic party had slipped in popularity since July because of factionalism and lack of progress.

93. Foreign Ministry statement, *op. cit.*, p. 47: "One group of 13 businessmen alone have publicly admitted evading the Hwan equivalent of more than $33,449,924.00 dollars in income taxes . . . through massive bribery of public officials." For details of the sale of a tungsten company to a business friend of Premier Chang, see *Korea Times*, March 22, 1961.

94. Stephen Bradner, "Korea: Experiment and Instability," *Japan Quarterly*, 8.4:414 (Oct.–Dec. 1961). The Foreign Ministry statement, *op. cit.*, p. 65, lists 1,835 demonstrations involving 969,630 individuals, or some

7.3 a day. Approximately 471,779 students, 50 percent of the national student body, are thought to have participated. About 675 labor demonstrations involved some 219,303 individuals. *Korea Annual* (Hapdong News Agency: Seoul, 1966), p. 283, cuts these demonstration figures considerably to 51 demonstrations by university students and 117 by high school and younger students with a total of 119,000 demonstrators, and 35 street demonstrations by labor unions with over 20,000 participants. Definitions of demonstrations and estimates of numbers involved inevitably differ but it is doubtful that the Hapdong figures cover all non-school and non-union demonstrations, of which there were then many (e.g., wives against concubines); on the other hand, the Bradner–Foreign Ministry estimates may reflect some tendency on the part of the coup regime to exaggerate the "chaos" that its leaders felt marked the Democratic regime.

95. The author's office during this period contained a grandstand view of the plaza fronting Seoul City Hall, on which most demonstrations in Seoul converged. From about May 1, 1960, to approximately February 15, 1961, I can remember no day on which I did not see or hear of a demonstration; thereafter, until the military coup, demonstrations continued only sporadically.

96. Such sensitivities were further aroused by rumors, partly confirmed by Home Minister Shin Hyŏn-don in a statement of February 23, 1961.

97. See *Kyŏnghyang Sinmun,* Jan. 31, 1961, and the trial records of the *Minjok Ilbo* case, 1960–61, as cited there and in other press reports of the period. The latter must be treated with great caution because it was, in large part, a trumped-up case conducted with improper court procedures and without the appearance in court of the key witness, who was in Japan. There is, however, considerable suspicion that some funds from distinctly leftist sources were secretly transmitted to this socialist newspaper.

98. John Kie-chang Oh, "Western Democracy in a Newly Emerging Eastern State: A Case Study of Korea" (unpub. diss., Georgetown University, 1963); *Report of the Central Election Committee,* pp. 281, 433–434.

99. Student polls, informally conducted, revealed high rates of doubt about democracy despite the stand taken in the April revolution. Scores on leaders most admired rated Napoleon and even Hitler high, Abraham Lincoln comparatively low.

100. *Tong-A Ilbo,* Dec. 8, 1960.

101. Many conversations were held at this period between senior Korean politicians and American Embassy officials in which the former expressed alarm at conditions but were unable to convince the latter that alarm was justified.

102. *Tong-A Ilbo,* Dec. 28, 1960.

103. For details concerning the instigators of the coup, see Chapter 13.

104. The forced announcement of support for the coup by Yi Han-lim, commanding general of the predominant First Army, came on the evening of May 17 (*Korea Times,* May 18, 1961). The reason so small a group of military men could so quickly and bloodlessly capture the government is a complex subject outside our inquiry. A coup was suspected before its occurrence, but its exact locus was not guessed until fairly shortly before the event. The Chief of Staff's effort to investigate was ineffective

and late. American intelligence did not further pursue inquiries on its own. The Chang government was extremely preoccupied with economic affairs, and its leaders were tired. One minister who knew something of the background failed to tell the Prime Minister. Once the coup had started, there was a very strong instinct on the part of the Chief of Staff and the President to avoid bloodshed. The Prime Minister escaped into a nunnery and was incommunicado for the crucial hours. The President, partly to avoid fighting, partly because of strong antipathy to the Chang government, refused to act even when pressed to do so. U.S. pressures were severely undercut by the concentration of all Washington policymakers on the Bay of Pigs trauma, April 16–19, which not only blinded other action but created strong antipathy to anything that might further "rock the boat."

105. Foreign Ministry statement, *op. cit.*, pp. 38–43.

106. Among others, see Yoshihashi Takehiko, *Conspiracy of Mukden* (Washington, D.C., 1963), pp. 96–97.

107. Foreign Ministry statement, *op. cit.*, pp. 2–3. See also C. I. Eugene Kim, *Korea: A Pattern of Political Development* (Ann Arbor, 1964), pp. 163–164.

108. A translation of this law appears in Reeve, *op. cit.*, Appendix I, pp. 179–185.

109. The Secretariat, Supreme Council for National Reconstruction, *Military Revolution in Korea* (Seoul, 1961), p. 81.

110. Kim, *op. cit.*, p. 164. Many of the "agencies" had not seriously operated.

111. Popular belief in democracy and the complete lack of an acceptable tradition of military rule dictated an external posture of support for democratic principle, however. The Foreign Ministry statement, *op. cit.*, read: "The temporary suspension of democratic government in the Republic of Korea does not imply the permanent destruction of democratic principles. Both the present leaders of the Government and the people are determined to establish Constitutional civilian Government as soon as possible. Democracy is revered in Korea . . . Unfortunately . . . real democracy has never existed in this country" (pp. 2–3).

112. A certain senior general, once acquitted, was then immediately retried on identical charges. When his counsel asked the judge why the general had been subjected to double jeopardy, the judge replied that his answer to this question would have to be deferred until the end of court when he would give it privately. Though the Court Martial Law itself stated that evidence obtained under duress was inadmissible, evidence obtained by torture clearly was admitted in the trials of Col. Chŏng Chin and Lt. Gen. Kim Tong-ha, the court martial ruling that "even if the accused might have been tortured . . . they cannot be believed to have made false confessions in consideration of their former positions and career." For further evidence of governmental pressure on the courts, see the handling of the "People's Reform party" case, *Korea Times*, Sept. 13, 1964. *Korea Annual, op. cit.*, p. 285, gives 679 persons as those tried in the special revolutionary courts alone between July 29, 1961, and May 10, 1962, and notes that 324 of these were retried in the court's appellate panel.

113. Reeve, *op. cit.*, p. 152.

114. New York *Times,* Oct. 8, 1961.

115. Not only did the CIA itself have thousands of places, but it sponsored entrants into every ministry; for example, twenty-five young former officers entered the Foreign Ministry under its sponsorship in 1962.

116. Carl Berger, *The Korea Knot,* rev. ed. (Washington, D.C., 1964), pp. 208–209; New York *Times,* June 13, 1961.

117. The constitution and other principal laws are now available from the Korean Legal Center in English in *Laws of the Republic of Korea* (Seoul, 1964).

118. Examples are given in Kim Kwan-bong, "Politics in Korea: Report of a Young Man" (unpub. MS, University of Pennsylvania, 1965), p. 28. Mr. Kim was himself a government candidate and CIA employee.

119. A recent poll among 377 students specializing in social science showed that 86 percent thought Western democracy inapplicable or unsuitable for Korea because of the cultural gaps between Korea and the West. Robert Scalapino, "Which Route for Korea?" *Asian Survey* 2.7:2 (Sept. 1962).

120. *Korea Times,* April 20, 1965. Demonstrations endangered the government in May and June of 1964 and caused severe disquiet in Seoul in both April and August of 1965, several major universities being temporarily closed on these occasions.

121. The government announced in early October 1965 its intention of increasing the national police by 3,000 to a total of 38,000 to cope with internal and Communist infiltration threats (New York *Times,* Oct. 24, 1965). Many observers feel that actual police strength already exceeded this figure.

CHAPTER 7

Centralization and Political Mobility

1. For example, the Japanese-established Shokusan Ginkō (Industrial Bank) had 67 branches throughout the provinces and the credit cooperatives (*kinyū kumiai*) showed an immense growth from 10 with 6,616 members in 1907 to 723 with a membership of 1,934,000 by the end of 1939. Andrew Grajdanzev, *Modern Korea* (New York, 1944), pp. 204, 278–279. Cooperatives, although locally organized, were channels both into banking and the administrative-control systems. There were also 189 irrigation associations by 1938, branches of the Central Agricultural Experiment Station in Suwŏn, and a Movement of Rural Revival, launched by Governor-General Ugaki on January 1, 1934. Except for the last — which had its recent counterpart in the military government's National Reconstruction Movement — these organizations survive today, under Koreanized and sometimes somewhat different names. See Grajdanzev, pp. 95–99, 204–208; Hoon K. Lee, *Land Utilization and Rural Economy in Korea* (Chicago, 1936), pp. 124–131. A 4-H Club movement, started by USAMGIK in 1946, has grown to one of the largest in the world, with 7,324 local clubs by 1958 and 720,000 members in South Korea alone in 1966, reportedly in some 22,000 clubs (American–Korean Foundation, New York).

2. W. D. Reeve, *The Republic of Korea: A Political and Economic Study* (London, 1963), p. 129; Robert T. Oliver, *Syngman Rhee: The Man behind the Myth* (New York, 1954), p. 284, gives 1,709,320 acres for sale to 1,236,558 tenants.

3. A Korean strongly arguing the damage to leadership implicit in land reform is Pyun Yung-tae (Pyŏn Yŏng-t'ae) in *Korea, My Country* (Seoul, 1949). He is one of very few. Most Koreans have immense appetite for change and a corresponding indifference to the past.

4. An exception is the Yuhan Chemical Company, whose Korean owners had become United States citizens.

5. Innumerable disclosures of such practices were revealed in the investigations and trials following the overthrow of the regime. See Reeve, *op. cit.*, pp. 96–99, and the U.S. House of Representatives Sub-Committee for Review of Mutual Security Programs, Staff Survey Team, *Report . . . on Economic Assistance to Korea, Thailand and Iran* (Washington, D.C., 1960).

6. Unless one includes scholarly "retirement" and teaching in a local *sŏwŏn* (Confucian school) for those few with both the talent and the disposition.

7. Gari Keith Ledyard, "The Korean Language Reform of 1446: The Origin, Background and Early History of the Korean Alphabet" (unpub. diss., Columbia University, 1965), p. 79.

8. Ministry of Education and National Commission for UNESCO, *Education in Korea* (Seoul, 1962), p. 35.

9. The National Academy was called Sŏnggyun-gwan; this name and the remaining original buildings of the old academy are incorporated in another university whose function in the state system does not, however, correspond with the academy's. The heir to the modern function is Seoul National University.

10. Students had an autonomous academy residents' meeting known as Chaehoe in which they decided on action by mass opinion or by a majority. The meeting could punish fellow students or take part in government politics by sending a memorial in the name of the body. Sometimes strikes were called. See Yi Sang-baek, *Han'guk-sa Kŭnse chŏn'gip'yŏn* (History of Korea: early modern period; Seoul, 1962), pp. 271–272.

11. Kim Sa-yŏp, *Chosŏn munhak-sa* (History of Korean literature; Seoul, 1950), p. 175.

12. Edward W. Wagner, "The Literati Purges" (unpub. diss., Harvard University, 1959), pp. 97–99, 372–373, closely following the dynastic annals.

13. Cho Ching-yang, "The Decade of the Taewŏn'gun" (unpub. diss., Harvard University, 1960), pp. 506–507. In this instance, the students were more conservatively indignant at the memorializer's accusation averring "destruction of the principle of human relationships." Punishment other than banishment for accused students included being barred from taking the examinations.

14. The importance of influencing the examination result, either by special training relating to the questions it asked or by influencing the examiners, is illustrated in factional incidents of the period, especially in that of 1575, which is often taken as the starting point of full factional

struggle. Key P. Yang and Gregory Henderson, "An Outline History of Korean Confucianism," Pt. I, 18.1:96 *JAS* (Nov. 1958); Pt. II, 18.2:272–273 (Feb. 1959).

15. See also Yu Hyŏng-jin (Yoo Hyung-jin), "Intellectual History of Korea from Ancient Times to the Impact of the West with Special Emphasis on Education" (unpub. diss., Harvard University, 1958). In sequestering lands from taxation and in draft-evasion functions, Yu believes, the *sŏwŏn* may have given significant impetus to a tradition of civil irresponsibility. *Sŏwŏn* were fairly common even in the North where there were few *yangban*.

16. The quotation from Yi Su-gwang, cited in Chapter 2, n. 22, refers to the extensive mobility taking place as a result of the Hideyoshi invasion as observed by a man living through it and the three decades that followed.

17. These hundreds of reform resolutions of 1894–1895 could, in the absence of continual Japanese control from 1894 on, clearly have been successful only when they reflected processes already informally introduced into the body politic. Abolition of class distinctions in hiring is a particularly important case in point. W. H. Wilkinson, in *The Korean Government: Constitutional Changes, July, 1894, to October, 1895* (Shanghai, 1897), details all the reforms and much of their background.

18. O Chae-sik, *Hang-Il sun'guk ŭiyŏlsa-jŏn* (History of the martyred who fought against the Japanese; Seoul, 1959), p. 193.

19. Kamada Sawaichirō *Chōsen shinwa* (A new story of Korea; Tokyo, 1951), p. 285. There is conflicting evidence about the status of Song's father, for whom *yangban* ancestry has been claimed. There is no question, however, concerning his descent from an unmarried *kisaeng* mother, which technically would place him in the lower classes.

20. *Tōyō rekishi daijiten* (Encyclopedia of Far Eastern history; Tokyo, 1937), V, 374; Ri Sei-gen (Yi Ch'ŏng-wŏn), *Chōsen kindai-shi* (Modern history of Korea; Tokyo, 1956), p. 304. It should, however, be pointed out that genealogical charts, if untampered with, support Song's claim to be a descendant of the famed seventeenth-century scholar-official, Song Si-yŏl. Whether the claim of descent from Song, founder of the Noron faction, would have been one factor in his lower-class descendant's access to the Min, a Noron clan, remains to be determined.

21. Kamada, *op. cit.*, p. 285.

22. *Tōyō rekishi daijiten*, V, 374.

23. *Ibid.*

24. Fred H. Harrington, *God, Mammon, and the Japanese* (Madison, Wis., 1944), pp. 165, 304; F. A. McKenzie, *The Tragedy of Korea* (London, 1908), p. 100; *Chōsen jimmei jisho* (Biographical dictionary of Koreans; Keijō, 1937), p. 1994; *Tōyō rekishi daijiten* (Tokyo, 1938), VIII, 473. There is no longer any trace of Yi Yong-ik's family or, except for the institutions he founded, of his fortune.

The Songs, however, continue to prosper. The "founder's" daughter became the wife of a high Korean official of Japan's Central Korean Bank, after Liberation a member of Hodge's advisory committee, later Governor of the Bank of Korea, still later Minister of Finance under Rhee. Their fortune remains larger, by far, than that of the impoverished descendants of Song's princely patron.

25. Kamada, *op. cit.*, p. 265; *Chōsen jimmei jisho*, p. 1997. Yi Pŏm-jin is, however, also listed as an exam-passer in 1879, before the *émeute*, another sign of the breaching of the system. His rapid promotions seem owed to the queen's favor.

26. Hosoi Hajime, *Joō Binbi* (Queen Min; Tokyo, 1931), pp. 225–226; *Hanguk-sa sajŏn* (Dictionary of Korean history; Seoul, 1959), p. 137. Yi did come of a military family, his father, grandfather, and great-grandfather having passed the military exams. The family had fallen to this estate after long descent from King Sŏngjong.

27. William Kornhauser, *The Politics of Mass Society* (Glencoe, Ill., 1959), p. 106; I have drawn on this work for a number of the above formulations. Song fits the thesis with uncanny closeness.

28. Cited *ibid.*, p. 35.

29. Raymond Asquith, quoted in John Buchan, *Pilgrim's Way* (Boston, 1940), p. 54.

30. Methodist-Episcopal North Report for 1886, cited in L. George Paik, *The History of Protestant Missions in Korea, 1832–1910* (P'yŏngyang, 1929), pp. 292–299. See also pp. 120, 218.

31. *Ibid.*, p. 193.

32. David Chung (Chŏng Tae-ŭi), "A Narrative of Christianity in Social Change in Korea since the 17th Century," *Journal of Social Sciences and Humanities* (Seoul), 14:26–27 (June 1961).

33. Paik, *op. cit.*, p. 222.

34. Mary Scranton, "Women's Work in Korea," *Korean Repository*, 3.1:3–4 (Jan. 1896), cited in *ibid.*, p. 119.

35. Paik, *op. cit.*, p. 155.

36. It should not be implied, however, that all these joined the Christian church simply because of its career ladders. Korea had a severe spiritual vacuum at the time and, with the passing of national independence, a spiritual crisis. Motives for conversion were in origin probably no more selfish than they might be elsewhere.

37. Ch'ŏndogyo, appealing to a similar class but originally stronger in the south, had a somewhat similar development and role within the Independence Movement. First signer Son Pyŏng-hŭi and leader-signer Ch'oe In were Ch'ŏndogyo leaders.

38. Cho Pyŏng-ok, *Minju-juŭi wa na* (Democracy and I; Seoul, 1959), esp. pp. 353–356. Though only about 1 percent of the Korean population was Christian at the time, 18 percent of all persons arrested were Christian, and churches served as one of the chief vehicles for the distribution of the Independence Declaration. Lee Chong-Sik, *The Politics of Korean Nationalism* (Berkeley, 1963), pp. 112–117.

39. A Korean version of "back," in the sense of "backing." The term, though not the institution, is a product of post-Liberation years that gained ubiquitous currency during the Korean War.

40. These relationships were partly based on adoption, with which the Min clan was then rife.

41. McKenzie, *op. cit.*, pp. 137–138, from which much of this description is taken.

42. Alexis de Tocqueville, *The Old Regime and the French Revolution* (New York, 1955), p. 204.

43. *Korea Review*, 6.1:6 (Jan. 1906).

44. *Yi Kyu-wan ong paeng nyŏn-sa* (The hundred years of venerable Yi Kyu-wan; Seoul, 1958), pp. 2, 32–33, 38, 76–78. Yi, though admittedly impoverished, claimed honorable descent — but then, most Koreans do.

45. Long periods of exile — in Japan for pro-Japanese, in Shanghai or Vladivostock for others — were common. Some continued to be banished within the country. Cho Chung-ŭng was banished to Posŏng, Chŏlla-do, in 1883, for example, simply for recommending that the court "close the North" (i.e., northern borders) and "open the south."

46. Kamada, *op. cit.*, pp. 201–202.

47. *Ibid.*

48. The only daughter married Yi Si-yŏng, one of the few high aristocrats in the Independence Movement, who became the first Vice-President of the Republic of Korea in 1948. The family now shares the obscurity of most ancient Korean court *yangban.*

49. Hodge blunderingly admitted on September 11, 1945, to reporters, "As a matter of fact, the Japanese are my most reliable source of information" (*Tong-A Ilbo*, Sept. 12).

50. Mark Gayn, *Japan Diary* (New York, 1948), pp. 292–293. Mr. Gayn was a well-known correspondent in Japan and Korea at this time.

51. *Tong-A Ilbo*, August 7, 1948.

52. GAOR, 3rd Session, Supplement 9 (A/575), 1948, p. 10. Such criticisms, especially inside Korea, were chronic. Many are recorded in the UN reports.

53. Figures of officials by May 1953 are variously given as 304,000 or 326,591, excluding members of the armed forces but including 58,000 civilian employees of the Ministry of National Defense.

54. During the three and a half years that I was cultural attaché, my opposite numbers within the Korean government changed twenty-one times. Many were able and eager to make progress, but countless programs of admitted benefit to Korea could not be undertaken because tenures were too short and jockeying for the next position too time-consuming.

55. The Americans took over the Japanese radio system and programmed through it. They did not, however, utilize the chance to take over the Japanese official newspaper, the *Keijō Nippō*, and run it in Korean as an official American organ. They were thus at a disadvantage in their own zone vis-à-vis the Communists, who influenced much of the press and made virtually an official organ of two newspapers in succession. This serious mistake was one aspect of American unpreparedness in Korea.

56. Elton Mayo, *The Human Problems of an Industrial Civilization* (New York, 1933), esp. pp. 119–121; Mayo, *The Social Problems of an Industrial Civilization* (Cambridge, Mass., 1945), pp. 61–67, 72ff.

57. Somewhat similar role-playing trauma for the aristocrat is, of course, familiar to many societies. The United States, even, passed through it around the period of the 1830's when the difficulty or awkwardness of electioneering before large crowds was a comparatively common theme of complaint among "gentlemen" candidates. Many members of the American upper stratum also backed away from politics. But American — and English — upper-class behavior was more reconcilable with democratic political behavior than real *yangban* behavior was. Here again there was a distinction with regard to *hyangban,* whose behavior was less picayune and self-conscious and therefore far more adapted to politics.

58. Even in Andong, for example, most noted rural seat of *yangban*, the man most consistently elected was of *ajŏn* stock.

59. Regarding higher education's expansion and concentration, see above, Chapter 6. In 1966–1968, the Vietnamese War and industrial expansion may slightly have eased this situation.

60. Grajdanzev, *op. cit.*, p. 262, points out that nearly half of all Japanese of high school age in Chōsen were in high school, in contrast to only 5 percent of Koreans of the same age.

61. USAMGIK Summation No. 7, April 1946, p. 31.

62. Ministry of Education, *Mun'gyo t'onggye yoran* (Annual survey of education; Seoul, 1962). These annual surveys are the basic sources for Korean educational statistics.

63. Korean Ministry of Education statistics and *Korea Times,* Jan. 9, 1965, and Nov. 26, 1964. According to Ministry of Education statistics reported in the *Korea Times* of Feb. 27, 1966, 69 colleges and universities gave about 22,500 degrees in February 1966, and roughly 14,000 degrees were granted by junior colleges and technical schools in the same month.

64. *Mun'gyo t'onggye yoran* (1964), pp. 65–67.

65. Marion L. Edman, *Primary Teachers of Korea Look at Themselves* (Seoul, 1962), p. 12. Dr. Edman, Professor of Education, Wayne State University, was a Fulbright Research Scholar in Seoul.

66. *The Europa Yearbook, 1967* (London, 1967), II, 726; *Korea Times,* August 28, 1964.

67. *Education in Korea*, pp. 42–43.

68. *Mun'gyo t'onggye yoran* (1964), p. 196.

69. Often a younger son. The oldest son in the Confucian-influenced countryside is obligated to help with the process of giving his younger brothers every advantage he can — even those he himself has never had. The younger sons are trained to ask or demand of others and given far less training in responsibility than the eldest brother. The presence of many younger brothers in colleges is one factor in student demonstrations.

70. I find materials on child-training in the Korean family still insufficient to permit more than a few speculations on the subject. It appears reasonable, however, to assume that family solidarity behind the child in education should not be taken as implying that the Korean home is free of divisions and tensions. Crowded urbanization has caused a fairly abrupt substitution of the small nuclear family for the classic extended one. This has brought considerable change to the parents' role in child-rearing, which frequently can no longer be so widely shared as formerly with grandparents and others. On the one hand, this means that the child, less often trained by the grandparents than in the past, is freed from the hand of influences two generations old instead of one. On the other, it means that strain and often dissatisfaction with the new role are felt by the parents and perceived by the child. Added to this is the environment of isolation and dissatisfaction of urban life (see Chapter 10), which is also subconsciously perceived by the child. These perceptions constitute obstacles to the child's acceptance of the models of behavior and value his parents give him and, if these models are rather extreme, as in upper-class Confucian traditions, often lead to direct and even violent rejection. Such factors cause extreme gaps between different generations that are compounded, in the last generations, by the sharpness of the historical changes

of 1910 and 1945. Though these factors probably compound social and political instability, they, plus surging education, also lead to an openness to change and innovation that could be, and now is being, harnessed for comparatively rapid development.

71. The 1964 struggle between the president of Sungmyŏng Women's College and a portion of his faculty over his unilateral admission of students can be cited as a case in point. Maintaining that "secrecy" was needed, the president and several faculty members were forced to resign over the incident.

72. *Korea Times*, Nov. 26, 1964.

73. *Korea Times* article Oct. 13, 1965, by Lee Chang-gun, a staff member of the institute, and private letter of Dec. 2, 1965, from him to the author. The new Institute of Science and Technology, however, is now (1968) starting to pay salaries many times this—up to the equivalent of $400 a month.

74. Pak Song-yong, "Prospects for the Export of Labor from Korea," *Korea Journal*, 5.3:10 (March 1965), based on latest statistics of the Economic Planning Board. Of these, 604,000 are listed as totally unemployed, 2,118,000 as underemployed. Unemployment statistics have lacked much exactness but have long run at about these levels. Recent economic and export gains seem thus far to have made few inroads into the unemployment total. Increased army recruitment has dented the unemployment market since 1965.

75. The government claims the literacy rate in *han'gŭl* is 90 percent or over, but most obeservers believe that *effective* literacy is far lower, perhaps 70 percent or, recently, a little higher. With the vast educational expansion since 1945, it advances steadily. The 1944 census of the government-general lists 19,642,775 uneducated out of a total population of 22,793,766 — thus 3,150,000 "educated." Only 7,374 were at university or graduate school level beyond the gymnasium-level high school, and only 22,064 more were graduates of colleges or technical schools. John Kie-chang Oh, "Western Democracy in a Newly Emerging Eastern State: A Case Study of Korea" (unpub. diss., Georgetown University, 1963).

CHAPTER 8

Functional and Organizational Diffusion

1. This section is based largely on the many trips the author made to the countryside over a seven-year period, often staying in villages; all but one of the counties of Korea were thus visited. I am grateful to Dr. Maner Thorpe for his oral reportage of his rich experience of living for a year and a half in a Korean village.

Other sources on Korean villages include Yi Man-gap, *Han'guk nongch'on ŭi sahoe kujo* (The social structure of Korean villages; Korean Studies Series, No. 5, Korean Research Center, 1960); John E. Mills, "Ethno-Sociological Reports of Four Korean Villages" (U.S. Operations Mission, Community Development Division, Seoul, 1960); Cornelius Osgood, *The Koreans and Their Culture* (Tokyo, 1954).

2. Herbert Passin, "The Paekchŏng of Korea," *Monumenta Nipponica,* 12.3–4:27–72 (Oct. 1956).

3. Maner Thorpe, "A Study in the Logic of Ethnography" (unpub. MS, 1965), describes such characteristics in a village near Chinju, Kyŏngsang Namdo, where he spent many months.

4. Herbert R. Barringer in "Increasing Social Scale and Changing Social Character in Korea" (unpub. MS, 1965), pp. 21–26, gives a good description of the cliques of a mountain village. Most inter-family squabbles, recruitment of labor for road service, etc., were handled by the clique leaders and "the police chief found it impossible to 'catch criminals' or to enforce the national curfew because families within the various groups protected offenders."

5. The author knows of no special study on the great markets. The following material has been gathered from those working in the market or concerned with it and from personal observation.

6. Note the strong parallel to the attitude of persons or groups within a Korean political party. The Korean market seems to be less devoted to common interests than were the corporate communities of the European Middle Ages.

7. This interpretation places the full brunt of ineffective cohesion on adult society. It can be asked whether child-training habits within the Korean home should not bear some of the blame. The Korean child is comparatively carefully trained regarding — and made excessively reliant upon — his relationship to a warm, extended family circle. He is, however, given little supervision or training regarding behavior or choice of companions outside the home — again a contrast with Japan. This may contribute to a pattern whereby he seeks in later life a close, fairly small group but feels insecure within a larger group operating more impersonally.

8. *Chosa pogo-sŏ* (Research report; Taegu, 1963), p. 62. This research report on a poor Taegu neighborhood was prepared by sociologists of Kyŏngbuk University for the Kyŏngsang Pukto provincial government.

9. Actual starvation, though recorded fairly frequently in Korean history and occasionally reported recently, has become quite rare in the last fifty years thanks to better distribution of grains and, since 1945, their charitable provision by the United States. The feeling of not having enough to eat, of carrying through life a belly almost always on the edge of emptiness, is, however, quite common.

10. Taegu survey, *op. cit.,* p. 254. Rich neighborhoods lack many of even these bonds and are still more isolated.

11. Dr. Herbert Barringer in a survey by questionnaire found that Taegu lower-class respondents ranked lowest of all surveyed in "theoretical" orientation (17.1 percent as opposed to 74.5 percent for national ministry officials), indicating low social participation and small capability of resolving problems in a rational-theoretical framework.

12. The reverse of this coin is the community building of Pak T'ae-sŏn, a defrocked Presbyterian minister, who has founded a new and rather fanatic religious sect that has built two communities near Seoul. These are extremely integrated, have their own factories, set their own standards of behavior, allow no fences, and have marked community pride, a commodity otherwise hard to find in Korea. The fanaticism of these communi-

ties, however, can be regarded as a reflection of their conscious antagonism to the high order of incohesiveness of most Korean urban communities.

13. Loyalty and obedience within the family or to the sovereign or to specially sworn friend-brothers is frequently found in Korean history. Where it is rare is in larger and, especially, more impersonal groups.

14. Published in the newspaper *Kyŏnghyang Sinmun* (Seoul), 1956–1957, after Gen. Kim's assassination.

15. Professional painting, for example, was connected on the whole with the socially less exalted specialist; however, amateur painting, especially of bamboo and landscape, was a well-known avocation of the Chinese literatus. It is difficult to imagine a Chinese scholar saying, in regard to paintings of the amateur type, what the Korean literatus Kang Hŭi-an, 1419–1465, is quoted as saying: "Painting is lowly expertise; if a painting of mine remains for later times, it will only bring stigma on my name." Robert T. Paine, ed., *Masterpieces of Korean Art* (Boston, 1957), p. 21.

16. Son Po-gi, "Social History of the Early Yi Dynasty, 1392–1592" (unpub. diss., University of California, Berkeley, 1963), pp. 137, 412. Some of these changes, of course, had other motives beside spreading access to power. Kings wished by Censorate changes to prevent or blunt attacks on themselves. Some censors were appointed and resigned five or six times, thus providing no new access.

17. Cho Ching-yang, "The Decade of the Taewŏn'gun" (unpub. diss., Harvard University, 1960), p. 495. The Taewŏn'gun used this instrument to weaken the Censorate.

18. Kim Kyŏng-t'ak, *Yulgok ŭi yŏn'gu* (A study of Yulgok; Korean Research Center, 1960), pp. 6–8.

19. Historical Compilation Committee, *Hyangt'o Seoul* (Seoul's native ground; Seoul, 1957), I, 160–179, records all the names. The position, one of the most administratively demanding in the kingdom, was not held concurrently with other posts.

20. Cho Ching-yang, *op. cit.*, p. 66.

21. W. H. Wilkinson, *The Korean Government: Constitutional Changes, July, 1894, to October, 1895* (Shanghai, 1897), p. 36. A Home Office Order of April 4, 1895, forbade this practice, thus advertising it. The so-called *sa man* system of the time encouraged it by actually limiting some offices to a certain number of days.

22. Hosoi Hajime, *Chōsen kōsho* (A series on Korea; Seoul, 1936), II, 154; *Tōyō rekishi daijiten* (Encyclopedia of Far Eastern history; Tokyo, 1938), VIII, 25.

23. *Tong-A Ilbo*, Jan. 30, 1961.

24. See, for example, the passage from the Ming philosopher Lu K'un quoted in C. K. Yang, "Chinese Bureaucratic Behavior," in David Nivison and Arthur Wright, eds., *Confucianism in Action* (Stanford, 1959), p. 150.

25. Chŏng To-jŏn, *Sambong-jip* (Collected works of Sambong [Chŏng To-jŏn]; woodlock ed., Taegu, 1791), Book 8; reprinted in Kuksa P'yŏnch'an Wiwŏnhoe (Committee for the Compilation of Korean History), ed., *Han'guk saryo ch'ongsŏ* (Korean historical materials), No. 13 (Seoul, 1961).

26. E. Grant Meade, *American Military Government* (New York,

1951), p. 132. There were abortive attempts to found law schools during the last years of the Yi Dynasty, and a few Koreans graduated from Japanese law schools, Korea's first lawyer hanging out his shingle in 1906 and six more graduates of Japanese law schools becoming instructors in 1905. *Korea Review*, 1905, p. 477, and other occasional notices in the news columns of the *Korea Review*, 1904–1906. These early attempts, however, were without much permanent effect.

27. Rates of acquittal during the colonial period dropped to 7 percent in cases before examining magistrates and 2.5 percent in trial courts even in Japan; they were lower in Korea. From 1916 on, the tradition grew that prosecutors "do not institute proceedings unless they themselves have a firm belief in the guilt of the defendant." Arthur von Mehren, *Law in Japan* (Cambridge, Mass., 1963), p. 298. Cases of judicial independence like the Otsu conspiracy case in Meiji Japan never occurred in Korea.

28. For examples, see Meade, *op. cit.*, pp. 133–136; George M. McCune, *Korea Today* (Cambridge, Mass., 1950), p. 86.

29. Robert K. Sawyer, *Military Advisors in Korea: KMAG in War and Peace* (Washington, D.C., 1962), p. 26.

30. For an especially good statement by a foreign-trained scientist, see Lee Chang-gun (Yi Ch'ang-gŭn), research member of the Atomic Energy Research Institute, Seoul, in an article in the *Korea Times*, Oct. 8, 1965. Dr. Lee points out that there has been a 70 percent turnover of staff in the short history of this institute and that most remaining members would leave and go abroad to work if they could. A new national Institute for Science and Technology, which could favorably encourage scientific research, is, with American help, in process of formation.

31. Gregory Henderson, "Foreign Students: Exchange or Immigration?" *International Development Review*, 6.4:19–20 (Dec. 1964).

CHAPTER 9

Factionalism and the Council Pattern

1. Edward W. Wagner, "Korea" (hectographed, Cambridge, Mass., 1961), p. 87; Wagner, "A Symposium: Korean Modernization — Some Historical Considerations," *Korea Journal*, 3:27–28 (August 1963).

2. Among them *to pyŏngma-sa* and *to p'yŏngŭisa-sa;* also called *hapchwa* (joint sitting). For this description of committee rule in Koryŏ, I am much indebted to Son Po-gi, "Social History of the Early Yi Dynasty, 1392–1592" (unpub. diss., University of California, Berkeley, 1963), pp. 130–131. There was also a Board of Civil Affairs (Munhasa) that in turn consisted of the Supreme Council, the Board of Economic Affairs, and the Board of Military Affairs. See Cho Ching-yang, "The Decade of the Taewŏn'gun" (unpub. diss., Harvard University, 1960), p. 133.

3. The original Korean State Council, though theoretically modeled on the Ming Secretariat, later the grand Secretariat and the Ch'ing Grand Council, in fact until 1519 had authority greatly exceeding that of any Chinese body, and the same was true of succeeding bodies after the Taewŏn'gun's reforms. The Koreans never claimed to model their govern-

ment after the Ch'ing, and their relations with the Manchus were distinctly cooler than with the Ming. Indeed, one of the late Yi critics, Pak Che-ga (1750–1805) criticized the Yi Dynasty of his day for its disregard of the changes and, he felt, progress made in China during Ch'ing times.

4. As the annals for the reign of T'aejong put it, "A State without remonstrance cannot stand as a State" (quoted in Son Po-gi, *op. cit.*, p. 347). The translation "remonstrance" has misleading connotations, however, for this function was a prestigious but almost routine duty in which personal grievance was improper and reproof not necessary. The location of this critical function in the aristocracy and the enlargement of its role through the Korean pattern, however, help to account for the often-noted criticism and back-biting indulged in by Koreans about their leaders. In this instance, upper-class values spread downward, whereas in political behavior and manners lower-class norms moved up.

5. This summary of the Censorate and its function is derived from the excellent and far fuller description given by Edward W. Wagner, "The Literati Purges" (unpub. diss., Harvard University, 1959). I have ignored here certain formal divisions within the Censorate bodies that seem not to have been essential to the operation of the censoring function as a whole.

6. *Ibid.*, p. 26. The emphasis on documentary forgery and fraudulence seems to have been important largely because of the prevalence of covert mobility.

7. The theological attacks on Mary Queen of Scots, Lord Darnley, and their circle by John Knox offer in diverse dress an interesting comparison.

8. Son Po-gi, *op. cit.*, pp. 211ff, contains an eloquent and extensive exposition of the significance and power of historians.

9. As a senior councilor put it, "When the Censorate speaks out, then the Office of Special Counselors follows suit, and, when the Office of Special Counselors has spoken, then the National Academy students follow up in turn — A sings and B harmonizes, together thus forming a chorus" (quoted in Wagner, "The Literati Purges," p. 108). The capacity of the Censorate to assemble and maintain such alliances says much for the group character of Korean government.

10. The dynasty's second king (1398–1400) complained of physical suffering from lack of exercise, whereupon the Censorate grudgingly acceded that proprieties would permit him to play ball so long as he did so in the presence of the court historian. This monarch was later permitted to retire while still in the prime of life, a grace by no means always acceded to by the literati. See Son Po-gi, *op. cit.*, p. 221.

11. Suematsu Yasukazu, "Chōsen giseifu kō" (Study of the cabinet system in the Yi Dynasty), *Chōsen Gakuhō* (Journal of the Academic Association of Koreanology in Japan), 9:12–26 (March 1956). Professor Suematsu is an outstanding authority on Korean history. The power of the State Council to supervise the activities of the bureaucracy and serve as the channel between the Six Boards and the throne was removed by Sejo (1455–1468). This act, in effect permanent, can be regarded historically as having stimulated the power-access and broad-surfaced council patterns by removing a most important hierarchical step and exposing the Six Boards and, therewith, much of the bureaucracy more or less directly to the throne. From then on, in fact, the tendency of increasing numbers

of subordinate offices and subordinate officials to address the throne directly mounts palpably.

12. Son Po-gi, *op. cit.*, p. 26.

13. Cho Ching-yang, *op. cit.*, pp. 53, 116. The inefficiency and lack of defined authority of these groups was criticized with some trenchancy by reformist scholars like Yu Hyŏng-wŏn (1622–1674).

14. Son Po-gi, *op. cit.*, pp. 126–127.

15. This summary of later Yi administrative difficulties follows largely the lines laid out in Cho Ching-yang, *op. cit.*, pp. 1–30, with additional reference to the *Han'guk-sa* (History of Korea), sponsored by the Chindan Society, and other standard works. As an example of somewhat similar paralysis of oligarchic council rule, Holland in the eighteenth century might be cited. A Dutch historian of this period cited by Everett E. Hogan, "National Differences in Personality and the Industrial Revolution: The Historical Evidence" (unpub. paper, 1965), p. 35, writes of this time: "Action always lagged far behind the roar of oratorical protest. The absurd contrast between the energy spent in words and that spent in deeds was so great that often, as in 1747 and 1787, the effect is tragi-comical." The Dutch army and navy both declined because each had their supporters, who discussed the matter for years without being able to agree on a compromise.

16. Cho Ching-yang, *op. cit.*, p. 245.

17. The *Korean Government Gazette*, Jan. 22, 1895, observed that every twenty years a surveyor-general ought to have been sent from Seoul to reassess the field tax, but this system "has long fallen into disuse and the condition of the land tenures has not been worse than at present these hundred years."

18. One vignette, drawn from Cho Ching-yang, *op. cit.*, pp. 41, 86–95, will give the flavor of Korean council rule. On the eve of the Taewŏn'gun's coming to power in 1864, there was great support within the bureaucracy for reform of the long corrupt grain and tax system. "The king summoned, on July 8 [1862] the entire regiment of government officials, as well as prominent scholars (except those of the military classes), and asked them to present essays on 'Rectification of the Defects of the Three Systems.' Appointed as reader of the essays was the grand old autocrat, Chŏng Wŏn-yong. Each essayist was given ten days to compose his thoughts at home. Furthermore, the king ordered the government to circulate the title of the essay throughout the provinces so that each locality could make known its specific problems. The high-ranking officials were especially asked to offer the king their oral opinions on the reforms." A Committee of Reforms was established, a plan drafted and submitted to the throne on September 23. On October 4, senior members of the Committee met for a final debate on the plan. They were divided into supporters and opposers of the abolition of the relief grain system. Chŏng, the senior member, seventy-eight years old, opposed change on the grounds that the system "has existed for many years." A majority opposed him, but decision had to be taken by consensus, not by vote. Chŏng was then asked to draft a new plan, which was essentially his own, including little change. Though a minority view, it was accepted because he was senior and had the king's trust. No essential reform was made, and the Committee was abolished.

This minuet took place against a background of chronic and violent uprisings in the southern provinces.

19. The Taewŏn'gun reconstituted but did not end government councils. They persisted with some, though reduced, powers. After the reforms of 1895 and the mounting control of Japan, however, council rule in the formal sense ended.

20. On KILA, see the USAMGIK and SKIG Summations from October 1946 on and the *Korea Times,* Dec. 1946–May 1948. KILA members were mostly unaware of parallels between themselves and their Censorate predecessors and certainly did not consciously imitate them. The fact that the parallel was completely unconscious makes it, in my opinion, of greater relevance for revealing fundamental Korean political instincts.

21. Activities No. 20, May 1947, p. 15.

22. The government has often accused politicians and assemblymen of master-minding student protest demonstrations. Students have virulently denied the charge. In general, student opinion and protest is and has been, since 1959, an essentially independent force. Opposition assemblymen and politicians had little part in the student revolution; some students carried signs attacking both the Liberal party and the opposition. It is apparent, however, that such incidents as the forced entry of students into the National Assembly in October 1960 in support of *ex post facto* legislation against those held responsible for the excesses of the Rhee regime were influenced by opposition assemblymen.

23. No Sa-sin was a chief state councilor of King Yŏnsan'gun in 1495. Denounced, without much ground, by the Censorate, he went into seclusion and, on submitting his resignation, observed: "The Confucian sages of yore have said: Political authority must not for even one day fail to reside in the administrative hierarchy, for if it does not reside in the administrative hierarchy then it resides in the Censorate, and if it does not reside in the Censorate then it resides in the palace. If political authority resides in the administrative hierarchy then there is good government; if it resides in the Censorate then there is turmoil; if it resides in the palace then there is ruin." From the Yi Dynasty Annals for 1495, cited and translated in Wagner, "The Literati Purges," pp. 108–109.

24. Resignation of the cabinet was demanded by the Assembly on June 2, 1949, by a vote of 82 to 61 on charges that the cabinet had not enforced regulations regarding autonomy in provincial and municipal elections. See *Voice of Korea,* June 15, 1949, p. 392. The disruption of the executive and the legislative branches could have been minimized by a provision similar to ones wisely operative in the legislatures of some former British colonies (e.g., Nigeria) whereby interrogations are limited to one particular time during the week.

25. With regard to the "Special Investigation Incident," see the *Korea Times* of May 29–June 20, 1949. Also GAOR, 4th Session, Supplement 9 (A/936), 1949, which gives an account and translates the National Traitors Law, pp. 26–27.

26. Among other stratagems, an enemy of Cho's is described in a traditional source as having "caused a bug to eat out a leaf of a tree in the palace garden so as to form the four characters 'the running image [i.e., Cho] will become King.' Then he had the leaf discovered and brought to

the King's attention . . . In these and myriad other ways it was sought to perturb the King's mind." Wagner, "The Literati Purges," p. 413.

27. *Yŏktae kukhoe ŭiwŏn sŏn'gŏ sanghwang* (Historical National Assembly committee election conditions; compiled by the Central Election Management Committee, Seoul, 1963), p. 173. W. D. Reeve, *The Republic of Korea: A Political and Economic Study* (London, 1963), p. 42, claims that supporters fell to twelve but overstates the fall since many on Rhee's side were under youth group as well as National Society labels. Many moderates ran as independents, who gained 126 seats out of 210. Again Reeve's figures do not accord with those of the Central Election Committee. The election was, however, a setback for Rhee.

28. General Wŏn, a founder of the constabulary, had been dismissed therefrom after the Yŏsu rebellion, had found the outside world cold, needed support for a comeback, and was willing to pay for it by unquestioning loyalty.

29. Had the military not been so preoccupied with active fighting on distant fronts, so recently reformed after early defeats, so much under American supervision and headed by a Chief of Staff strongly opposed to military intervention in politics, a coup might well have occurred.

30. For both statements, see Department of State Publication 7084, *Record on Korean Unification, 1943–1960* (Washington, D.C., 1960), pp. 125–126.

31. No constitutional provision for the "recall" of assemblymen existed. When the Assembly protested Rhee's "recall" campaign of the spring of 1952, Rhee replied that the constitution could not only be amended but also "supplemented" in accordance with "popular will."

32. The lower house was enlarged to 235 members, and the upper house numbered 58, more than three times the 90 members with which KILA had started fourteen years before. The trend toward increasing both numbers in council and numbers of councils likewise characterized the Yi period.

33. See also pp. 296–298. In March 1954, for example, Yi Ki-bung was out-maneuvred at the National Convention by the "old faction" in the contest for seats on the Central Committee despite the use of some force and threats by strong-arm party elements. Rhee restored support to Yi by publishing on March 18 a "revised" list removing three "old faction" leaders and replacing them with pliant Presidential followers (*Tong-A Ilbo*, March 19, 1954).

34. For a brief but pithy description of the stock market defrauding as well as other scandals of the period — imported "Bluebird" automobiles from Japan, Walker Hill (the tourist center), pinball machine licensing — see *Korea Annual* (Hapdong News Agency: Seoul, 1966), p. 288. As an example of recruiting for government agencies, through the CIA twenty-five young officers entered the Foreign Ministry at one time in 1962.

35. Several members of the CIA had had backgrounds in the South Korea Labor party, and most of its leaders were, through intelligence work, extremely familiar with North Korean Communist organizations. In a manner reminiscent of the circle and organizations of Ngo Dhin Nhu in Vietnam, they had been influenced by Communist techniques while retaining anti-Communist motivations.

36. CIA's leadership picture is more complex than that of the Liberal party. Kim Chong-p'il, unlike Yi Ki-bung, has not remained formally its leader, and his two terms in exile eroded, temporarily, some of his grey eminence powers. Analysis of real power is hindered by the organization's secrecy, but most leadership appears to have remained consistently in Kim's eighth class G-2 circle.

37. Composed of the Noron (the Old Doctrine), the Soron (the Young Doctrine), the Namin (the Southerners), and the Pugin (the Northerners). Such geographical distinctions as arose between these factions were not the result of their origin but derived from the social network fashioned by their power struggle.

38. For a summary of factional history, see Key P. Yang and Gregory Henderson, "An Outline History of Korean Confucianism," Pt. I: "The Early Period and Yi Factionalism," *JAS*, 18:94–99 (Nov. 1958).

39. In the 1670's hundreds, perhaps thousands, of scholars devoted their energies to the mourning question.

40. Not only did lines die out, but adoption seems to have become increasingly necessary by the end of the Yi period. There are still some families who will not permit marriage of their children to the descendants of factional opponents or who ascribe current conduct to factional ancestry. Such expressions remain in the private area, however.

41. Other roots of factionalism may some day be traced within the family pattern, especially in the way in which sibling claims are arbitrated. In the older pattern, the extended family lived together under the authoritarian control of the senior male but with the senior female in fact frequently deciding home issues. Married sons or their wives would then bring conflicting claims to the parent. If the decision-maker was strong and established clear rules, quarreling was brought under control, but if he (or she) was weak, strife got out of hand and splits occurred. Large families in which all married sons live under one roof, although the ideal, were probably always the exception and are now extremely rare, especially in urban life. Their decline may have some healing effect on factionalism. But the combination of strong interdependence of family members with attempts at authoritarian control, which still occurs, may bring rivalry and quarrels even when there is no cohabitation.

42. For factionalism within the Liberal party, see *Kyŏnghyang Sinmun*, Supplement, Sept. 4 and 5, 1958; also issues of March 25, 1957; March 29, 1957; and Sept. 5, 1958.

43. Few of Yi's followers have ever regained place. One of his most powerful secretaries became a chicken farmer.

44. Factional division over treatment of one's political opposition and over expulsion from post, party, or capital are classics of Korean politics. It was the specific cause of the division of the Tongin faction in 1591 into the Pugin and Namin factions; the blocking of an opponent's appointment caused the incident of 1575 from which the first factions are held to come (Yang and Henderson, *op. cit.*, pp. 96–97).

45. Cf. Reeve, *op. cit.*, p. 158.

46. Carl Berger, *The Korea Knot*, rev. ed. (University Park, Pa., 1964), p. 213.

CHAPTER 10

Political Parties

1. Two relevant analyses appear in C. I. Eugene Kim, ed., *Korea: A Pattern of Political Development* (Seoul, 1964). They are Shin Sang-ch'o, "Interest Articulation: Pressure Groups," pp. 41–47, and Yim Kyŏng-il, "Interest Aggregation: Political Parties," pp. 75–96. See also Oh Byung-hun (O Pyŏng-hŏn), "Party System in Korea," *Journal of Social Sciences and Humanities* (Seoul), 21:58 (Dec. 1964), pp. 58–67; and, for factual material, Korean Central Election Committee, *Taehan Min'guk chŏngdang-sa* (History of Korean political parties; Seoul, 1964).

2. James Bryce, *The American Commonwealth* (New York, 1908), II, 20.

3. Yim Kyŏng-il, "A Study of Korean Political Parties: An Analysis of Their Behavior Patterns," in Kim, ed., *op. cit.*, pp. 87–88.

4. Koreans have been reluctant to articulate this background or foreigners to study it because of general denigration of clan and interest groups and the shame connected with the term *ajŏn*. The information here comes from years of visits with a wide spectrum of local Korean families and with their Seoul representatives, years that provided much opportunity for cross-checking.

5. Song Chin-u, first head of the Korean Democratic party, was one such scholarship recipient; his own family was not well off.

6. Although Kim would certainly have been reckoned wealthy anywhere, the extreme wealth known in the upper ranks of many emerging Asian nations has not characterized Korea at, so far as we know, any time and is just beginning to appear in very recent years.

7. William R. Langdon, conversation, 1950. Mr. Langdon was the senior investigator.

8. Kang Chin-hwa, *Taihan Min'guk kun-guk shinnyŏn-chi* (Ten-year record of the founding of the Korean Republic; Seoul, 1956), pp. 186–187.

9. Song was rumored to be favoring a certain period of tutelage by the U.S. before Korea attained complete independence. See Han T'ae-su, *Han'guk chŏngdang-sa* (Korean political party history; Seoul, 1961), p. 70. Richard D. Robinson, "Korea: The Betrayal of a Nation" (unpub. MS, 1947), pp. 64–65, states that Police Chief Cho Pyŏng-ok later asserted, under the influence of liquor, that he knew Kim Ku had engineered the killing out of fear of Song's growing moderate influence on the right wing. On November 2, 1946, a second top KDP leader, Chang Tŏk-su, was murdered at his own front door under circumstances sufficiently implicating Kim Ku to warrant his being called as a witness in the trial.

10. Rhee was never a member of the KDP and was, of course, later its enemy. His alliance with it from the end of 1945 until 1949 was, however, crucial to the rise of both.

11. Robinson, *op. cit.*, p. 60. The basic elements of the Rhee story can also be found in Robert T. Oliver, *Syngman Rhee: The Man behind the Myth* (New York, 1954).

12. Rhee, "To the Korean Communist Element," *Korean Open Letter,*

Nov. 30, 1946, p. 12, as cited in Koh Kwang-il, "In Quest of National Unity and Power: Political Ideas and Practices of Syngman Rhee" (unpub. diss., Rutgers University, 1963), p. 32.

13. At a speech at a Foreign Policy Association Forum, New York, Oct. 20, 1945. See John Carter Vincent, "The Postwar Period in the Far East," *Department of State Bulletin,* Oct. 21, 1945, p. 646.

14. Robinson, *op. cit.,* p. 62. Capt. Robinson was present in person with his interpreter at this meeting and claims that ¥200 million (about $2 million) was pledged.

15. *Tong-A Ilbo,* Feb. 7, 1946, cited in Koh Kwang-il, *op. cit.* For a translation of this program (which Oliver claims that Rhee formulated in the United States), see Oliver, *op. cit.,* pp. 365–367. Programs being of even less importance to Korean than to American politics, Rhee paid scant attention to these promises.

16. For example, in his inaugural speech of August 15, 1948, he declared: "We should place our full trust and faith in democracy," "protect civil rights and fundamental freedom," "understand, respect and protect liberalism." *Korea's Fight for Freedom: Selected Address by Korean Statesmen* (Korean Pacific Press: Washington, D.C., 1951) pp. 8–9, a book that makes available in translation many of Rhee's important speeches.

17. Some Koreans felt that Rhee never really moved from the stand of his youth when he favored reforming, not abolishing, the monarchy.

18. Hodge had not only reported Korean opposition to trusteeship to Washington and strongly opposed its use in Korea but had been given no information regarding the American pro-trusteeship position at the Moscow Conference and was even reassured by Washington regarding his doubts and objections. He had good reason by the turn of the year to feel that Washington had pulled the rug out from under him.

19. There was talk of merger in January 1947 of the three major parties of the right: the KDP, NARRKI, and Kim Ku's Korea Independence party. No such merger took place.

20. *Korean Open Letter,* as quoted in Koh Kwang-il, *op. cit.,* p. 89.

21. The best description and analysis in English of *Il Min Chu I* is in Koh Kwang-il, *op. cit.,* pp. 63ff. As Dr. Koh observes, one of the most extensive analyses of *Il Min Chu I* occurs in Yang, U-jŏng, *Yi Taet'ongnyŏng kŏnguk chŏngch'i inyŏm, Il Min Chu I ŭi ironjŏk chŏn'gae* (A theoretical evolution of President Rhee's political ideal, Il Min Chu I; Seoul, 1949). Mr. Yang was, at the time he wrote, an important politician, youth-group leader, and newspaperman close to Rhee. He was considered one of the chief formulators of this doctrine, for which his newspaper, the *Yŏnhap Sinmun,* was one of the chief organs.

22. See, for example, "The Living Spirit of Korea," a Rhee speech of Dec. 15, 1948, translated in *Korea's Fight for Freedom,* pp. 11–12.

23. Its formulator, Yang U-jŏng, and his group fell from power in the purge of the Yi Pŏm-sŏk faction in 1952.

24. As, for example, when officials were told that "patriotism" required them to accept low salaries on which they could not possibly live or Foreign Ministry personnel were forced to serve overseas without their wives and families.

25. Even American officers observed that, in contrast to the left, "the

handbills and pamphlets of the conservatives have been inept and offer no concrete program or specific action" (SCAP Summation No. 1, Sept.–Oct. 1945, p. 179).

26. See, for example, his August 1949 speech (to the Assembly) warning against "those foolish [men] who hinder unity by striving for political power and self-interest under the protection of so-called parties and organizations or the Communist party or by seeking sectional rift." Kongboch'ŏ (Korean Government Office of Public Information), *Taet'ongnyŏng Yi Sŭng-man paksa tamhwa-jip* (Collected speeches of President Dr. Syngman Rhee; 1953), I, 4.

27. This summary of election patterns is drawn from the author's experience in observation of local elections and questioning of voters and represents more conservative rural opinion than urban views. Rural opinion, always a majority, was relatively more dominant in the early elections.

28. Despite landlord candidates, only 5–10 percent of Korean rural districts had a single obvious choice sufficiently superior in qualifications to insure his re-election on a continuing basis; not more than this percentage have an impressive record of returning a single candidate on the basis of his local position. Provinces differ considerably, however, in their capacity to do this, Chŏlla-do returning on the order of twice as many candidates to more than one term than does Kyŏngsang-do.

29. For a survey performed later, after parties were much stronger but still closely reflective of this pattern, see Yun Ch'ŏn-ju, "The Voting Behavior of Eup Inhabitants," *Journal of Asiatic Studies*, 4.1:1–59 (June 1961). Dr. Maner Thorpe, in his long residence in a Korean village near Chinju, also found that most inhabitants continued, in the 1960's, to vote for those they considered "great men" regardless of party. Urban areas developed a far greater consciousness of party voting, however, during the 1950's.

30. W. W. Reeve, *The Republic of Korea: A Political and Economic Study* (London, 1963), p. 42, gives 133 independents. Ample data on the Korean National Assembly have been published since its beginning in reports of that body, one of the latest being *Yŏktae kukhoe ŭiwŏn sŏngŏ sanghwang* (Historical National Assembly committee election conditions; compiled by the Central Election Management Committee, Seoul, 1963).

31. *Voice of Korea*, May 27, 1950, reported, for example, the arrests of seven campaigners or would-be candidates on May 7, including a professor at Seoul National University, on charges of violating the National Security Act. Two candidates were elected from jail.

32. Among many other examples, the brother of Kim Sŏng-su himself was arraigned under this bill.

33. For political events of the 1950's, see (besides Reeve, *op. cit.*) David M. Earl, "Korea: The Meaning of the Second Republic," *Far Eastern Survey*, 29.11:169–175 (Nov. 1960); Cho Pyŏng-ok, *Naŭi hoegorok* (My recollections; Seoul, 1959).

34. On the 1952 incident and events leading up to it see Cho Il-mun, "Chŏngch'i p'adong ŭi insik kwa pip'an" (Understanding and critique of the political crisis), *Shinch'ŏnji* (New universe), 3.1:32 (April 1953); Ŏm Sang-sŏp, *Kwŏllyŏk kwa chayu* (Authority and freedom; Seoul,

1957). I have also relied on daily newspapers and extensive personal notes.

35. The creation of an upper house was never supported by any statement other than a mention in Rhee's August 15, 1951, speech that bicameralism "would make the nation safe and sound for democracy." It was clear, however, that Rhee, a past master of the ancient art of divide and rule, intended to weaken the legislature by playing the lower and upper houses off against each other. The amendments were proposed, in the same speech, "in order to make it possible for the great masses of our people to assume their rightful place as the real basis of our government." For text of this speech, see Kongboch'ŏ, *op. cit.*, I, 58–61.

36. Independence Day address of President Rhee, August 15, 1951, *ibid.*, p. 61. Whether the massive buildup of the Korean Army also suggested to him the eventual need for a larger counterbalancing organization in the political field was not revealed. Army expansion was overlaid by more urgent political needs.

37. At the March 20, 1952, convention the Liberal party (so named in December 1951) was able to claim 2,654,250 members, most absorbed from the national organizations.

38. Widespread popular rumor credited this illiterate parvenu with having first placed his foot on the power ladder by fondling the infant son of an established politician at an inn. His power in the Kyŏngsang Namdo branch of the party caused major factional trouble in the 1957–1958 period.

39. For other analyses of the Liberal party, see Yi Chŏng-kŭk, "Ch'ong pip'an jayudang" (General criticism of the Liberal party), *Sasanggye* (World of thought), 4.2:237–249 (Feb. 1956); for a description of the Democratic party, see Shin To-sŏng, "Ch'ong pip'an minjudang" (General criticism of the Democratic party), *ibid.*, pp. 301–312.

40. Youth groups as major South Korean political forces did not survive the purge of Yi Pŏm-sŏk and his followers in 1952–1953. Rhee ordered the dissolution of all South Korean youth groups on September 10, 1953, and instructed the Liberal party "to see to it that no member of the Korean National Youth is elected to the assembly" (Kongboch'ŏ, *op. cit.*, p. 130).

41. The Foreign Ministry officially announced regarding Rhee and the Liberal party's attempt to pass the constitutional amendments of September 6, 1954: "Though they openly purchased the votes of thirty-four legislators . . ." *Han'guk kunsa hyŏngmyŏng* (The Korean military revolution; Seoul, 1961), p. 33.

42. Reeve, *op. cit.*, pp. 92–95, has a particularly good summary of the seesawing course of legislation regarding the election or appointment of local officials in the period. I have drawn on these data.

43. Conversation with former Finance Minister of Rhee's regime.

44. The government-operated *Korean Republic*, of January 1, 1959, in a statement emanating from government sources and perfectly reflective of the views of such senior Liberal officials as Chang Kyŏng-gŭn, gave on this matter the following trenchant views:

> Under the present law [the new law took effect a few days later] all heads of *dong* [blocks] and *ri* [villages] are to be elected directly by the local residents, but the head of the *dong* or *ri* is no more than a mere subsidary organ of the ward chief, mayor, head of *eup* [town] or *myŏn*

[township], and if he is to be chosen through the election system, it will be difficult to supervise or control him. This will not only cause a decrease of efficiency in the administration but also produce bad effects on the whole field administration, because it will split the unity of local residents and the spirit of mutual help among themselves on account of the difference of opinion over the elections of the head of *dong* or *ri*. In view of the above, an amendment is proposed to make all heads of *dong* or *ri* be appointed by the ward chief, mayor, head of *eup* or *myŏn*.

45. The pressures for specialization in this period are of interest and deserve further attention. Relative stability under an essentially one-party system protected competent specialization — at least under the ministerial or bureau chief level. The requirements of budgets, of bankers, of exchange rates, of aid, of the need to rival the competence of American experts on the Joint Economic Board and to report better statistics within Korea and abroad were also important inducements.

46. For example, little advance was made in all these years by the judiciary. A few comparatively feeble attempts to achieve greater independence were ventured, especially in the invalidating of several of the 1958 district elections, which had returned Liberal candidates. Rhee checkmated these tendencies, with the advice of such Liberal party leaders as Chang Kyŏng-gŭn, by refusing to reappoint the offending among the fifty judges who were up for reappointment in 1959. The constitutional committee provided for in the constitution had still not been established by the end of the regime, because of executive and party antipathy to its function and because its head would have been the Vice-President who, from 1956 to 1960, was Rhee's leading opponent. Trials like those of Cho Pong-am and his colleagues (1958–1959) remained on a level no higher than before.

47. For example, according to charges made in January 1955 against the Liberal Finance Deputy Chief, Sŏl Kyŏng-dong — by no accident one of the country's wealthiest men — his Taehan Industrial Company had been awarded sole export privileges for 110,000 tons of rice so that, as was remarked, "Sol may be able to offset a 300 million hwan loan he secured from various banks in order to finance the Liberal Party during the National Assembly debate on the Constitutional Amendment Bill" (UNCACK Report, Feb. 1955). The Liberal party not only had to buy votes during elections, purchase new members after them, and give regular subventions to its assemblymen, but it even had to give special payments to its members as well as independents to vote for crucial but less popular measures. Speaker Yi complained sorrowfully to me in 1959 of the "enormous expense of a representative form of government."

48. Reported to the author by a witness.

49. Chang Myŏn himself was not born in the province but in Inch'ŏn near Seoul. His family had originally come from the northwest, however, and Koreans believed that his associations were mostly from these provinces. From November 1951 to April 1952 he was Rhee's Acting Prime Minister, but he split from the old man so violently during the 1952 crisis that he had to hide on a foreign hospital ship to avoid arrest.

50. In a press statement of May 16, 1955, for example, Shin To-sŏng, former Secretary of Kim Sŏng-su, resigned from the DNP after criticizing the opposition for being under "outside" (i.e., U.S.) influences.

51. These amendments abolished the Prime Ministry with its vestigial Assembly appointative ratification and provided for an upper house (un-implemented until after Rhee's overthrow) designed to forward divide-and-rule tactics by Rhee. The amendments deprived the Assembly of al-most its last powers over the executive and were opposed even by some Liberals.

52. This incident also caused troubles within the U.S. government. Ambassador William Lacey was removed half a year after arrival and was never given another ambassadorial post.

53. In resigning as chief of the Propaganda Department of the DNP, for example, Shin To-sŏng stated that the Liberal party, with all its faults, was better than the "undemocratic forces" (i.e., those that would not fully accept his claims and stand) of the opposition. Similar sophistic appeals to Confucianism to sanction splits and withdrawals were common in Yi Dynasty politics.

54. Richard D. Allen (pseud.), *Korea's Syngman Rhee: An Unau-thorized Portrait* (Rutland, Vt., 1960), p. 213. The return of Shin's body to Seoul was the occasion of a demonstration by thousands of supporters — one of the first and largest spontaneous demonstrations that had, up to that time, taken place since the government's foundation.

55. Kim Yŏng-sŏn, "Kuhhoe sŏn'gŏ" (National Assembly, elections), *Sasanggye* (World of thought), 4.8:57–62 (August 1956), for example, hailed the rise of popular interest in elections and declared that Koreans proved "capable of rational judgment, of resisting pressure from the rul-ing group." (Kim later became Chang Myŏn's Finance Minister.)

56. A Socialist, later Progressive, party dating from September 1957 had been founded under Cho Pong-am after the failure of the Democratic party to include its future leaders in the united opposition forces in 1955. It had gained strength, and Cho received two million votes for President as the only important surviving opposition candidate in 1956. Cho and his top associates were arrested early in 1958, however, under security charges. Cho was executed, unjustly, in 1959, and his party was banned. It has not since effectively revived. During its brief existence, it, too, suffered factional struggles along cleavages caused by the subparties, like the Democratic Revolutionary party, which were its constituent units.

57. As the *Han'guk Ilbo* and *Korea Times*, p. 2, editorialized on April 20, 1965, in connection with the political troubles aroused by the effort to normalize relations with Japan: "One principal cause of the current crisis is the ineffective functioning of the National Assembly. The nor-malization debate is thus being carried into the streets." Such rebellious-ness has, however, since the early summer of 1965, receded, although there were temporary university closings by the government also in 1967.

58. Cf. William Kornhauser, *The Politics of Mass Society* (Glencoe, Ill., 1959), pp. 32, 41.

CHAPTER 11

Communism

1. Figures are somewhat uncertain. Lee Chong-Sik, *The Politics of Korean Nationalism* (Berkeley, 1963), p. 148, gives 40,000–50,000 for

the Korean community in Siberia around 1918, and Chung's figure of 300,000 (see note 2), cited from Walter Kolarz, *The Peoples of the Soviet Far East* (New York, 1954), pp. 32–35, apparently refers to a few years later, after the Red Army's occupation of the Ussuri region in October 1922 influenced Soviet Koreans; it implies a higher figure than Lee's for 1918. Robert A. Scalapino and Lee Chong-Sik, "The Origins of the Korean Communist Movement," *JAS*, 20.1:10 (Nov. 1960), gives "about 200,000" as living in the Siberian area by 1918.

2. Chung Kiwon, "The North Korean People's Army and the Party," *China Quarterly*, 14:105–106 (April–June 1963).

3. Suh Dae-Sook, *The Korean Communist Movement, 1918–1948* (Princeton, 1967), pp. 8–20. This book, based on an extensive use of source materials, is now the most detailed and authoritative source on its subject available. Scalapino and Lee Chong-Sik, *op. cit.*, pp. 10–11, 21; Lee Chong-Sik, *op. cit.*, p. 147. By the end of 1922, the Koryŏ Communist party claimed 6,812 members in 40 different places and helped the Japanese, Chinese, and Formosan Communist movements from Shanghai.

4. Lenin himself is said to have promised two million rubles, and the Comintern gave 600,000 for Communist propagation to a representative of Yi Tong-hwi, Premier of the Provisional Government and founder of the Korean Socialist and Koryŏ Communist parties. Yi used them only for Communist purposes and resigned from the Provisional Government. The incident made internal Provisional Government turmoil (and also Communist factionalism) still worse (Suh Dae-Sook, *op. cit.*, pp. 14–20; Lee Chong-Sik, *op. cit.*, p. 148).

5. Besides the descriptions in Suh Dae-Sook, *op. cit.*, pp. 29–34, Scalapino and Lee Chong-Sik, *op. cit.*, pp. 25–26, and Lee Chong-Sik, *op. cit.*, pp. 160–161, see also a speech by a leader of the Independence Corps of that time, General Kim Hong-il, made while he was Korean Ambassador to China in Taipei, August 15, 1957. General Kim described the incident as "the bitterest sacrifice in the whole history of the Korean Movement of Independence." The Korean Volunteer Army, though not Communist, supported the Irkutsk group's rival Yi Tong-hwi in Shanghai, and its defeat was also a defeat for Yi's Communist leadership.

6. General Kim Hong-il, *op. cit.*, observed that such recognition had been suggested as a joint effort of China, England, the United States, and other nations by Kuo Tai-chi, World War II Chinese Ambassador to Great Britain. It was reportedly supported by Wu Tieh-cheng (Secretary-General of the Kuomintang) and others.

7. The nationalism of such Marxists — later Communists prominent in North Korea's government — is well illustrated in the series of influential articles Paek wrote beginning April 1, 1946, in the newspaper *Seoul Sinmun* on "Korea, the nation-state." Paek, a noted social historian, became a prominent Minister of Education in the North Korean government. For the many Korean currents in and around communism see Suh Dae-Sook, *op. cit.*, Pt. I.

8. *Chosŏn yŏn'gam* (Korean annual; Seoul, 1948), pp. 457–473, shows that only two of sixty prominent Communists there listed were of proletarian or laborer background.

9. Otto Kuusinen, "O Koreiskom kommunisticheskom dvizhenii," *Revo-lyutsionnyi vostok,* Nos. 11–12:108 (1931); cited in Glenn D. Paige and Lee Dong-Jun, "The Postwar Politics of Communist Korea," *China Quarterly,* 14:20 (April–June 1963). For the Korean Communist party movement between 1925 and 1928, see Suh Dae-Sook, *op. cit.,* pp. 85–114. Suh does not believe that factionalism was as important or destructive an element within pre-World War II Korean communism as Kuusinen claims.

10. Conspiracy and the atmosphere it evokes can be one of the most adhesive of group agents. Perhaps the prevalence of a conspiratorial atmosphere as in Korea may be one manifestation of the incohesiveness of a society in its subconscious search for any sort of unity it can get.

11. This account of the background of the Korean Communist movement is drawn from Richard D. Robinson, "Korea: The Betrayal of a Nation" (unpub. MS, 1947), and from Justin Sloane, "The Communist Effort in South Korea, 1945–48" (M.A. thesis, Northwestern University, 1949). Mr. Sloane was for a time an American Military Government officer active in the consultation process before the Joint Commission. I have also made use of personal notes and many conversations in both urban and rural districts with those knowledgeable about local Communists, their beliefs and their roots.

12. Robinson, *op. cit.,* p. 38. It is interesting that USAMGIK officers believed Pak had strong Russian support. Suh Dae-Sook, *op. cit.,* p. 326, believes, probably on better grounds, that the domestic Korean Communist movement had long lost touch with the Russians.

13. The Communists ordered sudden reversal of many of their members' sentiments about New Year 1946, and announced support for trusteeship and the Moscow decision on January 3, 1946. George Lee Millikan and Sheldon Z. Kaplan, *Background Information on Korea: Report of the Committee on Foreign Affairs Pursuant to House Resolution 206,* House Report 2496, 81st Congress, 2nd Session (Washington, D.C., 1950), p. 5.

14. Sloane, *op. cit.,* p. 46.

15. General John R. Hodge, address before Chicago Council on Foreign Relations, Chicago, Oct. 23, 1948.

16. The Communist-controlled Democratic People's Front claimed 6,217,000 members when registering before the Joint Commission in June 1947 — a third of the population. Such claims, of course, were grossly inflated, but many front organizations were, in fact, active, influential, and quite large (Sloane, *op. cit.,* p. 65).

17. *Ibid.,* pp. 65–67.

18. E. Grant Meade, *American Military Government* (New York, 1951), p. 204, citing the case of the former Kanebo Textile Plant in Kwangju, Chŏlla Namdo.

19. Robinson, *op. cit.,* pp. 113–114.

20. In an interview with a reporter on October 31, 1945, Pak said: "We must cooperate fully with the U.S. Military Government in Korea. Cooperation is only right. We must not forget that the U.S. came to wipe out Japanese imperialism and guarantee Korean liberation" (*Korean Free Press,* Nov. 1, 1945). A Communist pamphlet of the same period reflected his views: "There is a rumor that the Korean Communist Party advocates

a proletarian revolution and the establishment of a socialist state. This is a misconception. The Party stands for and has always advocated the foundation of a bourgeois democracy as a necessary step toward full freedom for all classes."

Pak often disappeared to P'yŏngyang for instructions, not only in February 1946, but from June 10 to July 22 of the same year, after which he set about wrecking the moderate coalition.

21. Kim Sam-gyu, once a *Tong-A Ilbo* editor, now an advocate of a "neutral" Korea, in *Konnichi no Chōsen* (Korea today; Tokyo, 1956), pp. 51–103; cited in Lee Chong-Sik, "Land Reform, Collectivization, and the Peasants in North Korea," *China Quarterly,* 14:15 (April–June 1963).

22. Paige and Lee Dong-Jun, *op. cit.,* p. 21.

23. USAMGIK's 1946–1947 reiterations that Korean Communist strength lay primarily in terror supported by outside help strikingly parallel the similar assertions of American military and State Department sources about the Viet-Cong in South Vietnam, especially in the 1964–1965 period.

24. Son Pyŏng-hŭi, rising through Tonghak ranks, might have a prior claim.

25. Even high-ranking American observers privately noted that Communists were virtually the only people present on the 1945 scene who refused cooperation on grounds of principle and conviction and, by and large, stuck to this choice. Opportunism existed of course among Communist ranks, but it was less ubiquitous than elsewhere in the South Korea of that time.

26. T. R. Fehrenbach, *This Kind of War* (New York, 1963), p. 553, gives 36.

27. Kim was reportedly awarded the Stalin Medal and the rank of major in the Red Army for the part he and other, mostly Russian, Koreans played in the encircling operation on Stalingrad, January 1943. Other Red Army Korean officers were lieutenants or captains. Chung Kiwon, *op. cit.,* p. 106, citing Tsuboe Sengi, *Hokusen no kaihō jūnen* (Ten years of liberated North Korea; Tokyo, 1956), pp. 24–26. This chapter of Kim's career has yet to be satisfactorily explained, however.

28. Paige and Lee Dong-Jun, *op. cit.,* p. 20. This article, pp. 17–29, is one of the best recent published descriptions of its subject. For Kim's career, see Suh Dae-Sook, *op. cit.,* pp. 256–293, 311–324. George M. McCune, *Korea Today* (Cambridge, Mass., 1950), pp. 172–198, gives a description of the first years of the North Korean regime.

29. Paige and Lee Dong-Jun, *op. cit.,* p. 17.

30. Department of State Publication 7118, Far Eastern Series 103, "North Korea: A Case Study in the Techniques of Takeover" (Washington, 1961), p. 2.

31. Lee Chong-Sik, "Land Reform, Collectivization, and the Peasants in North Korea," pp. 73–74.

32. *Ibid.,* p. 74.

33. Key P. Yang and Chang-bo Chee, "North Korean Educational System: 1945 to Present," *China Quarterly,* 14:136 (April–June 1963). The number of North Korean students per 10,000 population when this article appeared was 90, compared with 57 for South Korea, 13 for Communist China, 73 for Japan, 107 for the U.S.S.R., and 180 for the United States.

34. For illustrations of oustings of technicians see "North Korea: A Case Study in the Techniques of Takeover," *op. cit.*, pp. 63–64.

35. Recent North Korean propaganda films betray a mass approach, an avoidance of any emphasis on individual performance which considerably surpasses that in comparable Soviet or even Chinese films.

36. Paige and Lee Dong-Jun, *op. cit.*, p. 19. Suh Dae-Sook, *op. cit.*, pp. 294ff, points out, however, that domestic communism had been essentially one movement segmented for security reasons and that the main body of this movement, around Pak Hŏn-yŏng, not understanding the influence of the U.S. and Soviet occupations, made a tactical mistake in remaining in South Korea. Pak's group hopelessly gambled for national unity under communism instead of asserting their leadership in North Korea, where it would have counted.

37. Suh Dae-Sook, *op. cit.*, p. 49.

38. Suh Dae-Sook, "The Elite Group of North Korea," paper presented at a meeting of the Association of Asian Studies, Chicago, March 20, 1967.

39. For a generally accurate account, see the *Wall Street Journal*, Sept. 24, 1963.

40. Organization for Economic Cooperation and Development (OECD), *Planning Education for Economic and Social Development*, ed. Herbert S. Parnes (Paris, 1962), p. 18, cites the Korean and Vietnamese savings ratio at "below 5%," though the average in non-Communist Asia is "about 10–12%." Korea's ratio of savings to GNP is believed to have risen to about 8 percent by 1967 and perhaps a little over in 1968.

41. Yu Wan-sik, "Industry and Armament in North Korea," *Korea Journal*, 5.10:6 (Oct. 1965), claims "investment in heavy industry accounts for 60% of the total amount set aside for industry, a figure never achieved in other communist countries." Mr. Yu was a member of the research staff of the Institute of Strategic Study in Seoul.

42. New York *Times*, Jan. 27, 1967. ROK exports have risen from $33 million in 1960 to $350 million in 1967, with prospects of a $500 million level in 1968; industrial production rose 16 percent in 1965 and, by 1967, was double that of 1960.

43. Geneva Conference statement of ROK representative Y. T. Pyun, April 27, 1954, from Department of State Publication 5609, *The Korean Problem at the Geneva Conference* (Washington, 1954), pp. 38–39.

44. After the Hungarian revolt of 1956, North Korean students in eastern Europe were steadily reduced, partly out of fear of the influences they might bring home. In the last years they have been almost eliminated from the U.S.S.R. and Communist China as well. At the same time, visitors from Communist countries have been increasingly segregated and news, even from the U.S.S.R. and Peking, cut down. An atmosphere of narrow nationalism is now reported from P'yŏngyang.

45. Since North Korean factionalism endured until 1960–1961 and since our knowledge of the inner workings of the North Korean political system is remote, any prediction of an end to factionalism is premature. The best we can say is that in recent years there has been little external sign of it.

46. The former Korean residents of Japan who have taken advantage

of the "repatriation" agreement but have then sent back covert messages to their relatives still in Japan not to come to Korea have appeared to cut to a small trickle the once considerable emigration from Japan to North Korea.

CHAPTER 12

The Military

1. The navy and air force are relatively insignificant, though the latter is growing. The navy has some 40,000 men, including some 27,000 in the Marine Corps; the air force numbers about 25,000.

2. *Koryŏ-sa* (History of Koryŏ; Tokyo, 1909 edition) 81.639, cited by William E. Henthorn, "Some Notes on Koryŏ Military Units," *Transaction of the Royal Asiatic Society for Korea* (TRASK), 35:67–75 (1959).

3. Cited from the *Koryŏ-sa* in William E. Henthorn, *Korea: The Mongol Invasion* (Leyden, 1963), p. 10.

4. Lee Chong-Sik, *The Politics of Korean Nationalism* (Berkeley, 1963), pp. 79ff.

5. The "Kwangbok Liberation Army" in China had at its height only some 3,600 men and little continuity of operation (*ibid.*, pp. 223–225).

6. An exception was President Park Chŏng-hŭi, a poor boy from near Taegu, Kyŏngsang Pukto.

7. Lee Chong-Sik, *op. cit.*, p. 186.

8. *Ibid.*, p. 224.

9. The leftist one, known as the Chosŏn Hakpyŏng Tongmaeng (Korean Student Soldier Alliance) was dissolved by the military governor in January 1946 because of its militant, terroristic nature. It reappeared briefly in June 1947 to apply for consultation with the U.S.–U.S.S.R. Joint Commission, claiming, at the time, 1,370 members. It was not heard of after that time but was considered an "associate organization of the communist-led Democratic People's Front" (Justice Sloane, "The Communist Effort in South Korea, 1945–48" [M.A. thesis, Northwestern University, 1949], p. 147). Though claims of membership made to the Joint Commission had little meaning, the total number of *hakpyŏng* is estimated by some of their members at 3,000, of whom, however, very few were officers.

10. For much of this material on 1945, I am indebted to Lt. Gen. (ret.), now Ambassador Kang Mun-bong, a member of one of the last Manchurian–Tokyo classes, who attended and then broke with this group.

11. Robert K. Sawyer, *Military Advisors in Korea: KMAG in War and Peace* (Washington, D.C., 1962), p. 26.

12. *Ibid.*, pp. 9–15.

13. For a muted expression of Hodge's outrage at not being permitted to build up a strong Korean Army in early Occupation days because "such a move might be misunderstood by the Russians," see *ibid.*, p. 21.

14. *Ibid.*, p. 26; see also p. 14.

15. *Ibid.*, pp. 11, 26, for example, still reflects such confusion when Sawyer mentions "private armies" and "14 quasi-military organizations"

that "had sprung up around the time of Japan's surrender." These appear to be the associations we have described, which were neither "private armies" nor, without considerable qualification, "quasi-military." Since Sawyer uses the best official documents available, it appears that Hodge and his staff possessed a most inaccurate picture of the sources from which they were drawing the new constabulary.

16. *Ibid.*, p. 20.
17. *Ibid.*, p. 16.
18. *Ibid.*, p. 12.
19. USAMGIK Summation No. 14, Nov. 1946, p. 5.
20. General Yi Hyŏng-gŭn, private letter to the author, June 26, 1964.
21. Sawyer, *op. cit.*, pp. 76–78.
22. There were exceptions. The second-generation Japanese-trained officers tended to be outside this system. Their language weakness and relative inability to adopt new American techniques plus Korean embarrassment at competing with seniors tended to place them outside the system.
23. Although the retainer system is a general pattern of the society, it is a particularly visible and striking part of the military scene and is hence here handled as part of it.
24. Like much else in the Korean world, the retainer has his strong parallel in Chinese culture and played a vital part in Chinese local administration as part of the staff of the magistrate, whose *fu-hsin* ("stomach and heart"), i.e., confidential aide, he was. "Nearly all . . . engaged in one or another form of corruption." Ch'ü T'ung-tsu, *Local Government in China under the Ch'ing* (Cambridge, Mass., 1962), p. 88; see also pp. 74–92.
25. Here I part with Ch'ü, who calls his chapter "Personal Servants." Far from being a man with whom one does not discuss personal things, the retainer is a man with whom one talks over things one discusses with no one else.
26. For much of this material I am indebted to a former G-4 of the Korean Army.
27. Bruce M. Russett *et al.*, *World Handbook of Political and Social Indicators* (New Haven, 1964), p. 77, lists South Korea with 4.85 percent of the population between 15 and 64 in the military as ranking fourth in this respect among all world nations. North Korea ranks second, with 7.16 percent. Some 2.00 percent of all South Koreans are in the military.
28. For an excellent inside description, see Lew Young-ick (Yu Yŏng-ik), "An Analysis of Bureaucratic Pathologies in the Korean Army Training Center" (unpublished term paper in sociology, Brandeis University, 1962). Mr. Lew was trained at Nonsan as a recruit in 1958 and personally experienced these hardships. As the author knows from many other friends in the Korean Army, such conditions were by no means confined to Nonsan, though their scale there was perhaps larger than normal. It should be stressed, however, that many officers tried with considerable personal risk and heroism to fight such tendencies. Their personal tragedies are the unsung stories of development.
29. Walter G. Hermes, *Truce Tent and Fighting Front* (Washington, D.C.: Office of the Chief of Military History, 1966), p. 440. The army had already grown to 463,000 men by November 1952 (p. 357). Hermes is another excellent and insufficiently used source.

30. See Chapter 6, n. 45.

31. Sawyer, *op. cit.*, pp. 48–49, 58.

32. For KMAG training of the ROK Army, see Sawyer, *op. cit.*, pp. 67–90. Only twelve Korean officers had completed training in U.S. schools before the war, and twenty-seven more were in training or on the way when war broke out (p. 88). Until the war's outbreak, many officers trained in Japan or China continued to train their troops in the way in which they were accustomed.

33. *Ibid.*, pp. 178–179.

34. *Ibid.*, p. 162.

35. Exactly the same feeling had played an important role in the Koryŏ military coup of 1170.

36. Foreign Ministry statement, July 1961, p. 43: "Original plans for the military coup were drawn after the notoriously rigged elections by the Syngman Rhee regime in 1960. However, the April 1960 Student's Revolution brought about the downfall of the corrupt administration and everyone, including the military leaders, expected that an era of honest and efficient government would follow."

37. Comparatively few of the Japanese- or Chinese-trained officers had substantial combat experience in World War II. From 1945 to June 1950, there was a little experience in guerrilla fighting but much more in warehouse guarding and police-reserve duties.

38. The ability to speak English played an appreciable role. Maj. Gen. Park Chŏng-hŭi was one of the very few senior Korean officers known for paucity of English and lack of communication with his American advisors. Similarly, almost none of the "young colonels" in the coup, unlike many of their colleagues, spoke English or communicated readily with Americans. Even after they were in power, many were unwilling to accept American invitations, including those of the American ambassador himself.

39. For neighboring precedents of this type of action, note the similar phenomenon in the Japanese Army between 1934 and 1941, known as *gekokujō*, "the overpowering of seniors by juniors." Like the Japanese officers of that time, these Koreans were self-styled patriots propelled by beliefs that in direct, extremist action lay the answer to their insistence on a perfect world. One of the Japanese leaders, Lt. Col. Hashimoto Kingorō, wrote *The Road to the Reconstruction of the World*; Park Chŏng-hŭi wrote *Our Nation's Path: The Ideology of Social Reconstruction*. Until after the start of the Manchurian incident, the young Japanese were also motivated, in part, by fears of threatened reductions in the armed forces of the kind being rumored in Korea in 1961.

40. Kim was, however, not among those who entered the Chief of Staff's room.

41. Foreign Ministry statement, July 1961, p. 43. The original "core" group is here officially described as nine. It was, apparently, for a while composed of a greater number. There had been a falling out among these "Sixteen Young Officers" even before the coup took place, and only about nine really stayed together. The core group was one whose associations were formed from years in intelligence together. This association was responsible for the creation of the Korean Central Intelligence Agency, which bore most of the regime's real powers for its first two years. Kim

headed this CIA, and his other associates occupied key places within it.

42. Native Korean governments had old civilian traditions. The military character of Japanese rule during the period 1910–1919 and from about 1938 to 1945 and the continual leadership of Japanese senior officers as governors-general cannot be forgotten, however, as an influential break in the indigenous pattern.

43. A group of the senior graduates of the first four-year class were briefly arrested shortly after the coup's outbreak when they tried to ascertain the opinion of their former Superintendent, then commanding general of the First Army, and give him their views. Separation of the army from politics had been strong in their training, particularly during his tenure as Superintendent.

44. The Korean Army as of January 1968 had some 48,000 men fighting in Vietnam, in addition to many thousands of civilians, a force from which future political leadership is not unlikely to arise after the Vietnamese engagement is over. The fact that rewards have, for almost the first time in Korean history, been rather quickly available to thousands of Koreans outside the peninsula and largely outside the Korean system may well constitute an added fulcrum for change.

45. Korean Army service in Vietnam provides temporary relief from this poverty. U.S. *per diem* for a second lieutenant is believed to be about $5.00, around four times his normal Korean salary. Pfc's, at $1.00 per day, get almost as much in a day as the Korean Army normally paid them in a month.

CHAPTER 13

The Choice: Cohesion through Decentralization

1. A partial exception of vast size may be China. Space does not permit exploration of any generalization in this regard acceptable for so vast a nation but much of the core area of China would appear to display related historical, social, and political difficulties. The difficulties in clearly defining the groups struggling from 1966 to 1968 for Communist power are difficulties closely associated with a mass society and with the consequent fevers of atomized mobility.

2. For example, the only railway linking Korea's populous southernmost provinces, 90 percent completed by the Japanese before Liberation, was, after twenty-two years and billions in aid, only finished as 1968 dawned. More than the cost needed to complete it was lost in July 1950, when American military equipment, because a means of transportation to the Pusan perimeter was lacking, had to be abandoned in Chŏlla Namdo.

3. See David E. Apter, *The Politics of Modernization* (Chicago, 1965), p. 23.

4. Park Chŏng-hŭi, *Our Nation's Path: The Ideology of Social Reconstruction* (Seoul, 1962), Foreword.

5. For a descriptive tableau of this social isolation and vindictiveness, see Richard E. Kim, "O My Korea," *Atlantic*, Feb. 1966, pp. 106–117.

6. Walt W. Rostow, "Unsolved Problems of International Development," *International Development Review*, 7:17 (Dec. 1965).

7. Considerable improvement in this respect has taken place in the last decade.

8. Robert K. Sawyer, *Military Advisors in Korea: KMAG in War and Peace* (Washington, D.C., 1962), p. 162. The Sino-Soviet split would seem to reduce the chances — never great since 1953 — of any renewal of large-scale armed adventures affecting the Republic of Korea. Temporarily, the Vietnamese War has increased armed threat — and some forays near and south of the Demilitarized Zone — but probably not decisively. Troop reductions on both sides of the Demilitarized Zone are the prerequisite for the reduction of tensions and for any hope of eventual solutions in Korea. Such reductions should follow closely on the end of or decrease in hostilities in Vietnam. So long as Vietnam hostilities continue, however, north-south tensions in Korea are likely to mount, though they are unlikely to result in any recurrence of invasion from the north.

9. Local or, in Seoul, non-governmental business and institutions.

10. Recent surveys among college women, for example, have revealed a shift toward business and away from politics as a criterion for the selection of husbands. The number of excellent ex-government officials now in business has greatly increased.

Index

Abe Nobuyuki, Gen., 113–114, 117, 120, 127

Acheson, Dean, 150–151

Administration, national: traditional, 17, 21 29, 32, 80, 235–238; under Taewŏn'gun, 60–63; under Japan, 72, 74, 79–81, 86–89, 101–103, 111; during Liberation, 115, 123–124, 127, 137–139; under Rhee, 158–162, 239–240, 255–261; under Chang, 178–179, 239; after coup, 183–185, 190, 239; in North Korea, 326–333. *See also* Local administration

Africa, 72, 111, 265, 361, 362–363, 382n13, 387n7

Agriculture, 75–77, 94, 96, 97, 101, 145, 156, 197, 251, 275

Aid, U.S. for Korea, 150, 197–198, 220, 243, 329, 369, 385n41

Ajŏn (local clerks): political role of, 34, 43–44, 46–50, 61, 188, 218–219, 283, 286; cohesiveness of, 46–50, 55, 68, 275–276, 278; origin of, 54; descendants of, 204, 294

Allen, Dr. Horace N., 121

American Military Government (USAMGIK), *see* Occupation of Korea

An Chae-hong, 93, 115, 133–134, 281; Chief Civil Administrator, 160

Annexation by Japan (1910–1945), 4, 6, 66, 70, 183; mobilization of support for, 67–71, 205–207; pensioning of Korean officials, 77; Korean attitudes toward, 118. *See also* Chōsen

Anti-communism: USAMGIK, 126, 141, 147, 150–152, 275–283, 320–324; Rhee's, 128–130, 152, 162–168; after coup, 182–183, 190; in military, 340, 447n35

Antonov, Gen. Aleksei I., 121

Appointments: in Silla, 21–22; in Yi, 29–30, 37–38, 42, 236–238, 286; under Taewŏn'gun and Kojong, 61–62, 203; under Hodge, 154, 212–214; under Rhee, 160–162, 215–216, 239; under Chang Myŏn, 178, 239; after coup, 239; in North Korea, 326, 328–329, 331–332

Archeology, 19, 21, 382n12

Army, *see* Military

Assembly, National: elections for 1963, 3, 384n26; People's (1896–1898), 65; Korean Provisional Government's, 85; of People's Republic, 119; KILA, 134, 153–154, 253–254; Assembly of 1948, 155, 162–167, 215, 256–258, 283, 291; general characteristics of, 157–159, 253–263, 269, 286, 289–290; Assembly of 1950, 167–168, 258–261, 291–295; Assembly of 1954 and 1958, 173, 295–296, 299; Assembly after 1960, 177, 181, 183, 187–191,

Publications Written under the Auspices
of the Center for International Affairs
Harvard University

Created in 1958, the Center for International Affairs fosters advanced study of basic world problems by scholars from various disciplines and senior officials from many countries. The research at the Center focuses on economic, social, and political development, the management of force in the modern world, and the evolving roles of Western Europe and the Communist bloc. The published results appear here in the order in which they have been issued. The research programs are supervised by Professors Robert R. Bowie (Director of the Center), Hollis B. Chenery, Samuel P. Huntington, Alex Inkeles, Henry A. Kissinger, Seymour Martin Lipset, Edward S. Mason, Gustav F. Papanek, Thomas C. Schelling, and Raymond Vernon.

BOOKS

The Soviet Bloc, by Zbigniew K. Brzezinski (jointly with the Russian Research Center), 1960. Harvard University Press. Revised edition, 1967.

The Necessity for Choice, by Henry A. Kissinger, 1961. Harper & Bros.

Strategy and Arms Control, by Thomas C. Schelling and Morton H. Halperin, 1961. Twentieth Century Fund.

Rift and Revolt in Hungary, by Ferenc A. Váli, 1961. Harvard University Press.

United States Manufacturing Investment in Brazil, by Lincoln Gordon and Engelbert L. Grommers, 1962. Harvard Business School.

The Economy of Cyprus, by A. J. Meyer, with Simos Vassiliou (jointly with the Center for Middle Eastern Studies), 1962. Harvard University Press.

Entrepreneurs of Lebanon, by Yusif A. Sayigh (jointly with the Center for Middle Eastern Studies), 1962. Harvard University Press.

Communist China 1955–1959: Policy Documents with Analysis, with a Foreword by Robert R. Bowie and John K. Fairbank (jointly with the East Asian Research Center), 1962. Harvard University Press.

In Search of France, by Stanley Hoffmann, Charles P. Kindleberger, Laurence Wylie, Jesse R. Pitts, Jean-Baptiste Duroselle, and François Goguel, 1963. Harvard University Press.

Somali Nationalism, by Saadia Touval, 1963. Harvard University Press.

The Dilemma of Mexico's Development, by Raymond Vernon, 1963. Harvard University Press.

Limited War in the Nuclear Age, by Morton H. Halperin, 1963. John Wiley & Sons.

The Arms Debate, by Robert A. Levine, 1963. Harvard University Press.

Africans on the Land, by Montague Yudelman, 1964. Harvard University Press.

Counterinsurgency Warfare, by David Galula, 1964. Frederick A. Praeger, Inc.

People and Policy in the Middle East, by Max Weston Thornburg, 1964. W. W. Norton & Co.

Shaping the Future, by Robert R. Bowie, 1964. Columbia University Press.

Foreign Aid and Foreign Policy, by Edward S. Mason (jointly with the Council on Foreign Relations), 1964. Harper & Row.

Public Policy and Private Enterprise in Mexico, by M. S. Wionczek, D. H. Shelton, C. P. Blair, and R. Izquierdo, ed. Raymond Vernon, 1964. Harvard University Press.

How Nations Negotiate, by Fred Charles Iklé, 1964. Harper & Row.

China and the Bomb, by Morton H. Halperin (jointly with the East Asian Research Center), 1965. Frederick A. Praeger, Inc.

Democracy in Germany, by Fritz Erler (Jodidi Lectures), 1965. Harvard University Press.

The Troubled Partnership, by Henry A. Kissinger (jointly with the Council on Foreign Relations), 1965. McGraw-Hill Book Co.

The Rise of Nationalism in Central Africa, by Robert I. Rotberg, 1965. Harvard University Press.

Pan-Africanism and East African Integration, by Joseph S. Nye, Jr., 1965. Harvard University Press.

Communist China and Arms Control, by Morton H. Halperin and Dwight H. Perkins (jointly with the East Asian Research Center), 1965. Frederick A. Praeger, Inc.

Problems of National Strategy, ed. Henry Kissinger, 1965. Frederick A. Praeger, Inc.

Deterrence before Hiroshima: The Airpower Background of Modern Strategy, by George H. Quester, 1966. John Wiley & Sons.

Containing the Arms Race, by Jeremy J. Stone, 1966. M.I.T. Press.

Germany and the Atlantic Alliance: The Interaction of Strategy and Politics, by James L. Richardson, 1966. Harvard University Press.

Arms and Influence, by Thomas C. Schelling, 1966. Yale University Press.

Political Change in a West African State, by Martin Kilson, 1966. Harvard University Press.

Planning without Facts: Lessons in Resource Allocation from Nigeria's Development, by Wolfgang F. Stolper, 1966. Harvard University Press.

Export Instability and Economic Development, by Alasdair I. MacBean, 1966. Harvard University Press.

Foreign Policy and Democratic Politics, by Kenneth N. Waltz (jointly with the Institute of War and Peace Studies, Columbia University), 1967. Little, Brown & Co.

Contemporary Military Strategy, by Morton H. Halperin, 1967. Little, Brown & Co.

Sino-Soviet Relations and Arms Control, ed. Morton H. Halperin (jointly with the East Asian Research Center), 1967. M.I.T. Press.

Africa and United States Policy, by Rupert Emerson, 1967. Prentice-Hall.

Europe's Postwar Growth, by Charles P. Kindleberger, 1967. Harvard University Press.

The Rise and Decline of the Cold War, by Paul Seabury, 1967. Basic Books.

Student Politics, ed. S. M. Lipset, 1967. Basic Books.

Pakistan's Development: Social Goals and Private Incentives, by Gustav F. Papanek, 1967. Harvard University Press.

Strike a Blow and Die: A Narrative of Race Relations in Colonial Africa, by George Simeon Mwase, ed. Robert I. Rotberg, 1967. Harvard University Press.

Aid, Influence, and Foreign Policy, by Joan M. Nelson, 1968. The Macmillan Company.

International Regionalism, by Joseph S. Nye, 1968. Little, Brown & Co.

The TFX Tangle: The Politics of Innovation, by Robert J. Art, 1968. Little, Brown & Co.

Korea: The Politics of the Vortex, by Gregory Henderson, 1968. Harvard University Press.

OCCASIONAL PAPERS, PUBLISHED BY THE CENTER FOR INTERNATIONAL AFFAIRS

1. *A Plan for Planning: The Need for a Better Method of Assisting Underdeveloped Countries on Their Economic Policies,* by Gustav F. Papanek, 1961.*
2. *The Flow of Resources from Rich to Poor,* by Alan D. Neale, 1961.
3. *Limited War: An Essay on the Development of the Theory and an Annotated Bibliography,* by Morton H. Halperin, 1962.*
4. *Reflections on the Failure of the First West Indian Federation,* by Hugh W. Springer, 1962.*
5. *On the Interaction of Opposing Forces under Possible Arms Agreements,* by Glenn A. Kent, 1963.
6. *Europe's Northern Cap and the Soviet Union,* by Nils Örvik, 1963.
7. *Civil Administration in the Punjab: An Analysis of a State Government in India,* by E. N. Mangat Rai, 1963.
8. *On the Appropriate Size of a Development Program,* by Edward S. Mason, 1964.
9. *Self-Determination Revisited in the Era of Decolonization,* by Rupert Emerson, 1964.
10. *The Planning and Execution of Economic Development in Southeast Asia,* by Clair Wilcox, 1965.
11. *Pan-Africanism in Action,* by Albert Tevoedjre, 1965.
12. *Is China Turning In?* by Morton H. Halperin, 1965.
13. *Economic Development in India and Pakistan,* by Edward S. Mason, 1966.
14. *The Role of the Military in Recent Turkish Politics,* by Ergun Özbudun, 1966.
15. *Economic Development and Individual Change: A Social-Psychological Study of the Comilla Experiment in Pakistan,* by Howard Schuman, 1967.
16. *A Select Bibliography on Students, Politics, and Higher Education,* by Philip Altbach, 1967.
17. *Europe's Political Puzzle: A Study of the Fouchet Negotiations and the 1963 Veto,* by Alessandro Silj, 1967.
18. *The Cap and the Straits: Problems of Nordic Security,* by Jan Klenberg, 1968.

* Out of print.